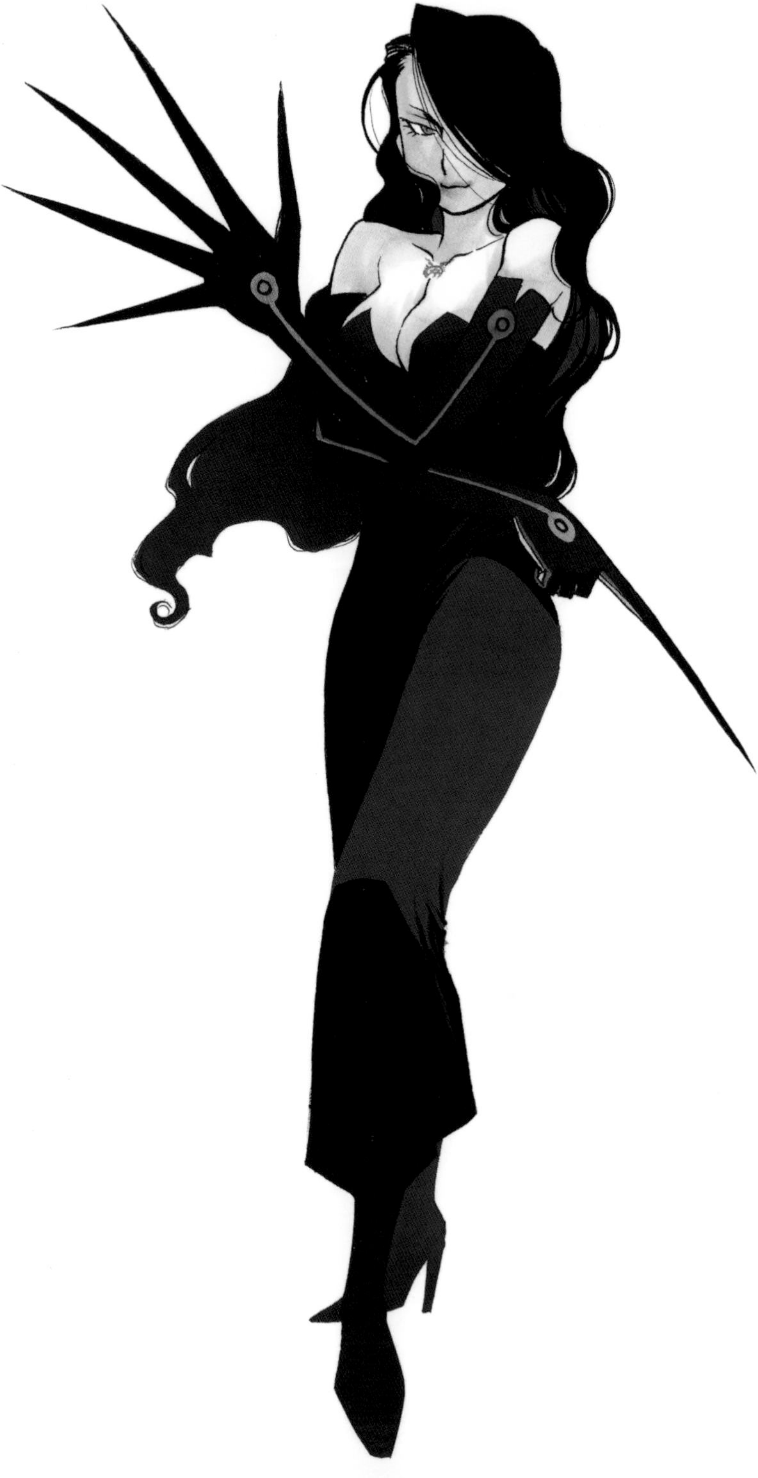

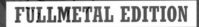

FULLMETAL ALCHEMIST

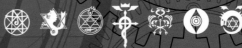

06
CONTENTS

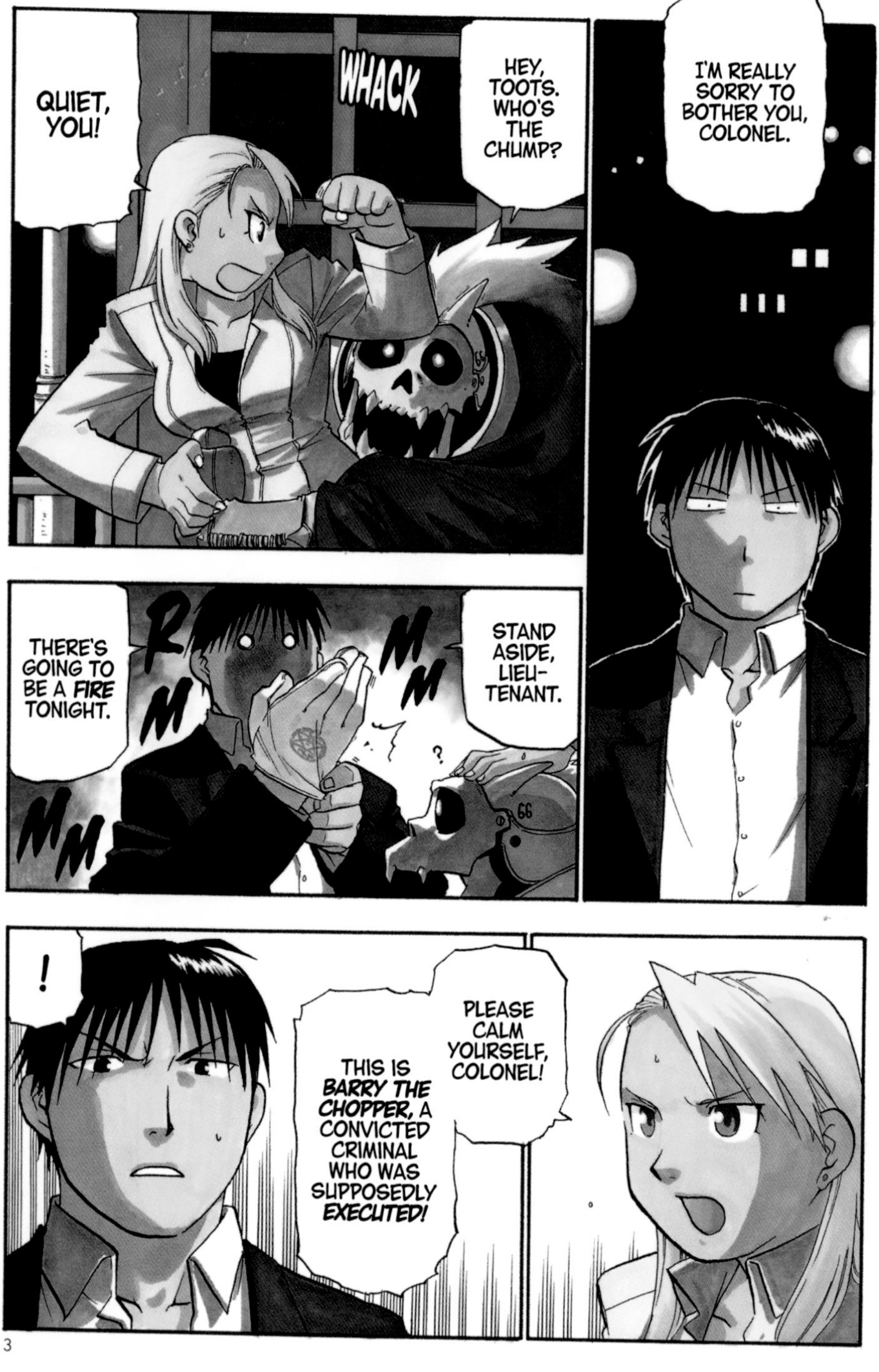
I'M REALLY SORRY TO BOTHER YOU, COLONEL.
HEY, TOOTS. WHO'S THE CHUMP?
WHACK
QUIET, YOU!
STAND ASIDE, LIEU-TENANT.
THERE'S GOING TO BE A **FIRE** TONIGHT.
PLEASE CALM YOURSELF, COLONEL!
THIS IS ***BARRY THE CHOPPER***, A CONVICTED CRIMINAL WHO WAS SUPPOSEDLY ***EXECUTED!***
!

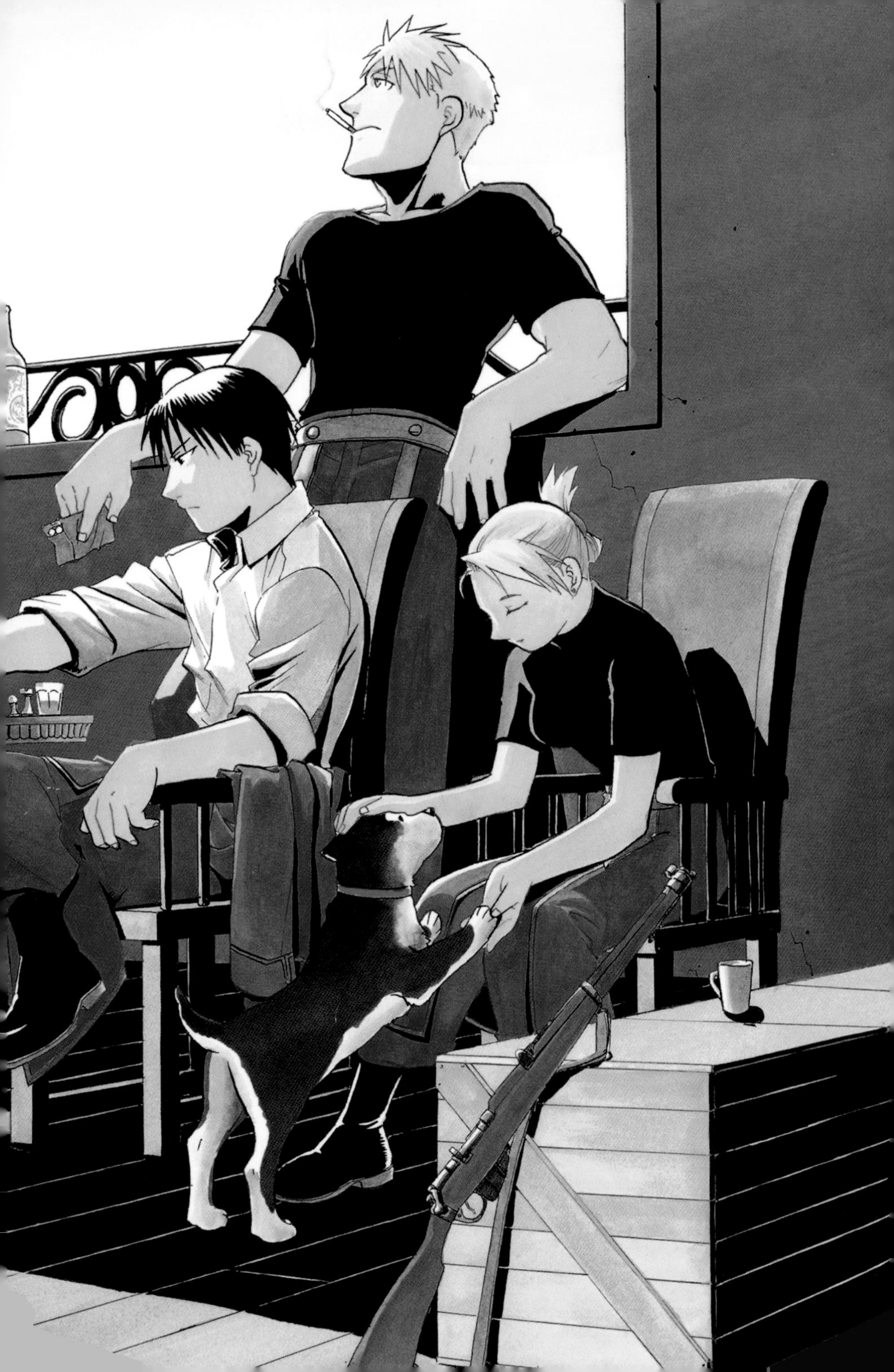

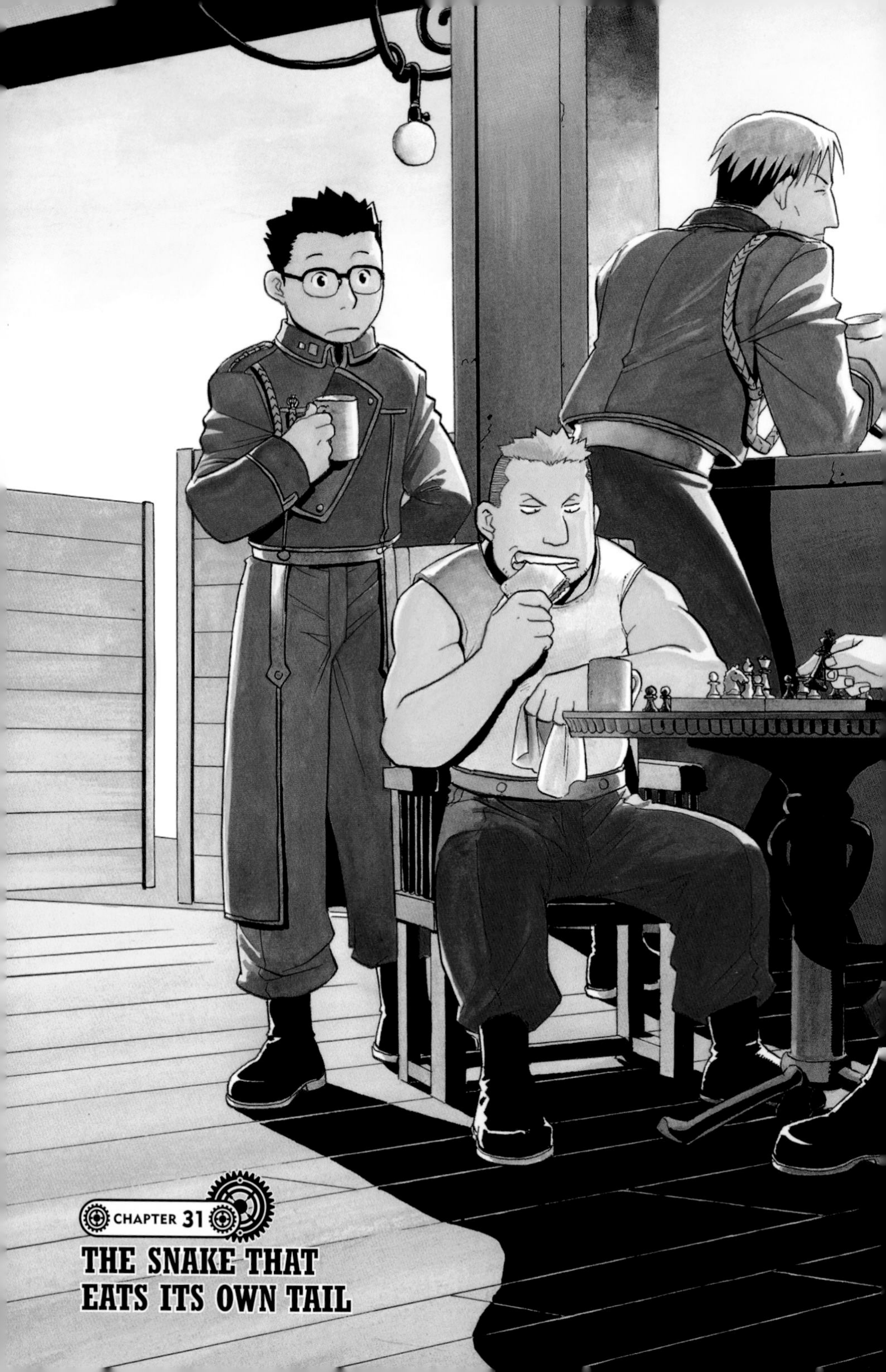
CHAPTER 31
THE SNAKE THAT
EATS ITS OWN TAIL

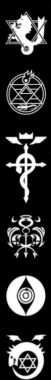

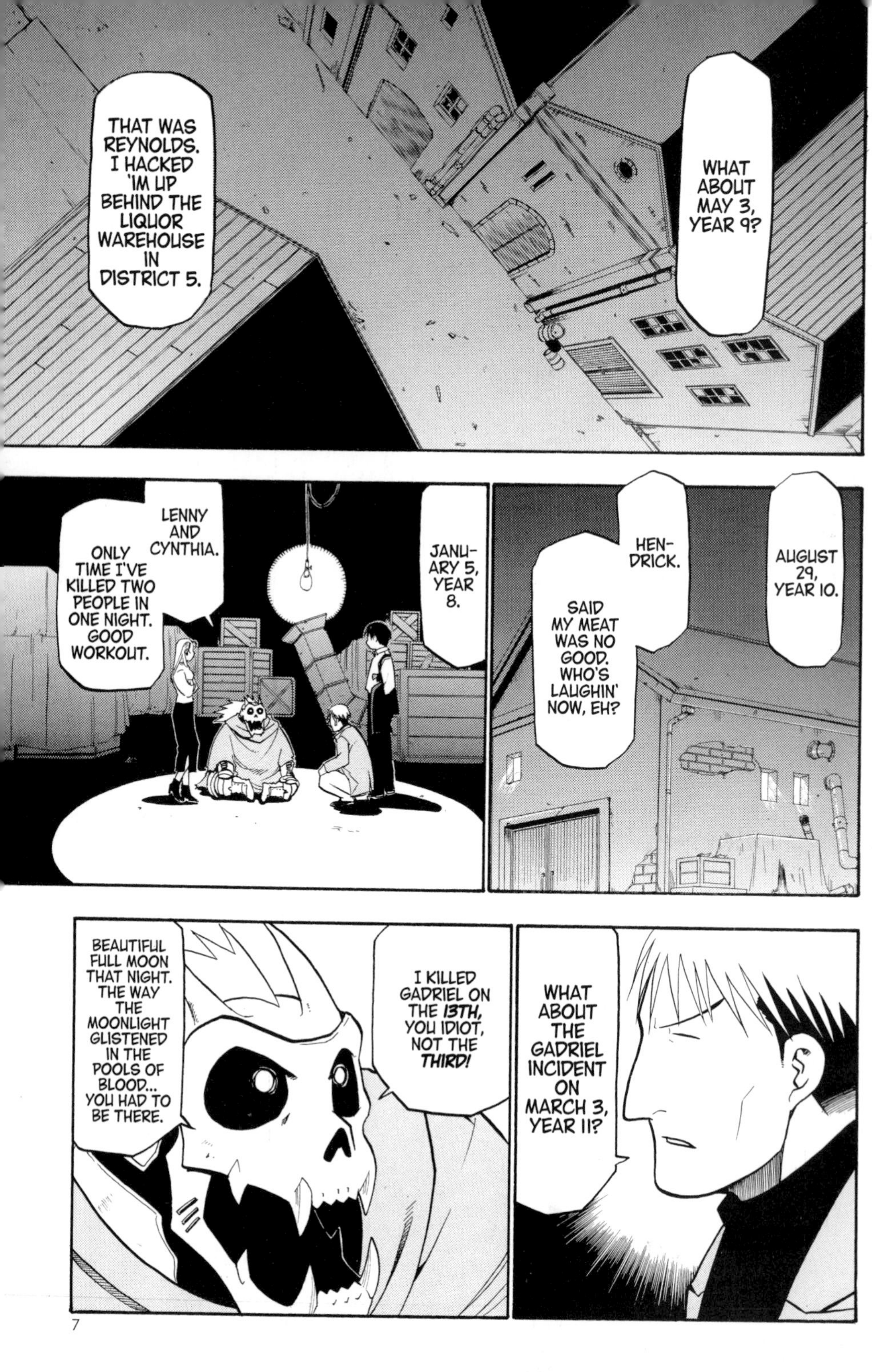
WHAT ABOUT MAY 3, YEAR 9?
THAT WAS REYNOLDS. I HACKED 'IM UP BEHIND THE LIQUOR WAREHOUSE IN DISTRICT 5.
AUGUST 29, YEAR 10.
HEN-DRICK.
SAID MY MEAT WAS NO GOOD. WHO'S LAUGHIN' NOW, EH?
JANU-ARY 5, YEAR 8.
LENNY AND CYNTHIA.
ONLY TIME I'VE KILLED TWO PEOPLE IN ONE NIGHT. GOOD WORKOUT.
WHAT ABOUT THE GADRIEL INCIDENT ON MARCH 3, YEAR 11?
I KILLED GADRIEL ON THE *13TH,* YOU IDIOT, NOT THE *THIRD!*
BEAUTIFUL FULL MOON THAT NIGHT. THE WAY THE MOONLIGHT GLISTENED IN THE POOLS OF BLOOD... YOU HAD TO BE THERE.

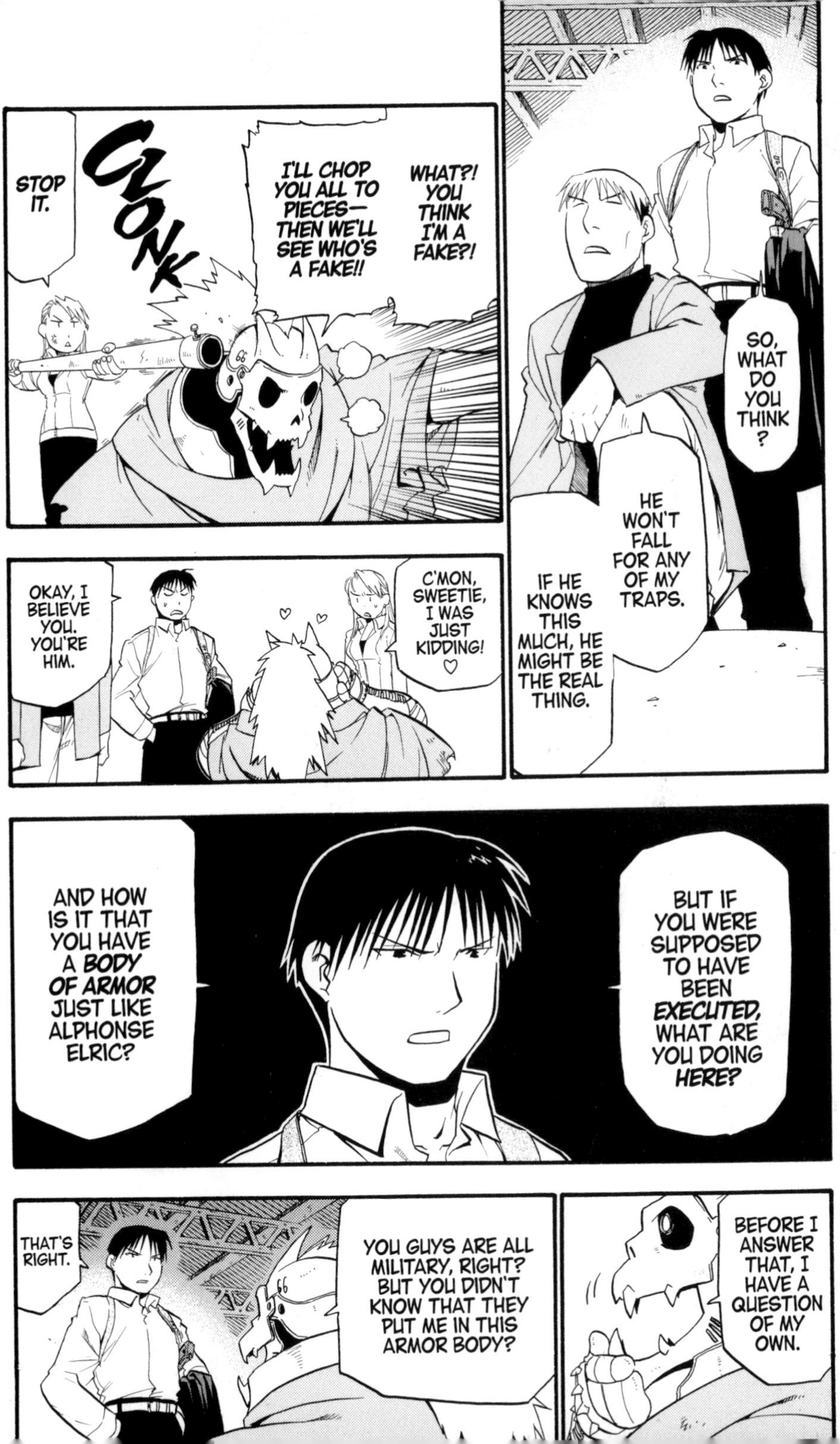
SO, WHAT DO YOU THINK?
HE WON'T FALL FOR ANY OF MY TRAPS.
IF HE KNOWS THIS MUCH, HE MIGHT BE THE REAL THING.
WHAT?! YOU THINK I'M A FAKE?!
I'LL CHOP YOU ALL TO PIECES—THEN WE'LL SEE WHO'S A FAKE!!
CLONK
STOP IT.
C'MON, SWEETIE, I WAS JUST KIDDING! ♡
OKAY, I BELIEVE YOU. YOU'RE HIM.
BUT IF YOU WERE SUPPOSED TO HAVE BEEN EXECUTED, WHAT ARE YOU DOING HERE?
AND HOW IS IT THAT YOU HAVE A BODY OF ARMOR JUST LIKE ALPHONSE ELRIC?
BEFORE I ANSWER THAT, I HAVE A QUESTION OF MY OWN.
YOU GUYS ARE ALL MILITARY, RIGHT? BUT YOU DIDN'T KNOW THAT THEY PUT ME IN THIS ARMOR BODY?
THAT'S RIGHT.

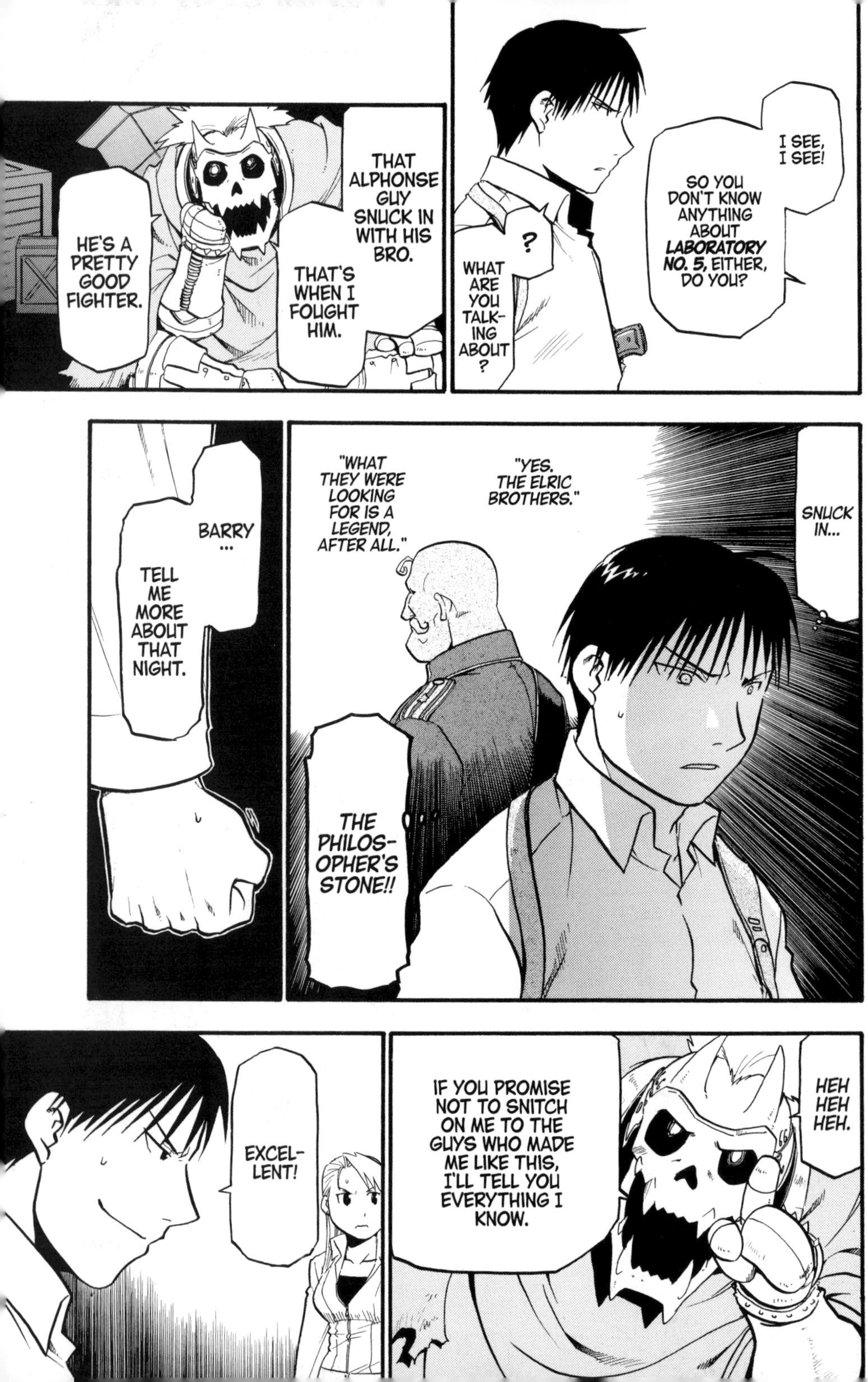
I SEE, I SEE!
SO YOU DON'T KNOW ANYTHING ABOUT **LABORATORY NO. 5,** EITHER, DO YOU?
?
WHAT ARE YOU TALKING ABOUT?
THAT ALPHONSE GUY SNUCK IN WITH HIS BRO.
THAT'S WHEN I FOUGHT HIM.
HE'S A PRETTY GOOD FIGHTER.
SNUCK IN...
"YES. THE ELRIC BROTHERS."
"WHAT THEY WERE LOOKING FOR IS A LEGEND, AFTER ALL."
THE PHILOSOPHER'S STONE!!
BARRY...
TELL ME MORE ABOUT THAT NIGHT.
HEH HEH HEH.
IF YOU PROMISE NOT TO SNITCH ON ME TO THE GUYS WHO MADE ME LIKE THIS, I'LL TELL YOU EVERYTHING I KNOW.
EXCELLENT!

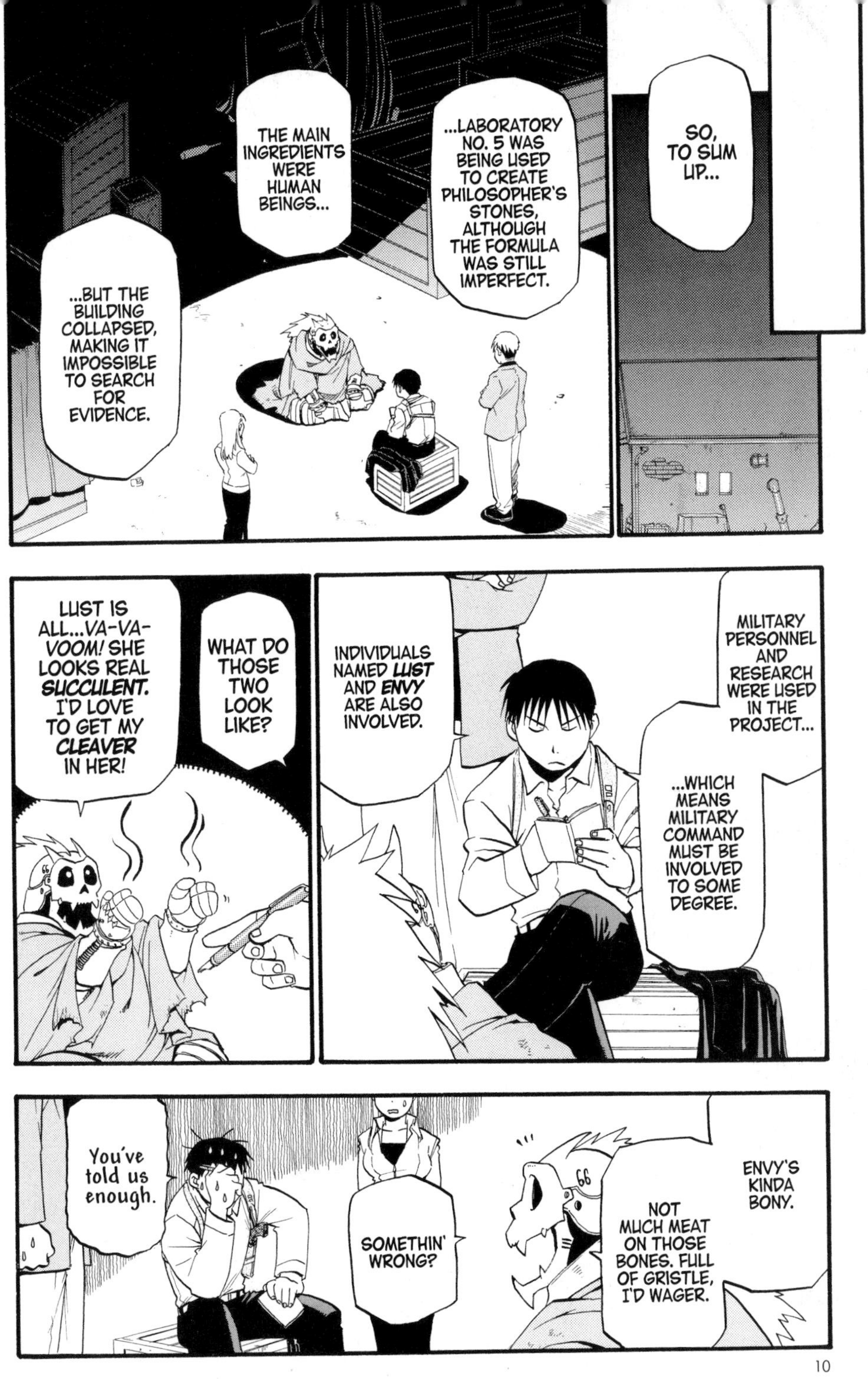
SO, TO SUM UP...
...LABORATORY NO. 5 WAS BEING USED TO CREATE PHILOSOPHER'S STONES, ALTHOUGH THE FORMULA WAS STILL IMPERFECT.
THE MAIN INGREDIENTS WERE HUMAN BEINGS...
...BUT THE BUILDING COLLAPSED, MAKING IT IMPOSSIBLE TO SEARCH FOR EVIDENCE.
MILITARY PERSONNEL AND RESEARCH WERE USED IN THE PROJECT...
...WHICH MEANS MILITARY COMMAND MUST BE INVOLVED TO SOME DEGREE.
INDIVIDUALS NAMED **LUST** AND **ENVY** ARE ALSO INVOLVED.
WHAT DO THOSE TWO LOOK LIKE?
LUST IS ALL...*VA-VA-VOOM!* SHE LOOKS REAL ***SUCCULENT.*** I'D LOVE TO GET MY ***CLEAVER*** IN HER!
ENVY'S KINDA BONY.
NOT MUCH MEAT ON THOSE BONES. FULL OF GRISTLE, I'D WAGER.
SOMETHIN' WRONG?
You've told us enough.

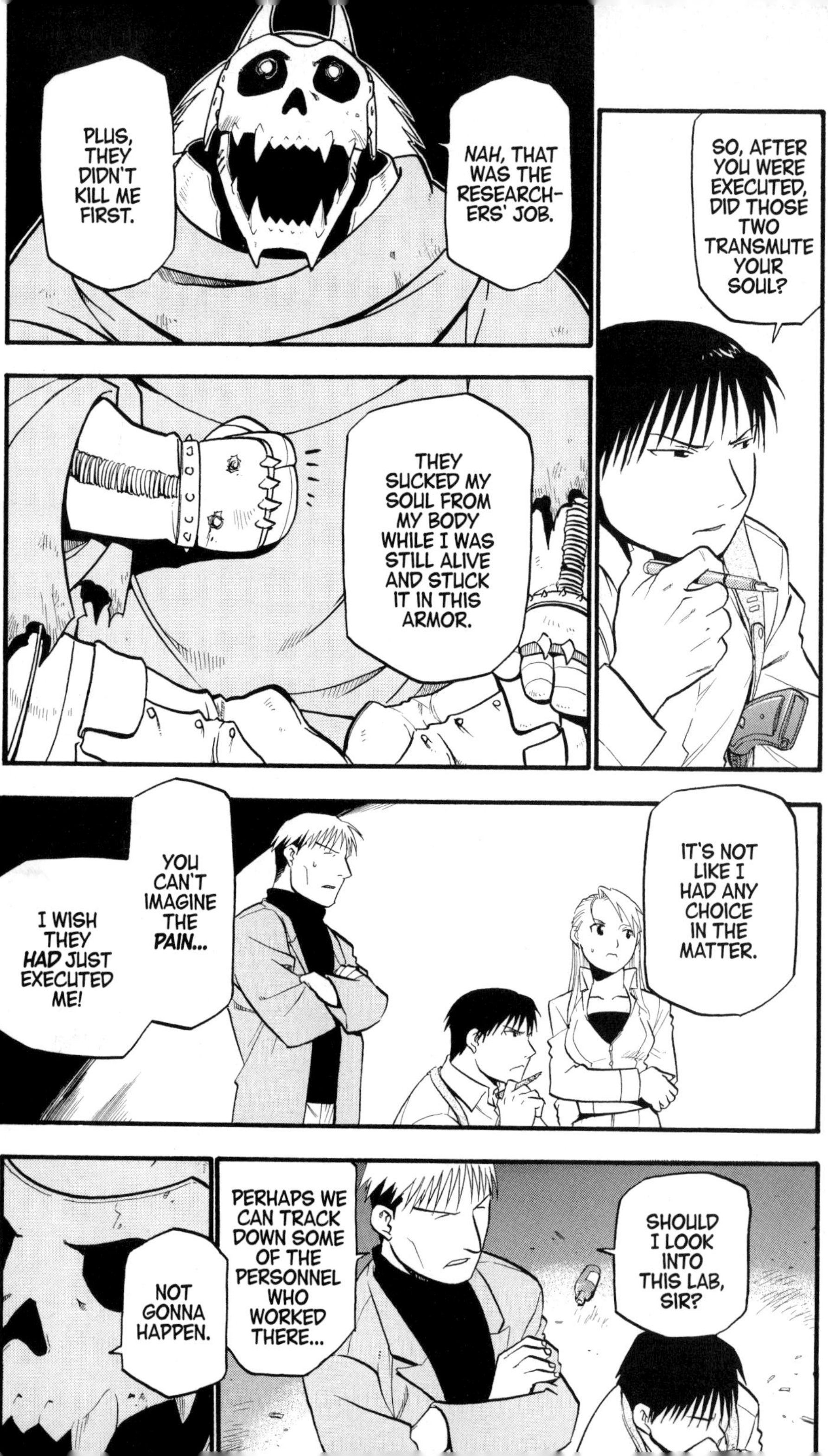
SO, AFTER YOU WERE EXECUTED, DID THOSE TWO TRANSMUTE YOUR SOUL?
NAH, THAT WAS THE RESEARCHERS' JOB.
PLUS, THEY DIDN'T KILL ME FIRST.
THEY SUCKED MY SOUL FROM MY BODY WHILE I WAS STILL ALIVE AND STUCK IT IN THIS ARMOR.
IT'S NOT LIKE I HAD ANY CHOICE IN THE MATTER.
YOU CAN'T IMAGINE THE PAIN...
I WISH THEY HAD JUST EXECUTED ME!
SHOULD I LOOK INTO THIS LAB, SIR?
PERHAPS WE CAN TRACK DOWN SOME OF THE PERSONNEL WHO WORKED THERE...
NOT GONNA HAPPEN.

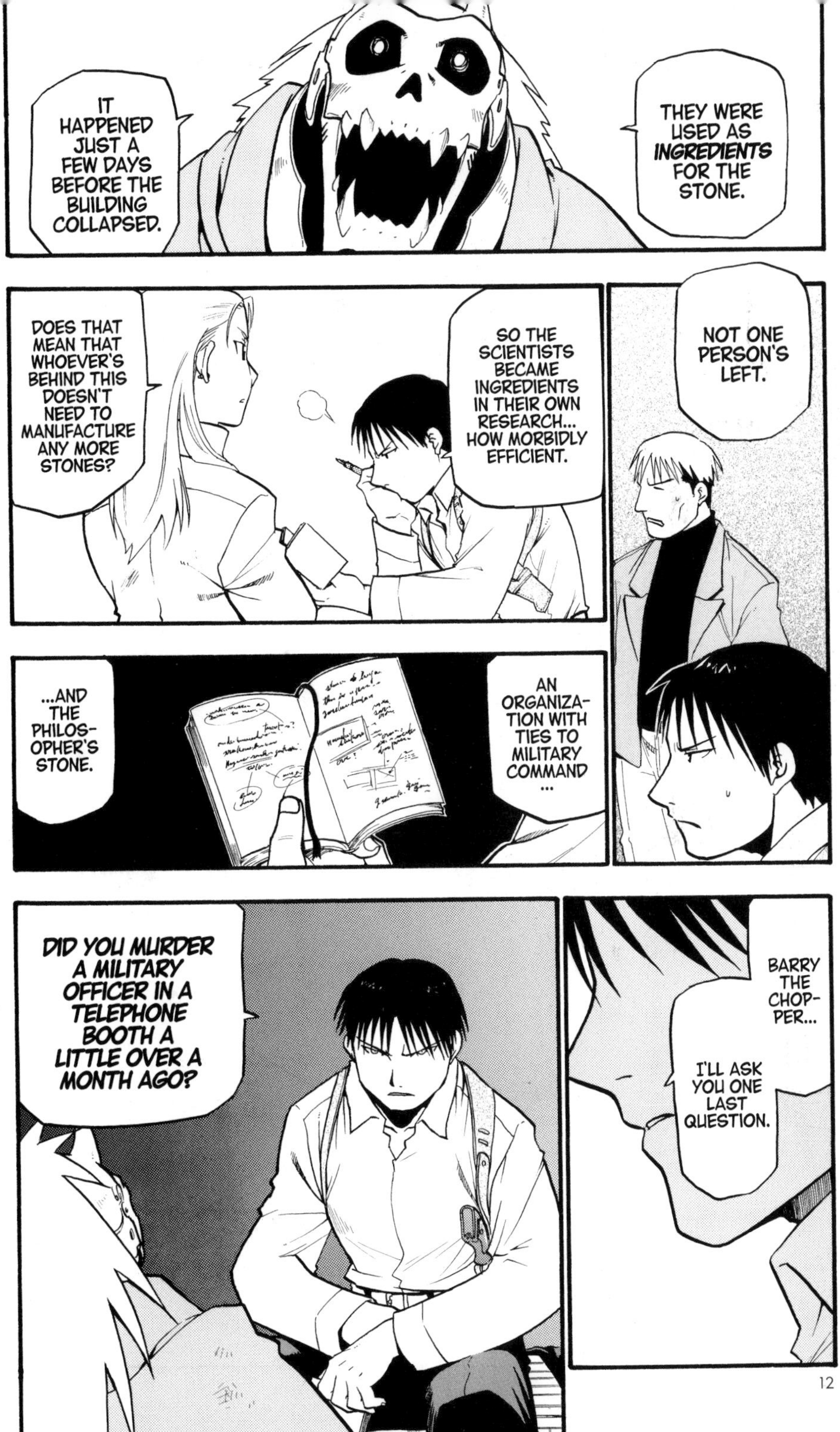
THEY WERE USED AS INGREDIENTS FOR THE STONE.
IT HAPPENED JUST A FEW DAYS BEFORE THE BUILDING COLLAPSED.
NOT ONE PERSON'S LEFT.
SO THE SCIENTISTS BECAME INGREDIENTS IN THEIR OWN RESEARCH... HOW MORBIDLY EFFICIENT.
DOES THAT MEAN THAT WHOEVER'S BEHIND THIS DOESN'T NEED TO MANUFACTURE ANY MORE STONES?
AN ORGANIZATION WITH TIES TO MILITARY COMMAND...
...AND THE PHILOSOPHER'S STONE.
BARRY THE CHOPPER...
I'LL ASK YOU ONE LAST QUESTION.
DID YOU MURDER A MILITARY OFFICER IN A TELEPHONE BOOTH A LITTLE OVER A MONTH AGO?

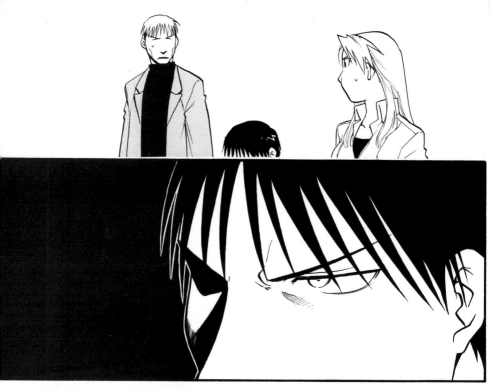

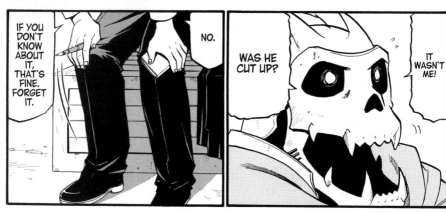

IF YOU DON'T KNOW ABOUT IT, THAT'S FINE. FORGET IT.

NO.

WAS HE CUT UP?

IT WASN'T ME!

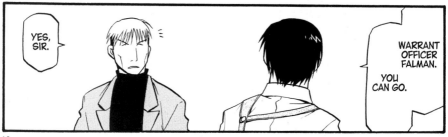

YES, SIR.

WARRANT OFFICER FALMAN.

YOU CAN GO.

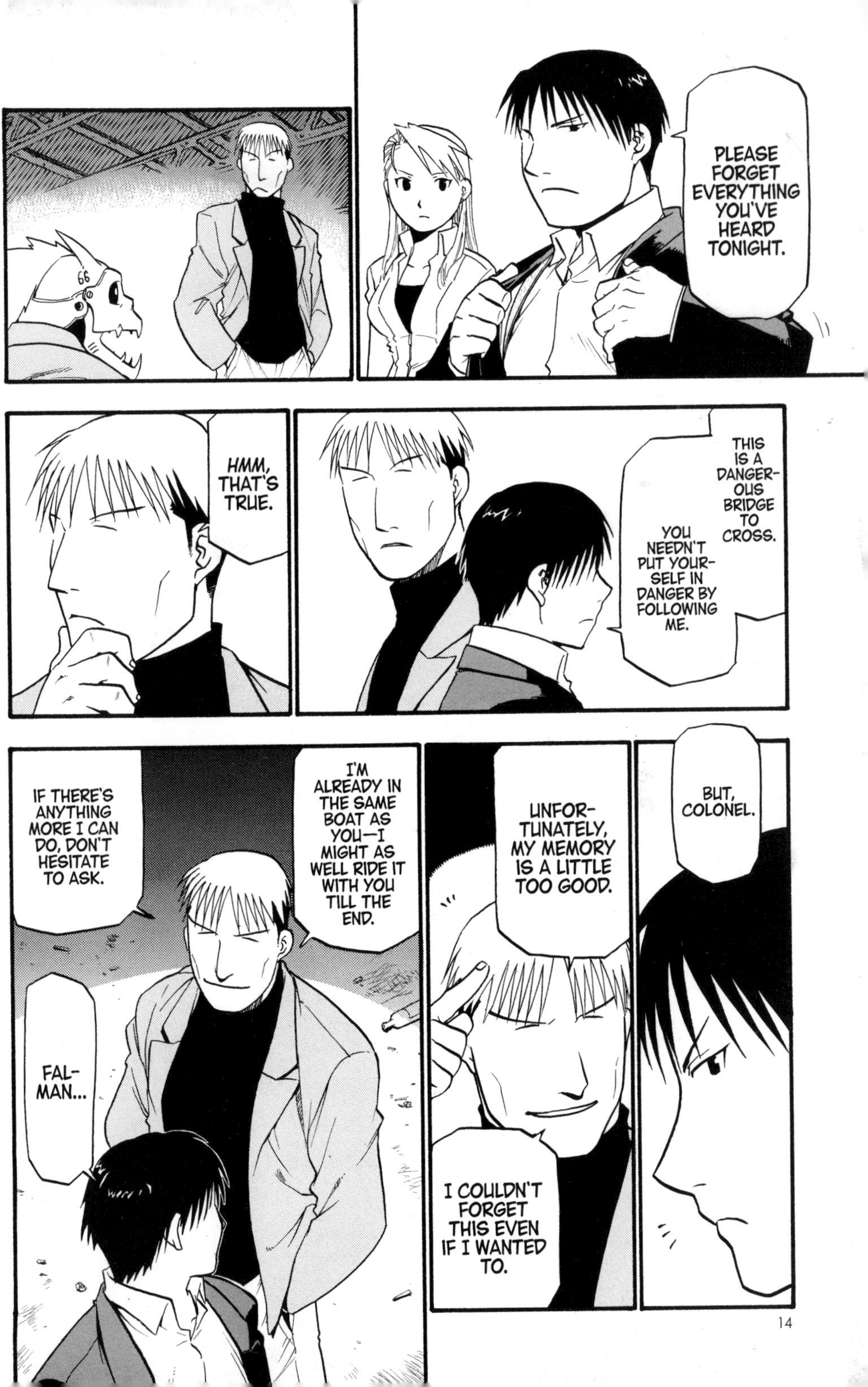
PLEASE FORGET EVERYTHING YOU'VE HEARD TONIGHT.
THIS IS A DANGER-OUS BRIDGE TO CROSS.
YOU NEEDN'T PUT YOUR-SELF IN DANGER BY FOLLOWING ME.
HMM, THAT'S TRUE.
BUT, COLONEL.
UNFOR-TUNATELY, MY MEMORY IS A LITTLE TOO GOOD.
I COULDN'T FORGET THIS EVEN IF I WANTED TO.
I'M ALREADY IN THE SAME BOAT AS YOU—I MIGHT AS WELL RIDE IT WITH YOU TILL THE END.
IF THERE'S ANYTHING MORE I CAN DO, DON'T HESITATE TO ASK.
FAL-MAN...

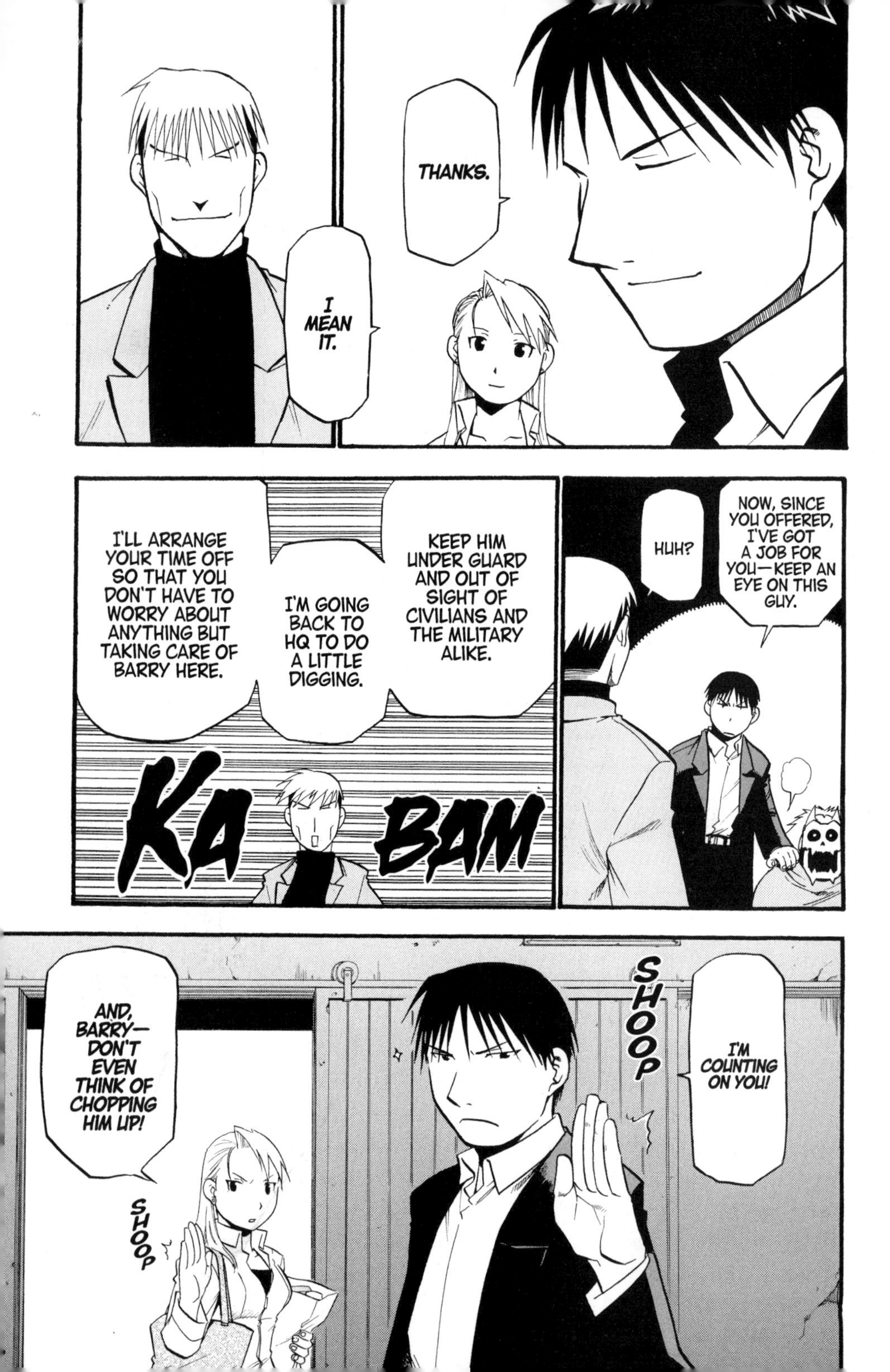
THANKS.
I MEAN IT.
NOW, SINCE YOU OFFERED, I'VE GOT A JOB FOR YOU—KEEP AN EYE ON THIS GUY.
HUH?
KEEP HIM UNDER GUARD AND OUT OF SIGHT OF CIVILIANS AND THE MILITARY ALIKE.
I'M GOING BACK TO HQ TO DO A LITTLE DIGGING.
I'LL ARRANGE YOUR TIME OFF SO THAT YOU DON'T HAVE TO WORRY ABOUT ANYTHING BUT TAKING CARE OF BARRY HERE.
KA BAM
SHOOP
I'M COUNTING ON YOU!
AND, BARRY—DON'T EVEN THINK OF CHOPPING HIM UP!
SHOOP

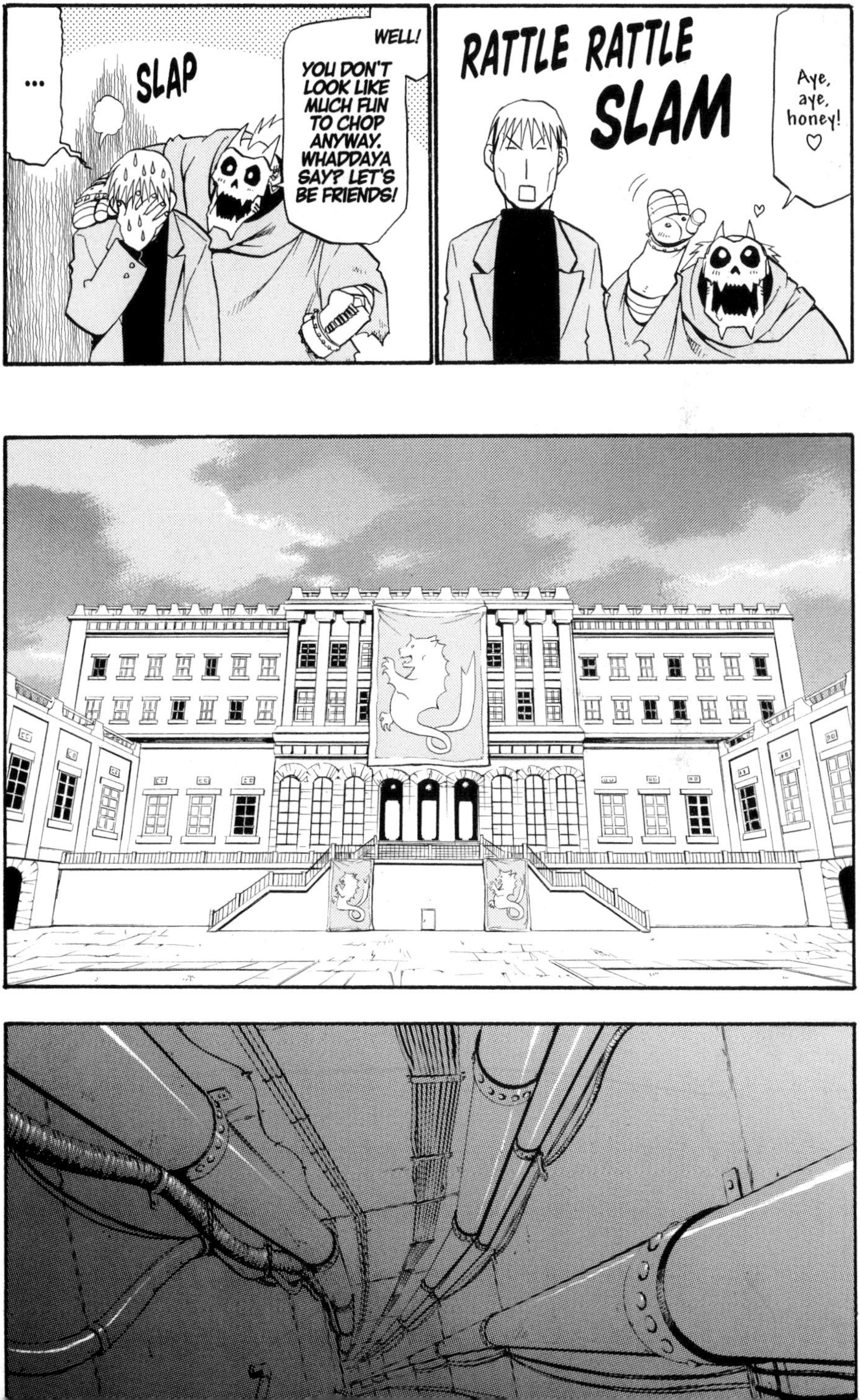
Aye, aye, honey! ♡
RATTLE RATTLE
SLAM
WELL!
YOU DON'T LOOK LIKE MUCH FUN TO CHOP ANYWAY. WHADDAYA SAY? LET'S BE FRIENDS!
SLAP
...

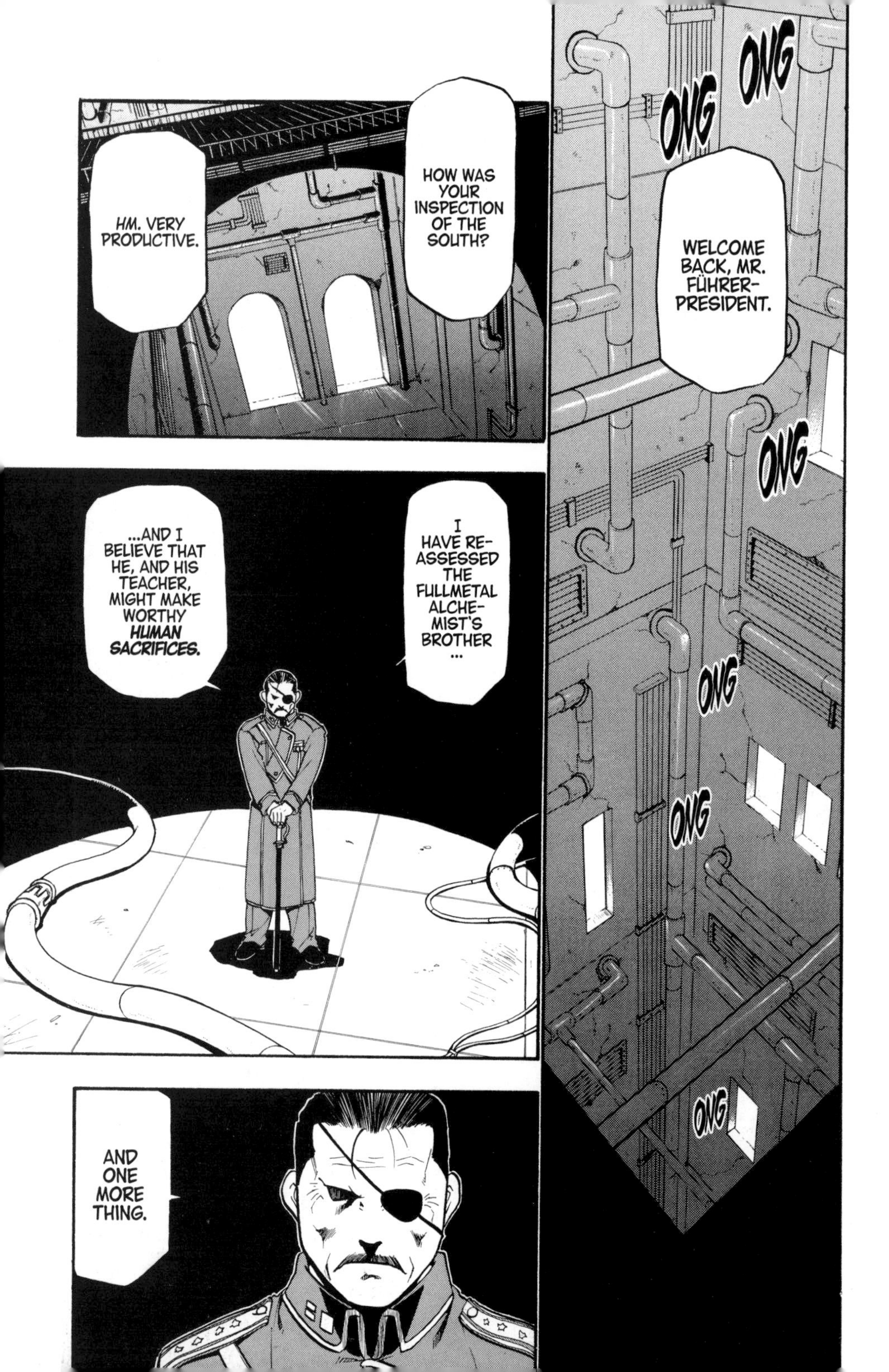
ONG ONG
WELCOME BACK, MR. FÜHRER-PRESIDENT.
ONG
ONG
ONG
ONG
HOW WAS YOUR INSPECTION OF THE SOUTH?
HM. VERY PRODUCTIVE.
I HAVE RE-ASSESSED THE FULLMETAL ALCHE-MIST'S BROTHER...
...AND I BELIEVE THAT HE, AND HIS TEACHER, MIGHT MAKE WORTHY **HUMAN SACRIFICES.**
AND ONE MORE THING.

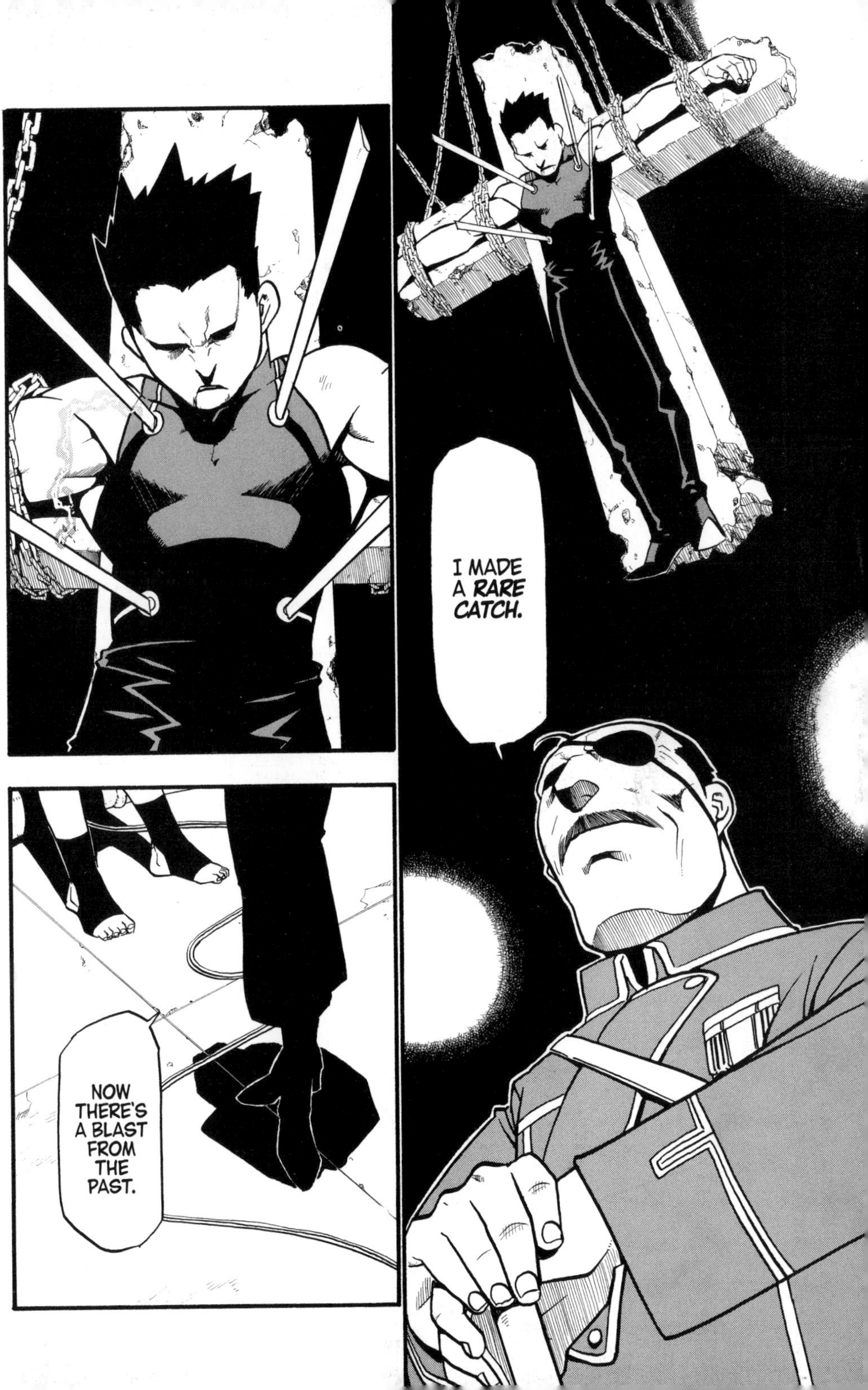
I MADE A *RARE* CATCH.
NOW THERE'S A BLAST FROM THE PAST.

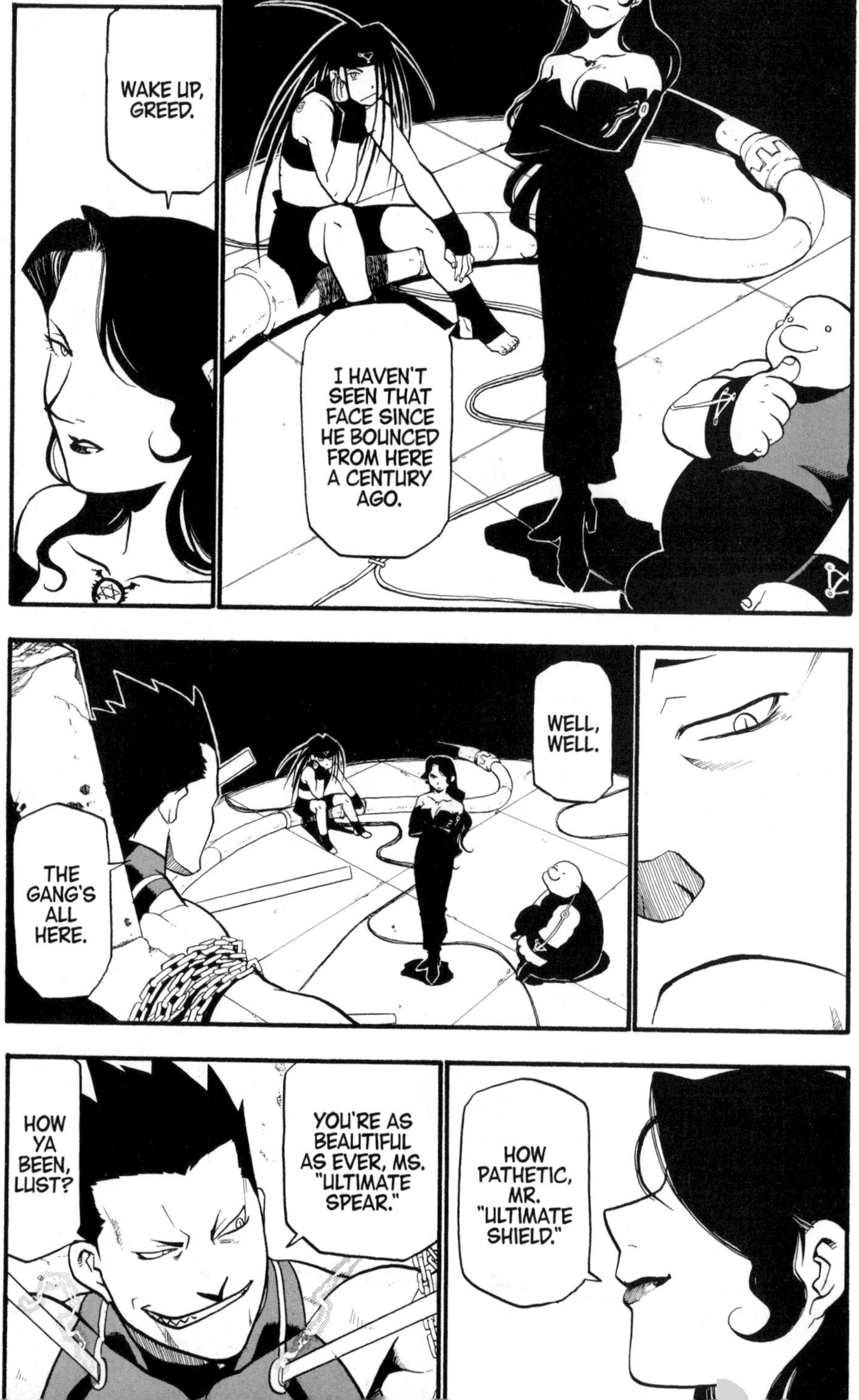
I HAVEN'T SEEN THAT FACE SINCE HE BOUNCED FROM HERE A CENTURY AGO.
WAKE UP, GREED.
WELL, WELL.
THE GANG'S ALL HERE.
HOW PATHETIC, MR. "ULTIMATE SHIELD."
YOU'RE AS BEAUTIFUL AS EVER, MS. "ULTIMATE SPEAR."
HOW YA BEEN, LUST?

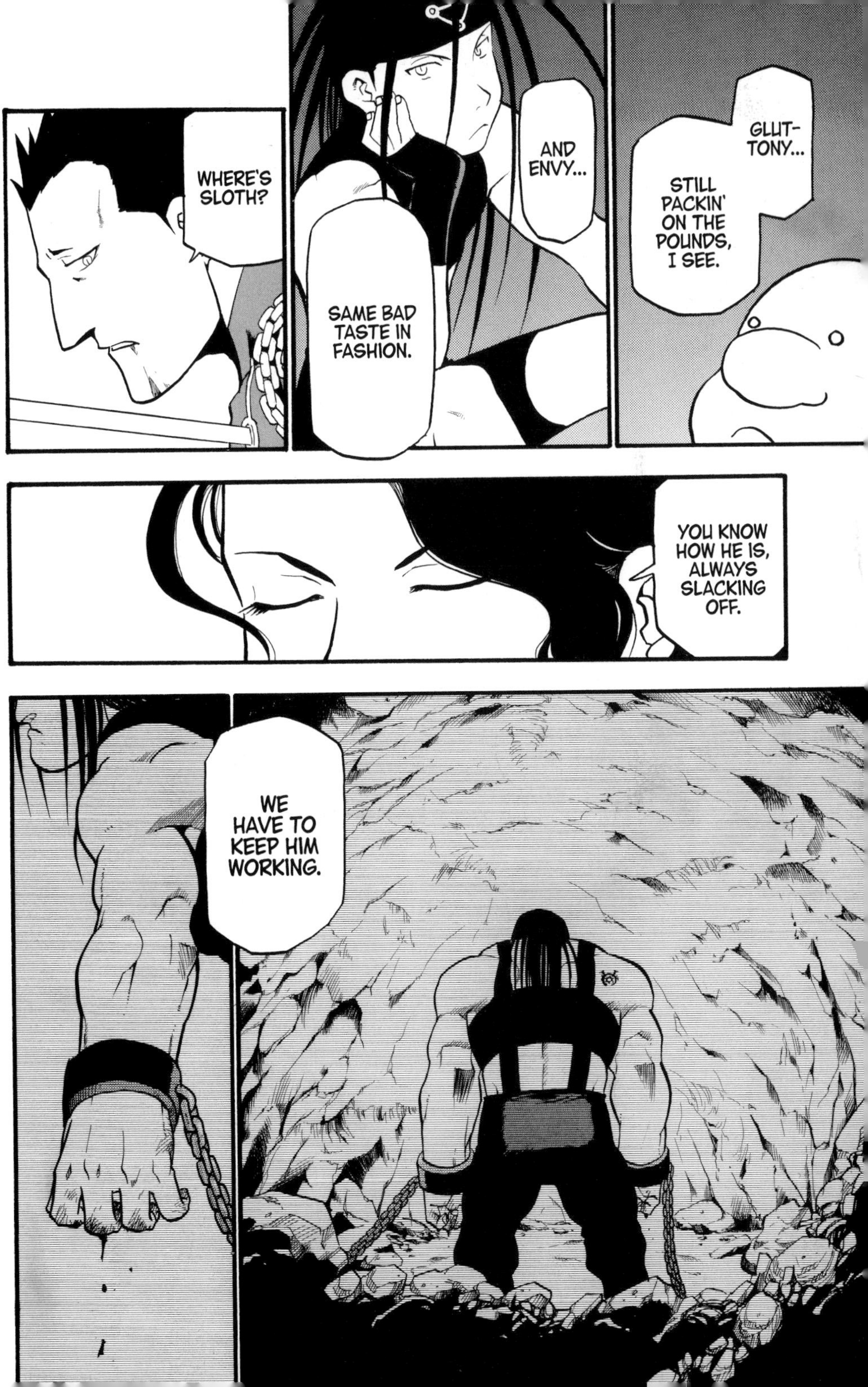
GLUTTONY...
STILL PACKIN' ON THE POUNDS, I SEE.
AND ENVY...
SAME BAD TASTE IN FASHION.
WHERE'S SLOTH?
YOU KNOW HOW HE IS, ALWAYS SLACKING OFF.
WE HAVE TO KEEP HIM WORKING.

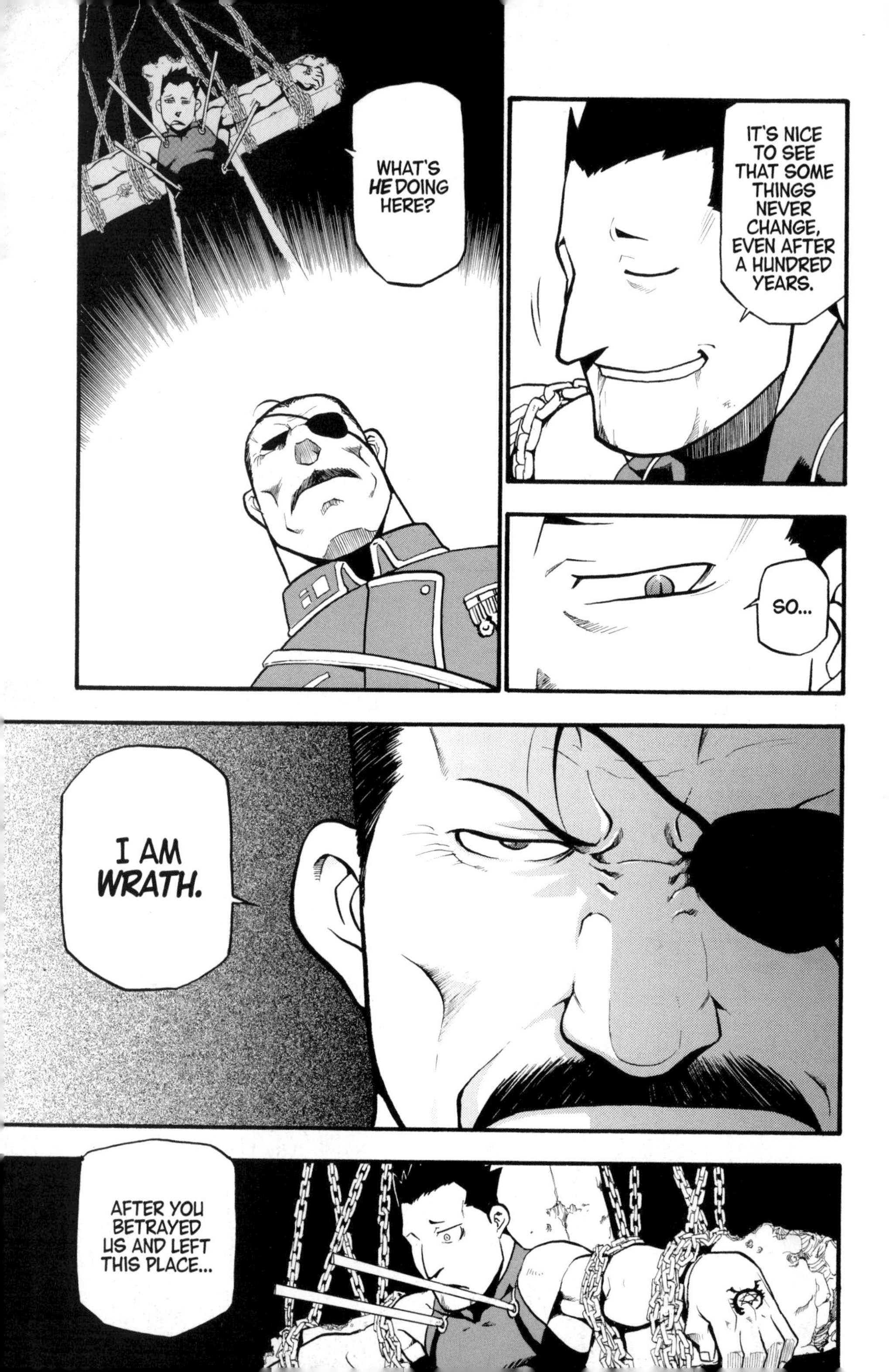
IT'S NICE TO SEE THAT SOME THINGS NEVER CHANGE, EVEN AFTER A HUNDRED YEARS.
SO...
WHAT'S HE DOING HERE?
I AM WRATH.
AFTER YOU BETRAYED US AND LEFT THIS PLACE...

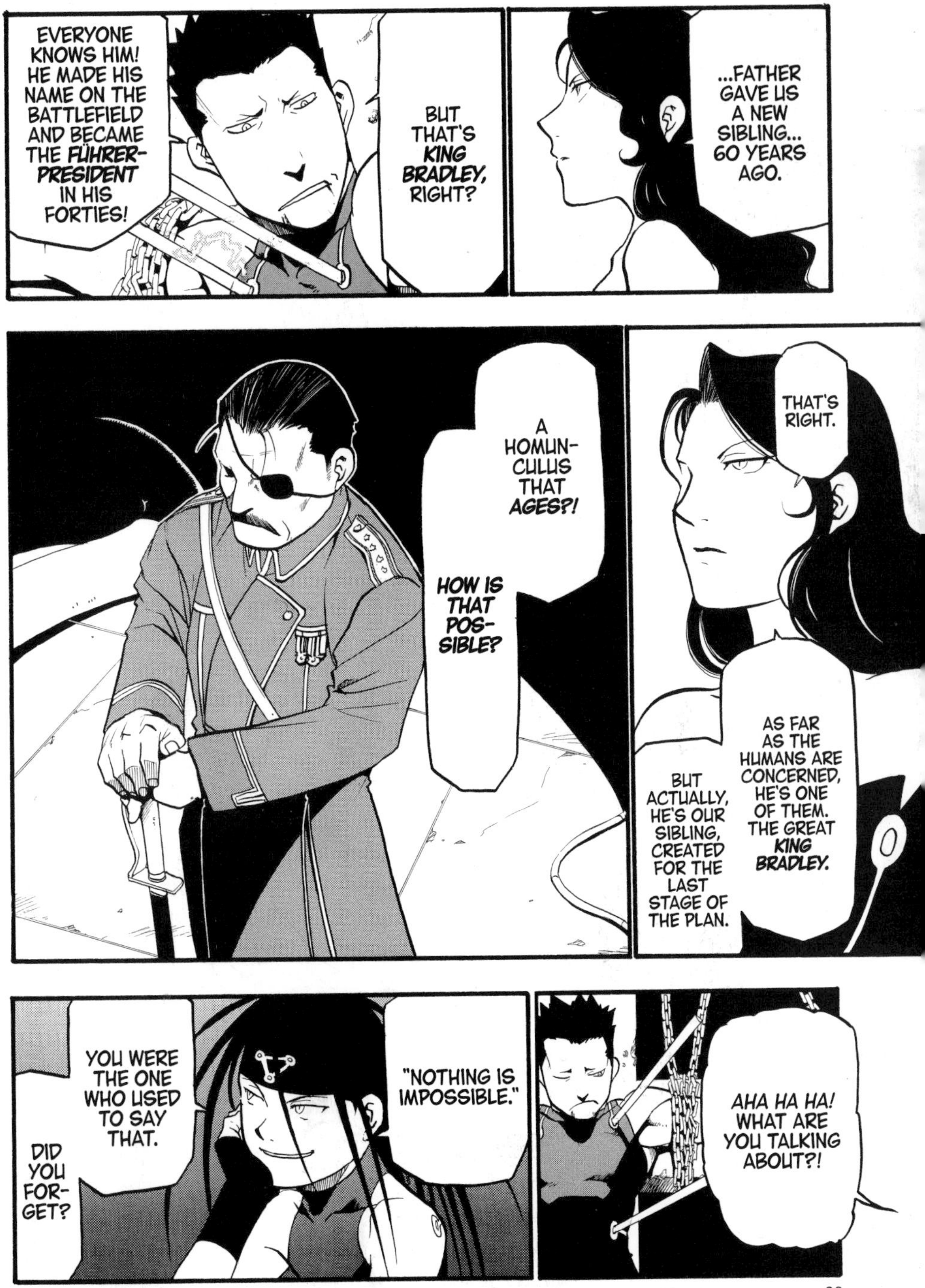
...FATHER GAVE US A NEW SIBLING... 60 YEARS AGO.
BUT THAT'S KING BRADLEY, RIGHT?
EVERYONE KNOWS HIM! HE MADE HIS NAME ON THE BATTLEFIELD AND BECAME THE FÜHRER-PRESIDENT IN HIS FORTIES!
THAT'S RIGHT.
AS FAR AS THE HUMANS ARE CONCERNED, HE'S ONE OF THEM. THE GREAT KING BRADLEY.
BUT ACTUALLY, HE'S OUR SIBLING, CREATED FOR THE LAST STAGE OF THE PLAN.
A HOMUN-CULUS THAT AGES?!
HOW IS THAT POS-SIBLE?
AHA HA HA! WHAT ARE YOU TALKING ABOUT?!
"NOTHING IS IMPOSSIBLE."
YOU WERE THE ONE WHO USED TO SAY THAT.
DID YOU FOR-GET?

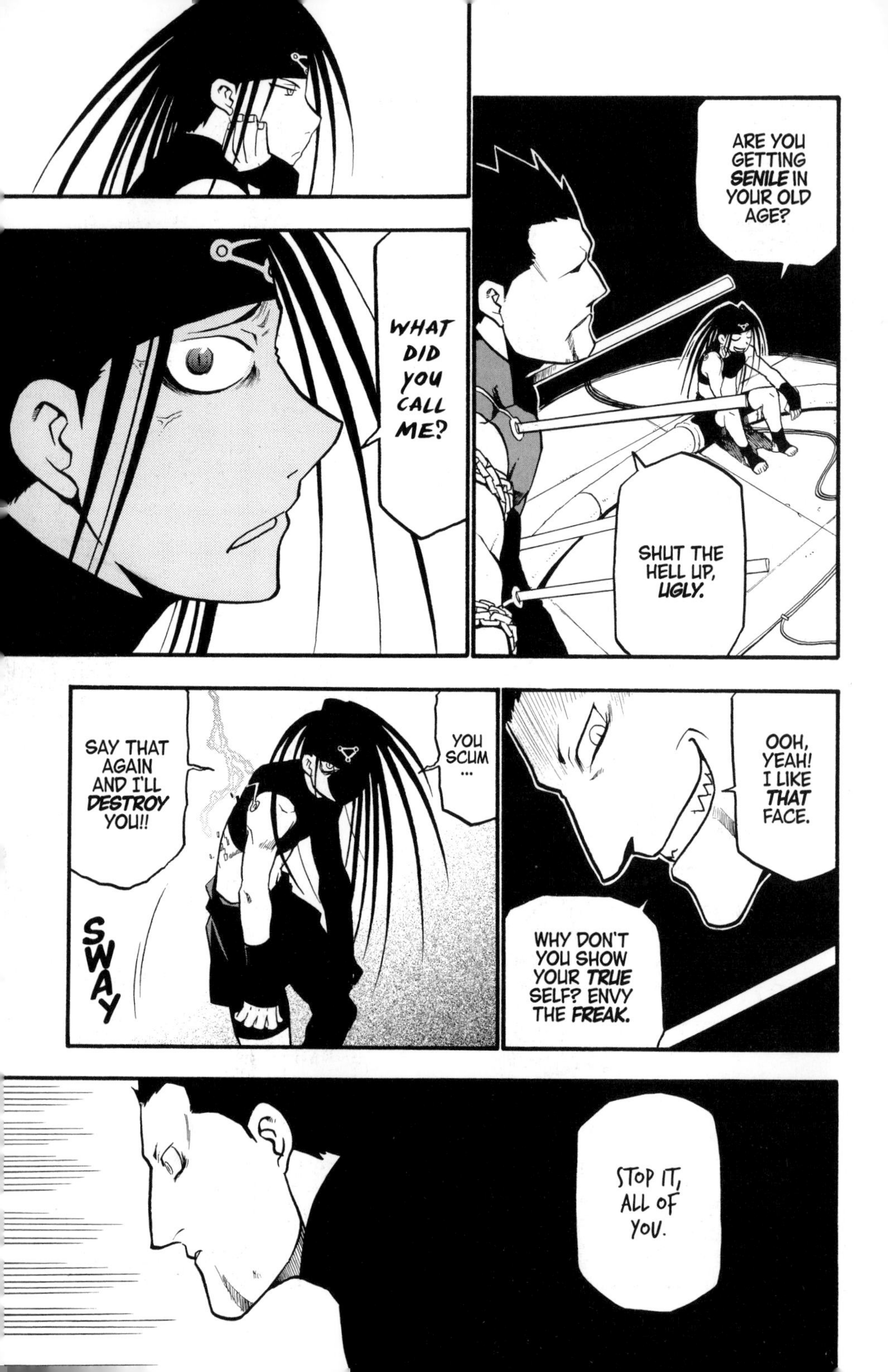
ARE YOU GETTING SENILE IN YOUR OLD AGE?
SHUT THE HELL UP, UGLY.
WHAT DID YOU CALL ME?
OOH, YEAH! I LIKE THAT FACE.
WHY DON'T YOU SHOW YOUR TRUE SELF? ENVY THE FREAK.
YOU SCUM...
SAY THAT AGAIN AND I'LL DESTROY YOU!!
SWAY
STOP IT, ALL OF YOU.

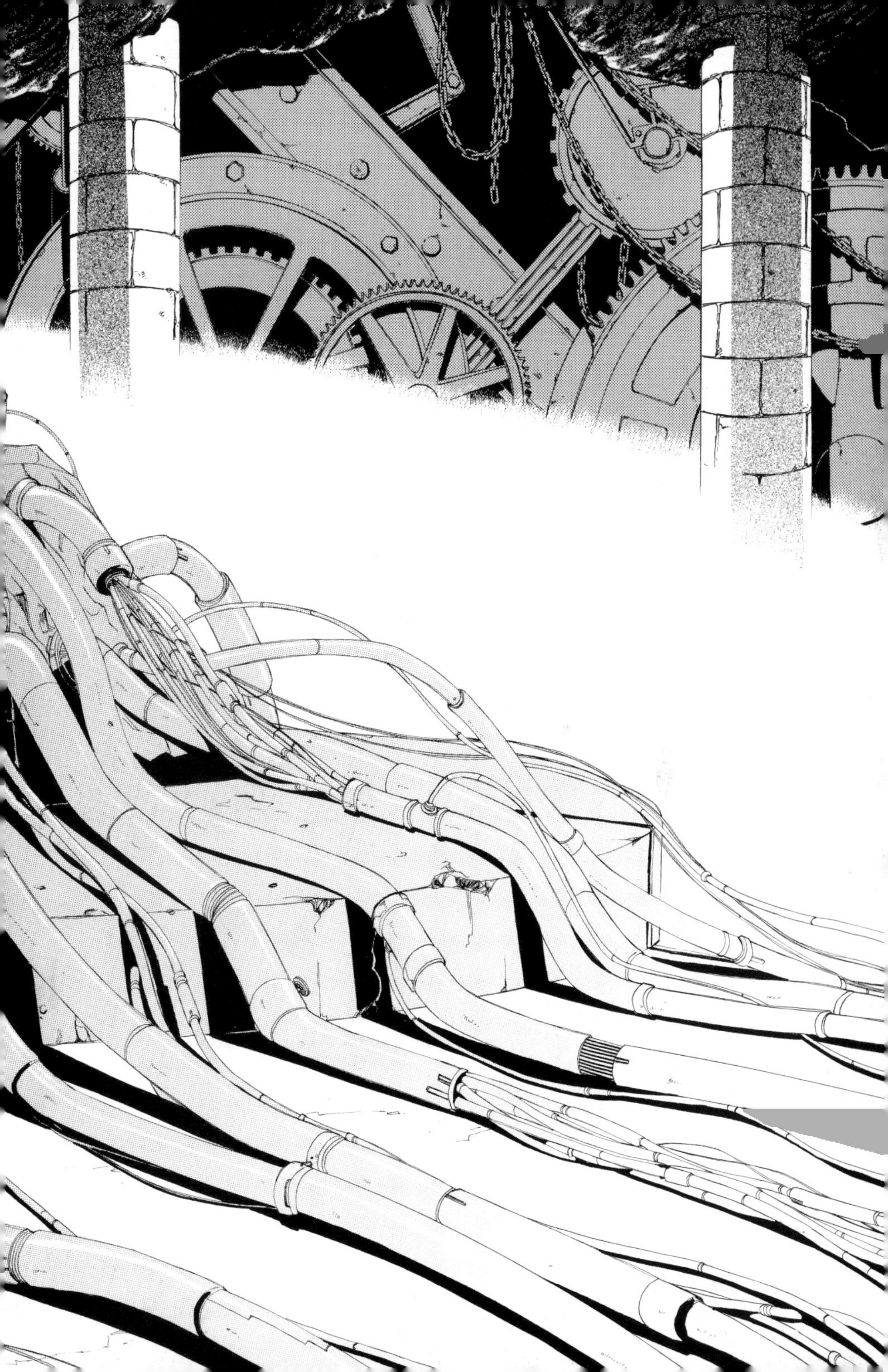

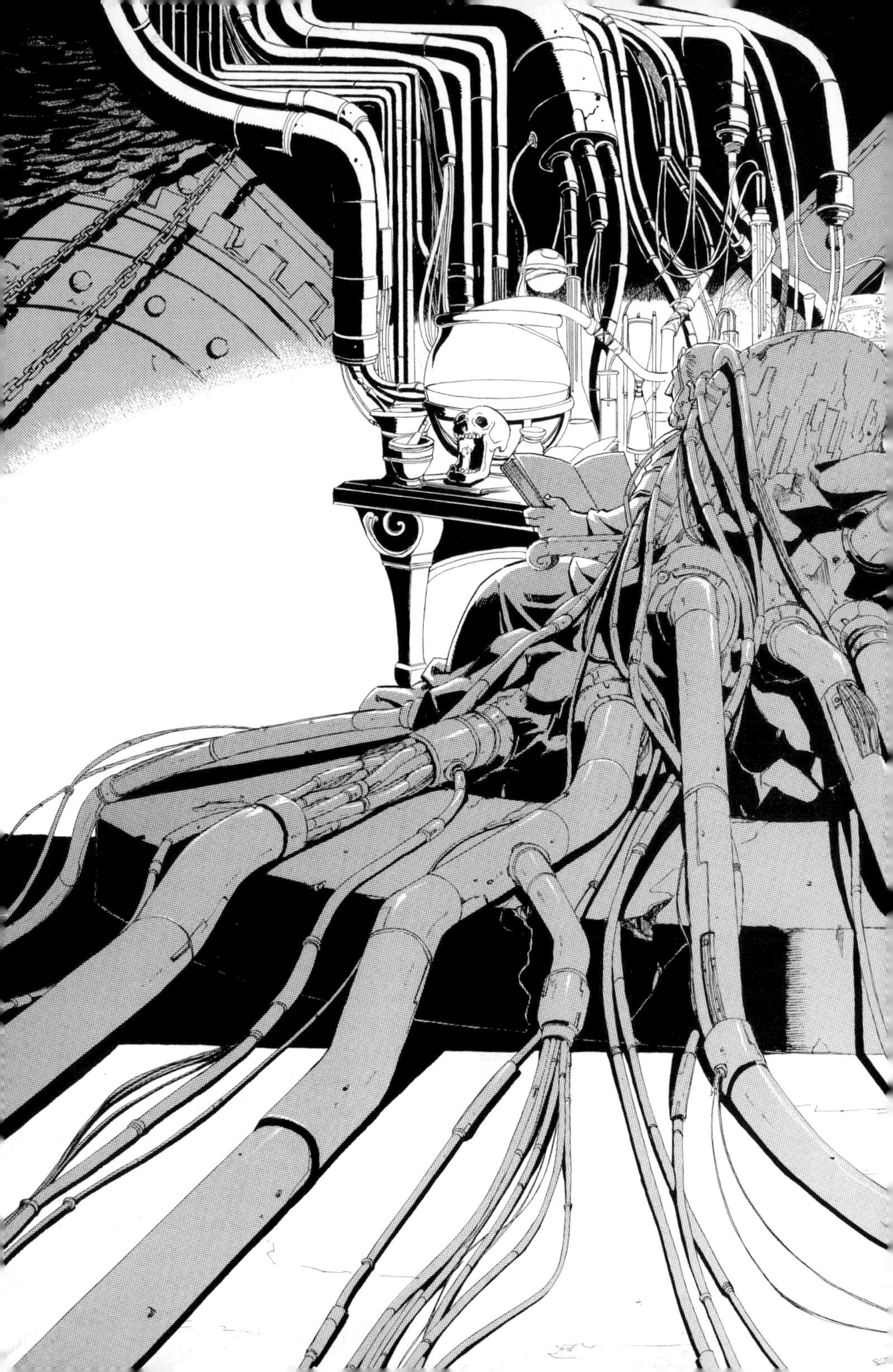

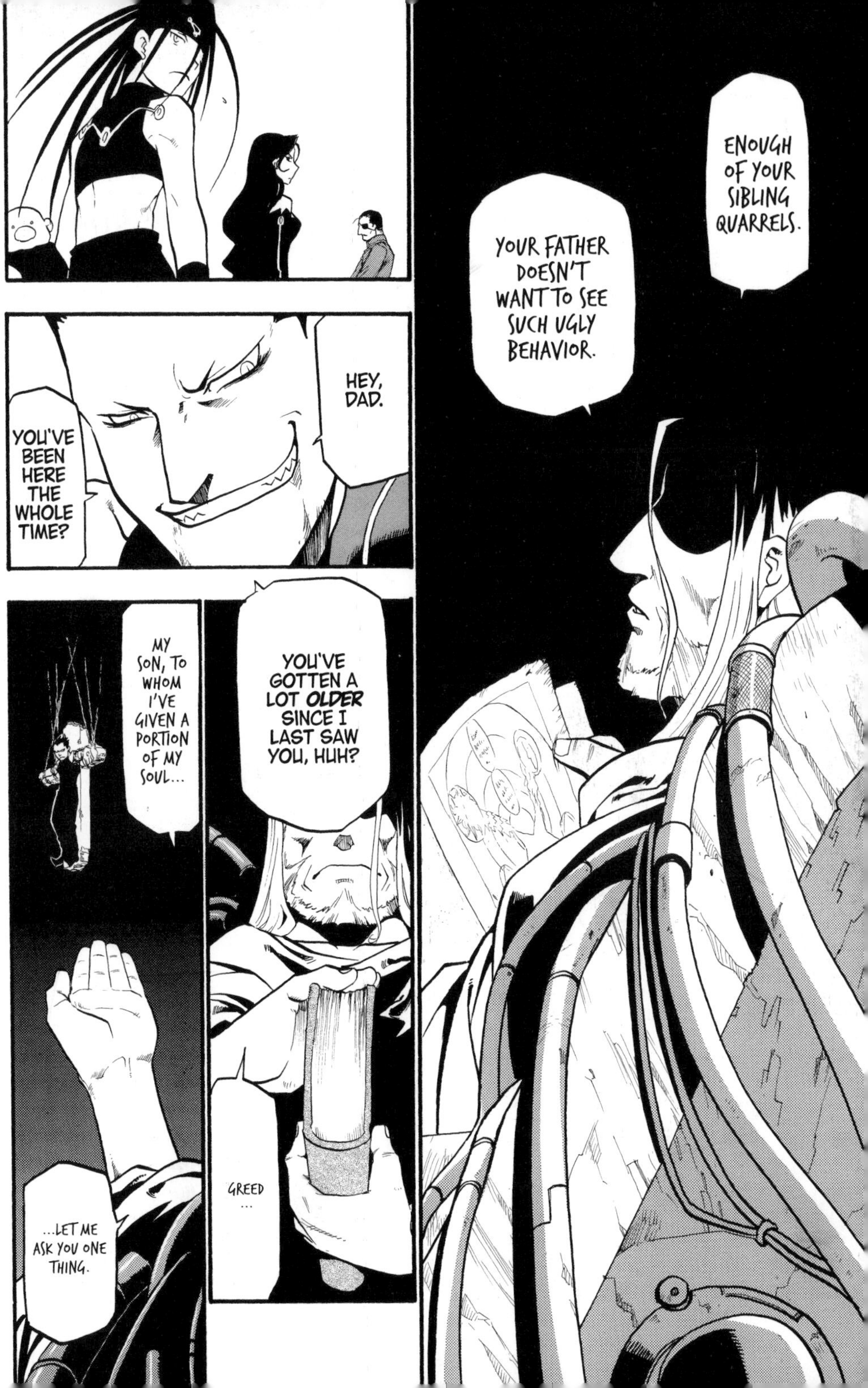
ENOUGH OF YOUR SIBLING QUARRELS.
YOUR FATHER DOESN'T WANT TO SEE SUCH UGLY BEHAVIOR.
HEY, DAD.
YOU'VE BEEN HERE THE WHOLE TIME?
YOU'VE GOTTEN A LOT *OLDER* SINCE I LAST SAW YOU, HUH?
GREED ...
MY SON, TO WHOM I'VE GIVEN A PORTION OF MY SOUL...
...LET ME ASK YOU ONE THING.

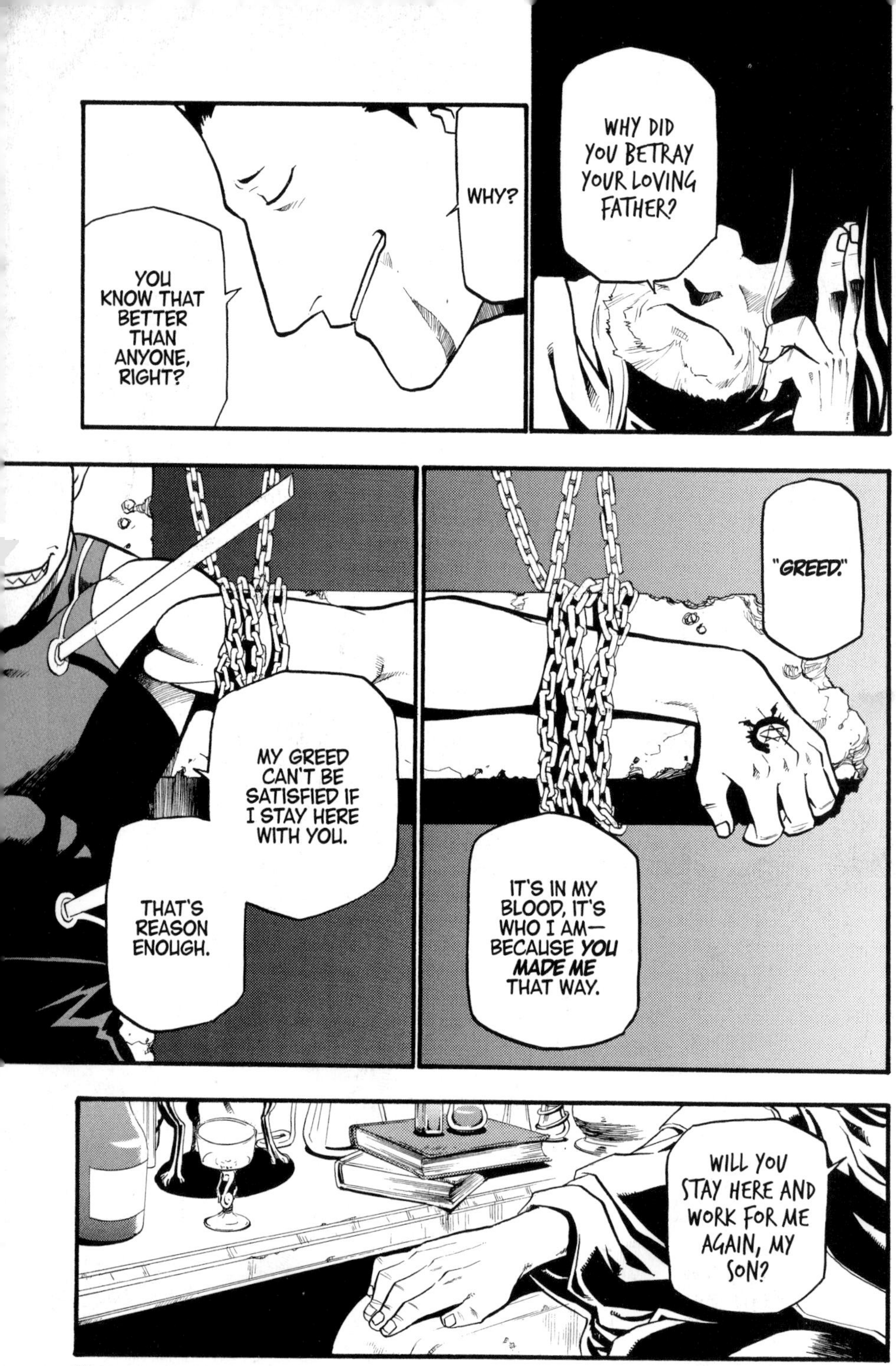
WHY DID YOU BETRAY YOUR LOVING FATHER?
WHY?
YOU KNOW THAT BETTER THAN ANYONE, RIGHT?
"GREED."
IT'S IN MY BLOOD, IT'S WHO I AM— BECAUSE *YOU MADE ME* THAT WAY.
MY GREED CAN'T BE SATISFIED IF I STAY HERE WITH YOU.
THAT'S REASON ENOUGH.
WILL YOU STAY HERE AND WORK FOR ME AGAIN, MY SON?

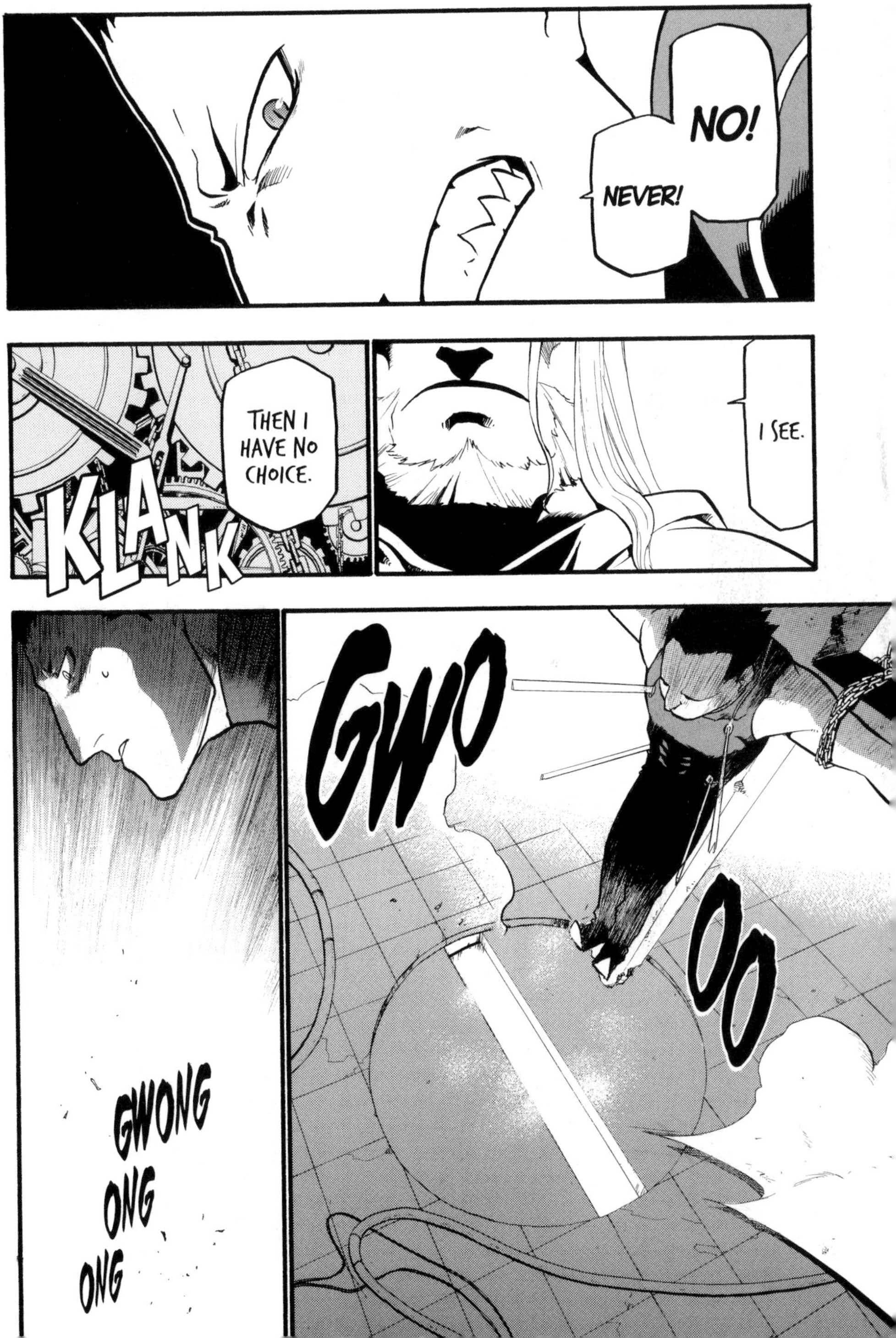
NO!
NEVER!
I SEE.
THEN I HAVE NO CHOICE.
KLANK
GWOOO
GWONG ONG ONG

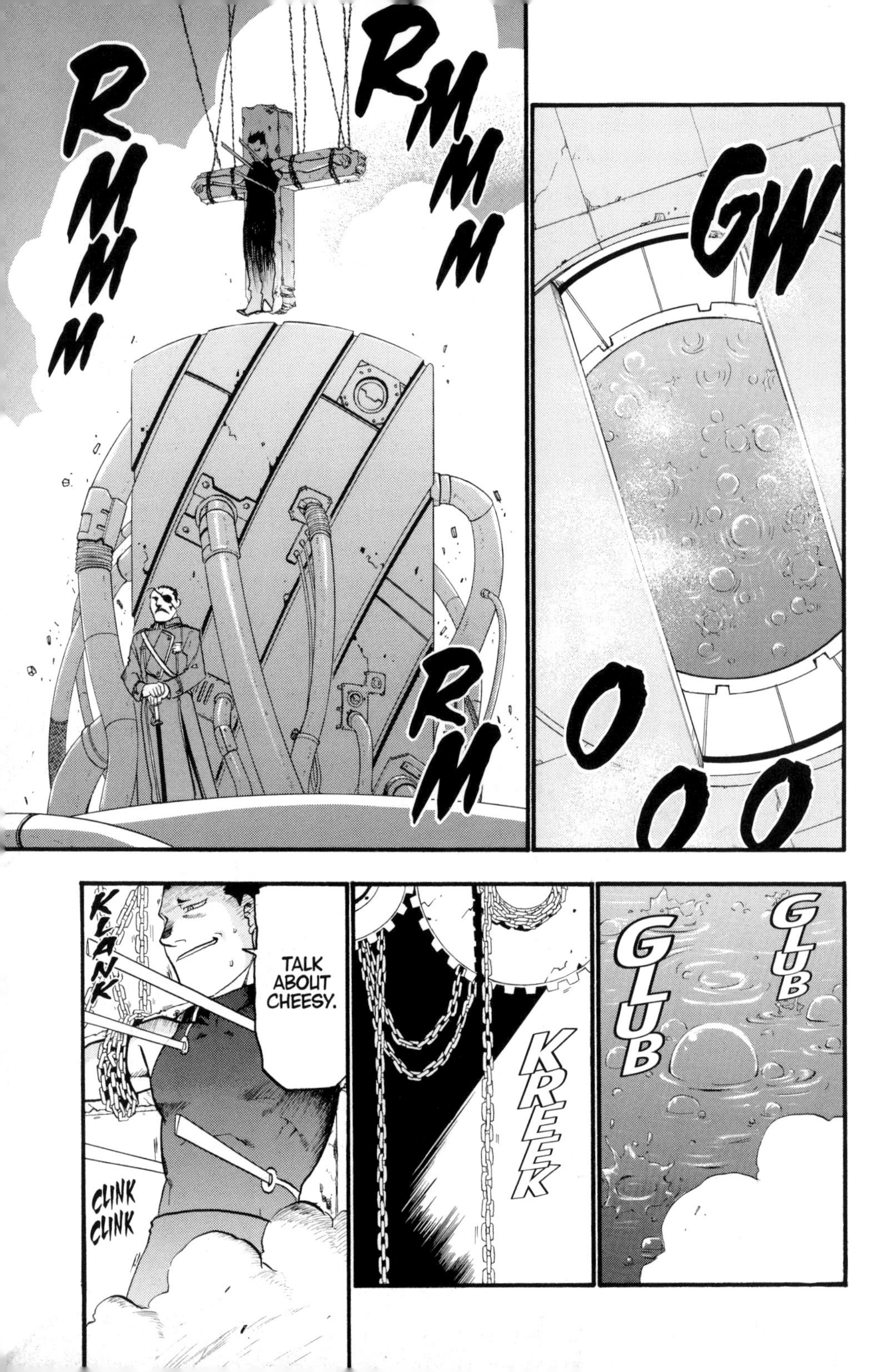
GWOOO
RMMMM
RMMMM
RM
GLUB
GLUB
KREEK
TALK ABOUT CHEESY.
KLANK
CLINK CLINK

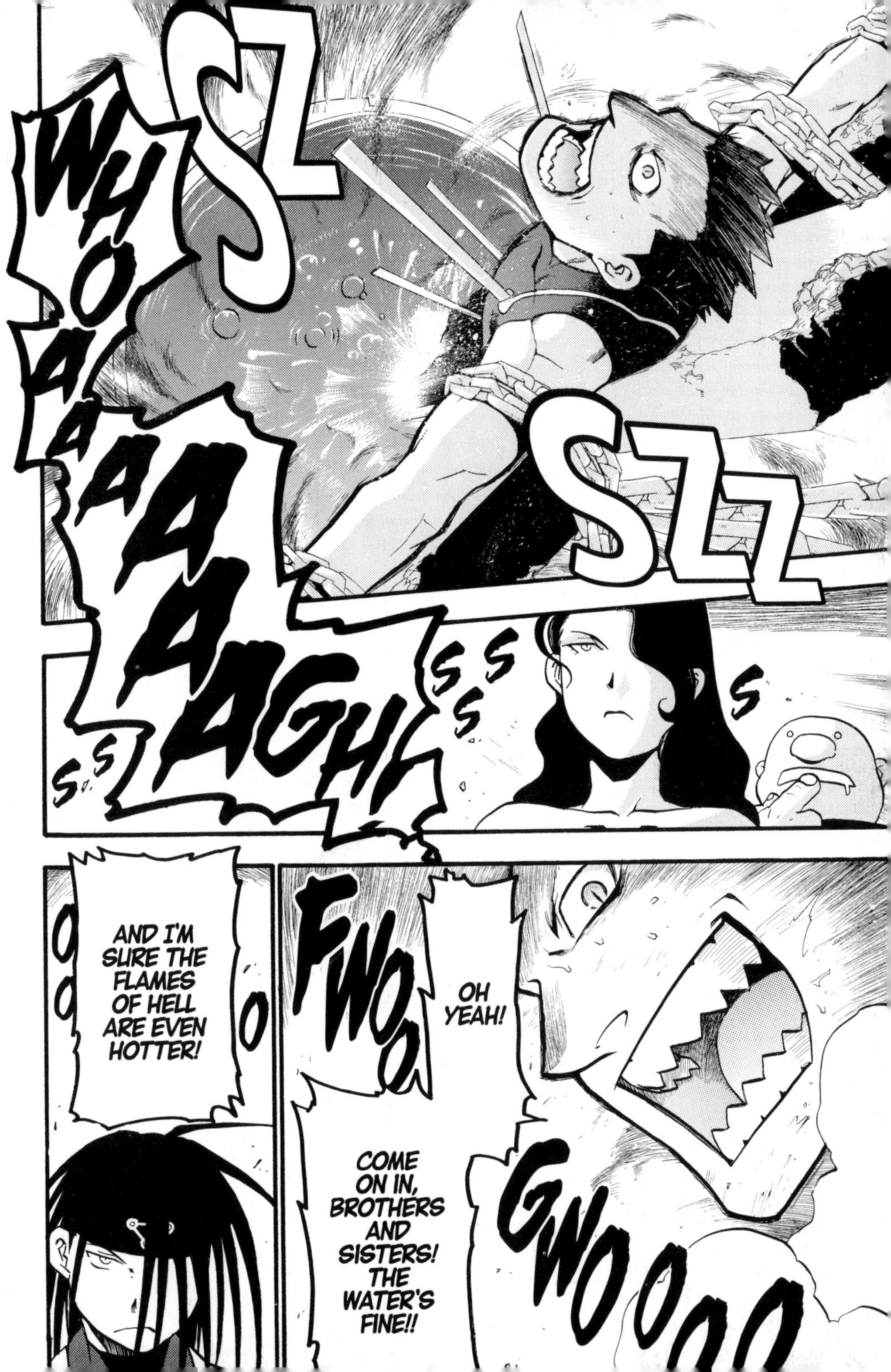
SZ
SZZ
WHOAAAAAAAAGH!
S S S S S
S S
OH YEAH!
FWOOO
COME ON IN, BROTHERS AND SISTERS! THE WATER'S FINE!!
GWOOOOO
AND I'M SURE THE FLAMES OF HELL ARE EVEN HOTTER!
OOOO

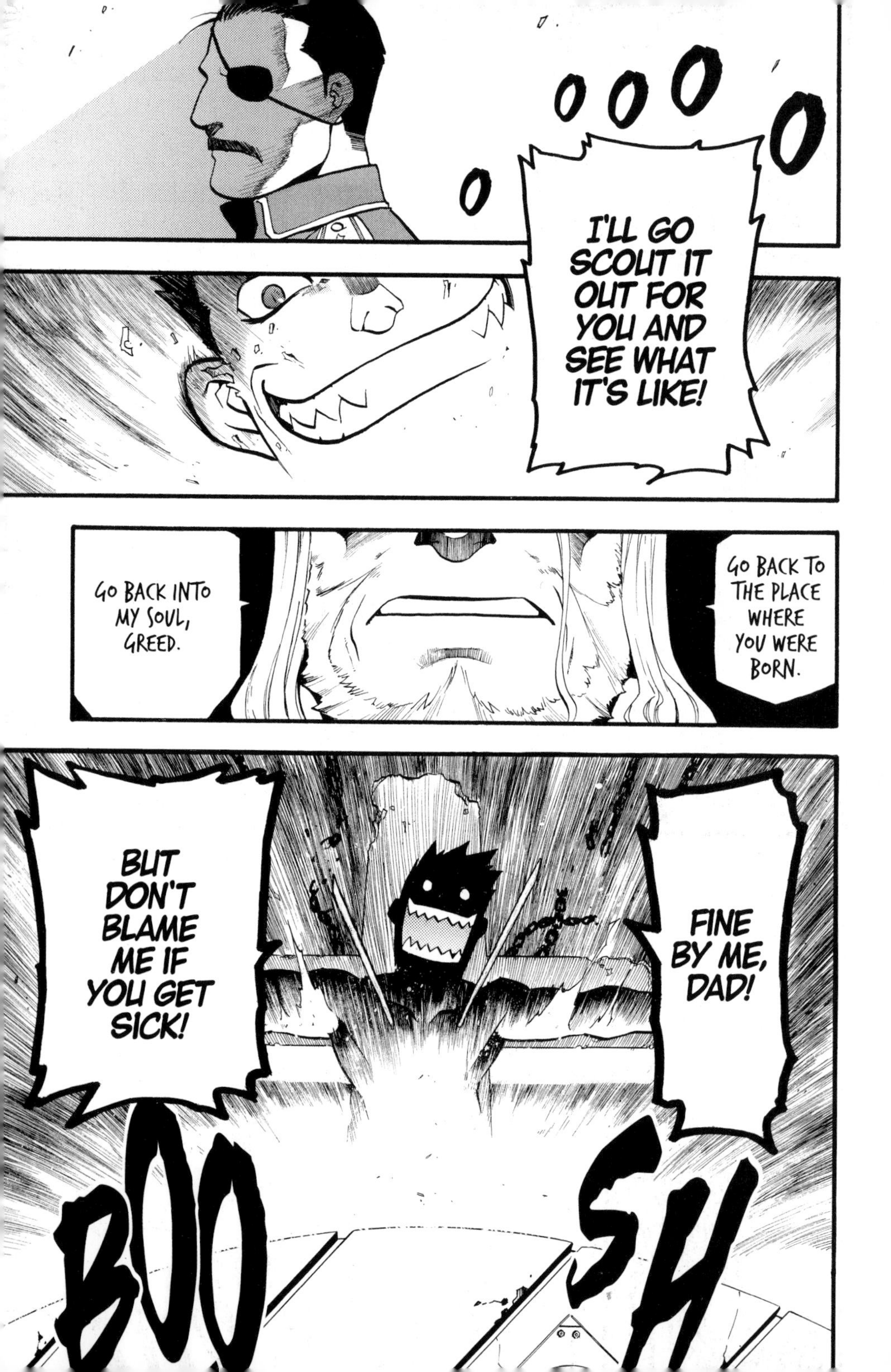

I'LL GO SCOUT IT OUT FOR YOU AND SEE WHAT IT'S LIKE!
OOOOO
GO BACK TO THE PLACE WHERE YOU WERE BORN.
GO BACK INTO MY SOUL, GREED.
FINE BY ME, DAD!
BUT DON'T BLAME ME IF YOU GET SICK!
BOOSH

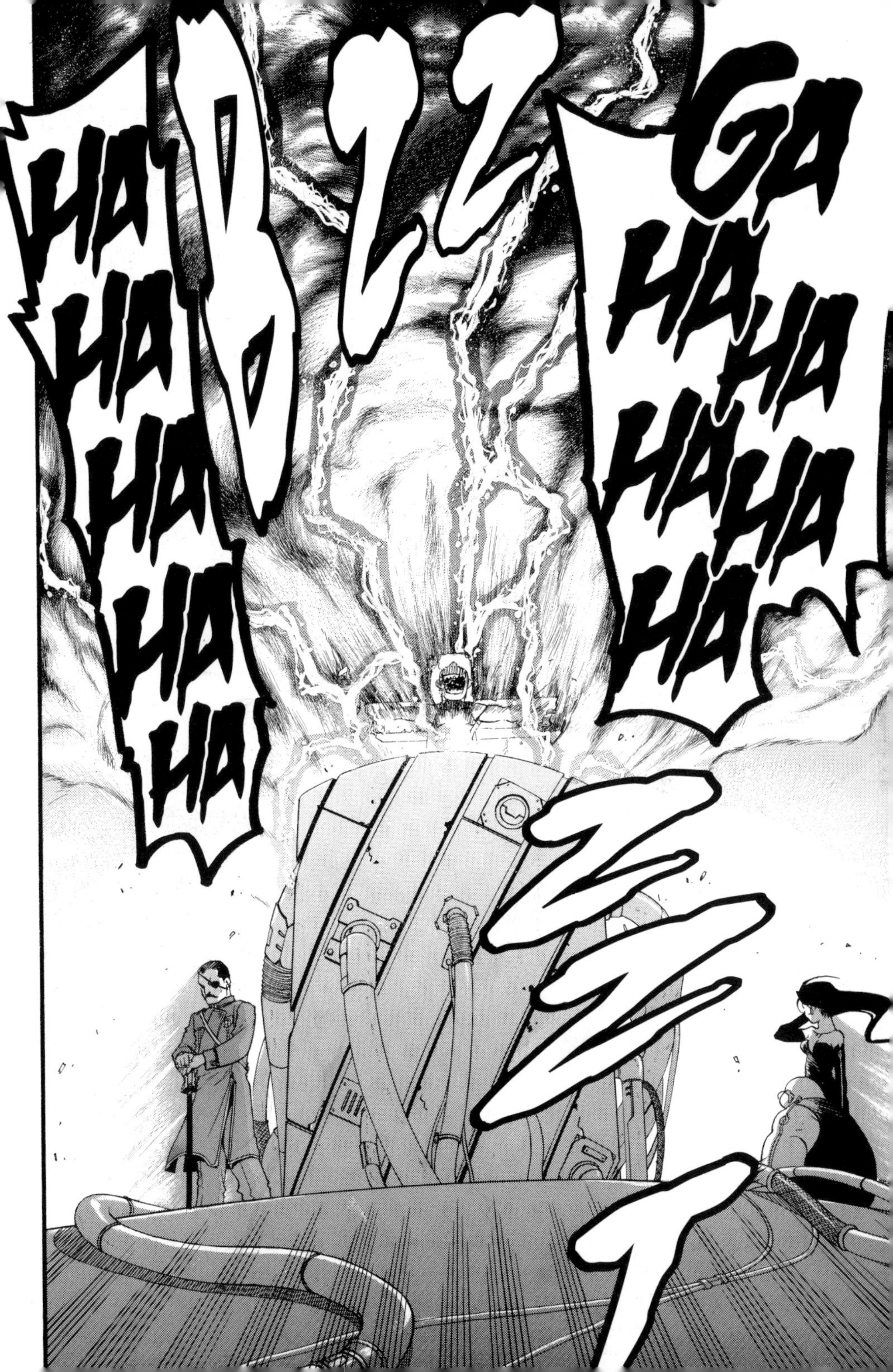
GA HA HA HA HA HA HA HA
BZZ
HA HA HA HA HA HA

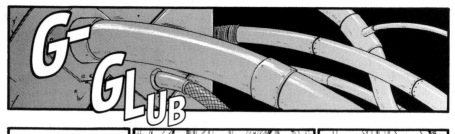

G-GLUB

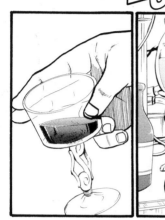

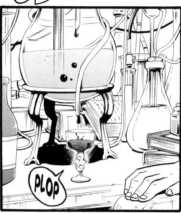

PLOP

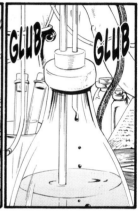

GLUB GLUB

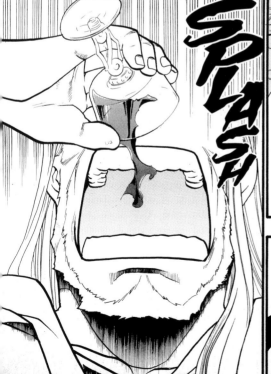

SPLASH

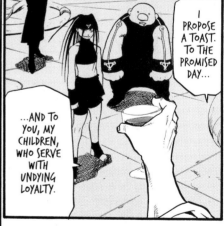

I PROPOSE A TOAST. TO THE PROMISED DAY...

...AND TO YOU, MY CHILDREN, WHO SERVE WITH UNDYING LOYALTY.

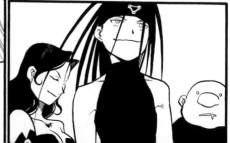

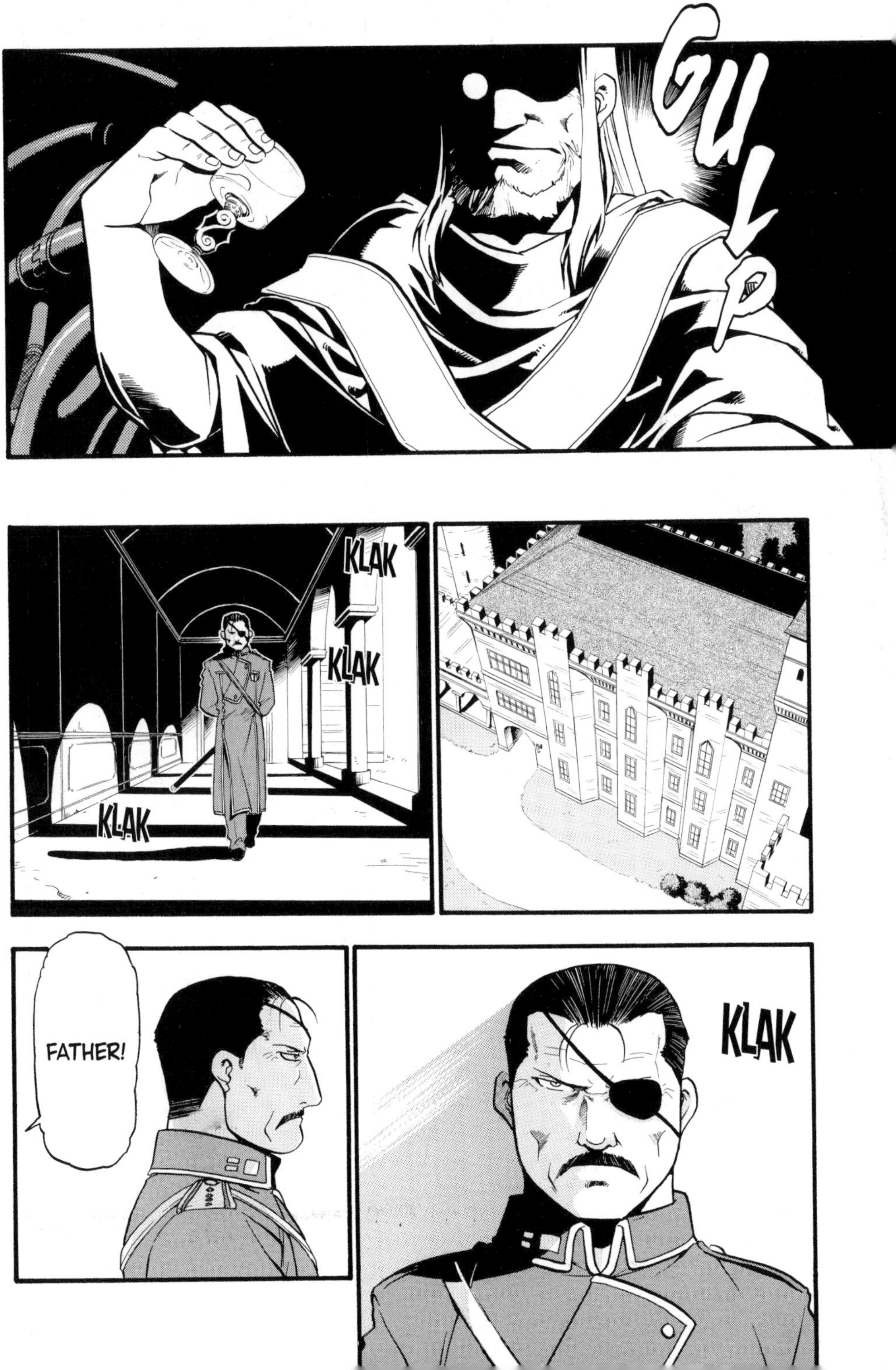
GULP
KLAK
KLAK
KLAK
KLAK
FATHER!

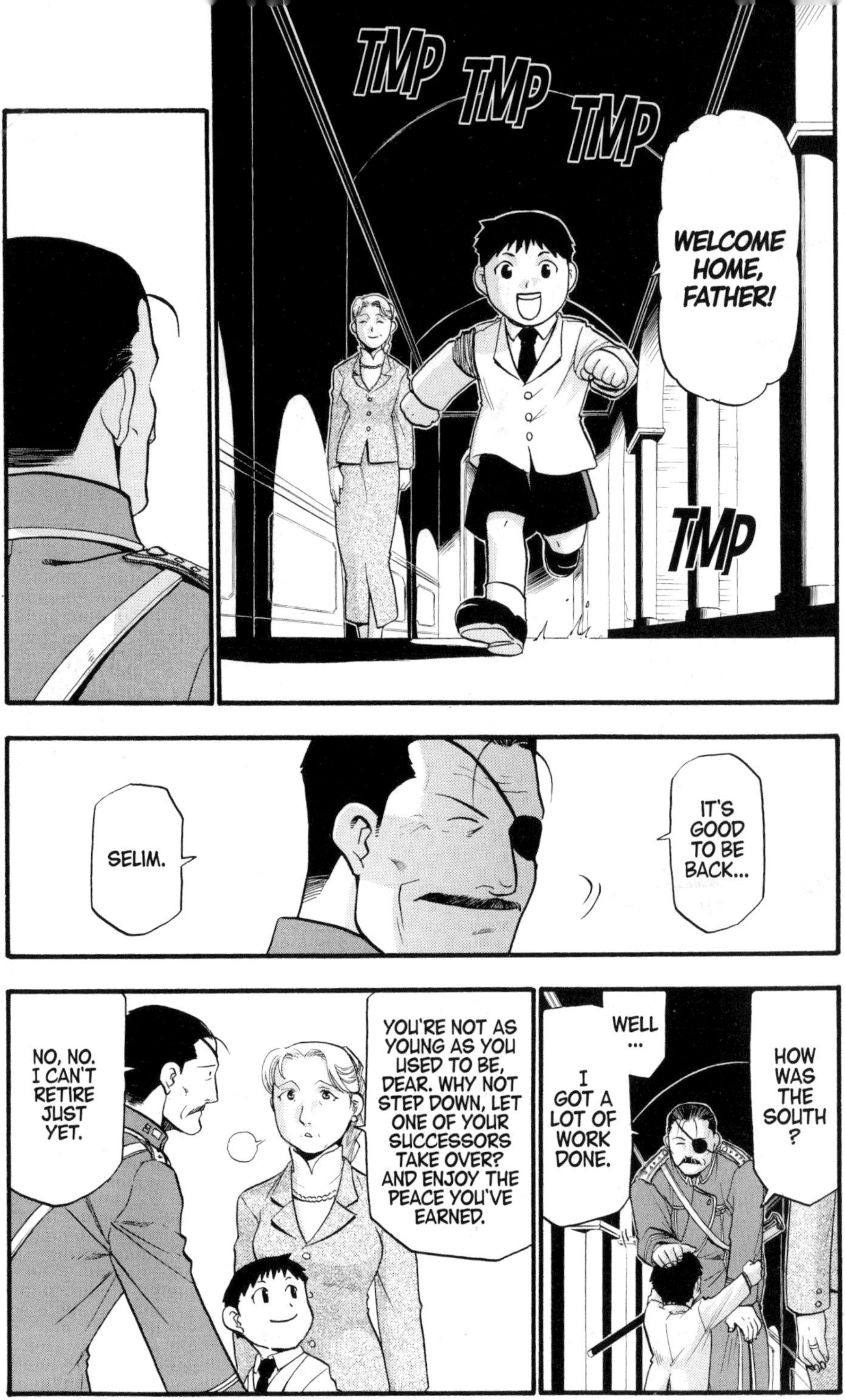
TMP TMP TMP
WELCOME HOME, FATHER!
TMP
IT'S GOOD TO BE BACK...
SELIM.
HOW WAS THE SOUTH?
WELL...
I GOT A LOT OF WORK DONE.
YOU'RE NOT AS YOUNG AS YOU USED TO BE, DEAR. WHY NOT STEP DOWN, LET ONE OF YOUR SUCCESSORS TAKE OVER? AND ENJOY THE PEACE YOU'VE EARNED.
NO, NO. I CAN'T RETIRE JUST YET.

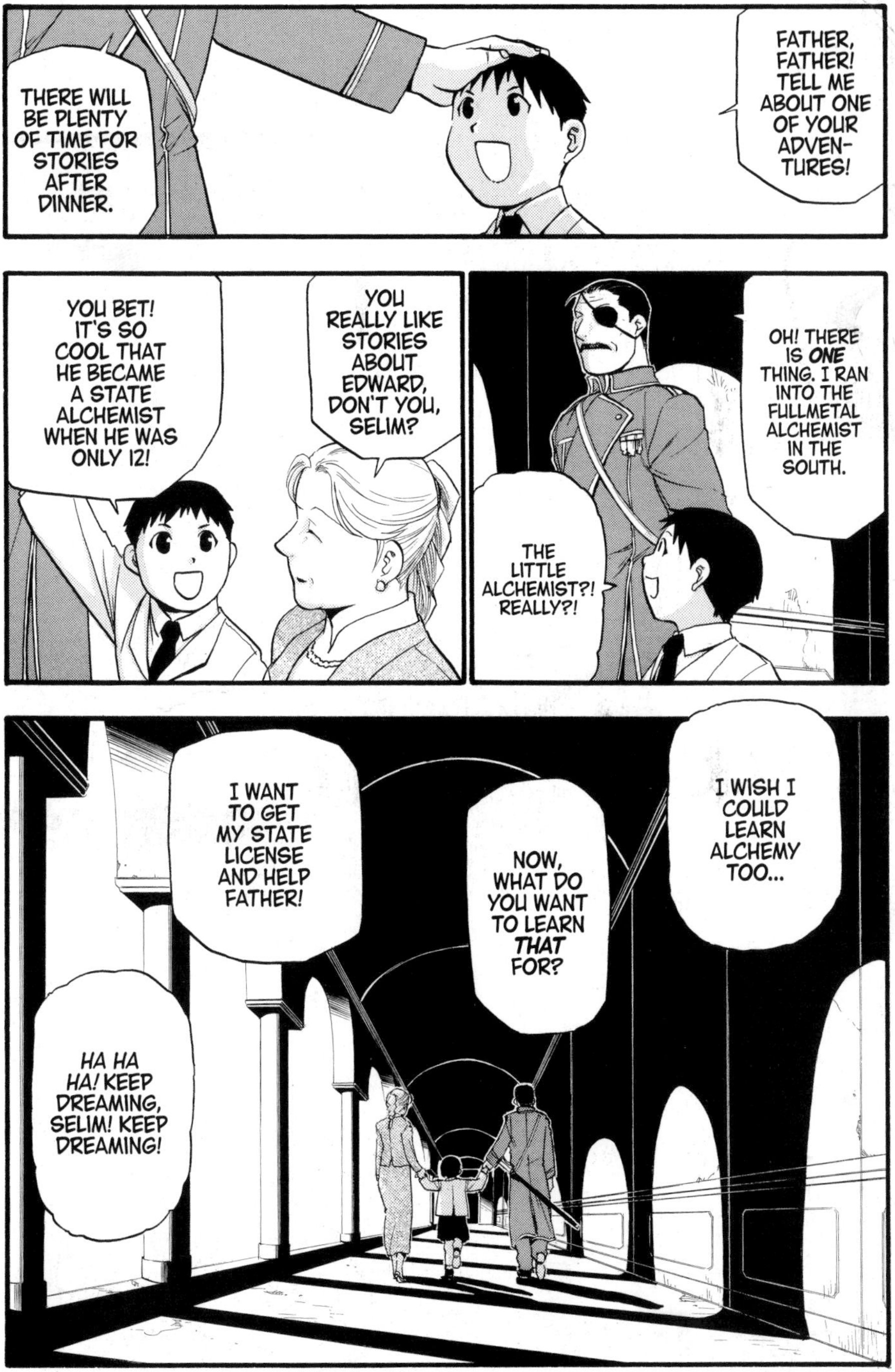
FATHER, FATHER! TELL ME ABOUT ONE OF YOUR ADVENTURES!
THERE WILL BE PLENTY OF TIME FOR STORIES AFTER DINNER.
OH! THERE IS *ONE* THING. I RAN INTO THE FULLMETAL ALCHEMIST IN THE SOUTH.
THE LITTLE ALCHEMIST?! REALLY?!
YOU REALLY LIKE STORIES ABOUT EDWARD, DON'T YOU, SELIM?
YOU BET! IT'S SO COOL THAT HE BECAME A STATE ALCHEMIST WHEN HE WAS ONLY 12!
I WISH I COULD LEARN ALCHEMY TOO...
NOW, WHAT DO YOU WANT TO LEARN *THAT* FOR?
I WANT TO GET MY STATE LICENSE AND HELP FATHER!
HA HA HA! KEEP DREAMING, SELIM! KEEP DREAMING!

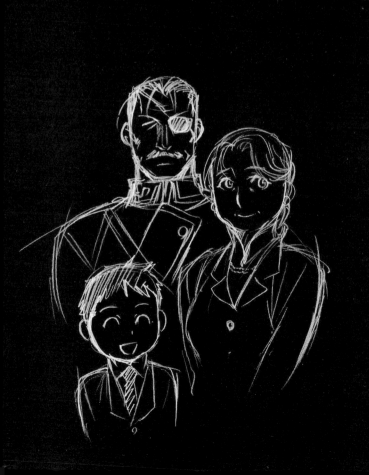

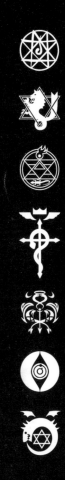

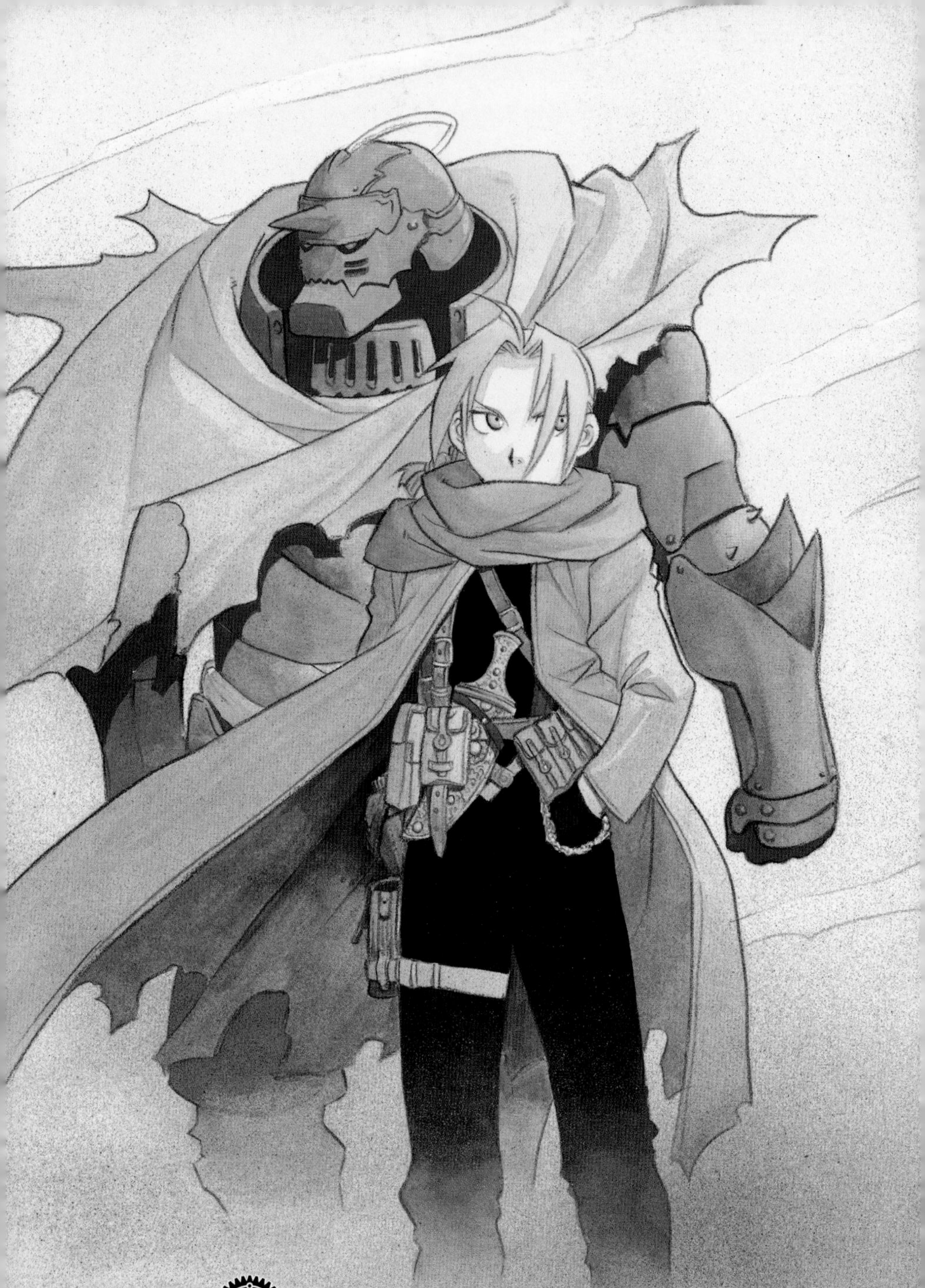

CHAPTER 32 EMISSARY FROM THE EAST

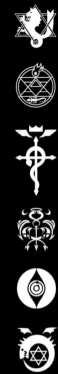

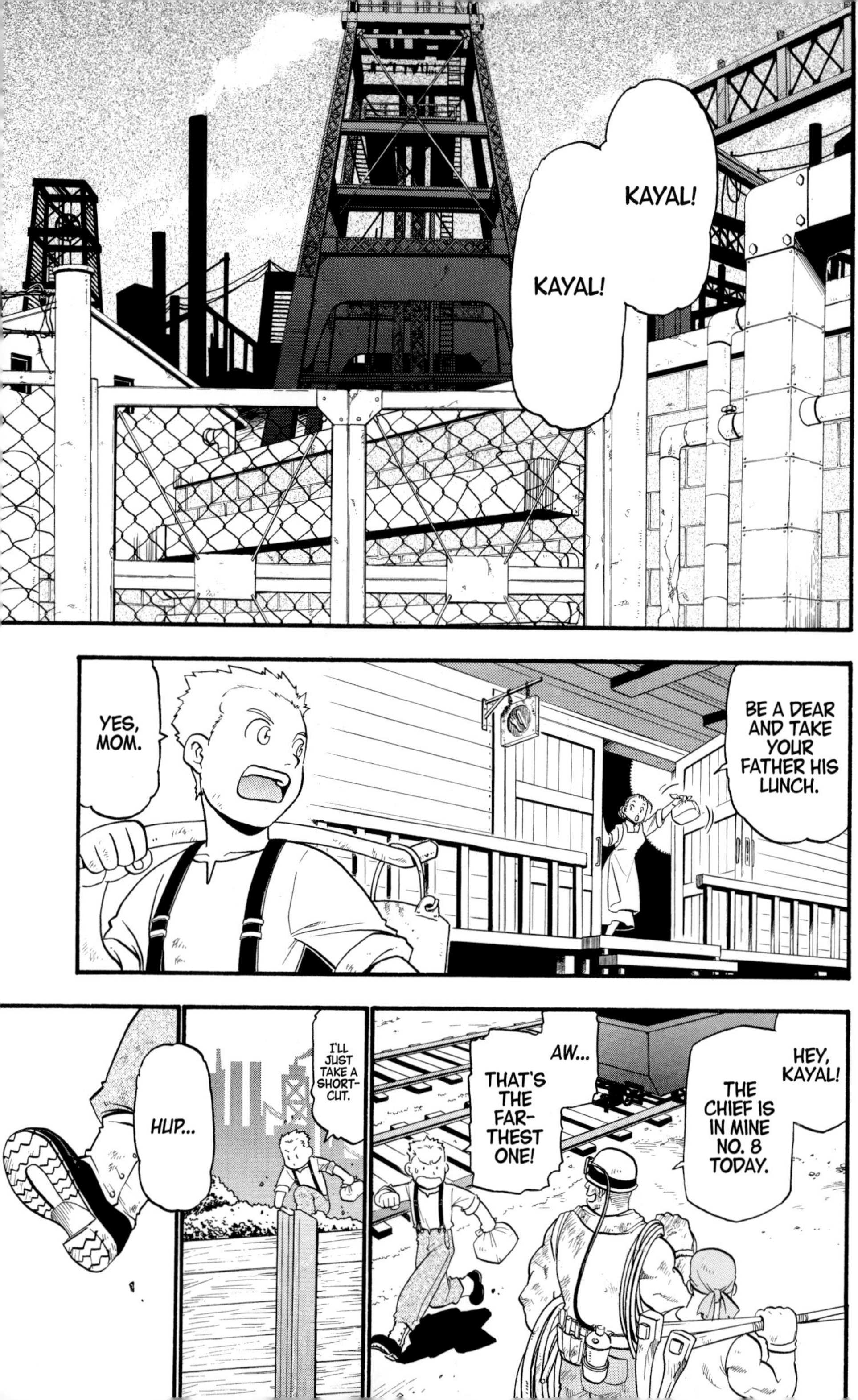
KAYAL!
KAYAL!
BE A DEAR AND TAKE YOUR FATHER HIS LUNCH.
YES, MOM.
HEY, KAYAL!
THE CHIEF IS IN MINE NO. 8 TODAY.
AW...
THAT'S THE FAR-THEST ONE!
I'LL JUST TAKE A SHORT-CUT.
HUP...

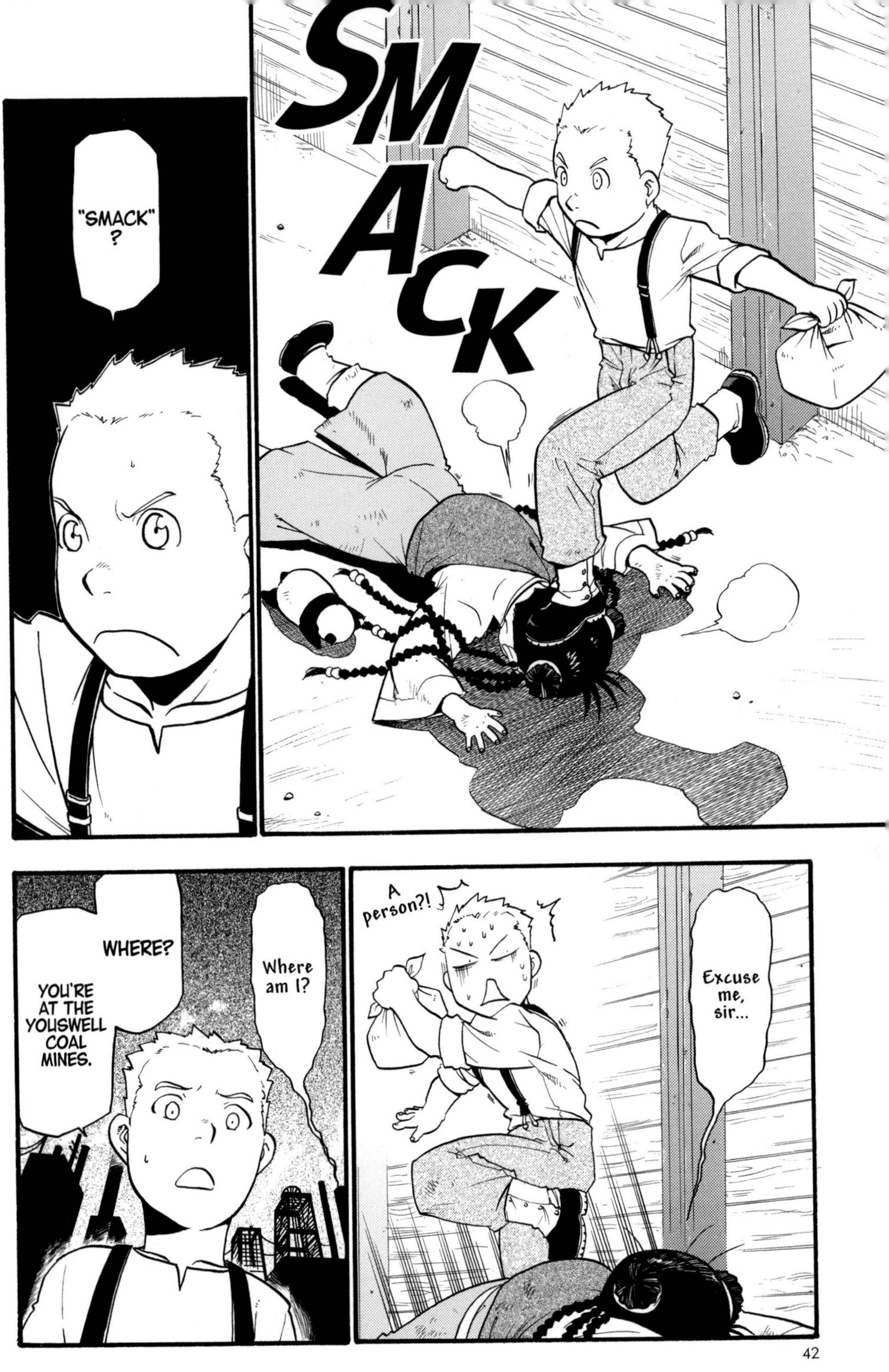
SMACK
"SMACK"?
Excuse me, sir...
A person?!
Where am I?
WHERE?
YOU'RE AT THE YOUSWELL COAL MINES.

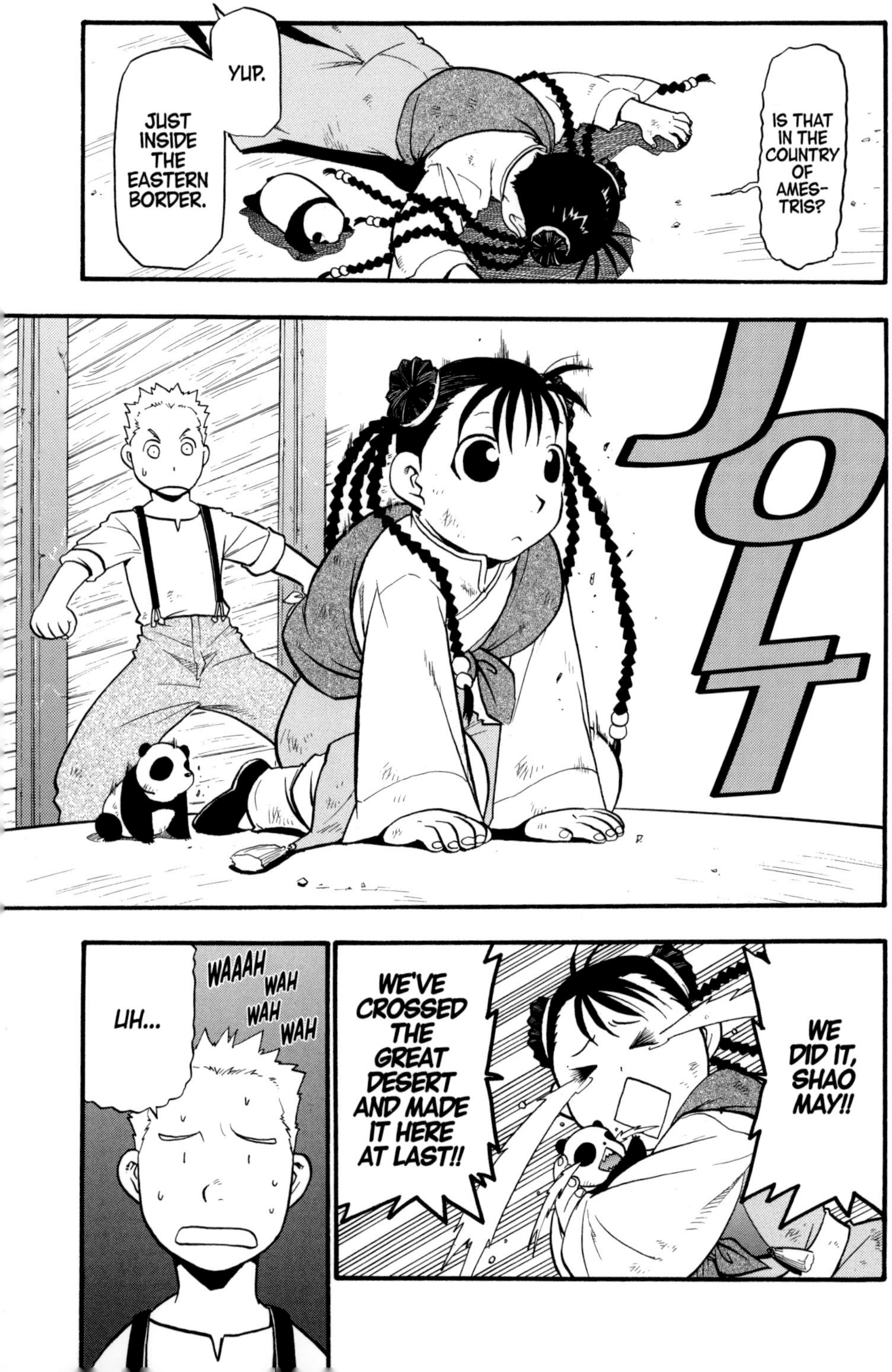
IS THAT IN THE COUNTRY OF AMES-TRIS?
YUP.
JUST INSIDE THE EASTERN BORDER.
JOLT
WE DID IT, SHAO MAY!!
WE'VE CROSSED THE GREAT DESERT AND MADE IT HERE AT LAST!!
WAAAH WAH WAH WAH
UH...

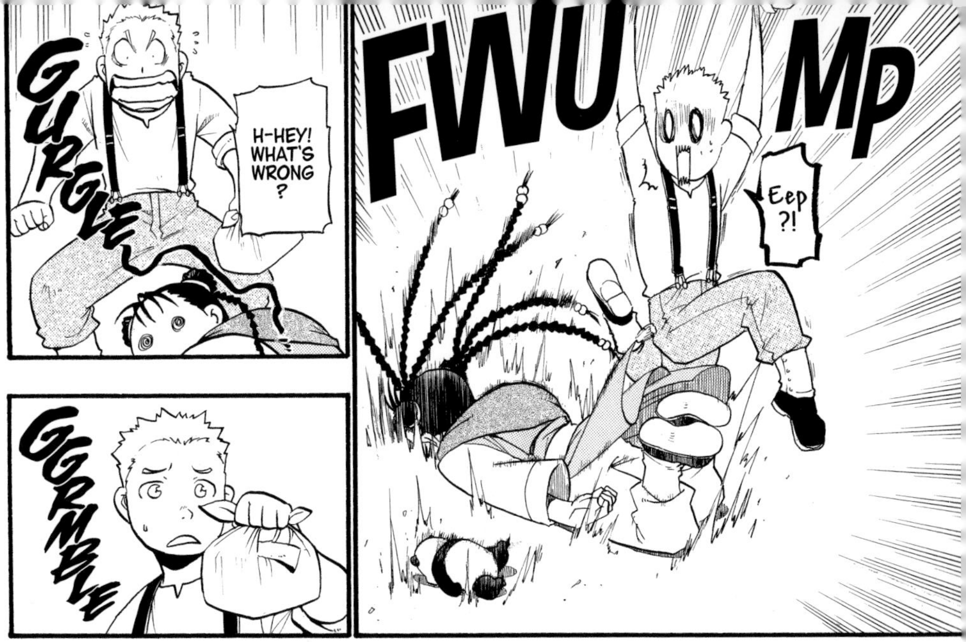
FWUMP
Eep?!
GURGLE
H-HEY! WHAT'S WRONG?
GGRMBLE

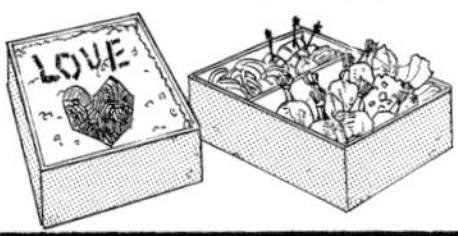
LOVE
Chicken and Seaweed Lunch Box (extra large)

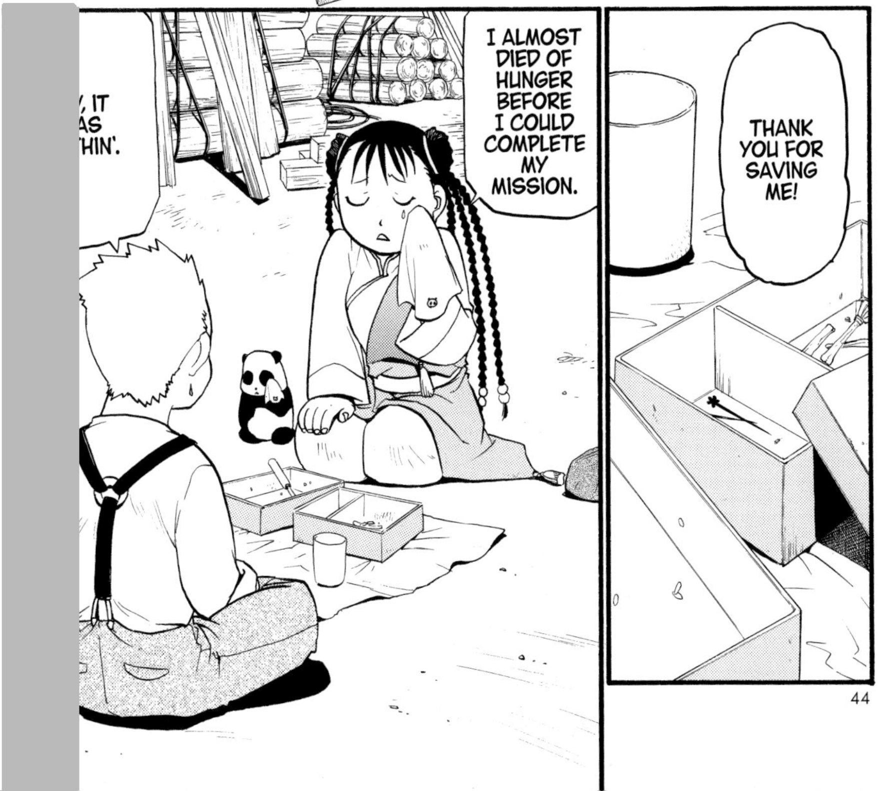
THANK YOU FOR SAVING ME!
I ALMOST DIED OF HUNGER BEFORE I COULD COMPLETE MY MISSION.
, IT AS THIN'.

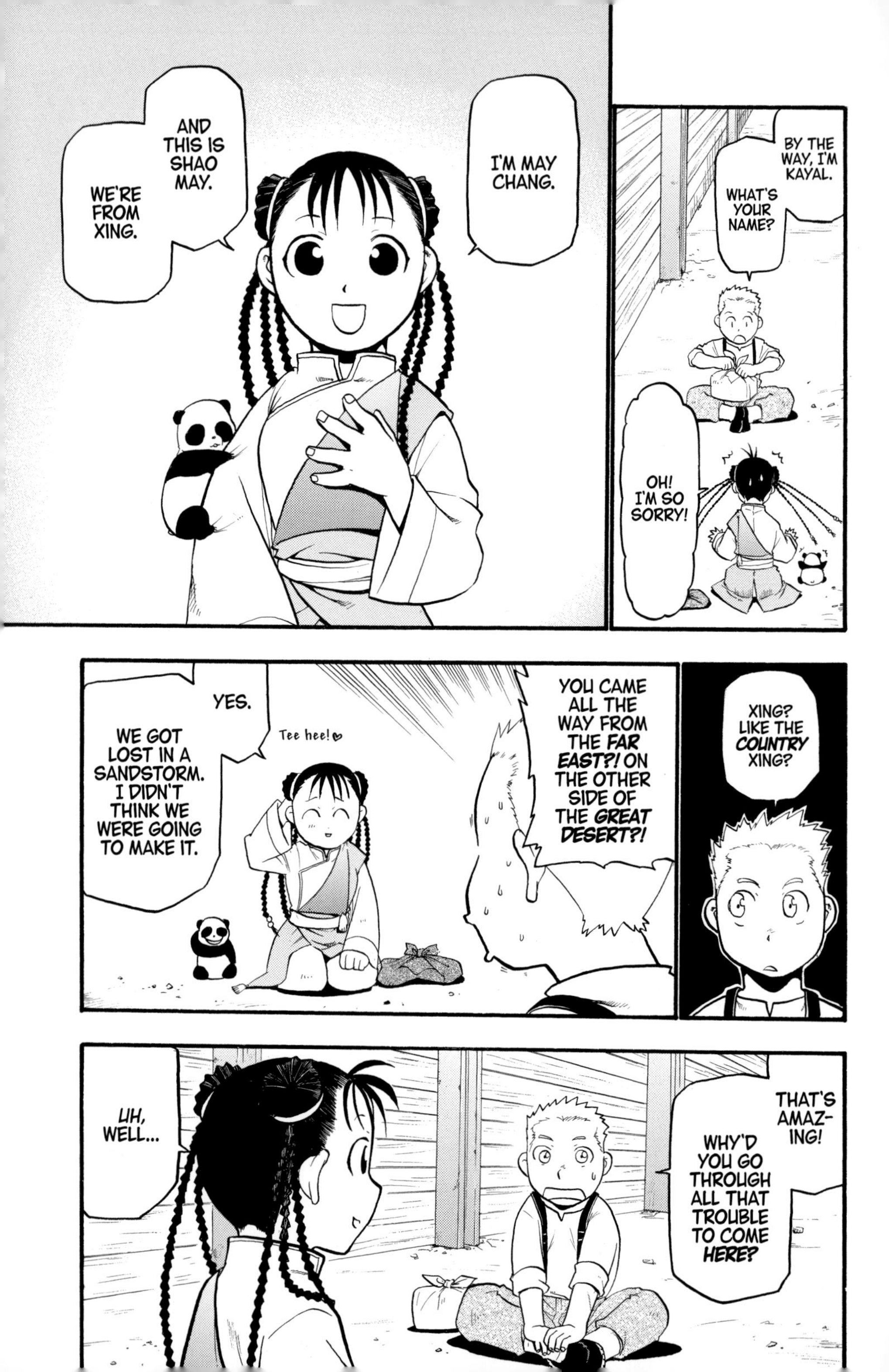
BY THE WAY, I'M KAYAL.
WHAT'S YOUR NAME?
OH! I'M SO SORRY!
I'M MAY CHANG.
AND THIS IS SHAO MAY.
WE'RE FROM XING.
XING? LIKE THE COUNTRY XING?
YOU CAME ALL THE WAY FROM THE FAR EAST?! ON THE OTHER SIDE OF THE GREAT DESERT?!
YES.
WE GOT LOST IN A SANDSTORM. I DIDN'T THINK WE WERE GOING TO MAKE IT.
Tee hee!♡
THAT'S AMAZ-ING!
WHY'D YOU GO THROUGH ALL THAT TROUBLE TO COME HERE?
UH, WELL...

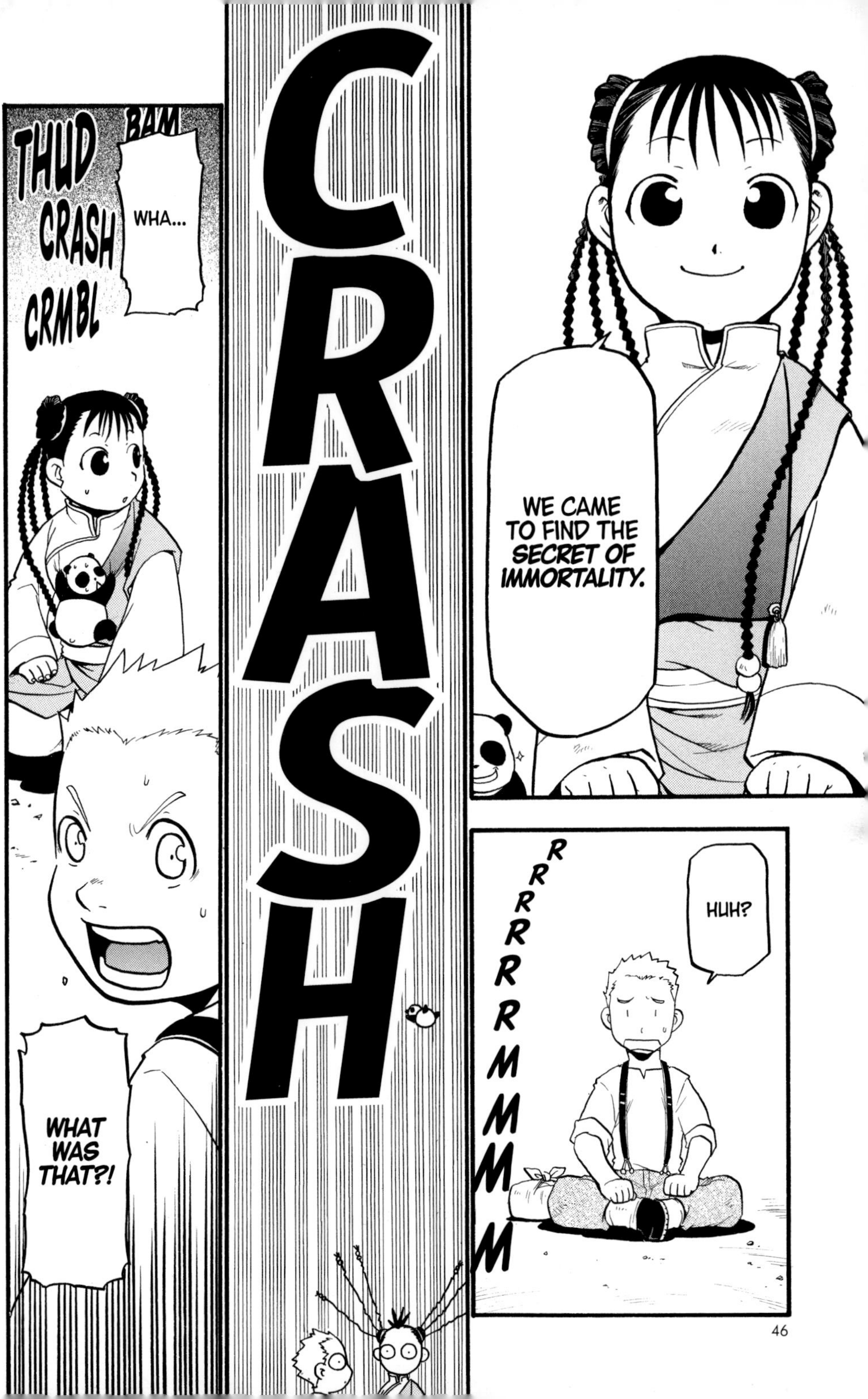

WE CAME TO FIND THE SECRET OF IMMORTALITY.
RRRRRRRMMMMMM
HUH?
CRASH
THUD
BAM
CRASH
CRMBL
WHA...
WHAT WAS THAT?!

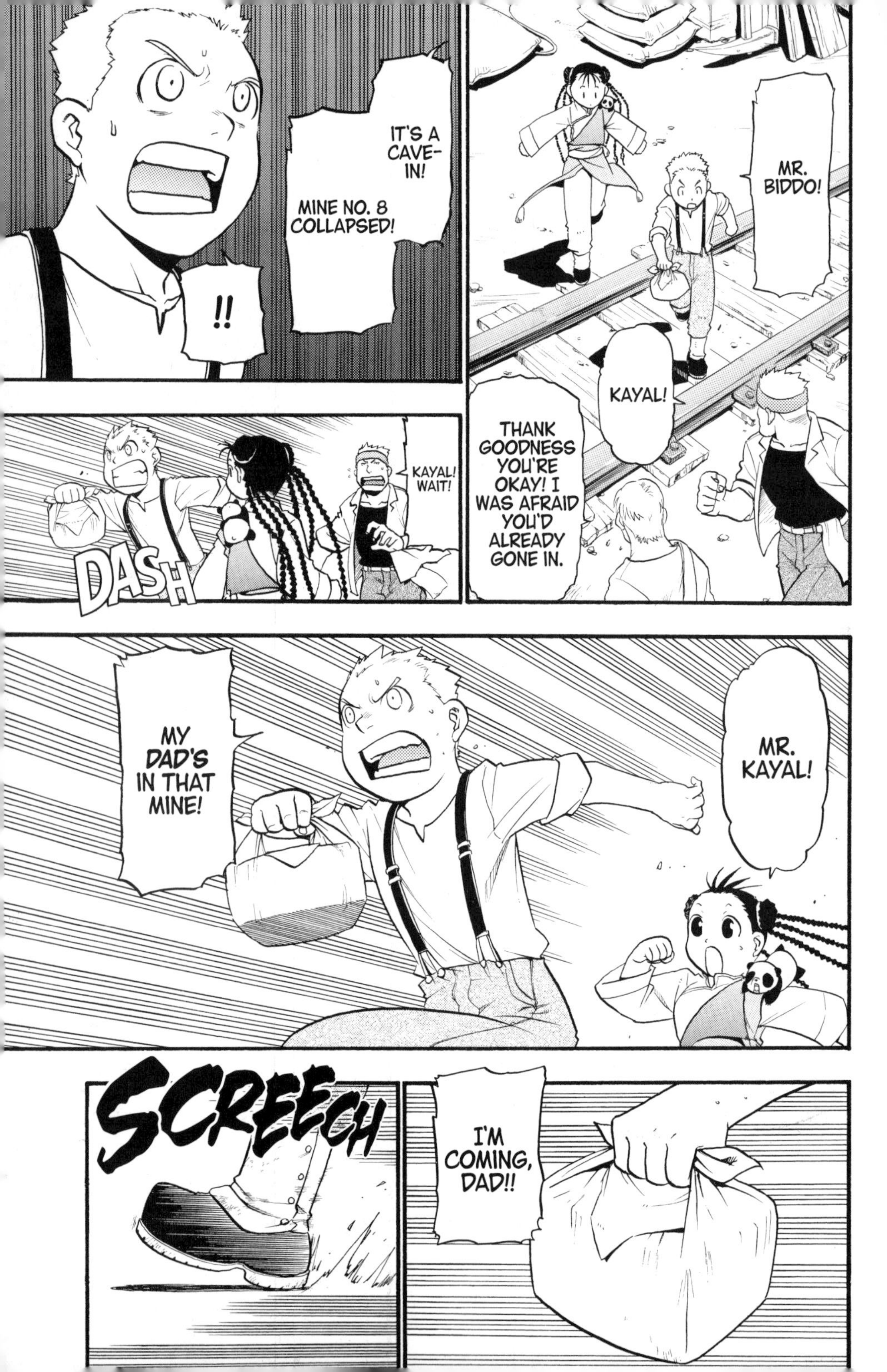
MR. BIDDO!
KAYAL!
THANK GOODNESS YOU'RE OKAY! I WAS AFRAID YOU'D ALREADY GONE IN.
IT'S A CAVE-IN!
MINE NO. 8 COLLAPSED!
!!
KAYAL! WAIT!
DASH
MR. KAYAL!
MY DAD'S IN THAT MINE!
I'M COMING, DAD!!
SCREECH

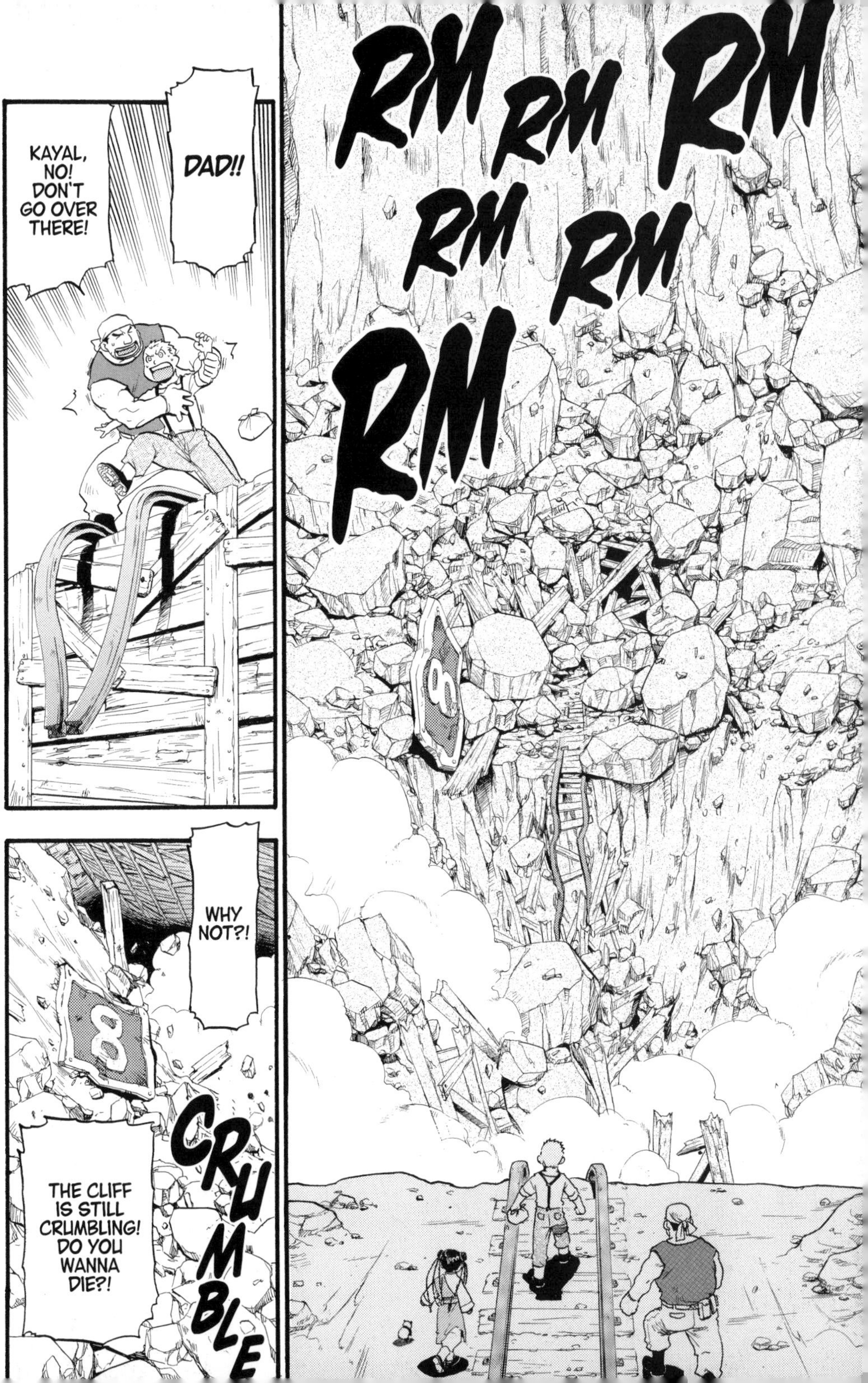
RM RM RM
RM RM
RM
DAD!!
KAYAL, NO! DON'T GO OVER THERE!
WHY NOT?!
CRUMBLE
THE CLIFF IS STILL CRUMBLING! DO YOU WANNA DIE?!

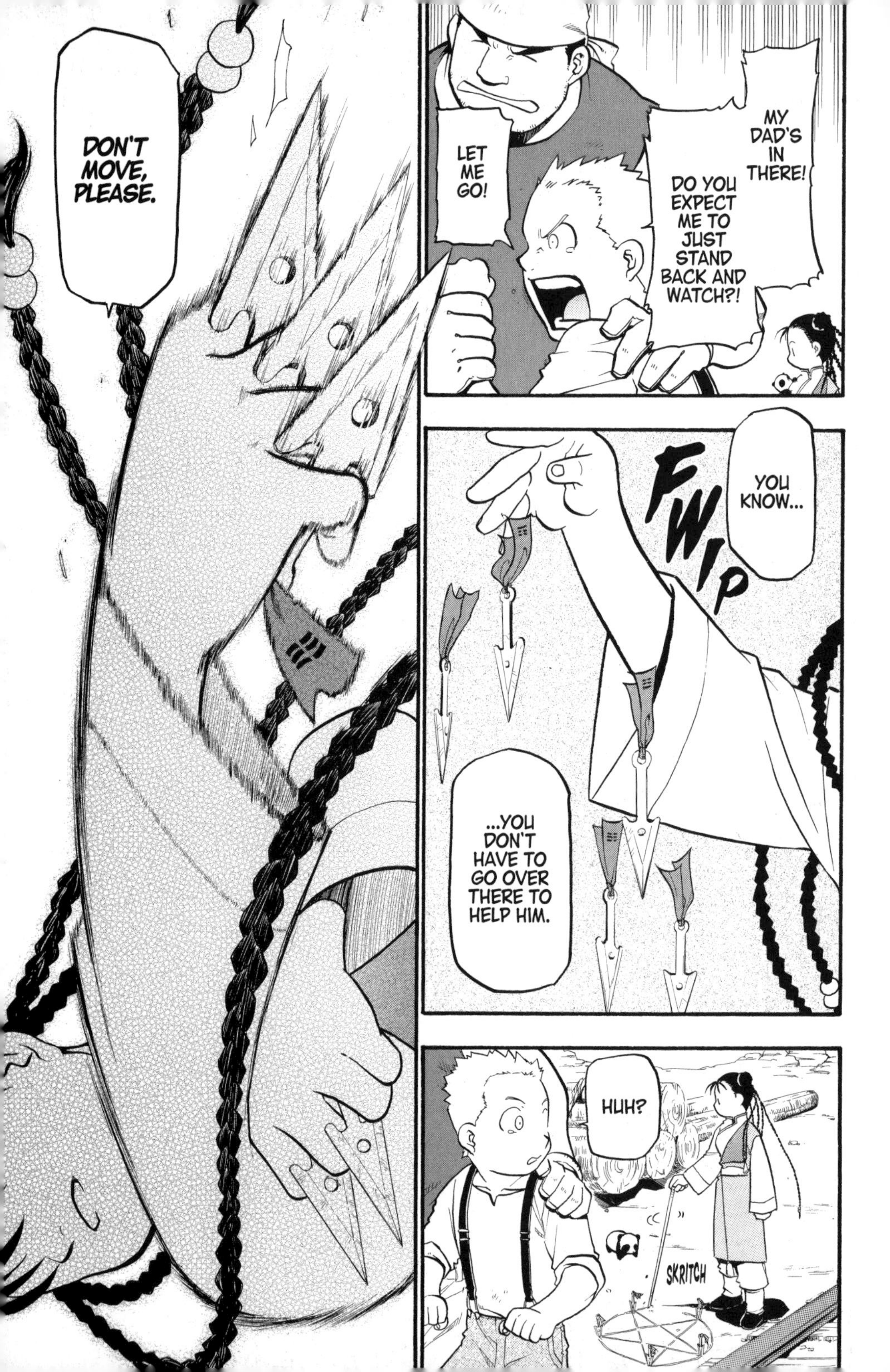
MY DAD'S IN THERE!
DO YOU EXPECT ME TO JUST STAND BACK AND WATCH?!
LET ME GO!
YOU KNOW...
FWIP
...YOU DON'T HAVE TO GO OVER THERE TO HELP HIM.
HUH?
SKRITCH
DON'T MOVE, PLEASE.

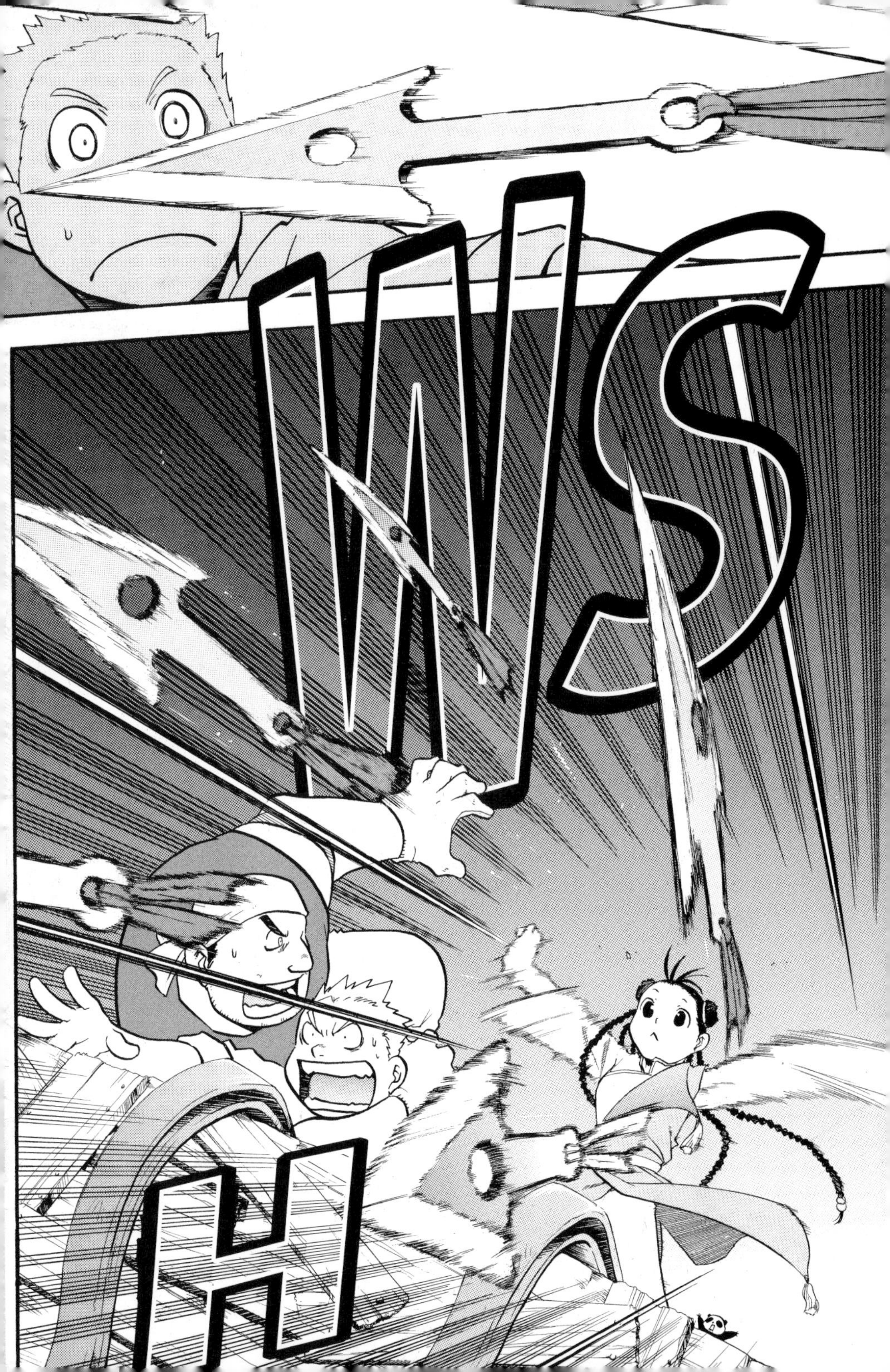
WS
H

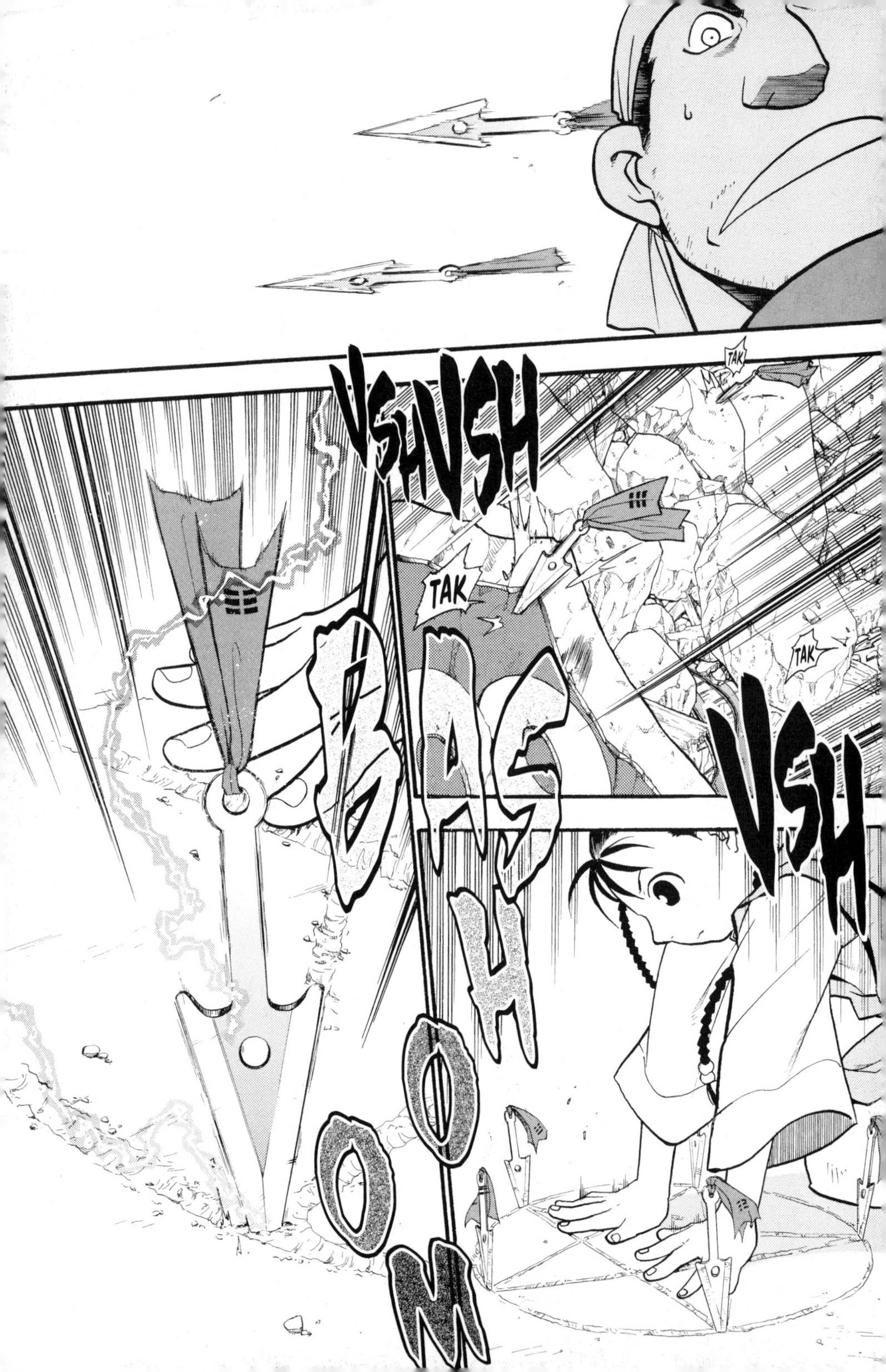
TAK
VSHVSH
TAK
TAK
BASHOOOM
VSH

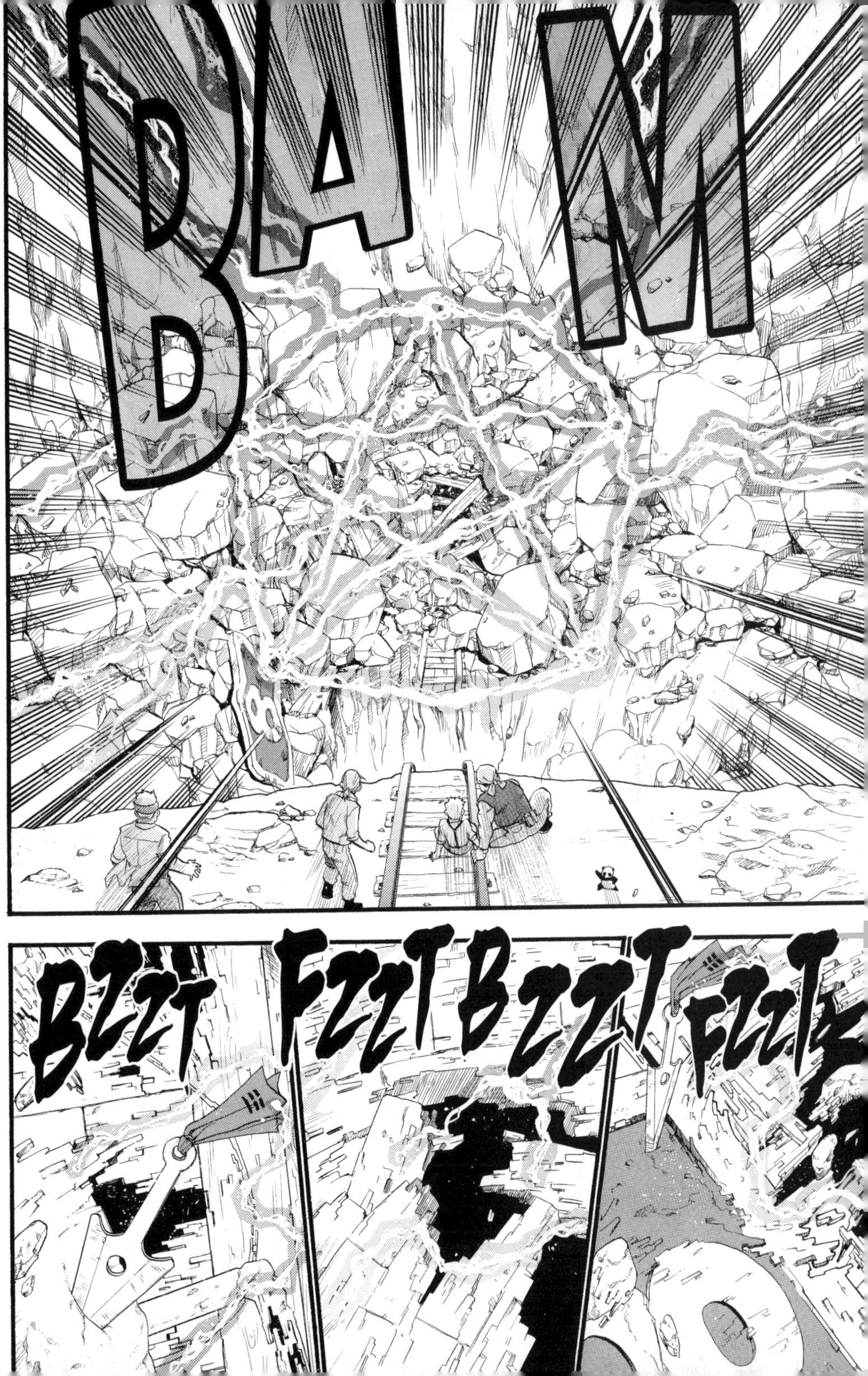
BAM
FZZT
FZZT BZZT
BZZT

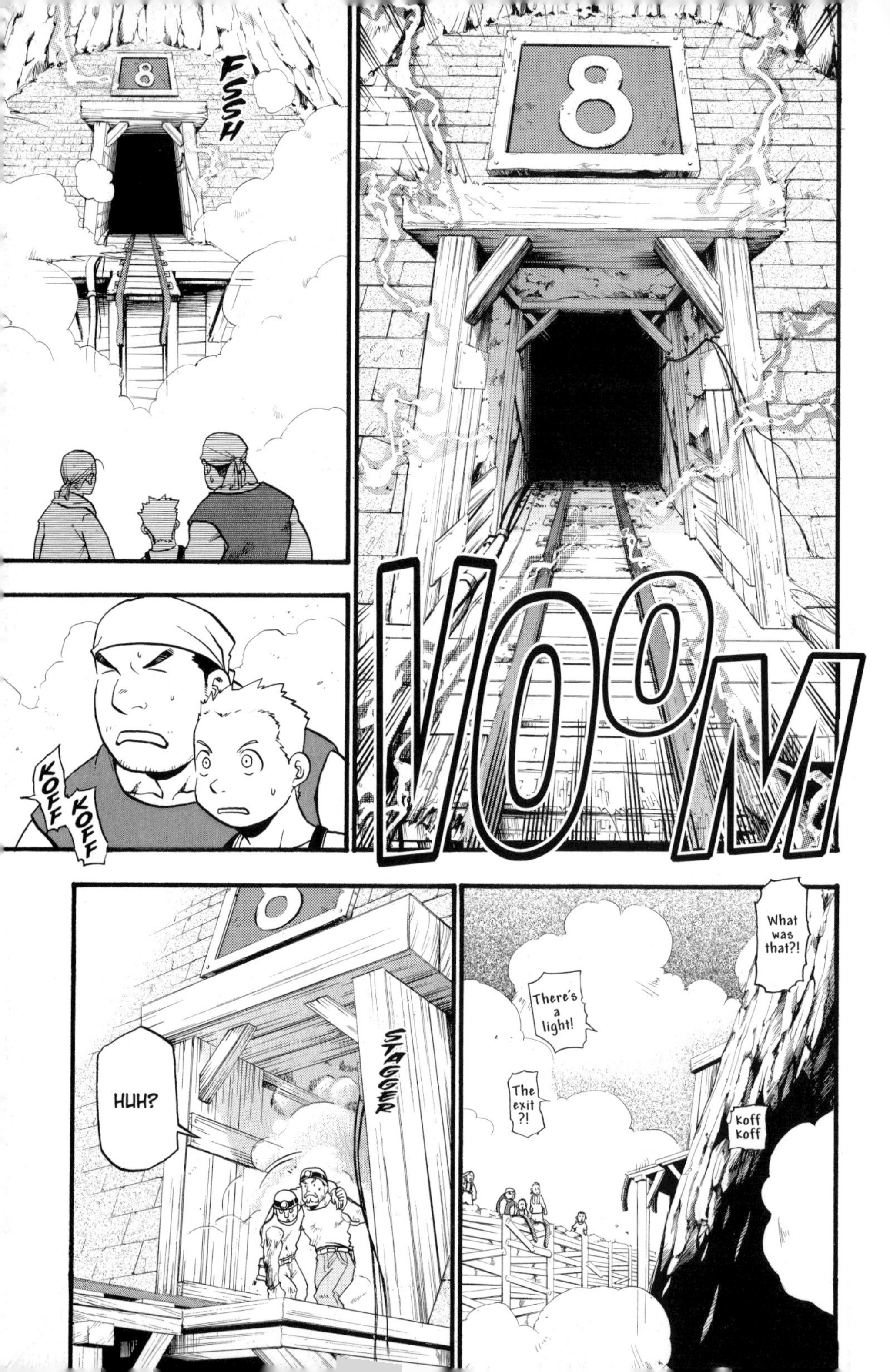
VOOM
FSSH
KOFF KOFF
What was that?!
There's a light!
The exit?!
Koff koff
HUH?
STAGGER

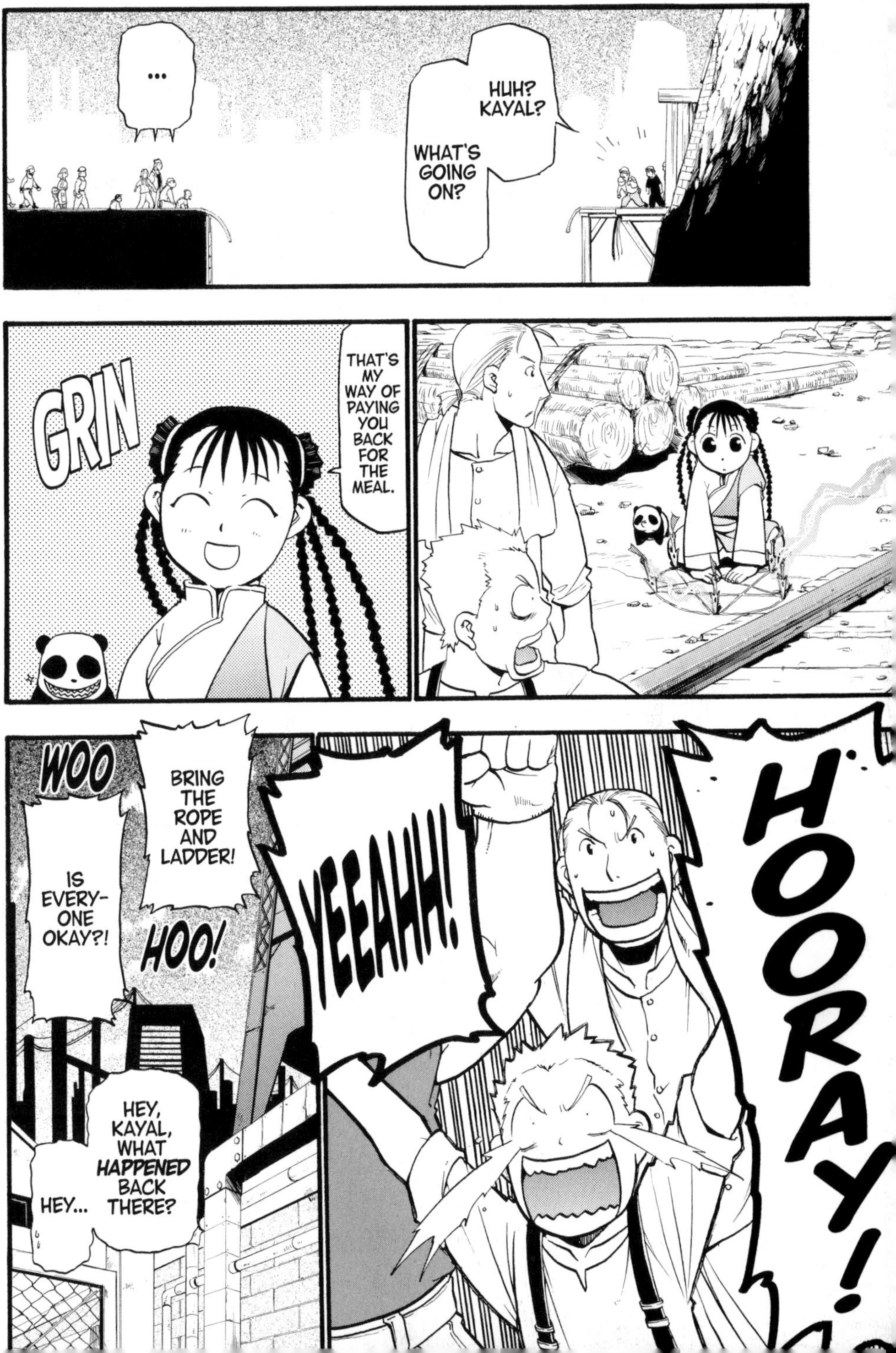
HUH? KAYAL?
WHAT'S GOING ON?
...
THAT'S MY WAY OF PAYING YOU BACK FOR THE MEAL.
GRIN
HOORAY!
YEEAHH!
BRING THE ROPE AND LADDER!
WOO
IS EVERYONE OKAY?!
HOO!
HEY, KAYAL, WHAT HAPPENED BACK THERE?
HEY...

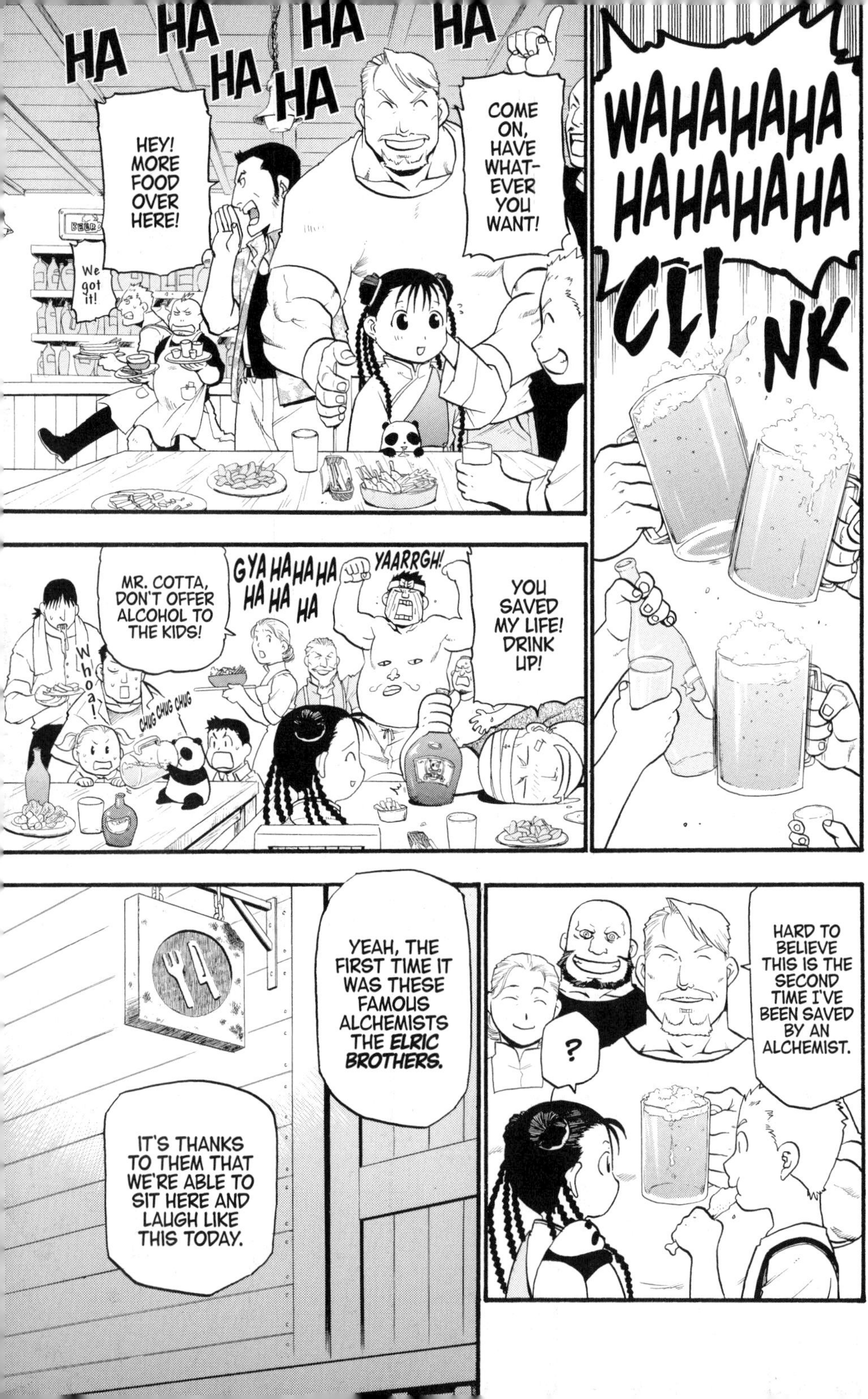
WAHAHAHAHA
HAHAHAHAHA
CLINK
HA HA HA HA HA HA
COME ON, HAVE WHATEVER YOU WANT!
HEY! MORE FOOD OVER HERE!
BEER
We got it!
YOU SAVED MY LIFE! DRINK UP!
YAARRGH!
GYA HA HA HA HA HA HA
MR. COTTA, DON'T OFFER ALCOHOL TO THE KIDS!
CHUG CHUG CHUG
Whoa!
HARD TO BELIEVE THIS IS THE SECOND TIME I'VE BEEN SAVED BY AN ALCHEMIST.
?
YEAH, THE FIRST TIME IT WAS THESE FAMOUS ALCHEMISTS THE ELRIC BROTHERS.
IT'S THANKS TO THEM THAT WE'RE ABLE TO SIT HERE AND LAUGH LIKE THIS TODAY.

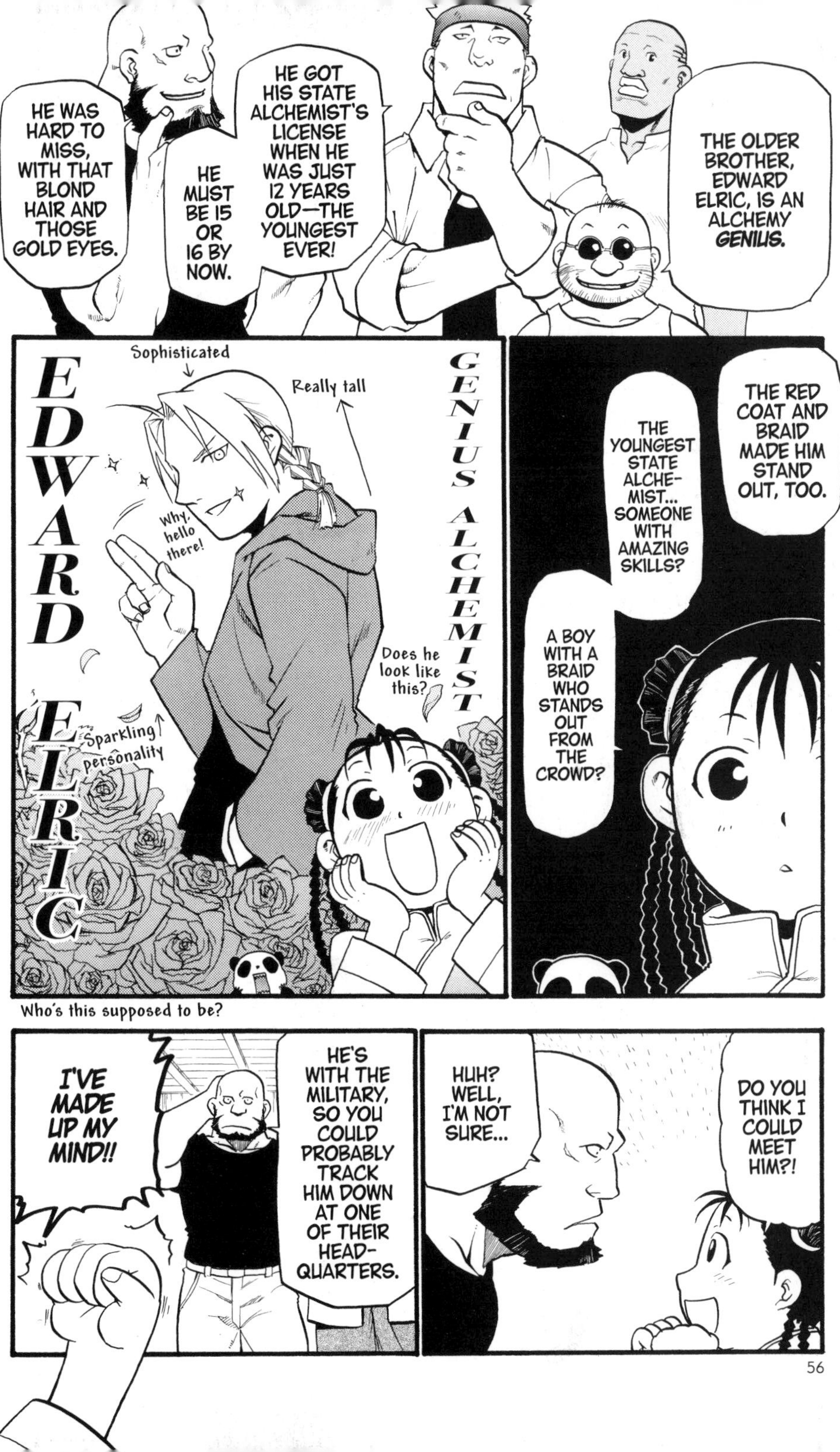
THE OLDER BROTHER, EDWARD ELRIC, IS AN ALCHEMY GENIUS.
HE GOT HIS STATE ALCHEMIST'S LICENSE WHEN HE WAS JUST 12 YEARS OLD—THE YOUNGEST EVER!
HE MUST BE 15 OR 16 BY NOW.
HE WAS HARD TO MISS, WITH THAT BLOND HAIR AND THOSE GOLD EYES.
THE RED COAT AND BRAID MADE HIM STAND OUT, TOO.
THE YOUNGEST STATE ALCHEMIST... SOMEONE WITH AMAZING SKILLS?
A BOY WITH A BRAID WHO STANDS OUT FROM THE CROWD?
GENIUS ALCHEMIST
EDWARD ELRIC
Sophisticated
Really tall
Why, hello there!
Does he look like this?
Sparkling personality
Who's this supposed to be?
DO YOU THINK I COULD MEET HIM?!
HUH? WELL, I'M NOT SURE...
HE'S WITH THE MILITARY, SO YOU COULD PROBABLY TRACK HIM DOWN AT ONE OF THEIR HEAD-QUARTERS.
I'VE MADE UP MY MIND!!

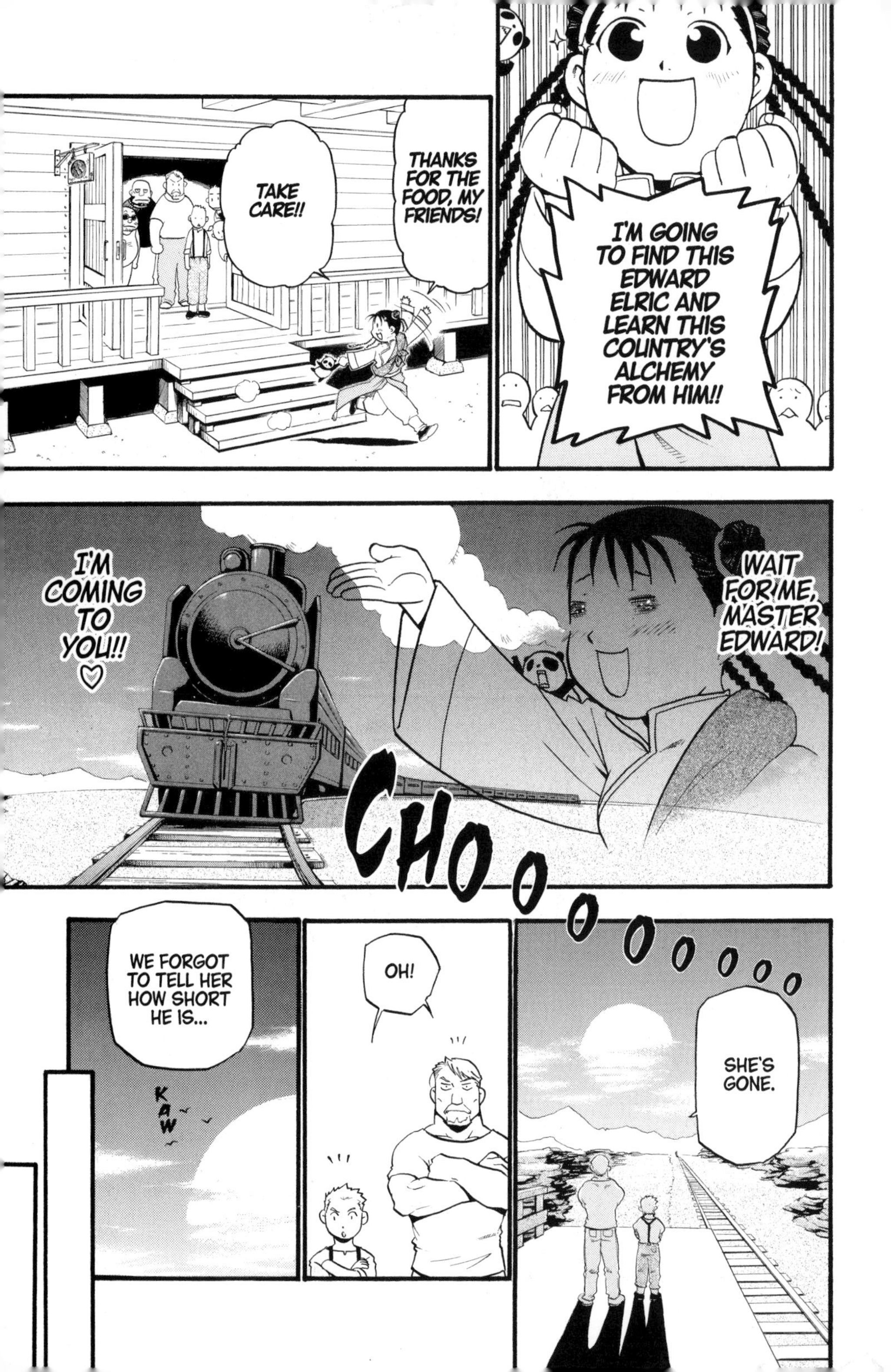
I'M GOING TO FIND THIS EDWARD ELRIC AND LEARN THIS COUNTRY'S ALCHEMY FROM HIM!!
THANKS FOR THE FOOD, MY FRIENDS!
TAKE CARE!!
WAIT FOR ME, MASTER EDWARD!
I'M COMING TO YOU!! ♡
CHOOOOOOOOO
SHE'S GONE.
OH!
WE FORGOT TO TELL HER HOW SHORT HE IS...
KAW

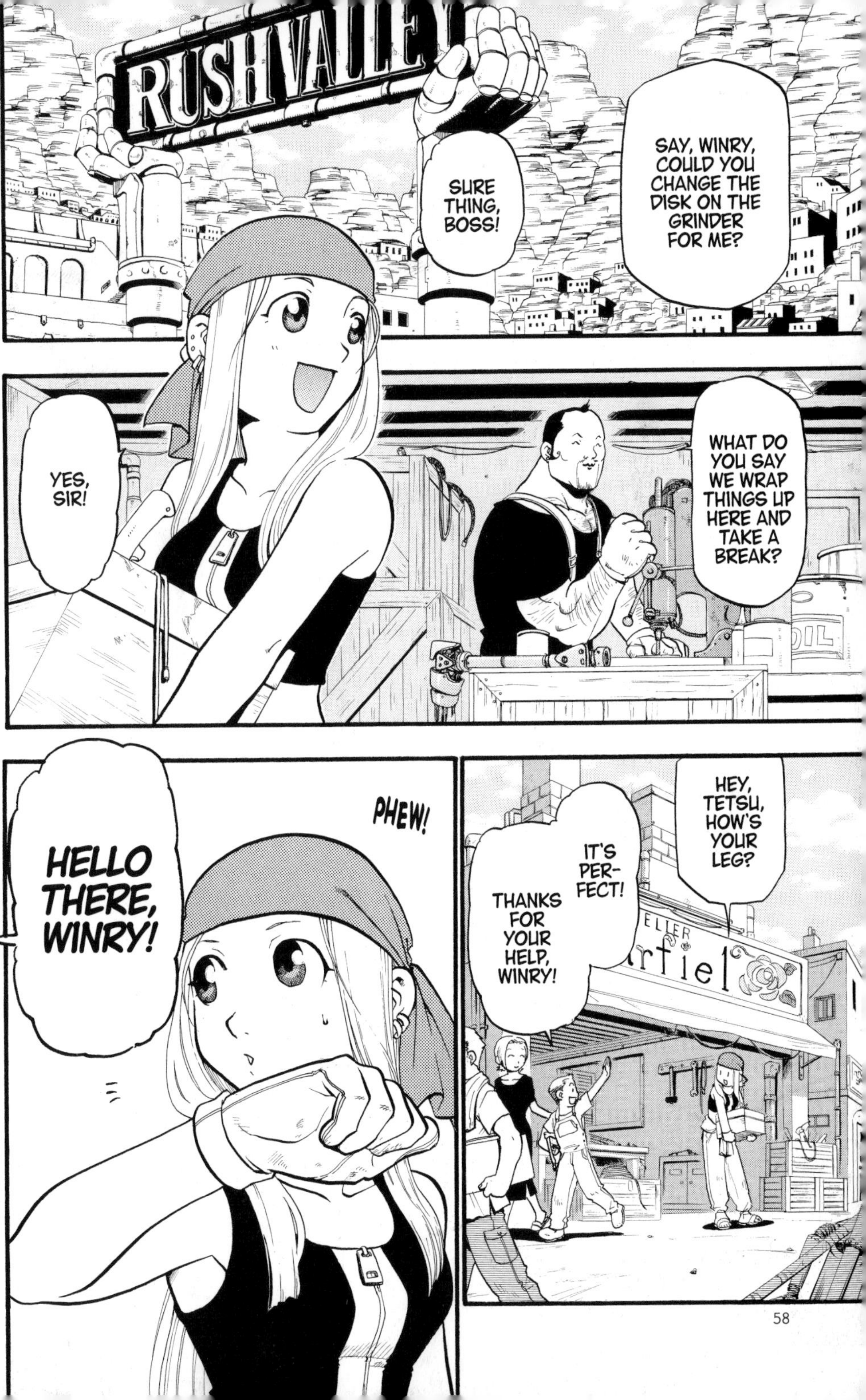
RUSH VALLEY
SAY, WINRY, COULD YOU CHANGE THE DISK ON THE GRINDER FOR ME?
SURE THING, BOSS!
WHAT DO YOU SAY WE WRAP THINGS UP HERE AND TAKE A BREAK?
YES, SIR!
HEY, TETSU, HOW'S YOUR LEG?
IT'S PER-FECT!
THANKS FOR YOUR HELP, WINRY!
PHEW!
HELLO THERE, WINRY!

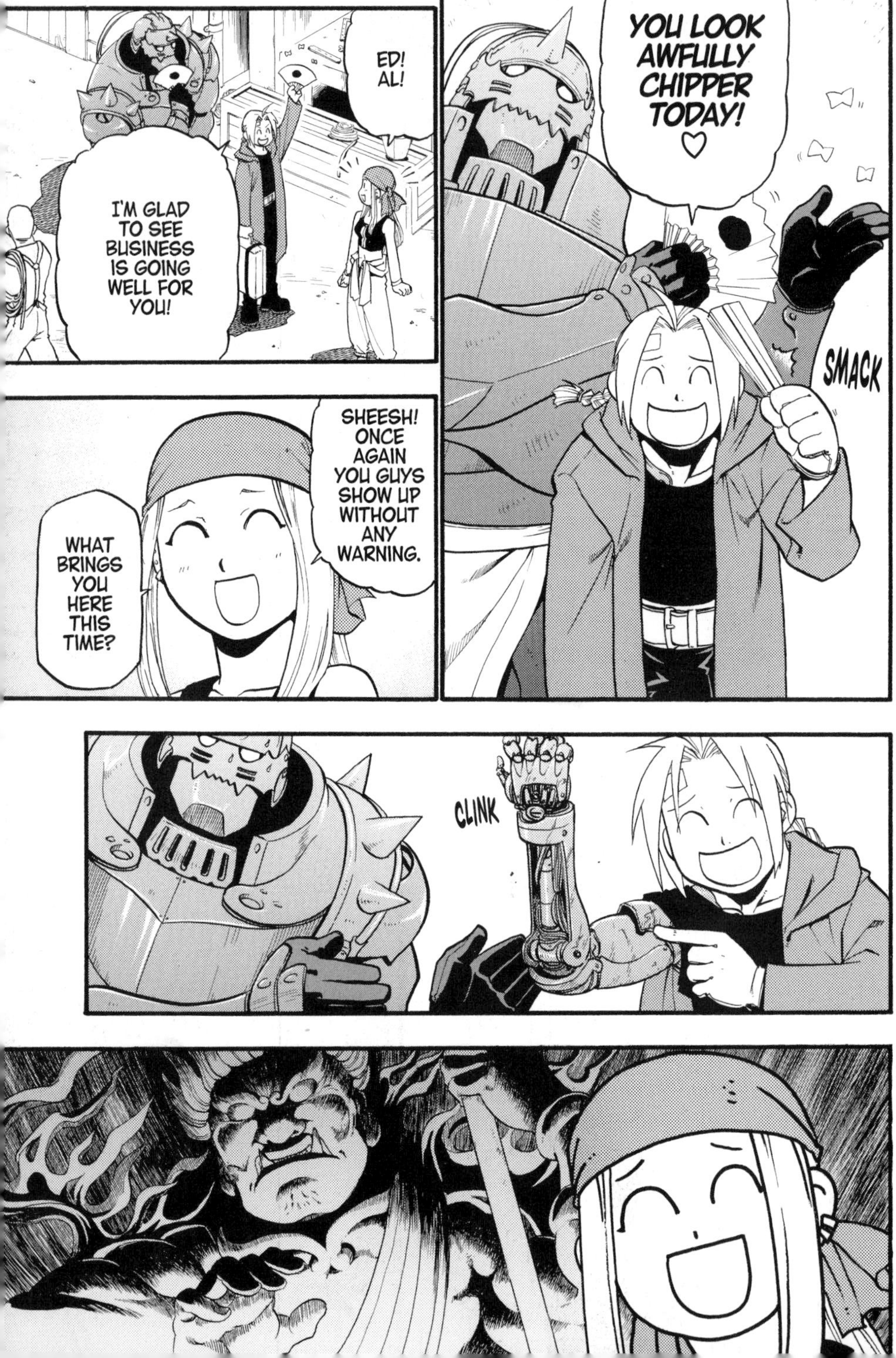
YOU LOOK AWFULLY CHIPPER TODAY! ♡
SMACK
ED! AL!
I'M GLAD TO SEE BUSINESS IS GOING WELL FOR YOU!
SHEESH! ONCE AGAIN YOU GUYS SHOW UP WITHOUT ANY WARNING.
WHAT BRINGS YOU HERE THIS TIME?
CLINK

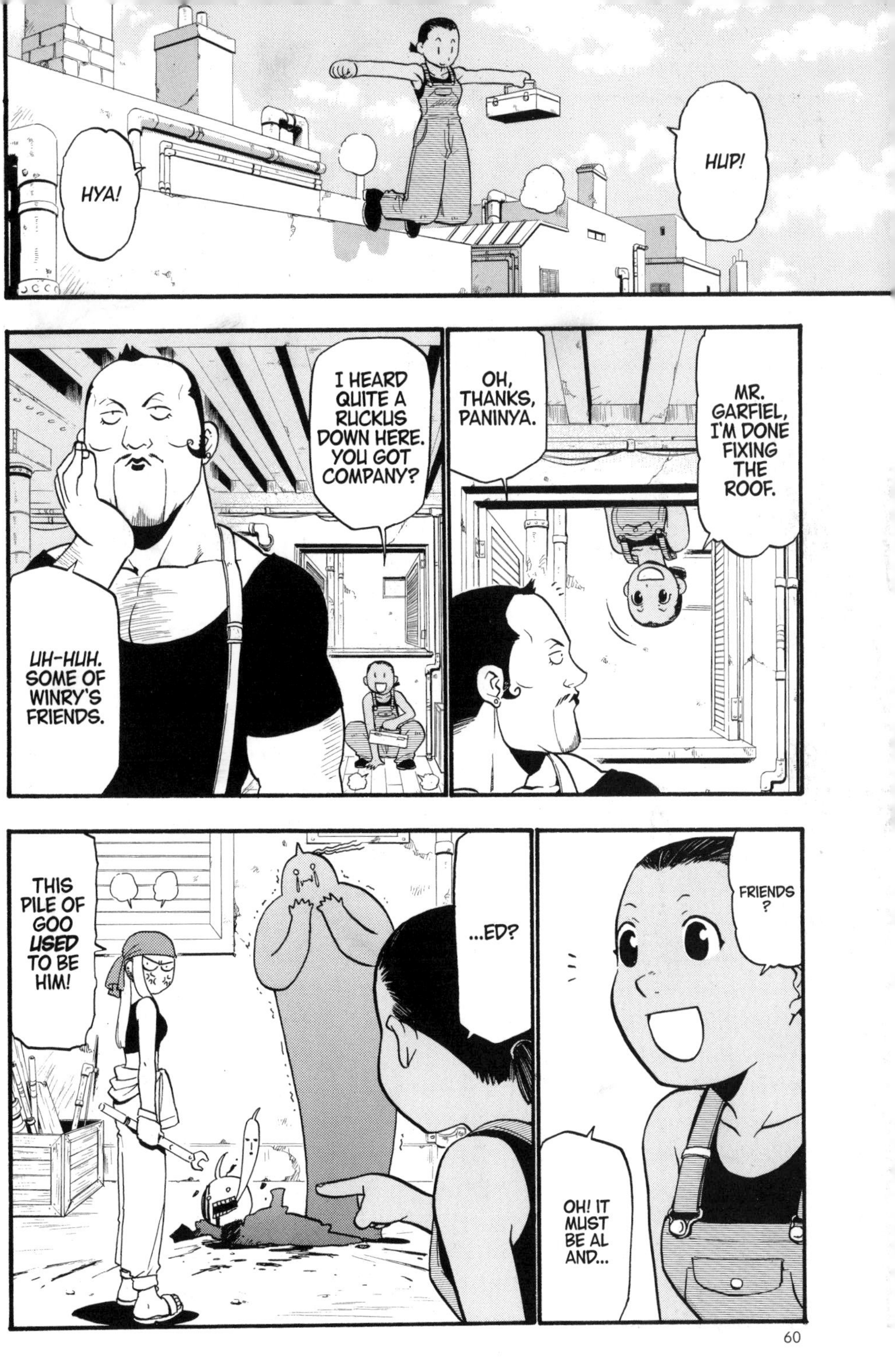
HUP!
HYA!
MR. GARFIEL, I'M DONE FIXING THE ROOF.
OH, THANKS, PANINYA.
I HEARD QUITE A RUCKUS DOWN HERE. YOU GOT COMPANY?
UH-HUH. SOME OF WINRY'S FRIENDS.
FRIENDS?
OH! IT MUST BE AL AND...
...ED?
THIS PILE OF GOO USED TO BE HIM!

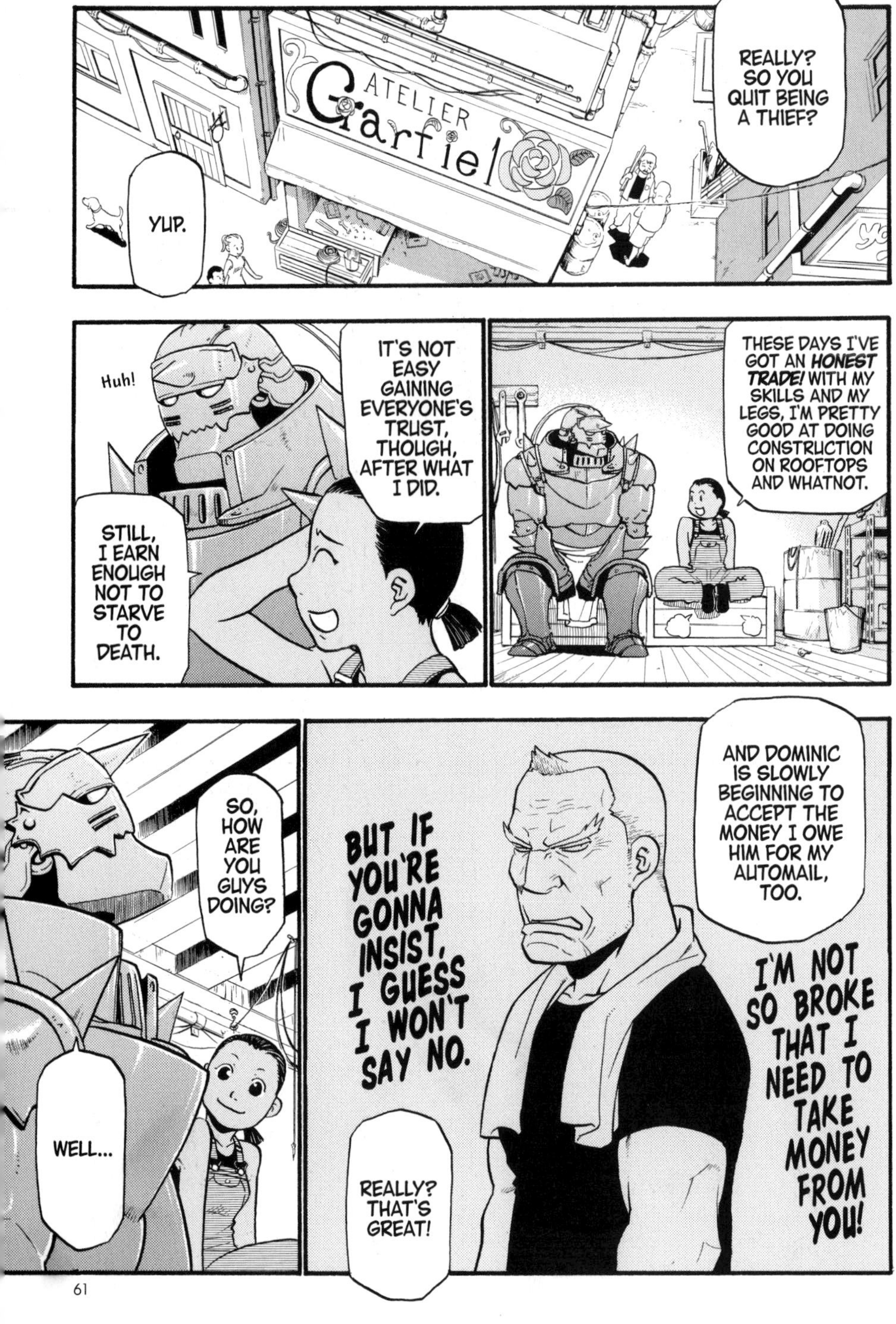
REALLY? SO YOU QUIT BEING A THIEF?
ATELIER Garfiel
YUP.
THESE DAYS I'VE GOT AN *HONEST TRADE!* WITH MY SKILLS AND MY LEGS, I'M PRETTY GOOD AT DOING CONSTRUCTION ON ROOFTOPS AND WHATNOT.
IT'S NOT EASY GAINING EVERYONE'S TRUST, THOUGH, AFTER WHAT I DID.
Huh!
STILL, I EARN ENOUGH NOT TO STARVE TO DEATH.
AND DOMINIC IS SLOWLY BEGINNING TO ACCEPT THE MONEY I OWE HIM FOR MY AUTOMAIL, TOO.
I'M NOT SO BROKE THAT I NEED TO TAKE MONEY FROM YOU!
BUT IF YOU'RE GONNA INSIST, I GUESS I WON'T SAY NO.
REALLY? THAT'S GREAT!
SO, HOW ARE YOU GUYS DOING?
WELL...

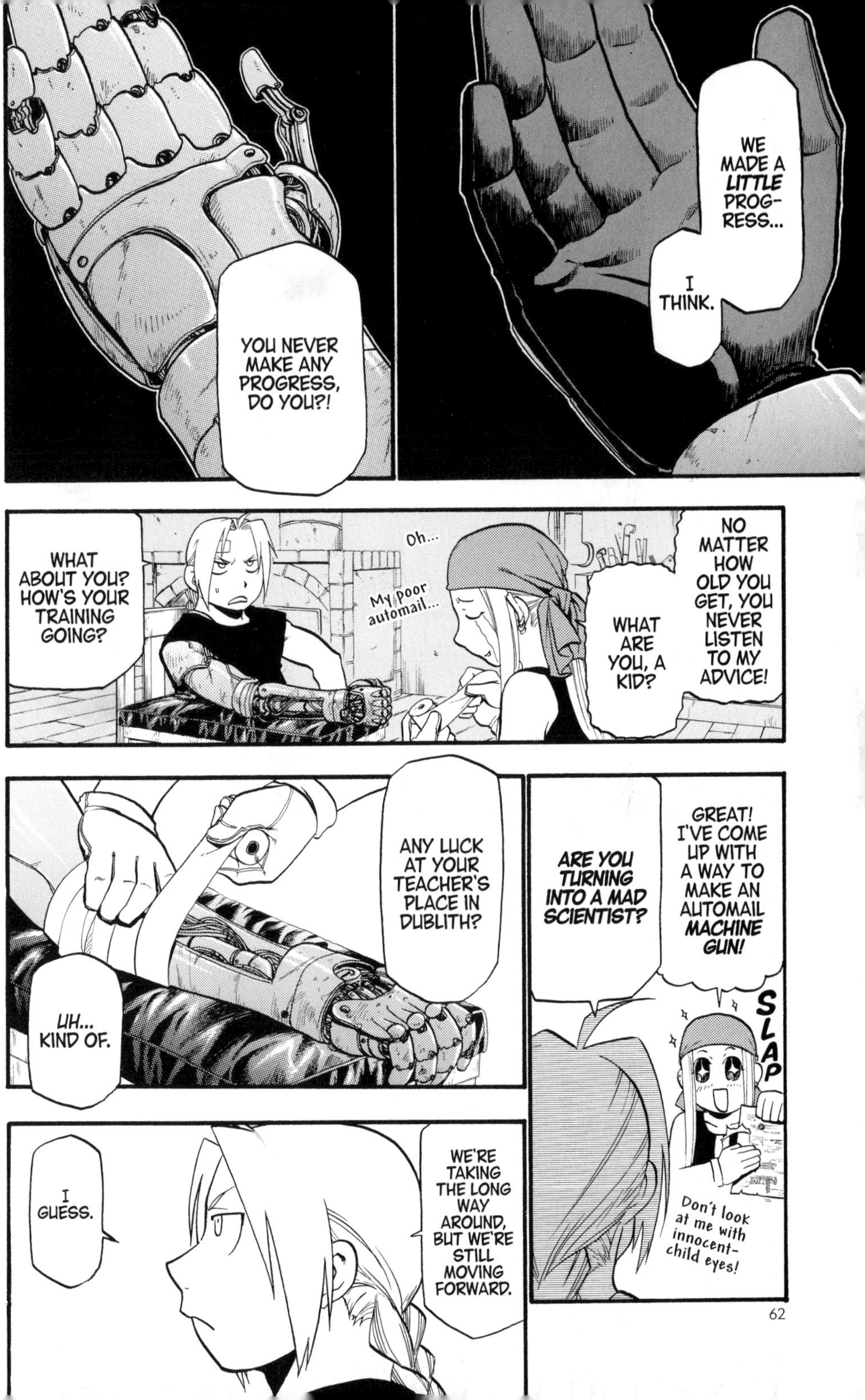
WE MADE A LITTLE PROGRESS...
I THINK.
YOU NEVER MAKE ANY PROGRESS, DO YOU?!
NO MATTER HOW OLD YOU GET, YOU NEVER LISTEN TO MY ADVICE!
WHAT ARE YOU, A KID?
My poor automail...
Oh...
WHAT ABOUT YOU? HOW'S YOUR TRAINING GOING?
GREAT! I'VE COME UP WITH A WAY TO MAKE AN AUTOMAIL MACHINE GUN!
ARE YOU TURNING INTO A MAD SCIENTIST?
SLAP
Don't look at me with innocent-child eyes!
ANY LUCK AT YOUR TEACHER'S PLACE IN DUBLITH?
UH... KIND OF.
WE'RE TAKING THE LONG WAY AROUND, BUT WE'RE STILL MOVING FORWARD.
I GUESS.

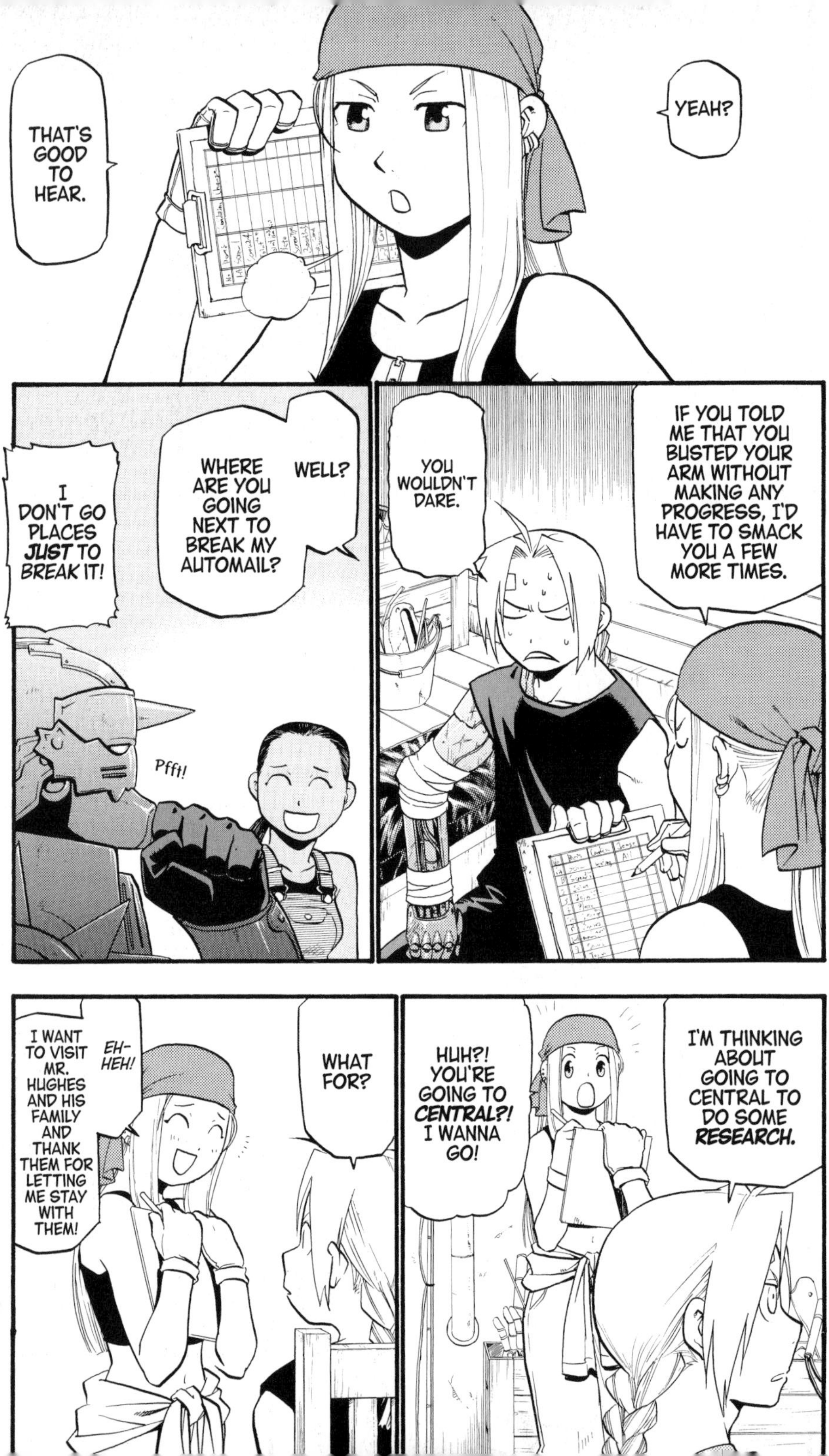
YEAH?
THAT'S GOOD TO HEAR.
IF YOU TOLD ME THAT YOU BUSTED YOUR ARM WITHOUT MAKING ANY PROGRESS, I'D HAVE TO SMACK YOU A FEW MORE TIMES.
YOU WOULDN'T DARE.
WELL?
WHERE ARE YOU GOING NEXT TO BREAK MY AUTOMAIL?
I DON'T GO PLACES JUST TO BREAK IT!
Pfft!
I'M THINKING ABOUT GOING TO CENTRAL TO DO SOME RESEARCH.
HUH?! YOU'RE GOING TO CENTRAL?! I WANNA GO!
WHAT FOR?
EH-HEH!
I WANT TO VISIT MR. HUGHES AND HIS FAMILY AND THANK THEM FOR LETTING ME STAY WITH THEM!

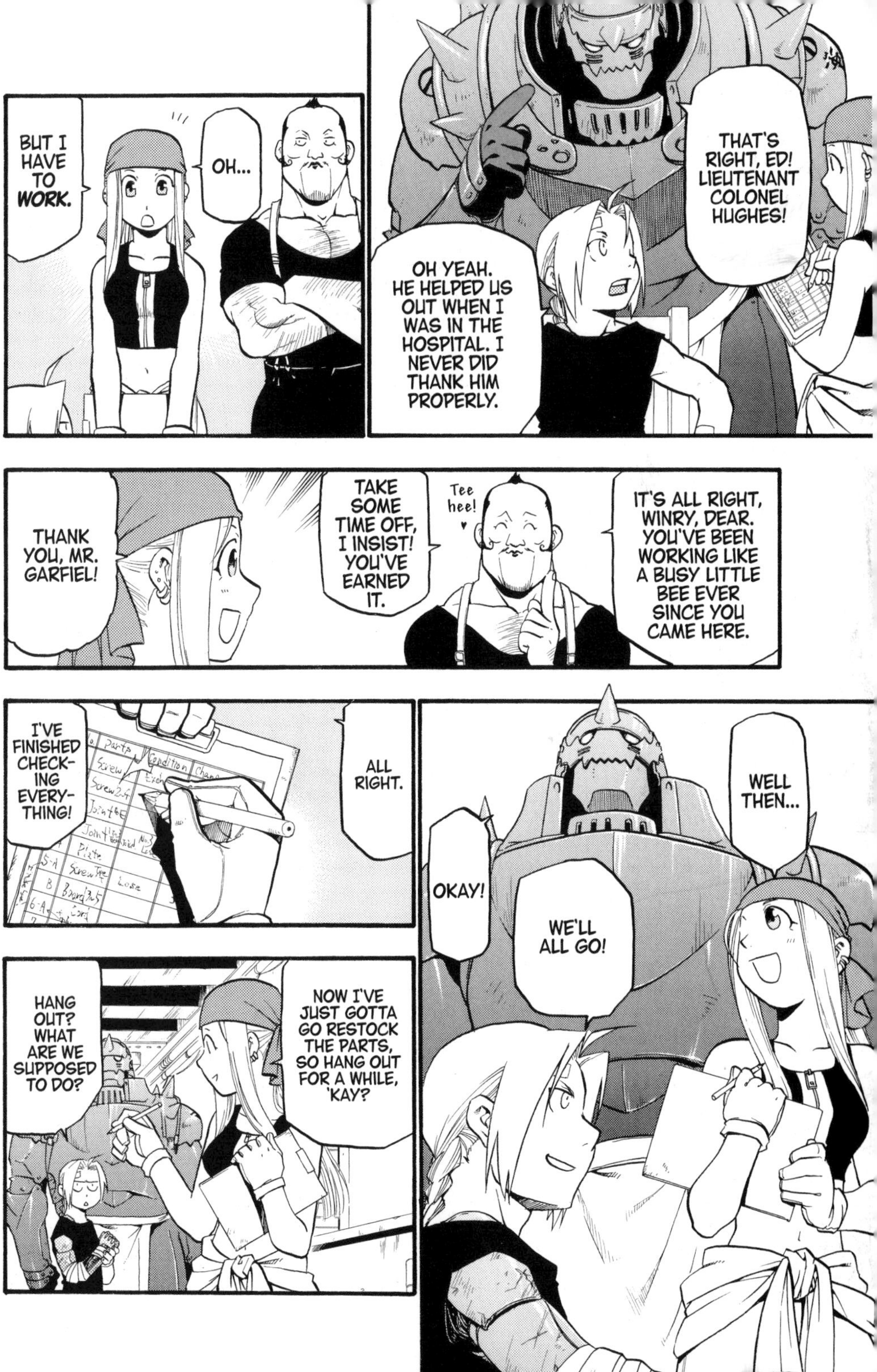
THAT'S RIGHT, ED! LIEUTENANT COLONEL HUGHES!
OH YEAH. HE HELPED US OUT WHEN I WAS IN THE HOSPITAL. I NEVER DID THANK HIM PROPERLY.
OH...
BUT I HAVE TO WORK.
IT'S ALL RIGHT, WINRY, DEAR. YOU'VE BEEN WORKING LIKE A BUSY LITTLE BEE EVER SINCE YOU CAME HERE.
Tee hee!
TAKE SOME TIME OFF, I INSIST! YOU'VE EARNED IT.
THANK YOU, MR. GARFIEL!
WELL THEN...
OKAY!
WE'LL ALL GO!
ALL RIGHT.
I'VE FINISHED CHECKING EVERYTHING!
NOW I'VE JUST GOTTA GO RESTOCK THE PARTS, SO HANG OUT FOR A WHILE, 'KAY?
HANG OUT? WHAT ARE WE SUPPOSED TO DO?

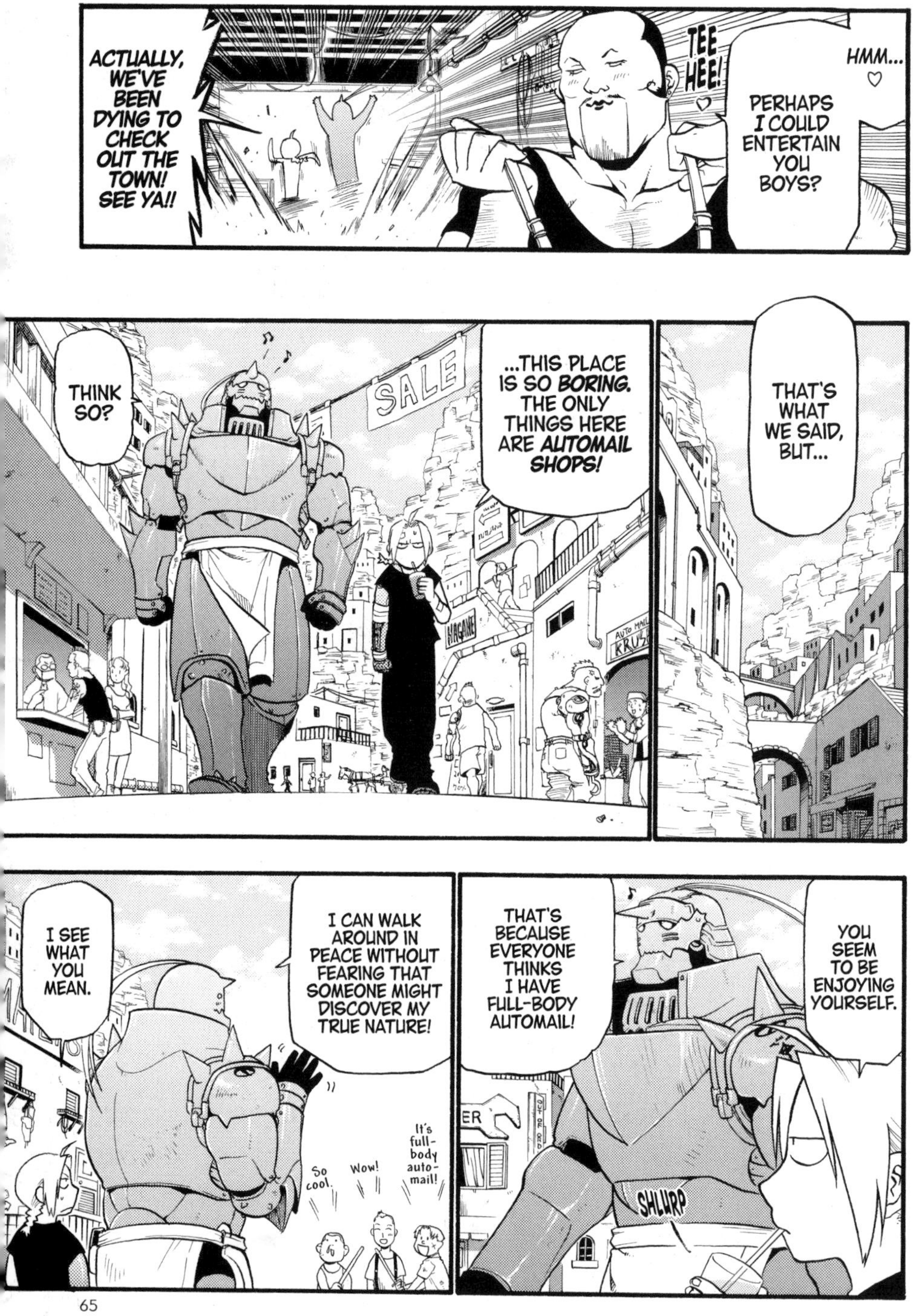
HMM... ♡
PERHAPS I COULD ENTERTAIN YOU BOYS?
TEE HEE! ♡
ACTUALLY, WE'VE BEEN DYING TO CHECK OUT THE TOWN! SEE YA!!
THAT'S WHAT WE SAID, BUT...
...THIS PLACE IS SO BORING. THE ONLY THINGS HERE ARE AUTOMAIL SHOPS!
SALE
THINK SO?
YOU SEEM TO BE ENJOYING YOURSELF.
THAT'S BECAUSE EVERYONE THINKS I HAVE FULL-BODY AUTOMAIL!
SHLURP
I CAN WALK AROUND IN PEACE WITHOUT FEARING THAT SOMEONE MIGHT DISCOVER MY TRUE NATURE!
It's full-body auto-mail!
Wow!
So cool.
I SEE WHAT YOU MEAN.

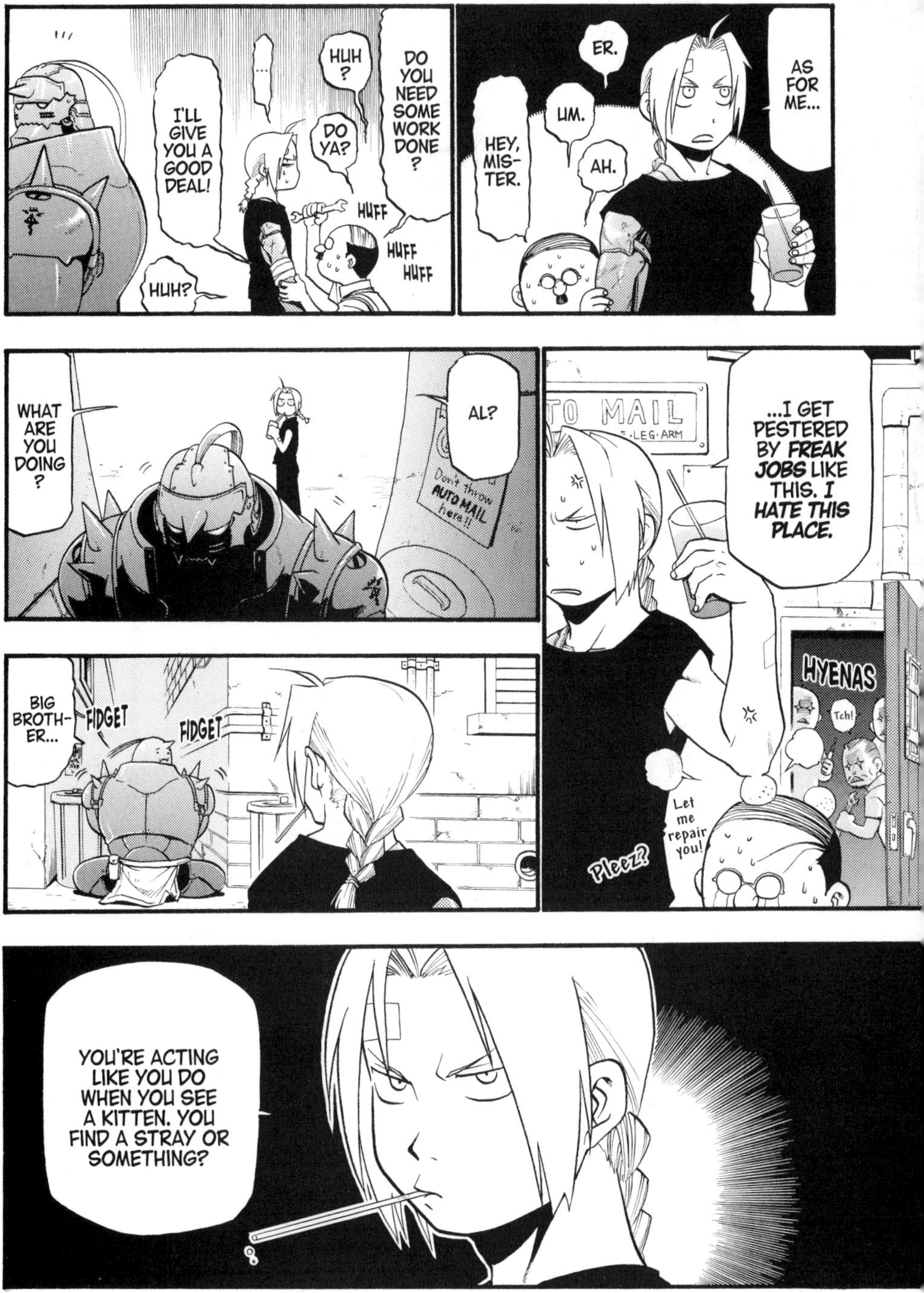
AS FOR ME...
ER.
UM.
AH.
HEY, MISTER.
DO YOU NEED SOME WORK DONE?
HUH?
DO YA?
HUFF
HUFF HUFF
...
I'LL GIVE YOU A GOOD DEAL!
HUH?
TO MAIL
E·LEG·ARM
...I GET PESTERED BY FREAK JOBS LIKE THIS. I HATE THIS PLACE.
HYENAS
Tch!
Let me repair you!
Pleez?
AL?
Don't throw AUTO MAIL here!!
WHAT ARE YOU DOING?
FIDGET
FIDGET
BIG BROTHER-ER...
YOU'RE ACTING LIKE YOU DO WHEN YOU SEE A KITTEN. YOU FIND A STRAY OR SOMETHING?

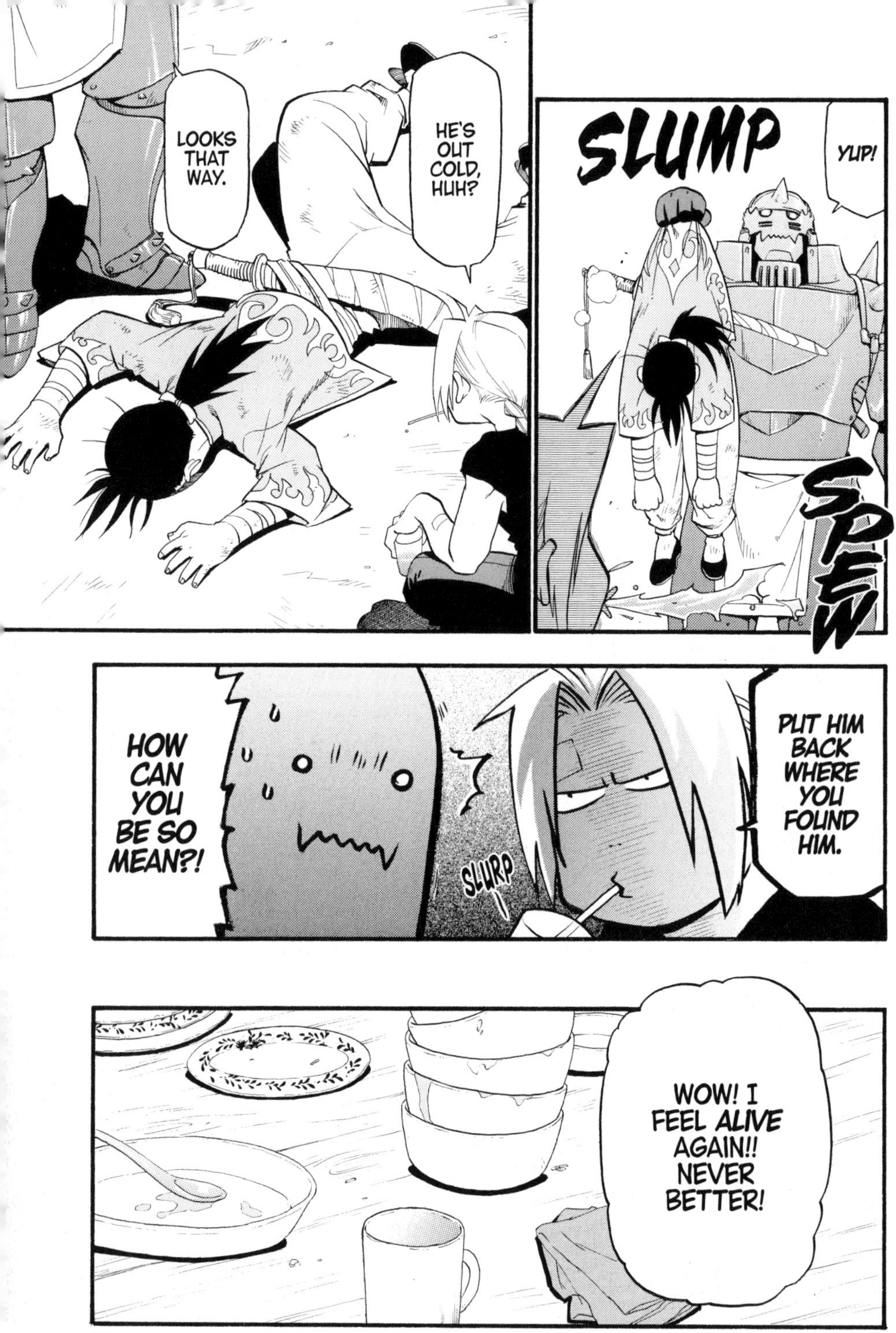
SLUMP
YUP!
SPEW
HE'S OUT COLD, HUH?
LOOKS THAT WAY.
PUT HIM BACK WHERE YOU FOUND HIM.
SLURP
HOW CAN YOU BE SO MEAN?!
WOW! I FEEL ALIVE AGAIN!! NEVER BETTER!

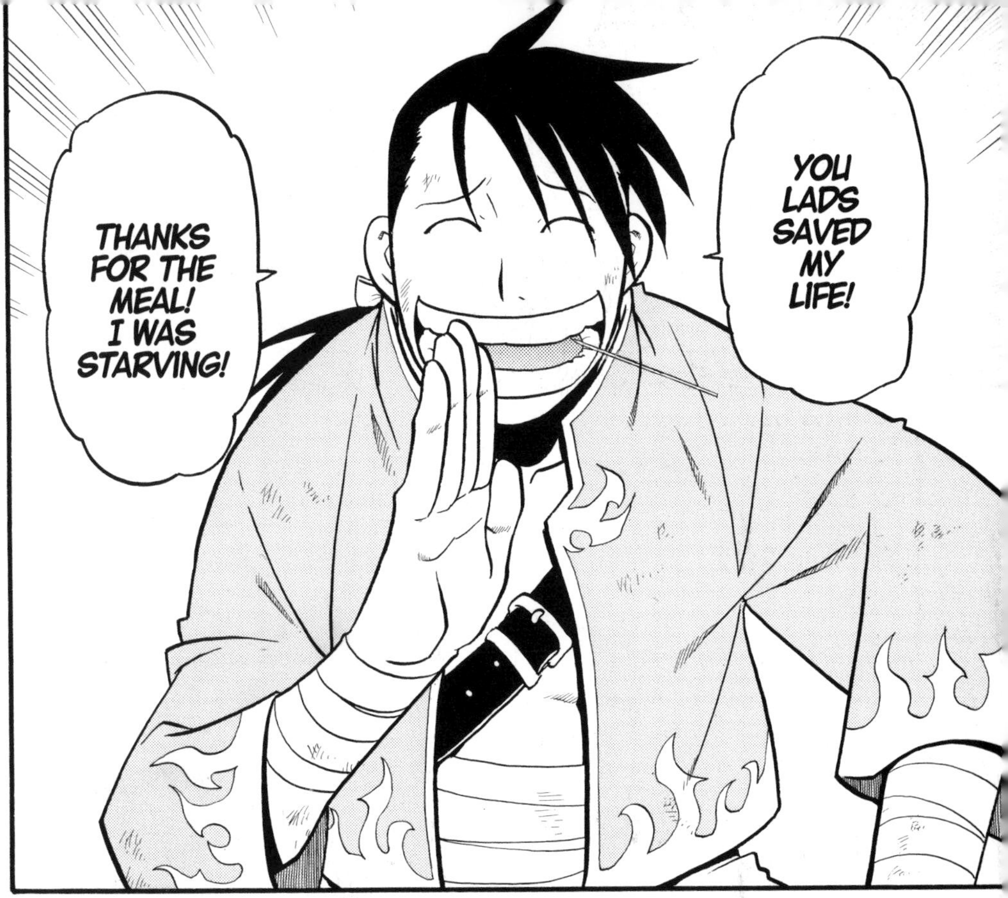
YOU LADS SAVED MY LIFE!
THANKS FOR THE MEAL! I WAS STARVING!

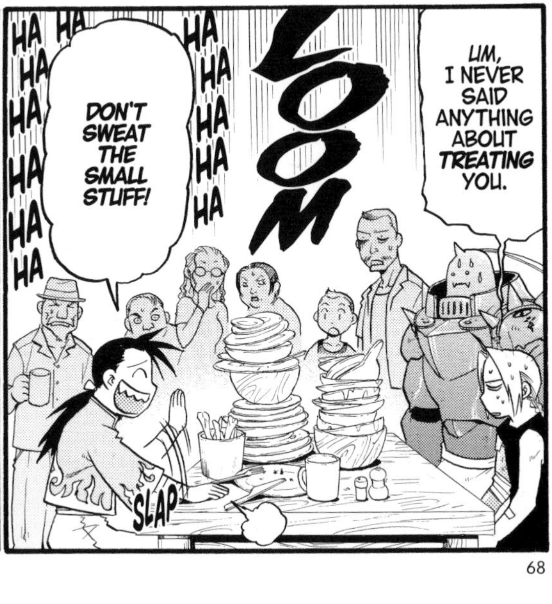
UM, I NEVER SAID ANYTHING ABOUT TREATING YOU.
VOOM
HA HA HA HA HA HA HA
HA HA HA HA HA HA HA HA
DON'T SWEAT THE SMALL STUFF!
SLAP

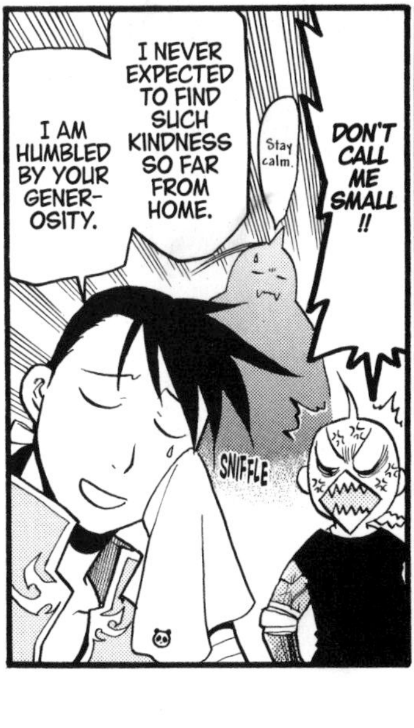
DON'T CALL ME SMALL!!
Stay calm.
I NEVER EXPECTED TO FIND SUCH KINDNESS SO FAR FROM HOME.
I AM HUMBLED BY YOUR GENER-OSITY.
SNIFFLE

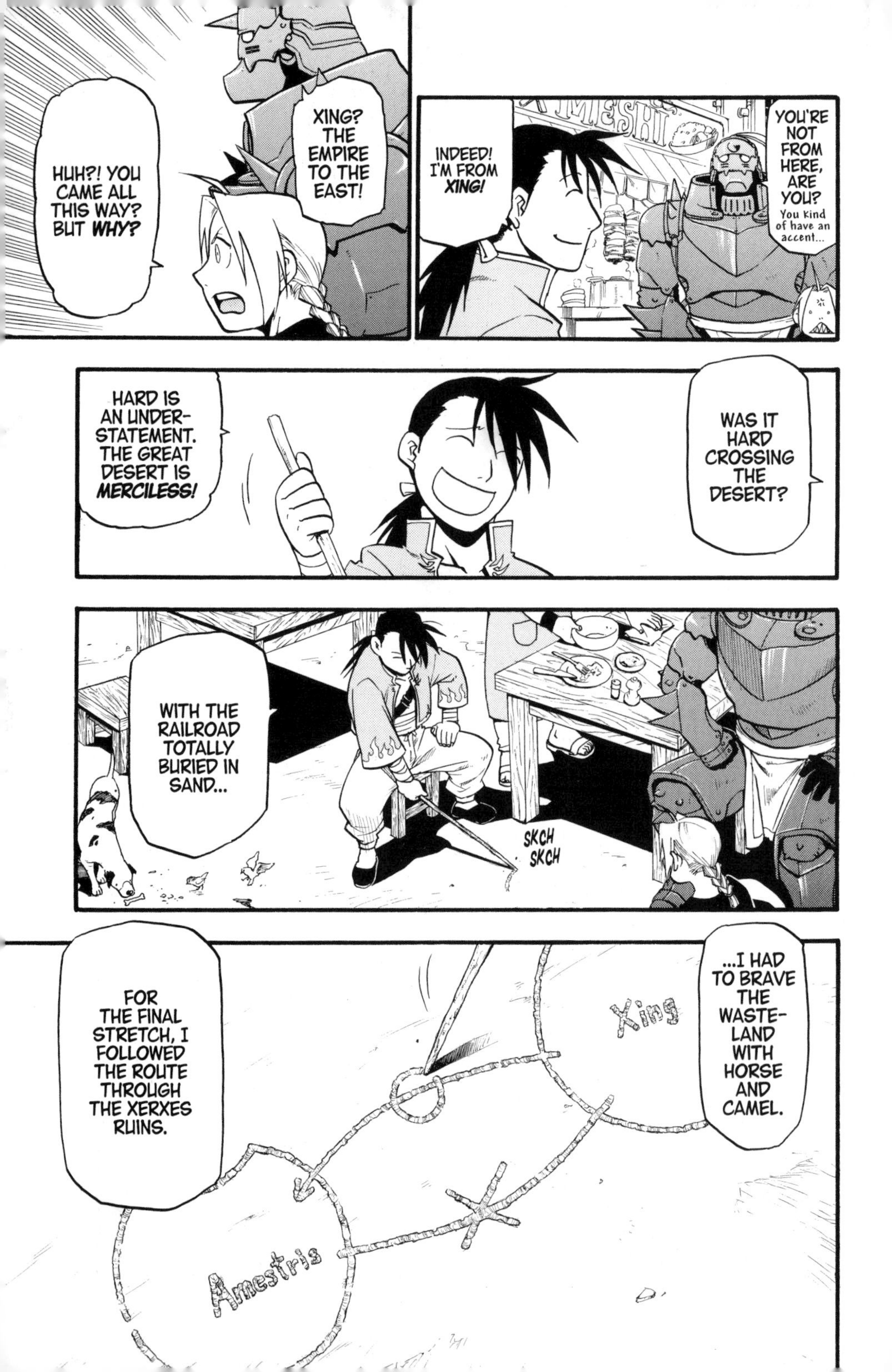
MESHI
YOU'RE NOT FROM HERE, ARE YOU? You kind of have an accent...
INDEED! I'M FROM XING!
XING? THE EMPIRE TO THE EAST!
HUH?! YOU CAME ALL THIS WAY? BUT WHY?
WAS IT HARD CROSSING THE DESERT?
HARD IS AN UNDER-STATEMENT. THE GREAT DESERT IS MERCILESS!
WITH THE RAILROAD TOTALLY BURIED IN SAND...
SKCH SKCH
...I HAD TO BRAVE THE WASTE-LAND WITH HORSE AND CAMEL.
Xing
FOR THE FINAL STRETCH, I FOLLOWED THE ROUTE THROUGH THE XERXES RUINS.
Amestris

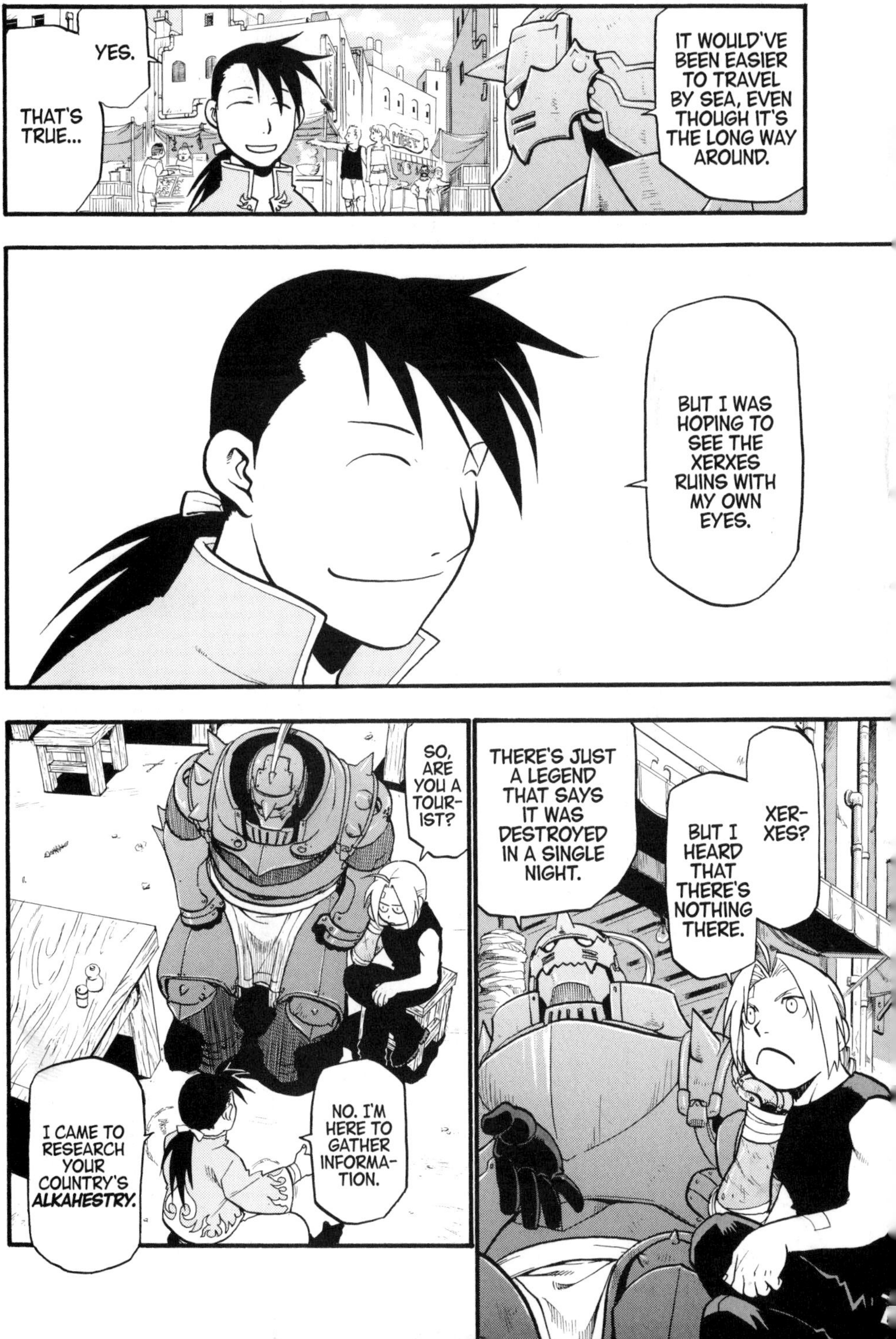
IT WOULD'VE BEEN EASIER TO TRAVEL BY SEA, EVEN THOUGH IT'S THE LONG WAY AROUND.
YES.
THAT'S TRUE...
BUT I WAS HOPING TO SEE THE XERXES RUINS WITH MY OWN EYES.
XER-XES?
BUT I HEARD THAT THERE'S NOTHING THERE.
THERE'S JUST A LEGEND THAT SAYS IT WAS DESTROYED IN A SINGLE NIGHT.
SO, ARE YOU A TOUR-IST?
NO. I'M HERE TO GATHER INFORMA-TION.
I CAME TO RESEARCH YOUR COUNTRY'S **ALKAHESTRY.**

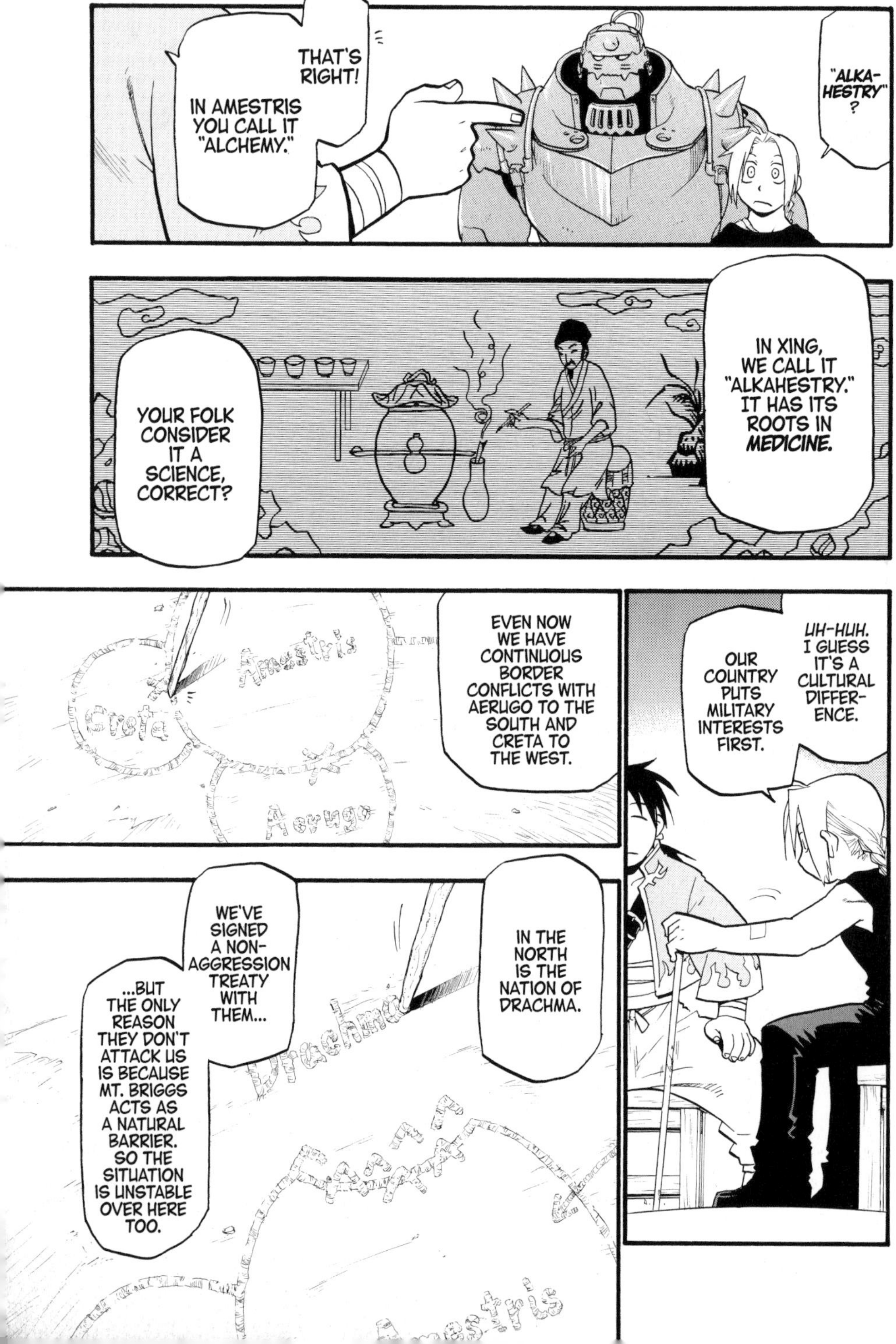
"ALKAHESTRY"?
THAT'S RIGHT!
IN AMESTRIS YOU CALL IT "ALCHEMY."
IN XING, WE CALL IT "ALKAHESTRY." IT HAS ITS ROOTS IN *MEDICINE.*
YOUR FOLK CONSIDER IT A SCIENCE, CORRECT?
UH-HUH. I GUESS IT'S A CULTURAL DIFFERENCE.
OUR COUNTRY PUTS MILITARY INTERESTS FIRST.
EVEN NOW WE HAVE CONTINUOUS BORDER CONFLICTS WITH AERUGO TO THE SOUTH AND CRETA TO THE WEST.
Amestris
Creta
Aerugo
IN THE NORTH IS THE NATION OF DRACHMA.
WE'VE SIGNED A NON-AGGRESSION TREATY WITH THEM...
...BUT THE ONLY REASON THEY DON'T ATTACK US IS BECAUSE MT. BRIGGS ACTS AS A NATURAL BARRIER. SO THE SITUATION IS UNSTABLE OVER HERE TOO.
Drachma
Amestris

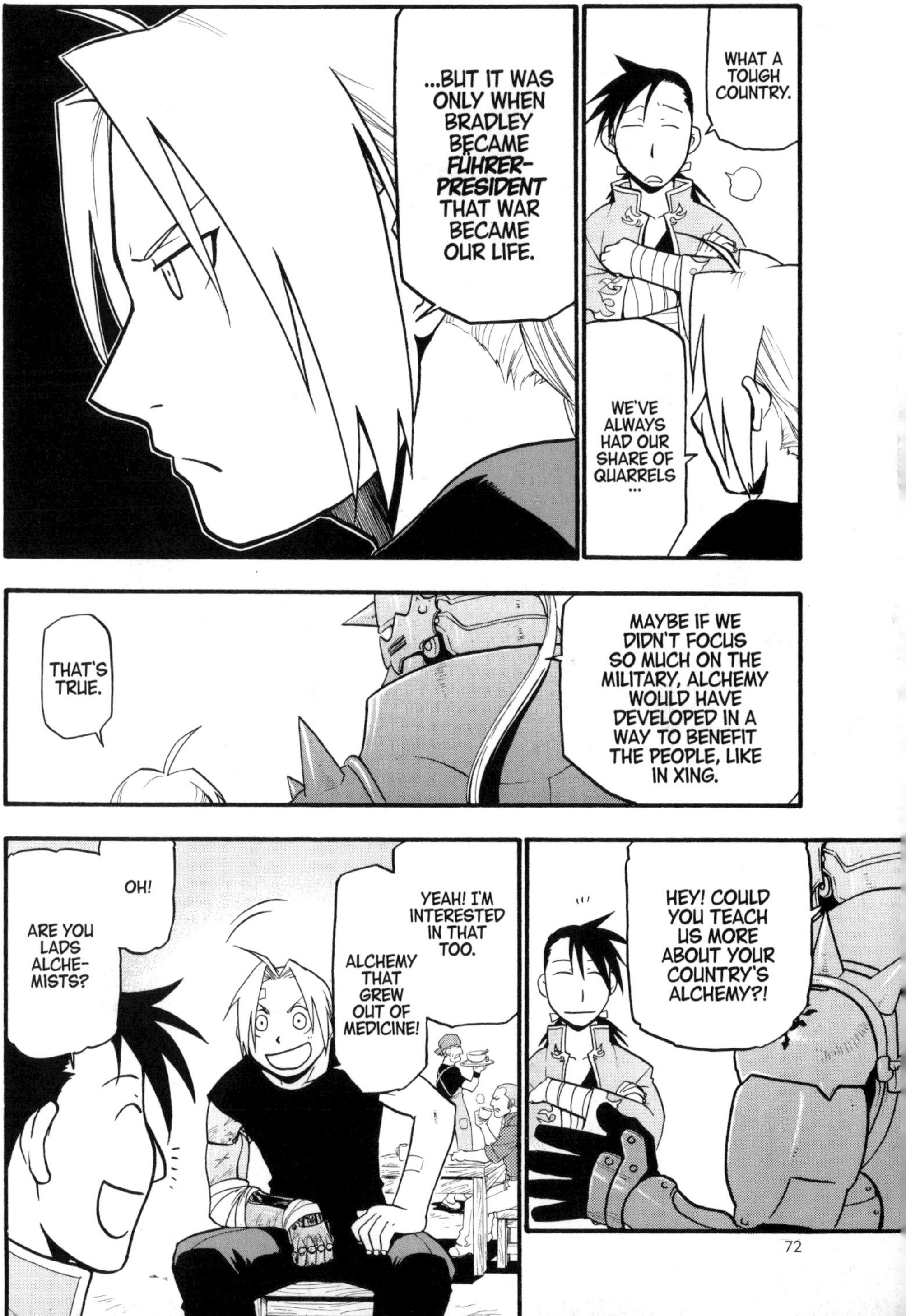
WHAT A TOUGH COUNTRY.
WE'VE ALWAYS HAD OUR SHARE OF QUARRELS...
...BUT IT WAS ONLY WHEN BRADLEY BECAME FÜHRER-PRESIDENT THAT WAR BECAME OUR LIFE.
MAYBE IF WE DIDN'T FOCUS SO MUCH ON THE MILITARY, ALCHEMY WOULD HAVE DEVELOPED IN A WAY TO BENEFIT THE PEOPLE, LIKE IN XING.
THAT'S TRUE.
HEY! COULD YOU TEACH US MORE ABOUT YOUR COUNTRY'S ALCHEMY?!
YEAH! I'M INTERESTED IN THAT TOO.
ALCHEMY THAT GREW OUT OF MEDICINE!
OH!
ARE YOU LADS ALCHE-MISTS?

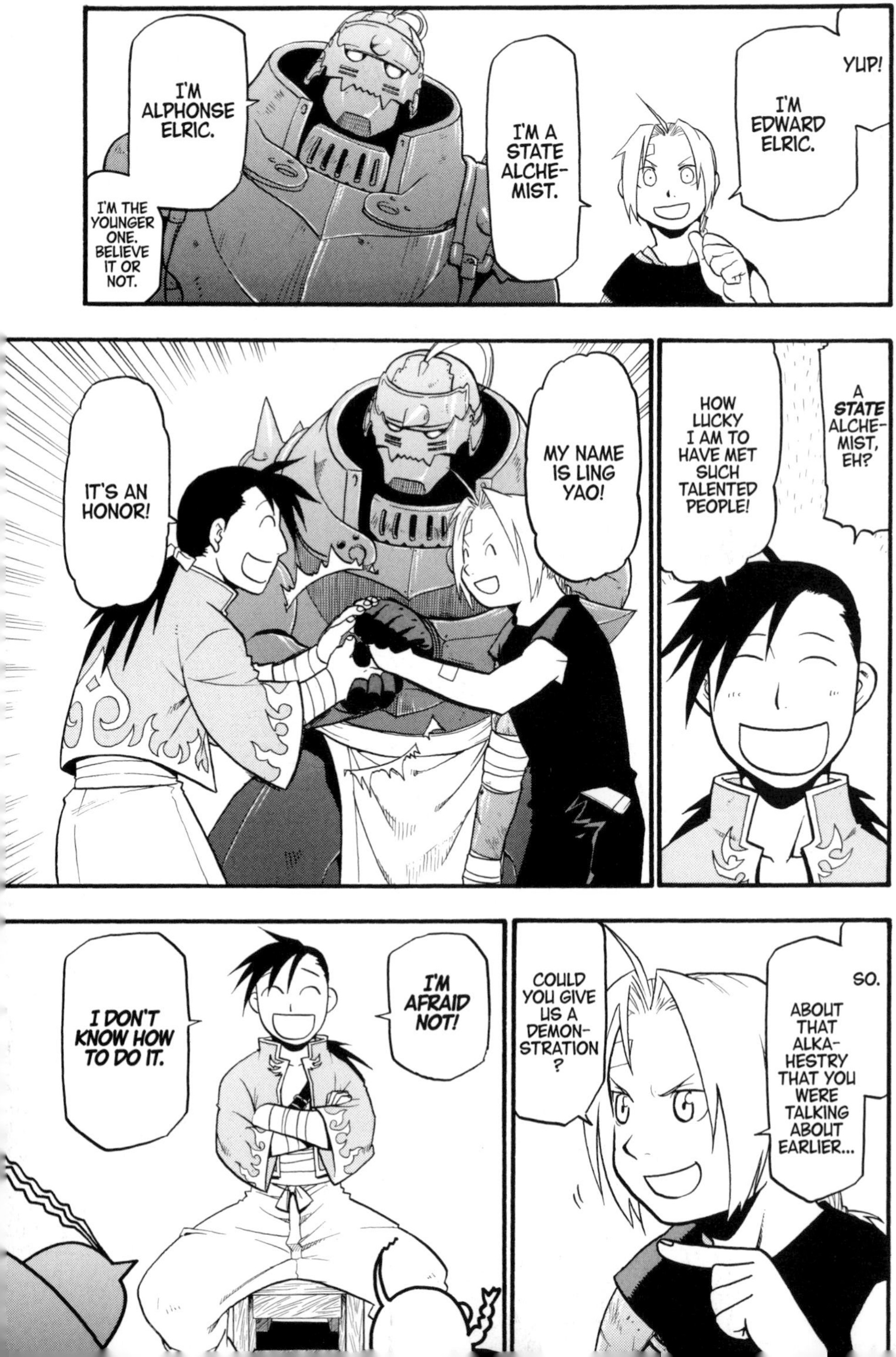
YUP!
I'M EDWARD ELRIC.
I'M A STATE ALCHEMIST.
I'M ALPHONSE ELRIC.
I'M THE YOUNGER ONE. BELIEVE IT OR NOT.
A STATE ALCHEMIST, EH?
HOW LUCKY I AM TO HAVE MET SUCH TALENTED PEOPLE!
MY NAME IS LING YAO!
IT'S AN HONOR!
SO.
ABOUT THAT ALKAHESTRY THAT YOU WERE TALKING ABOUT EARLIER...
COULD YOU GIVE US A DEMONSTRATION?
I'M AFRAID NOT!
I DON'T KNOW HOW TO DO IT.

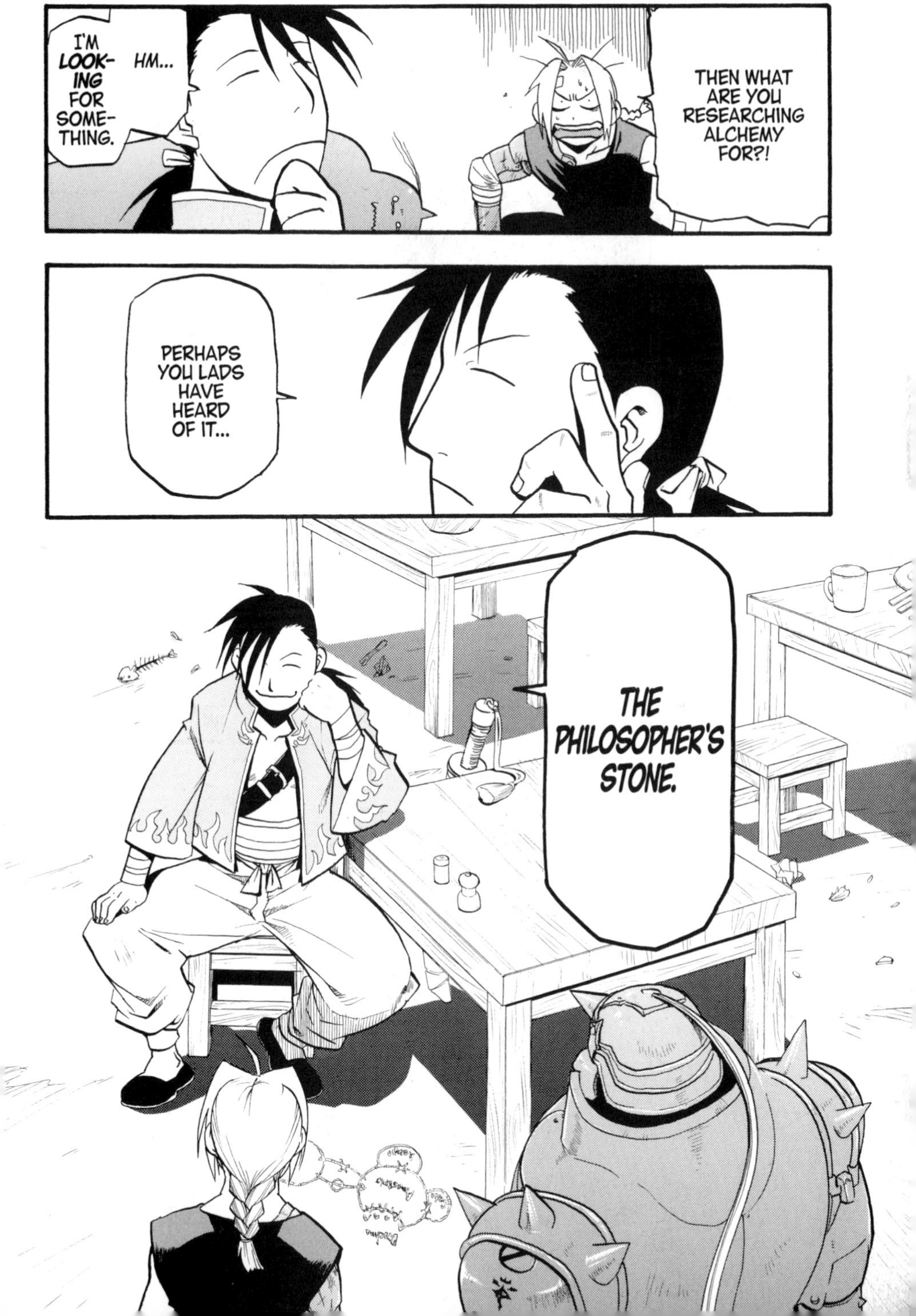
THEN WHAT ARE YOU RESEARCHING ALCHEMY FOR?!
HM...
I'M LOOKING FOR SOMETHING.
PERHAPS YOU LADS HAVE HEARD OF IT...
THE PHILOSOPHER'S STONE.

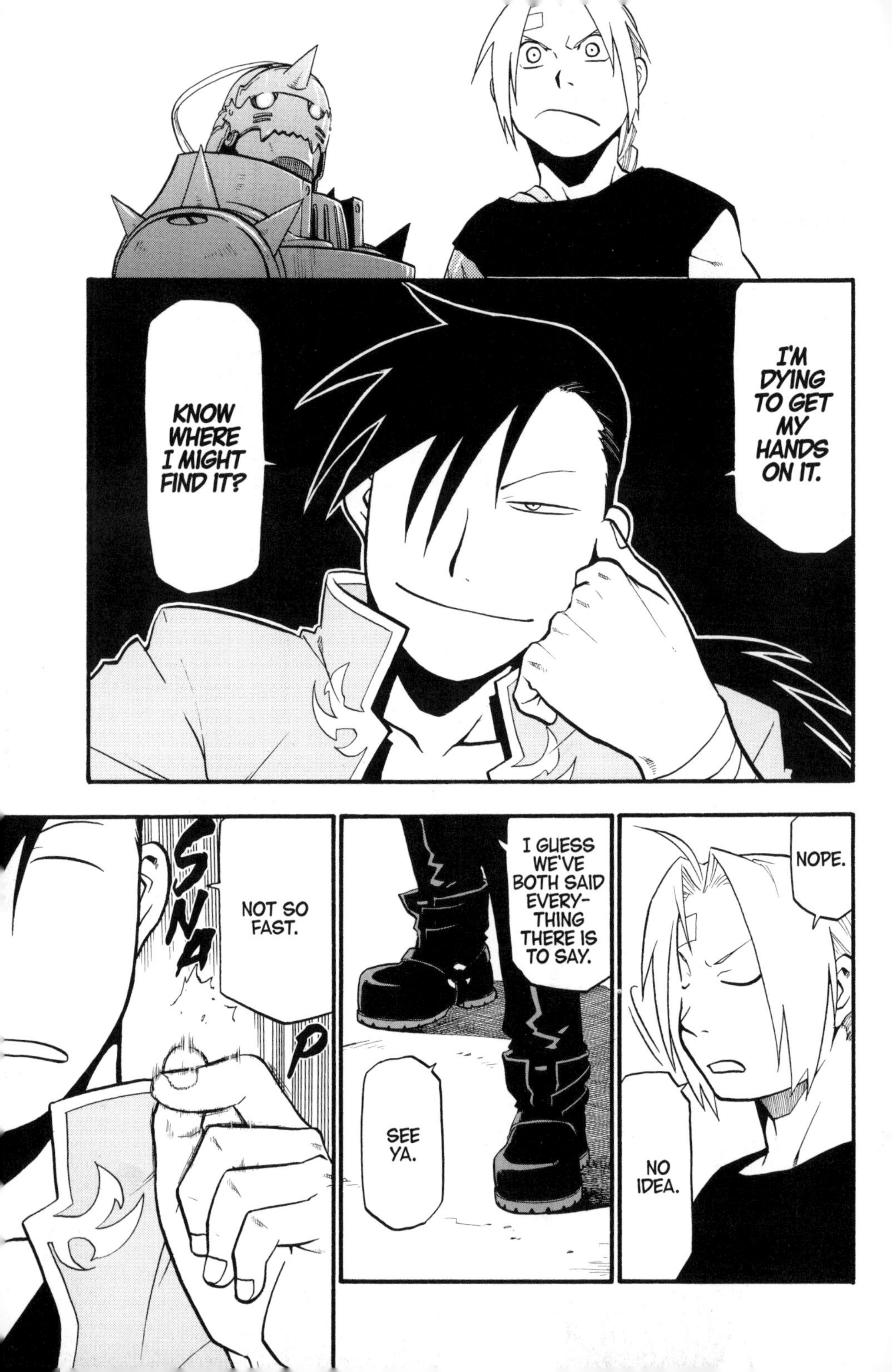
I'M DYING TO GET MY HANDS ON IT.
KNOW WHERE I MIGHT FIND IT?
NOPE.
NO IDEA.
I GUESS WE'VE BOTH SAID EVERY-THING THERE IS TO SAY.
SEE YA.
NOT SO FAST.
SNAP

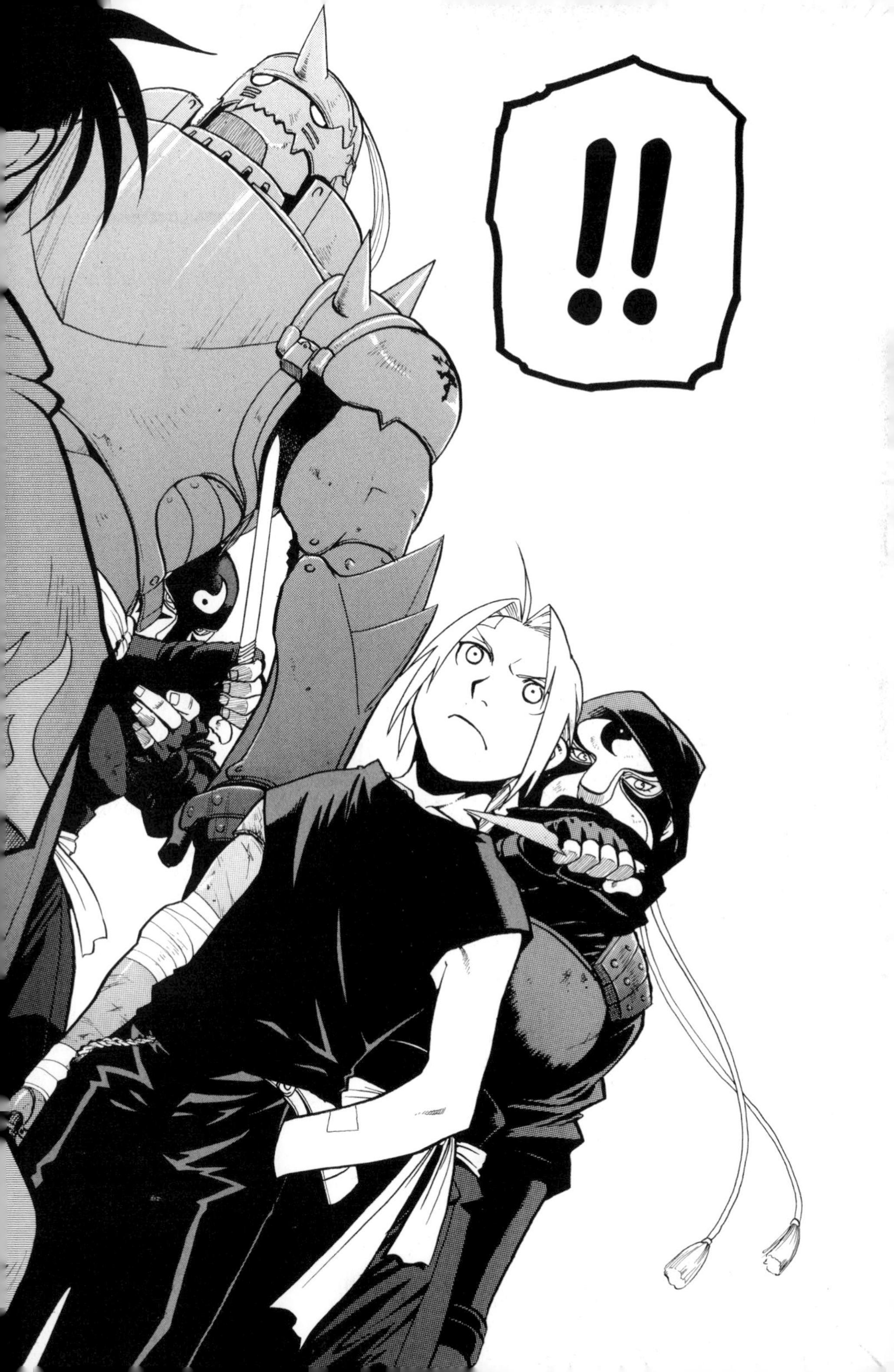
!!

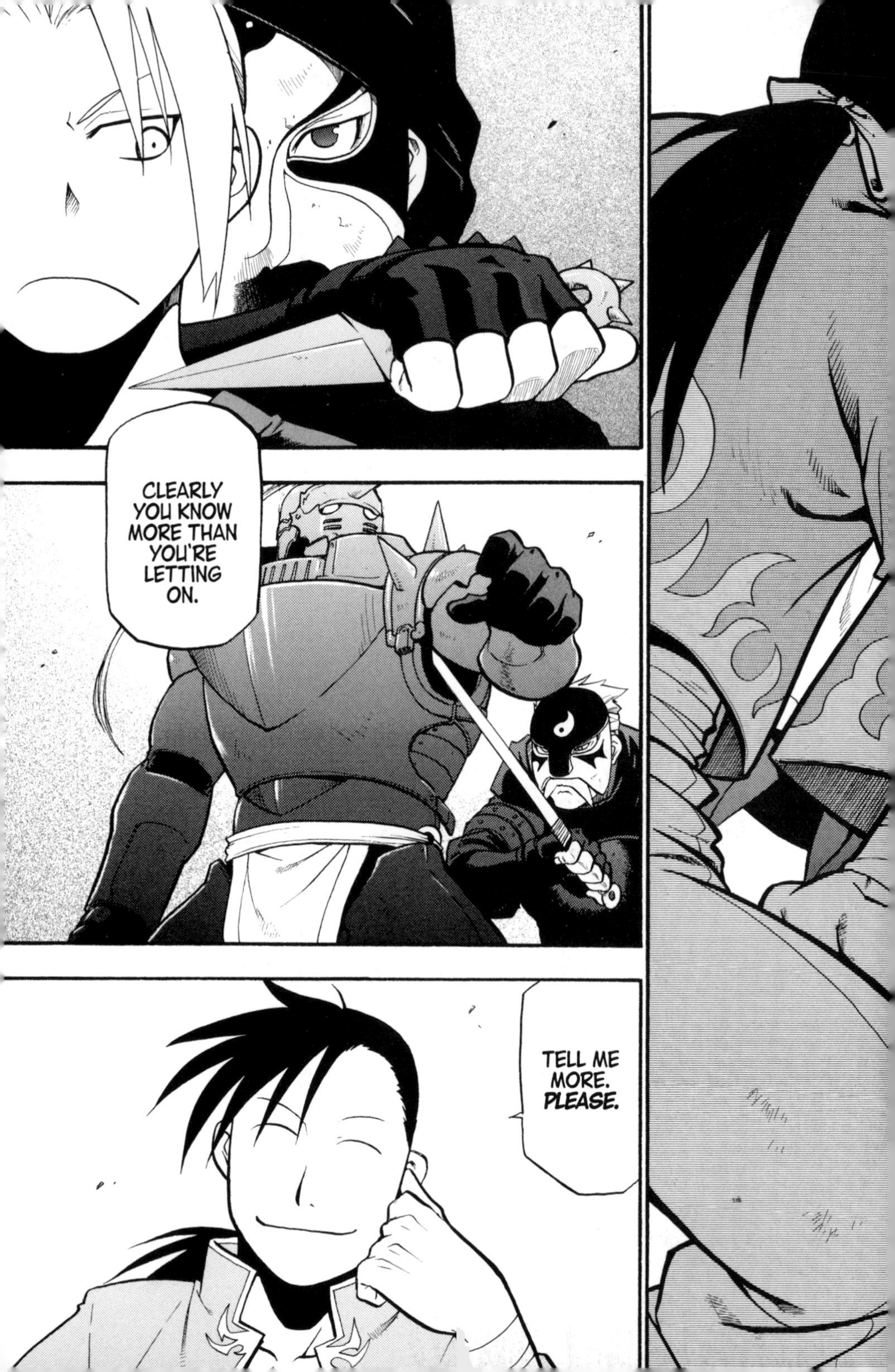
CLEARLY YOU KNOW MORE THAN YOU'RE LETTING ON.
TELL ME MORE. **PLEASE.**

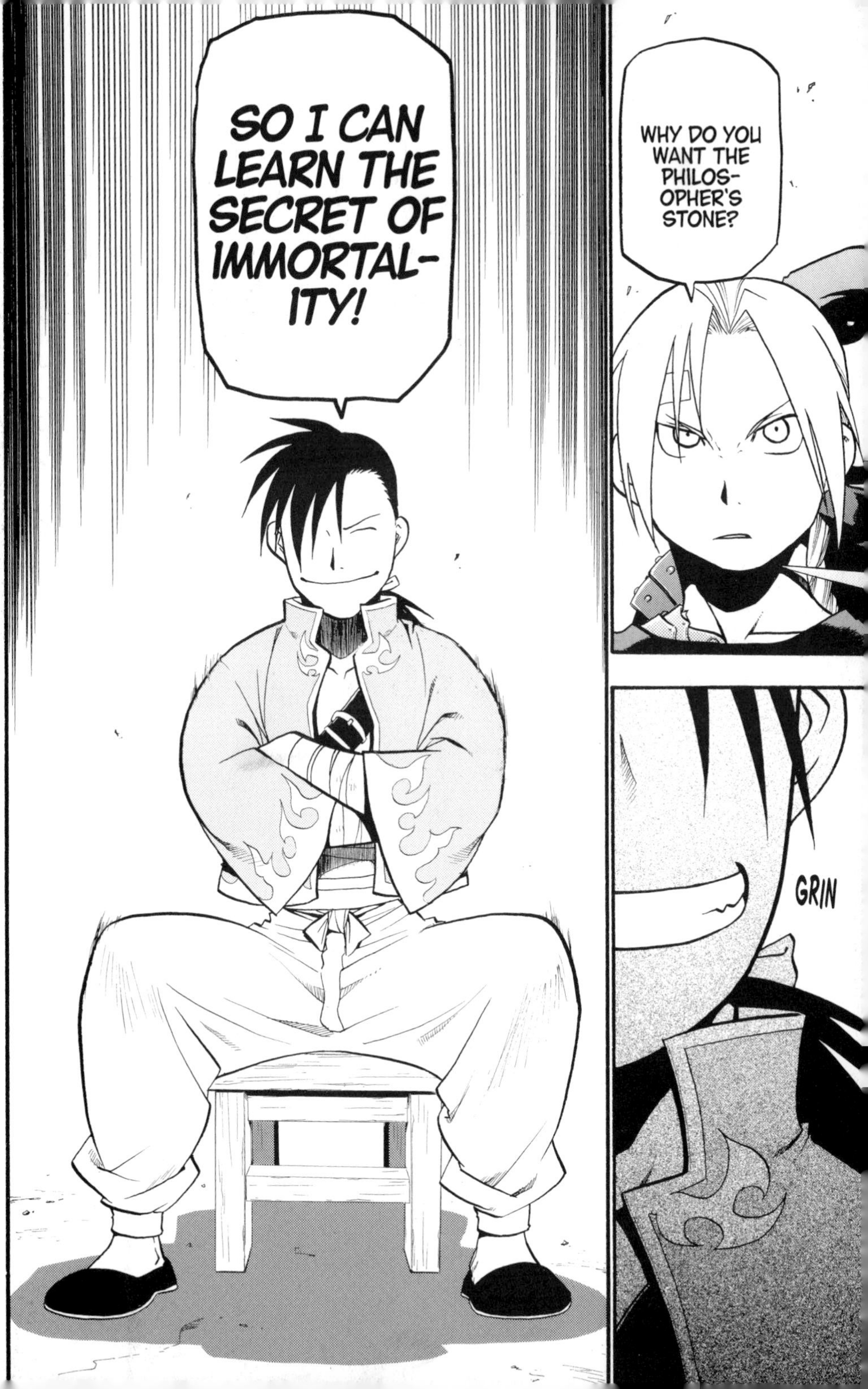
WHY DO YOU WANT THE PHILOS-OPHER'S STONE?
GRIN
SO I CAN LEARN THE SECRET OF IMMORTAL-ITY!

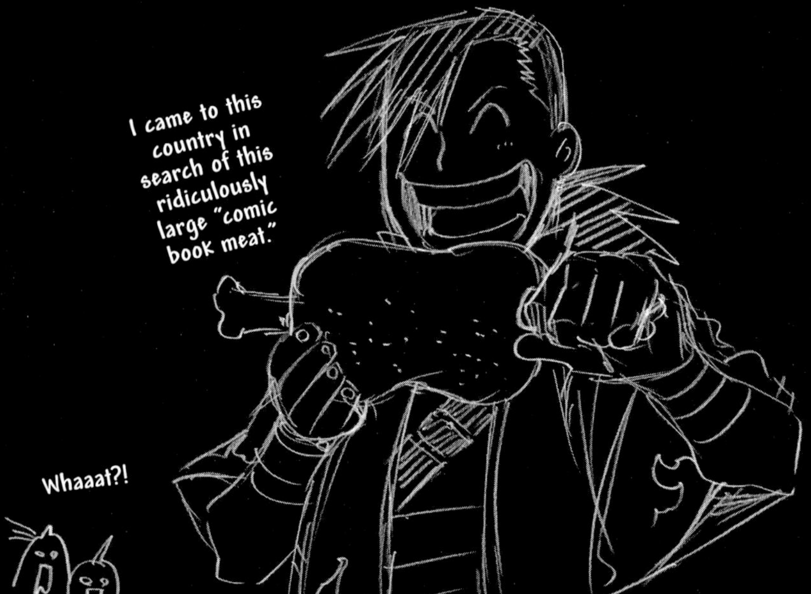
I came to this country in search of this ridiculously large "comic book meat."
Whaaat?!

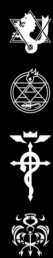

CHAPTER 33

SHOWDOWN IN RUSH VALLEY

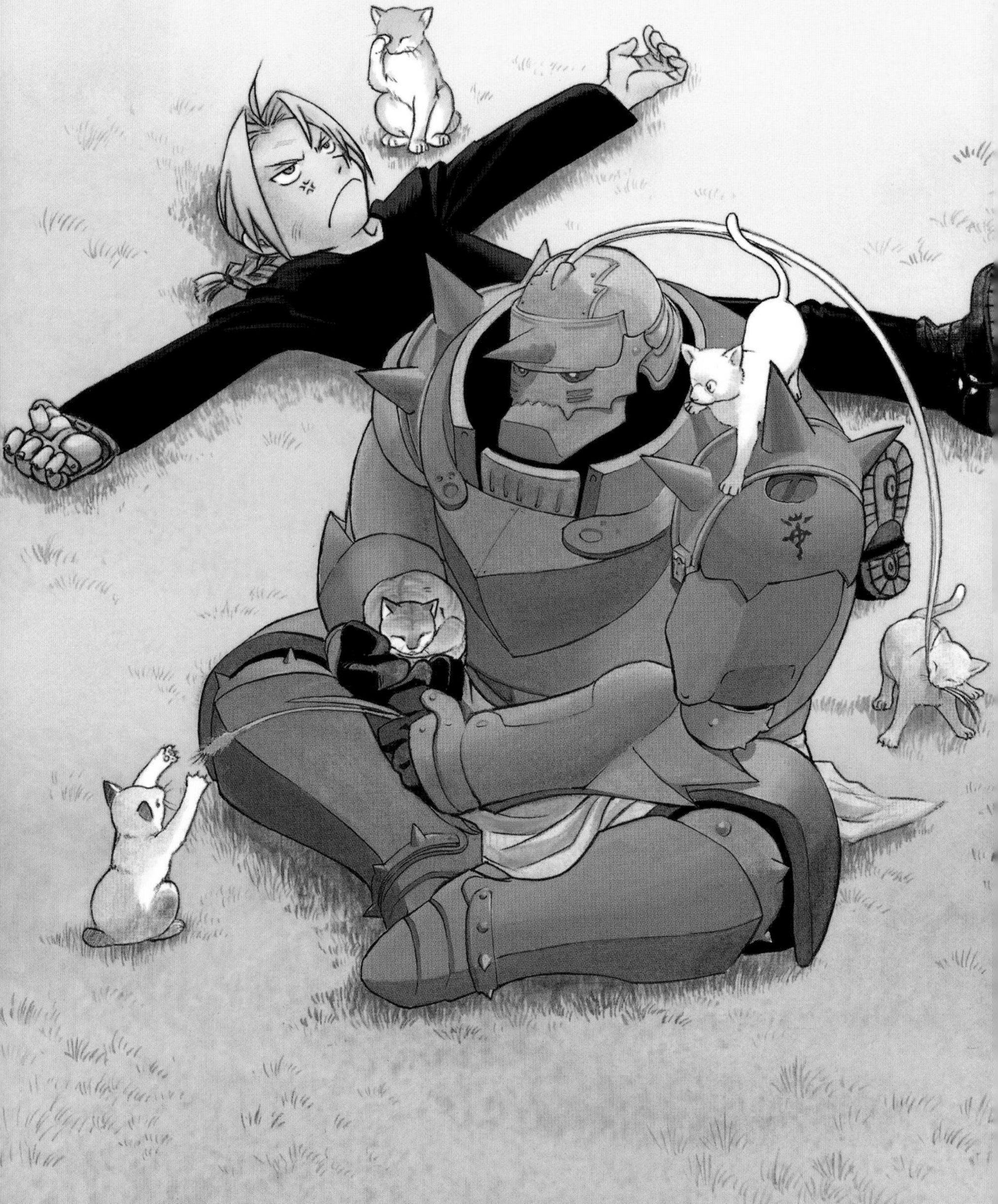

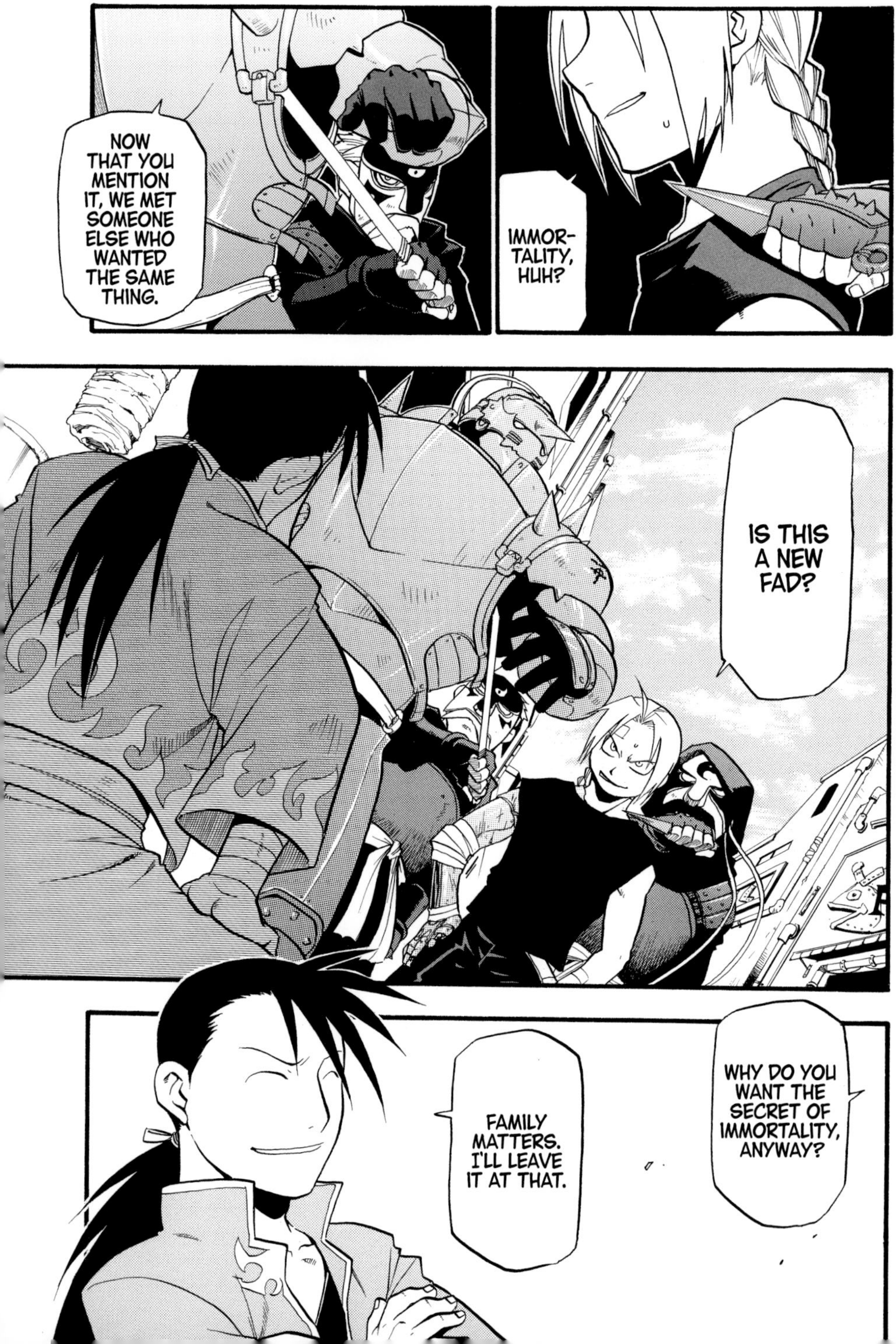
IMMOR-TALITY, HUH?
NOW THAT YOU MENTION IT, WE MET SOMEONE ELSE WHO WANTED THE SAME THING.
IS THIS A NEW FAD?
WHY DO YOU WANT THE SECRET OF IMMORTALITY, ANYWAY?
FAMILY MATTERS. I'LL LEAVE IT AT THAT.

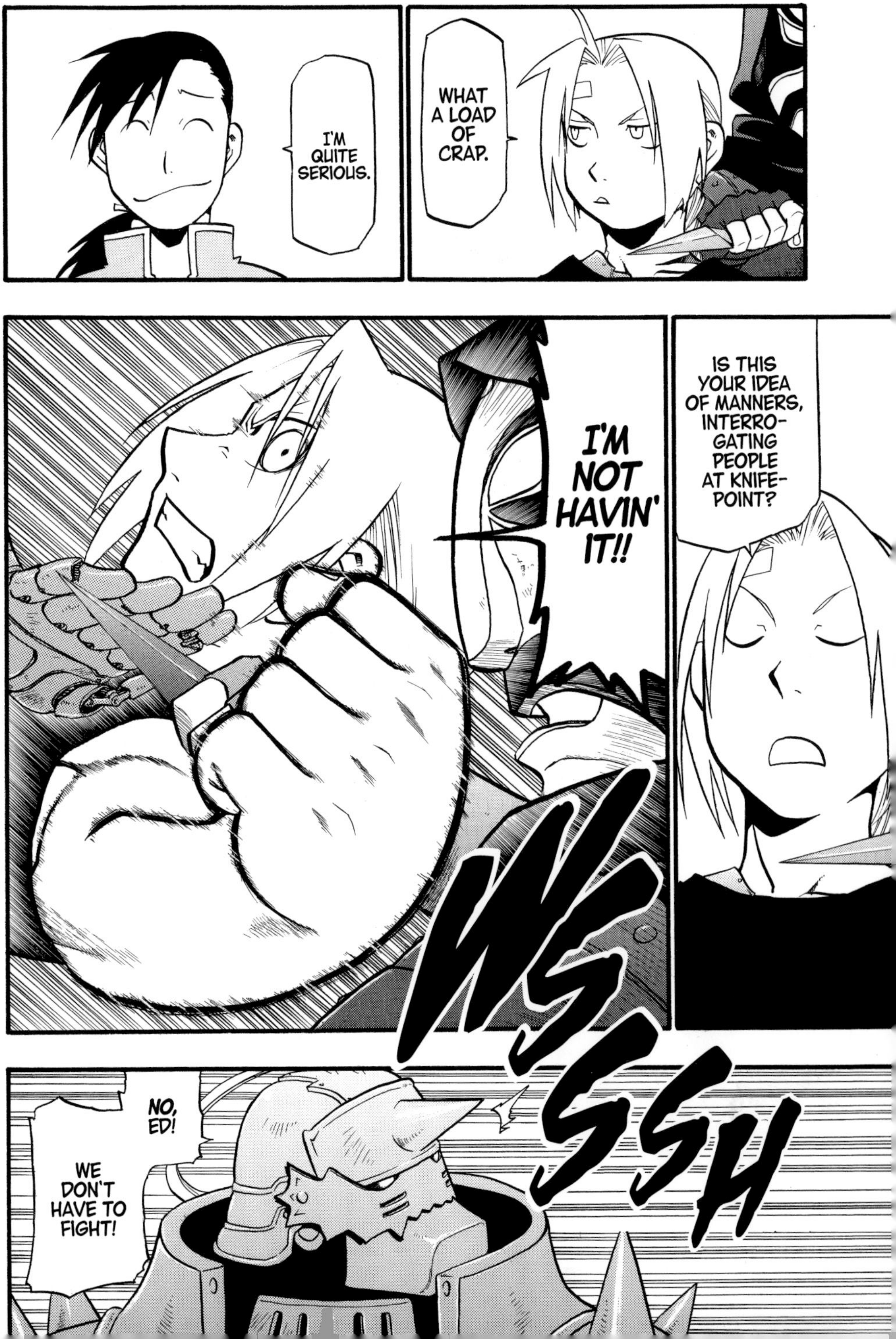
WHAT A LOAD OF CRAP.
I'M QUITE SERIOUS.
IS THIS YOUR IDEA OF MANNERS, INTERRO-GATING PEOPLE AT KNIFE-POINT?
I'M NOT HAVIN' IT!!
WSSSH
NO, ED!
WE DON'T HAVE TO FIGHT!

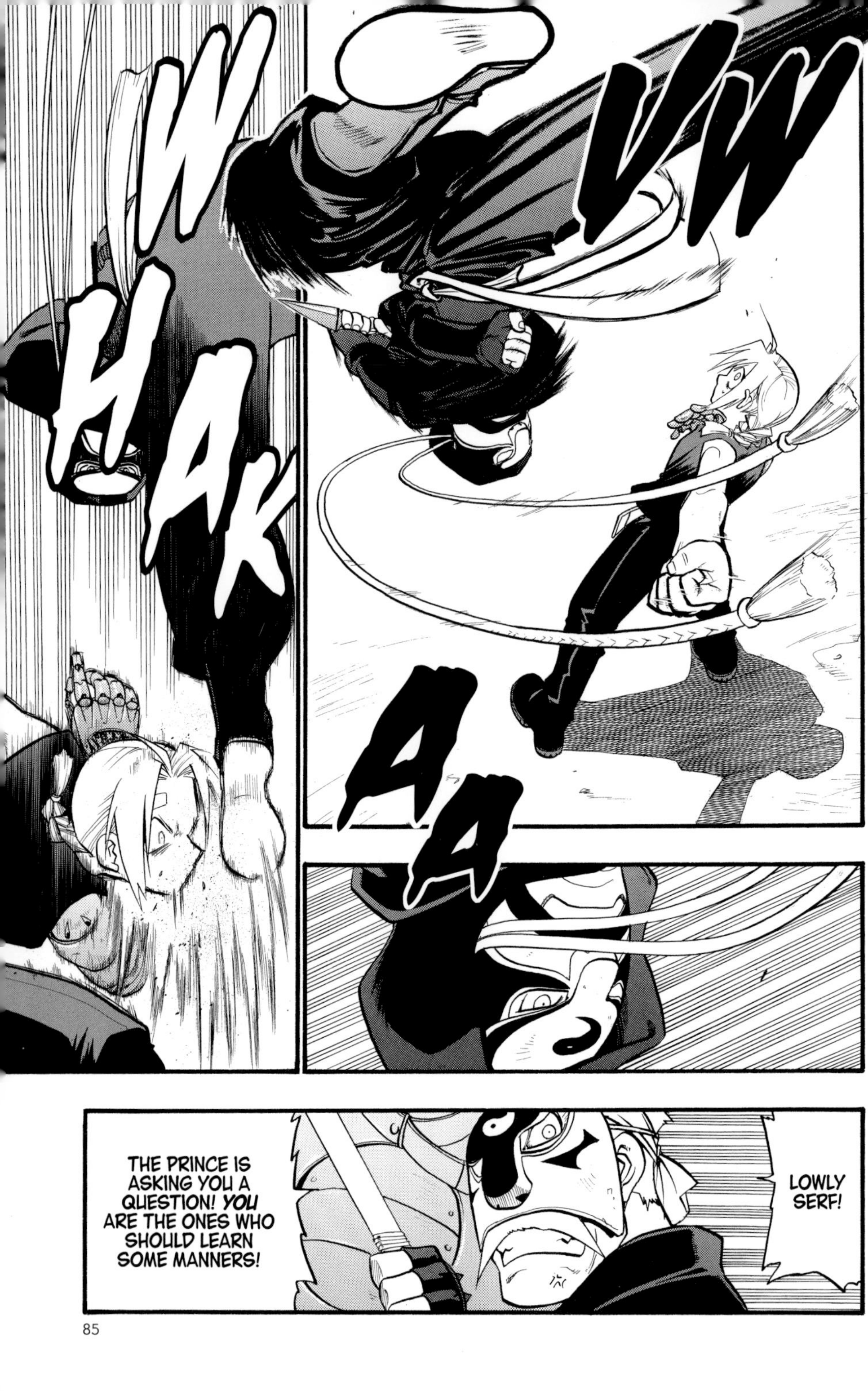
WHAK
LOWLY SERF!
THE PRINCE IS ASKING YOU A QUESTION! ***YOU*** ARE THE ONES WHO SHOULD LEARN SOME MANNERS!

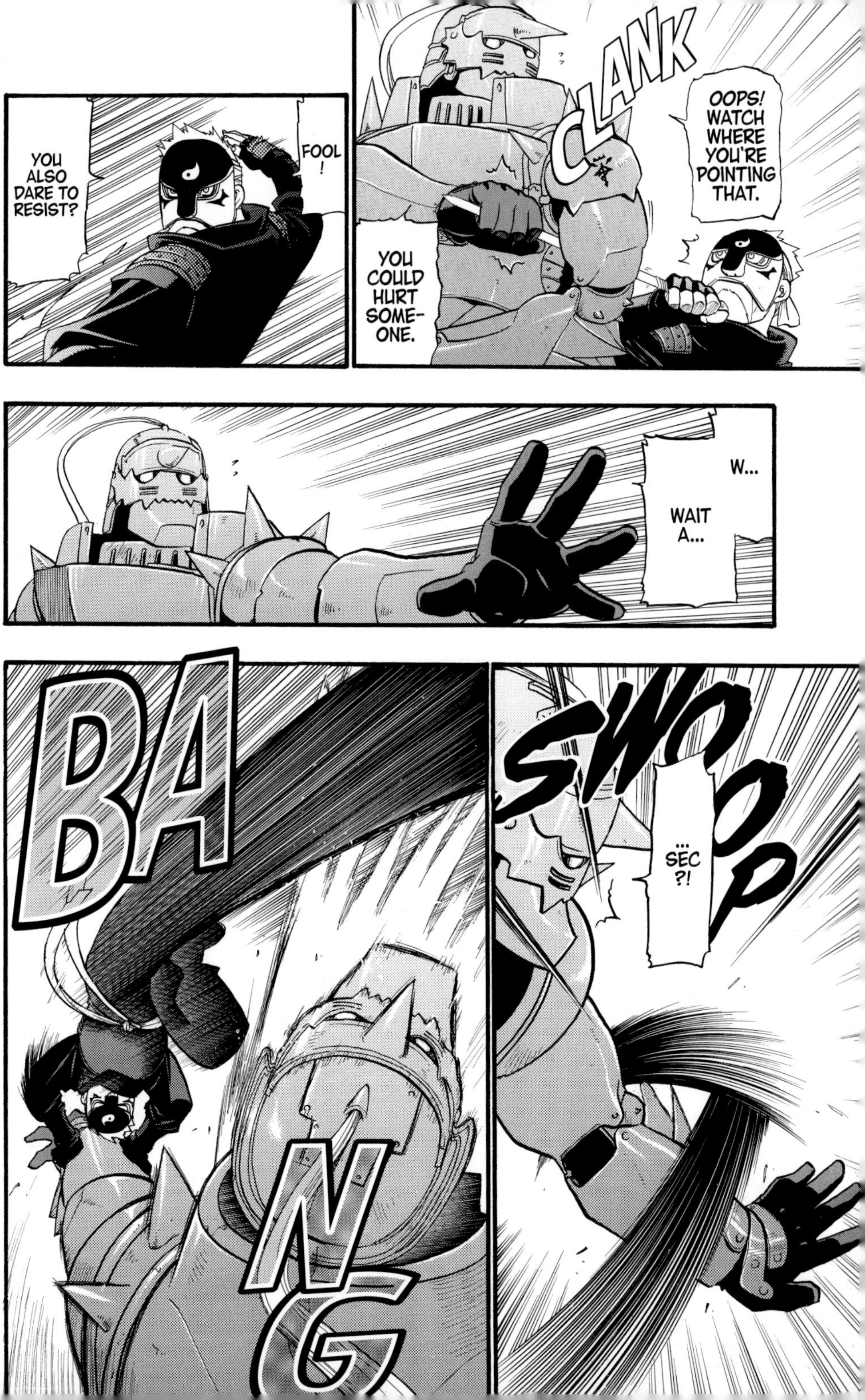
CLANK
OOPS! WATCH WHERE YOU'RE POINTING THAT.
YOU COULD HURT SOME-ONE.
FOOL!
YOU ALSO DARE TO RESIST?
W...
WAIT A...
SWOOP
...SEC?!
BANG

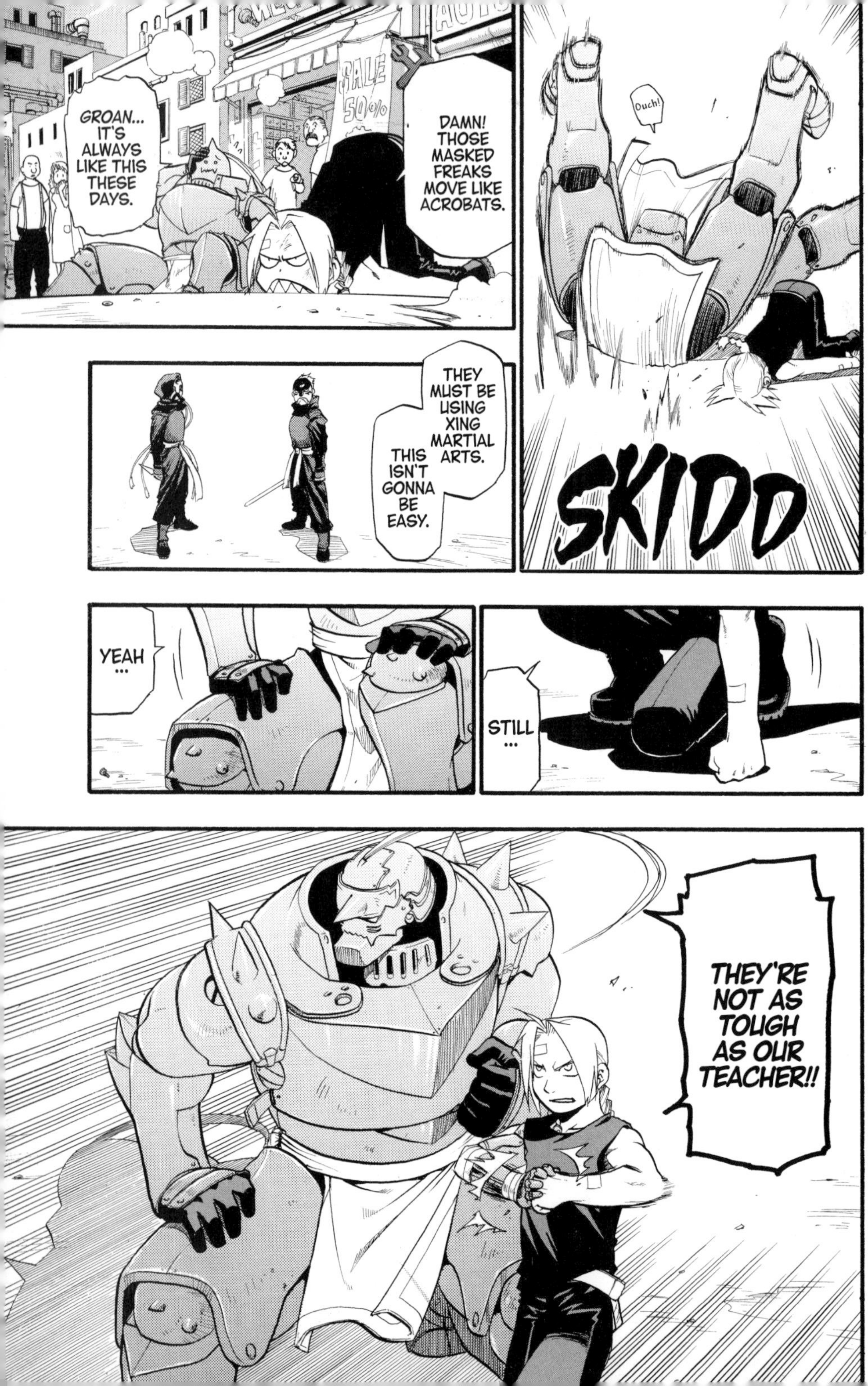
Ouch!
SKIDD
SALE 50%
DAMN! THOSE MASKED FREAKS MOVE LIKE ACROBATS.
GROAN... IT'S ALWAYS LIKE THIS THESE DAYS.
THEY MUST BE USING XING MARTIAL ARTS.
THIS ISN'T GONNA BE EASY.
STILL ...
YEAH ...
THEY'RE NOT AS TOUGH AS OUR TEACHER!!

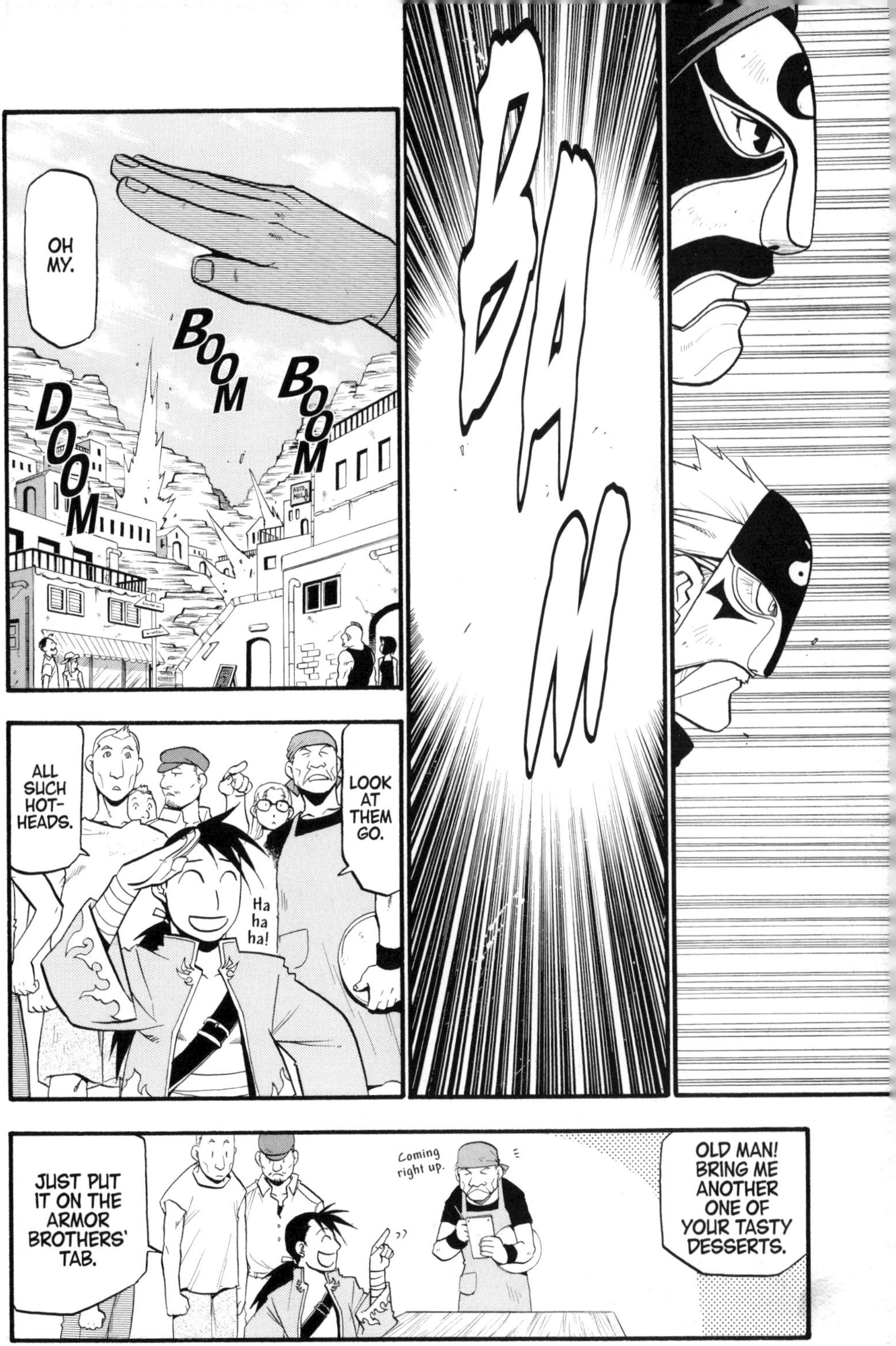

OH MY.
BOOM
BOOM
DOOM
LOOK AT THEM GO.
Ha ha ha!
ALL SUCH HOT-HEADS.
OLD MAN! BRING ME ANOTHER ONE OF YOUR TASTY DESSERTS.
Coming right up.
JUST PUT IT ON THE ARMOR BROTHERS' TAB.

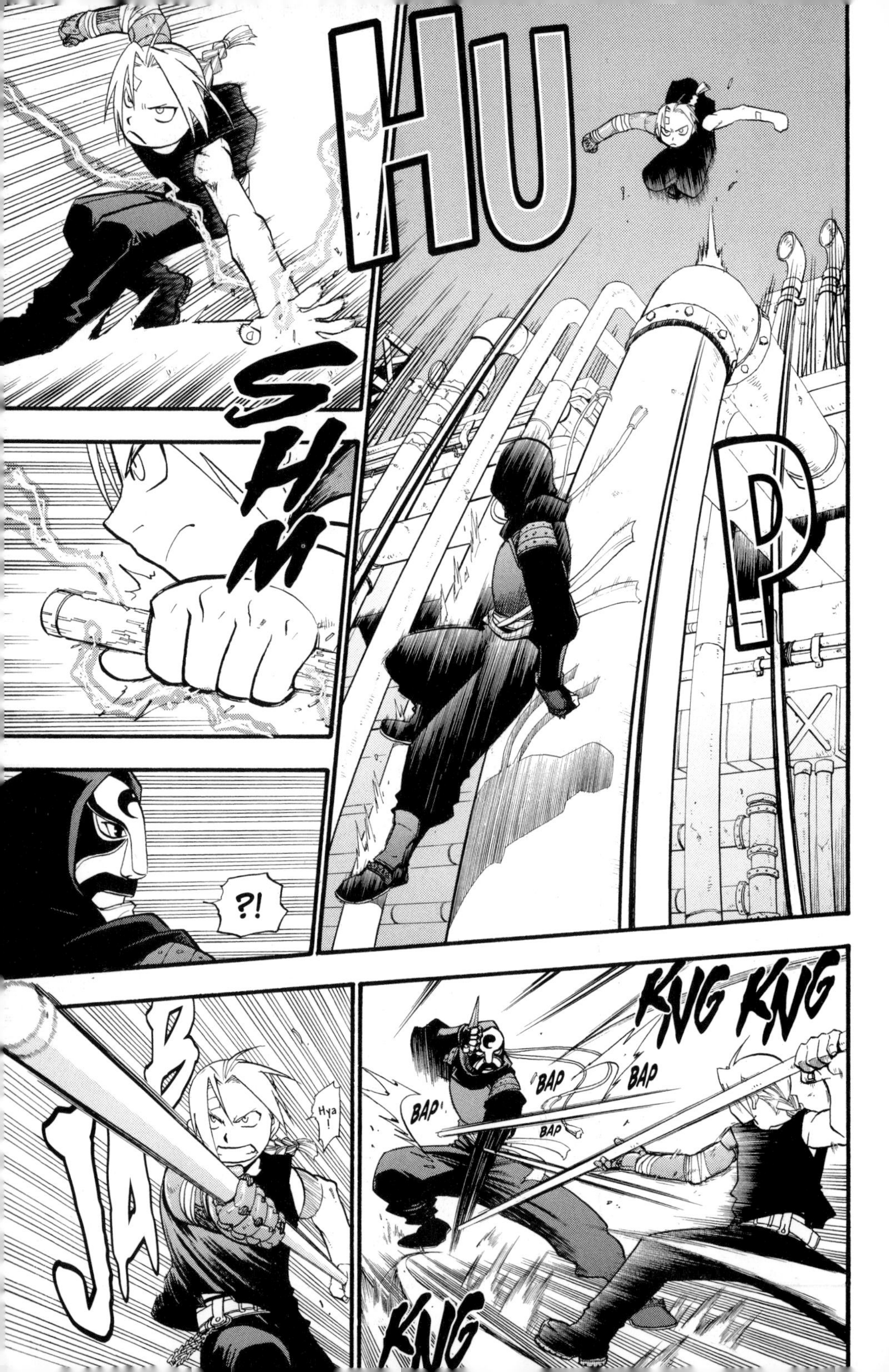
HUP
SHM
?!
KNG KNG
BAP
BAP
BAP
BAP
KNG
Hya!
JAB

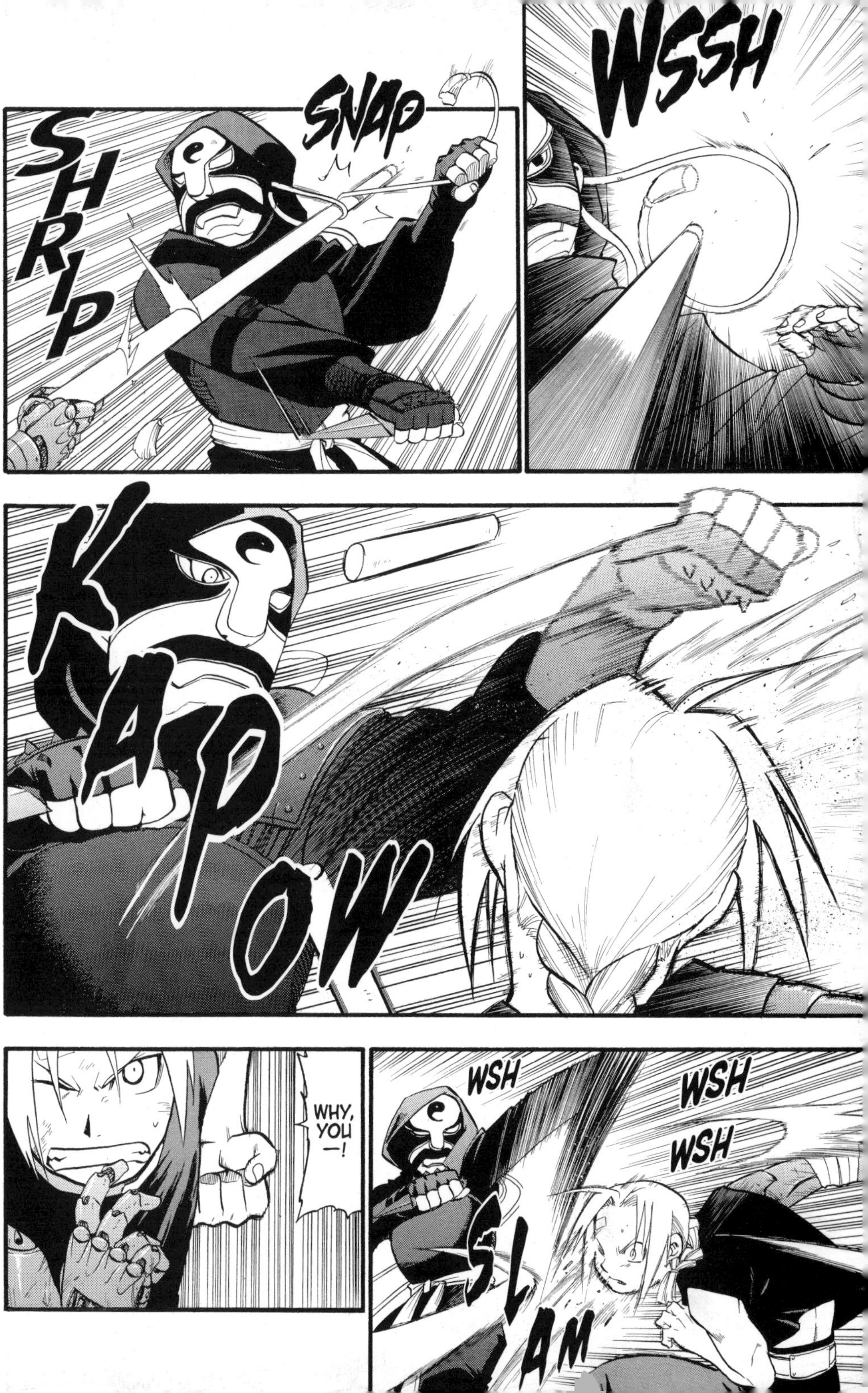
WSSH
SNAP
SHRIP
KAPOW
WSH
WSH
WSH
SLAM
WHY, YOU—!

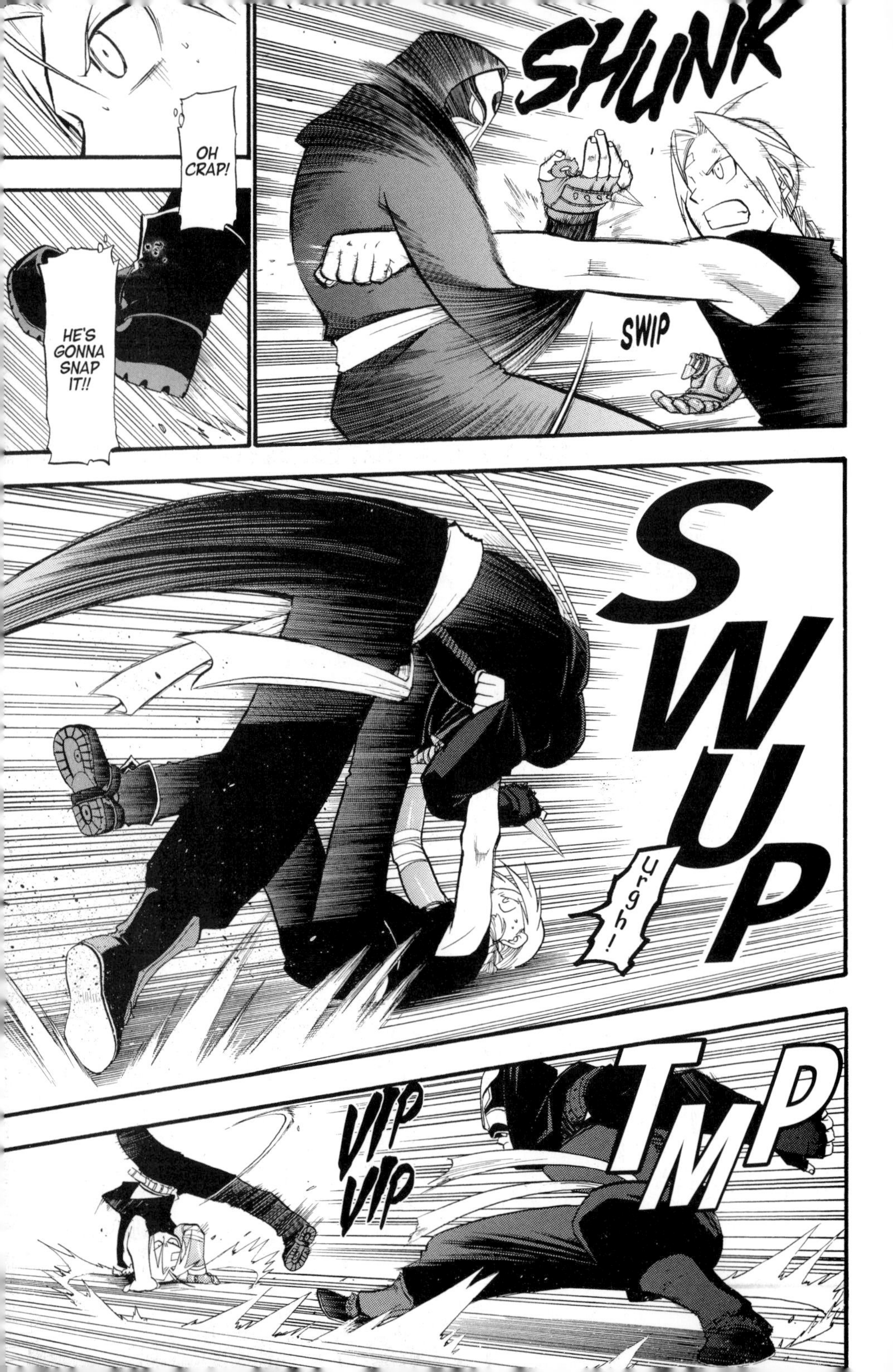
SHUNK
SWIP
OH CRAP!
HE'S GONNA SNAP IT!!
SWUP
Urgh!
TMP
VIP VIP

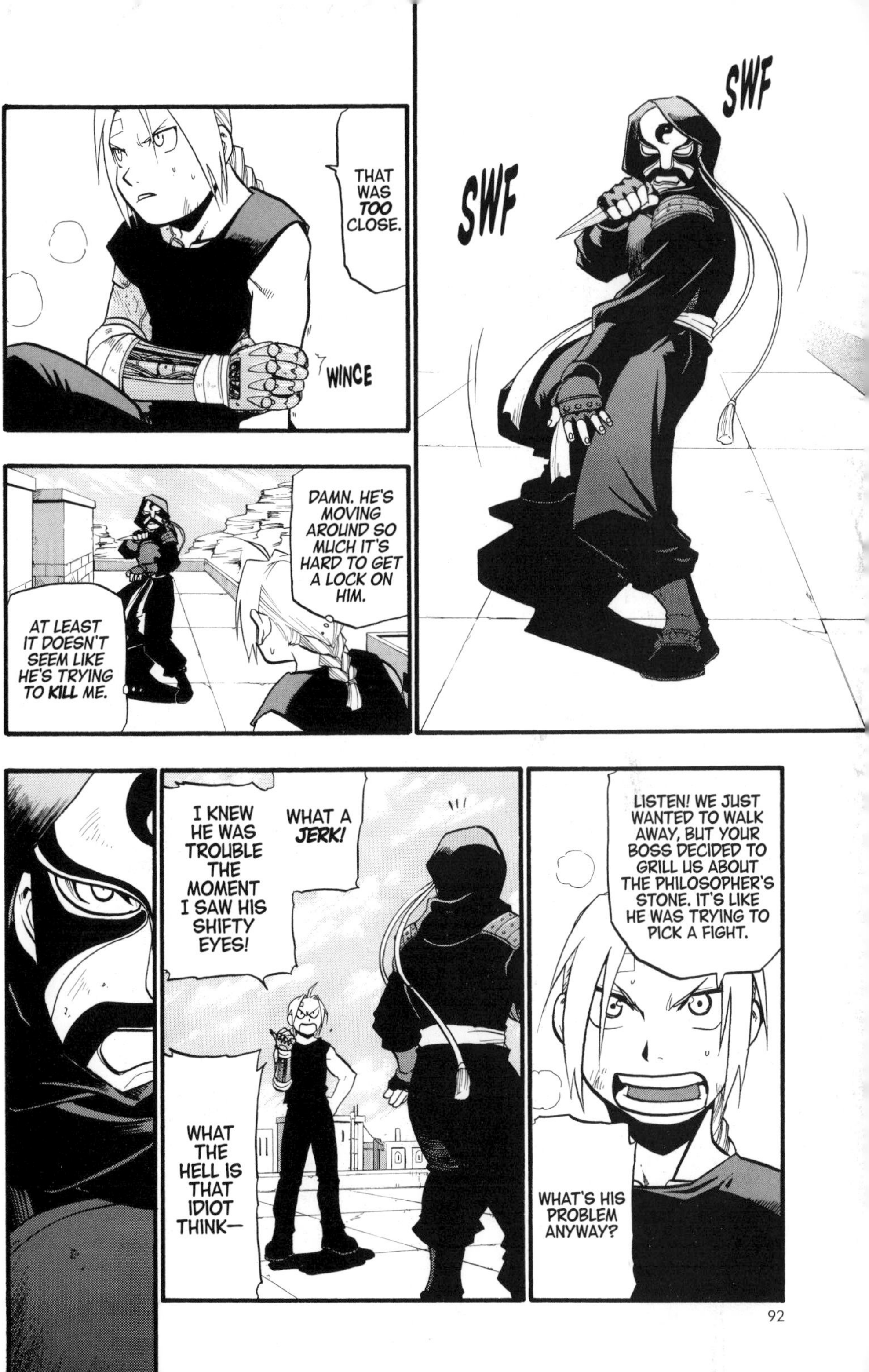
SWF
SWF
THAT WAS TOO CLOSE.
WINCE
DAMN. HE'S MOVING AROUND SO MUCH IT'S HARD TO GET A LOCK ON HIM.
AT LEAST IT DOESN'T SEEM LIKE HE'S TRYING TO KILL ME.
LISTEN! WE JUST WANTED TO WALK AWAY, BUT YOUR BOSS DECIDED TO GRILL US ABOUT THE PHILOSOPHER'S STONE. IT'S LIKE HE WAS TRYING TO PICK A FIGHT.
WHAT'S HIS PROBLEM ANYWAY?
WHAT A JERK!
I KNEW HE WAS TROUBLE THE MOMENT I SAW HIS SHIFTY EYES!
WHAT THE HELL IS THAT IDIOT THINK—

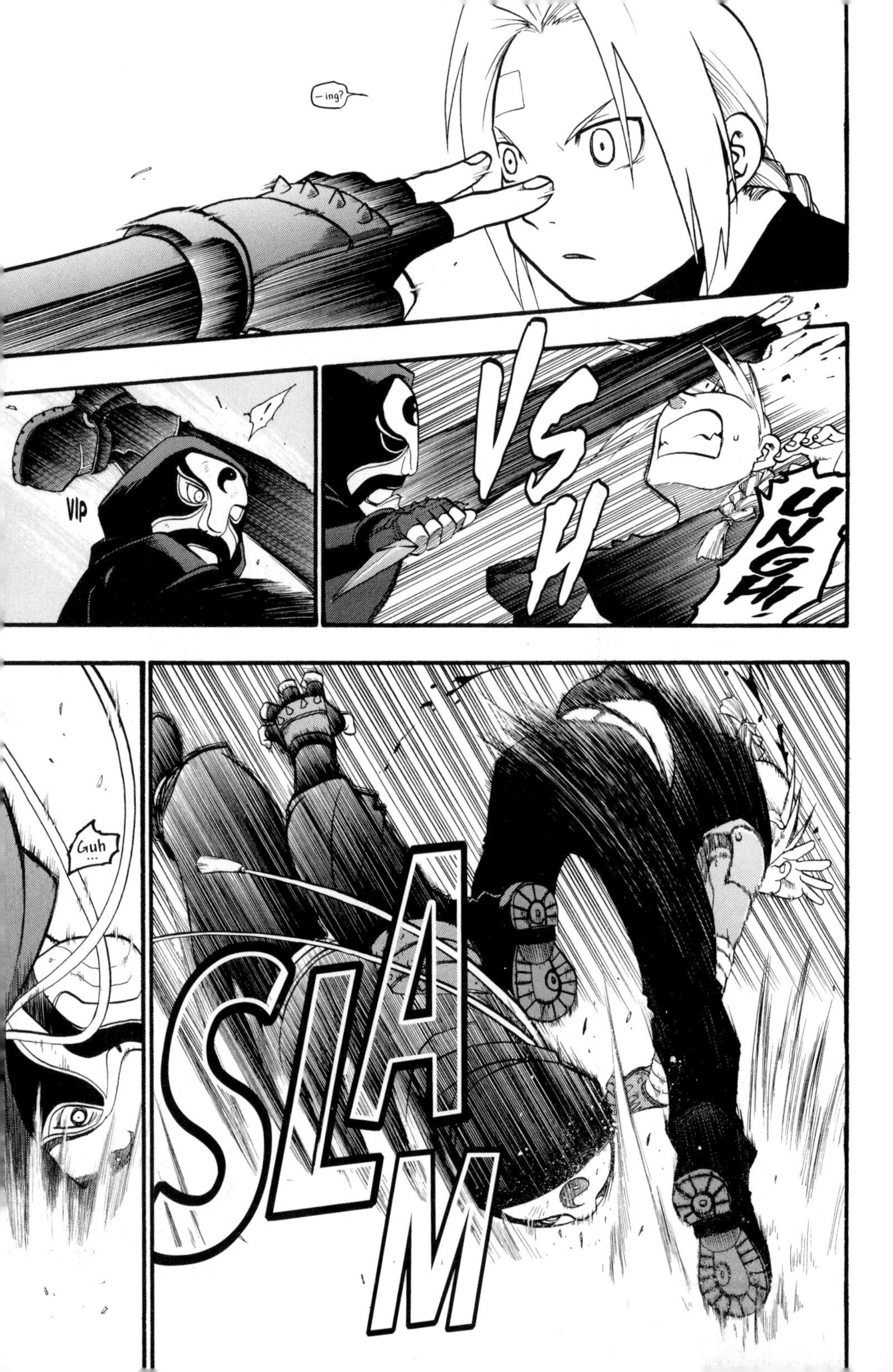
—ing?
VSH
UNGH!
VIP
SLAM
Guh...

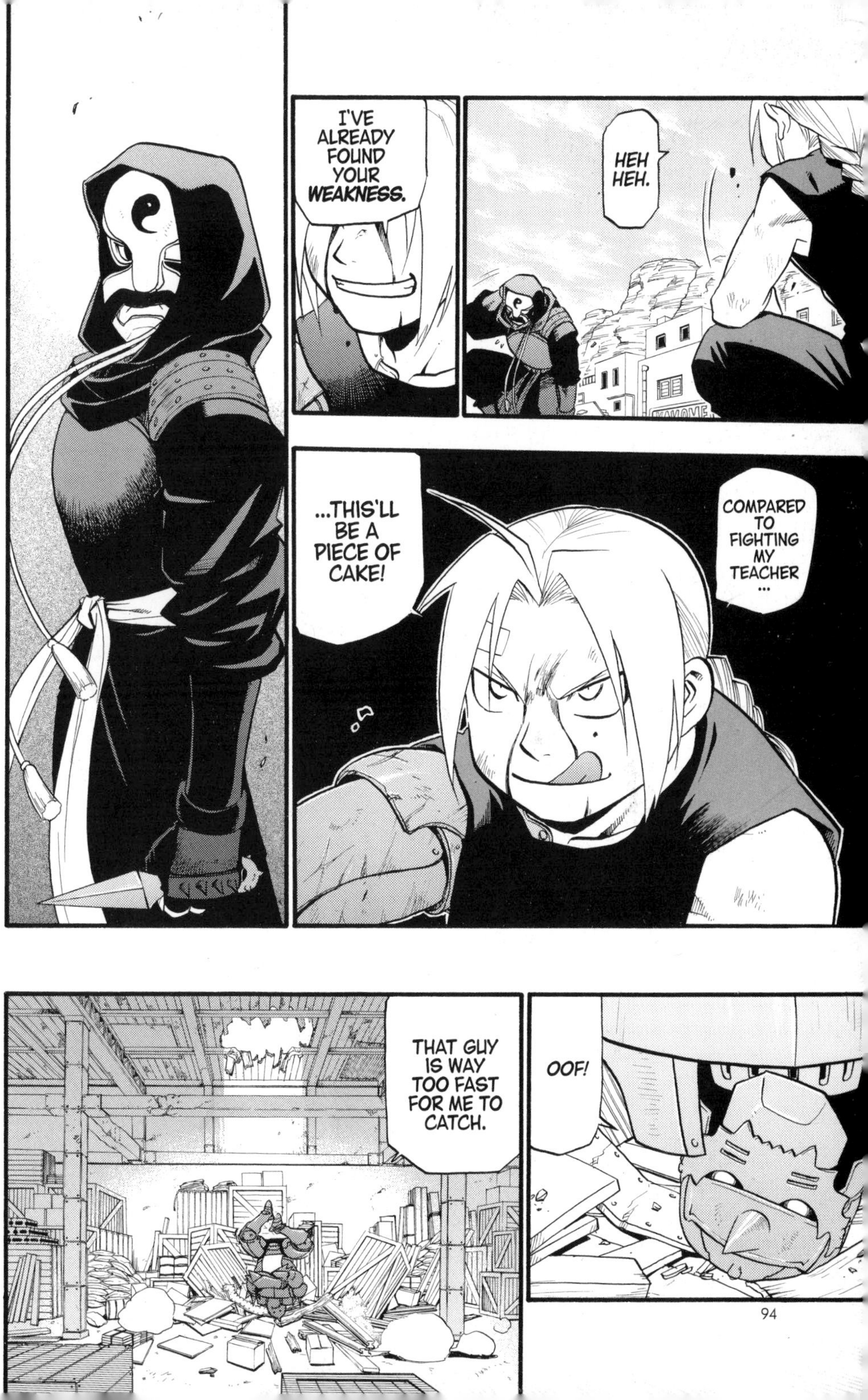
HEH HEH.
I'VE ALREADY FOUND YOUR WEAKNESS.
COMPARED TO FIGHTING MY TEACHER...
...THIS'LL BE A PIECE OF CAKE!
OOF!
THAT GUY IS WAY TOO FAST FOR ME TO CATCH.

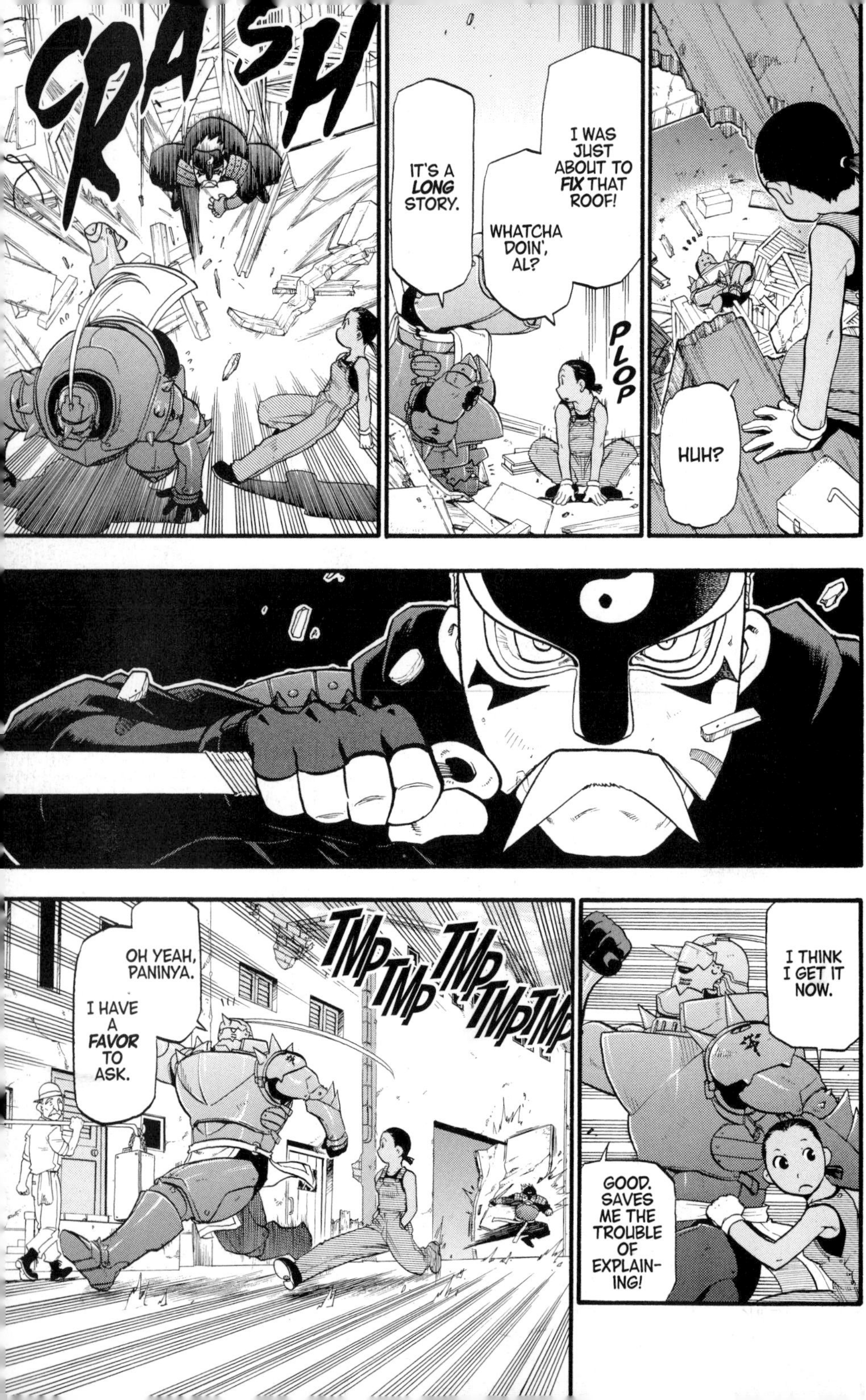
HUH?
I WAS JUST ABOUT TO FIX THAT ROOF!
WHATCHA DOIN', AL?
PLOP
IT'S A LONG STORY.
CRASH
I THINK I GET IT NOW.
GOOD. SAVES ME THE TROUBLE OF EXPLAINING!
TMP TMP TMP TMP TMP
OH YEAH, PANINYA.
I HAVE A FAVOR TO ASK.

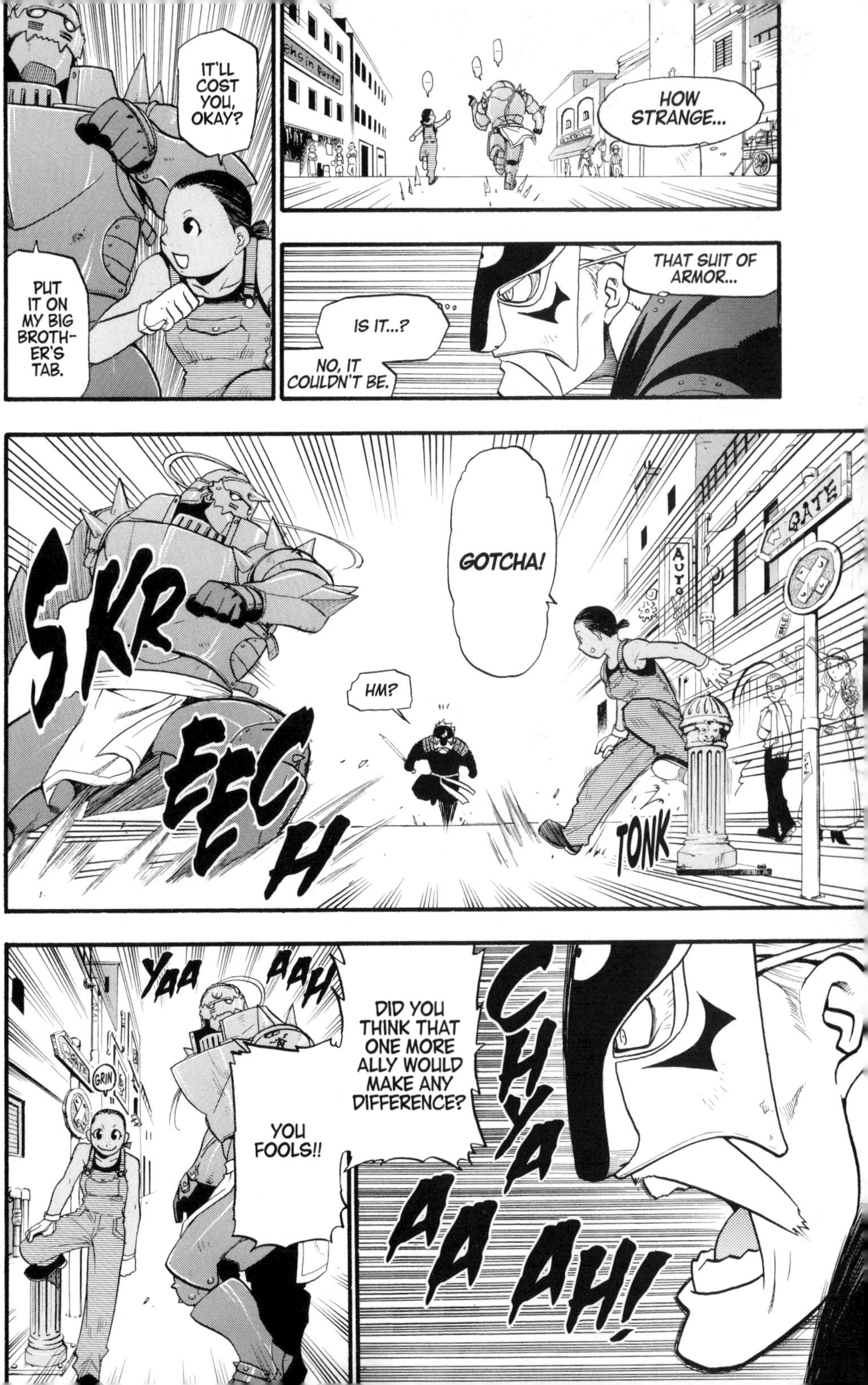
...
...
...
HOW STRANGE...
THAT SUIT OF ARMOR...
IS IT...?
NO, IT COULDN'T BE.
IT'LL COST YOU, OKAY?
PUT IT ON MY BIG BROTHER'S TAB.
GOTCHA!
HM?
TONK
SKREECH
GATE
CHYAAAAAH!
DID YOU THINK THAT ONE MORE ALLY WOULD MAKE ANY DIFFERENCE?
YOU FOOLS!!
YAAAAH
GRIN

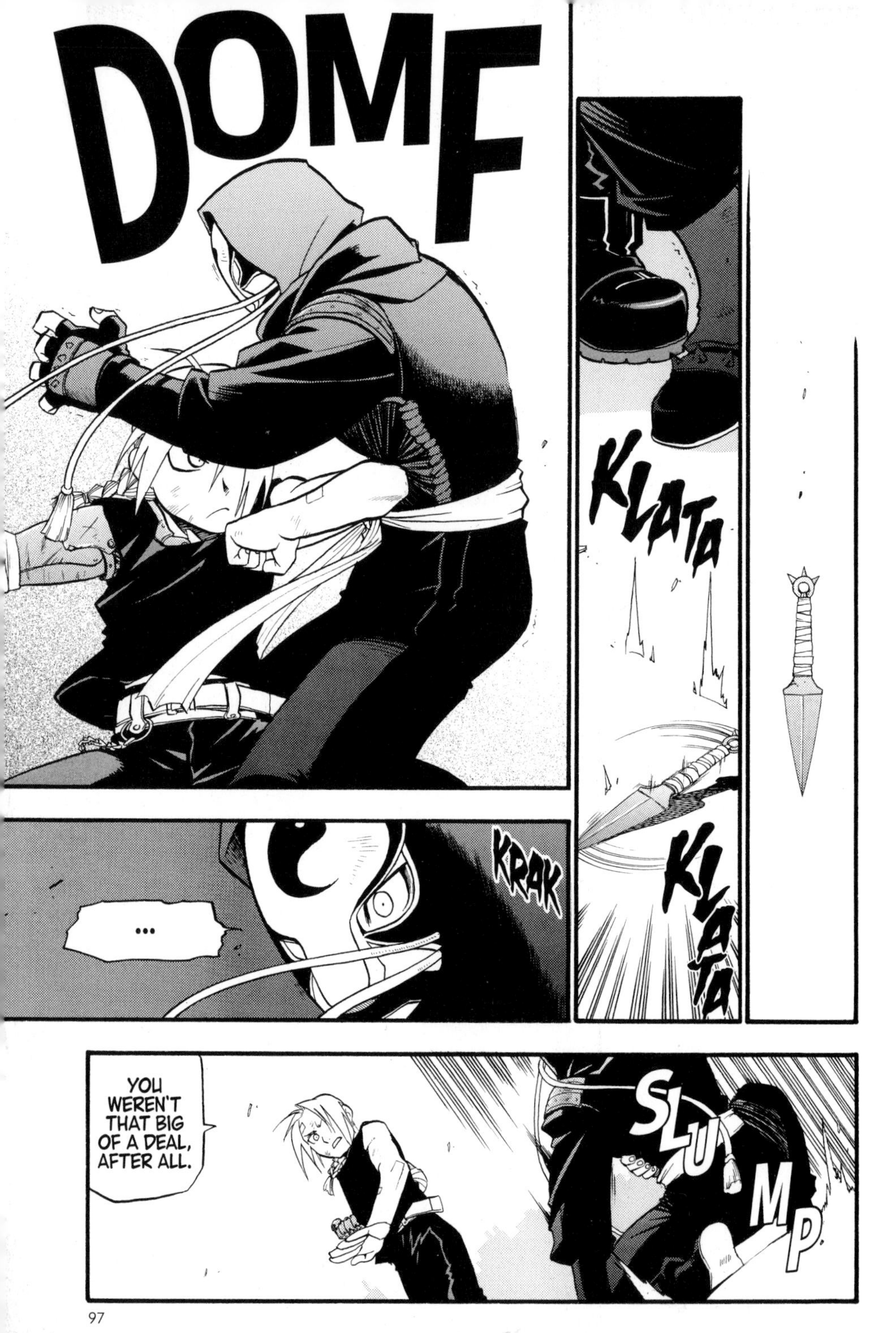
KLATATA
KLATA
DOMF
KRAK
...
SLUMP
YOU WEREN'T THAT BIG OF A DEAL, AFTER ALL.

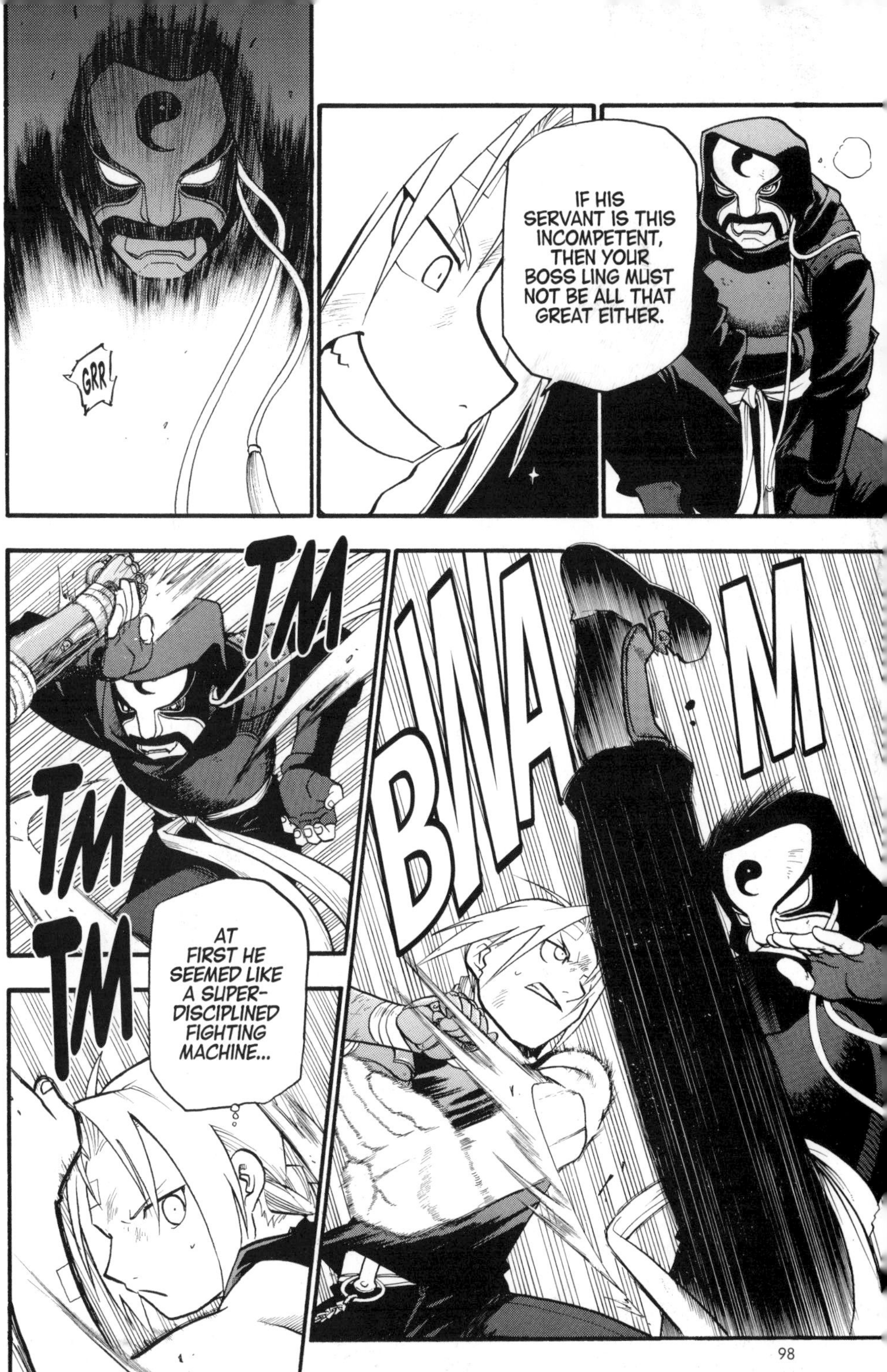
IF HIS SERVANT IS THIS INCOMPETENT, THEN YOUR BOSS LING MUST NOT BE ALL THAT GREAT EITHER.
GRR
BWA M
TM
TM TM
TM
AT FIRST HE SEEMED LIKE A SUPER-DISCIPLINED FIGHTING MACHINE...

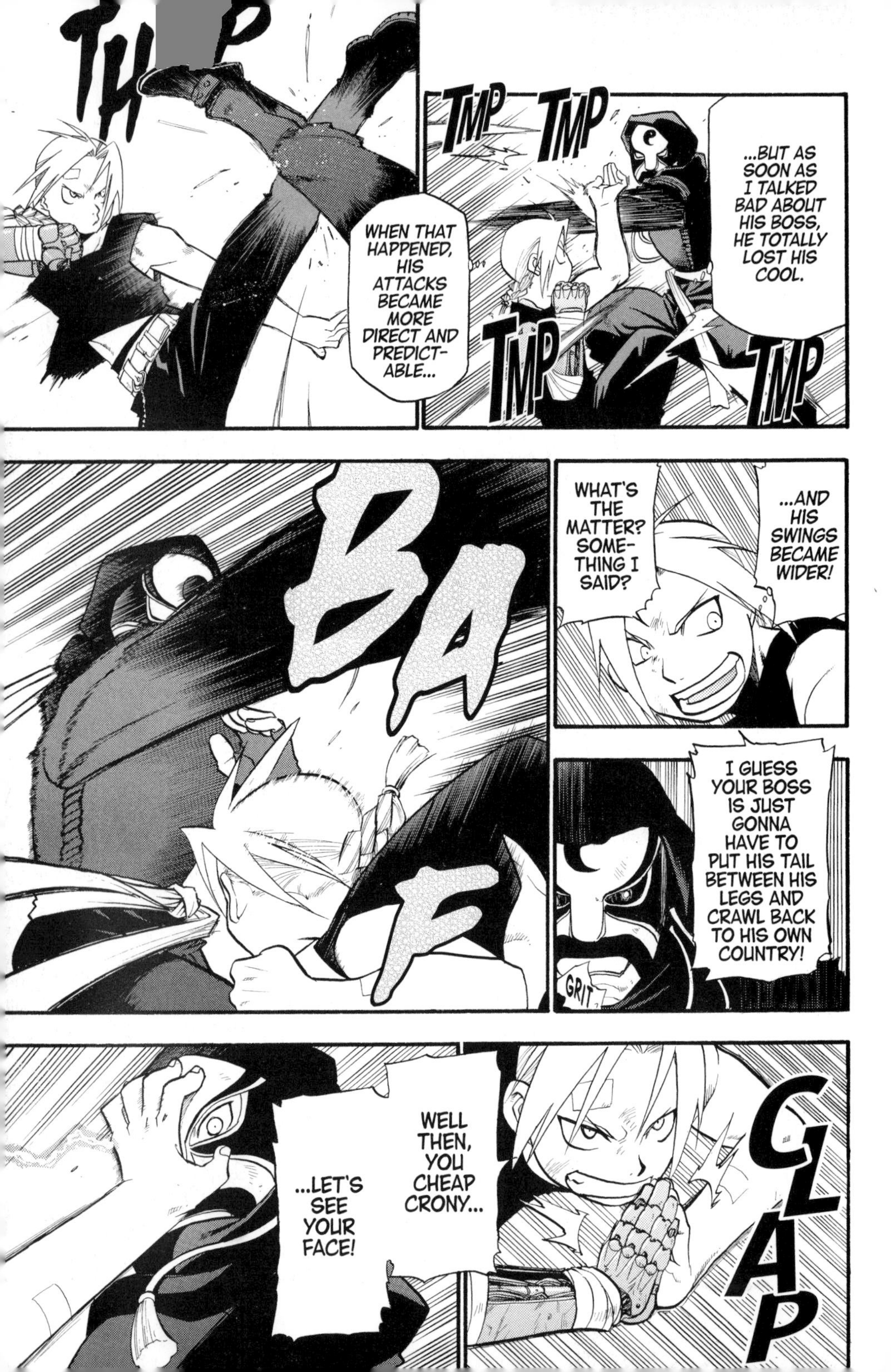
TMP TMP
...BUT AS SOON AS I TALKED BAD ABOUT HIS BOSS, HE TOTALLY LOST HIS COOL.
TMP
TMP
TH P
WHEN THAT HAPPENED, HIS ATTACKS BECAME MORE DIRECT AND PREDICT-ABLE...
...AND HIS SWINGS BECAME WIDER!
WHAT'S THE MATTER? SOME-THING I SAID?
I GUESS YOUR BOSS IS JUST GONNA HAVE TO PUT HIS TAIL BETWEEN HIS LEGS AND CRAWL BACK TO HIS OWN COUNTRY!
GRIT
BAF
CLAP
WELL THEN, YOU CHEAP CRONY...
...LET'S SEE YOUR FACE!

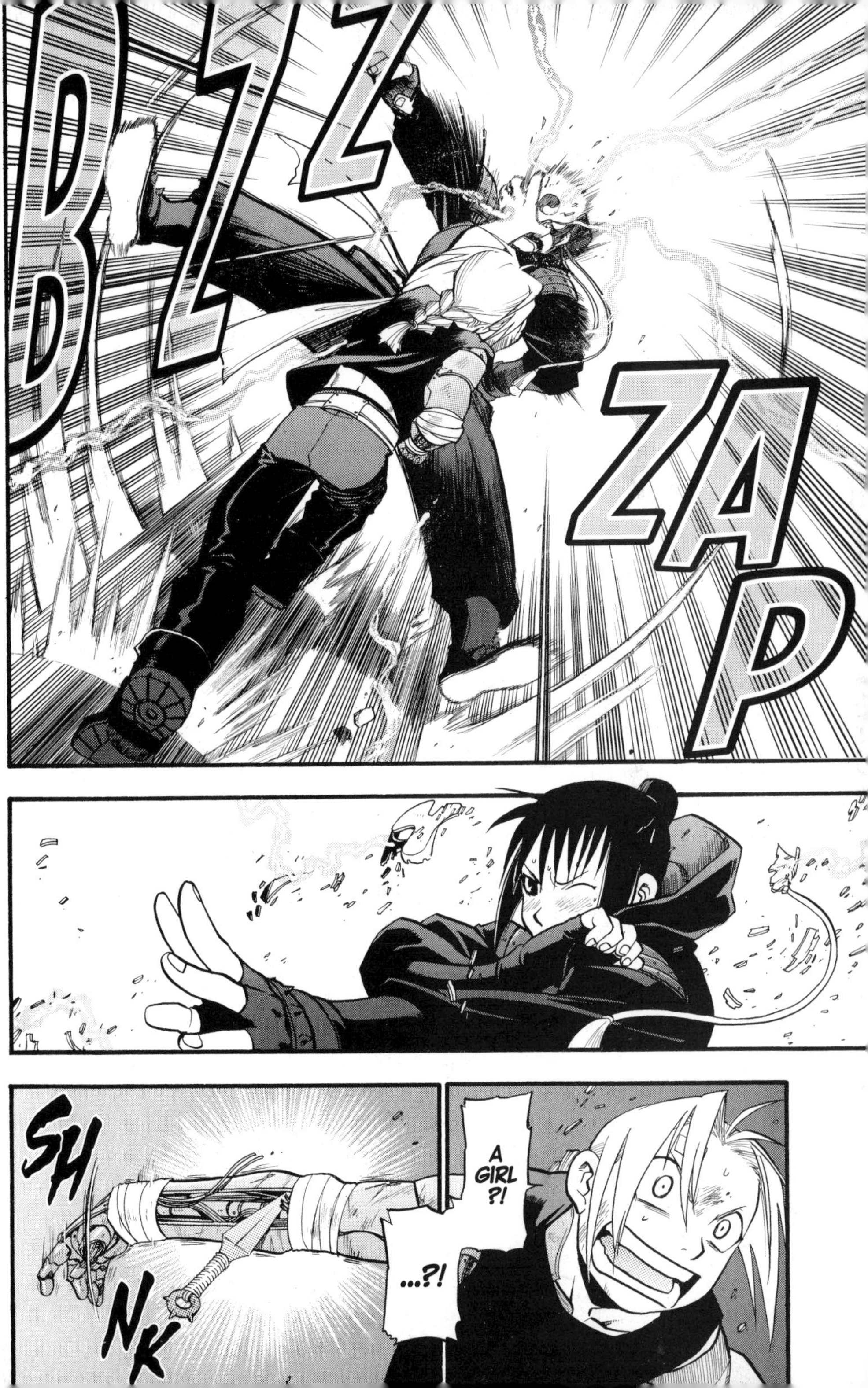
ZAP
BZZ
A GIRL ?!
...?!
SH
NK

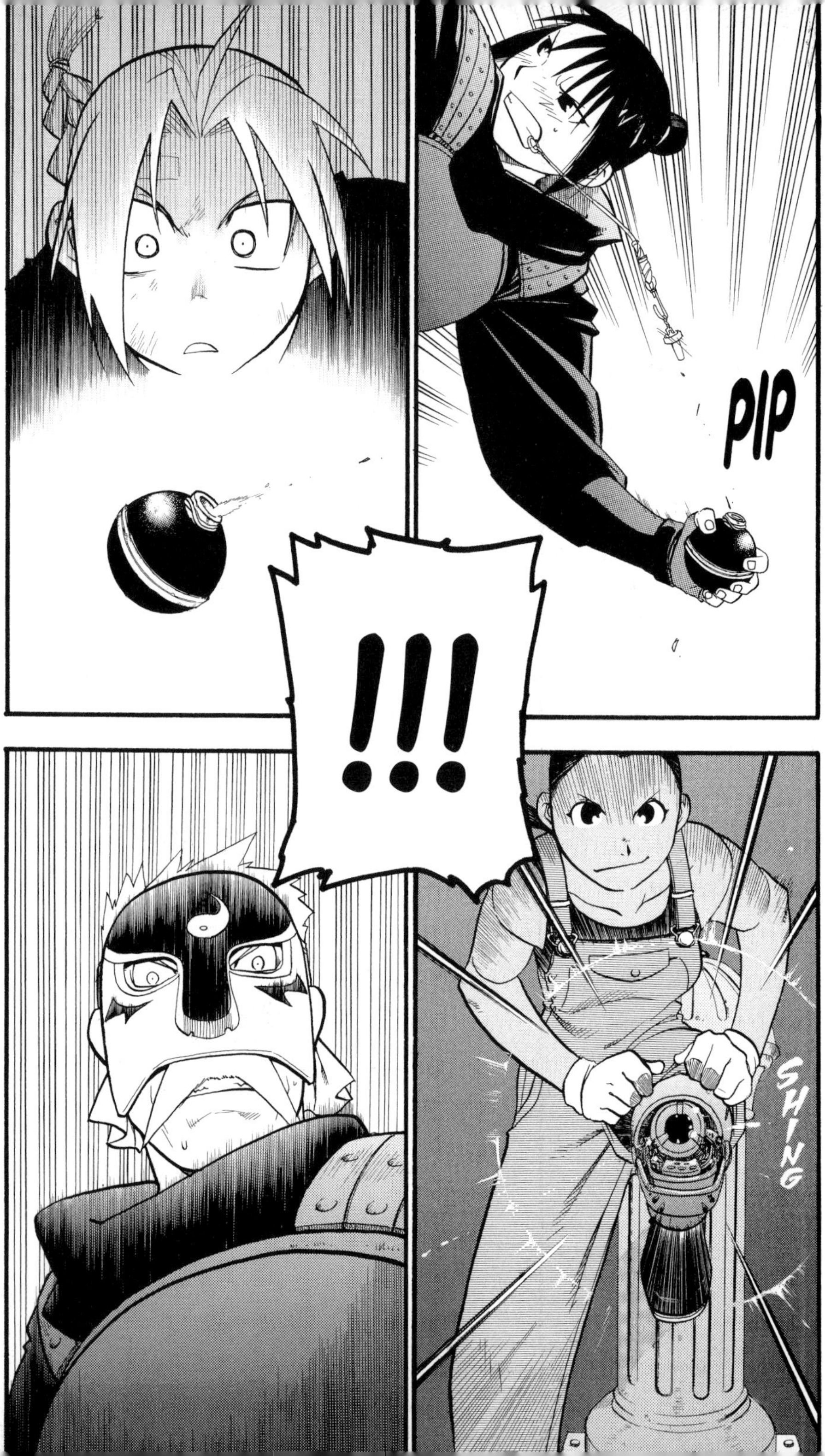
PIP
!!!
SHING

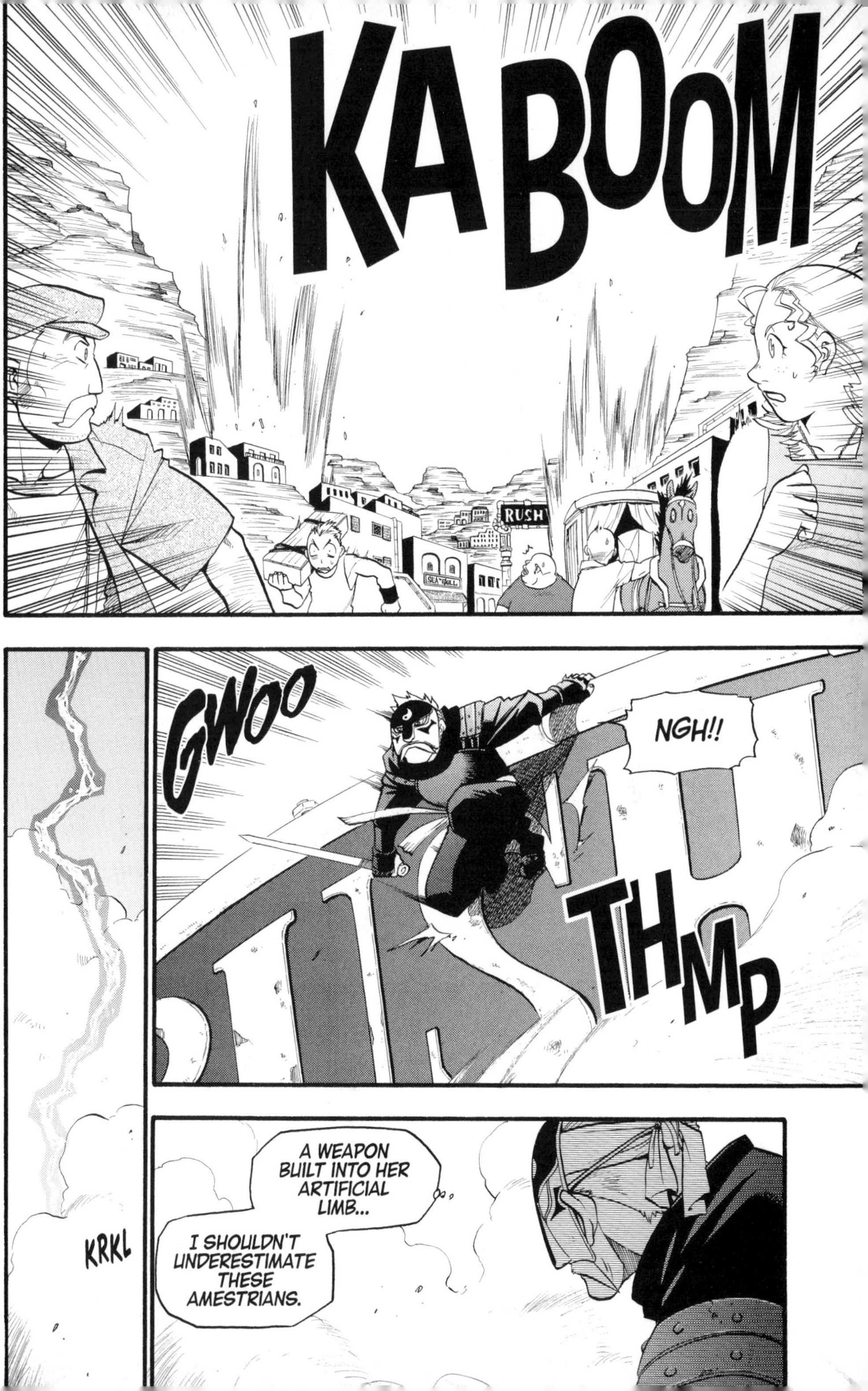
KABOOM
RUSH
SEA GULL
NGH!!
GWOO
THMP
A WEAPON BUILT INTO HER ARTIFICIAL LIMB...
I SHOULDN'T UNDERESTIMATE THESE AMESTRIANS.
KRKL

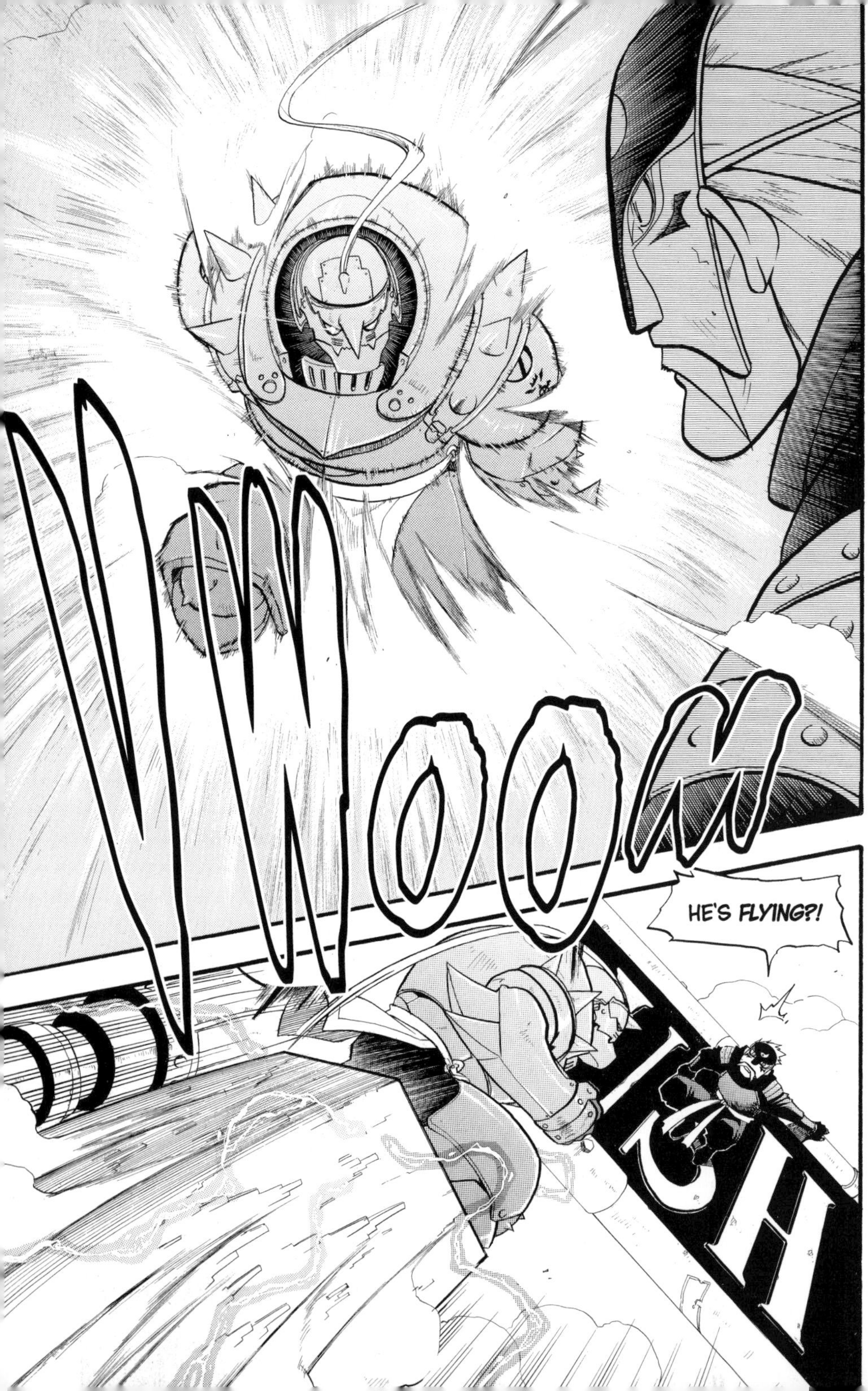
VWOOM
HE'S FLYING?!

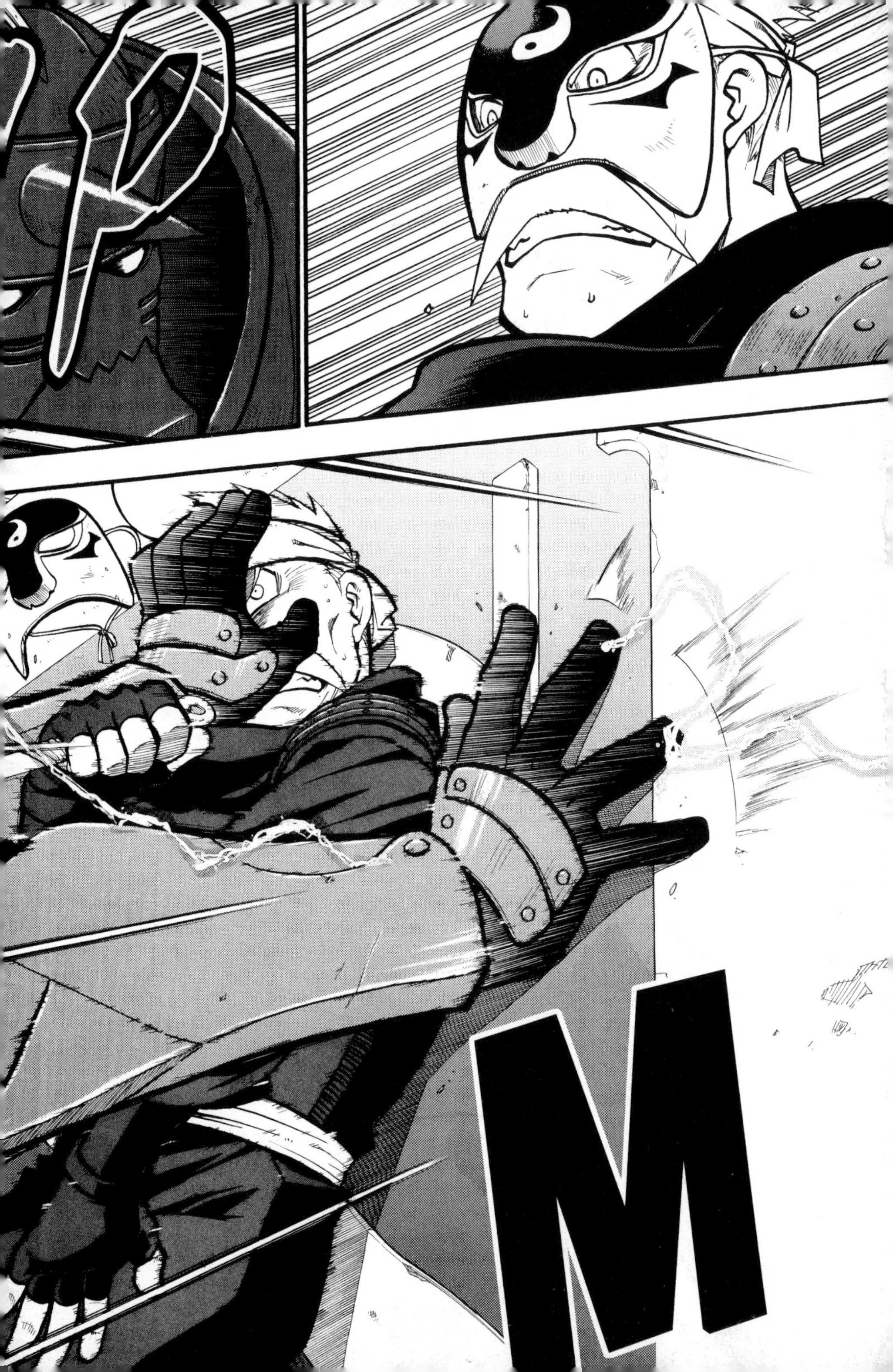
M

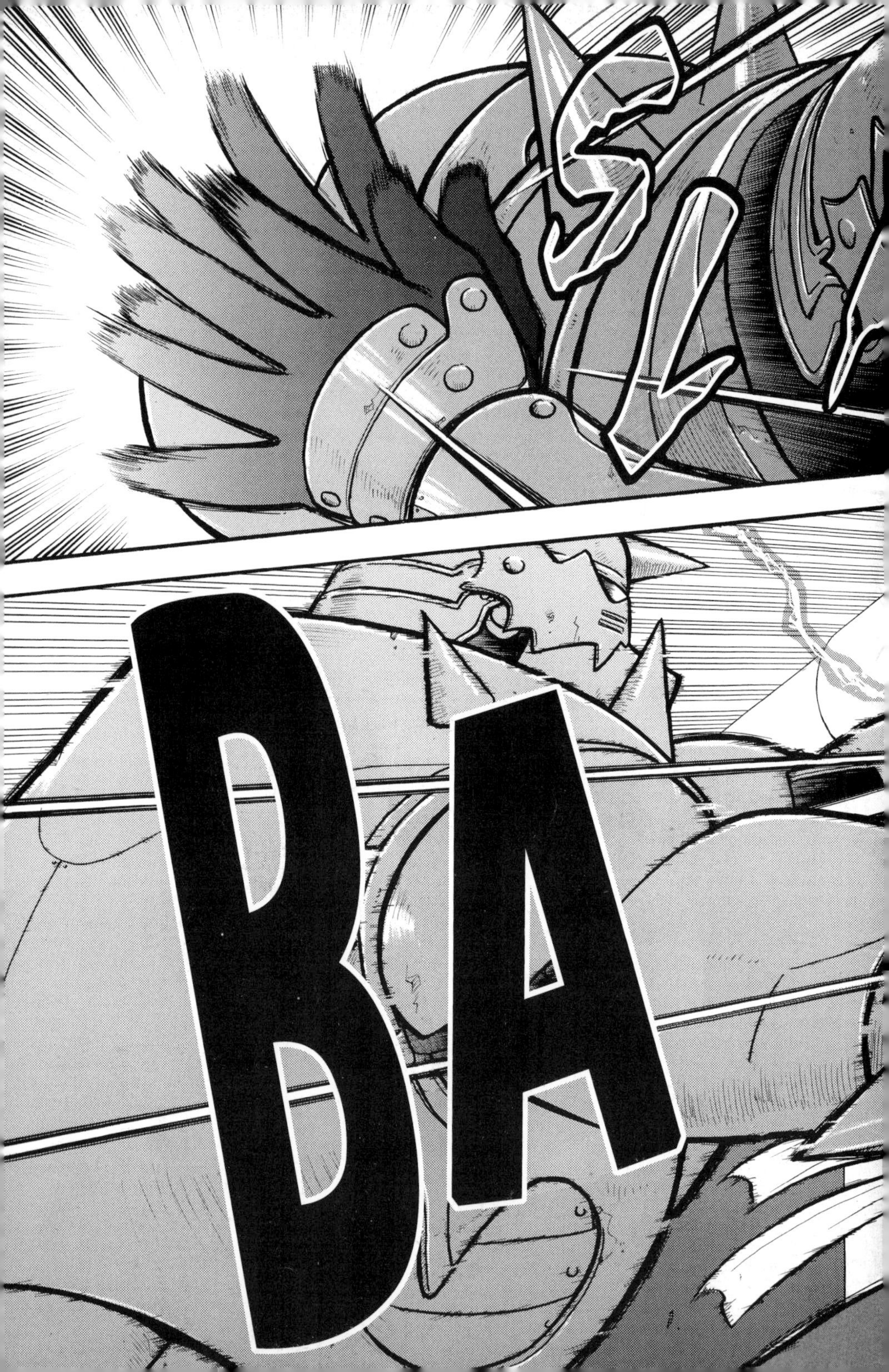
SL
BA

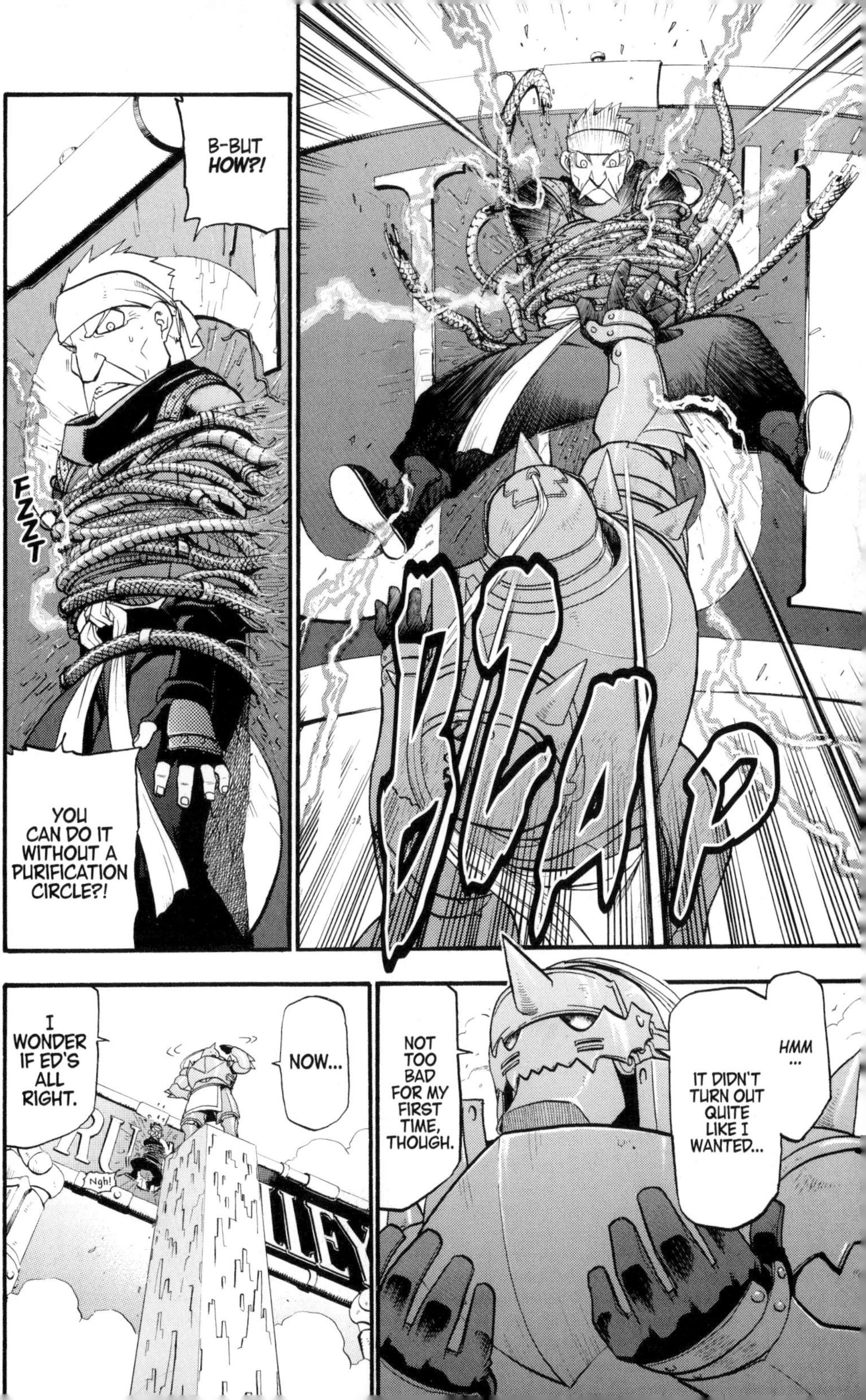
CLAP
B-BUT HOW?!
FZZZT
YOU CAN DO IT WITHOUT A PURIFICATION CIRCLE?!
HMM...
IT DIDN'T TURN OUT QUITE LIKE I WANTED...
NOT TOO BAD FOR MY FIRST TIME, THOUGH.
NOW...
I WONDER IF ED'S ALL RIGHT.
Ngh!

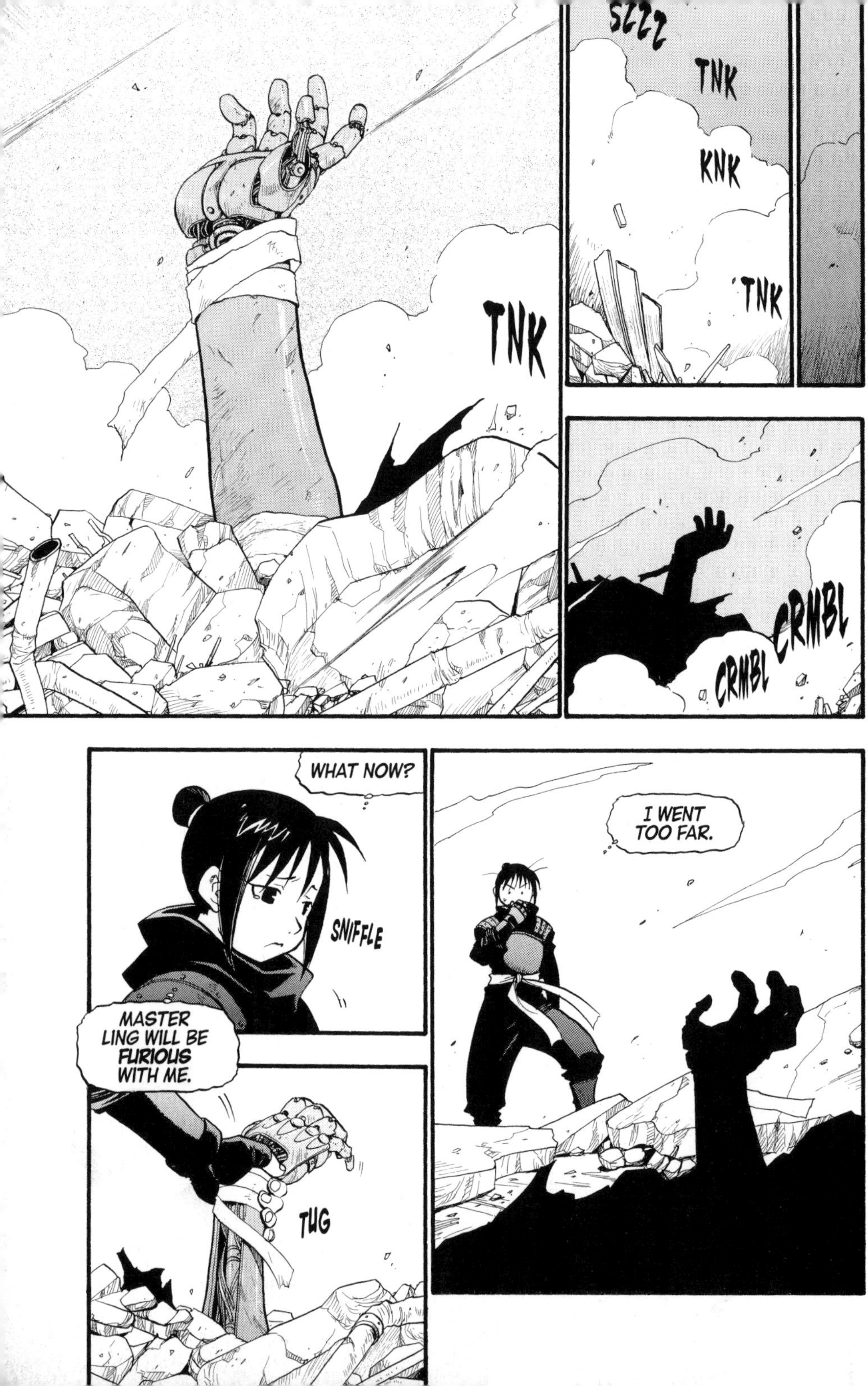
SZZZ
TNK
KNK
TNK
CRMBL
CRMBL
TNK
I WENT TOO FAR.
WHAT NOW?
SNIFFLE
MASTER LING WILL BE **FURIOUS** WITH ME.
TUG

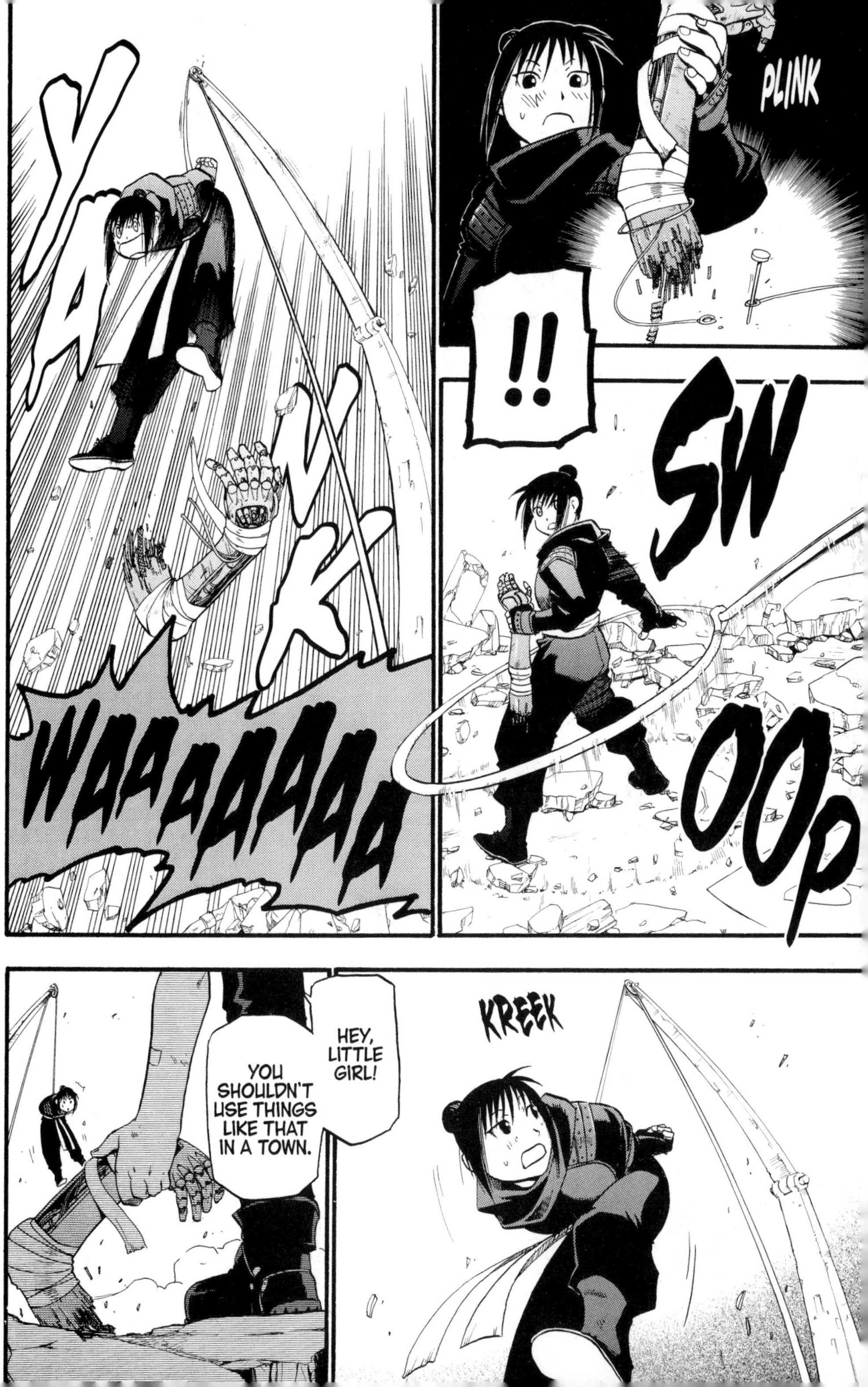
PLINK
!!
SWOOP
YANK
WAAAAAAA
KREEK
HEY, LITTLE GIRL!
YOU SHOULDN'T USE THINGS LIKE THAT IN A TOWN.

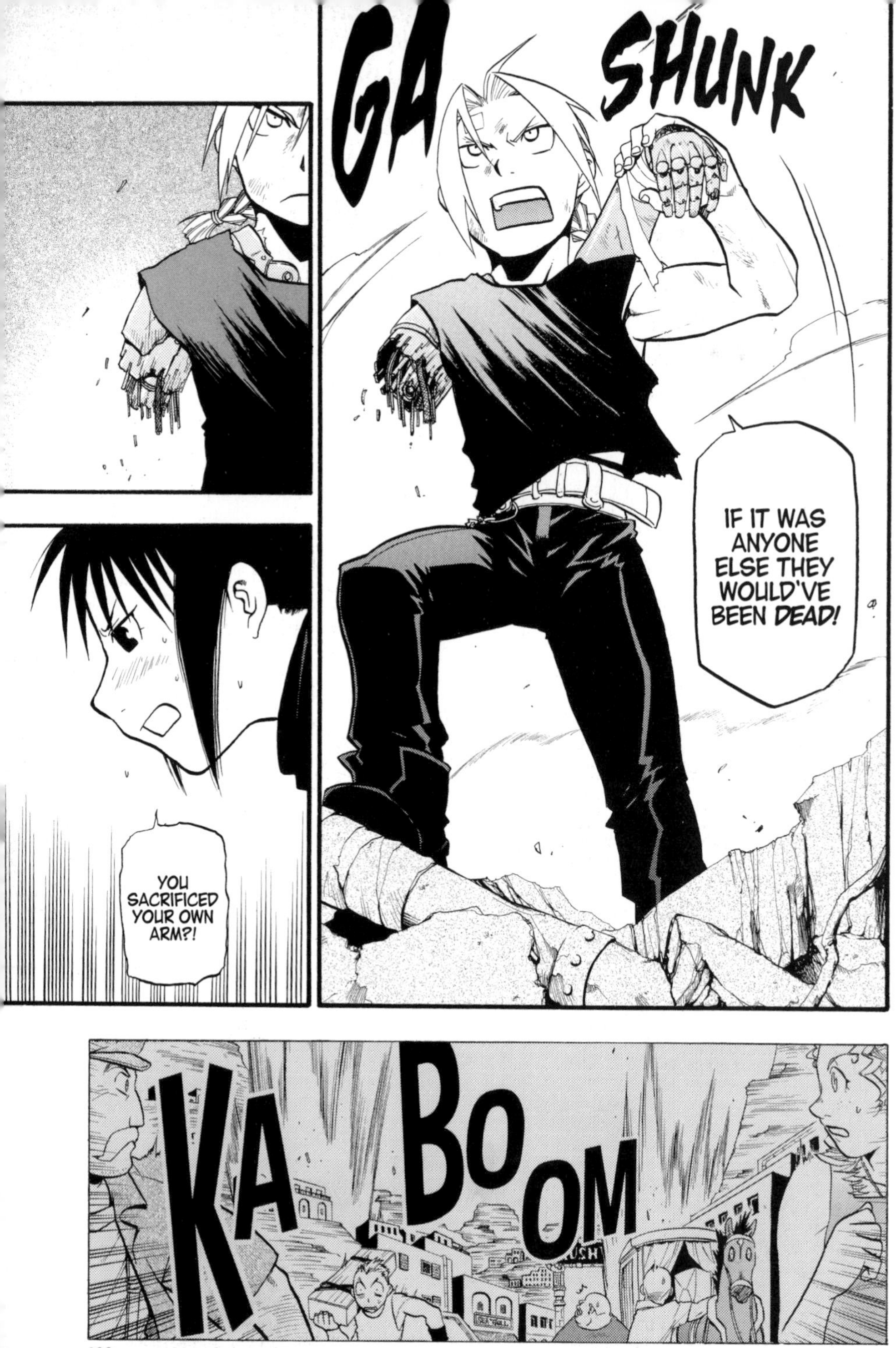
GA SHUNK
IF IT WAS ANYONE ELSE THEY WOULD'VE BEEN DEAD!
YOU SACRIFICED YOUR OWN ARM?!
KA BOOM

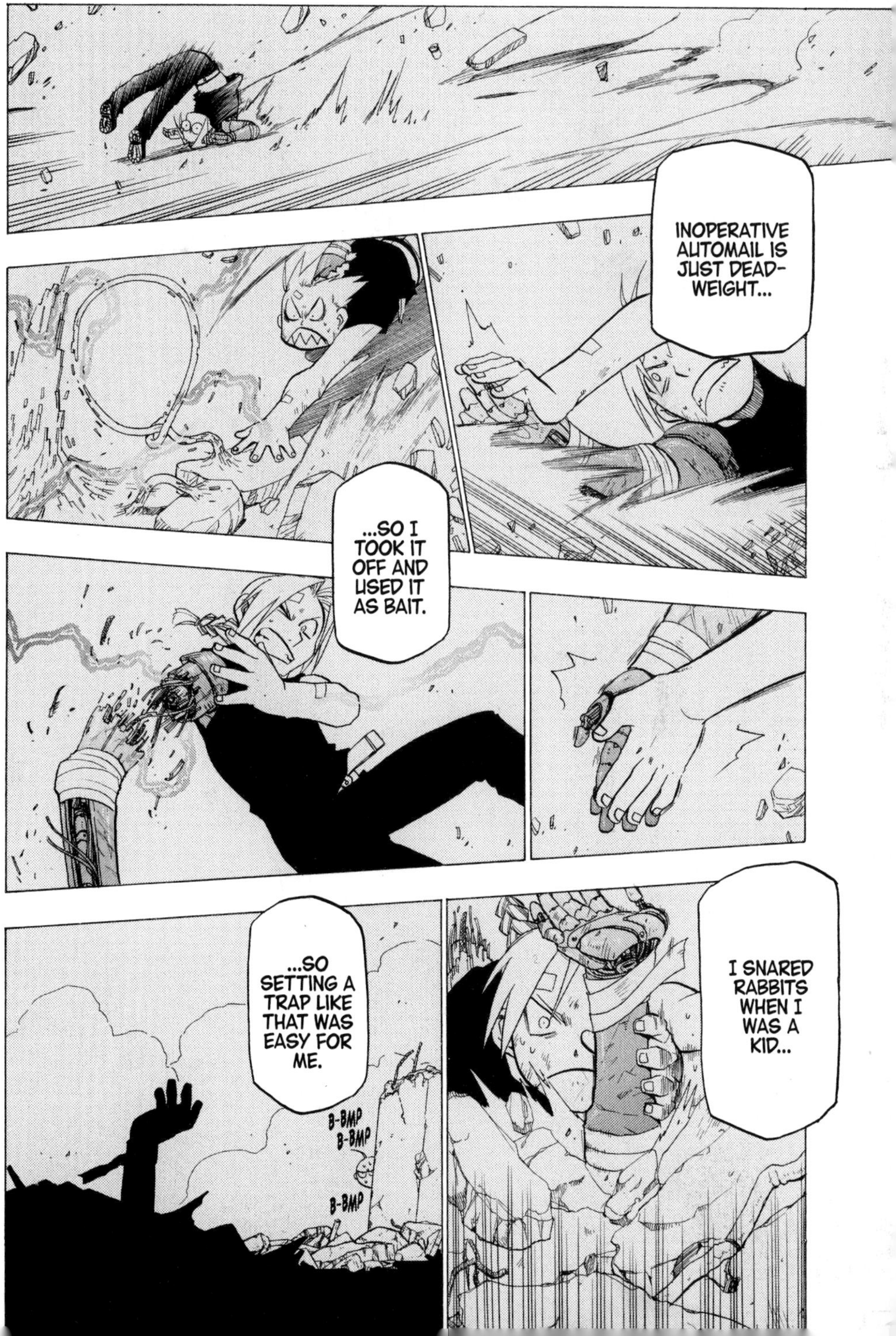
INOPERATIVE AUTOMAIL IS JUST DEAD-WEIGHT...
...SO I TOOK IT OFF AND USED IT AS BAIT.
I SNARED RABBITS WHEN I WAS A KID...
...SO SETTING A TRAP LIKE THAT WAS EASY FOR ME.
B-BMP
B-BMP
B-BMP

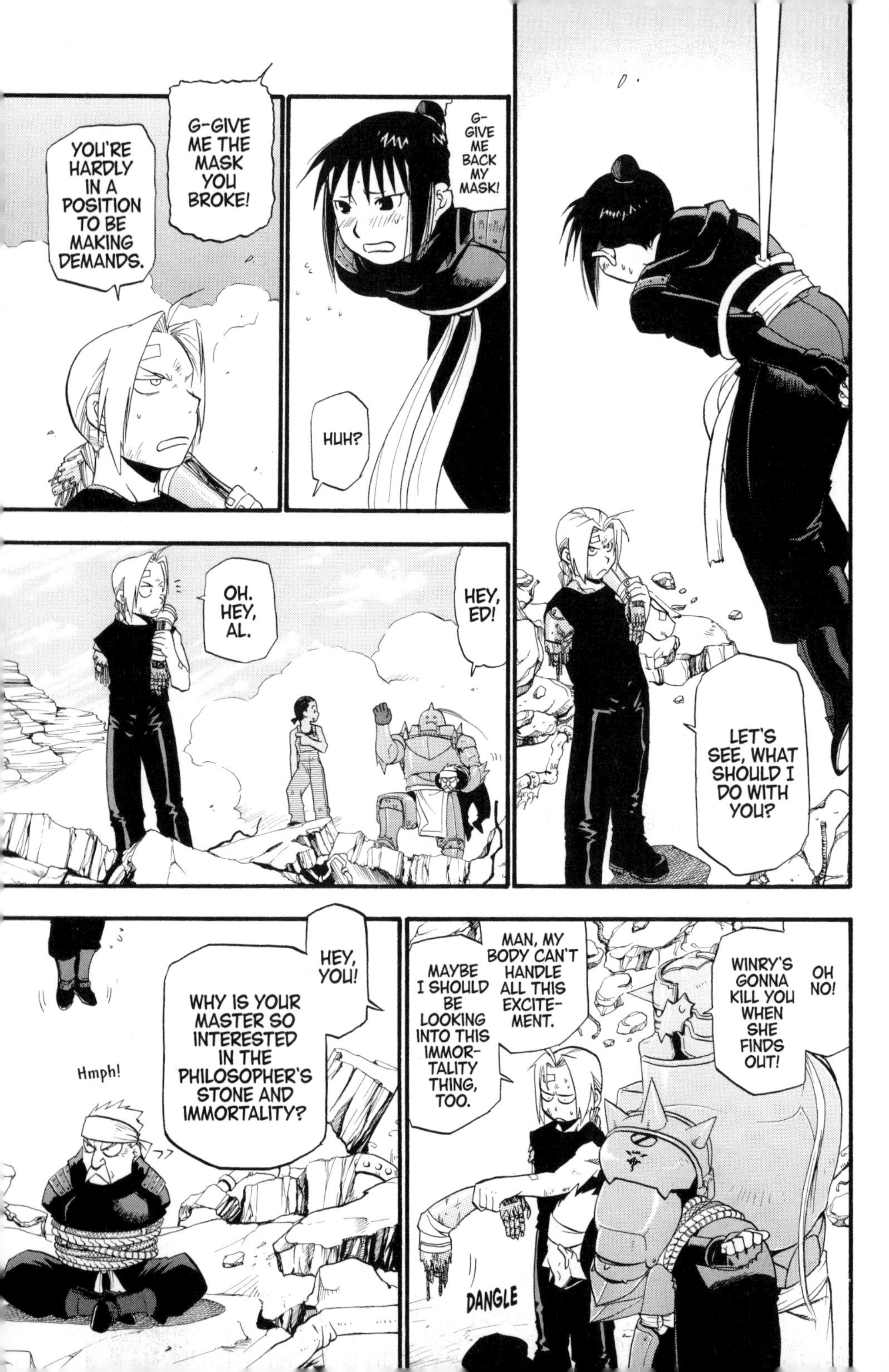
LET'S SEE, WHAT SHOULD I DO WITH YOU?
G-GIVE ME BACK MY MASK!
HUH?
G-GIVE ME THE MASK YOU BROKE!
YOU'RE HARDLY IN A POSITION TO BE MAKING DEMANDS.
HEY, ED!
OH. HEY, AL.
OH NO!
WINRY'S GONNA KILL YOU WHEN SHE FINDS OUT!
MAN, MY BODY CAN'T HANDLE ALL THIS EXCITEMENT.
MAYBE I SHOULD BE LOOKING INTO THIS IMMORTALITY THING, TOO.
DANGLE
HEY, YOU!
WHY IS YOUR MASTER SO INTERESTED IN THE PHILOSOPHER'S STONE AND IMMORTALITY?
Hmph!

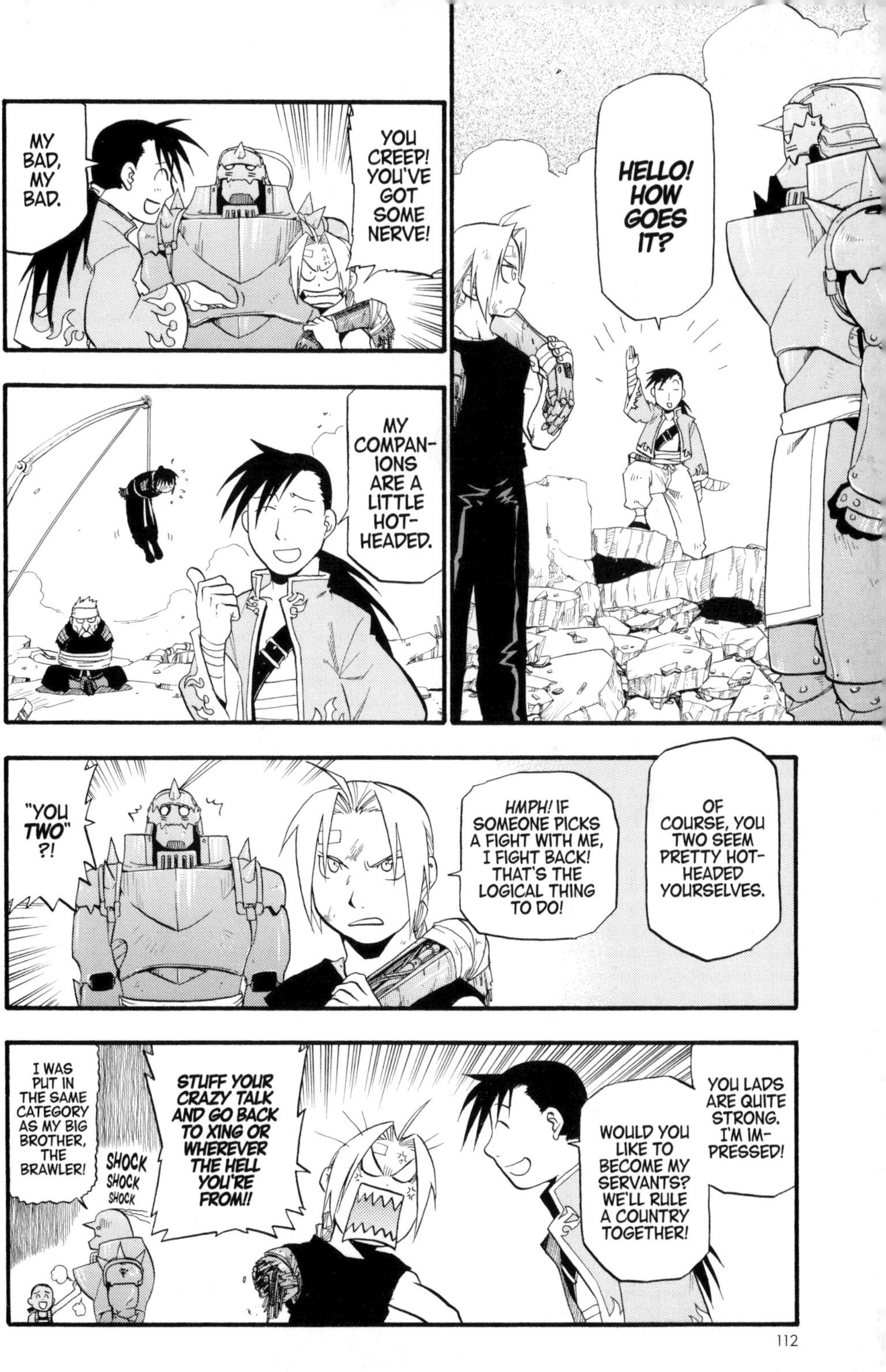
HELLO! HOW GOES IT?
YOU CREEP! YOU'VE GOT SOME NERVE!
MY BAD, MY BAD.
MY COMPANIONS ARE A LITTLE HOT-HEADED.
OF COURSE, YOU TWO SEEM PRETTY HOT-HEADED YOURSELVES.
HMPH! IF SOMEONE PICKS A FIGHT WITH ME, I FIGHT BACK! THAT'S THE LOGICAL THING TO DO!
"YOU TWO"?!
YOU LADS ARE QUITE STRONG. I'M IMPRESSED!
WOULD YOU LIKE TO BECOME MY SERVANTS? WE'LL RULE A COUNTRY TOGETHER!
STUFF YOUR CRAZY TALK AND GO BACK TO XING OR WHEREVER THE HELL YOU'RE FROM!!
SHOCK SHOCK SHOCK
I WAS PUT IN THE SAME CATEGORY AS MY BIG BROTHER, THE BRAWLER!

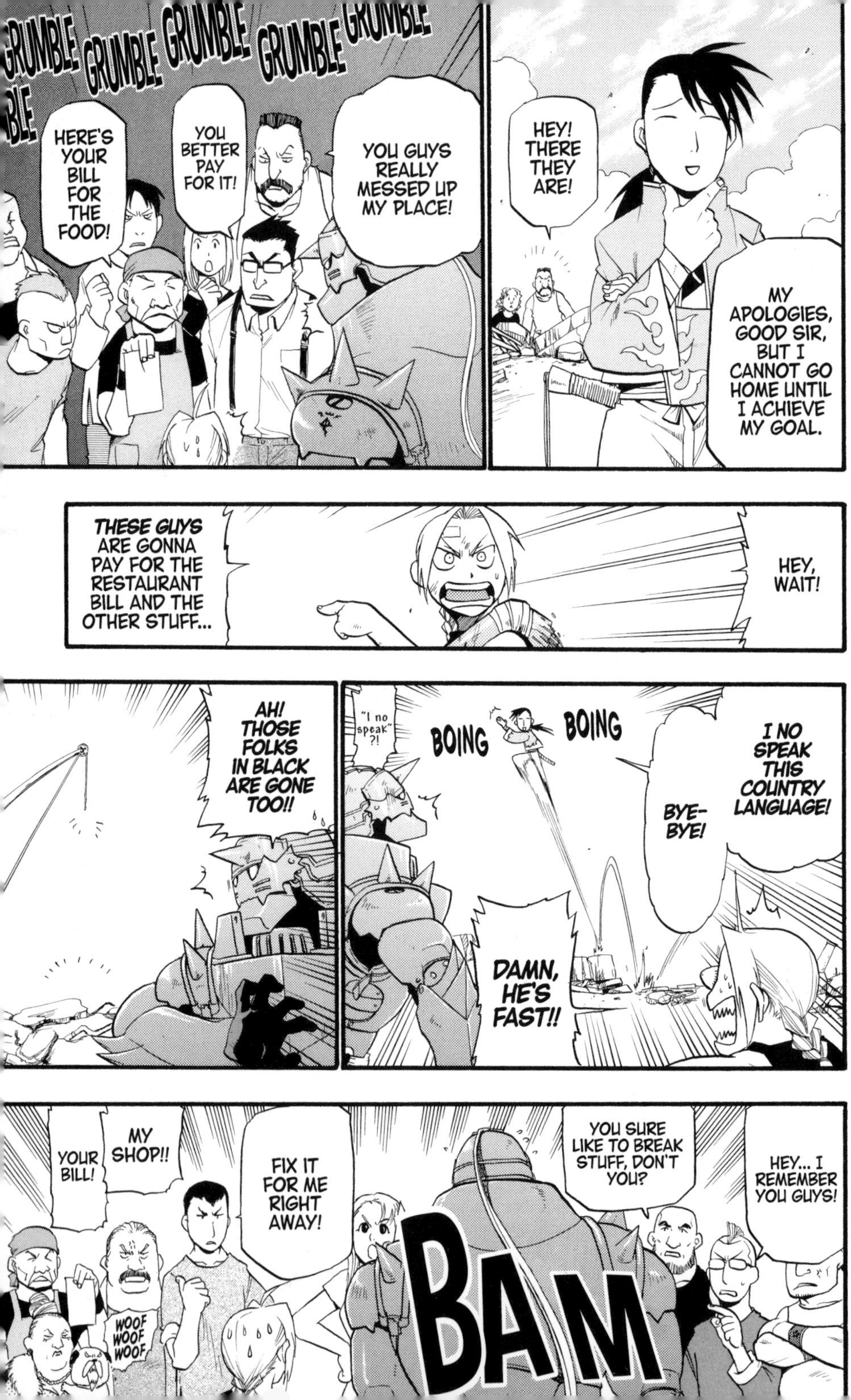
HEY! THERE THEY ARE!
MY APOLOGIES, GOOD SIR, BUT I CANNOT GO HOME UNTIL I ACHIEVE MY GOAL.
GRUMBLE GRUMBLE GRUMBLE GRUMBLE GRUMBLE
YOU GUYS REALLY MESSED UP MY PLACE!
YOU BETTER PAY FOR IT!
HERE'S YOUR BILL FOR THE FOOD!
HEY, WAIT!
THESE GUYS ARE GONNA PAY FOR THE RESTAURANT BILL AND THE OTHER STUFF...
I NO SPEAK THIS COUNTRY LANGUAGE!
BYE-BYE!
BOING
BOING
"I no speak"?!
DAMN, HE'S FAST!!
AH! THOSE FOLKS IN BLACK ARE GONE TOO!!
HEY... I REMEMBER YOU GUYS!
YOU SURE LIKE TO BREAK STUFF, DON'T YOU?
BAM
FIX IT FOR ME RIGHT AWAY!
MY SHOP!!
YOUR BILL!
WOOF WOOF WOOF

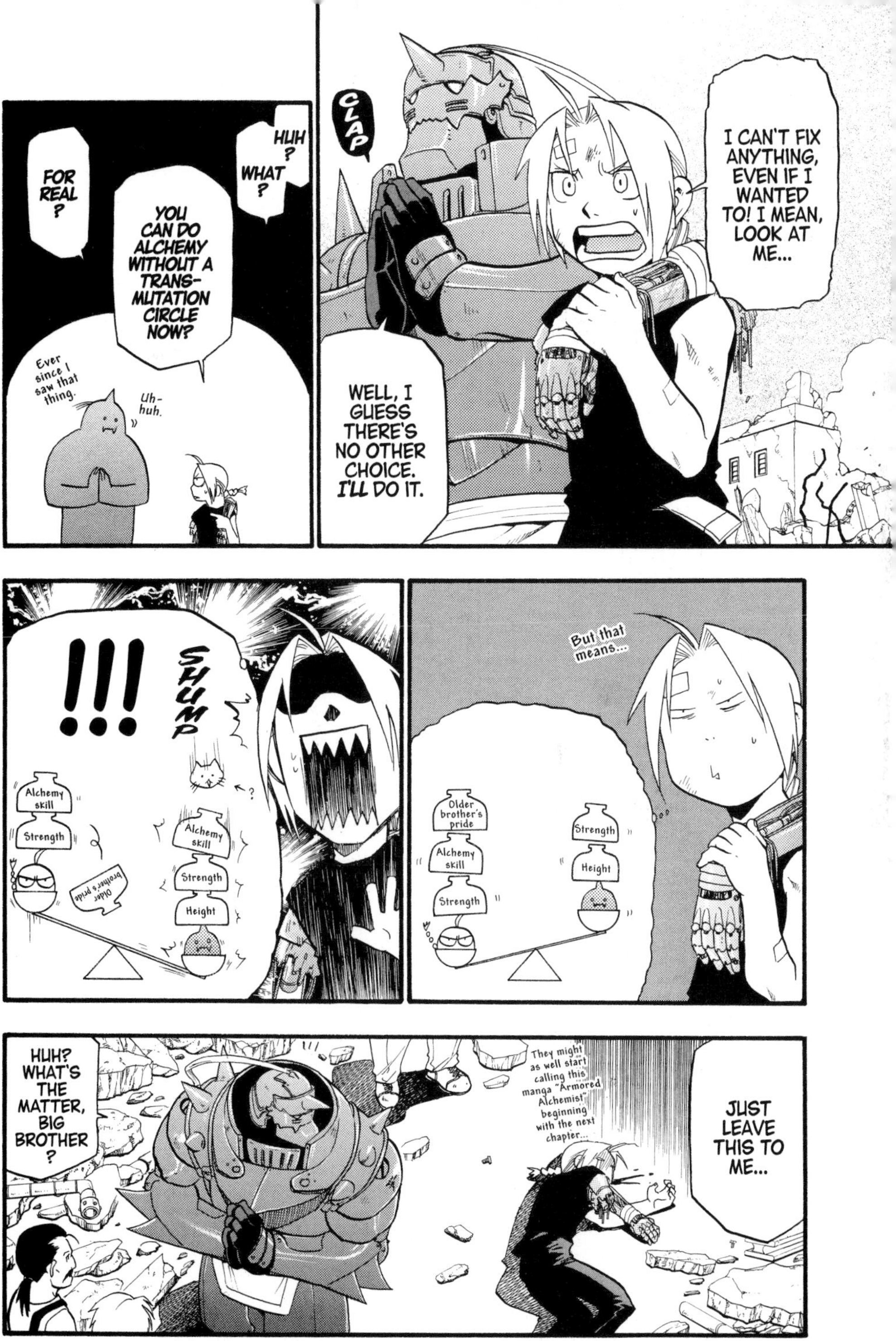
CLAP
I CAN'T FIX ANYTHING, EVEN IF I WANTED TO! I MEAN, LOOK AT ME...
WELL, I GUESS THERE'S NO OTHER CHOICE. I'LL DO IT.
HUH? WHAT?
FOR REAL?
YOU CAN DO ALCHEMY WITHOUT A TRANS-MUTATION CIRCLE NOW?
Ever since I saw that thing.
Uh-huh.
But that means...
Older brother's pride
Alchemy skill
Strength
Strength
Height
!!!
SHUMP
?
Alchemy skill
Strength
Older brother's pride
Alchemy skill
Strength
Height
JUST LEAVE THIS TO ME...
They might as well start calling this manga "Armored Alchemist" beginning with the next chapter...
HUH? WHAT'S THE MATTER, BIG BROTHER?

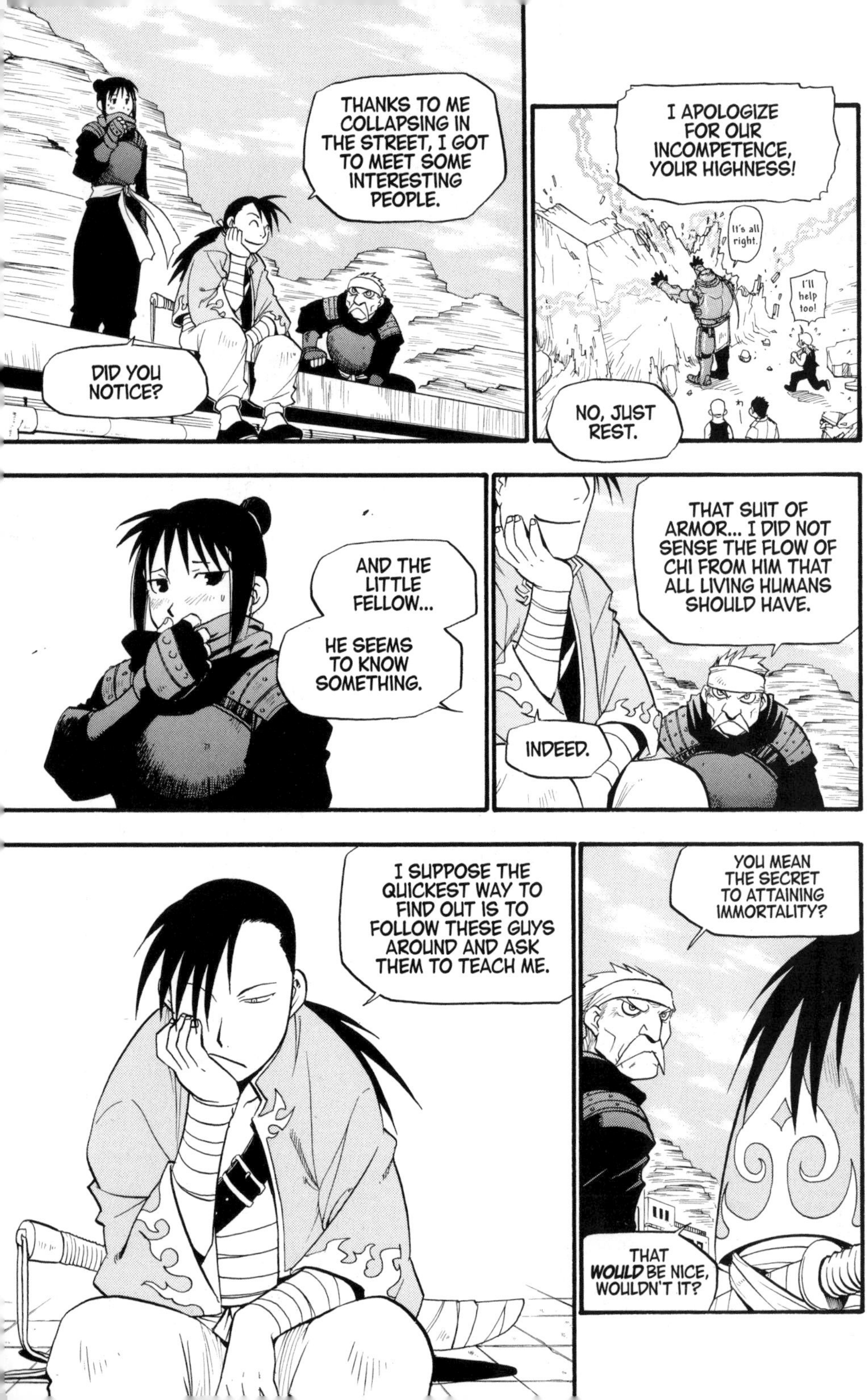
I APOLOGIZE FOR OUR INCOMPETENCE, YOUR HIGHNESS!
It's all right.
I'll help too!
NO, JUST REST.
THANKS TO ME COLLAPSING IN THE STREET, I GOT TO MEET SOME INTERESTING PEOPLE.
DID YOU NOTICE?
THAT SUIT OF ARMOR... I DID NOT SENSE THE FLOW OF CHI FROM HIM THAT ALL LIVING HUMANS SHOULD HAVE.
INDEED.
AND THE LITTLE FELLOW...
HE SEEMS TO KNOW SOMETHING.
YOU MEAN THE SECRET TO ATTAINING IMMORTALITY?
THAT *WOULD* BE NICE, WOULDN'T IT?
I SUPPOSE THE QUICKEST WAY TO FIND OUT IS TO FOLLOW THESE GUYS AROUND AND ASK THEM TO TEACH ME.

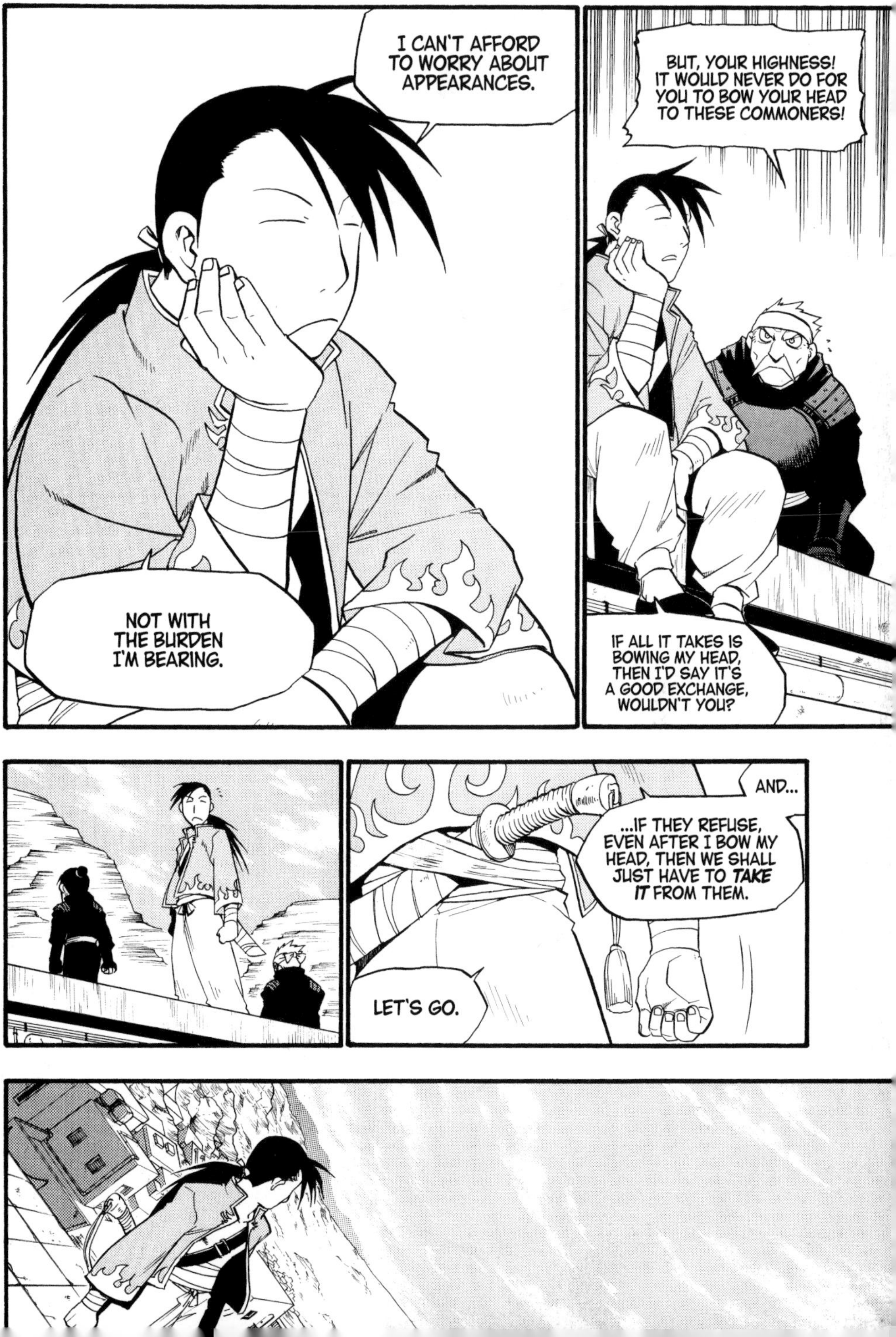
BUT, YOUR HIGHNESS! IT WOULD NEVER DO FOR YOU TO BOW YOUR HEAD TO THESE COMMONERS!
IF ALL IT TAKES IS BOWING MY HEAD, THEN I'D SAY IT'S A GOOD EXCHANGE, WOULDN'T YOU?
I CAN'T AFFORD TO WORRY ABOUT APPEARANCES.
NOT WITH THE BURDEN I'M BEARING.
AND...
...IF THEY REFUSE, EVEN AFTER I BOW MY HEAD, THEN WE SHALL JUST HAVE TO *TAKE IT* FROM THEM.
LET'S GO.

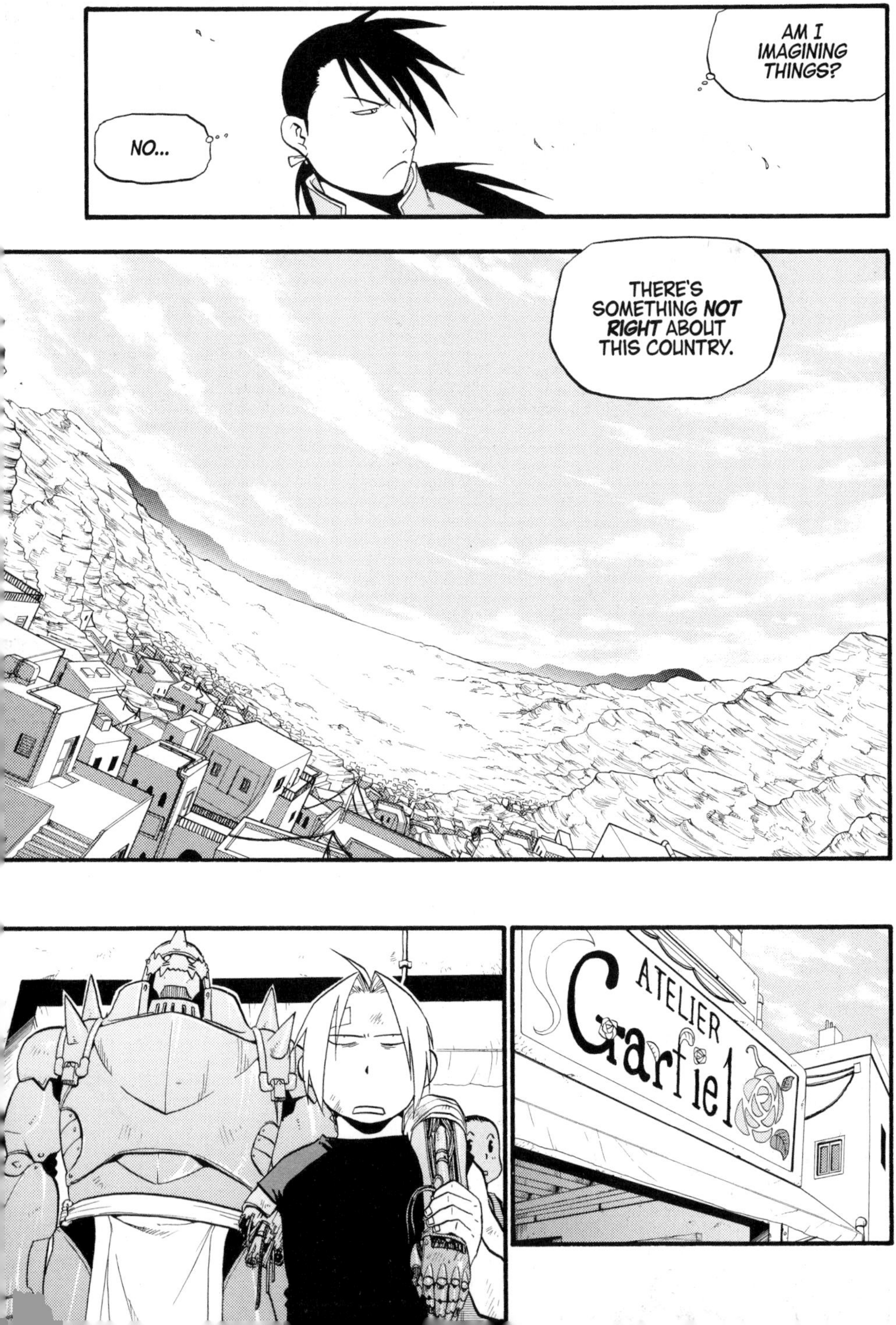
AM I IMAGINING THINGS?
NO...
THERE'S SOMETHING **NOT RIGHT** ABOUT THIS COUNTRY.
ATELIER
Garfiel

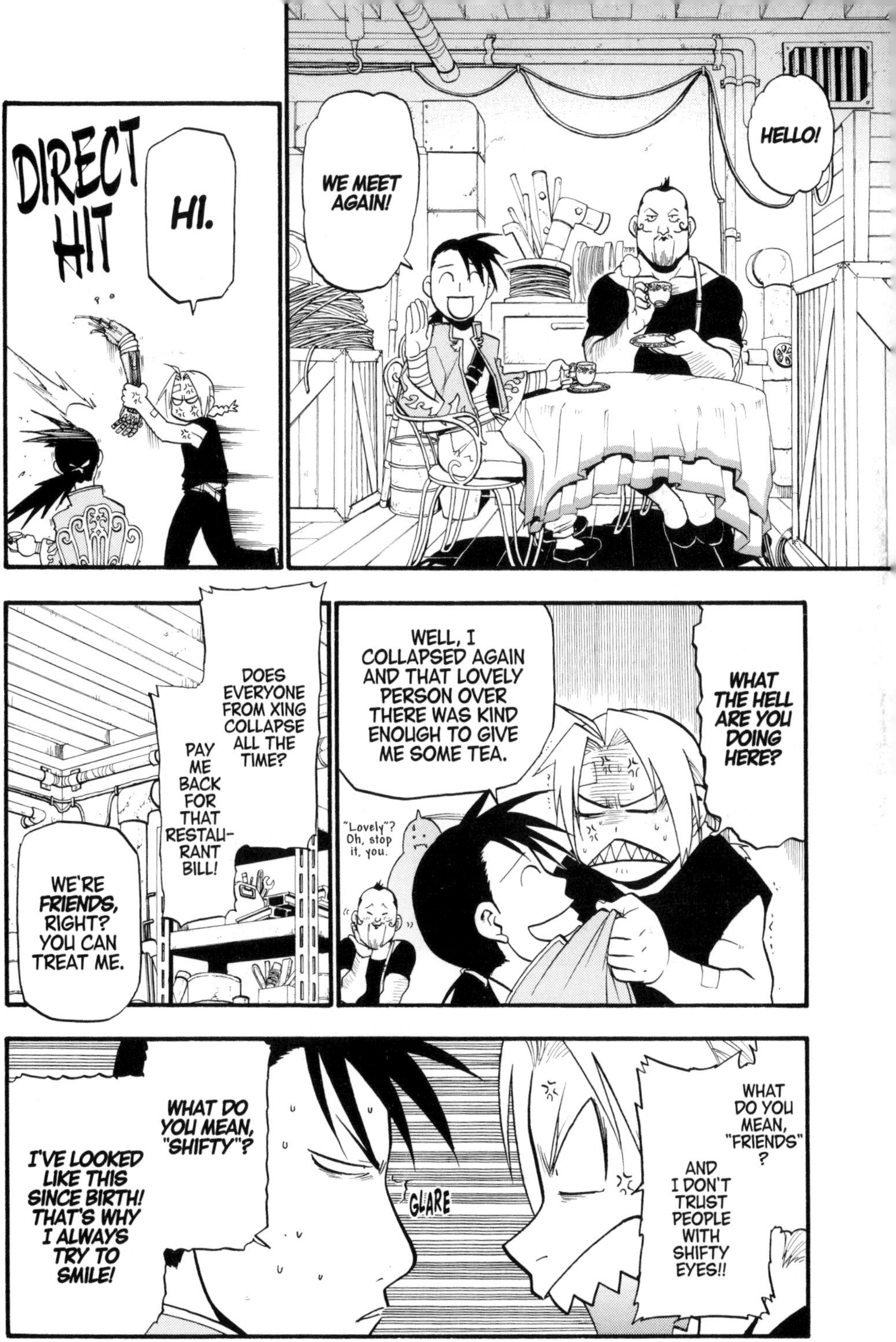
HELLO!
WE MEET AGAIN!
HI.
DIRECT HIT
WHAT THE HELL ARE YOU DOING HERE?
WELL, I COLLAPSED AGAIN AND THAT LOVELY PERSON OVER THERE WAS KIND ENOUGH TO GIVE ME SOME TEA.
"Lovely"? Oh, stop it, you.
DOES EVERYONE FROM XING COLLAPSE ALL THE TIME?
PAY ME BACK FOR THAT RESTAU-RANT BILL!
WE'RE FRIENDS, RIGHT? YOU CAN TREAT ME.
WHAT DO YOU MEAN, "FRIENDS"?
AND I DON'T TRUST PEOPLE WITH SHIFTY EYES!!
GLARE
WHAT DO YOU MEAN, "SHIFTY"?
I'VE LOOKED LIKE THIS SINCE BIRTH! THAT'S WHY I ALWAYS TRY TO SMILE!

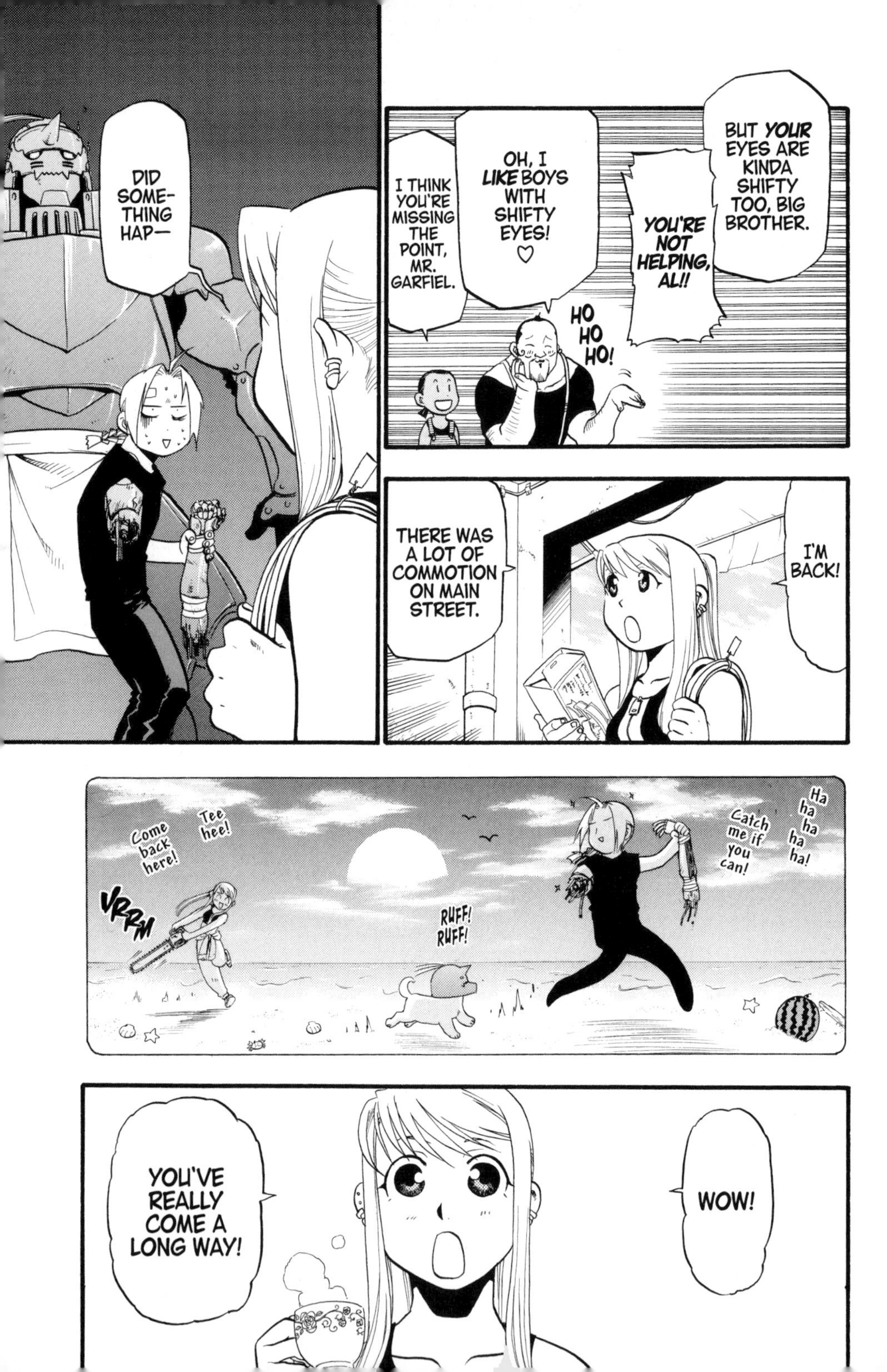
BUT YOUR EYES ARE KINDA SHIFTY TOO, BIG BROTHER.
YOU'RE NOT HELPING, AL!!
OH, I LIKE BOYS WITH SHIFTY EYES! ♡
HO HO HO!
I THINK YOU'RE MISSING THE POINT, MR. GARFIEL.
I'M BACK!
THERE WAS A LOT OF COMMOTION ON MAIN STREET.
DID SOMETHING HAP—
Ha ha ha ha ha!
Catch me if you can!
RUFF! RUFF!
Tee hee!
Come back here!
VRRM
WOW!
YOU'VE REALLY COME A LONG WAY!

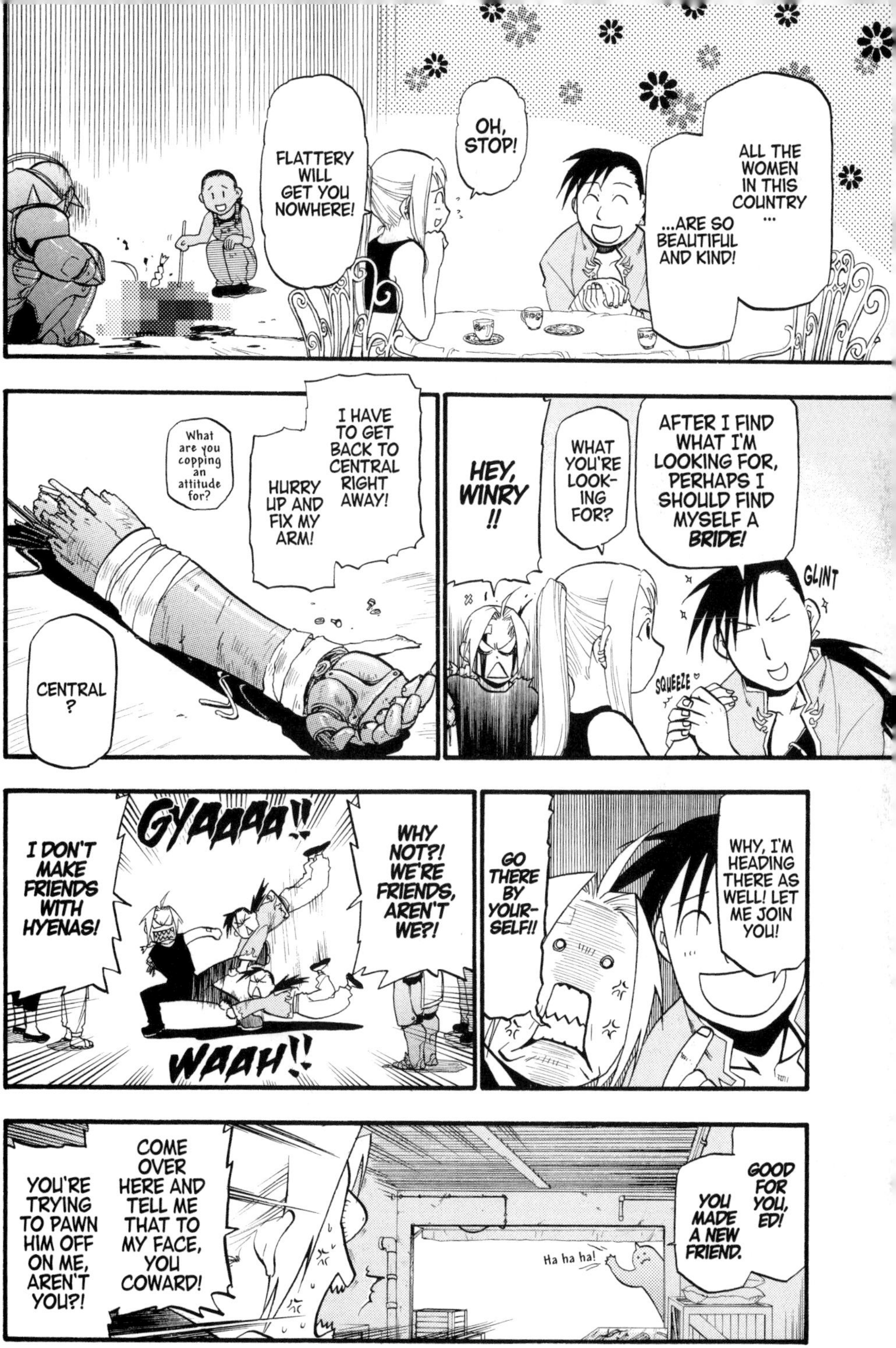
ALL THE WOMEN IN THIS COUNTRY ...
...ARE SO BEAUTIFUL AND KIND!
OH, STOP!
FLATTERY WILL GET YOU NOWHERE!
AFTER I FIND WHAT I'M LOOKING FOR, PERHAPS I SHOULD FIND MYSELF A BRIDE!
GLINT
WHAT YOU'RE LOOK-ING FOR?
HEY, WINRY!!
SQUEEZE
I HAVE TO GET BACK TO CENTRAL RIGHT AWAY!
HURRY UP AND FIX MY ARM!
What are you copping an attitude for?
CENTRAL?
WHY, I'M HEADING THERE AS WELL! LET ME JOIN YOU!
GO THERE BY YOUR-SELF!!
WHY NOT?! WE'RE FRIENDS, AREN'T WE?!
GYAAAA!!
I DON'T MAKE FRIENDS WITH HYENAS!
WAAH!!
GOOD FOR YOU, ED!
YOU MADE A NEW FRIEND.
Ha ha ha!
COME OVER HERE AND TELL ME THAT TO MY FACE, YOU COWARD!
YOU'RE TRYING TO PAWN HIM OFF ON ME, AREN'T YOU?!

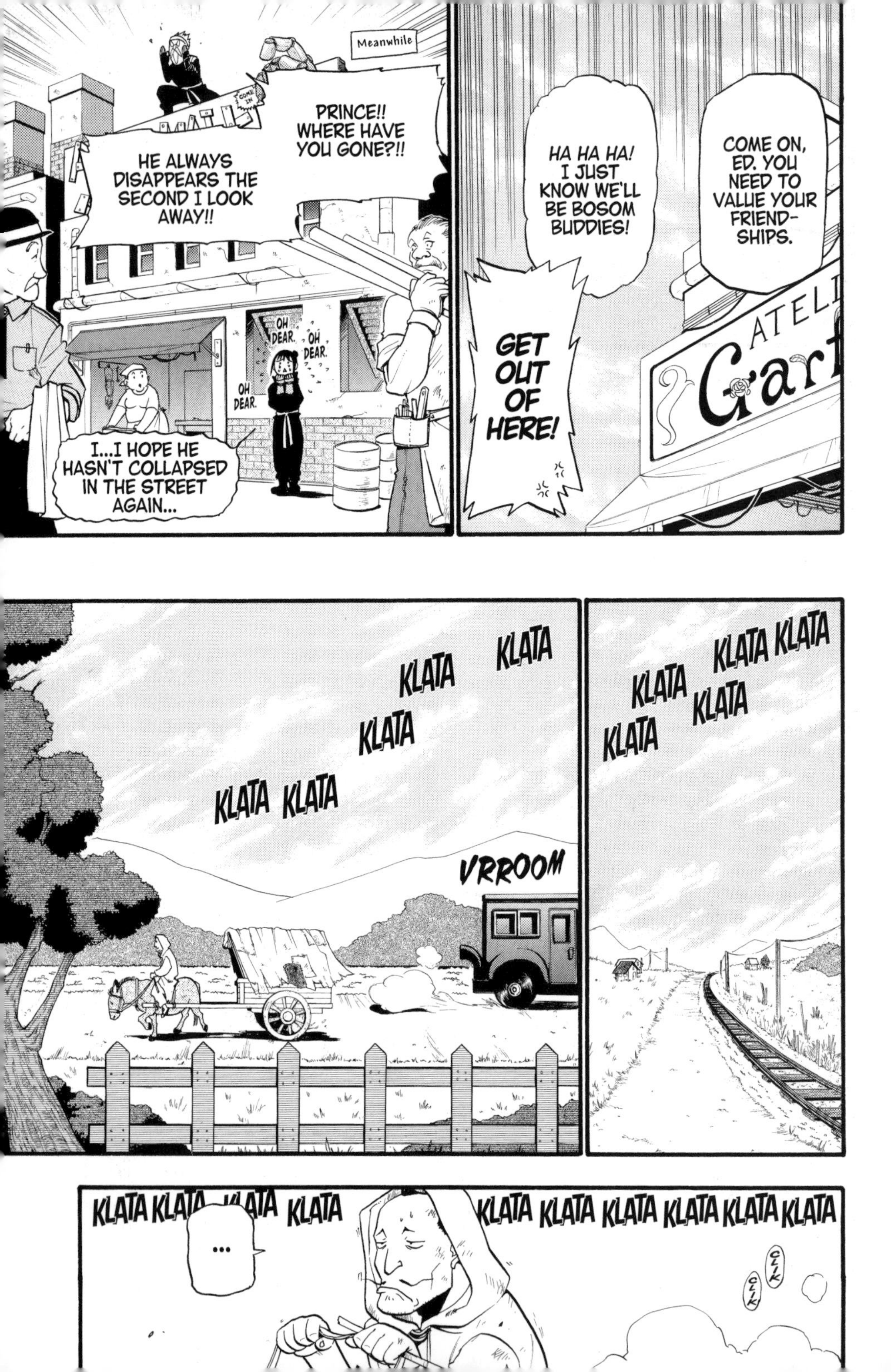
COME ON, ED. YOU NEED TO VALUE YOUR FRIEND-SHIPS.
HA HA HA! I JUST KNOW WE'LL BE BOSOM BUDDIES!
GET OUT OF HERE!
Meanwhile
COME IN
PRINCE!! WHERE HAVE YOU GONE?!!
HE ALWAYS DISAPPEARS THE SECOND I LOOK AWAY!!
OH DEAR.
OH DEAR.
OH DEAR.
I...I HOPE HE HASN'T COLLAPSED IN THE STREET AGAIN...
KLATA KLATA
KLATA KLATA
KLATA
KLATA
KLATA
KLATA
KLATA
KLATA
KLATA KLATA
VRROOM
KLATA KLATA KLATA KLATA KLATA KLATA
CLIK
CLIK
...
KLATA KLATA KLATA KLATA

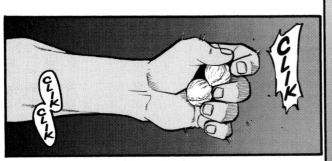

KLATA

EX- CUSE ME, SIR...

CLIK CLIK CLIK

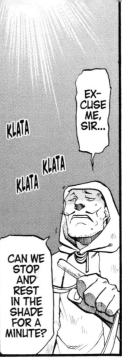

KLATA KLATA KLATA

CAN WE STOP AND REST IN THE SHADE FOR A MINUTE?

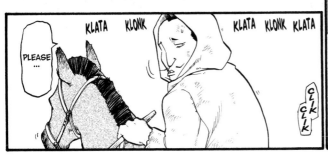

PLEASE ...

KLATA KLONK KLATA KLONK KLATA

CLIK CLIK

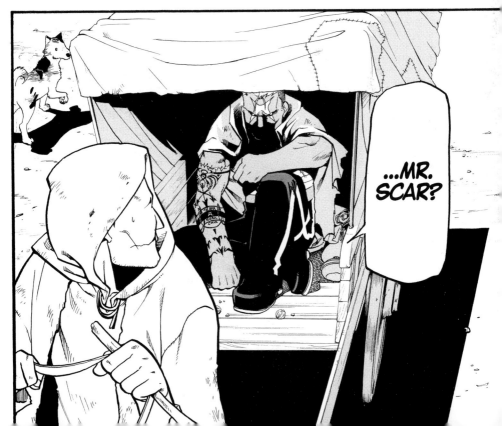

...MR. SCAR?

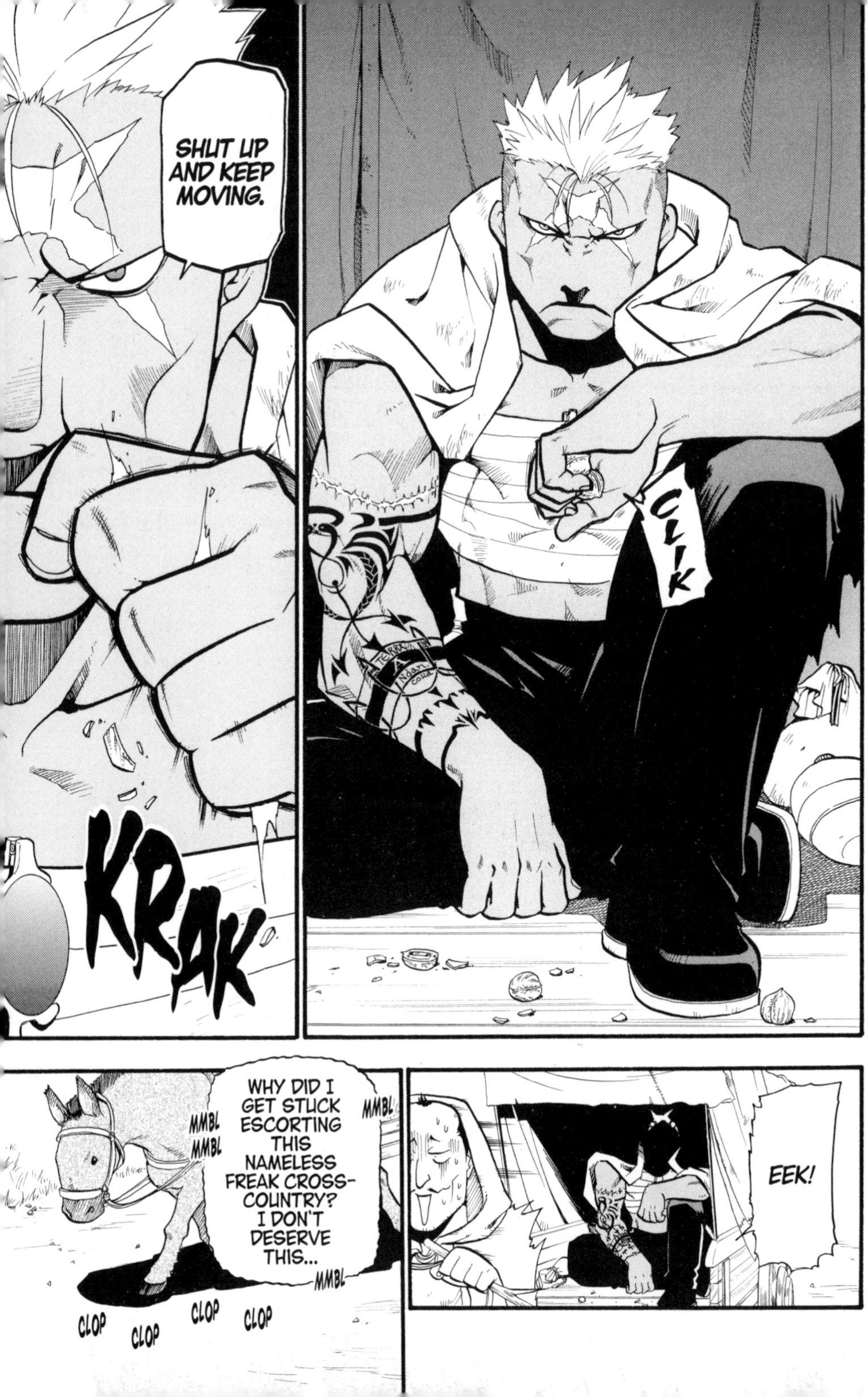
CLIK
SHUT UP AND KEEP MOVING.
KRAK
EEK!
MMBL
WHY DID I GET STUCK ESCORTING THIS NAMELESS FREAK CROSS-COUNTRY? I DON'T DESERVE THIS...
MMBL
MMBL
MMBL
CLOP
CLOP
CLOP
CLOP

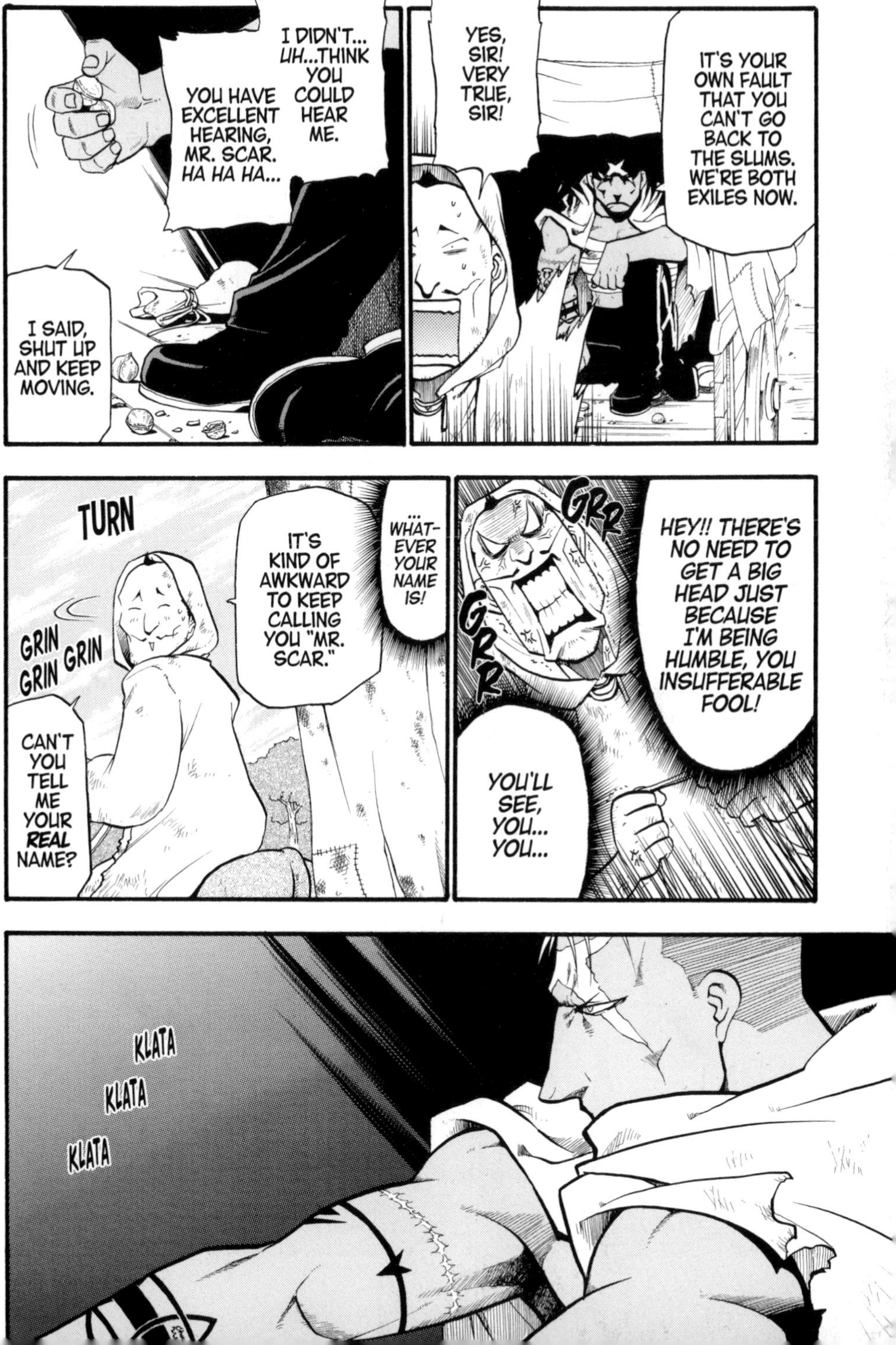
IT'S YOUR OWN FAULT THAT YOU CAN'T GO BACK TO THE SLUMS. WE'RE BOTH EXILES NOW.
YES, SIR! VERY TRUE, SIR!
I DIDN'T... UH...THINK YOU COULD HEAR ME.
YOU HAVE EXCELLENT HEARING, MR. SCAR. HA HA HA...
I SAID, SHUT UP AND KEEP MOVING.
GRR
HEY!! THERE'S NO NEED TO GET A BIG HEAD JUST BECAUSE I'M BEING HUMBLE, YOU INSUFFERABLE FOOL!
GRR
YOU'LL SEE, YOU... YOU...
...WHATEVER YOUR NAME IS!
TURN
IT'S KIND OF AWKWARD TO KEEP CALLING YOU "MR. SCAR."
GRIN GRIN GRIN
CAN'T YOU TELL ME YOUR *REAL* NAME?
KLATA
KLATA
KLATA

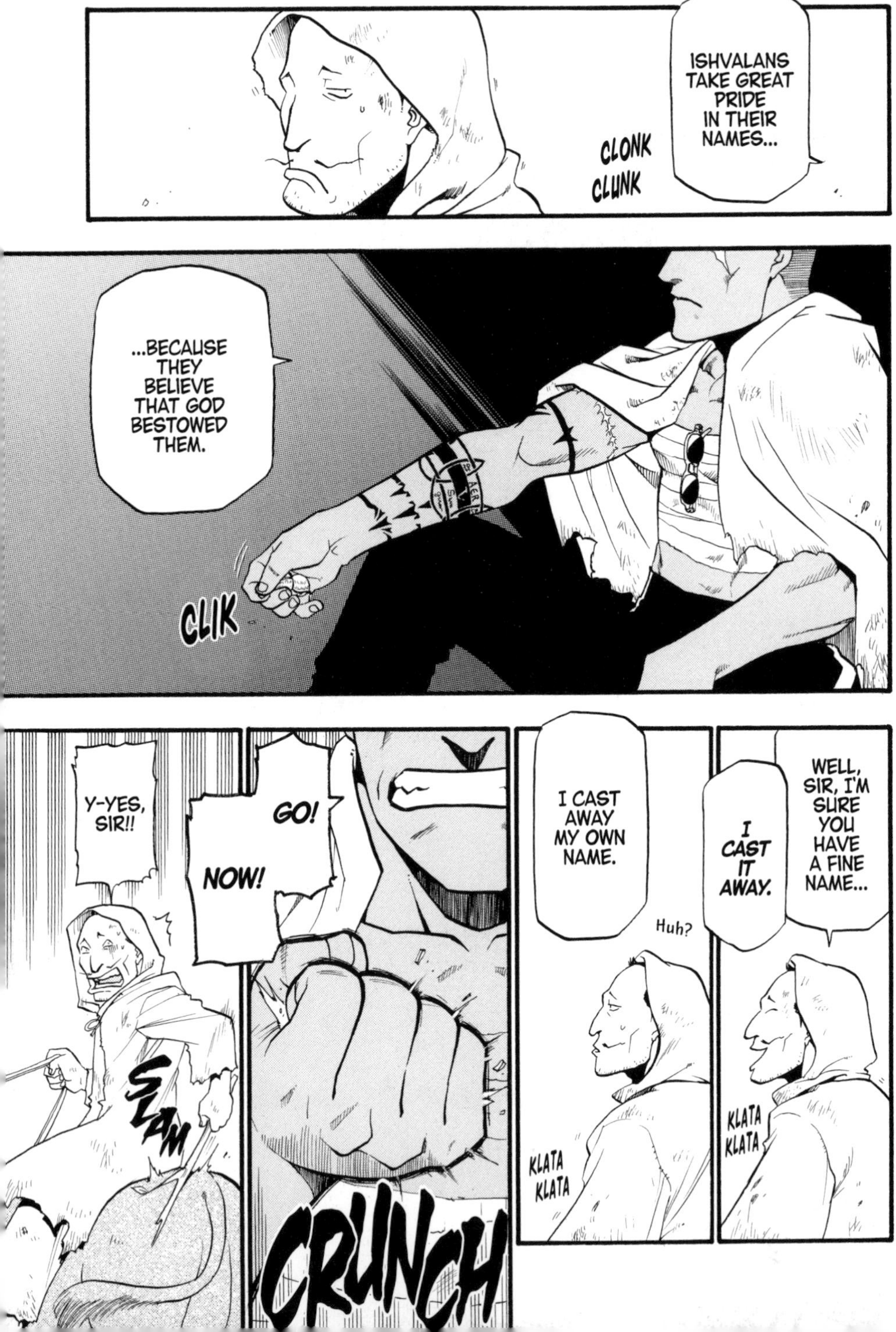
ISHVALANS TAKE GREAT PRIDE IN THEIR NAMES...
CLONK
CLUNK
...BECAUSE THEY BELIEVE THAT GOD BESTOWED THEM.
CLIK
WELL, SIR, I'M SURE YOU HAVE A FINE NAME...
I CAST IT AWAY.
KLATA KLATA
I CAST AWAY MY OWN NAME.
Huh?
KLATA KLATA
GO!
NOW!
CRUNCH
Y-YES, SIR!!
SLAM

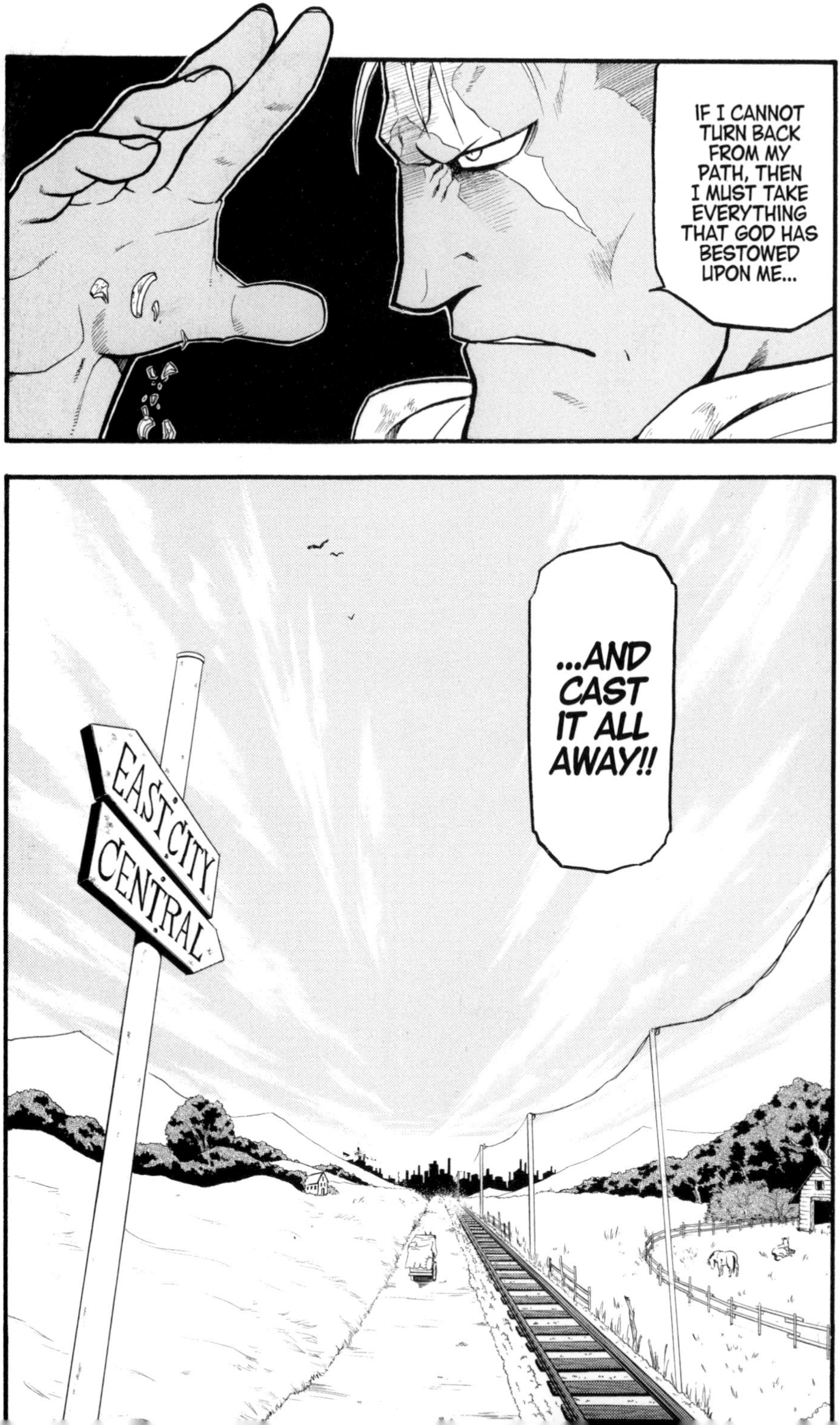
IF I CANNOT TURN BACK FROM MY PATH, THEN I MUST TAKE EVERYTHING THAT GOD HAS BESTOWED UPON ME...
...AND CAST IT ALL AWAY!!
EAST CITY
CENTRAL

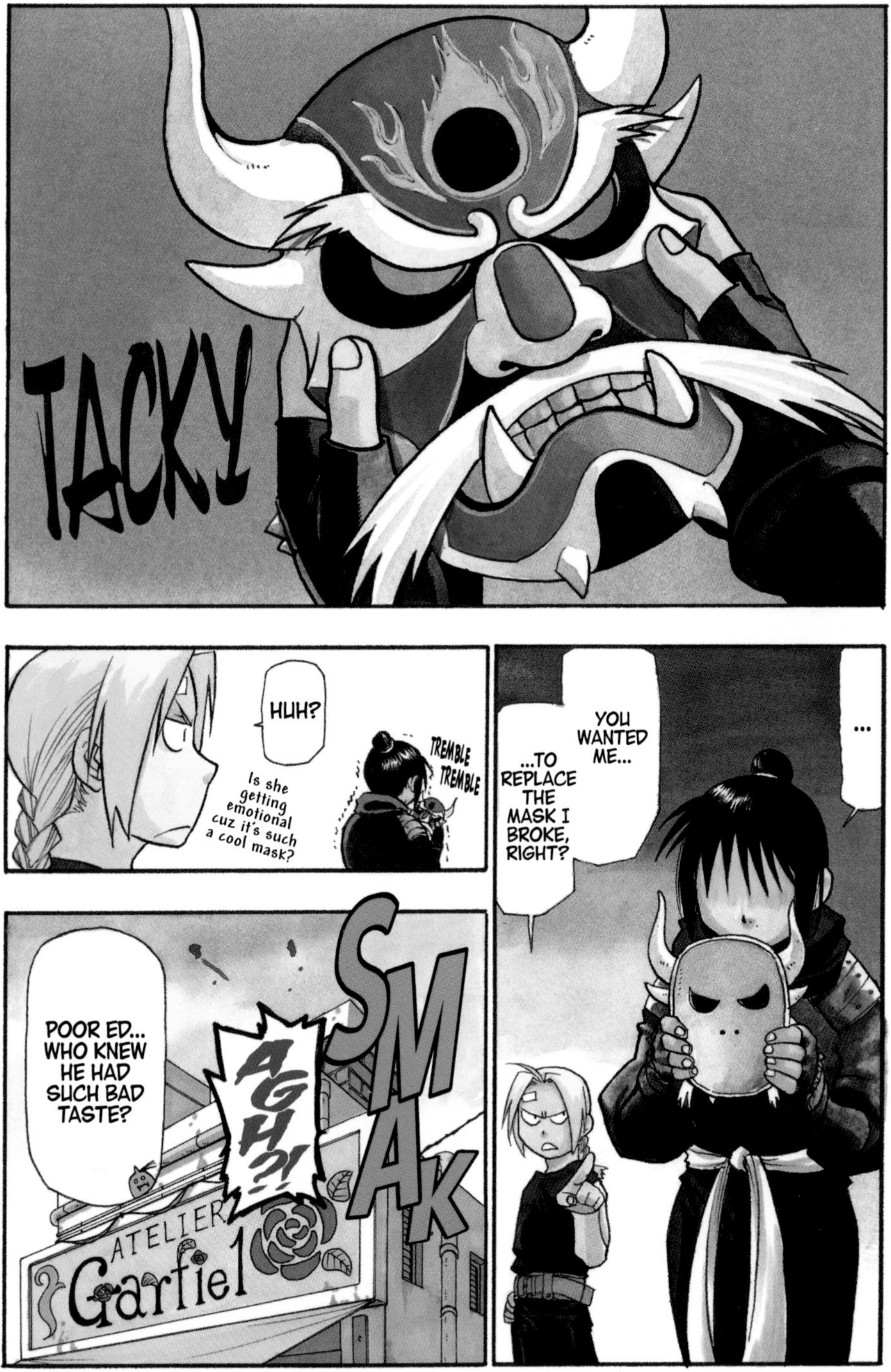
TACKY
...
YOU WANTED ME...
...TO REPLACE THE MASK I BROKE, RIGHT?
TREMBLE TREMBLE
HUH?
Is she getting emotional cuz it's such a cool mask?
SMAK
AGH?!
POOR ED... WHO KNEW HE HAD SUCH BAD TASTE?
ATELIER Garfiel

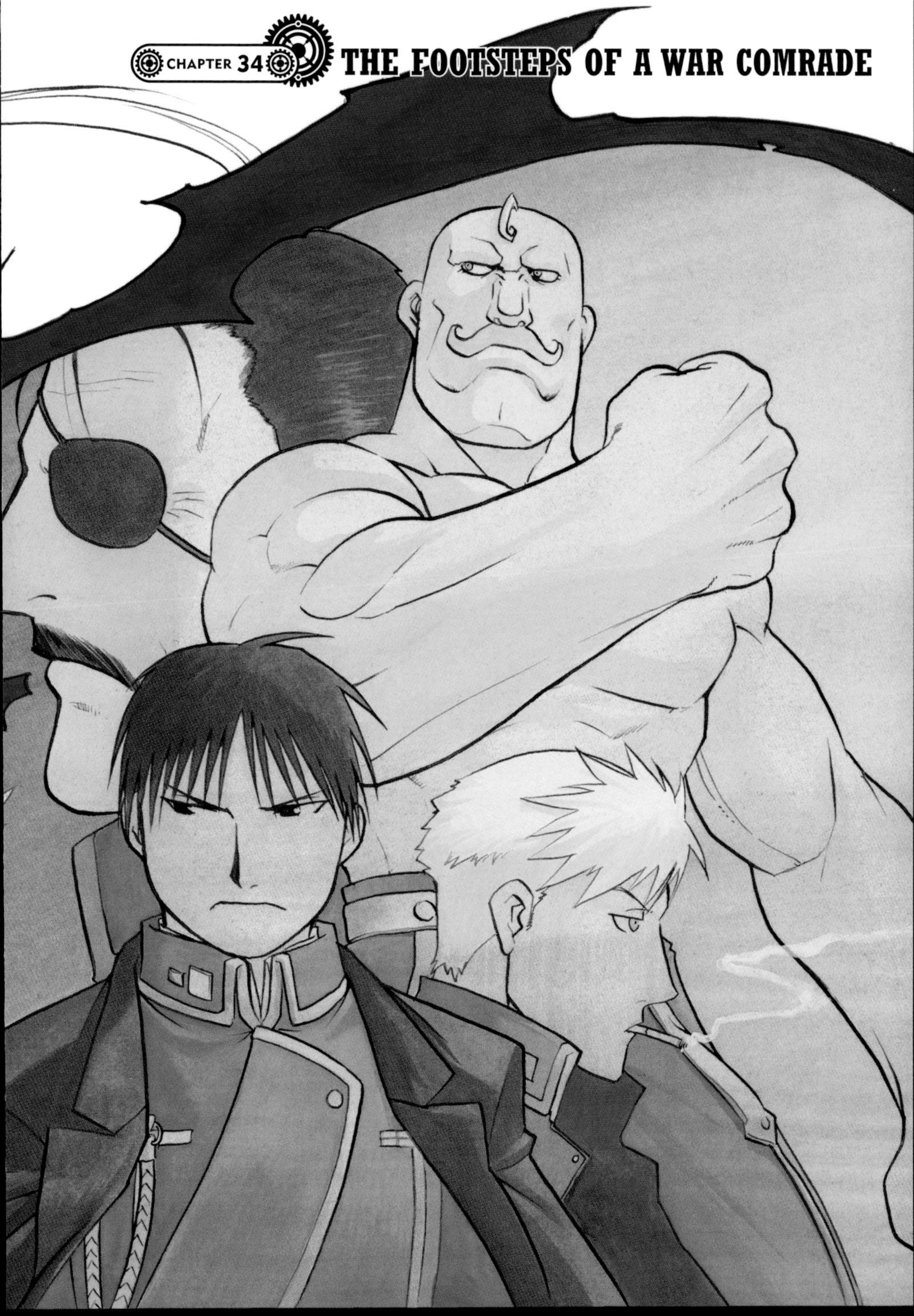
CHAPTER 34
THE FOOTSTEPS OF A WAR COMRADE

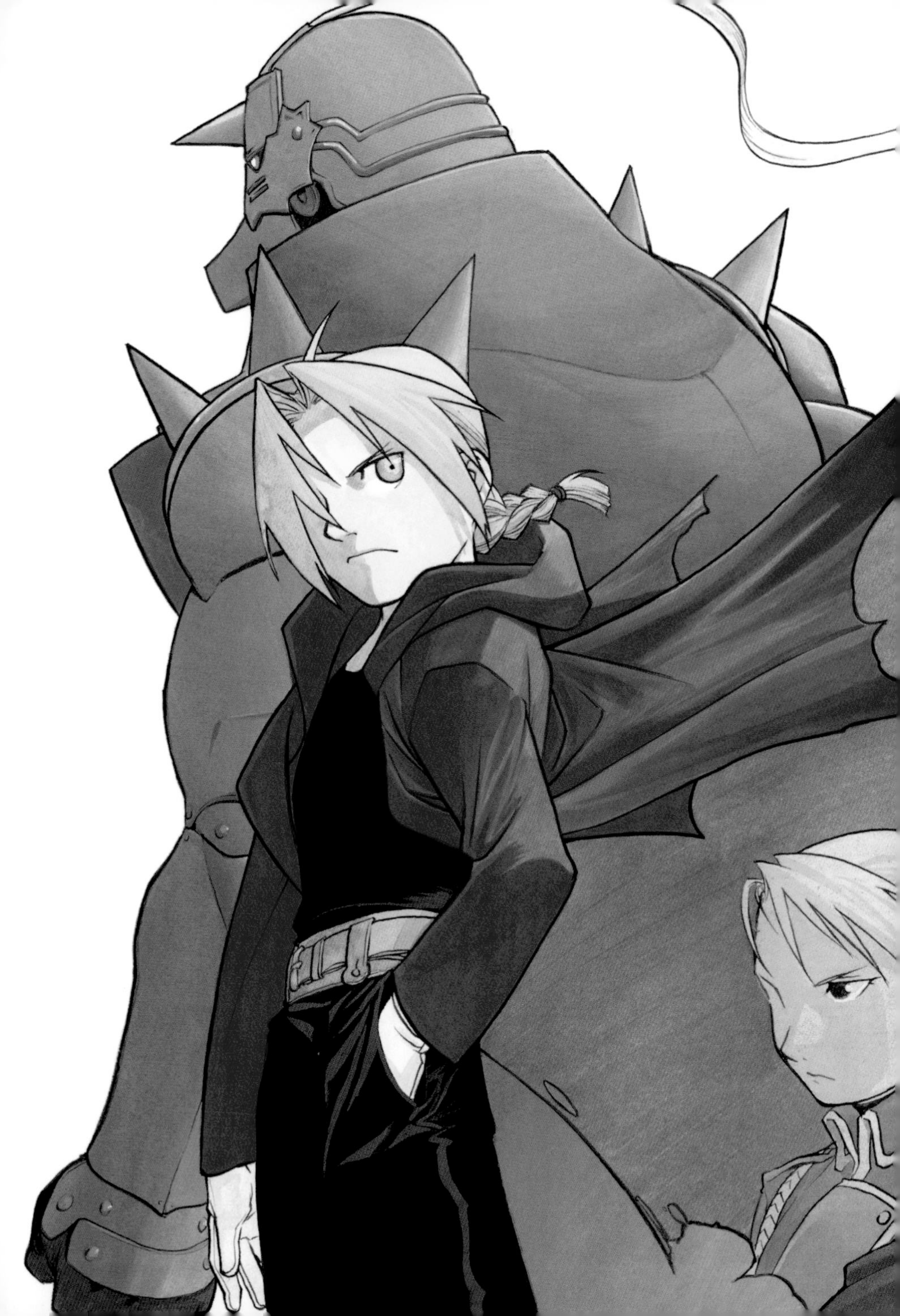

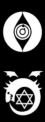

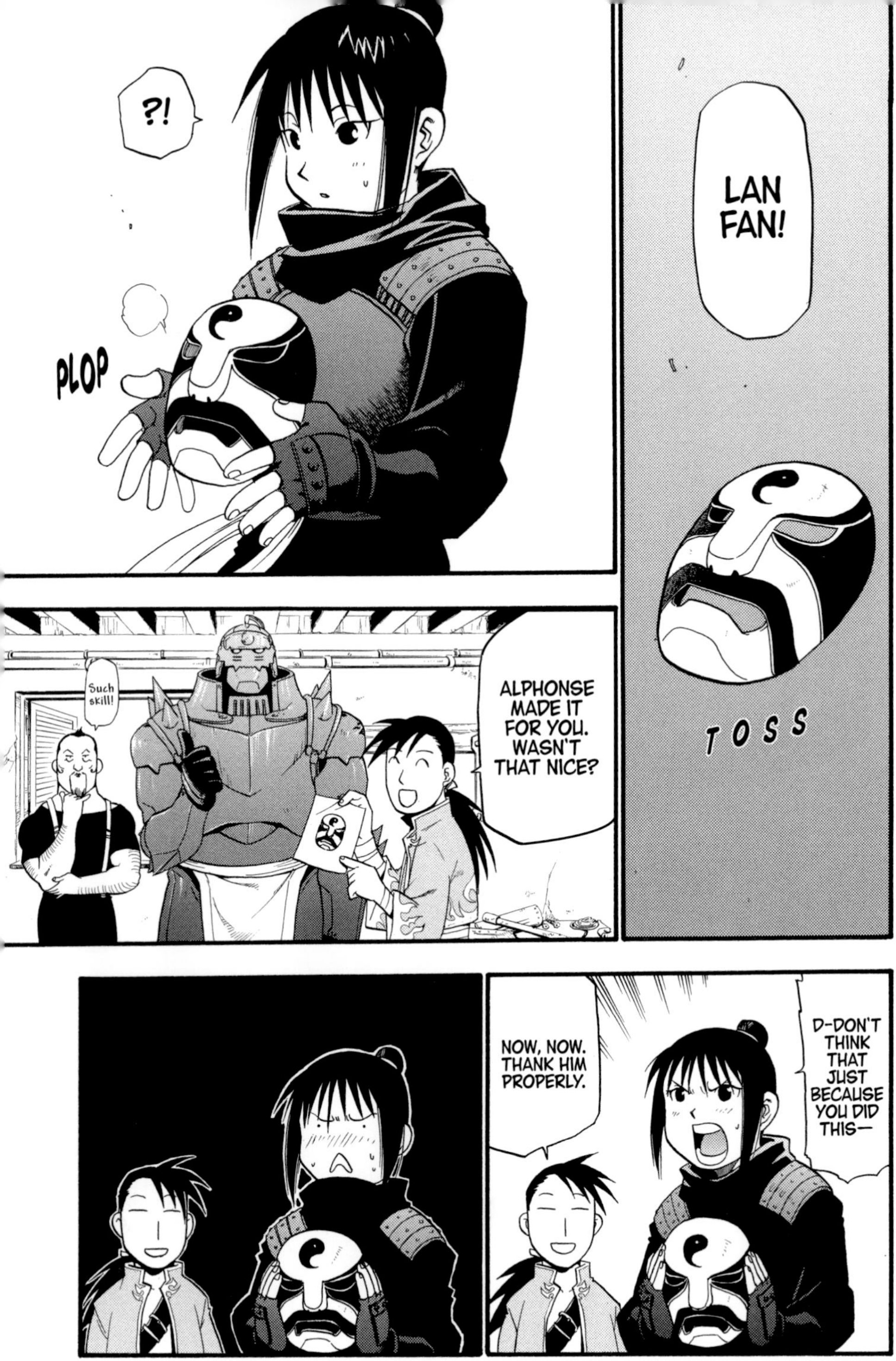
LAN FAN!
TOSS
?!
PLOP
ALPHONSE MADE IT FOR YOU. WASN'T THAT NICE?
Such skill!
D-DON'T THINK THAT JUST BECAUSE YOU DID THIS—
NOW, NOW. THANK HIM PROPERLY.

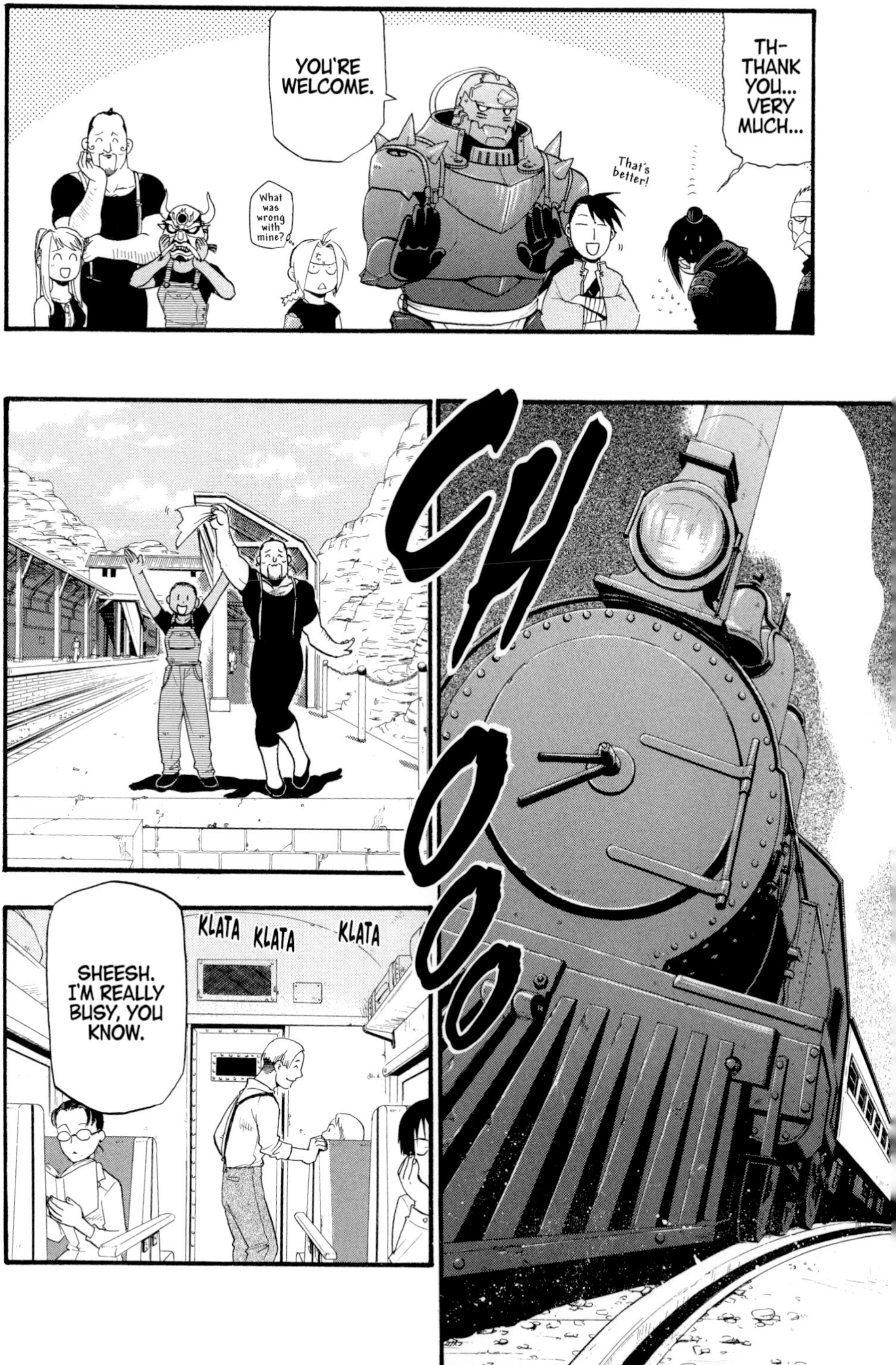
TH-THANK YOU... VERY MUCH...
That's better!
YOU'RE WELCOME.
What was wrong with mine?
CHOOOO
KLATA KLATA KLATA
SHEESH. I'M REALLY BUSY, YOU KNOW.

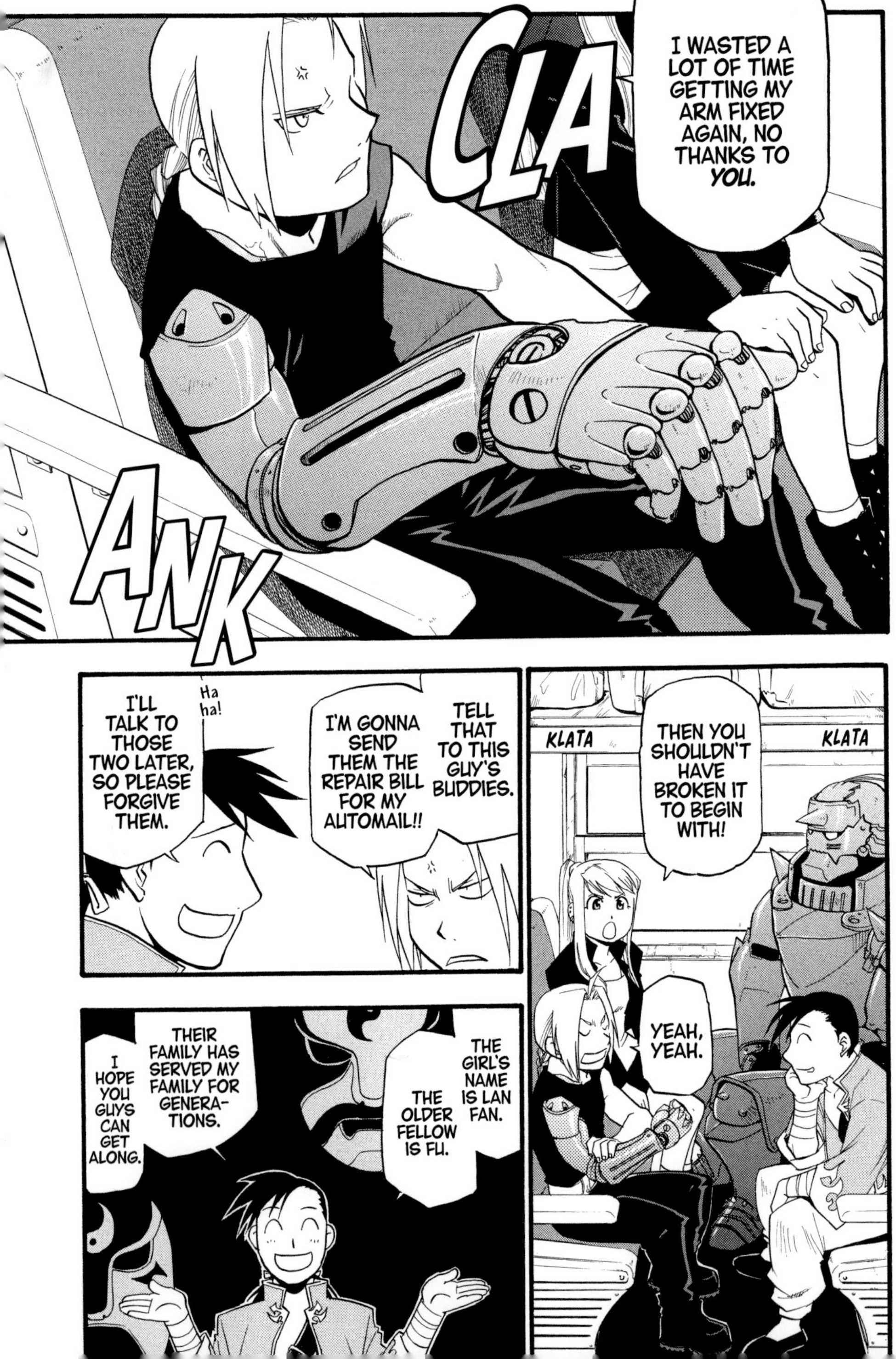
I WASTED A LOT OF TIME GETTING MY ARM FIXED AGAIN, NO THANKS TO YOU.
CLANK
KLATA
KLATA
THEN YOU SHOULDN'T HAVE BROKEN IT TO BEGIN WITH!
YEAH, YEAH.
TELL THAT TO THIS GUY'S BUDDIES.
I'M GONNA SEND THEM THE REPAIR BILL FOR MY AUTOMAIL!!
Ha ha!
I'LL TALK TO THOSE TWO LATER, SO PLEASE FORGIVE THEM.
THE GIRL'S NAME IS LAN FAN.
THE OLDER FELLOW IS FU.
THEIR FAMILY HAS SERVED MY FAMILY FOR GENERATIONS.
I HOPE YOU GUYS CAN GET ALONG.

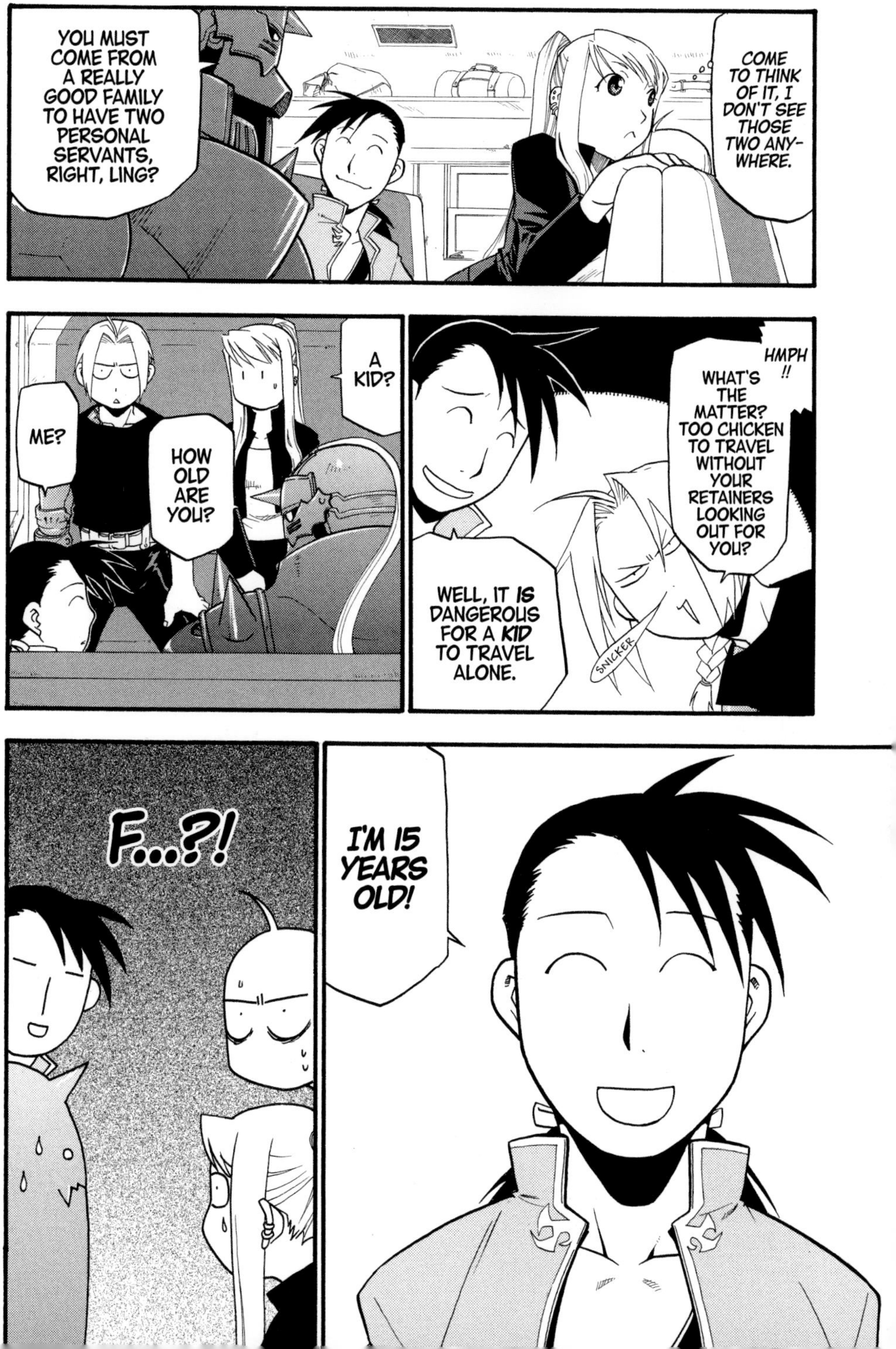
COME TO THINK OF IT, I DON'T SEE THOSE TWO ANYWHERE.
YOU MUST COME FROM A REALLY GOOD FAMILY TO HAVE TWO PERSONAL SERVANTS, RIGHT, LING?
HMPH !!
WHAT'S THE MATTER? TOO CHICKEN TO TRAVEL WITHOUT YOUR RETAINERS LOOKING OUT FOR YOU?
SNICKER
WELL, IT IS DANGEROUS FOR A KID TO TRAVEL ALONE.
A KID?
HOW OLD ARE YOU?
ME?
I'M 15 YEARS OLD!
F...?!

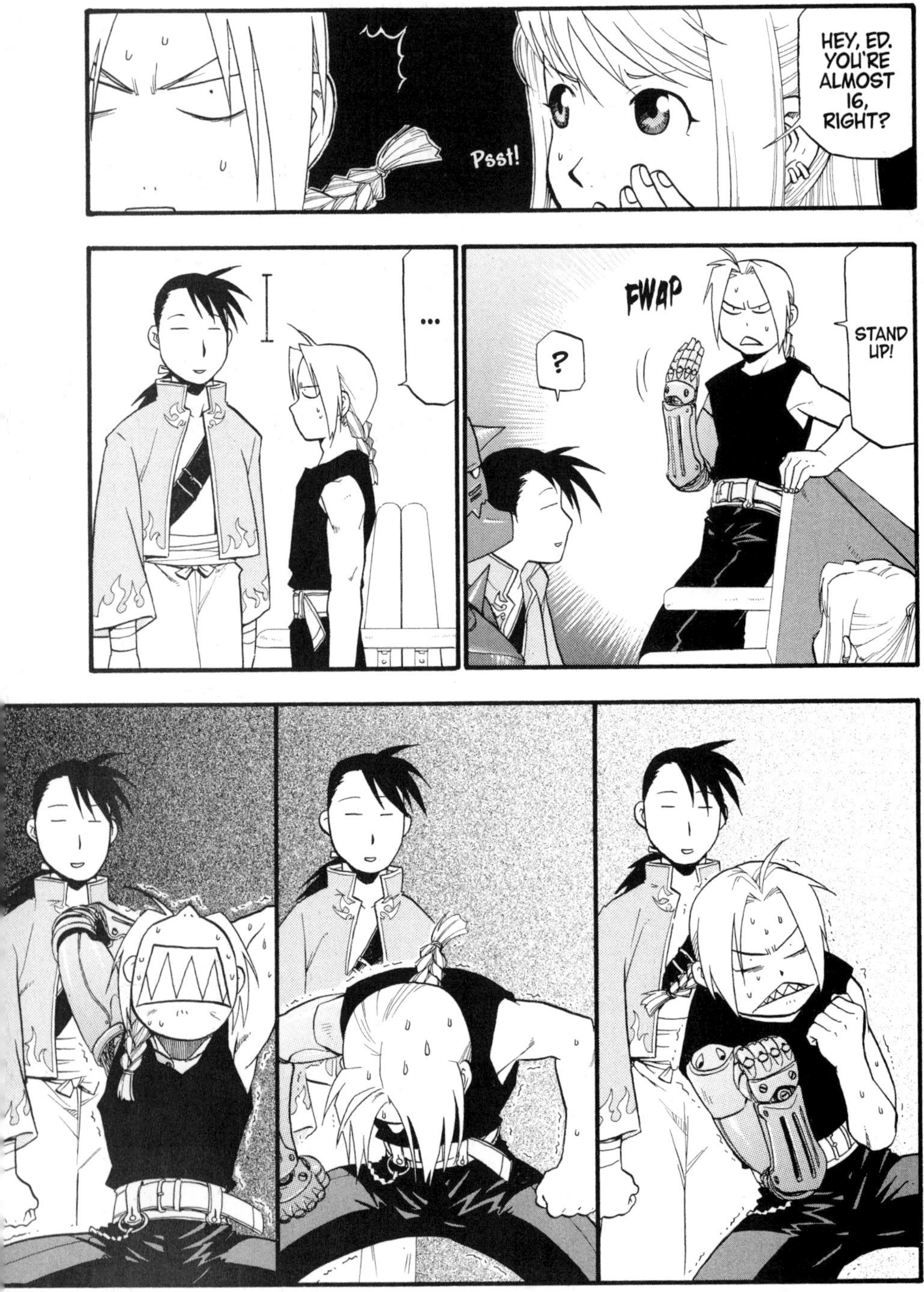
HEY, ED. YOU'RE ALMOST 16, RIGHT?
Psst!
STAND UP!
FWAP
?
...

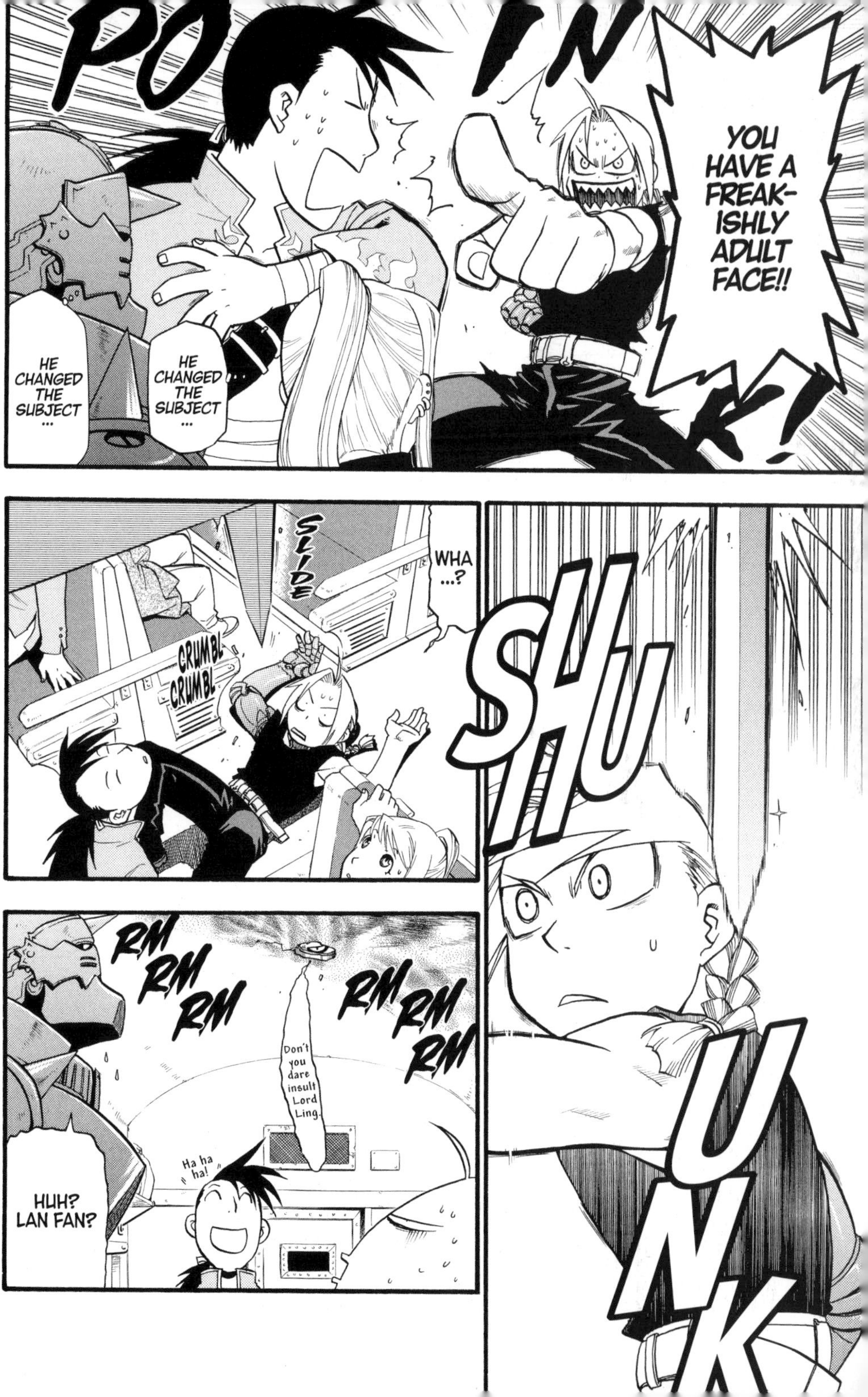
POINK!
YOU HAVE A FREAK-ISHLY ADULT FACE!!
HE CHANGED THE SUBJECT ...
HE CHANGED THE SUBJECT ...
SHUNK
WHA ...?
SLIDE
CRUMBL CRUMBL
RM RM RM
Don't you dare insult Lord Ling.
Ha ha ha!
HUH? LAN FAN?
RM RM RM

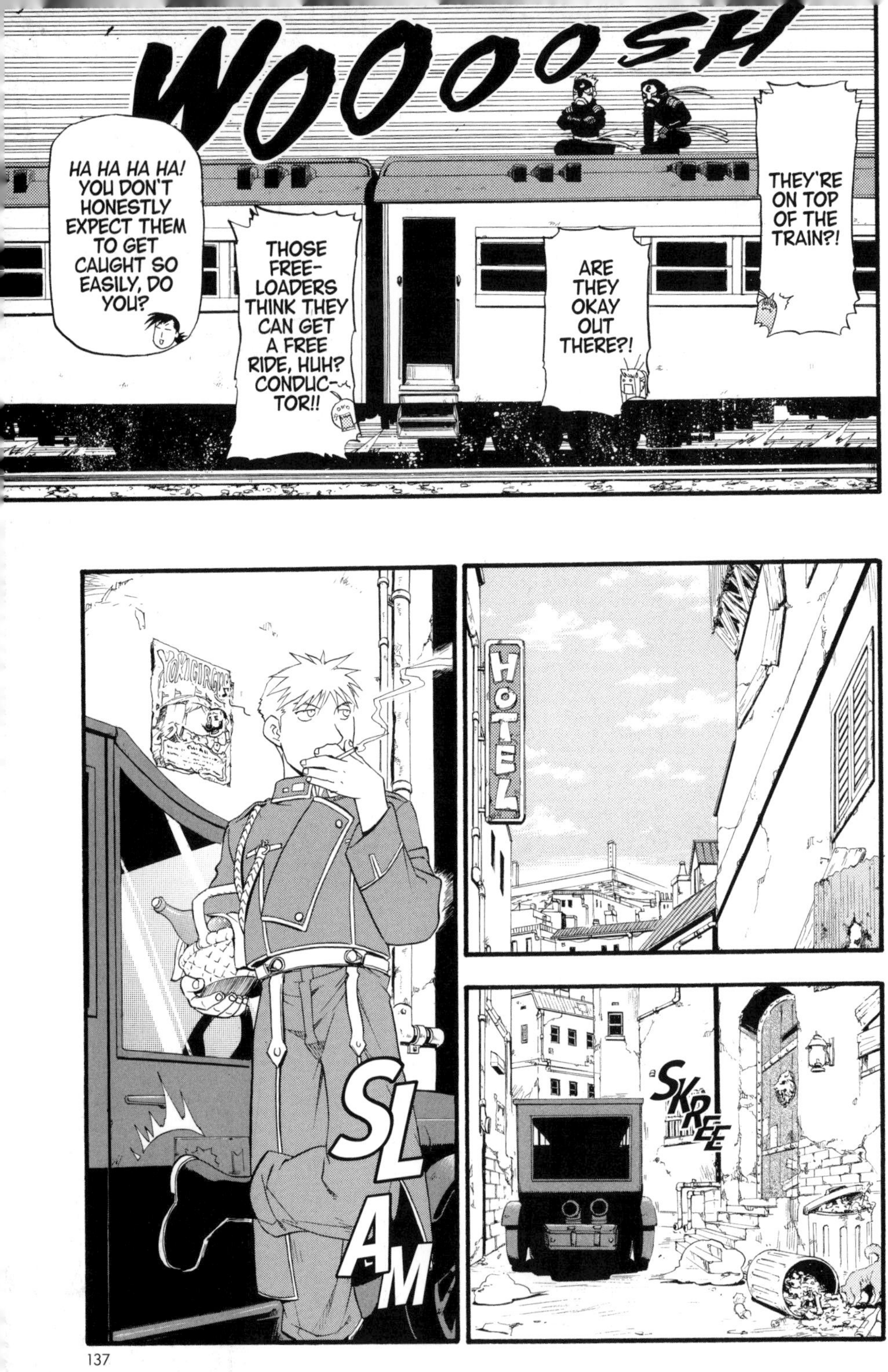
WOOOOOSH
THEY'RE ON TOP OF THE TRAIN?!
ARE THEY OKAY OUT THERE?!
THOSE FREE-LOADERS THINK THEY CAN GET A FREE RIDE, HUH? CONDUCTOR!!
HA HA HA HA! YOU DON'T HONESTLY EXPECT THEM TO GET CAUGHT SO EASILY, DO YOU?
HOTEL
SKREE
SLAM

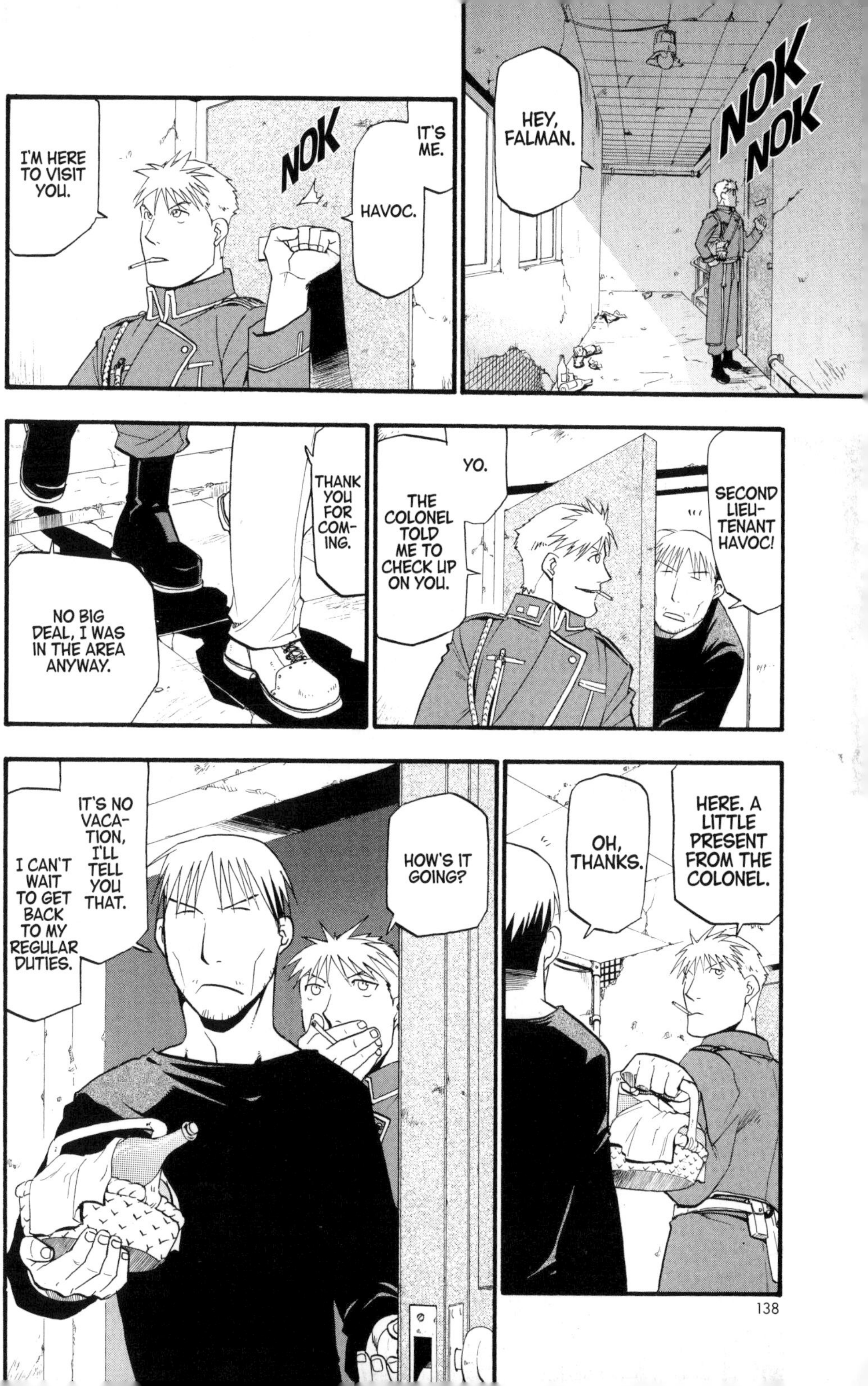
HEY, FALMAN.
NOK NOK
IT'S ME.
NOK
HAVOC.
I'M HERE TO VISIT YOU.
SECOND LIEUTENANT HAVOC!
YO.
THE COLONEL TOLD ME TO CHECK UP ON YOU.
THANK YOU FOR COMING.
NO BIG DEAL, I WAS IN THE AREA ANYWAY.
HERE. A LITTLE PRESENT FROM THE COLONEL.
OH, THANKS.
HOW'S IT GOING?
IT'S NO VACATION, I'LL TELL YOU THAT.
I CAN'T WAIT TO GET BACK TO MY REGULAR DUTIES.

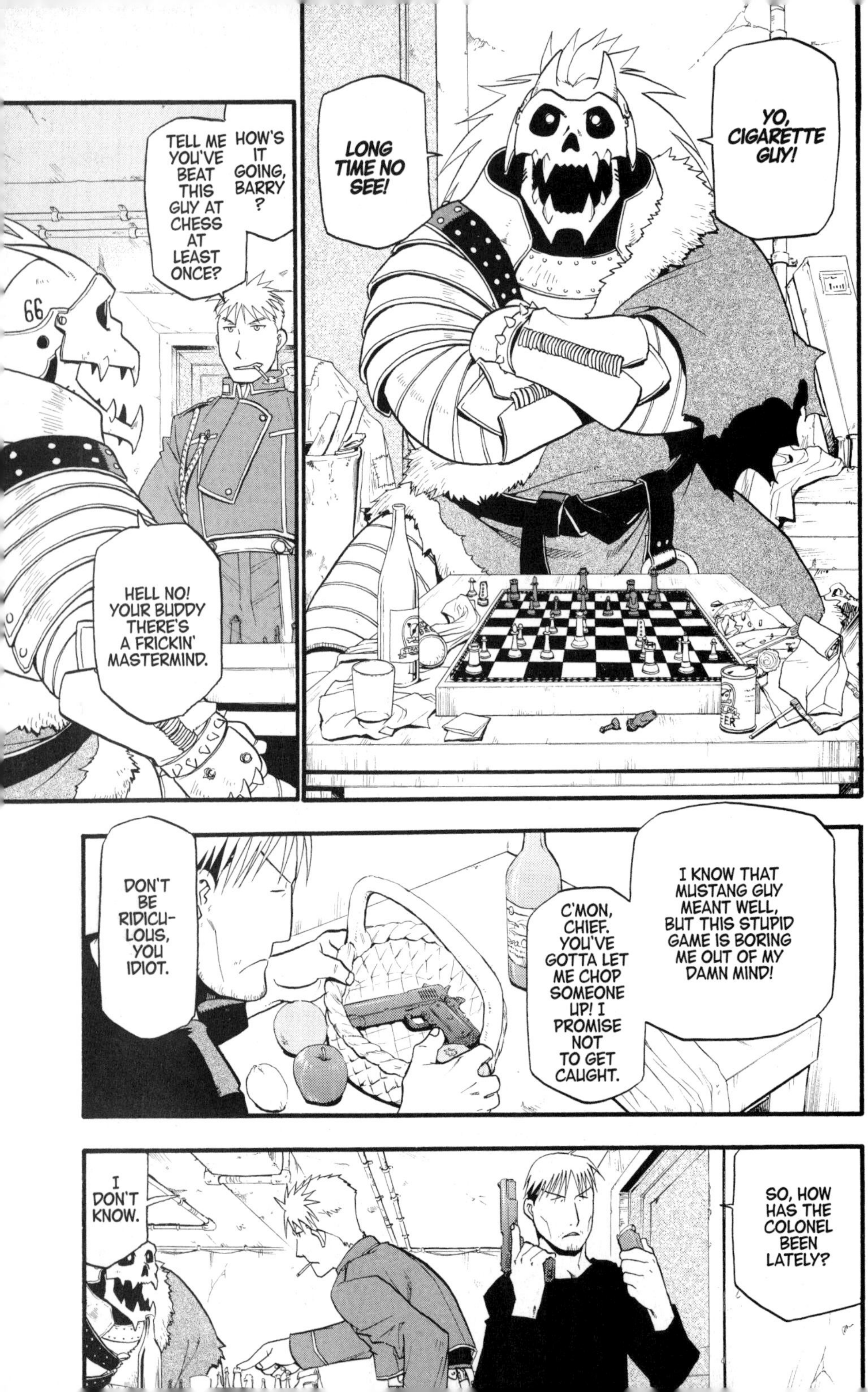
YO, CIGARETTE GUY!
LONG TIME NO SEE!
HOW'S IT GOING, BARRY?
TELL ME YOU'VE BEAT THIS GUY AT CHESS AT LEAST ONCE?
HELL NO! YOUR BUDDY THERE'S A FRICKIN' MASTERMIND.
I KNOW THAT MUSTANG GUY MEANT WELL, BUT THIS STUPID GAME IS BORING ME OUT OF MY DAMN MIND!
C'MON, CHIEF. YOU'VE GOTTA LET ME CHOP SOMEONE UP! I PROMISE NOT TO GET CAUGHT.
DON'T BE RIDICULOUS, YOU IDIOT.
SO, HOW HAS THE COLONEL BEEN LATELY?
I DON'T KNOW.

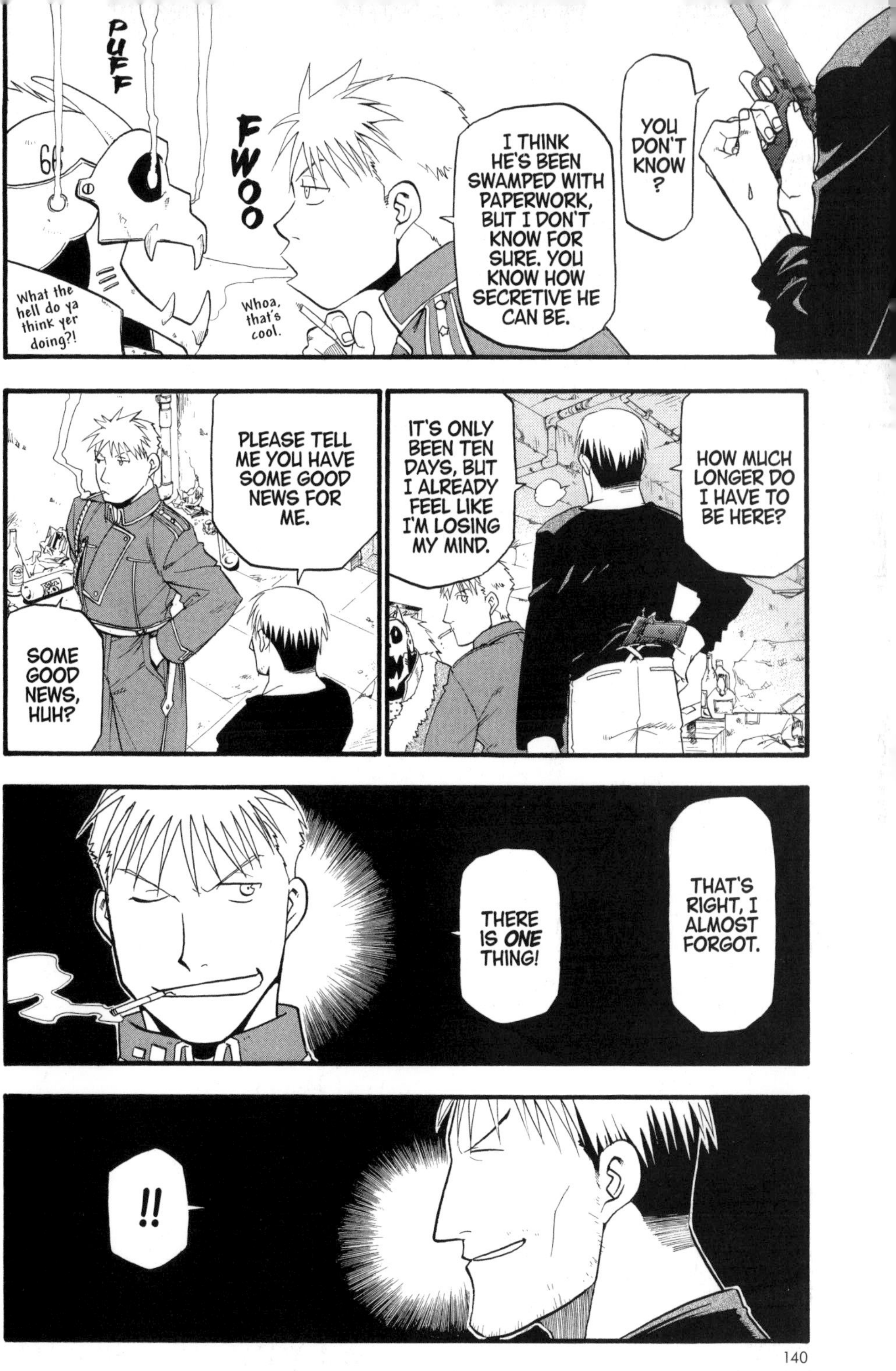
YOU DON'T KNOW?
I THINK HE'S BEEN SWAMPED WITH PAPERWORK, BUT I DON'T KNOW FOR SURE. YOU KNOW HOW SECRETIVE HE CAN BE.
FWOO
Whoa, that's cool.
PUFF
What the hell do ya think yer doing?!
HOW MUCH LONGER DO I HAVE TO BE HERE?
IT'S ONLY BEEN TEN DAYS, BUT I ALREADY FEEL LIKE I'M LOSING MY MIND.
PLEASE TELL ME YOU HAVE SOME GOOD NEWS FOR ME.
SOME GOOD NEWS, HUH?
THAT'S RIGHT, I ALMOST FORGOT.
THERE IS ONE THING!
!!

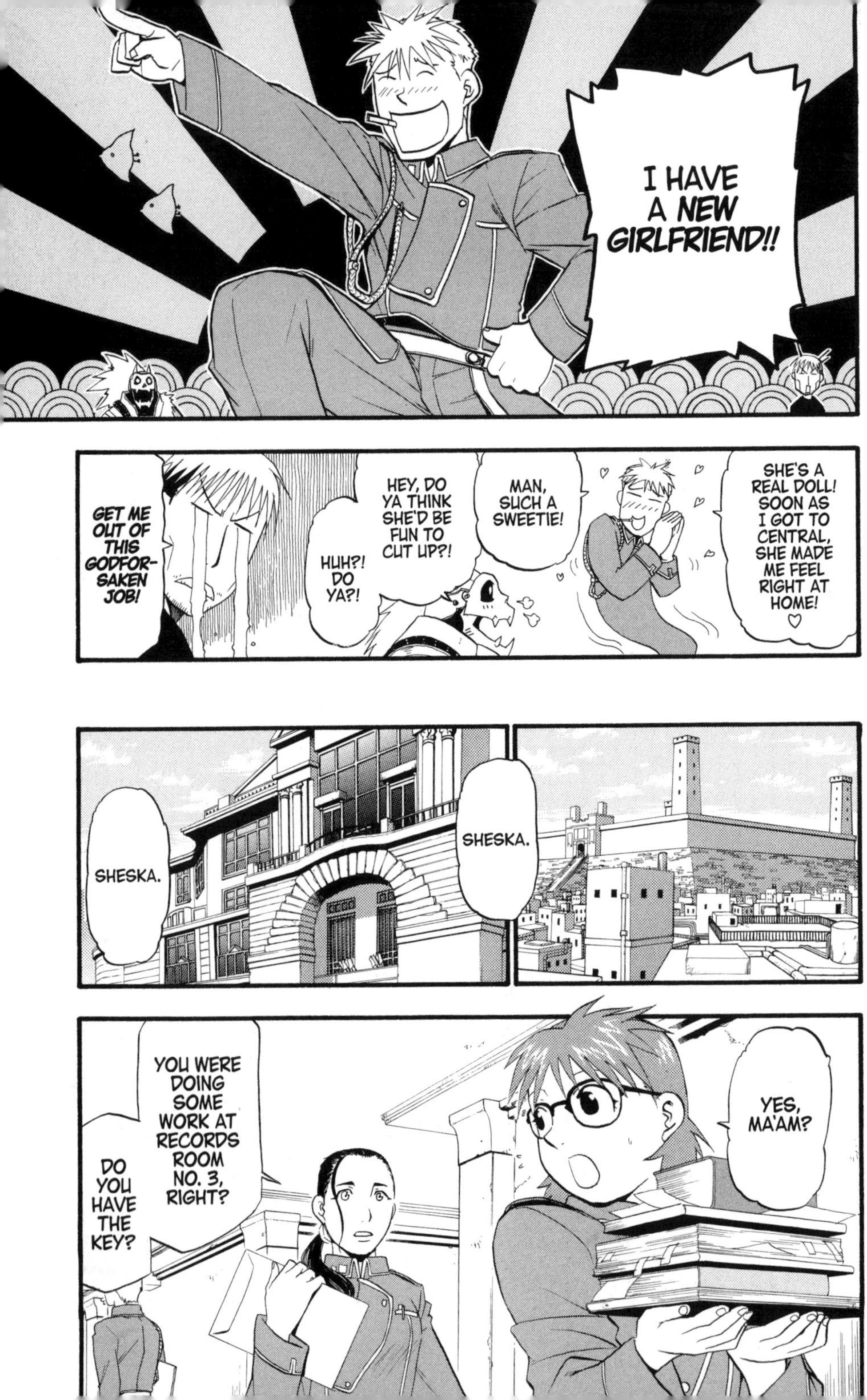
I HAVE A **NEW** GIRLFRIEND!!
SHE'S A REAL DOLL! SOON AS I GOT TO CENTRAL, SHE MADE ME FEEL RIGHT AT HOME! ♡
MAN, SUCH A SWEETIE!
HEY, DO YA THINK SHE'D BE FUN TO CUT UP?!
HUH?! DO YA?!
GET ME OUT OF THIS GODFORSAKEN JOB!
SHESKA.
SHESKA.
YES, MA'AM?
YOU WERE DOING SOME WORK AT RECORDS ROOM NO. 3, RIGHT?
DO YOU HAVE THE KEY?

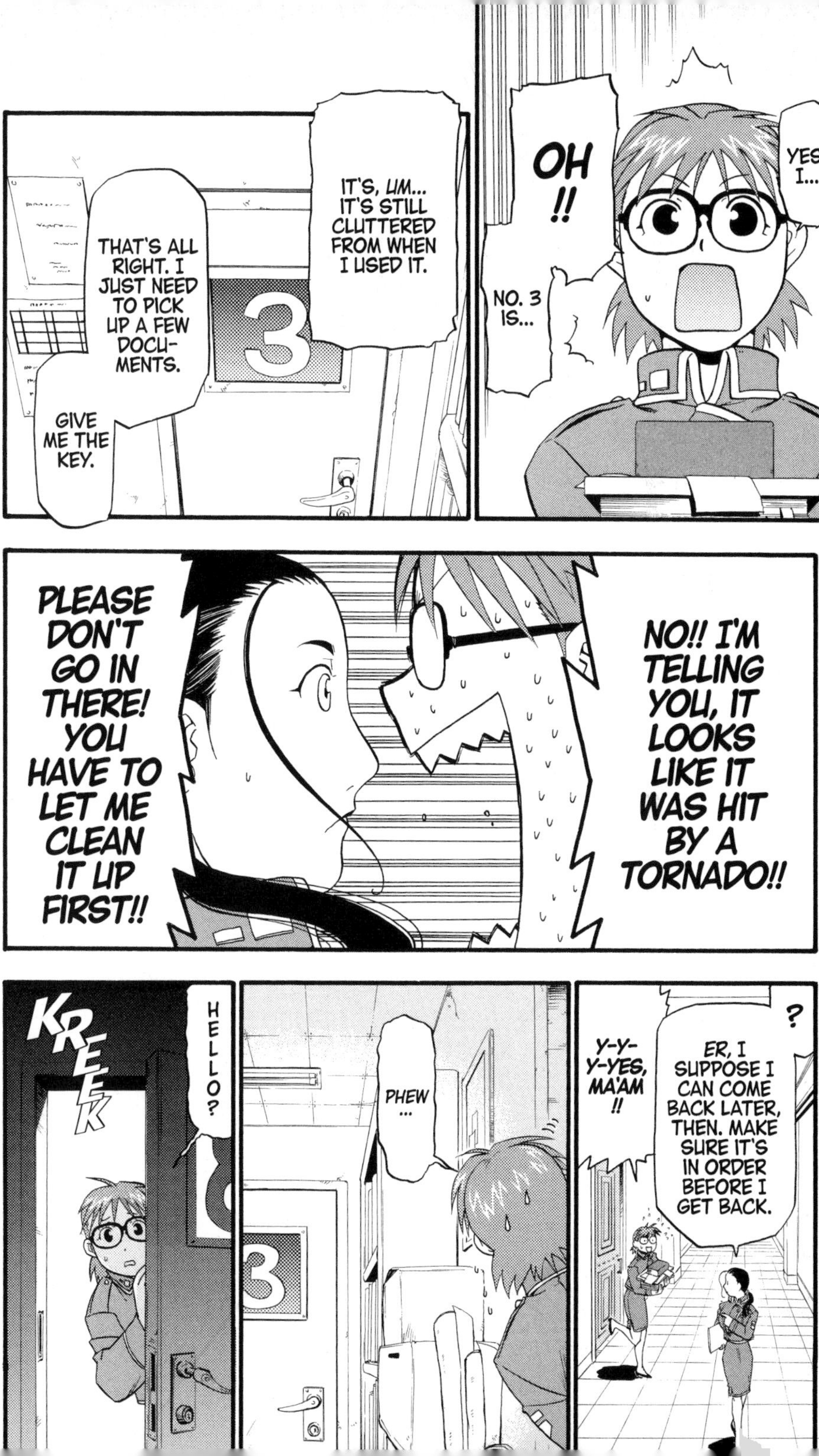
YES, I...
OH!!
NO. 3 IS...
IT'S, UM... IT'S STILL CLUTTERED FROM WHEN I USED IT.
THAT'S ALL RIGHT. I JUST NEED TO PICK UP A FEW DOCU-MENTS.
GIVE ME THE KEY.
NO!! I'M TELLING YOU, IT LOOKS LIKE IT WAS HIT BY A TORNADO!!
PLEASE DON'T GO IN THERE! YOU HAVE TO LET ME CLEAN IT UP FIRST!!
?
ER, I SUPPOSE I CAN COME BACK LATER, THEN. MAKE SURE IT'S IN ORDER BEFORE I GET BACK.
Y-Y-Y-YES, MA'AM!!
PHEW...
HELLO?
KREEEK

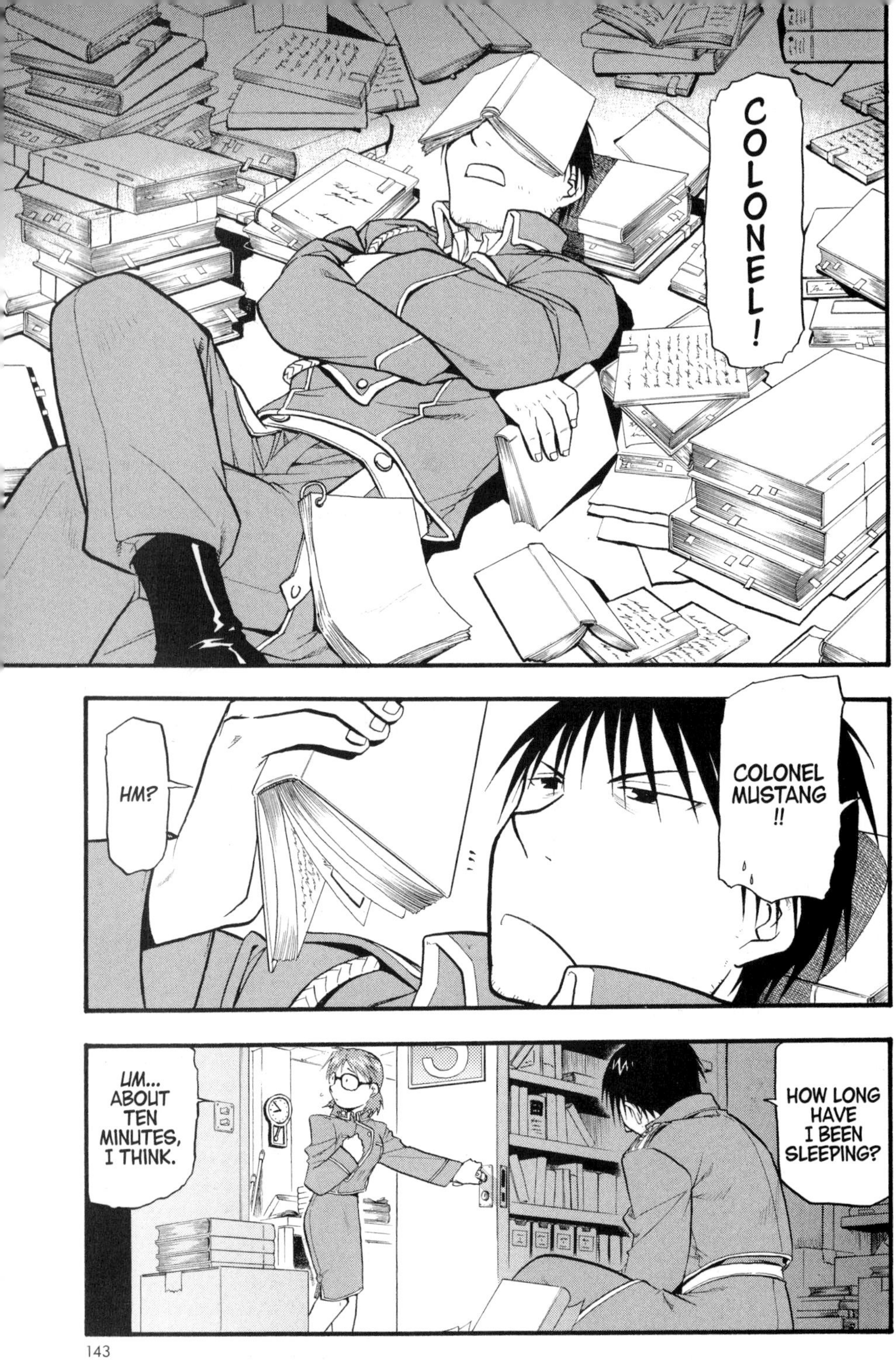

COLONEL!
COLONEL MUSTANG !!
HM?
HOW LONG HAVE I BEEN SLEEPING?
UM... ABOUT TEN MINUTES, I THINK.

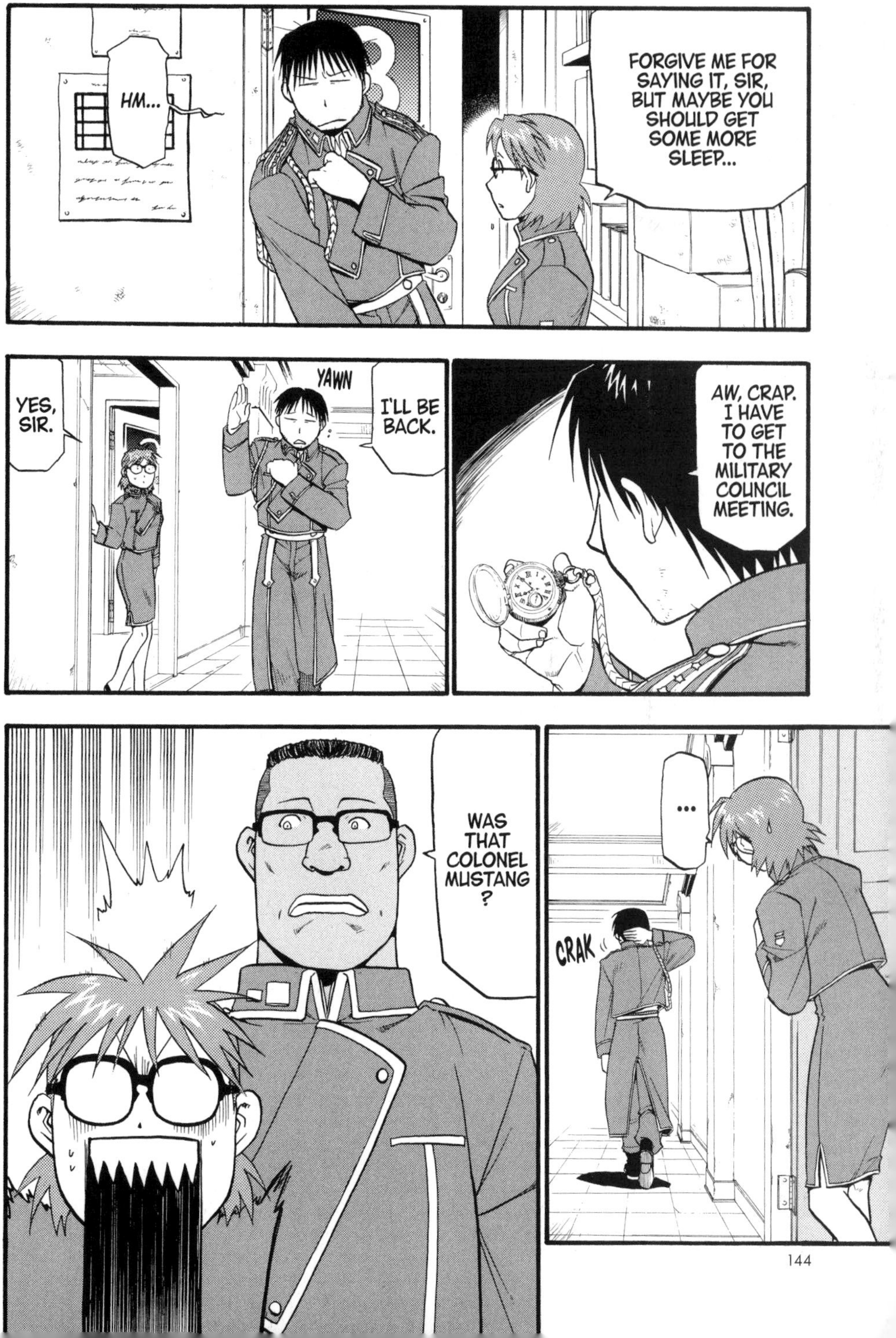
FORGIVE ME FOR SAYING IT, SIR, BUT MAYBE YOU SHOULD GET SOME MORE SLEEP...
HM...
AW, CRAP. I HAVE TO GET TO THE MILITARY COUNCIL MEETING.
I'LL BE BACK.
YAWN
YES, SIR.
...
CRAK
WAS THAT COLONEL MUSTANG?

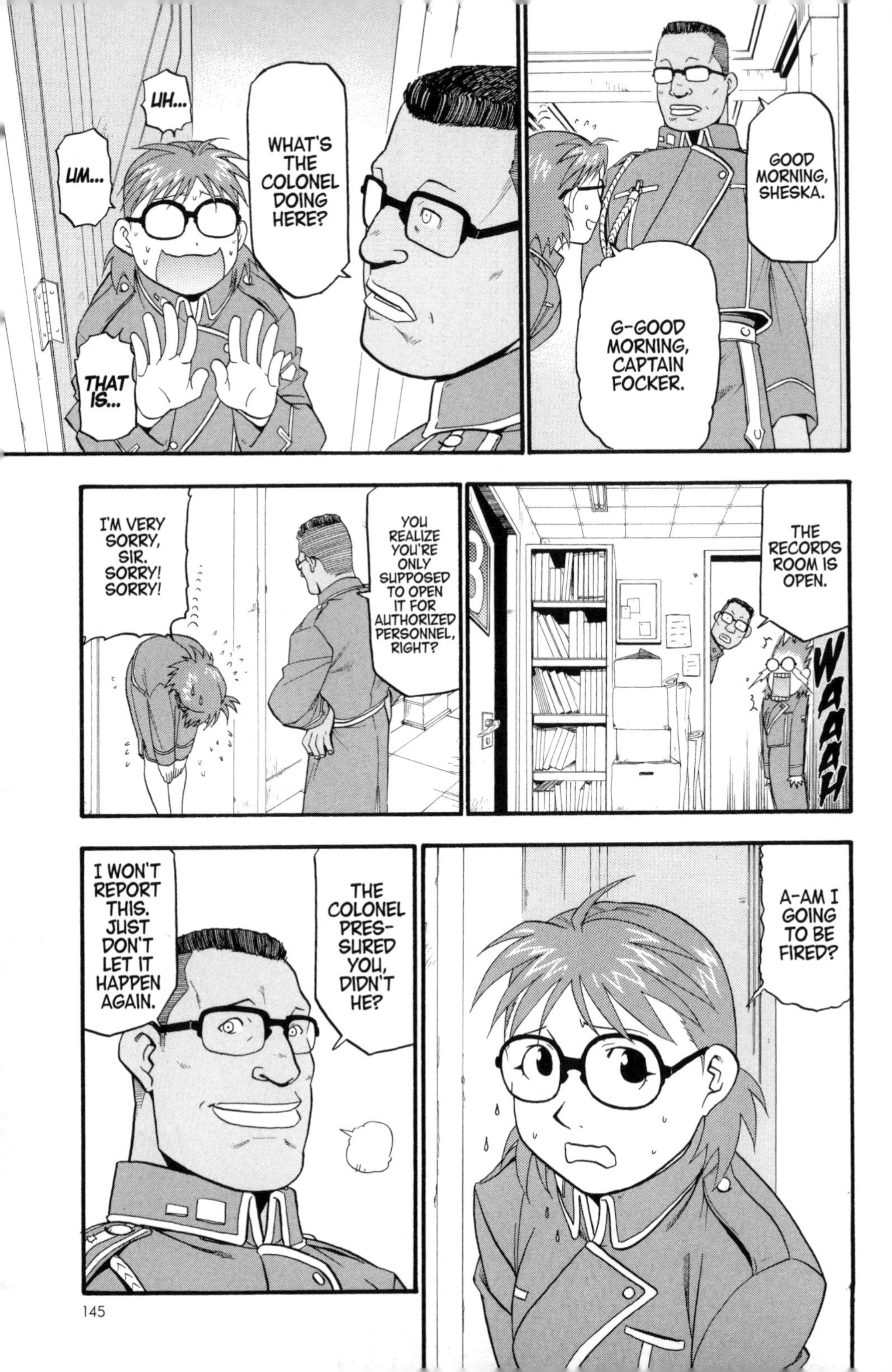
GOOD MORNING, SHESKA.
G-GOOD MORNING, CAPTAIN FOCKER.
WHAT'S THE COLONEL DOING HERE?
UH...
UM...
THAT IS...
THE RECORDS ROOM IS OPEN.
WAAAH
YOU REALIZE YOU'RE ONLY SUPPOSED TO OPEN IT FOR AUTHORIZED PERSONNEL, RIGHT?
I'M VERY SORRY, SIR. SORRY! SORRY!
A-AM I GOING TO BE FIRED?
THE COLONEL PRES-SURED YOU, DIDN'T HE?
I WON'T REPORT THIS. JUST DON'T LET IT HAPPEN AGAIN.

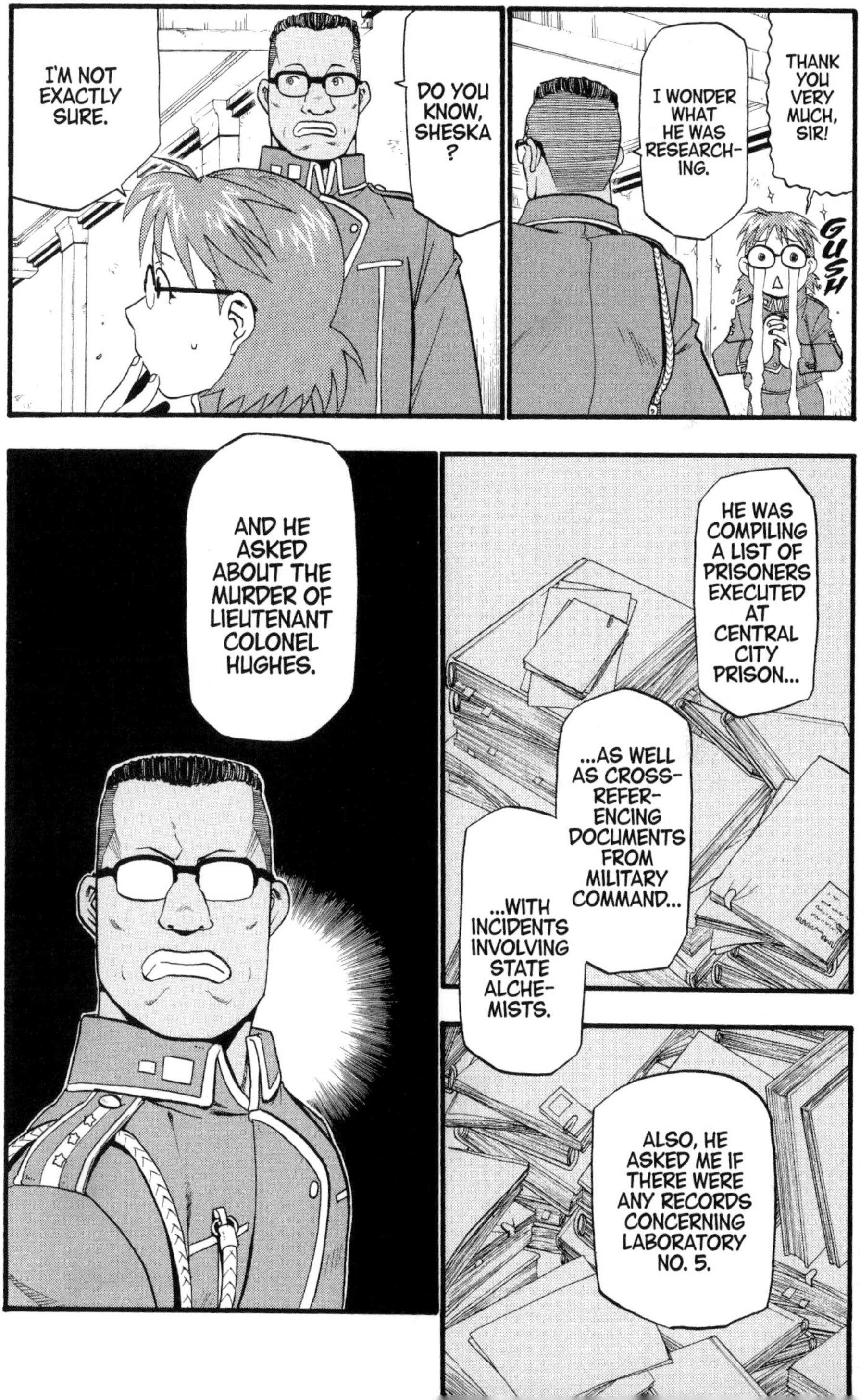
THANK YOU VERY MUCH, SIR!
GUSH
I WONDER WHAT HE WAS RESEARCHING.
DO YOU KNOW, SHESKA?
I'M NOT EXACTLY SURE.
HE WAS COMPILING A LIST OF PRISONERS EXECUTED AT CENTRAL CITY PRISON...
...AS WELL AS CROSS-REFERENCING DOCUMENTS FROM MILITARY COMMAND...
...WITH INCIDENTS INVOLVING STATE ALCHEMISTS.
ALSO, HE ASKED ME IF THERE WERE ANY RECORDS CONCERNING LABORATORY NO. 5.
AND HE ASKED ABOUT THE MURDER OF LIEUTENANT COLONEL HUGHES.

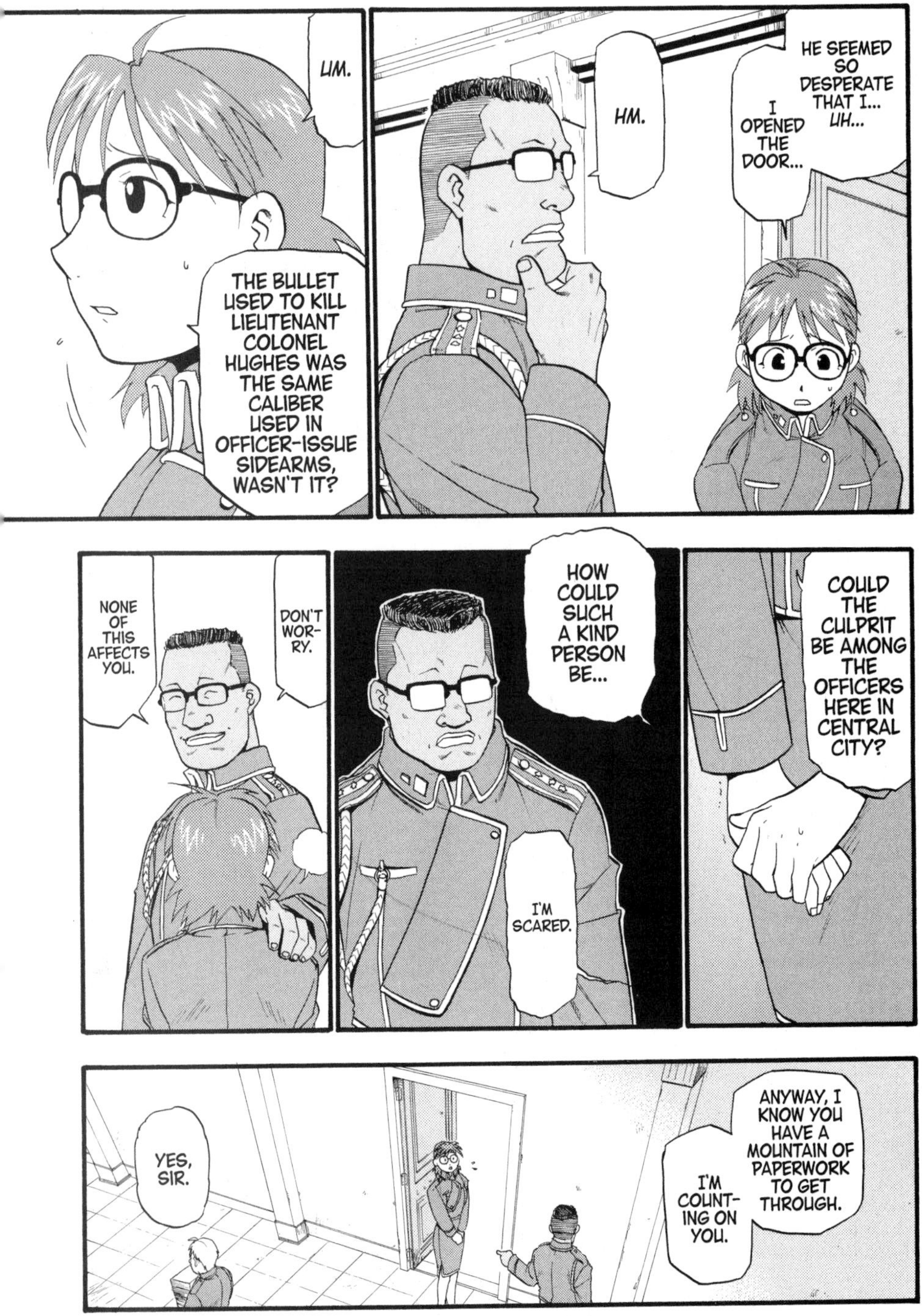
HE SEEMED SO DESPERATE THAT I... UH...
I OPENED THE DOOR...
HM.
UM.
THE BULLET USED TO KILL LIEUTENANT COLONEL HUGHES WAS THE SAME CALIBER USED IN OFFICER-ISSUE SIDEARMS, WASN'T IT?
COULD THE CULPRIT BE AMONG THE OFFICERS HERE IN CENTRAL CITY?
HOW COULD SUCH A KIND PERSON BE...
I'M SCARED.
DON'T WOR-RY.
NONE OF THIS AFFECTS YOU.
ANYWAY, I KNOW YOU HAVE A MOUNTAIN OF PAPERWORK TO GET THROUGH.
I'M COUNT-ING ON YOU.
YES, SIR.

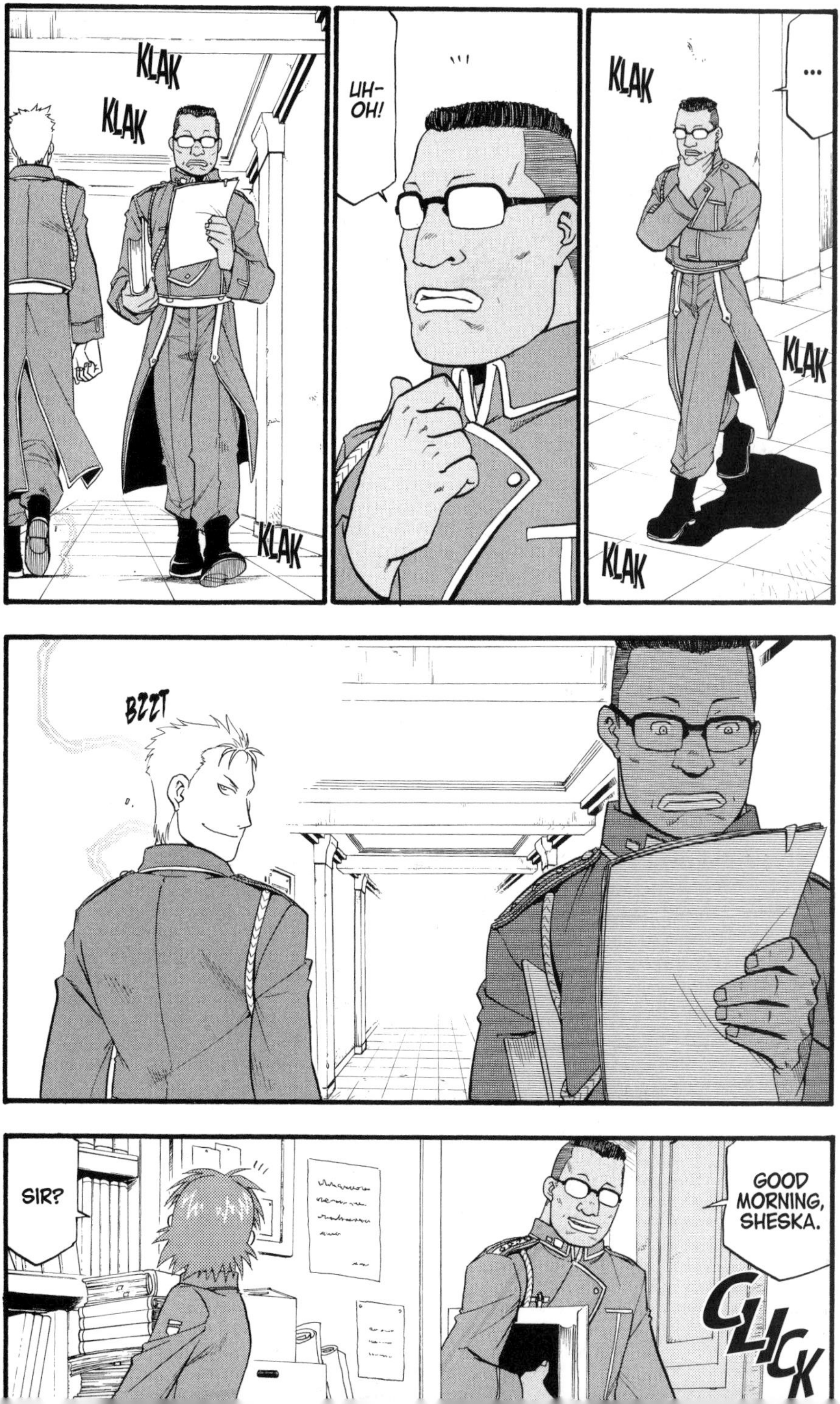
...
KLAK
KLAK
UH-OH!
KLAK
KLAK
KLAK
BZZT
GOOD MORNING, SHESKA.
CLICK
SIR?

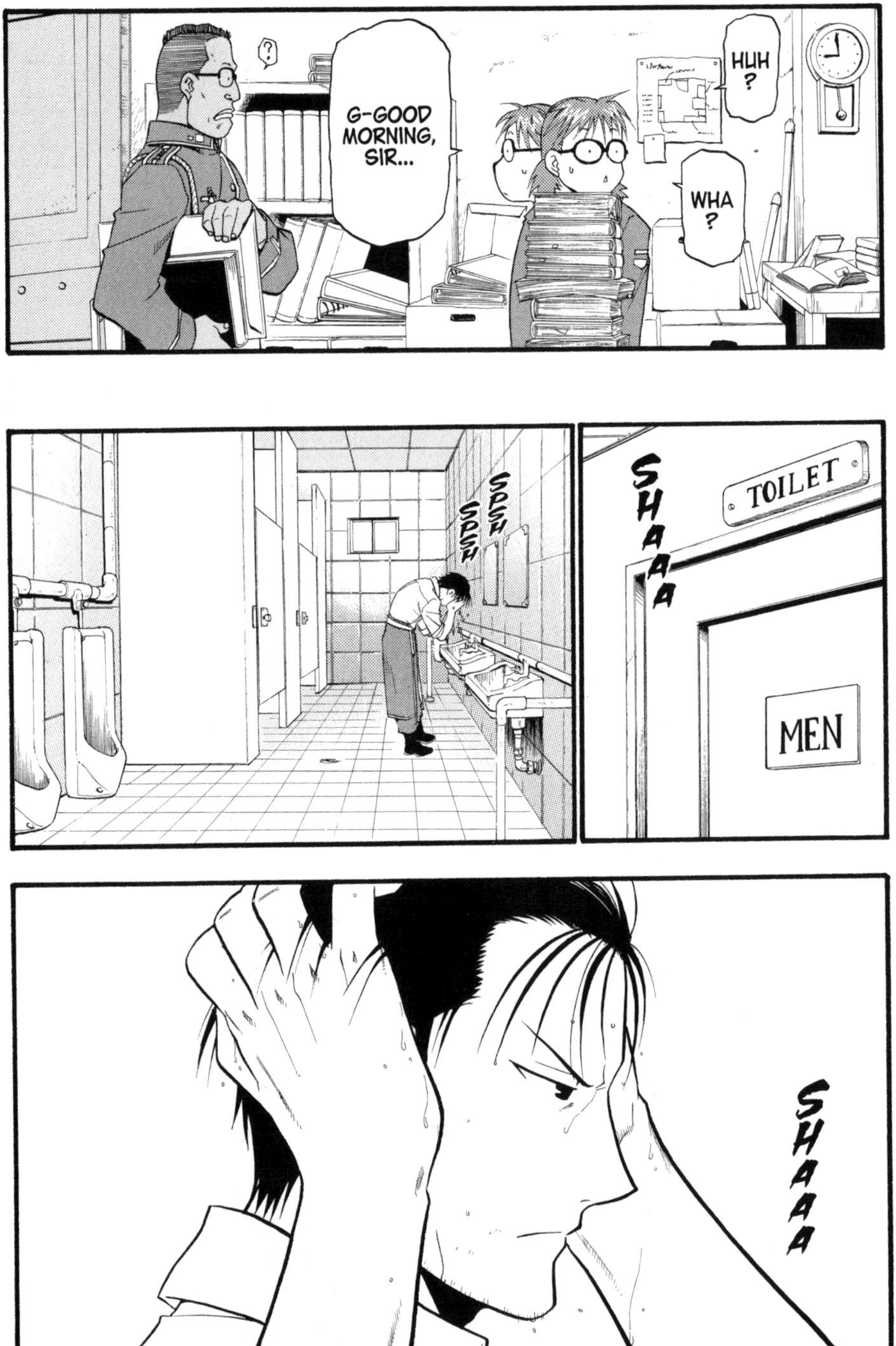
HUH?
WHA?
G-GOOD MORNING, SIR...
?
SHAAAA
TOILET
MEN
SPSH SPSH
SHAAAA

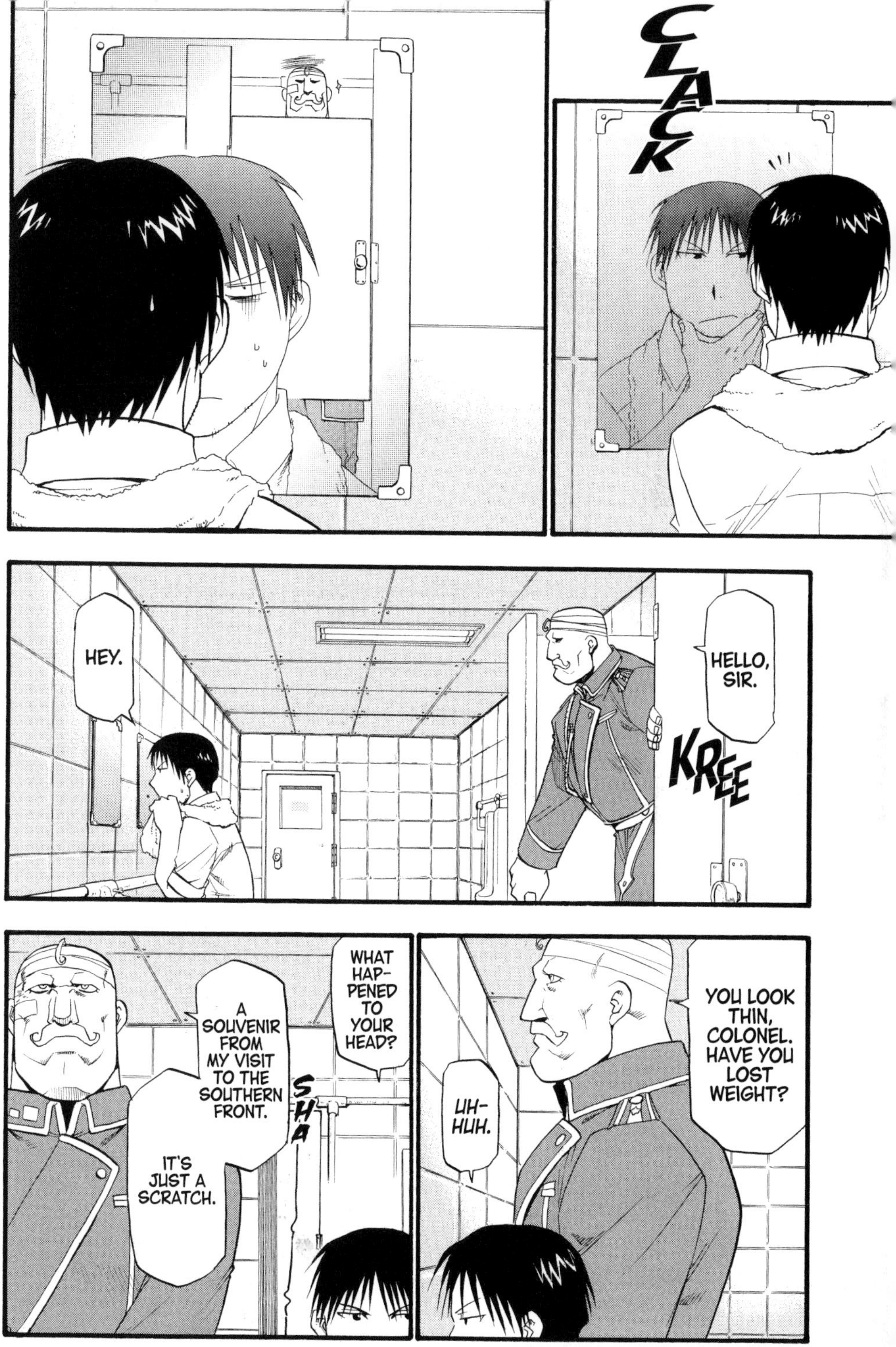
CLACK
HELLO, SIR.
KREE
HEY.
YOU LOOK THIN, COLONEL. HAVE YOU LOST WEIGHT?
UH-HUH.
WHAT HAPPENED TO YOUR HEAD?
A SOUVENIR FROM MY VISIT TO THE SOUTHERN FRONT.
SHA
IT'S JUST A SCRATCH.

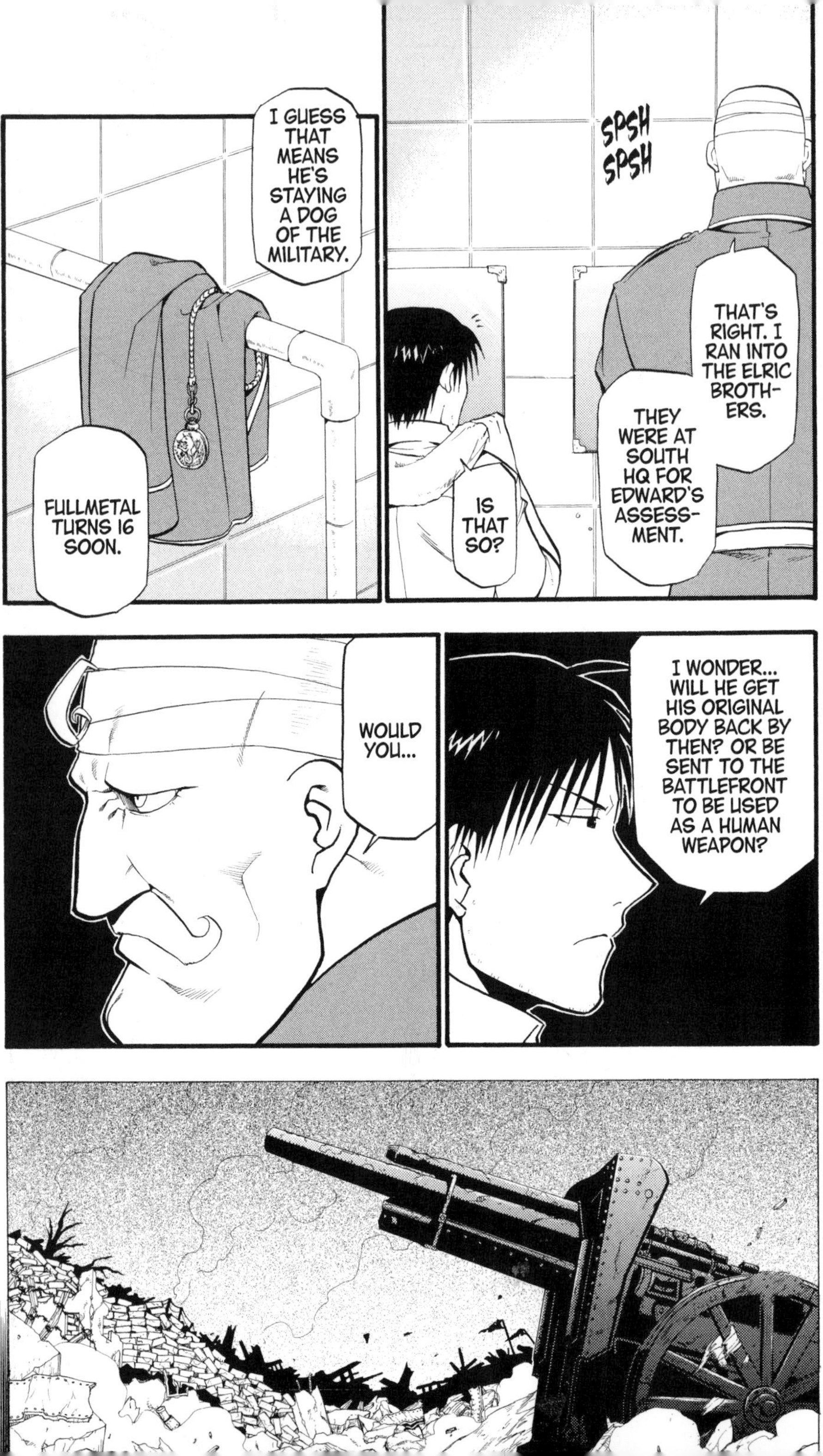
SPSH SPSH
THAT'S RIGHT. I RAN INTO THE ELRIC BROTHERS.
THEY WERE AT SOUTH HQ FOR EDWARD'S ASSESSMENT.
IS THAT SO?
I GUESS THAT MEANS HE'S STAYING A DOG OF THE MILITARY.
FULLMETAL TURNS 16 SOON.
I WONDER... WILL HE GET HIS ORIGINAL BODY BACK BY THEN? OR BE SENT TO THE BATTLEFRONT TO BE USED AS A HUMAN WEAPON?
WOULD YOU...

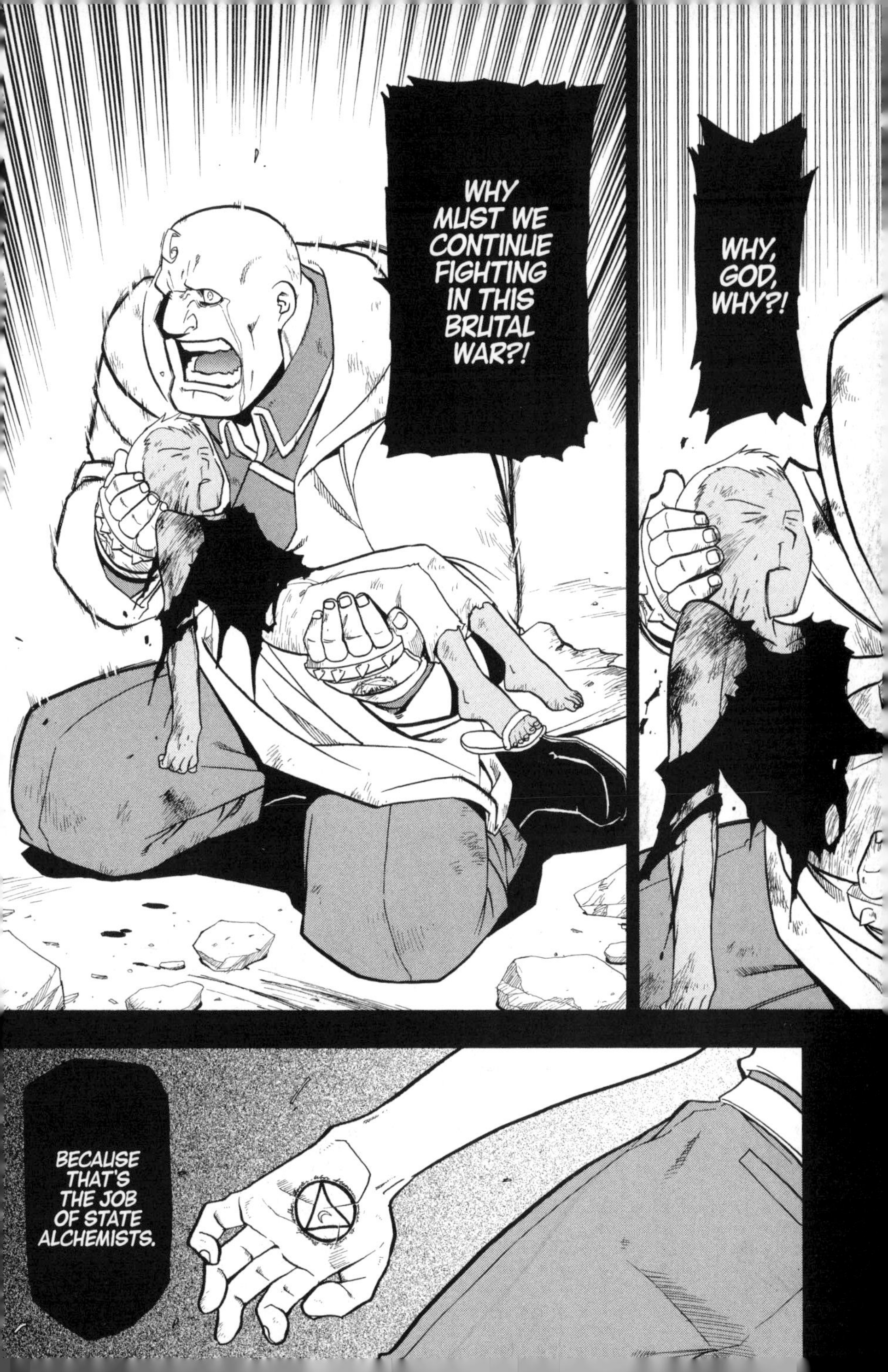
WHY, GOD, WHY?!
WHY MUST WE CONTINUE FIGHTING IN THIS BRUTAL WAR?!
BECAUSE THAT'S THE JOB OF STATE ALCHEMISTS.

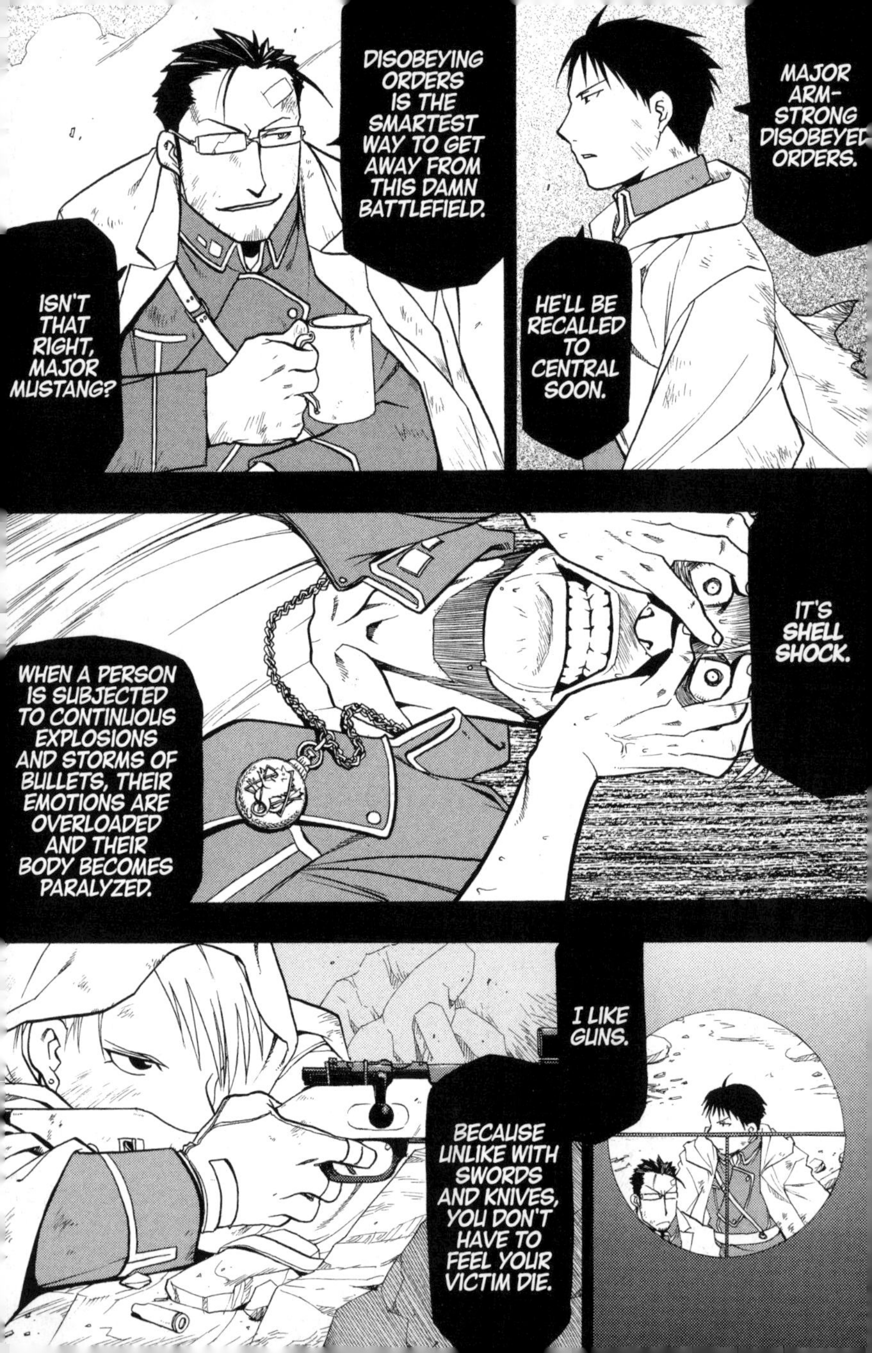
MAJOR ARM-STRONG DISOBEYED ORDERS.
HE'LL BE RECALLED TO CENTRAL SOON.
DISOBEYING ORDERS IS THE SMARTEST WAY TO GET AWAY FROM THIS DAMN BATTLEFIELD.
ISN'T THAT RIGHT, MAJOR MUSTANG?
IT'S SHELL SHOCK.
WHEN A PERSON IS SUBJECTED TO CONTINUOUS EXPLOSIONS AND STORMS OF BULLETS, THEIR EMOTIONS ARE OVERLOADED AND THEIR BODY BECOMES PARALYZED.
I LIKE GUNS.
BECAUSE UNLIKE WITH SWORDS AND KNIVES, YOU DON'T HAVE TO FEEL YOUR VICTIM DIE.

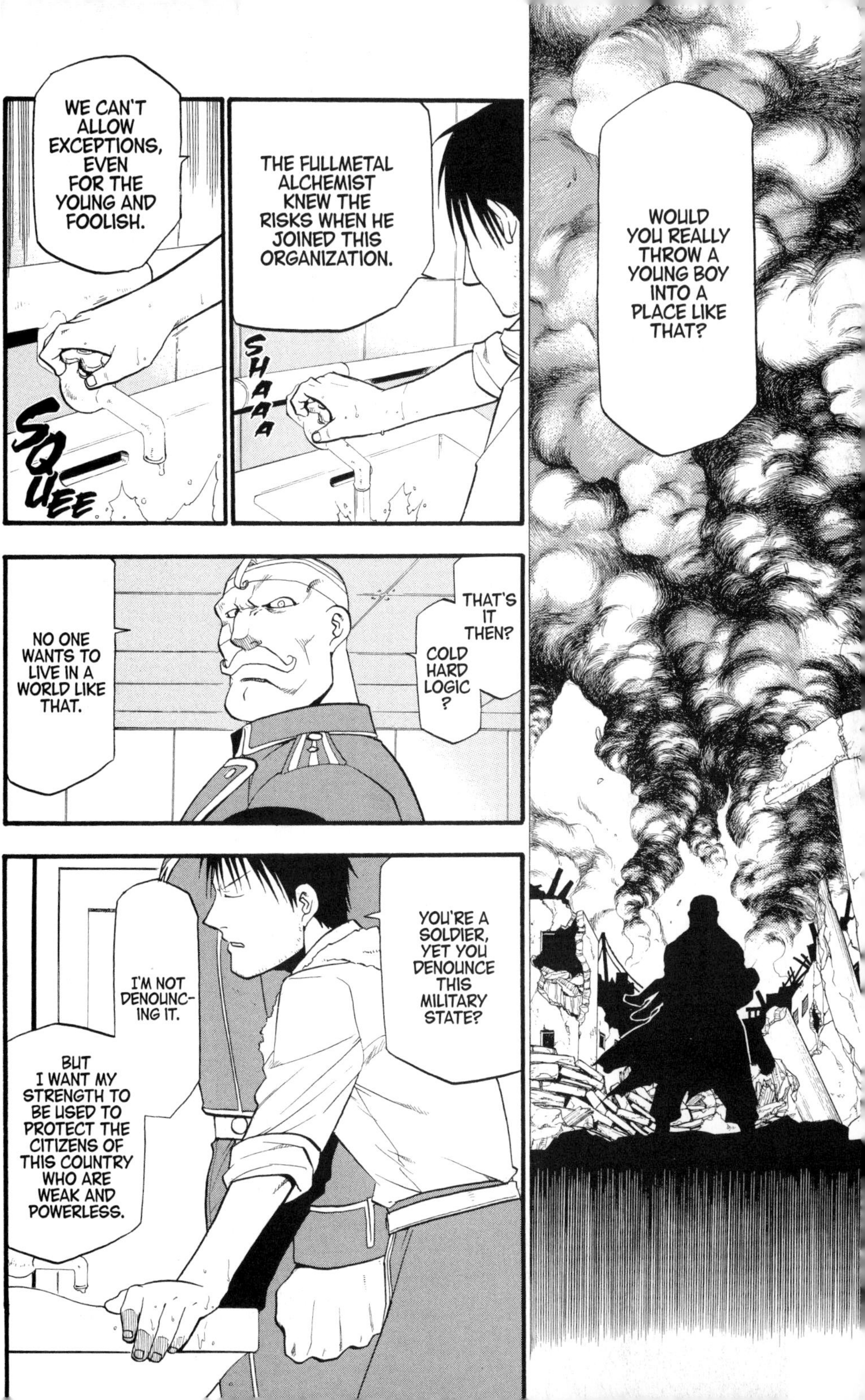
WOULD YOU REALLY THROW A YOUNG BOY INTO A PLACE LIKE THAT?
THE FULLMETAL ALCHEMIST KNEW THE RISKS WHEN HE JOINED THIS ORGANIZATION.
SHAAA
WE CAN'T ALLOW EXCEPTIONS, EVEN FOR THE YOUNG AND FOOLISH.
SQUEE
THAT'S IT THEN? COLD HARD LOGIC?
NO ONE WANTS TO LIVE IN A WORLD LIKE THAT.
YOU'RE A SOLDIER, YET YOU DENOUNCE THIS MILITARY STATE?
I'M NOT DENOUNCING IT.
BUT I WANT MY STRENGTH TO BE USED TO PROTECT THE CITIZENS OF THIS COUNTRY WHO ARE WEAK AND POWERLESS.

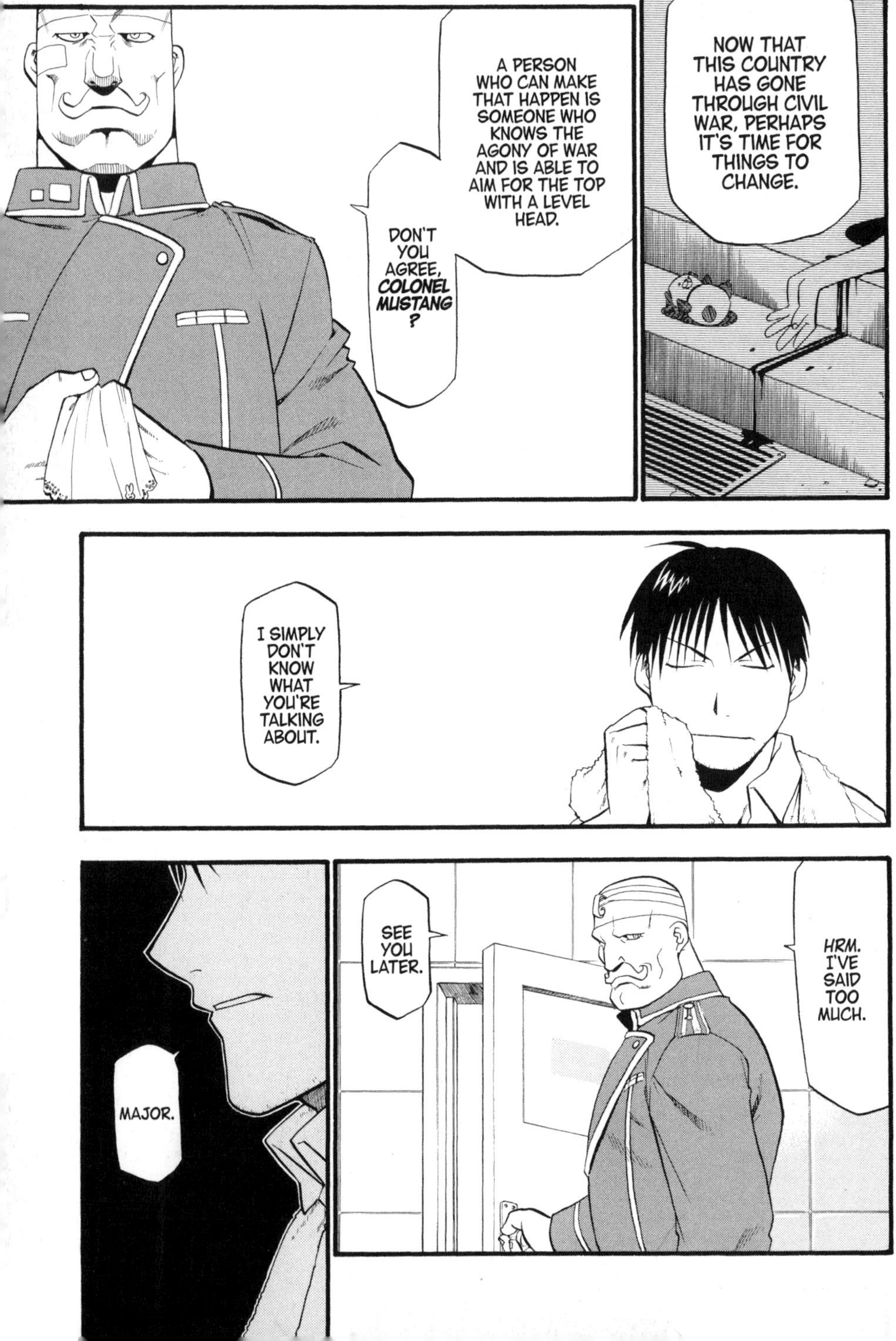
NOW THAT THIS COUNTRY HAS GONE THROUGH CIVIL WAR, PERHAPS IT'S TIME FOR THINGS TO CHANGE.
A PERSON WHO CAN MAKE THAT HAPPEN IS SOMEONE WHO KNOWS THE AGONY OF WAR AND IS ABLE TO AIM FOR THE TOP WITH A LEVEL HEAD.
DON'T YOU AGREE, **COLONEL MUSTANG**?
I SIMPLY DON'T KNOW WHAT YOU'RE TALKING ABOUT.
HRM. I'VE SAID TOO MUCH.
SEE YOU LATER.
MAJOR.

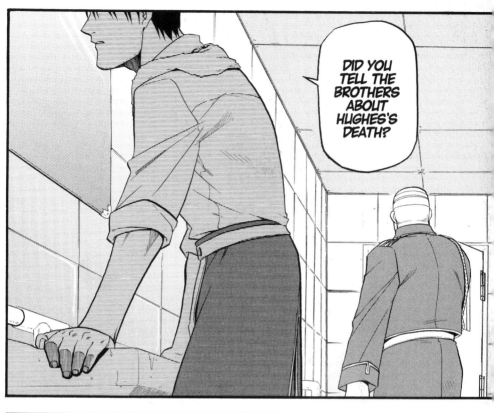

DID YOU TELL THE BROTHERS ABOUT HUGHES'S DEATH?

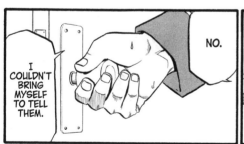

I COULDN'T BRING MYSELF TO TELL THEM.

NO.

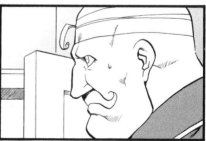

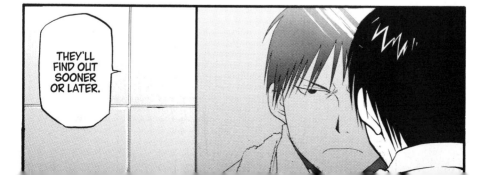

THEY'LL FIND OUT SOONER OR LATER.

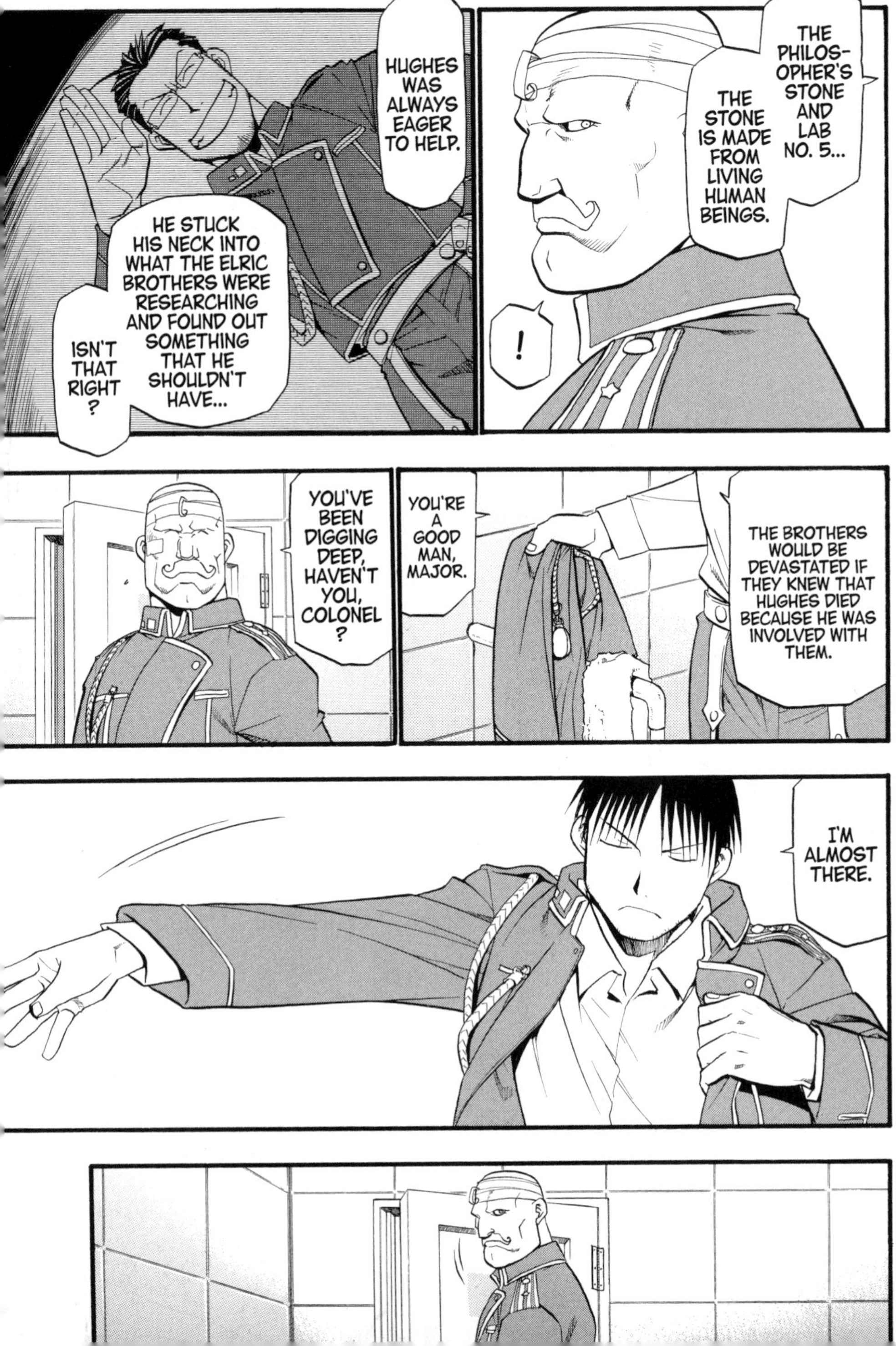
THE PHILOSOPHER'S STONE AND LAB NO. 5...
THE STONE IS MADE FROM LIVING HUMAN BEINGS.
!
HUGHES WAS ALWAYS EAGER TO HELP.
HE STUCK HIS NECK INTO WHAT THE ELRIC BROTHERS WERE RESEARCHING AND FOUND OUT SOMETHING THAT HE SHOULDN'T HAVE...
ISN'T THAT RIGHT?
THE BROTHERS WOULD BE DEVASTATED IF THEY KNEW THAT HUGHES DIED BECAUSE HE WAS INVOLVED WITH THEM.
YOU'RE A GOOD MAN, MAJOR.
YOU'VE BEEN DIGGING DEEP, HAVEN'T YOU, COLONEL?
I'M ALMOST THERE.

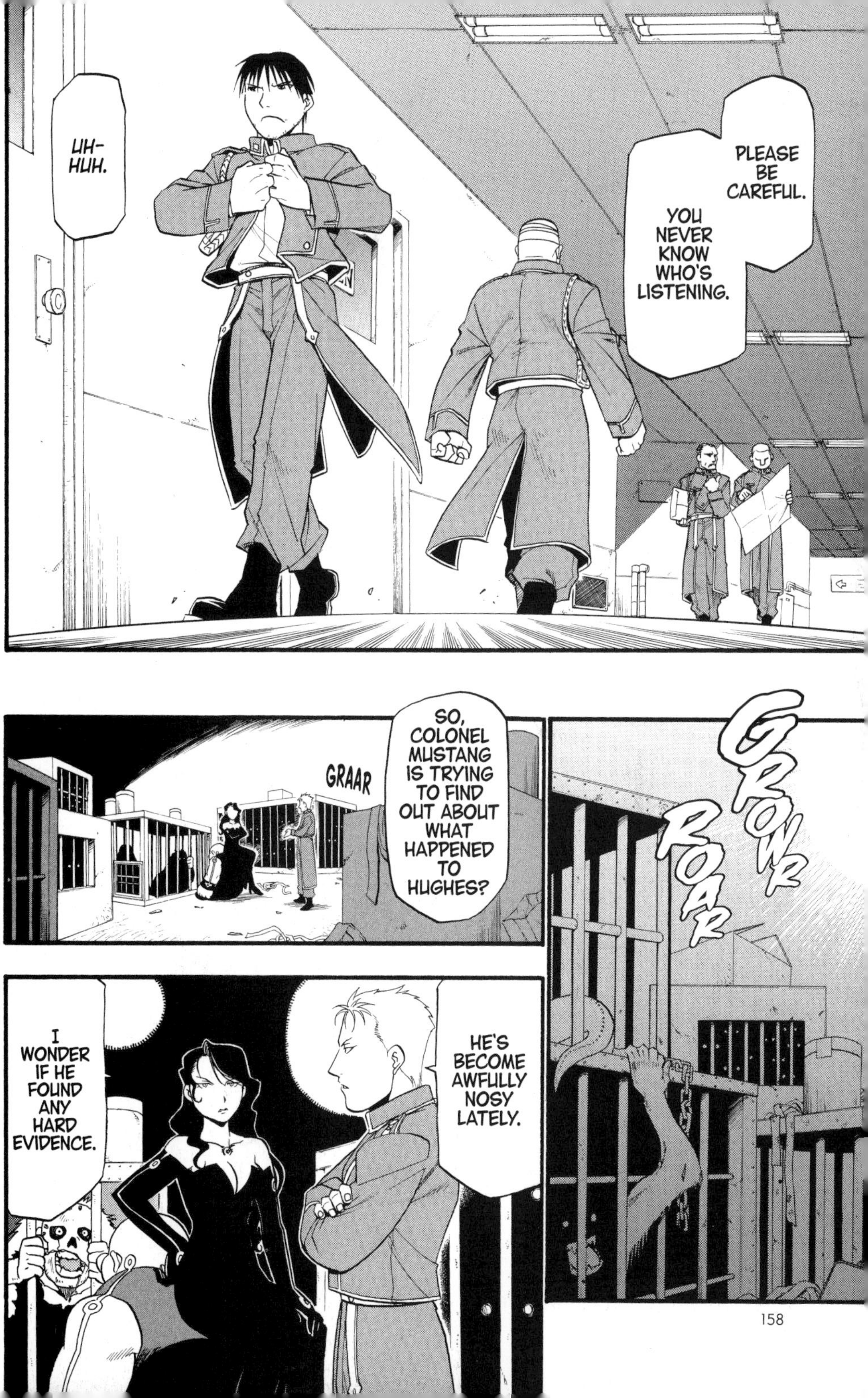
PLEASE BE CAREFUL.
YOU NEVER KNOW WHO'S LISTENING.
UH-HUH.
GROWR
ROAR
SO, COLONEL MUSTANG IS TRYING TO FIND OUT ABOUT WHAT HAPPENED TO HUGHES?
GRAAR
HE'S BECOME AWFULLY NOSY LATELY.
I WONDER IF HE FOUND ANY HARD EVIDENCE.

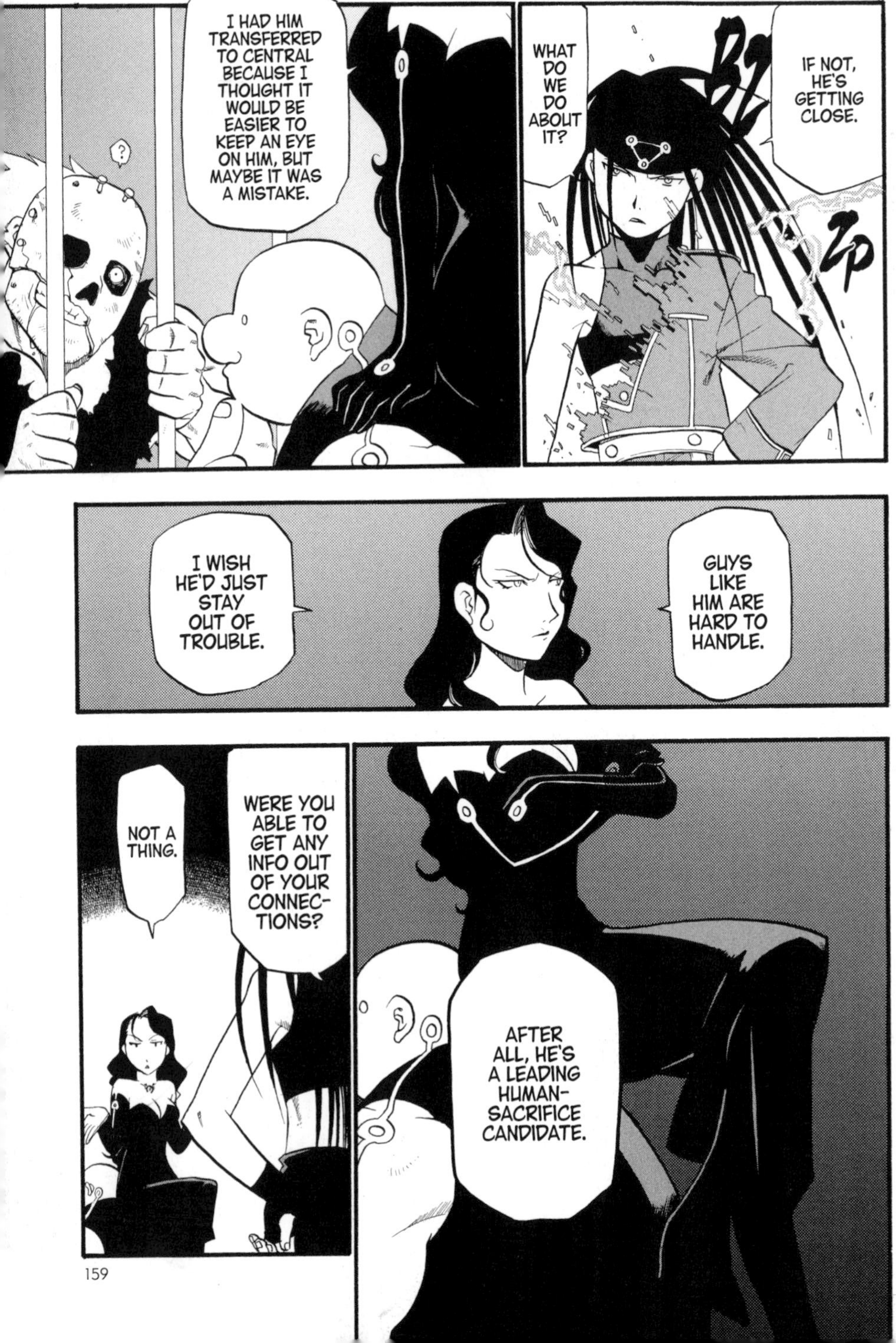
BZ
IF NOT, HE'S GETTING CLOSE.
WHAT DO WE DO ABOUT IT?
ZP
I HAD HIM TRANSFERRED TO CENTRAL BECAUSE I THOUGHT IT WOULD BE EASIER TO KEEP AN EYE ON HIM, BUT MAYBE IT WAS A MISTAKE.
?
GUYS LIKE HIM ARE HARD TO HANDLE.
I WISH HE'D JUST STAY OUT OF TROUBLE.
AFTER ALL, HE'S A LEADING HUMAN-SACRIFICE CANDIDATE.
WERE YOU ABLE TO GET ANY INFO OUT OF YOUR CONNEC-TIONS?
NOT A THING.

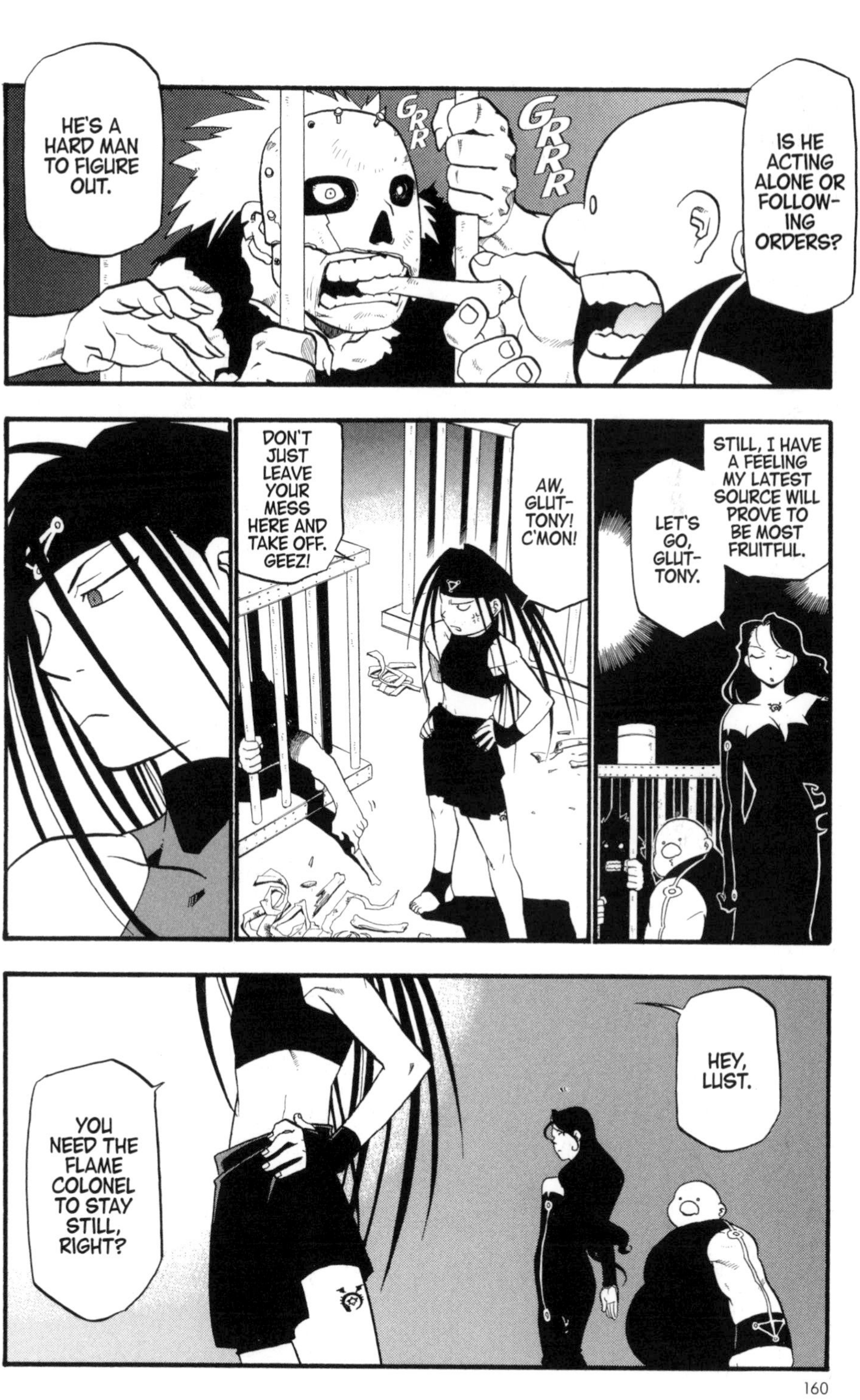
IS HE ACTING ALONE OR FOLLOW-ING ORDERS?
GRRR
GRR
HE'S A HARD MAN TO FIGURE OUT.
STILL, I HAVE A FEELING MY LATEST SOURCE WILL PROVE TO BE MOST FRUITFUL.
LET'S GO, GLUT-TONY.
AW, GLUT-TONY! C'MON!
DON'T JUST LEAVE YOUR MESS HERE AND TAKE OFF. GEEZ!
HEY, LUST.
YOU NEED THE FLAME COLONEL TO STAY STILL, RIGHT?

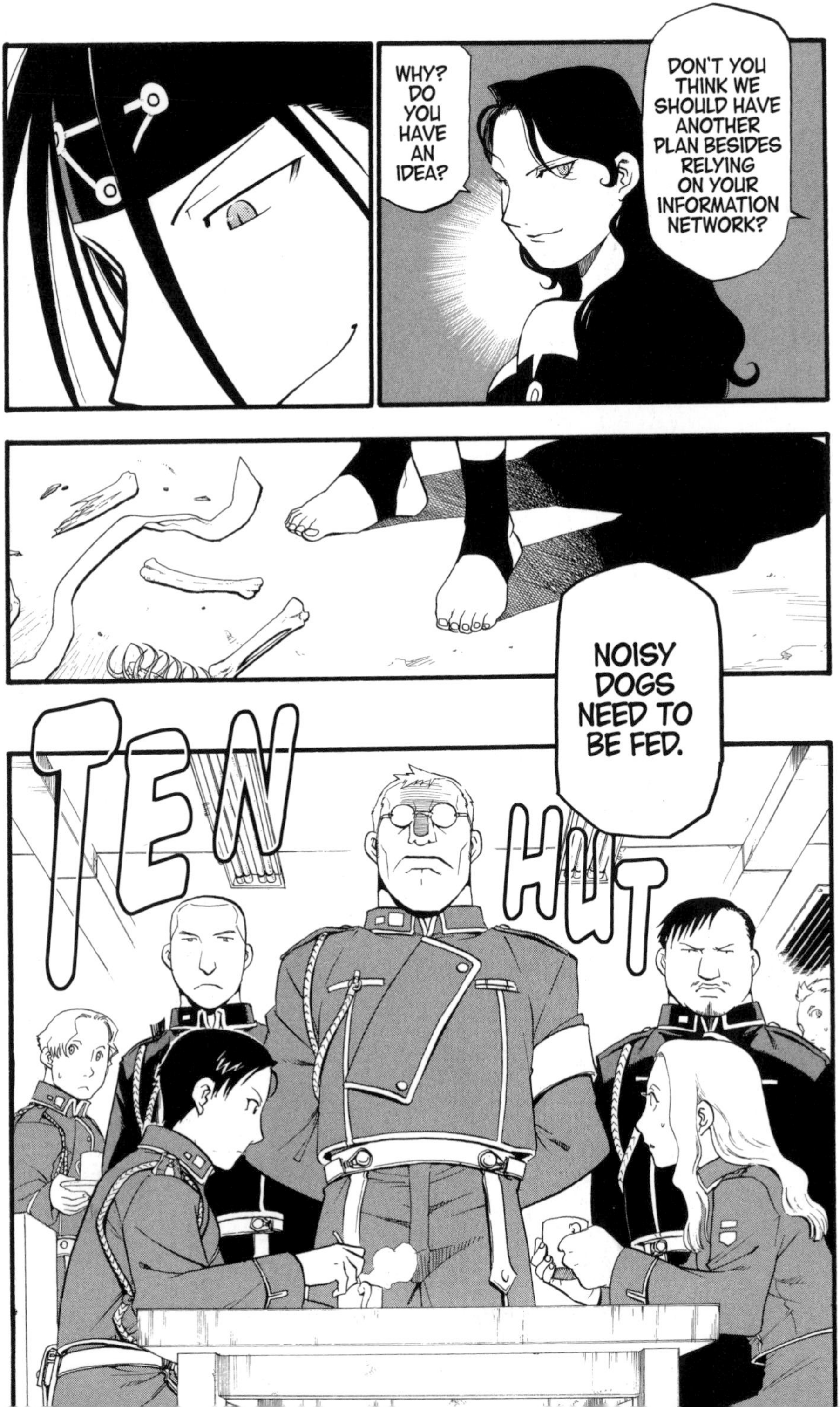
DON'T YOU THINK WE SHOULD HAVE ANOTHER PLAN BESIDES RELYING ON YOUR INFORMATION NETWORK?
WHY? DO YOU HAVE AN IDEA?
NOISY DOGS NEED TO BE FED.
TEN HUT

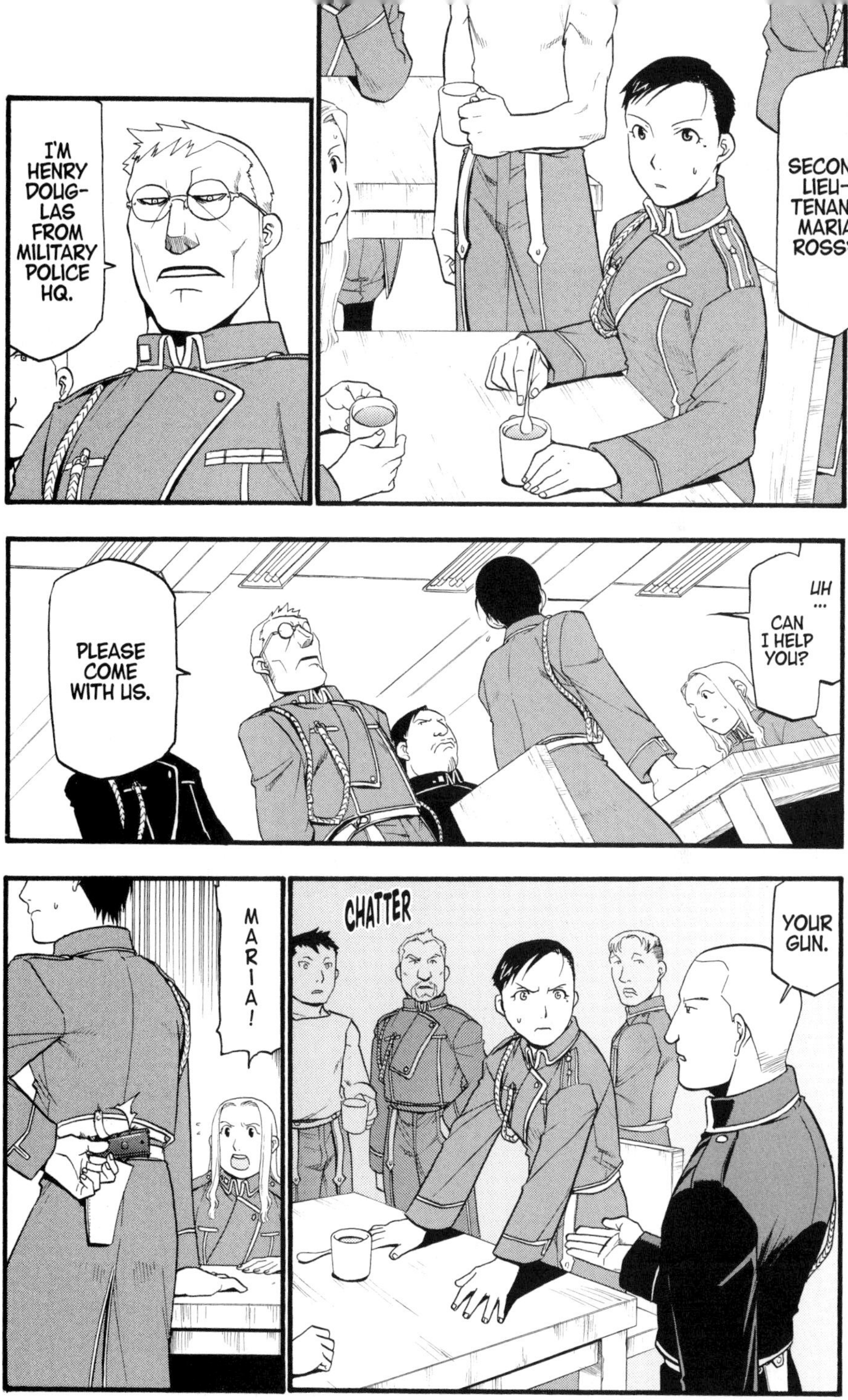
SECOND LIEUTENANT MARIA ROSS?
I'M HENRY DOUGLAS FROM MILITARY POLICE HQ.
UH... CAN I HELP YOU?
PLEASE COME WITH US.
YOUR GUN.
CHATTER
MARIA!

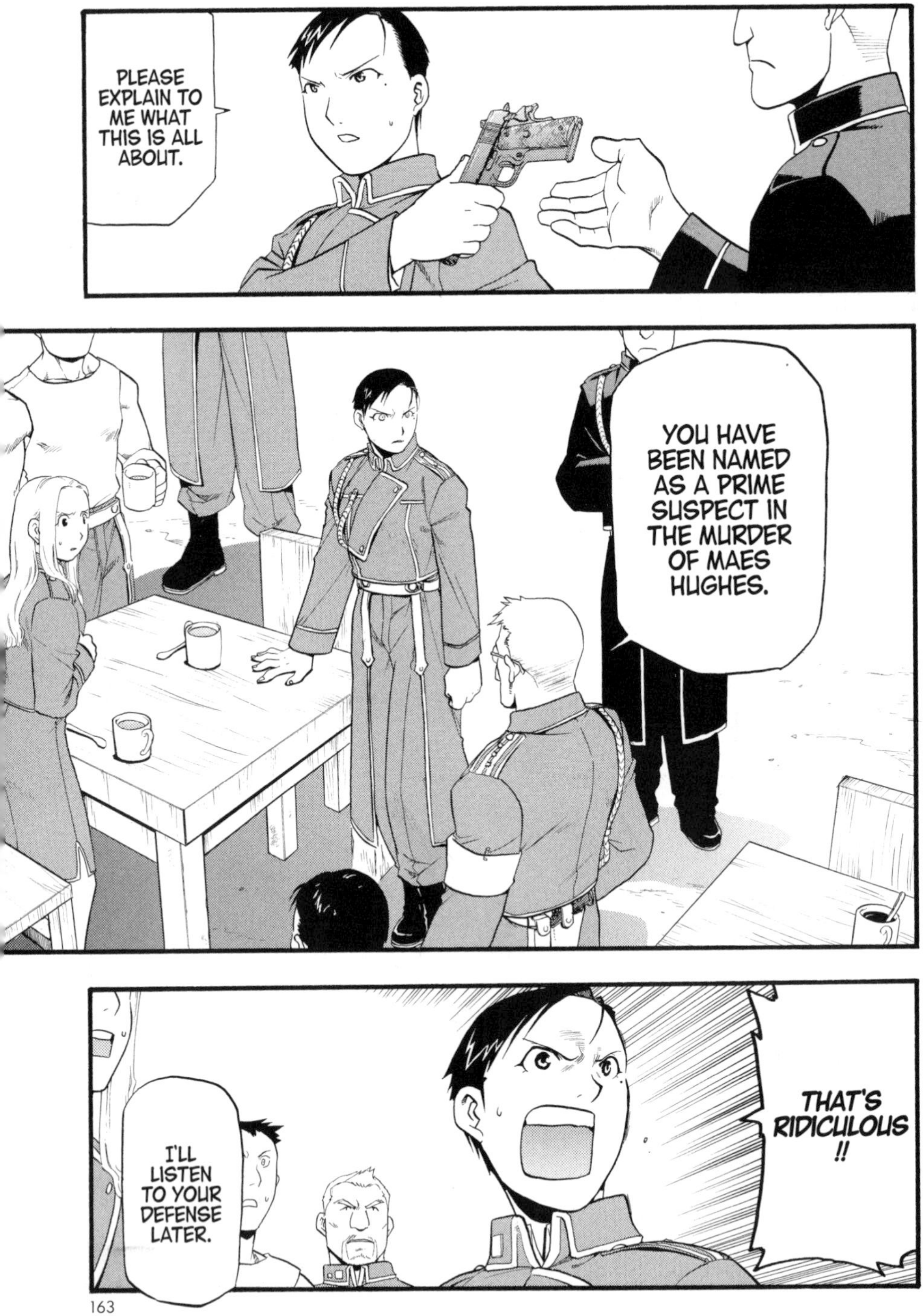
PLEASE EXPLAIN TO ME WHAT THIS IS ALL ABOUT.
YOU HAVE BEEN NAMED AS A PRIME SUSPECT IN THE MURDER OF MAES HUGHES.
THAT'S RIDICULOUS!!
I'LL LISTEN TO YOUR DEFENSE LATER.

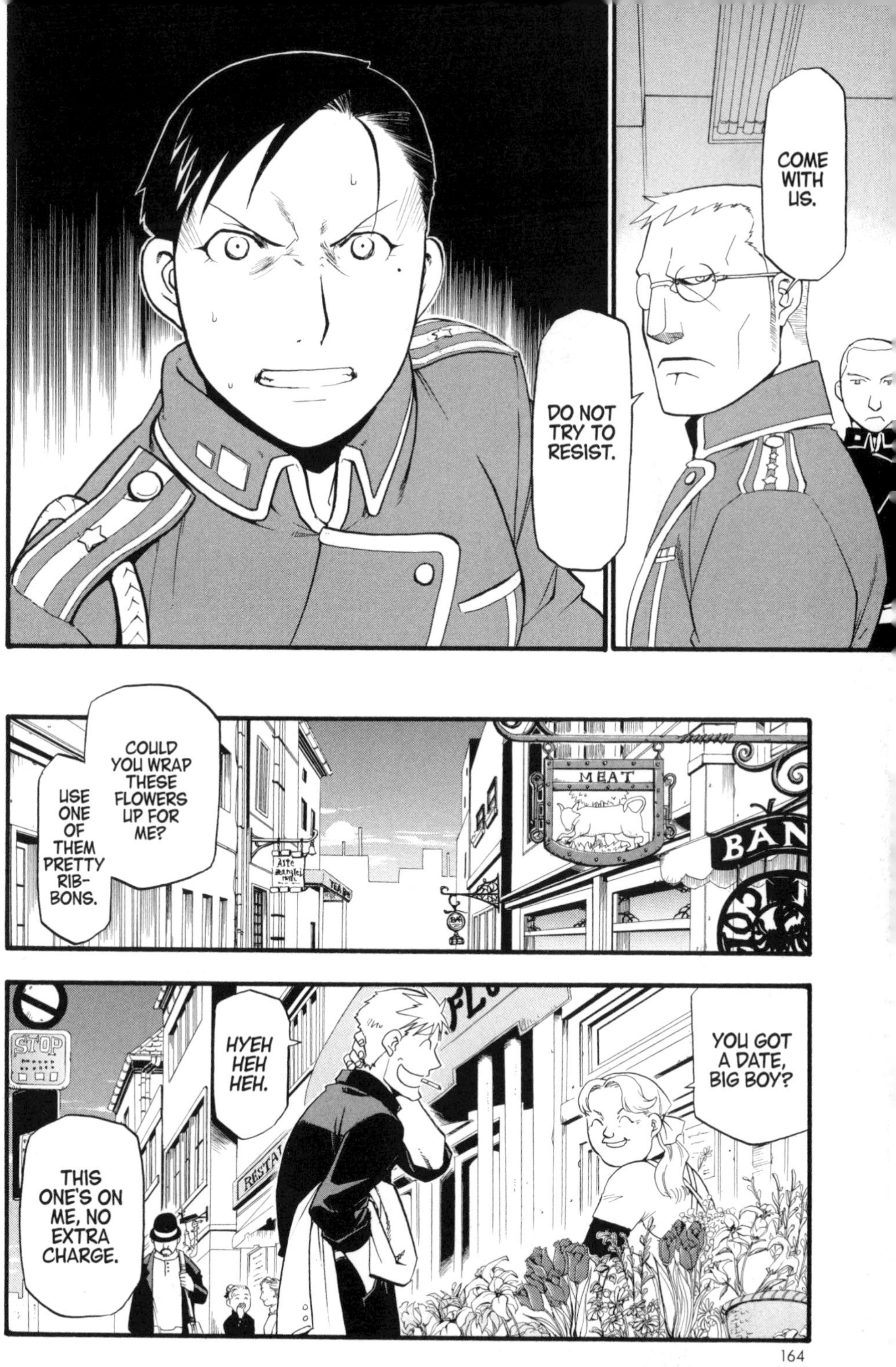
COME WITH US.
DO NOT TRY TO RESIST.
COULD YOU WRAP THESE FLOWERS UP FOR ME?
USE ONE OF THEM PRETTY RIB-BONS.
MEAT
YOU GOT A DATE, BIG BOY?
HYEH HEH HEH.
THIS ONE'S ON ME, NO EXTRA CHARGE.
STOP

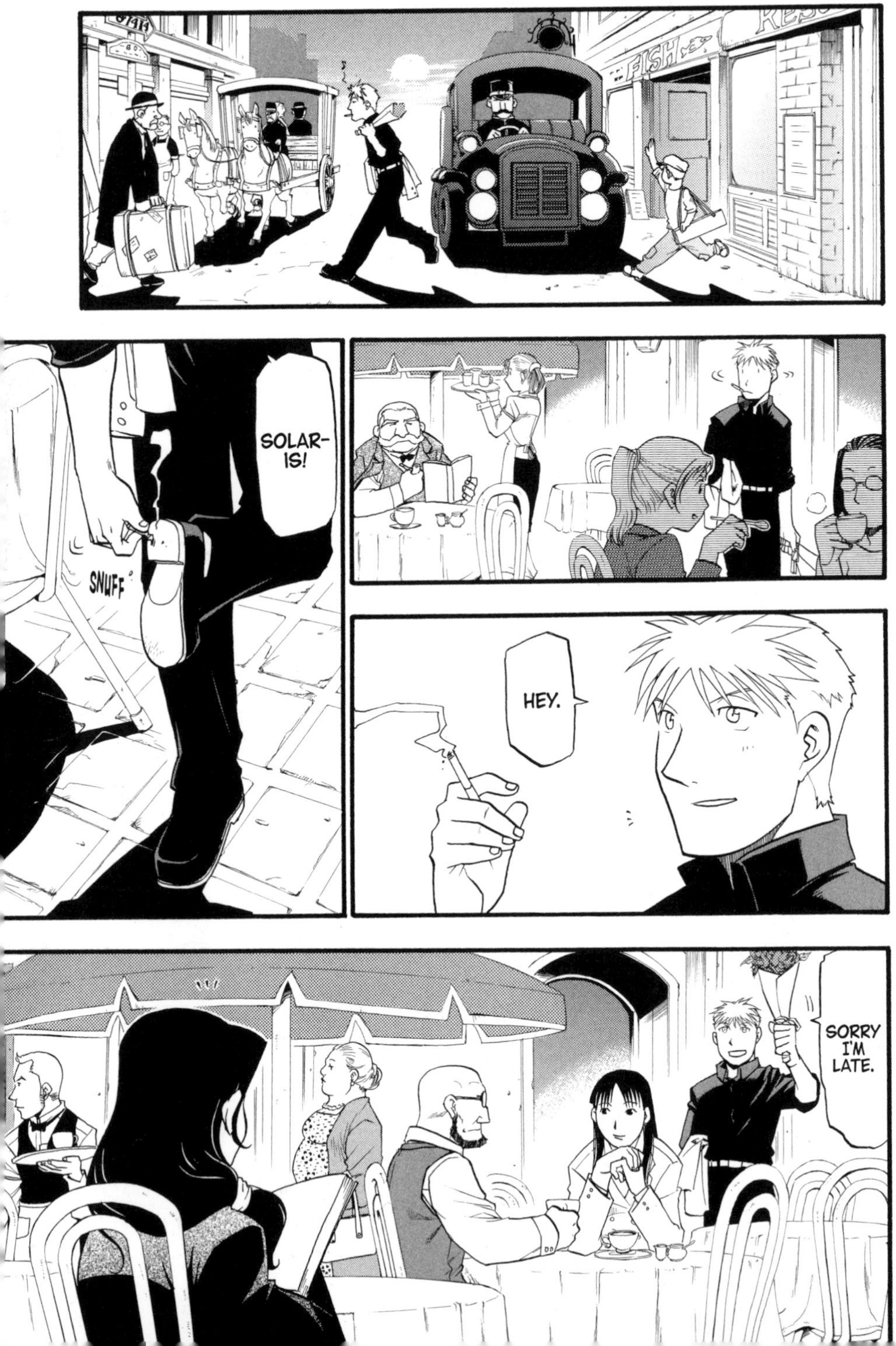
FISH
HEY.
SOLAR-IS!
SNUFF
SORRY I'M LATE.

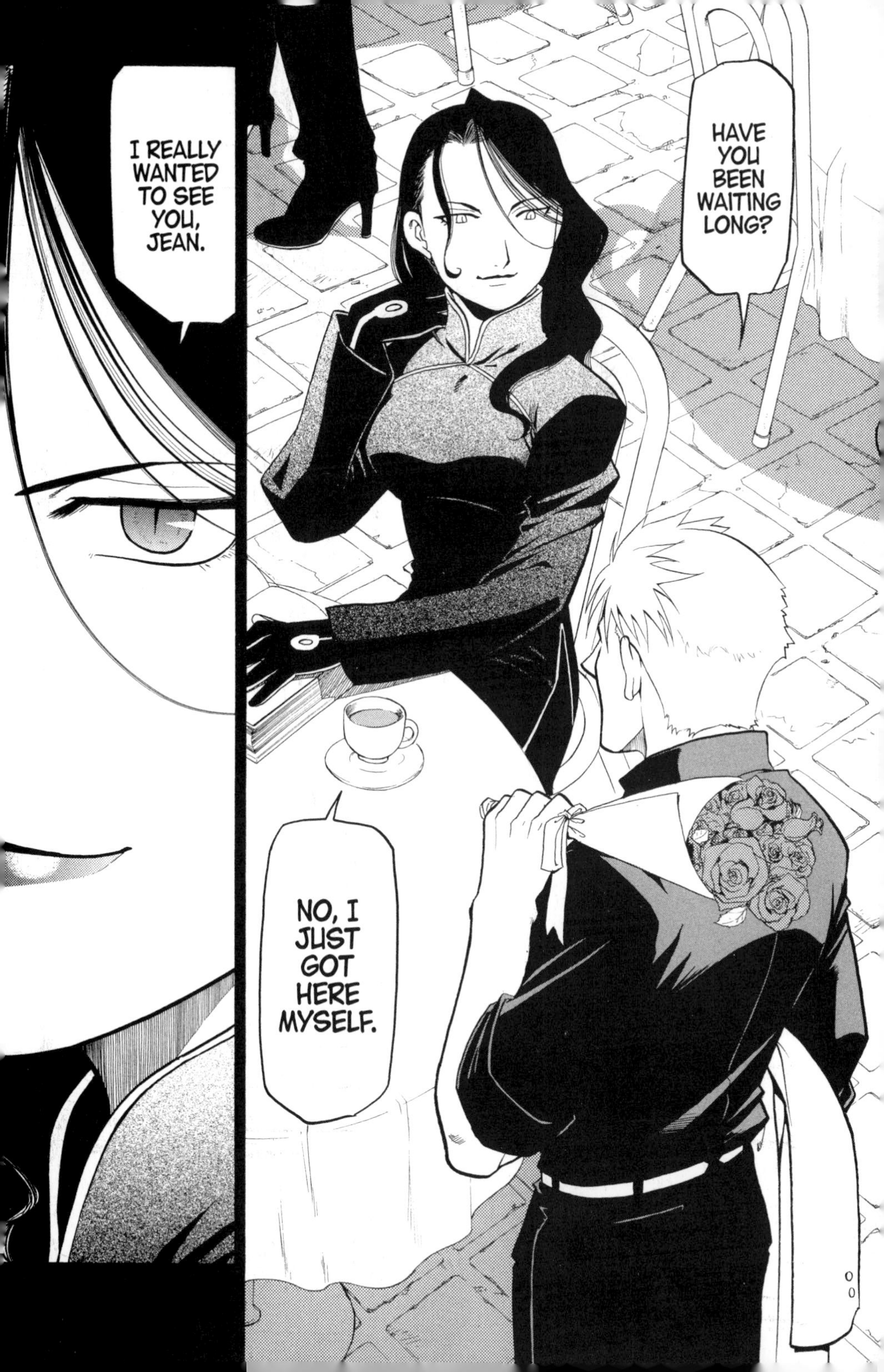
HAVE YOU BEEN WAITING LONG?
NO, I JUST GOT HERE MYSELF.
I REALLY WANTED TO SEE YOU, JEAN.

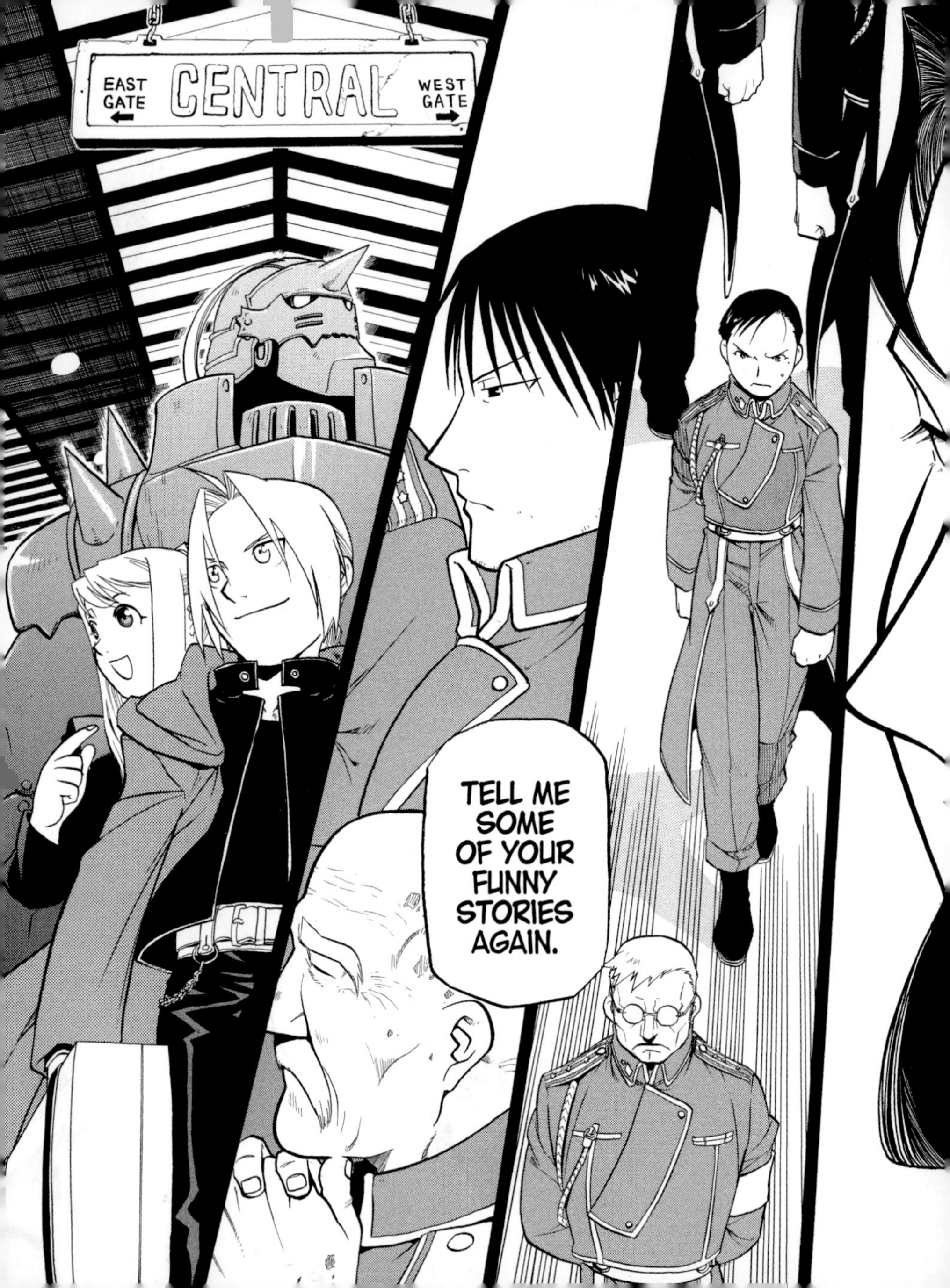
EAST GATE
CENTRAL
WEST GATE
TELL ME SOME OF YOUR FUNNY STORIES AGAIN.

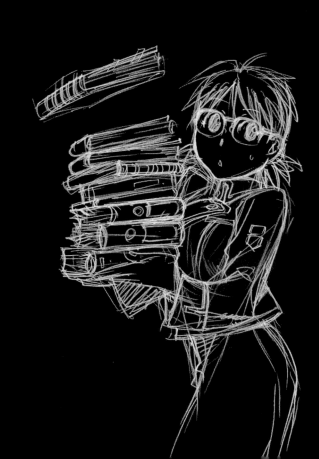

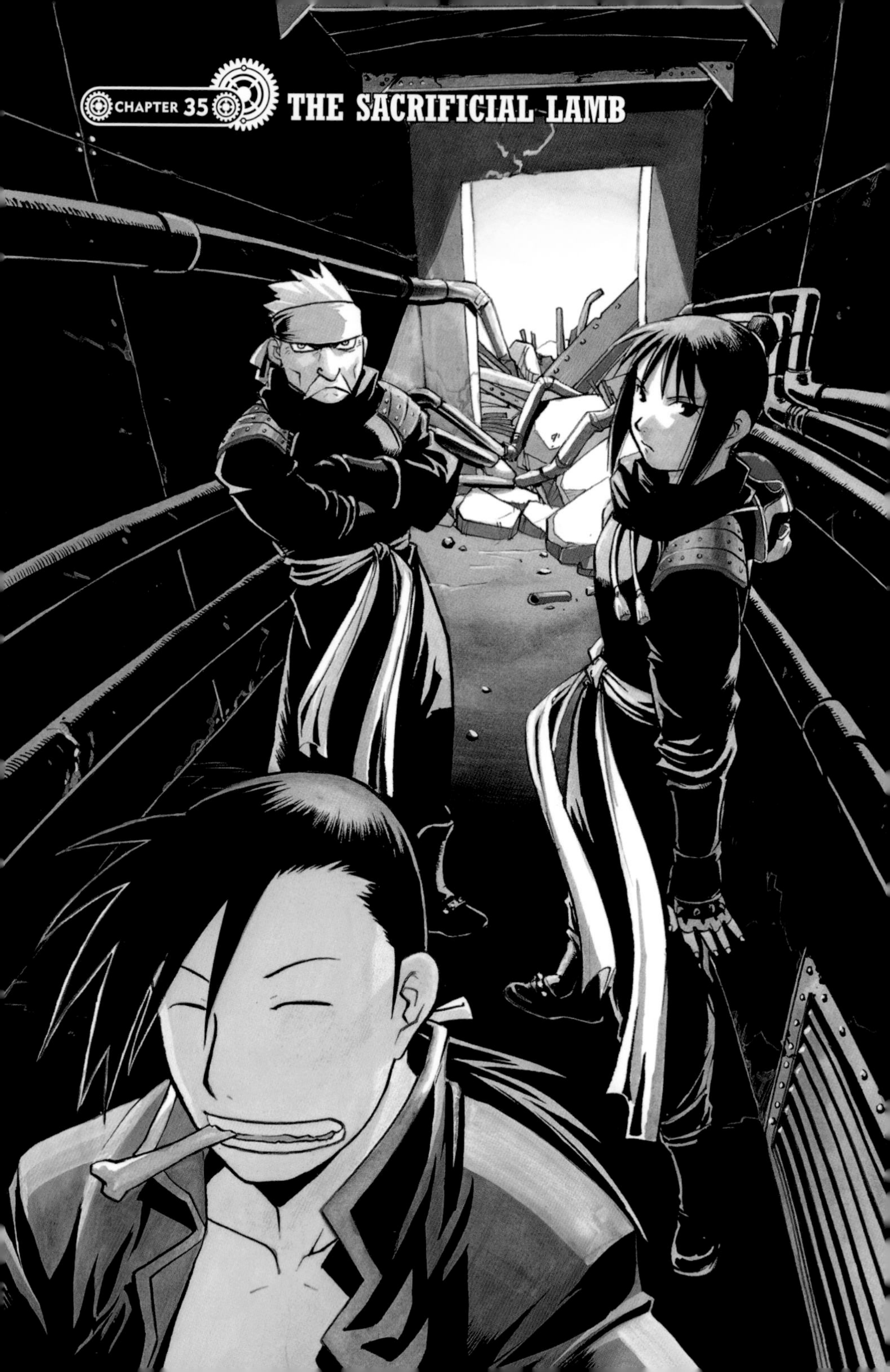
CHAPTER 35
THE SACRIFICIAL LAMB

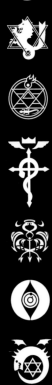

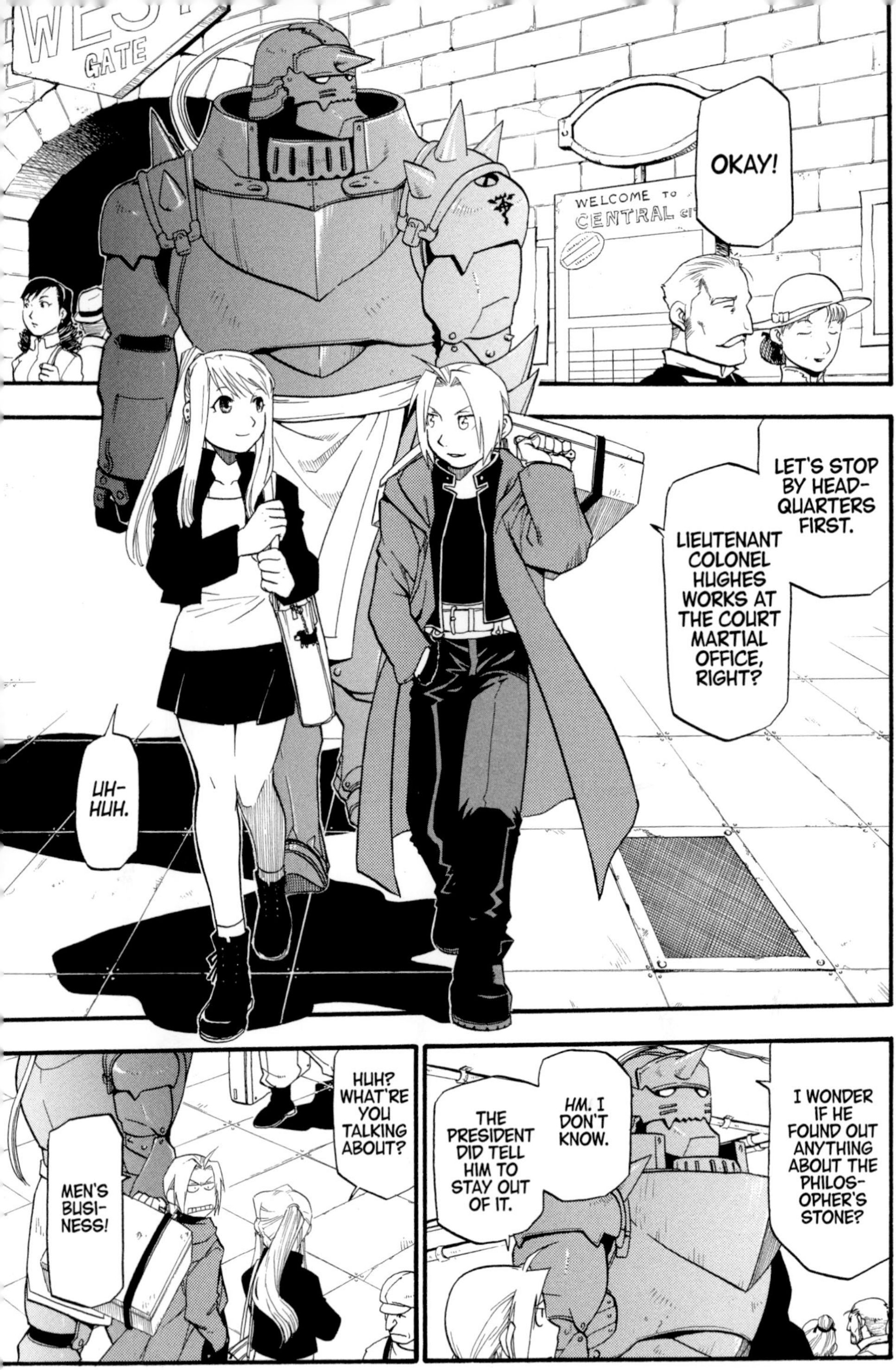
GATE
WELCOME TO
CENTRAL
OKAY!
LET'S STOP BY HEADQUARTERS FIRST.
LIEUTENANT COLONEL HUGHES WORKS AT THE COURT MARTIAL OFFICE, RIGHT?
UH-HUH.
I WONDER IF HE FOUND OUT ANYTHING ABOUT THE PHILOSOPHER'S STONE?
HM. I DON'T KNOW.
THE PRESIDENT DID TELL HIM TO STAY OUT OF IT.
HUH? WHAT'RE YOU TALKING ABOUT?
MEN'S BUSINESS!

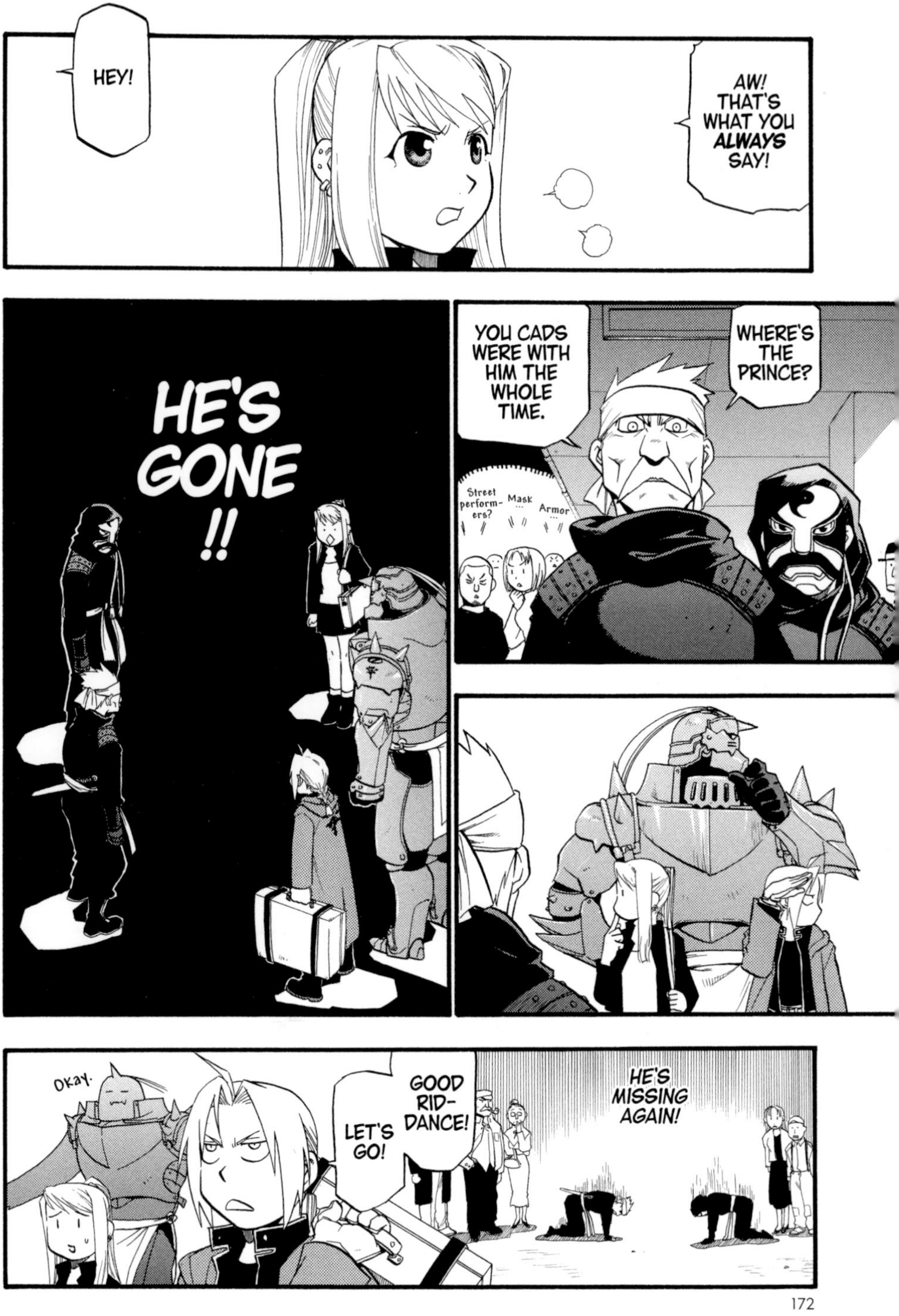
AW! THAT'S WHAT YOU ALWAYS SAY!
HEY!
WHERE'S THE PRINCE?
YOU CADS WERE WITH HIM THE WHOLE TIME.
Armor...
Mask...
Street perform-ers?
HE'S GONE!!
HE'S MISSING AGAIN!
GOOD RID-DANCE!
LET'S GO!
Okay.

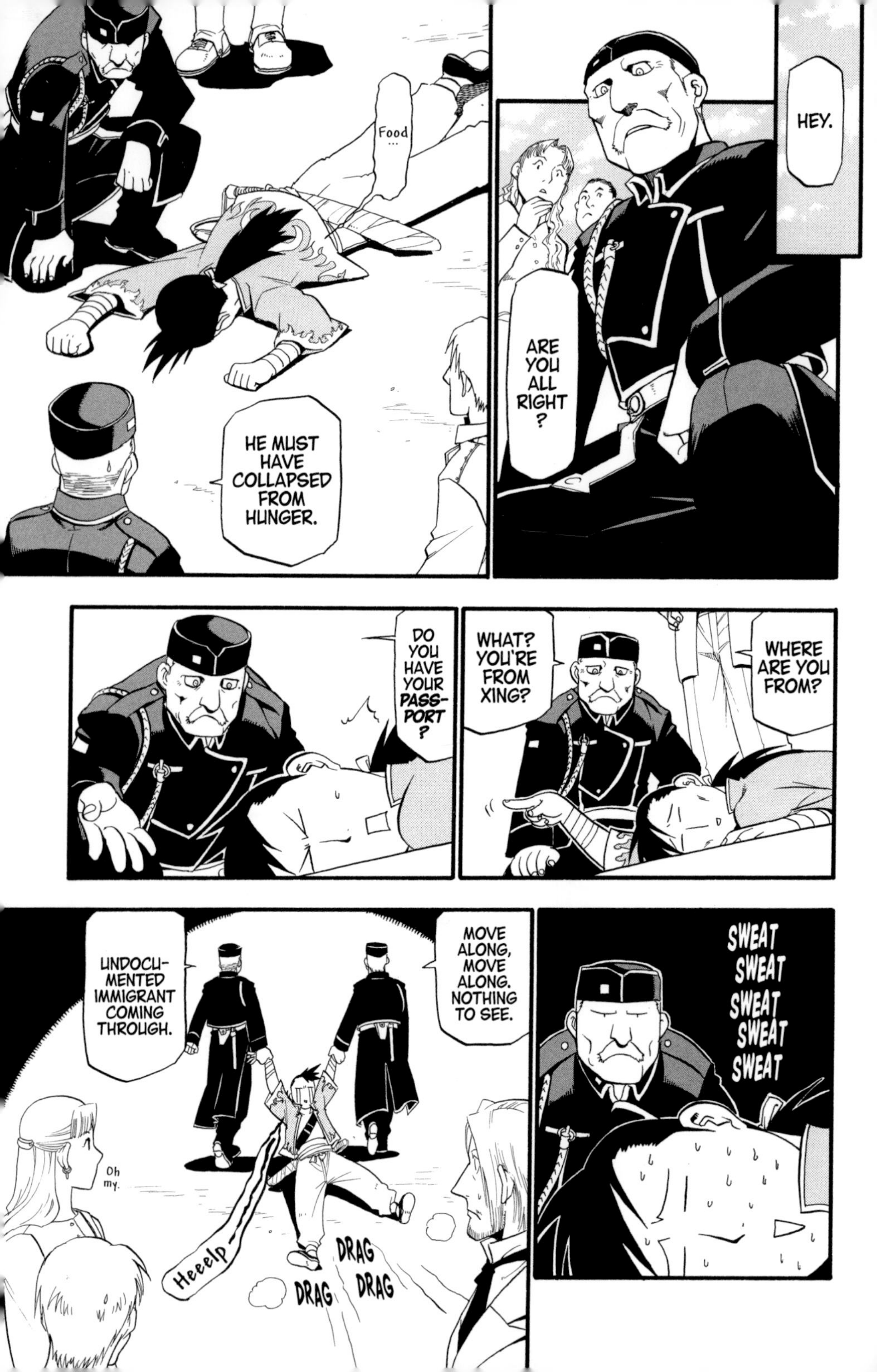
HEY.
ARE YOU ALL RIGHT?
Food...
HE MUST HAVE COLLAPSED FROM HUNGER.
WHERE ARE YOU FROM?
WHAT? YOU'RE FROM XING?
DO YOU HAVE YOUR PASSPORT?
SWEAT SWEAT SWEAT SWEAT SWEAT
MOVE ALONG, MOVE ALONG. NOTHING TO SEE.
UNDOCUMENTED IMMIGRANT COMING THROUGH.
Oh my.
Heeelp
DRAG DRAG DRAG

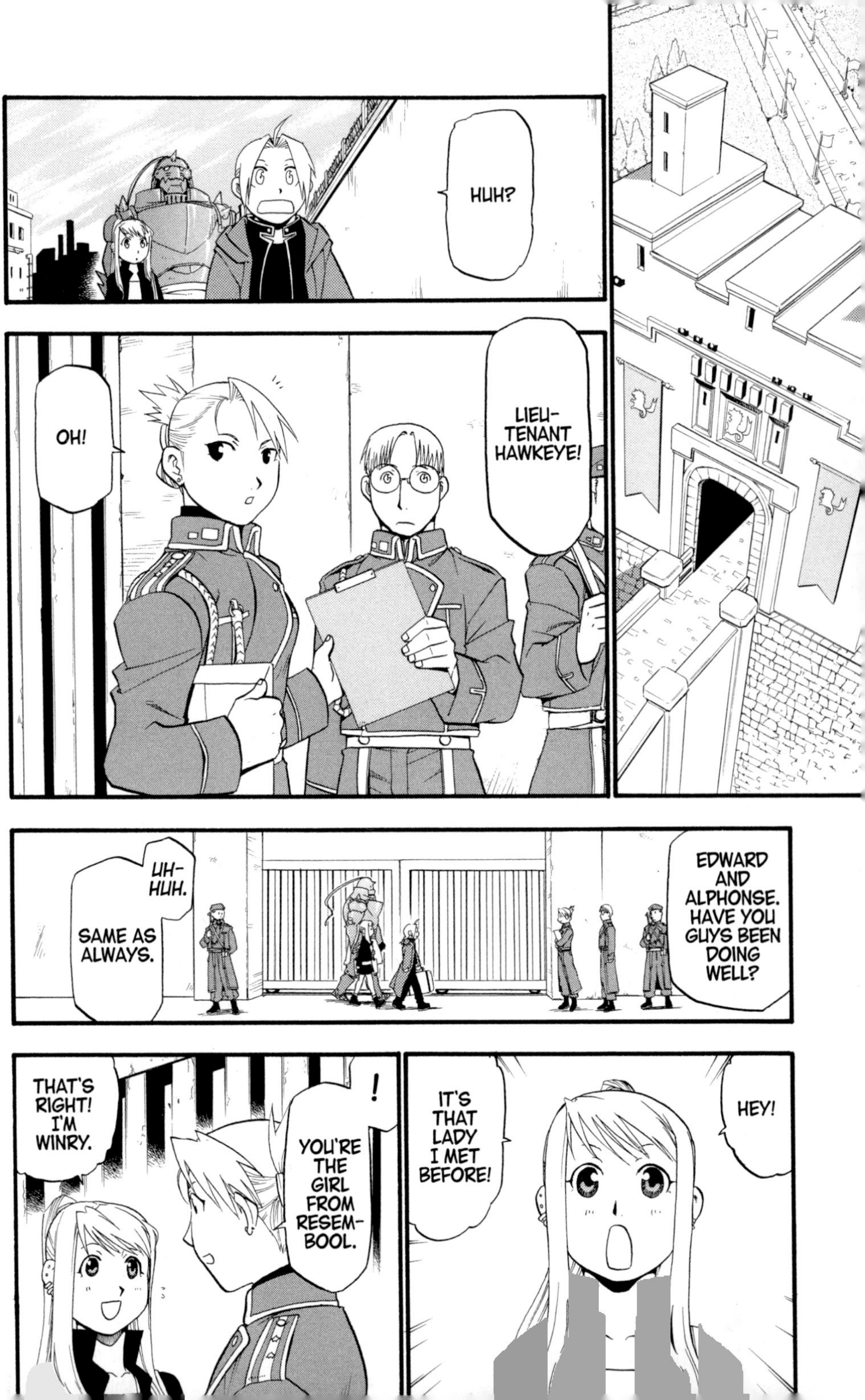
HUH?
LIEU-TENANT HAWKEYE!
OH!
EDWARD AND ALPHONSE. HAVE YOU GUYS BEEN DOING WELL?
UH-HUH.
SAME AS ALWAYS.
HEY!
IT'S THAT LADY I MET BEFORE!
!
YOU'RE THE GIRL FROM RESEM-BOOL.
THAT'S RIGHT! I'M WINRY.

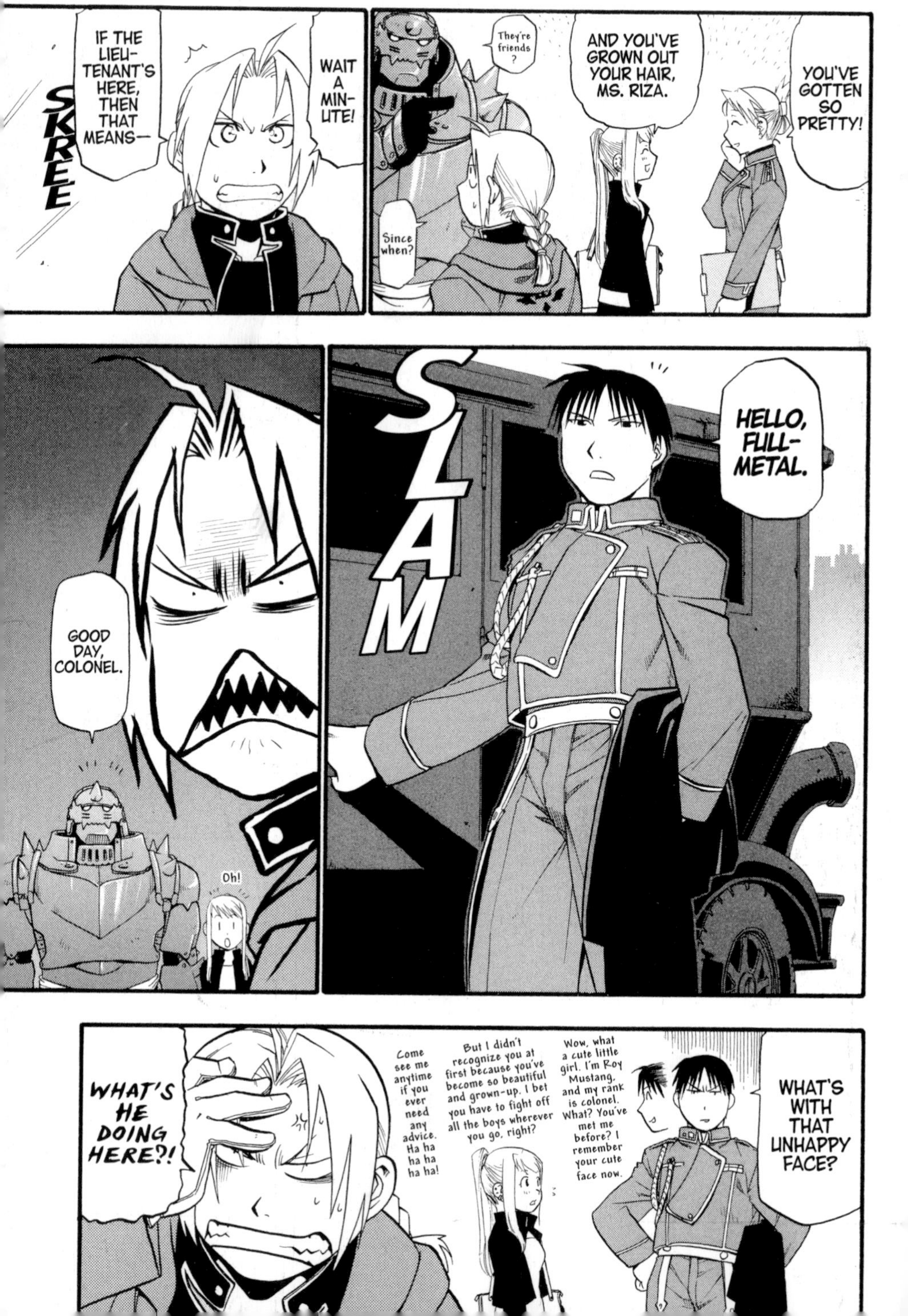
YOU'VE GOTTEN SO PRETTY!
AND YOU'VE GROWN OUT YOUR HAIR, MS. RIZA.
They're friends?
Since when?
WAIT A MINUTE!
IF THE LIEUTENANT'S HERE, THEN THAT MEANS—
SKREE
HELLO, FULLMETAL.
SLAM
GOOD DAY, COLONEL.
Oh!
WHAT'S WITH THAT UNHAPPY FACE?
Wow, what a cute little girl. I'm Roy Mustang, and my rank is colonel. What? You've met me before? I remember your cute face now.
But I didn't recognize you at first because you've become so beautiful and grown-up. I bet you have to fight off all the boys wherever you go, right?
Come see me anytime if you ever need any advice. Ha ha ha ha ha ha!
WHAT'S HE DOING HERE?!

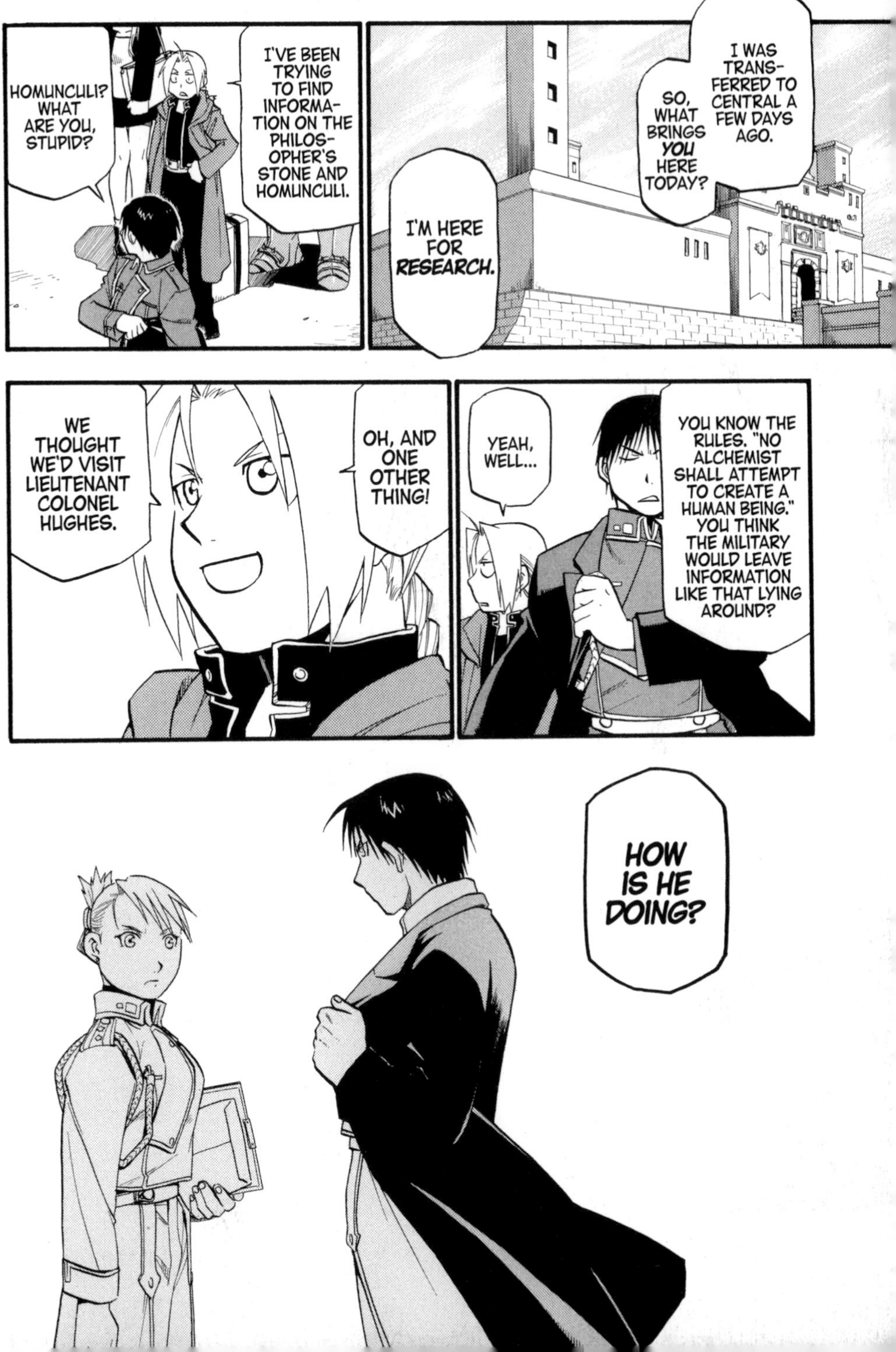
I WAS TRANSFERRED TO CENTRAL A FEW DAYS AGO.
SO, WHAT BRINGS *YOU* HERE TODAY?
I'M HERE FOR *RESEARCH.*
I'VE BEEN TRYING TO FIND INFORMATION ON THE PHILOSOPHER'S STONE AND HOMUNCULI.
HOMUNCULI? WHAT ARE YOU, STUPID?
YOU KNOW THE RULES. "NO ALCHEMIST SHALL ATTEMPT TO CREATE A HUMAN BEING." YOU THINK THE MILITARY WOULD LEAVE INFORMATION LIKE THAT LYING AROUND?
YEAH, WELL...
OH, AND ONE OTHER THING!
WE THOUGHT WE'D VISIT LIEUTENANT COLONEL HUGHES.
HOW IS HE DOING?

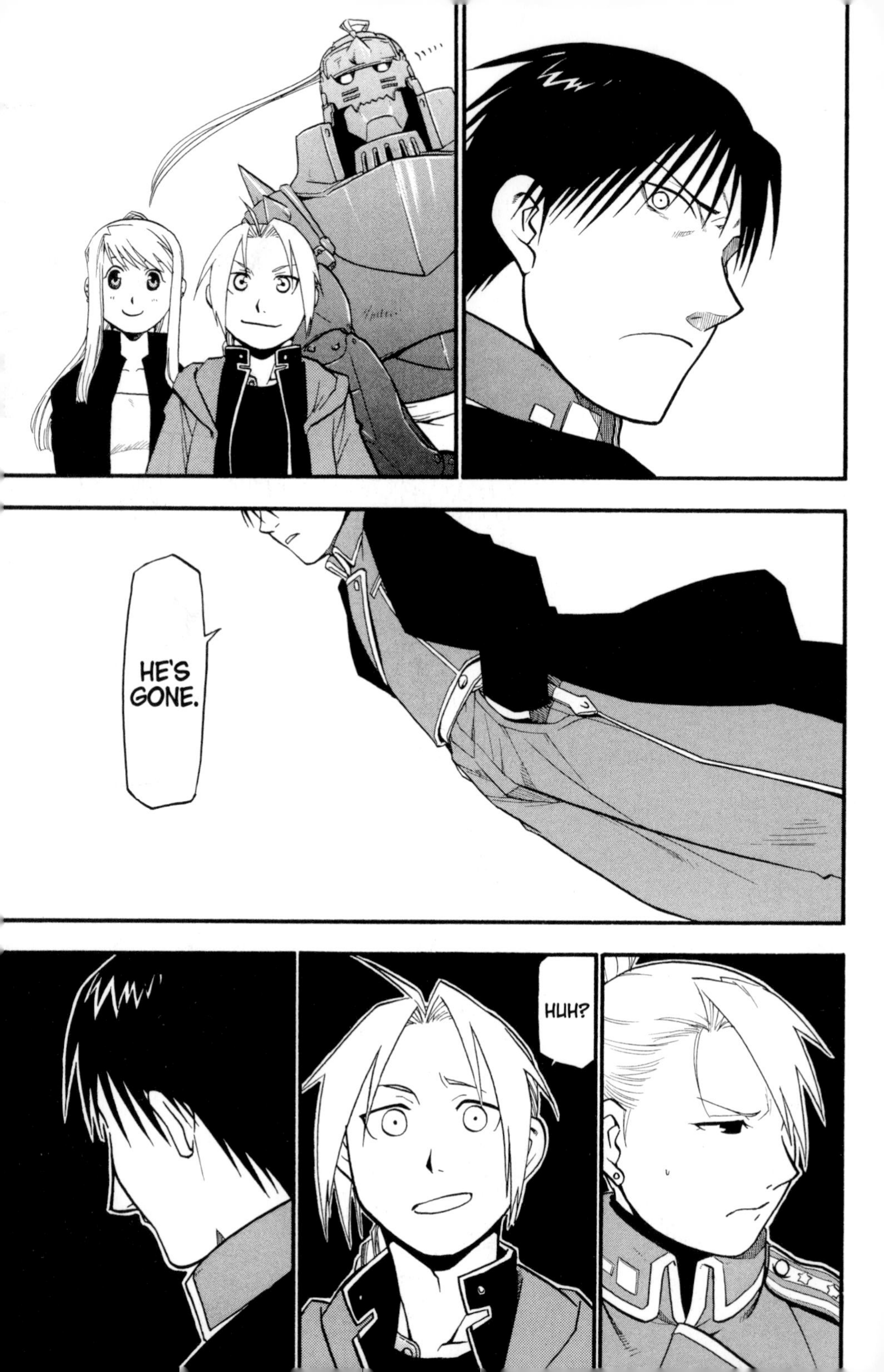
HE'S GONE.
HUH?

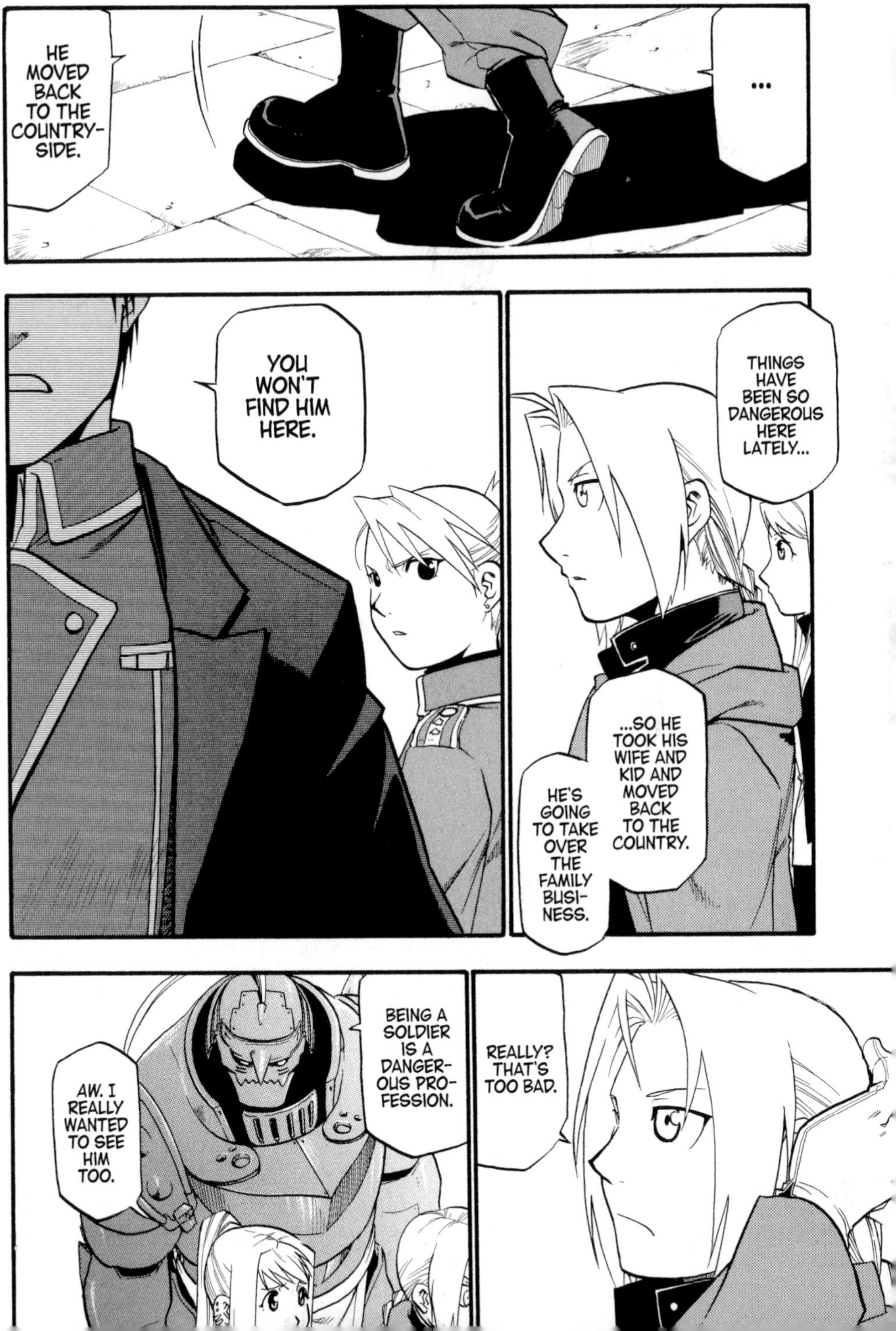
...
HE MOVED BACK TO THE COUNTRYSIDE.
THINGS HAVE BEEN SO DANGEROUS HERE LATELY...
...SO HE TOOK HIS WIFE AND KID AND MOVED BACK TO THE COUNTRY.
HE'S GOING TO TAKE OVER THE FAMILY BUSINESS.
YOU WON'T FIND HIM HERE.
REALLY? THAT'S TOO BAD.
BEING A SOLDIER IS A DANGEROUS PROFESSION.
AW. I REALLY WANTED TO SEE HIM TOO.

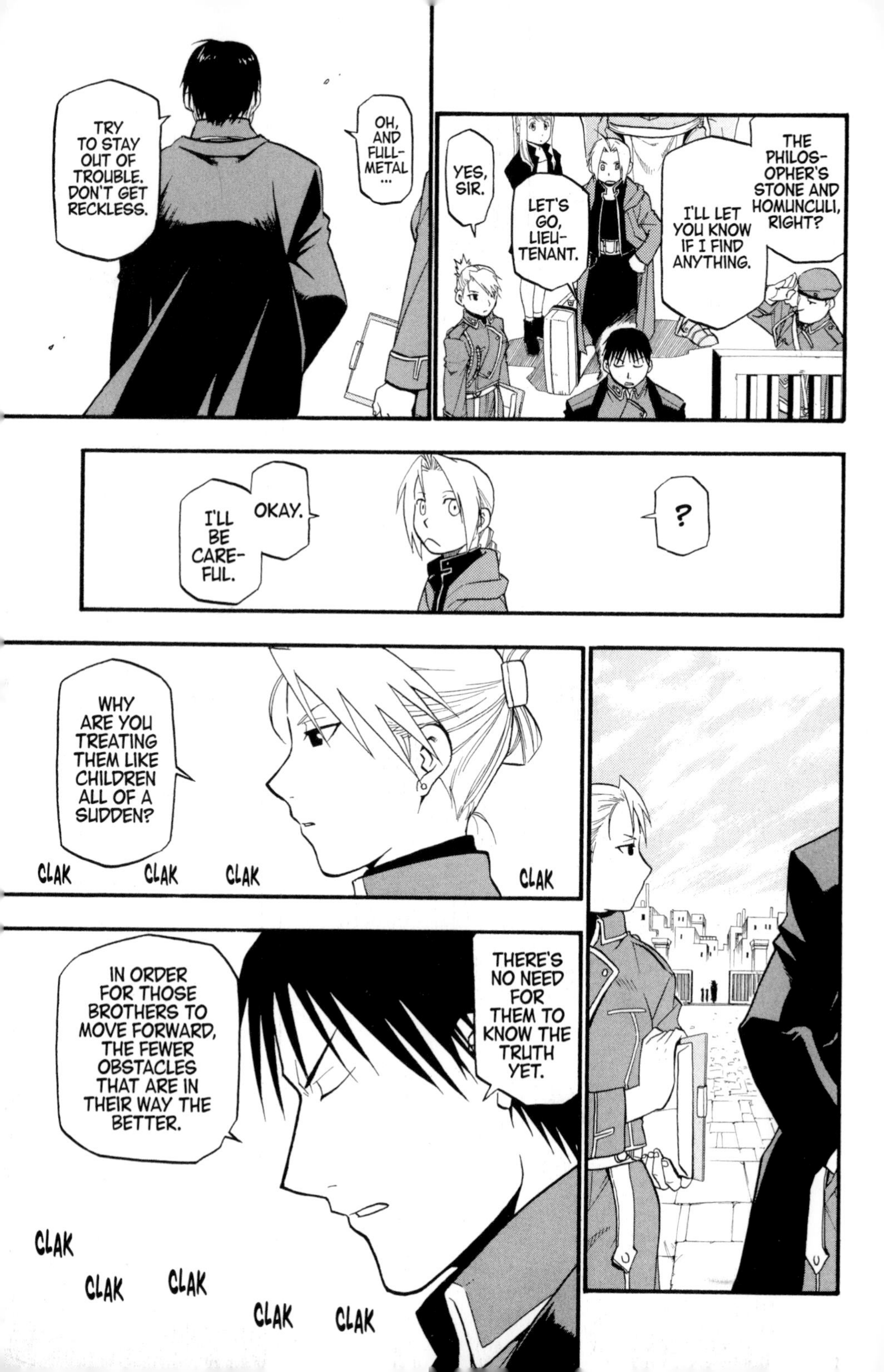
THE PHILOS-OPHER'S STONE AND HOMUNCULI, RIGHT?
I'LL LET YOU KNOW IF I FIND ANYTHING.
LET'S GO, LIEU-TENANT.
YES, SIR.
OH, AND FULL-METAL...
TRY TO STAY OUT OF TROUBLE. DON'T GET RECKLESS.
?
OKAY.
I'LL BE CARE-FUL.
THERE'S NO NEED FOR THEM TO KNOW THE TRUTH YET.
CLAK
CLAK
CLAK
CLAK
WHY ARE YOU TREATING THEM LIKE CHILDREN ALL OF A SUDDEN?
IN ORDER FOR THOSE BROTHERS TO MOVE FORWARD, THE FEWER OBSTACLES THAT ARE IN THEIR WAY THE BETTER.
CLAK
CLAK
CLAK
CLAK
CLAK

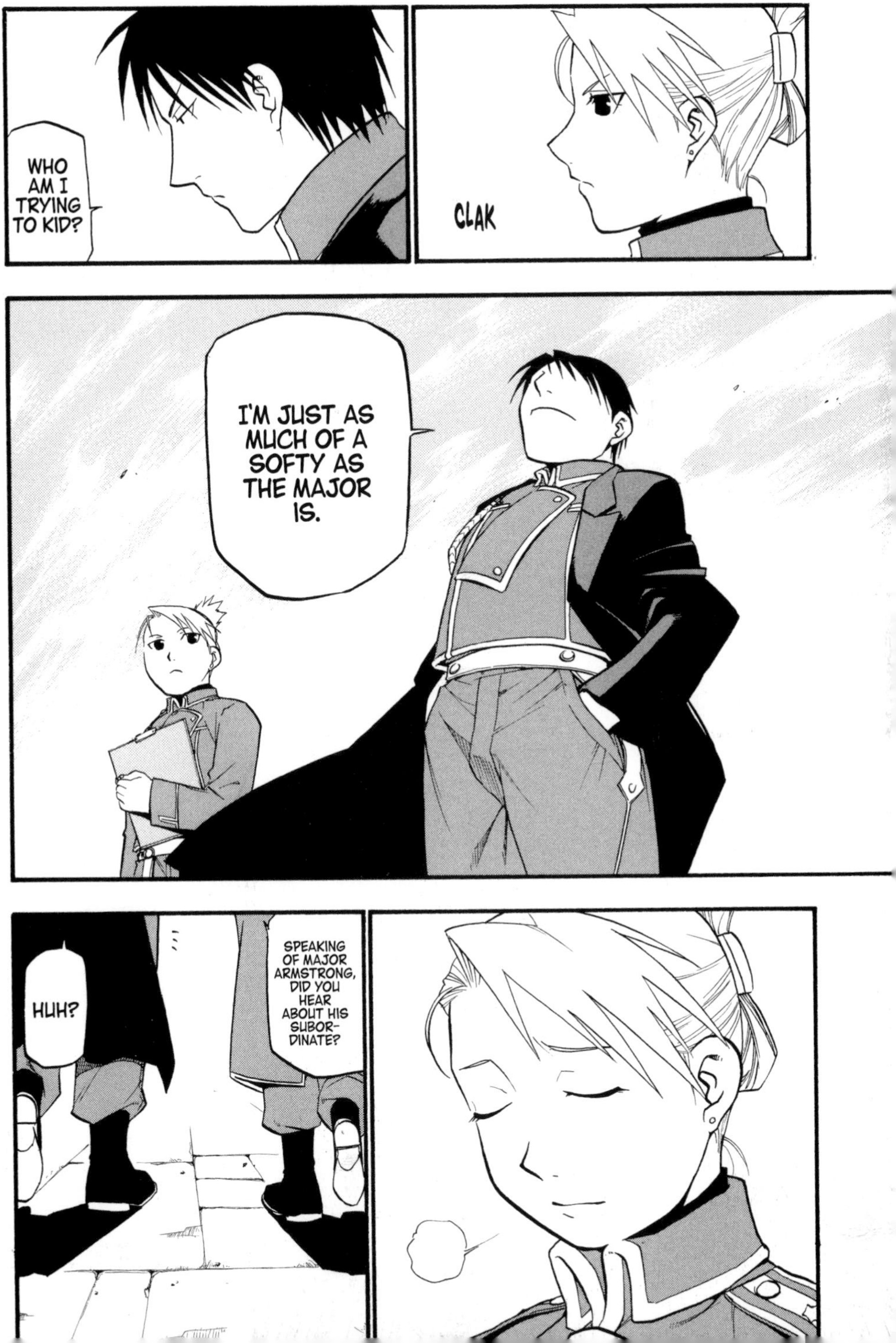
CLAK
WHO AM I TRYING TO KID?
I'M JUST AS MUCH OF A SOFTY AS THE MAJOR IS.
SPEAKING OF MAJOR ARMSTRONG, DID YOU HEAR ABOUT HIS SUBOR-DINATE?
HUH?

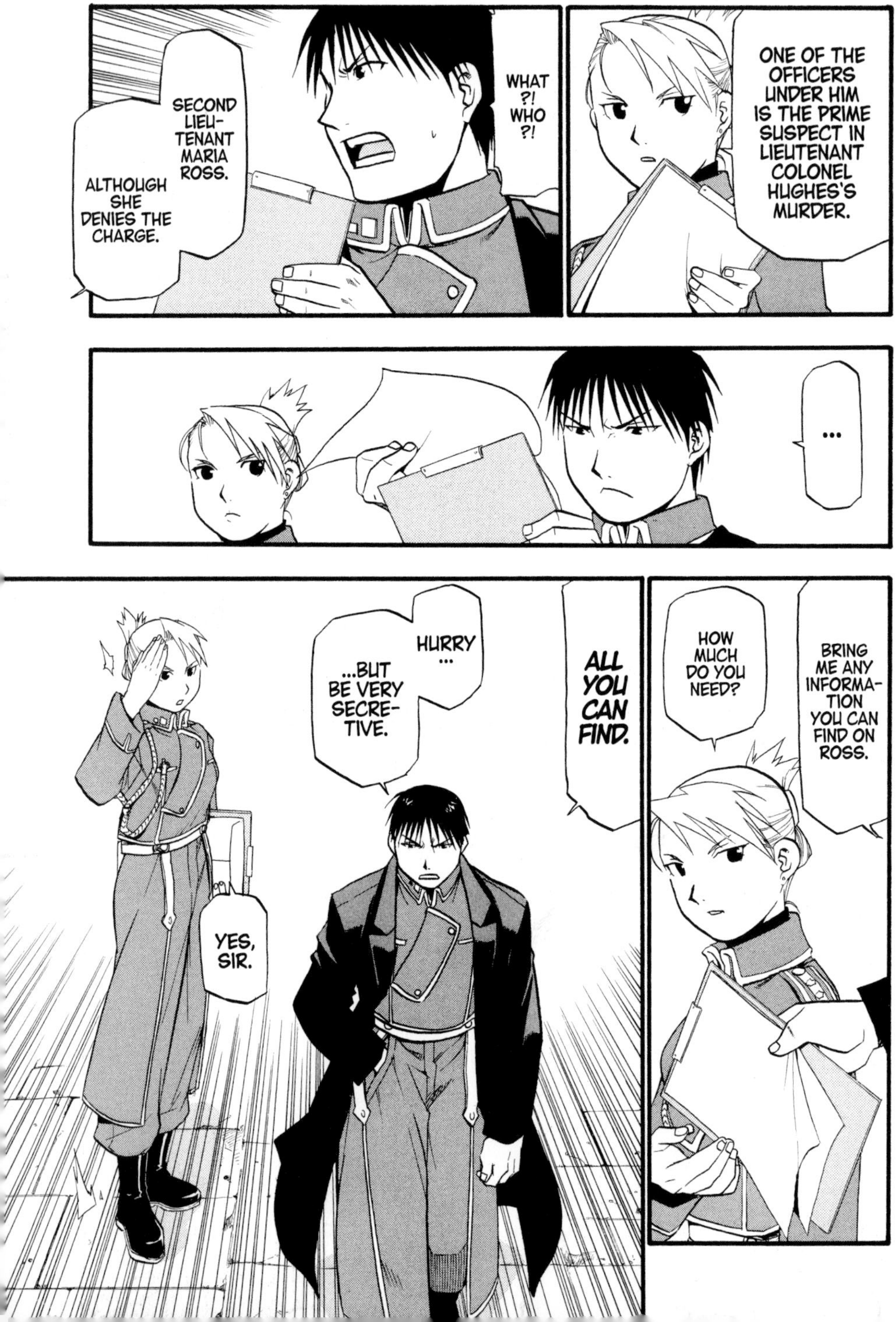
ONE OF THE OFFICERS UNDER HIM IS THE PRIME SUSPECT IN LIEUTENANT COLONEL HUGHES'S MURDER.
WHAT?! WHO?!
SECOND LIEU-TENANT MARIA ROSS.
ALTHOUGH SHE DENIES THE CHARGE.
...
BRING ME ANY INFORMA-TION YOU CAN FIND ON ROSS.
HOW MUCH DO YOU NEED?
ALL YOU CAN FIND.
HURRY...
...BUT BE VERY SECRE-TIVE.
YES, SIR.

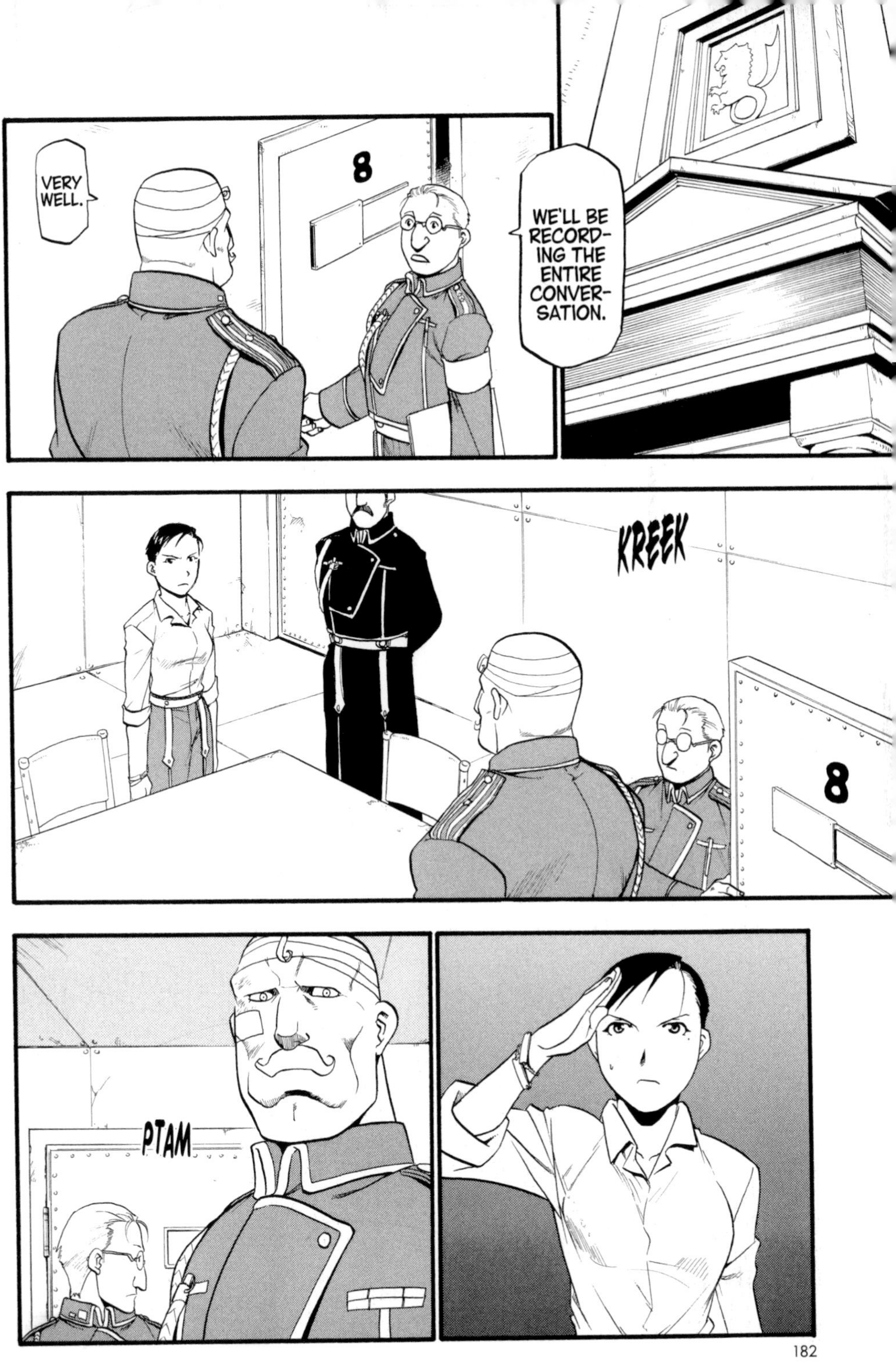
WE'LL BE RECORDING-ING THE ENTIRE CONVER-SATION.
VERY WELL.
KREEK
PTAM

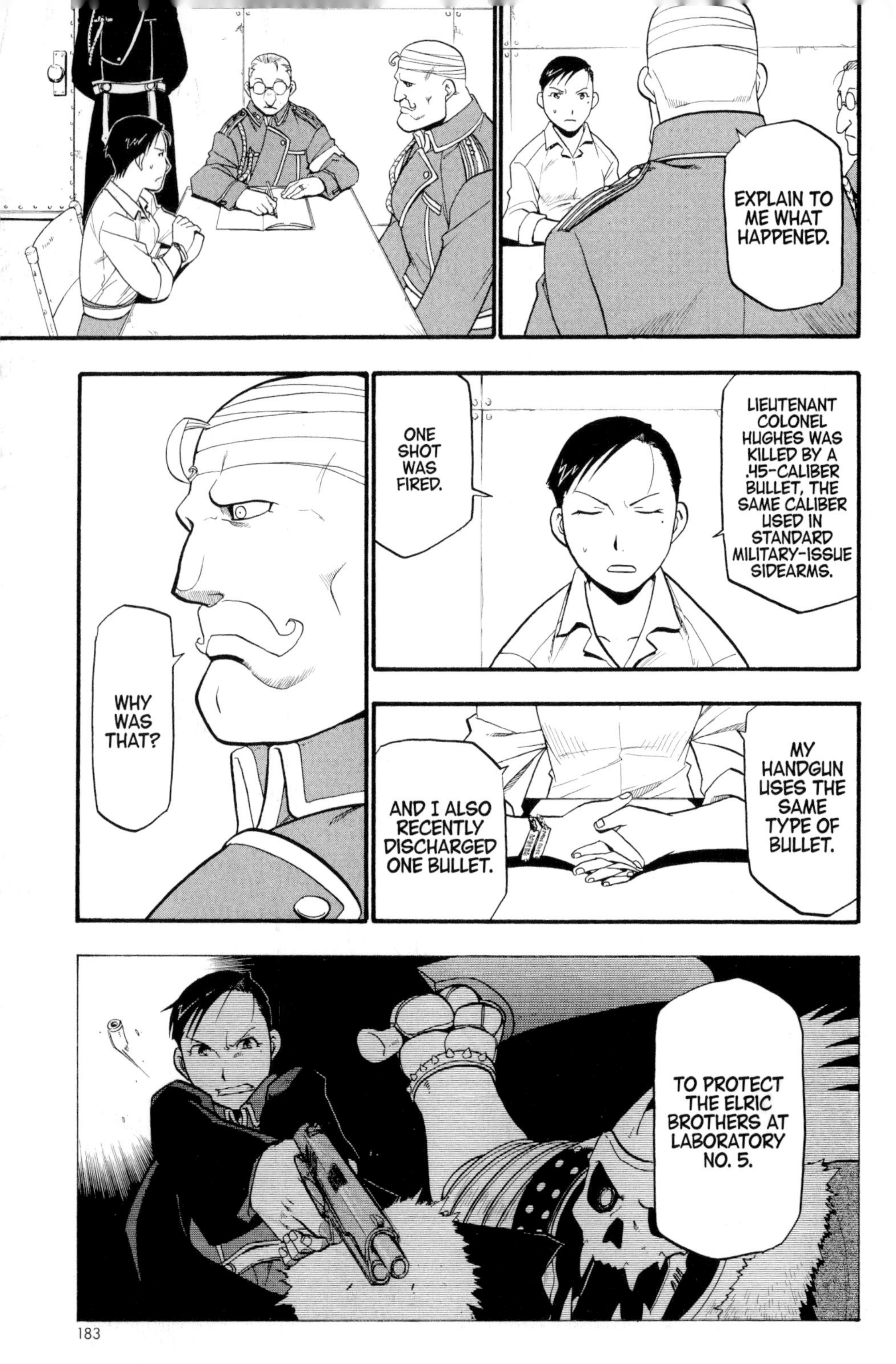
EXPLAIN TO ME WHAT HAPPENED.
LIEUTENANT COLONEL HUGHES WAS KILLED BY A .45-CALIBER BULLET, THE SAME CALIBER USED IN STANDARD MILITARY-ISSUE SIDEARMS.
ONE SHOT WAS FIRED.
MY HANDGUN USES THE SAME TYPE OF BULLET.
AND I ALSO RECENTLY DISCHARGED ONE BULLET.
WHY WAS THAT?
TO PROTECT THE ELRIC BROTHERS AT LABORATORY NO. 5.

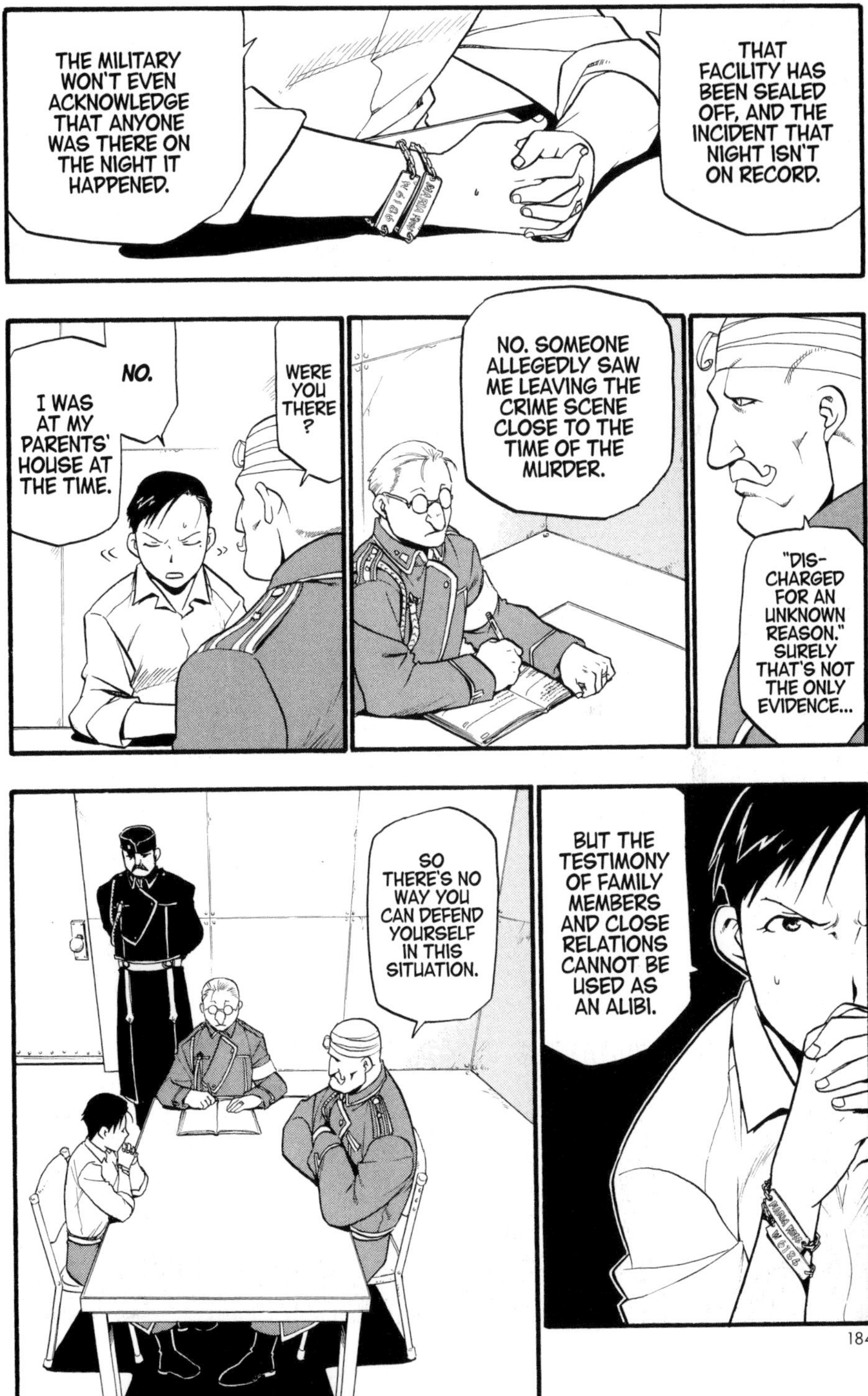
THAT FACILITY HAS BEEN SEALED OFF, AND THE INCIDENT THAT NIGHT ISN'T ON RECORD.
THE MILITARY WON'T EVEN ACKNOWLEDGE THAT ANYONE WAS THERE ON THE NIGHT IT HAPPENED.
"DIS-CHARGED FOR AN UNKNOWN REASON." SURELY THAT'S NOT THE ONLY EVIDENCE...
NO. SOMEONE ALLEGEDLY SAW ME LEAVING THE CRIME SCENE CLOSE TO THE TIME OF THE MURDER.
WERE YOU THERE?
NO.
I WAS AT MY PARENTS' HOUSE AT THE TIME.
BUT THE TESTIMONY OF FAMILY MEMBERS AND CLOSE RELATIONS CANNOT BE USED AS AN ALIBI.
SO THERE'S NO WAY YOU CAN DEFEND YOURSELF IN THIS SITUATION.

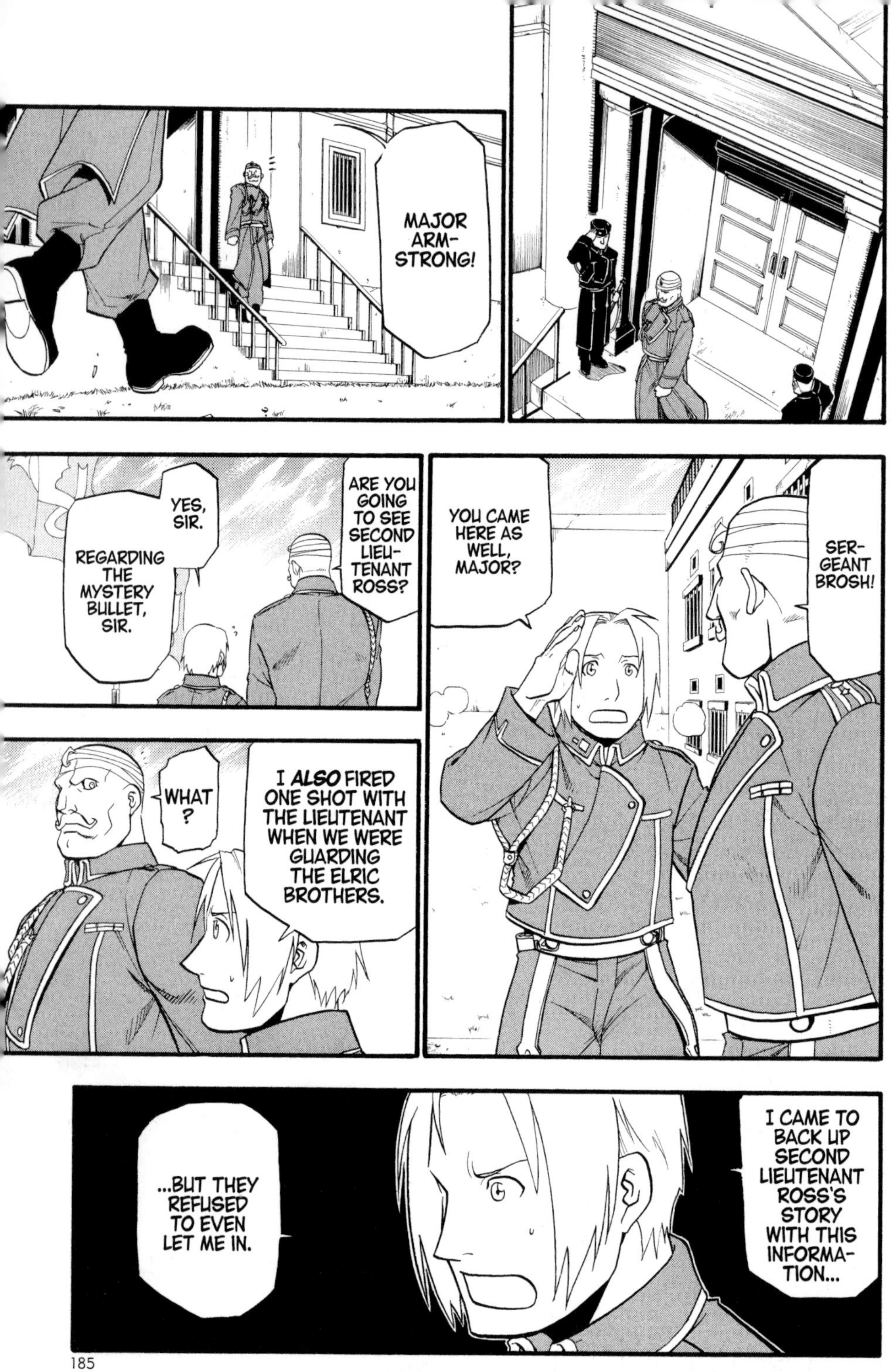
MAJOR ARM-STRONG!
SER-GEANT BROSH!
YOU CAME HERE AS WELL, MAJOR?
ARE YOU GOING TO SEE SECOND LIEU-TENANT ROSS?
YES, SIR.
REGARDING THE MYSTERY BULLET, SIR.
I *ALSO* FIRED ONE SHOT WITH THE LIEUTENANT WHEN WE WERE GUARDING THE ELRIC BROTHERS.
WHAT?
I CAME TO BACK UP SECOND LIEUTENANT ROSS'S STORY WITH THIS INFORMA-TION...
...BUT THEY REFUSED TO EVEN LET ME IN.

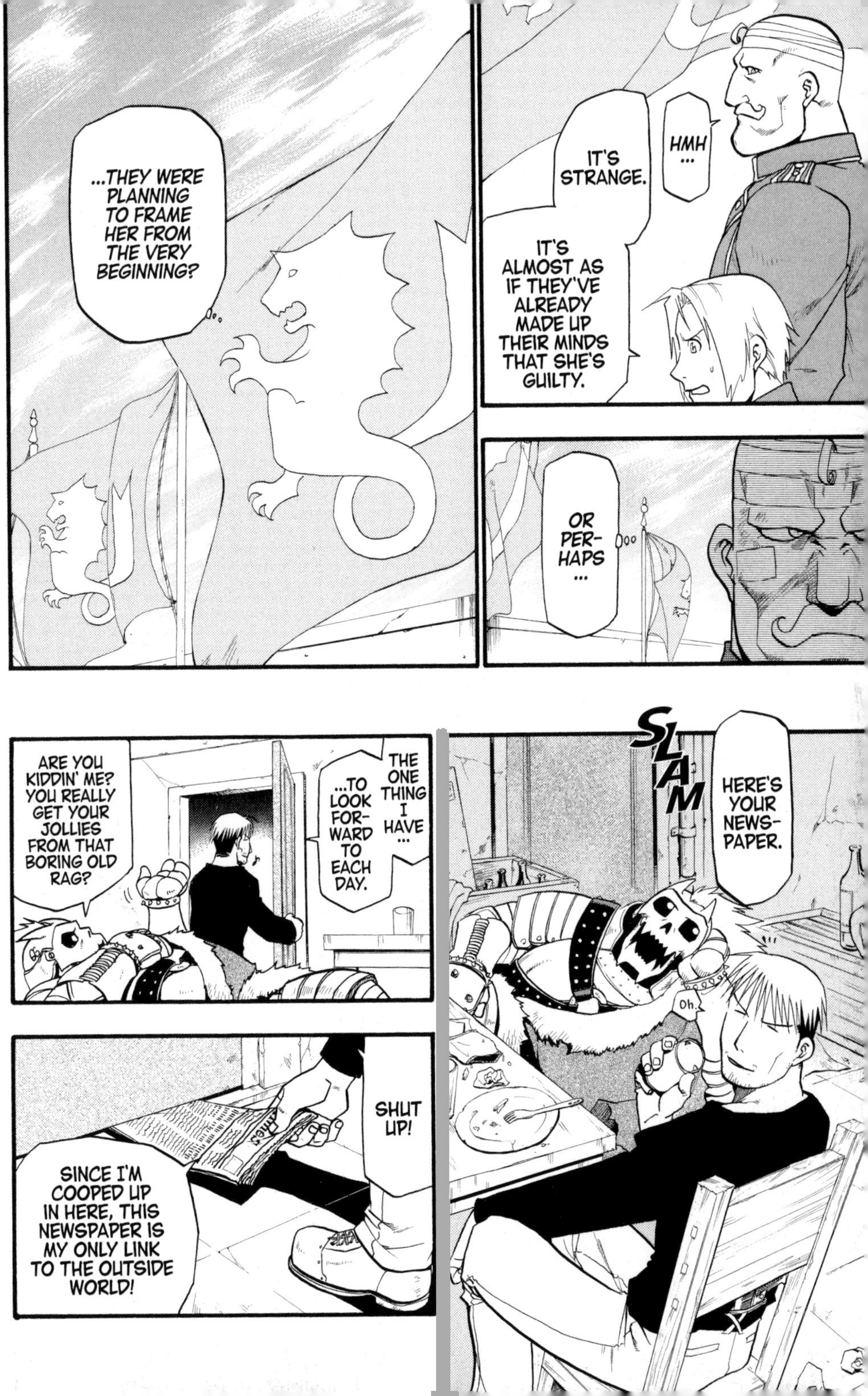
HMH...
IT'S STRANGE.
IT'S ALMOST AS IF THEY'VE ALREADY MADE UP THEIR MINDS THAT SHE'S GUILTY.
OR PER-HAPS...
...THEY WERE PLANNING TO FRAME HER FROM THE VERY BEGINNING?
SLAM
HERE'S YOUR NEWS-PAPER.
Oh.
THE ONE THING I HAVE...
...TO LOOK FOR-WARD TO EACH DAY.
ARE YOU KIDDIN' ME? YOU REALLY GET YOUR JOLLIES FROM THAT BORING OLD RAG?
SHUT UP!
SINCE I'M COOPED UP IN HERE, THIS NEWSPAPER IS MY ONLY LINK TO THE OUTSIDE WORLD!

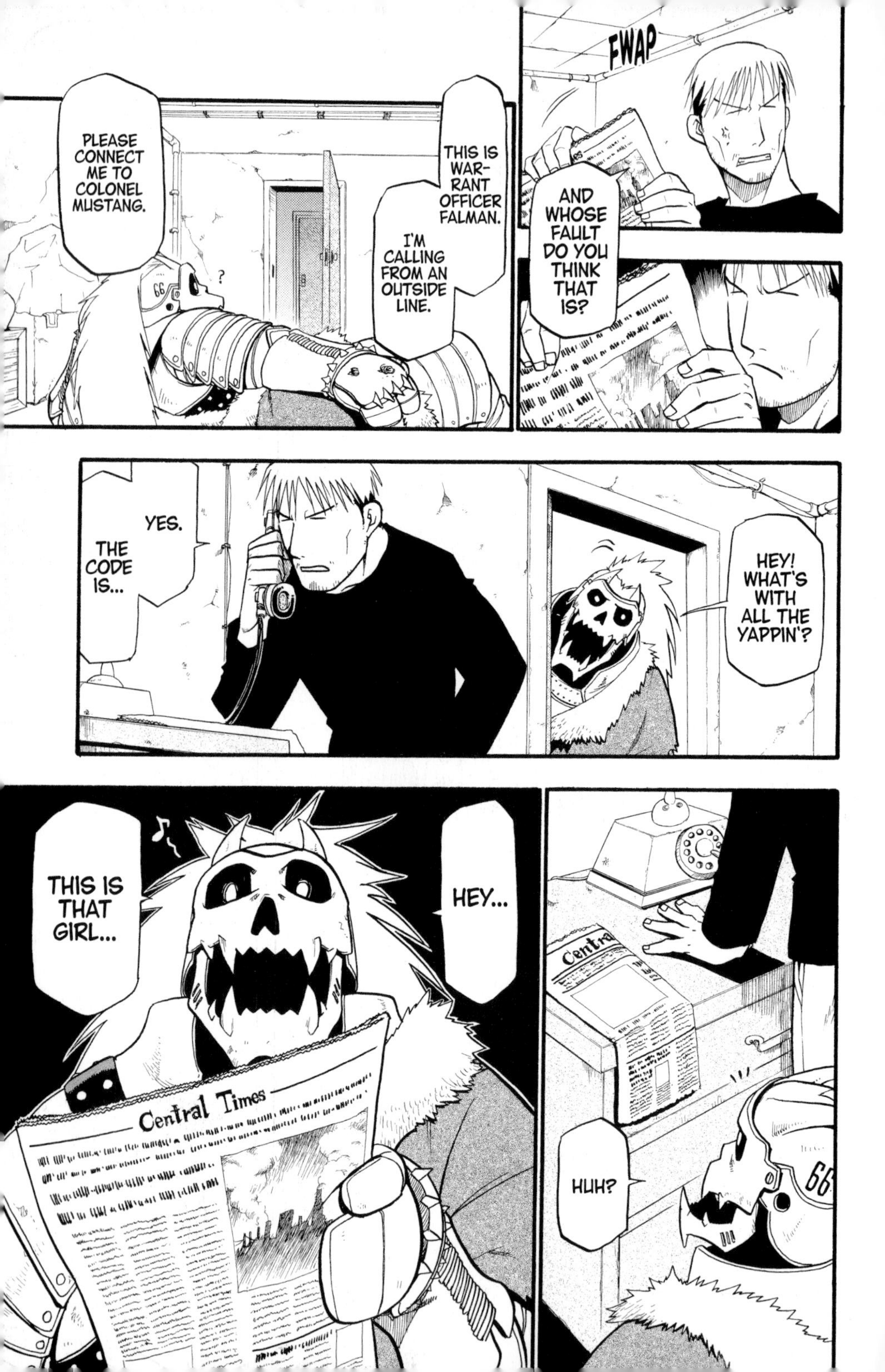
FWAP
AND WHOSE FAULT DO YOU THINK THAT IS?
THIS IS WAR-RANT OFFICER FALMAN.
I'M CALLING FROM AN OUTSIDE LINE.
PLEASE CONNECT ME TO COLONEL MUSTANG.
?
HEY! WHAT'S WITH ALL THE YAPPIN'?
YES.
THE CODE IS...
Central
HUH?
HEY...
THIS IS THAT GIRL...
Central Times

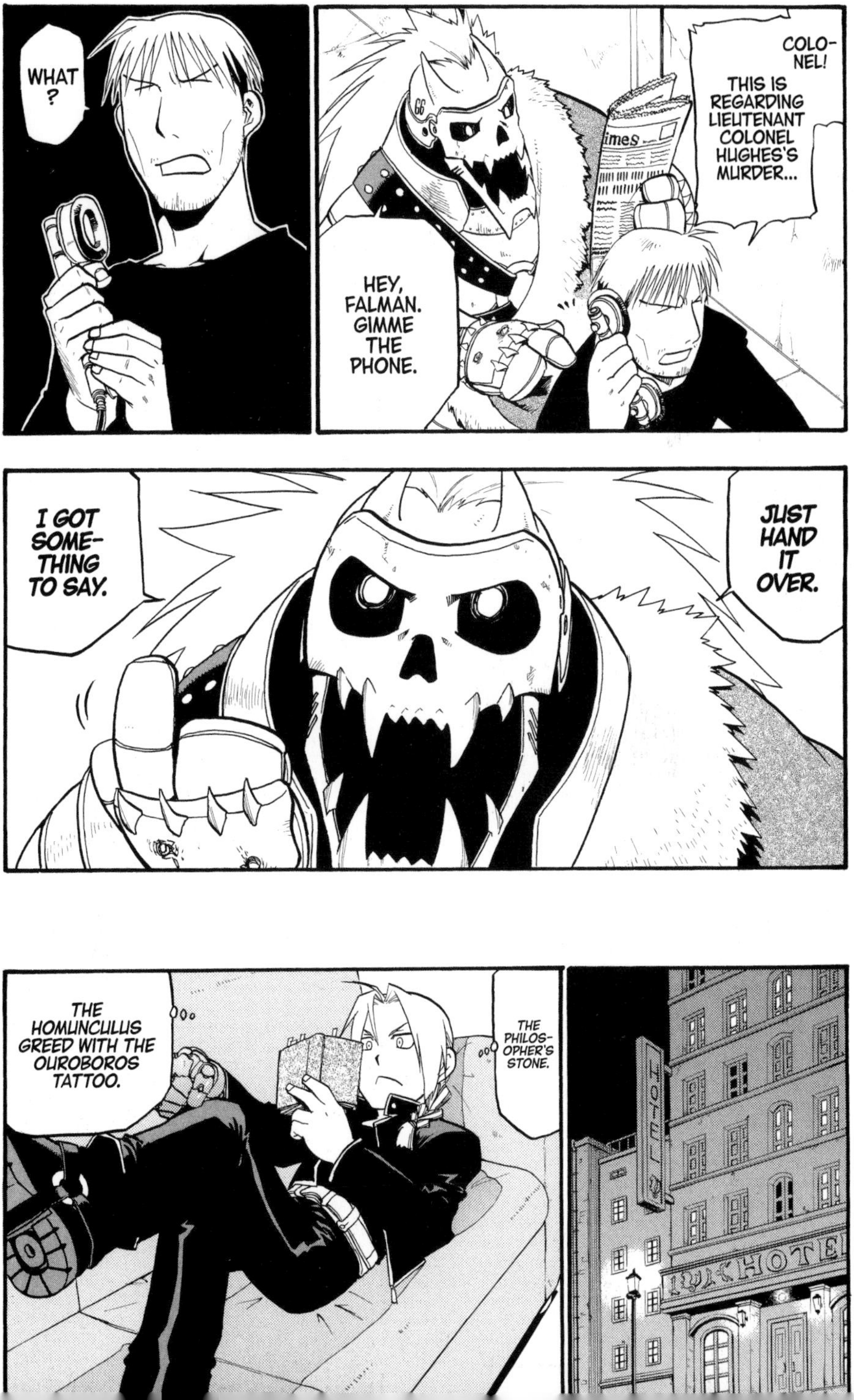
COLO-NEL! THIS IS REGARDING LIEUTENANT COLONEL HUGHES'S MURDER...
HEY, FALMAN. GIMME THE PHONE.
WHAT?
JUST HAND IT OVER.
I GOT SOME-THING TO SAY.
HOTEL
THE PHILOS-OPHER'S STONE.
THE HOMUNCULUS GREED WITH THE OUROBOROS TATTOO.

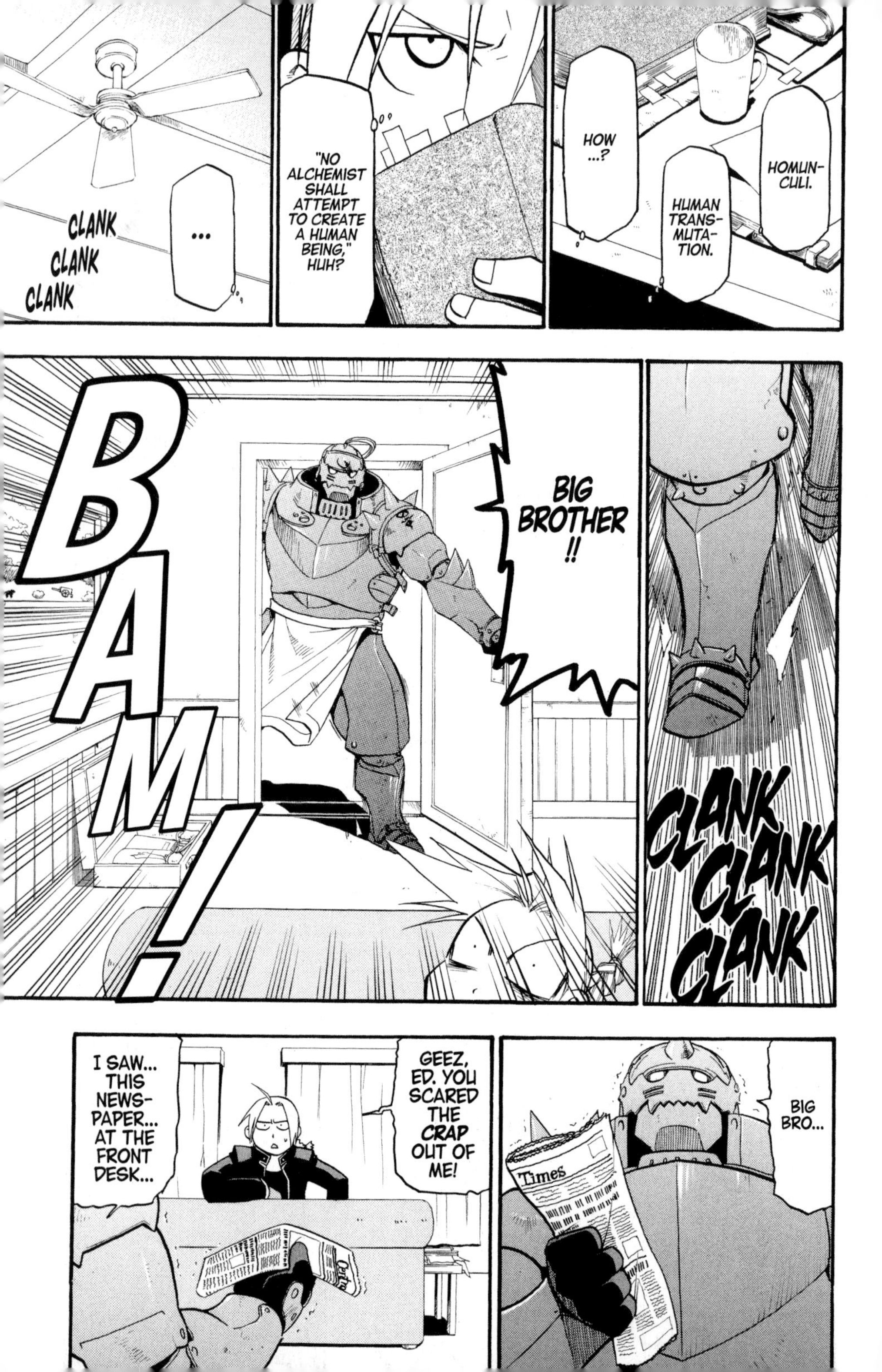
HOMUN-CULI.
HUMAN TRANS-MUTA-TION.
HOW ...?
"NO ALCHEMIST SHALL ATTEMPT TO CREATE A HUMAN BEING," HUH?
...
CLANK CLANK CLANK
CLANK CLANK CLANK
BIG BROTHER !!
BAM!
BIG BRO...
Times
GEEZ, ED. YOU SCARED THE **CRAP** OUT OF ME!
I SAW... THIS NEWS-PAPER... AT THE FRONT DESK...

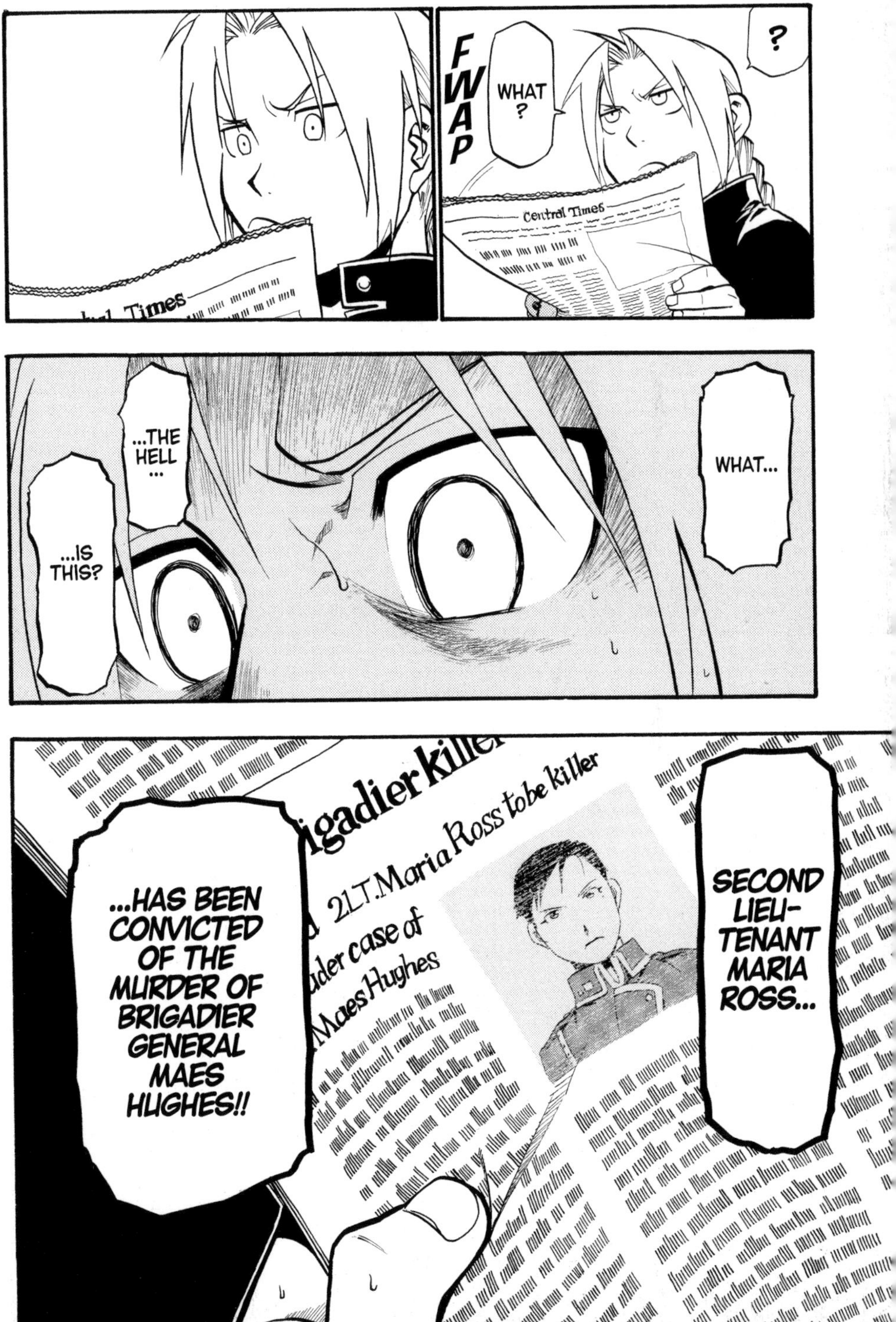
?
FWAP
WHAT ?
Central Times
WHAT...
...THE HELL ...
...IS THIS?
SECOND LIEU-TENANT MARIA ROSS...
2LT.Maria Ross tobe killer
Maes Hughes
...HAS BEEN CONVICTED OF THE MURDER OF BRIGADIER GENERAL MAES HUGHES!!

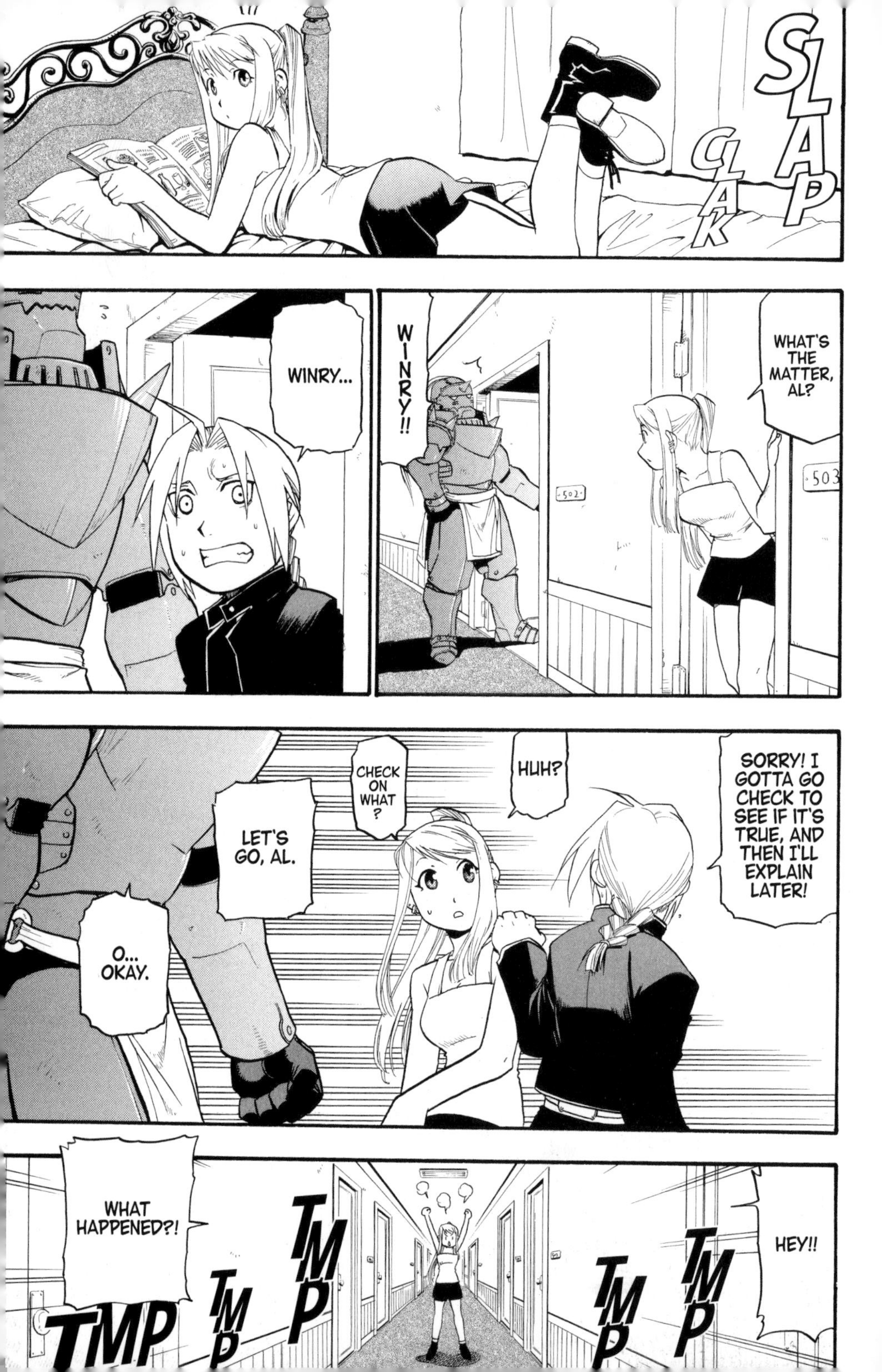
SLAP
CLAK
WHAT'S THE MATTER, AL?
WINRY!!
WINRY...
SORRY! I GOTTA GO CHECK TO SEE IF IT'S TRUE, AND THEN I'LL EXPLAIN LATER!
HUH?
CHECK ON WHAT?
LET'S GO, AL.
O... OKAY.
HEY!!
TMP
TMP
TMP
TMP
WHAT HAPPENED?!
TMP

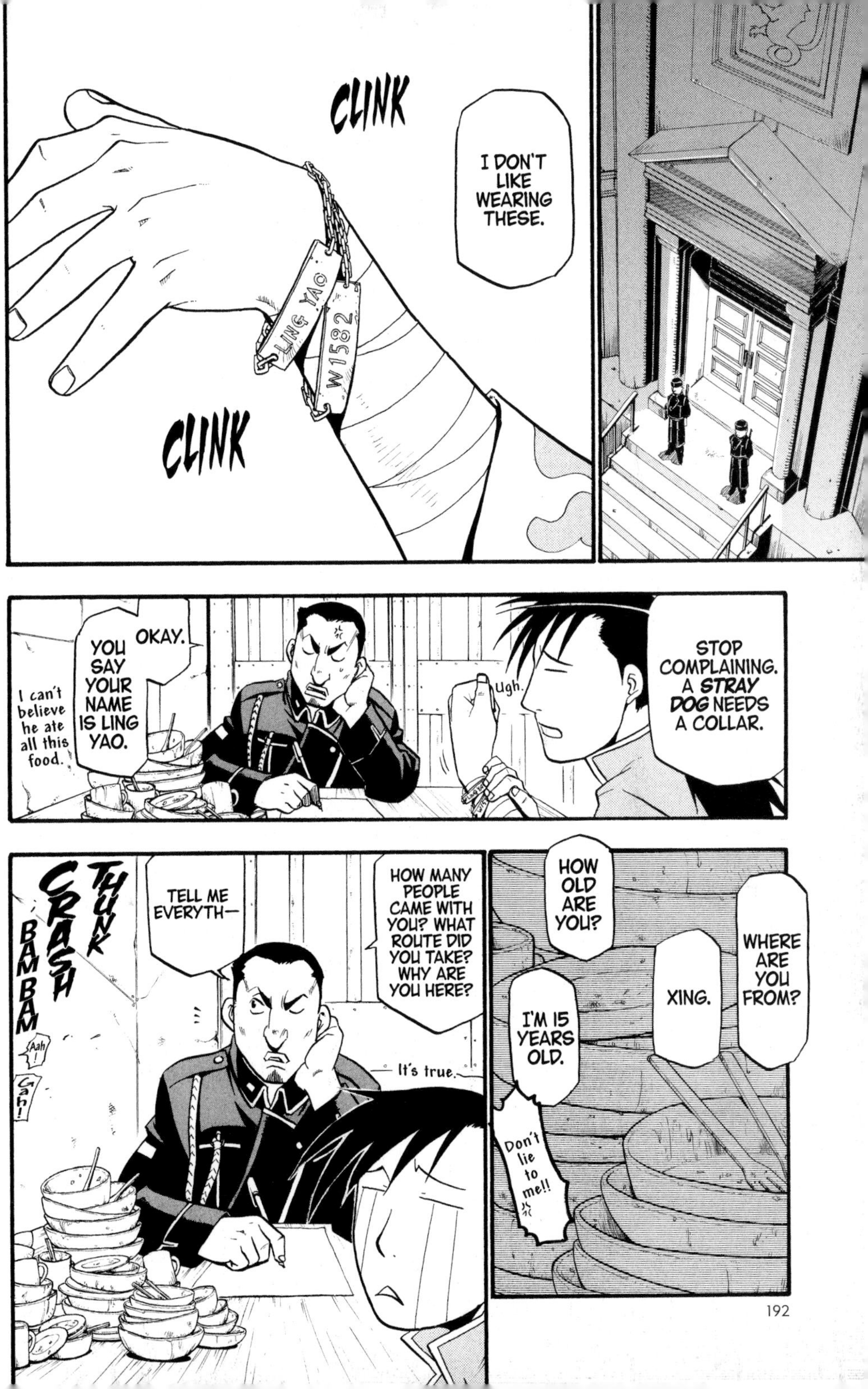
I DON'T LIKE WEARING THESE.
CLINK
LING YAO
W1582
CLINK
STOP COMPLAINING. A STRAY DOG NEEDS A COLLAR.
Ugh.
OKAY.
YOU SAY YOUR NAME IS LING YAO.
I can't believe he ate all this food.
WHERE ARE YOU FROM?
XING.
HOW OLD ARE YOU?
I'M 15 YEARS OLD.
Don't lie to me!!
HOW MANY PEOPLE CAME WITH YOU? WHAT ROUTE DID YOU TAKE? WHY ARE YOU HERE?
TELL ME EVERYTH—
THUNK
CRASH
BAM BAM
Aah!
Gah!
It's true.

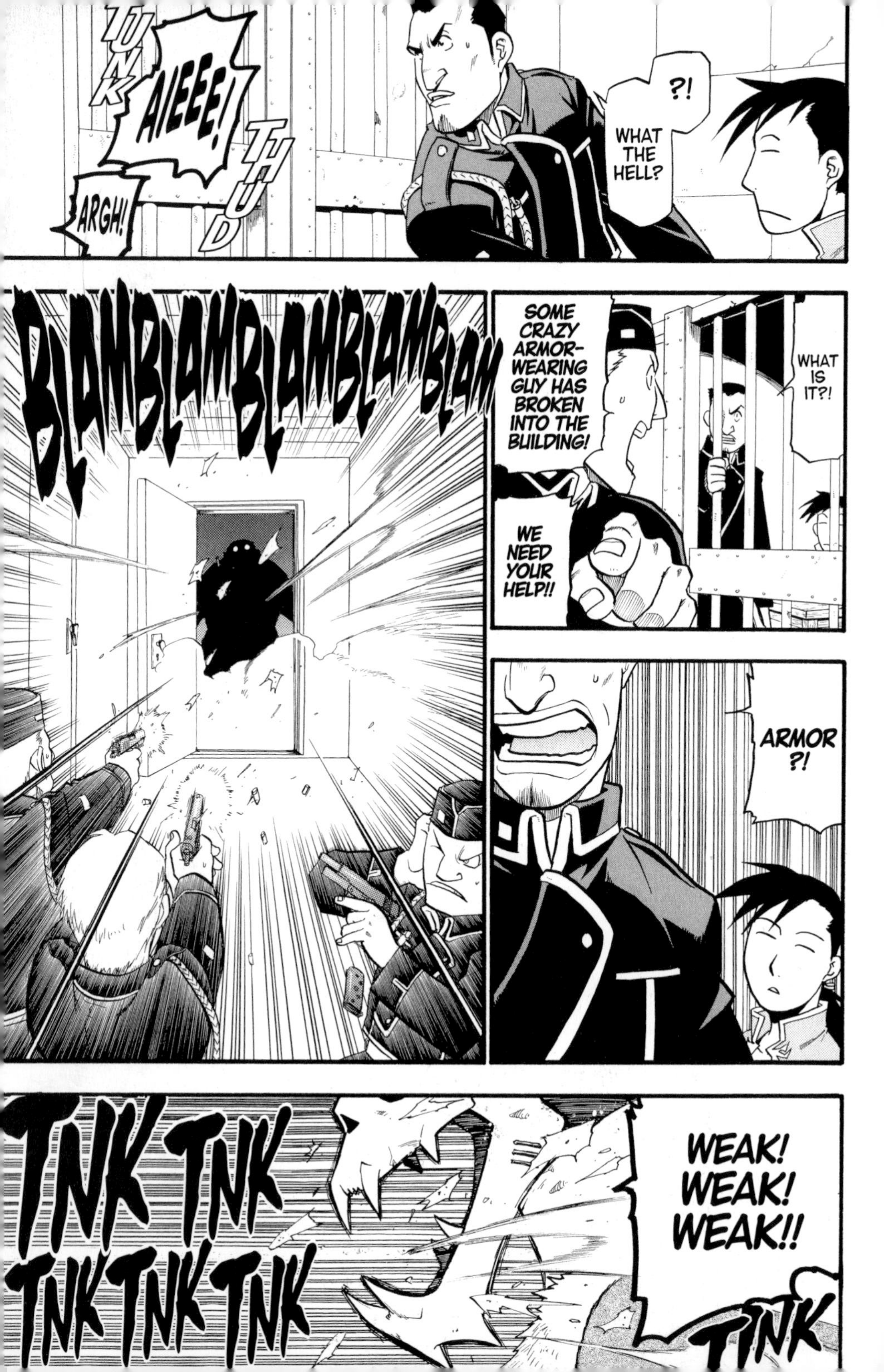
?!
WHAT THE HELL?
TUNK
AIEEE!
THUD
ARGH!
WHAT IS IT?!
SOME CRAZY ARMOR-WEARING GUY HAS BROKEN INTO THE BUILDING!
WE NEED YOUR HELP!!
ARMOR?!
BLAMBLAMBLAMBLAMBLAMBLAM
WEAK! WEAK! WEAK!!
TINK
TNK TNK
TNK TNK TNK

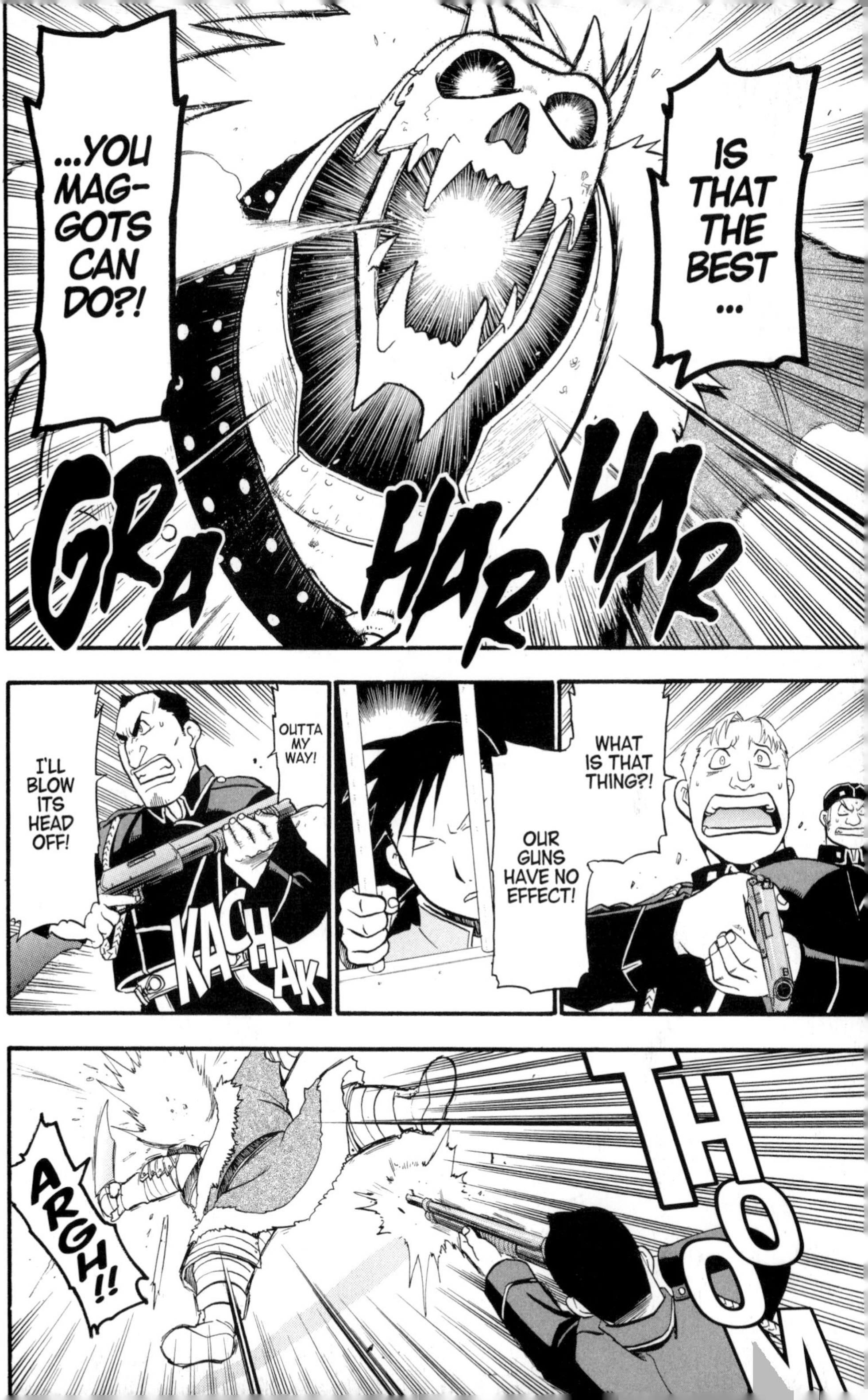
IS THAT THE BEST...
...YOU MAG-GOTS CAN DO?!
GRA HAR HAR
WHAT IS THAT THING?!
OUR GUNS HAVE NO EFFECT!
OUTTA MY WAY!
I'LL BLOW ITS HEAD OFF!
KACHAK
THOOM
ARGH!!

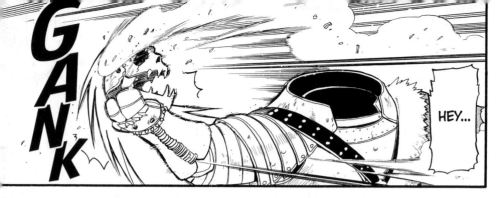

HEY...

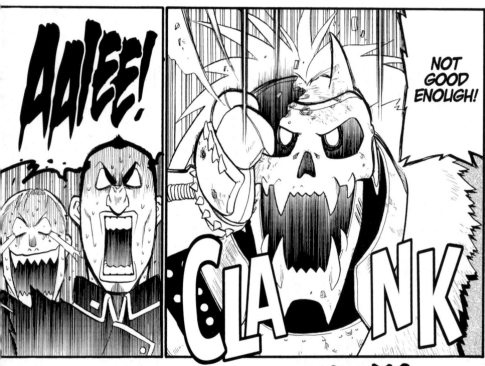

AAIEE!

NOT GOOD ENOUGH!

CLA NK

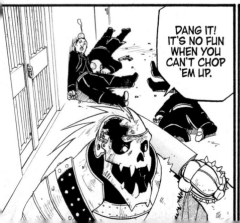

DANG IT! IT'S NO FUN WHEN YOU CAN'T CHOP 'EM UP.

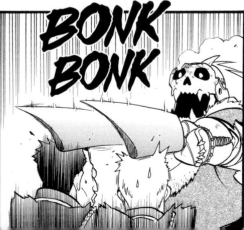

BONK BONK

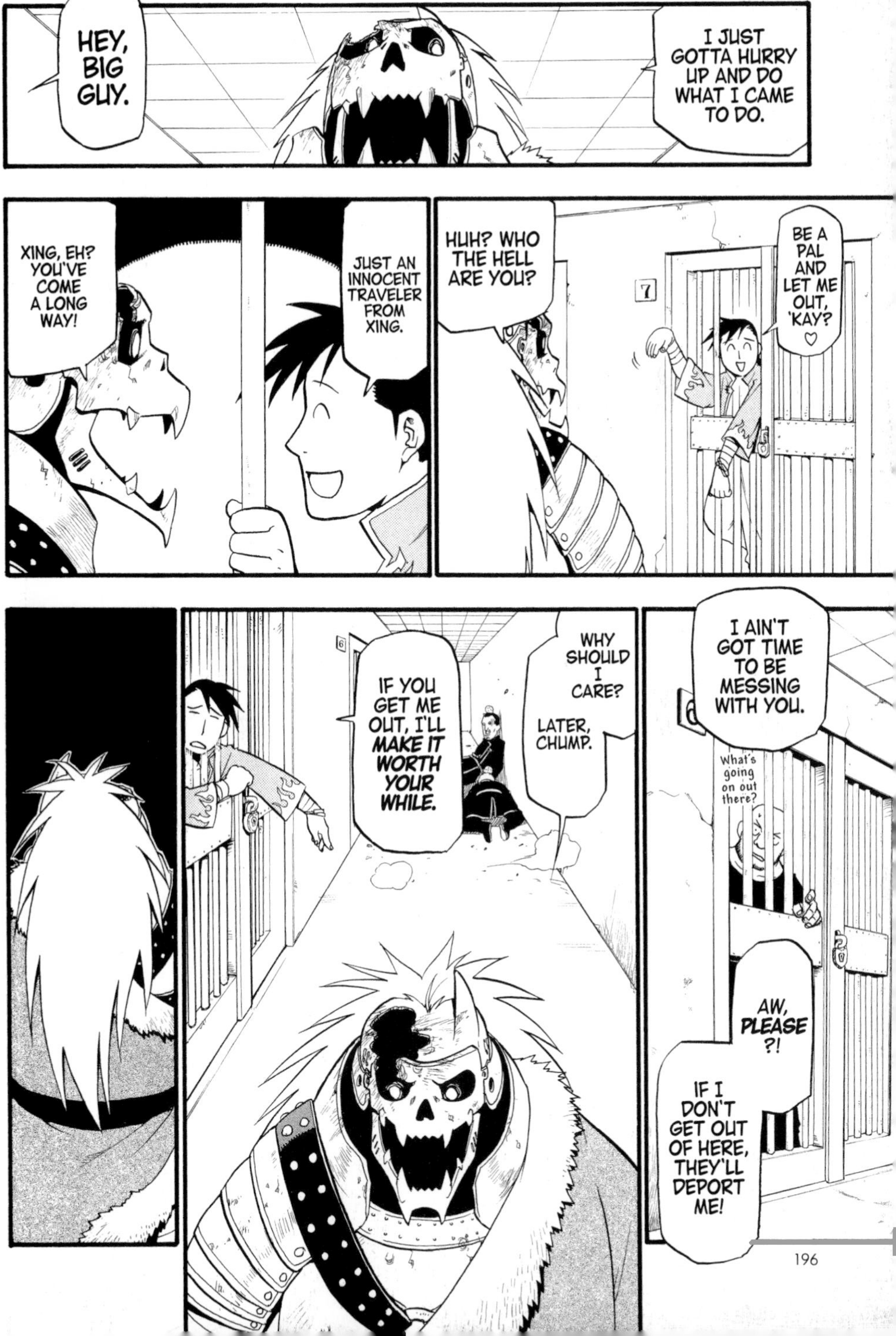

I JUST GOTTA HURRY UP AND DO WHAT I CAME TO DO.
HEY, BIG GUY.
BE A PAL AND LET ME OUT, 'KAY? ♡
HUH? WHO THE HELL ARE YOU?
JUST AN INNOCENT TRAVELER FROM XING.
XING, EH? YOU'VE COME A LONG WAY!
I AIN'T GOT TIME TO BE MESSING WITH YOU.
What's going on out there?
AW, **PLEASE**?!
IF I DON'T GET OUT OF HERE, THEY'LL DEPORT ME!
WHY SHOULD I CARE?
LATER, CHUMP.
IF YOU GET ME OUT, I'LL ***MAKE IT WORTH YOUR WHILE.***

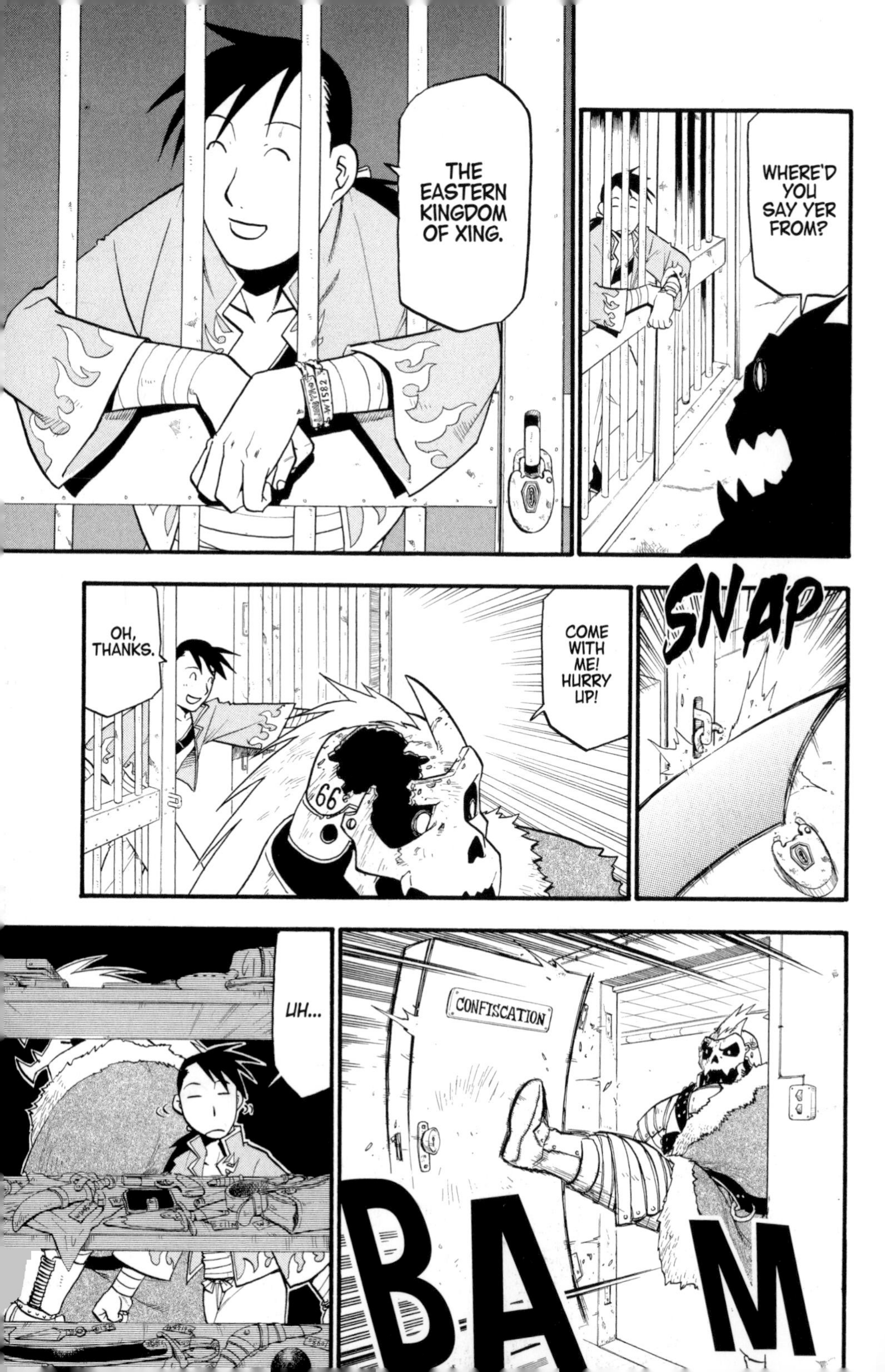
WHERE'D YOU SAY YER FROM?
THE EASTERN KINGDOM OF XING.
SNAP
COME WITH ME! HURRY UP!
OH, THANKS.
CONFISCATION
BAM
UH...

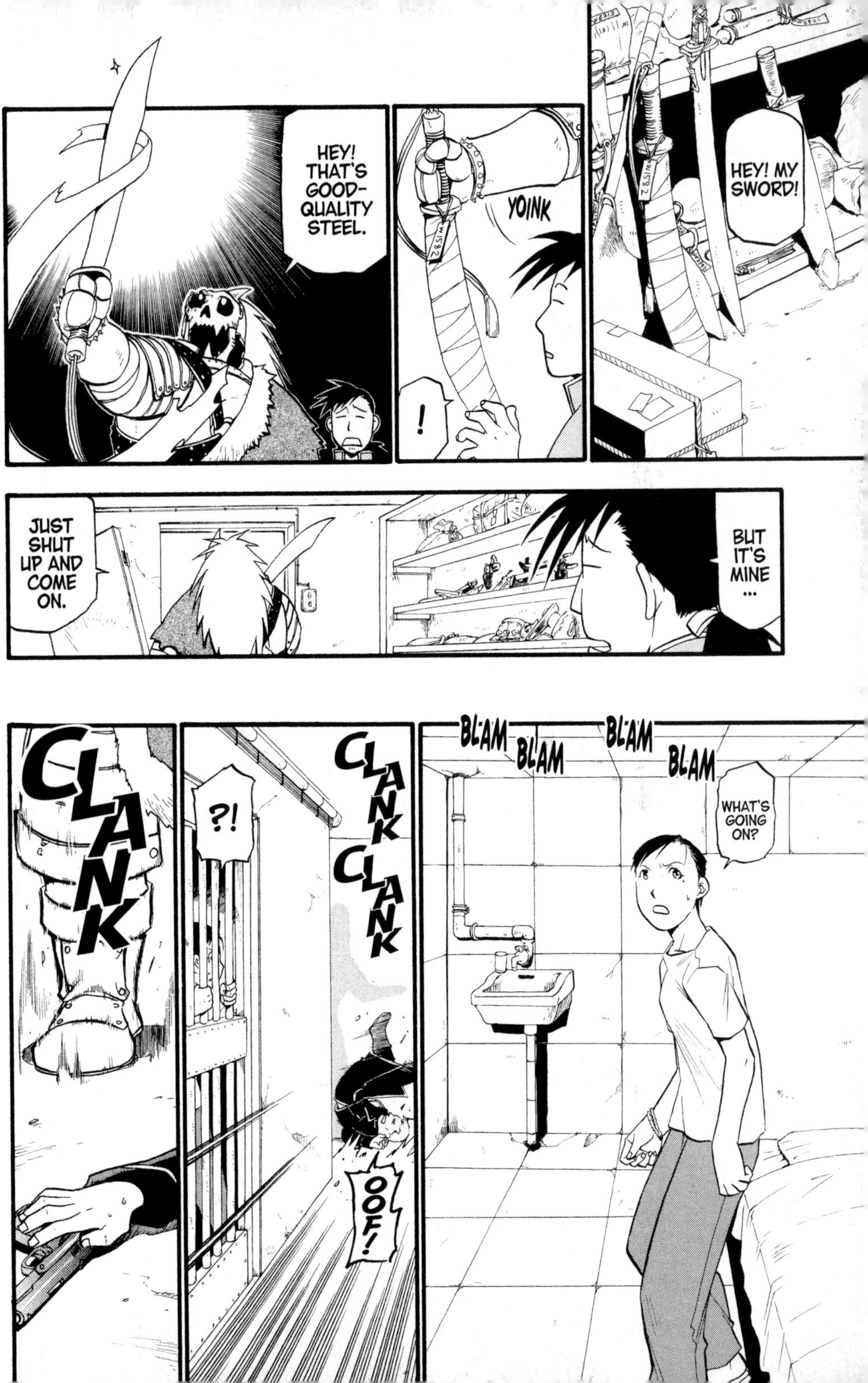
HEY! MY SWORD!
YOINK
!
HEY! THAT'S GOOD-QUALITY STEEL.
BUT IT'S MINE ...
JUST SHUT UP AND COME ON.
BLAM
BLAM
BLAM
BLAM
WHAT'S GOING ON?
CLANK
CLANK
?!
OOF!
CLANK

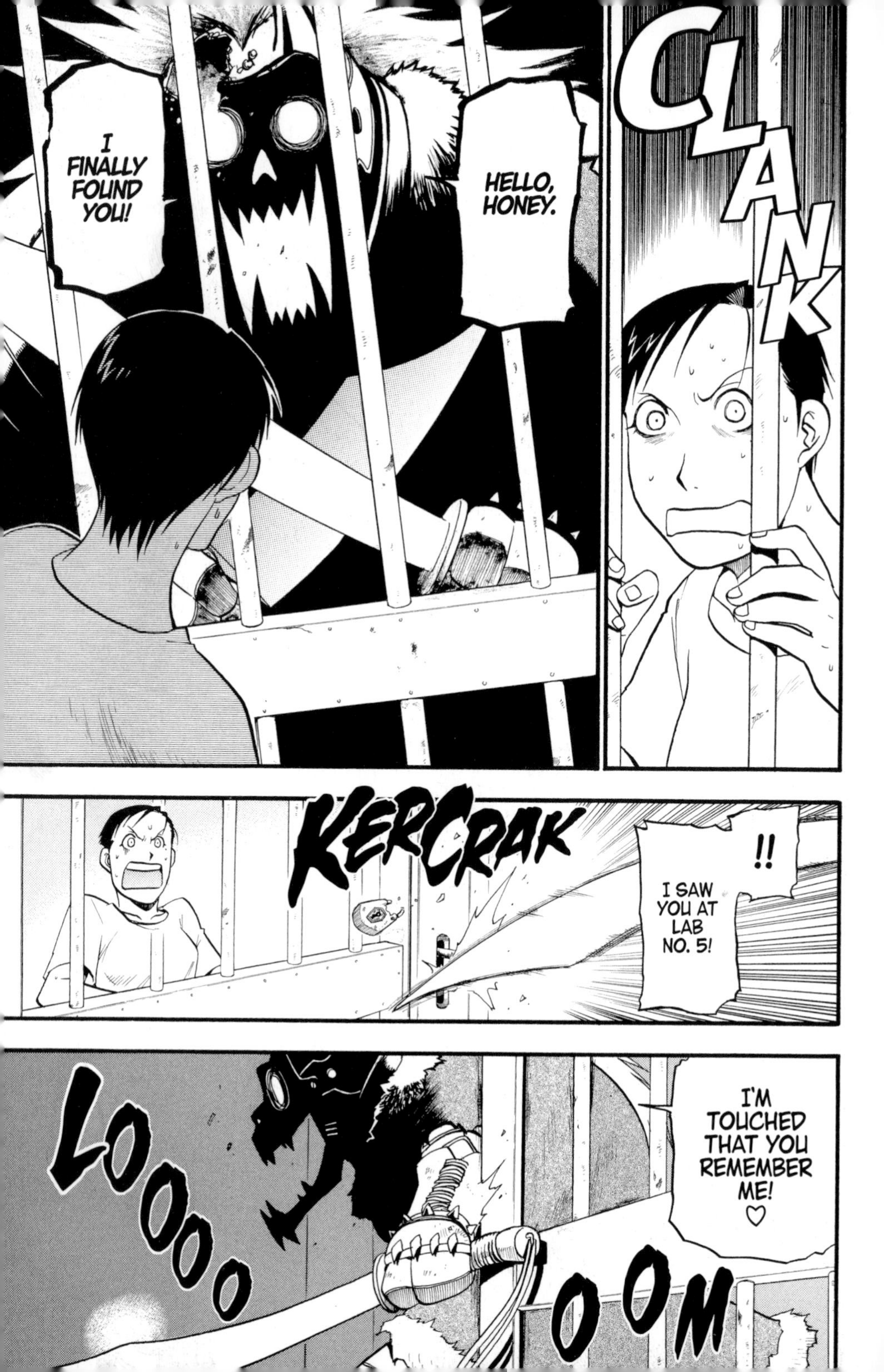
CLANK
HELLO, HONEY.
I FINALLY FOUND YOU!
!!
I SAW YOU AT LAB NO. 5!
KERCRAK
I'M TOUCHED THAT YOU REMEMBER ME! ♡
LOOOOOOOM

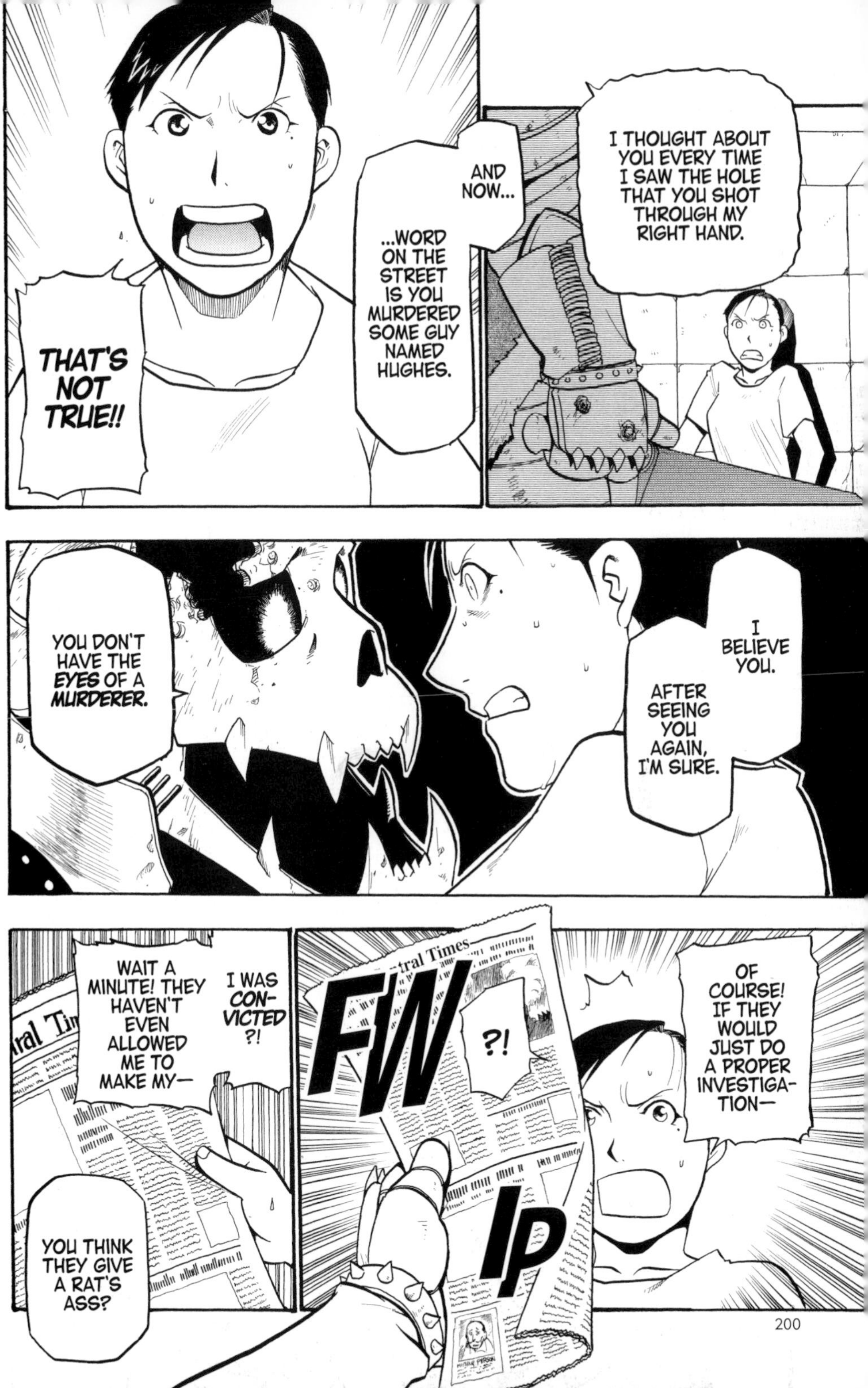
I THOUGHT ABOUT YOU EVERY TIME I SAW THE HOLE THAT YOU SHOT THROUGH MY RIGHT HAND.
AND NOW...
...WORD ON THE STREET IS YOU MURDERED SOME GUY NAMED HUGHES.
THAT'S NOT TRUE!!
I BELIEVE YOU.
AFTER SEEING YOU AGAIN, I'M SURE.
YOU DON'T HAVE THE EYES OF A MURDERER.
OF COURSE! IF THEY WOULD JUST DO A PROPER INVESTIGA-TION—
FWIP
?!
I WAS CON-VICTED?!
WAIT A MINUTE! THEY HAVEN'T EVEN ALLOWED ME TO MAKE MY—
YOU THINK THEY GIVE A RAT'S ASS?

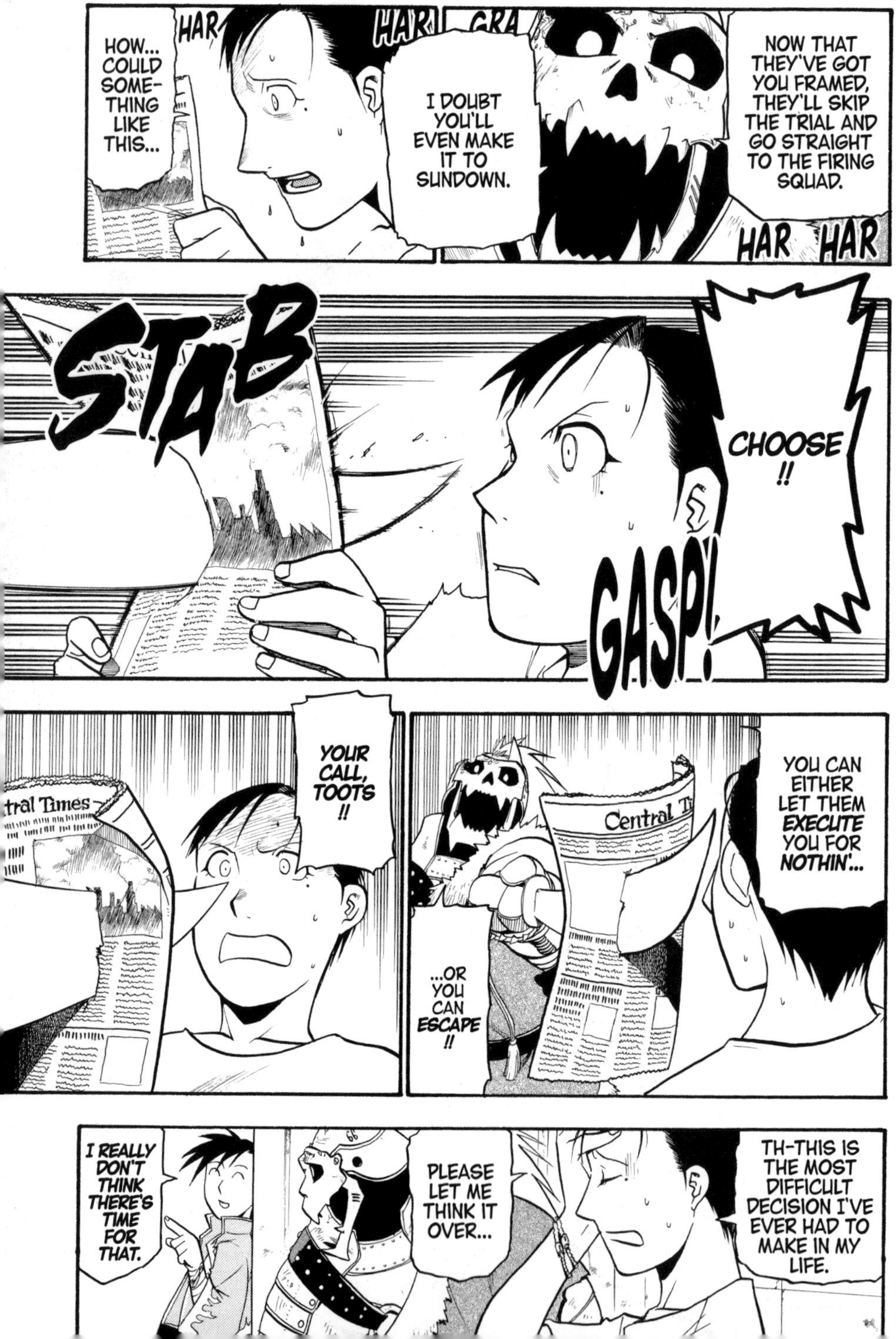
NOW THAT THEY'VE GOT YOU FRAMED, THEY'LL SKIP THE TRIAL AND GO STRAIGHT TO THE FIRING SQUAD.
HAR HAR
HAR
I DOUBT YOU'LL EVEN MAKE IT TO SUNDOWN.
HAR
HOW... COULD SOME-THING LIKE THIS...
CHOOSE!!
GASP!!
STAB
YOU CAN EITHER LET THEM EXECUTE YOU FOR NOTHIN'...
...OR YOU CAN ESCAPE!!
YOUR CALL, TOOTS!!
TH-THIS IS THE MOST DIFFICULT DECISION I'VE EVER HAD TO MAKE IN MY LIFE.
PLEASE LET ME THINK IT OVER...
I REALLY DON'T THINK THERE'S TIME FOR THAT.

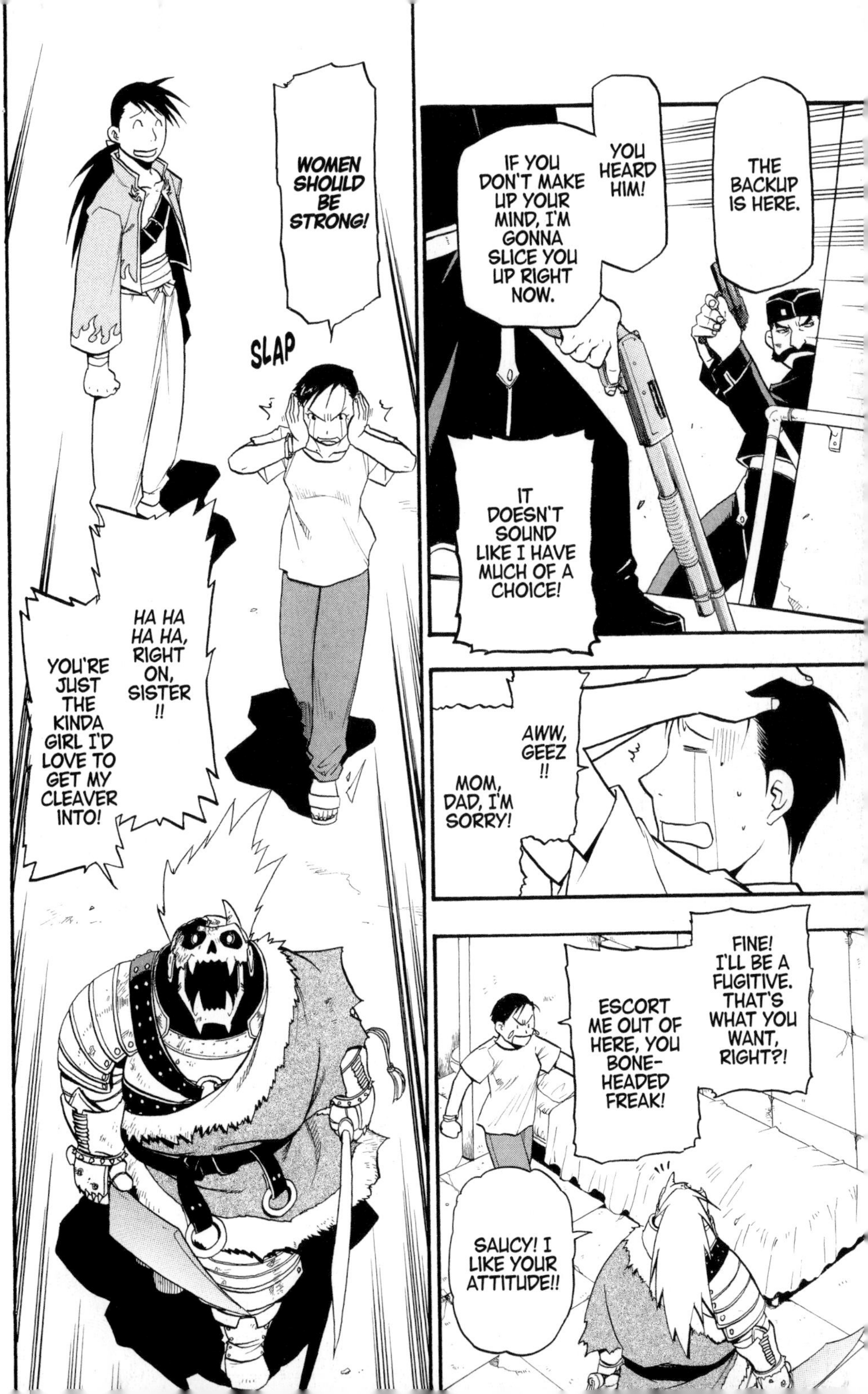
THE BACKUP IS HERE.
YOU HEARD HIM!
IF YOU DON'T MAKE UP YOUR MIND, I'M GONNA SLICE YOU UP RIGHT NOW.
IT DOESN'T SOUND LIKE I HAVE MUCH OF A CHOICE!
AWW, GEEZ!!
MOM, DAD, I'M SORRY!
FINE! I'LL BE A FUGITIVE. THAT'S WHAT YOU WANT, RIGHT?!
ESCORT ME OUT OF HERE, YOU BONE-HEADED FREAK!
SAUCY! I LIKE YOUR ATTITUDE!!
WOMEN SHOULD BE STRONG!
SLAP
HA HA HA HA, RIGHT ON, SISTER!!
YOU'RE JUST THE KINDA GIRL I'D LOVE TO GET MY CLEAVER INTO!

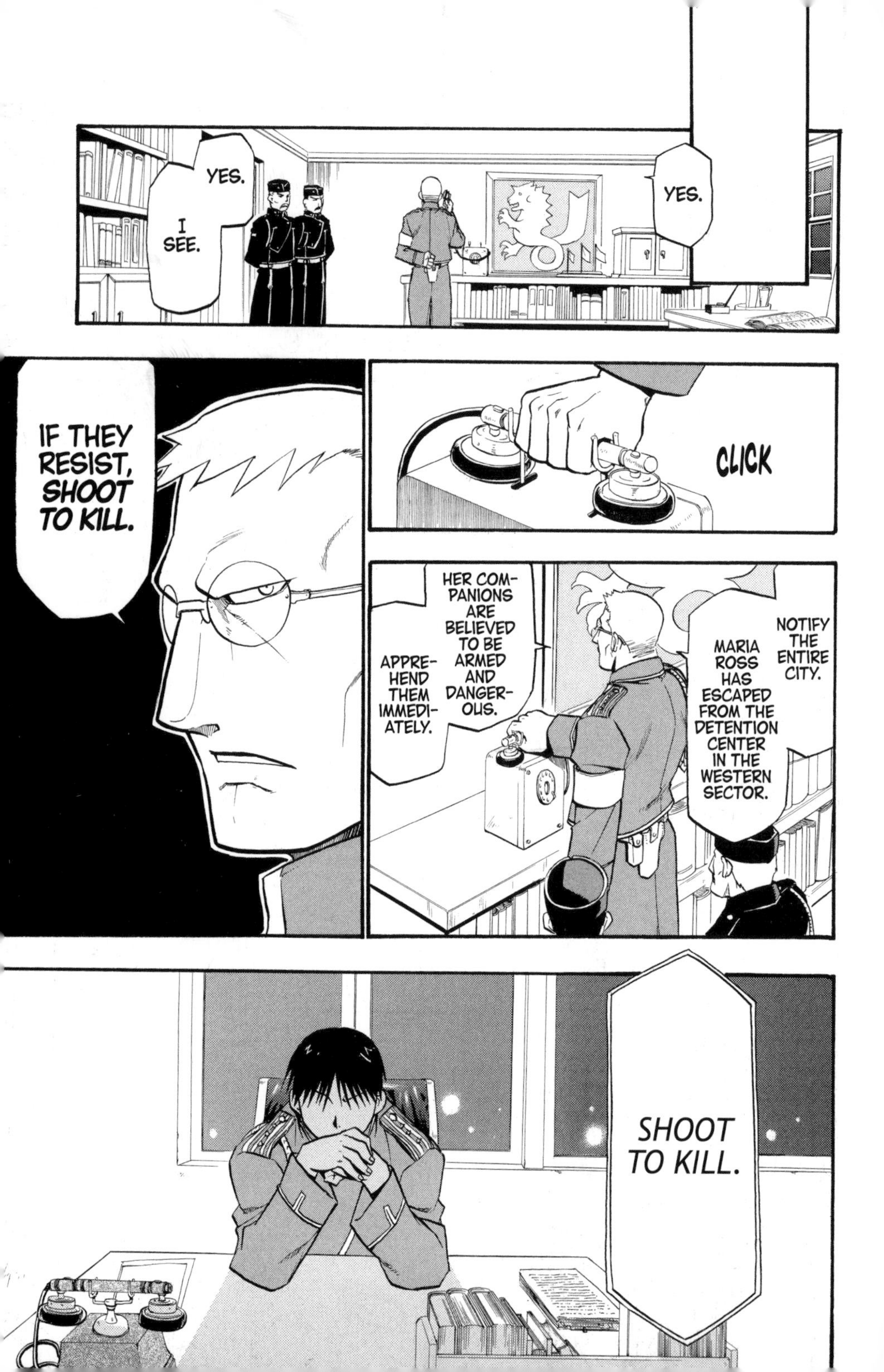
YES.
YES.
I SEE.
CLICK
NOTIFY THE ENTIRE CITY.
MARIA ROSS HAS ESCAPED FROM THE DETENTION CENTER IN THE WESTERN SECTOR.
HER COMPANIONS ARE BELIEVED TO BE ARMED AND DANGEROUS.
APPREHEND THEM IMMEDIATELY.
IF THEY RESIST, SHOOT TO KILL.
SHOOT TO KILL.

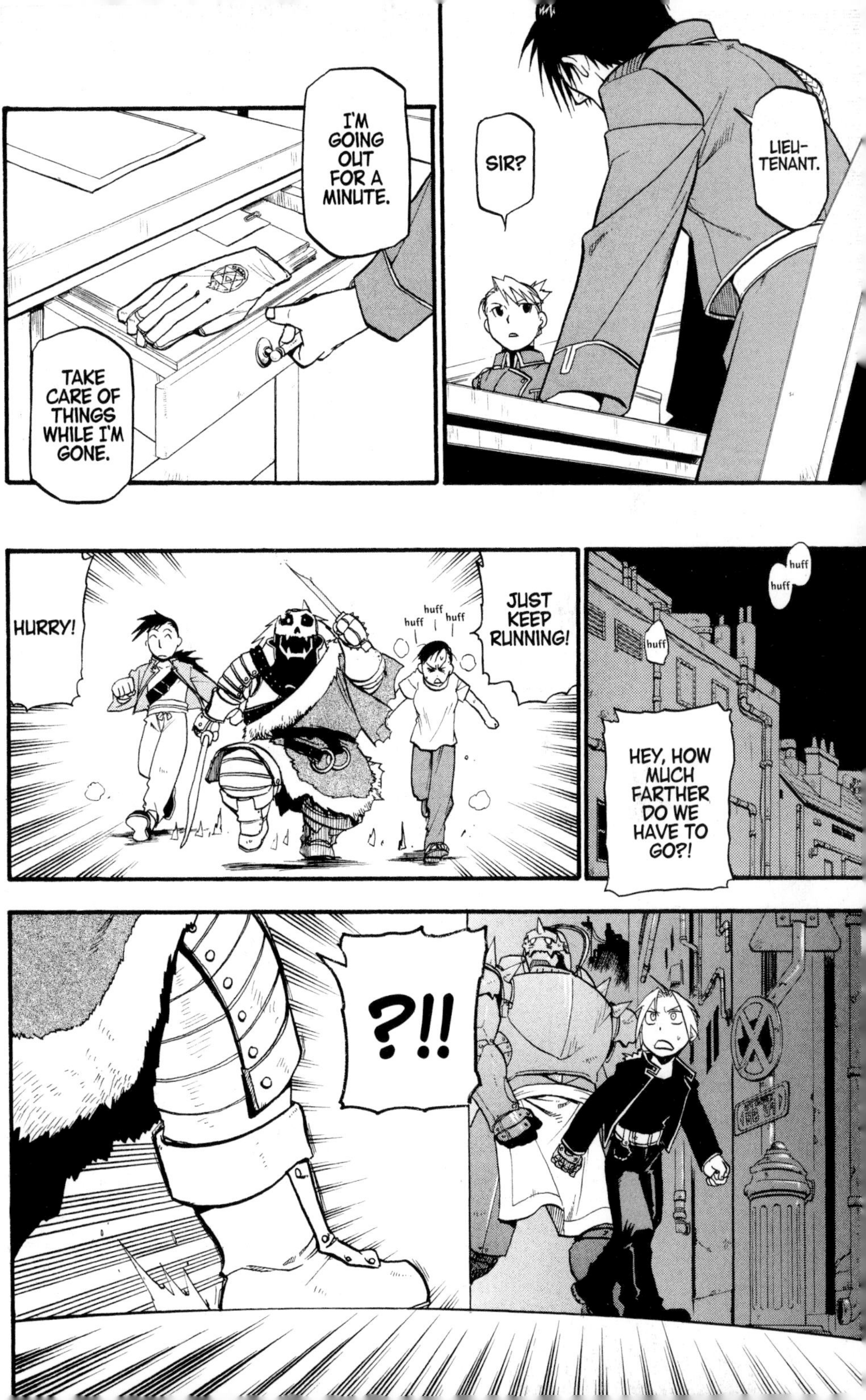
LIEU-TENANT.
SIR?
I'M GOING OUT FOR A MINUTE.
TAKE CARE OF THINGS WHILE I'M GONE.
huff
huff
huff
HEY, HOW MUCH FARTHER DO WE HAVE TO GO?!
JUST KEEP RUNNING!
huff huff huff
HURRY!
?!!

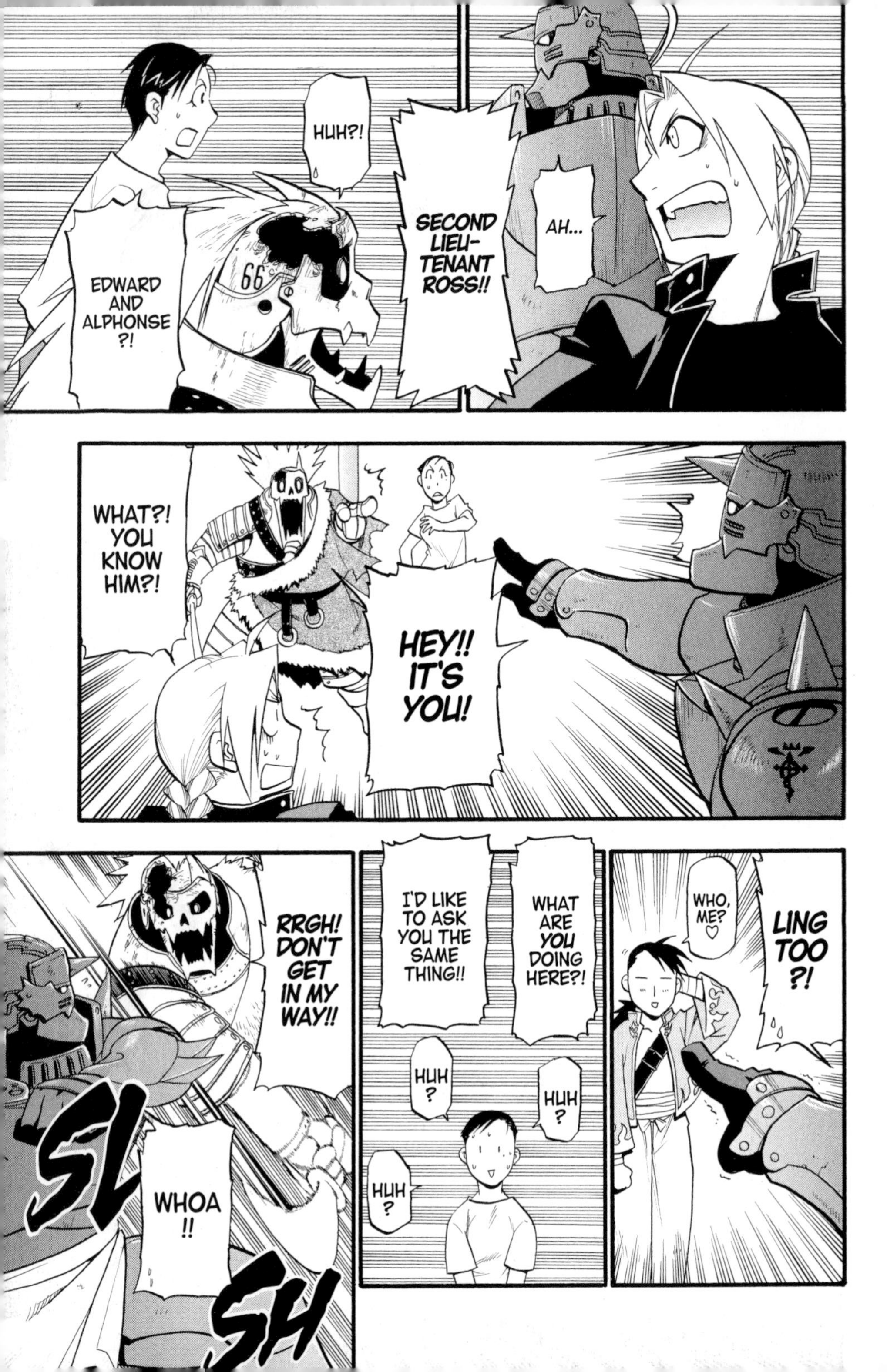
AH...
SECOND LIEUTENANT ROSS!!
HUH?!
EDWARD AND ALPHONSE ?!
HEY!! IT'S YOU!
WHAT?! YOU KNOW HIM?!
LING TOO ?!
WHO, ME? ♡
WHAT ARE YOU DOING HERE?!
I'D LIKE TO ASK YOU THE SAME THING!!
HUH ?
HUH ?
HUH ?
RRGH! DON'T GET IN MY WAY!!
SL
WHOA !!
SH

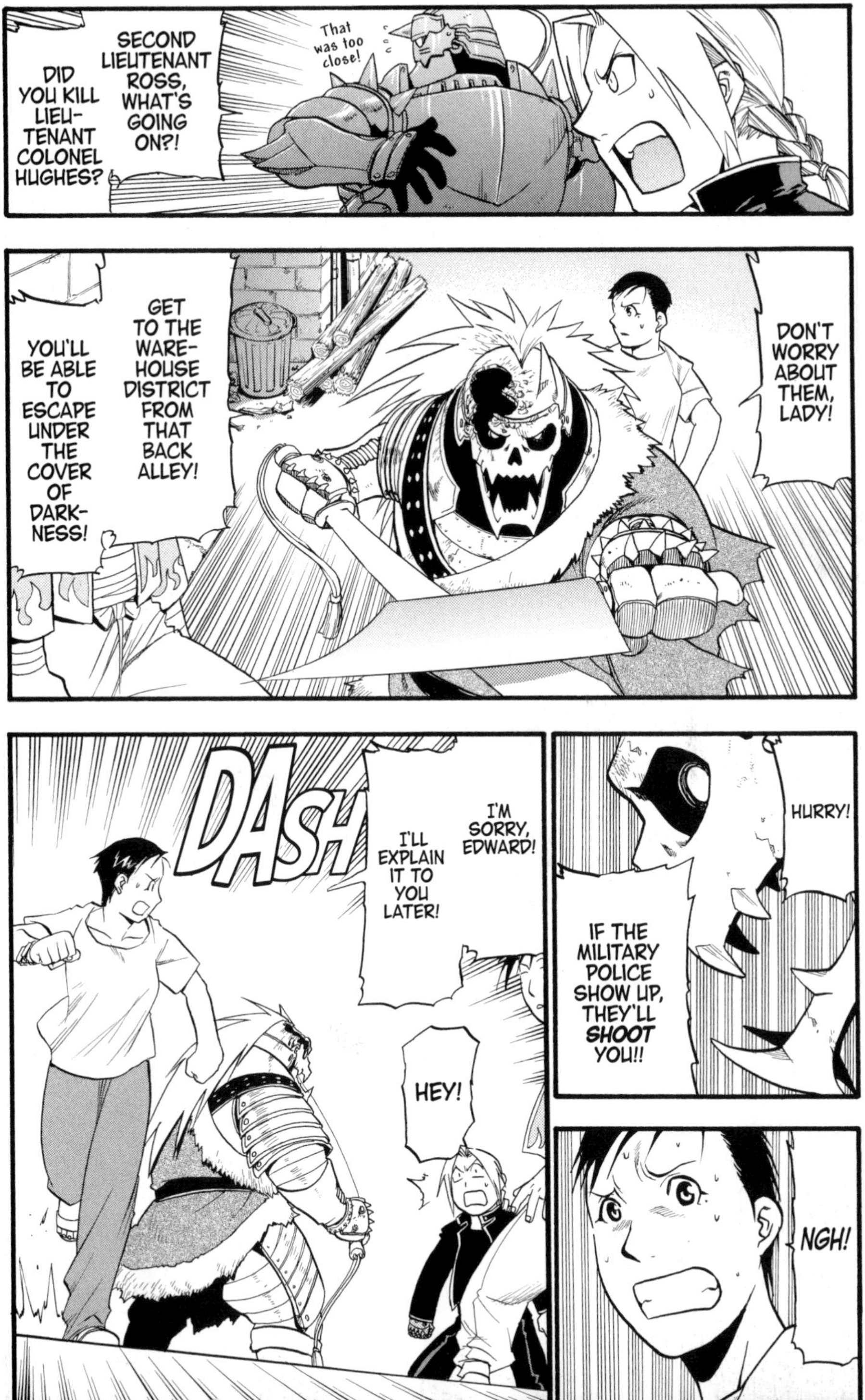
That was too close!
SECOND LIEUTENANT ROSS, WHAT'S GOING ON?!
DID YOU KILL LIEU-TENANT COLONEL HUGHES?
DON'T WORRY ABOUT THEM, LADY!
GET TO THE WARE-HOUSE DISTRICT FROM THAT BACK ALLEY!
YOU'LL BE ABLE TO ESCAPE UNDER THE COVER OF DARK-NESS!
HURRY!
IF THE MILITARY POLICE SHOW UP, THEY'LL SHOOT YOU!!
NGH!
I'M SORRY, EDWARD!
I'LL EXPLAIN IT TO YOU LATER!
DASH
HEY!

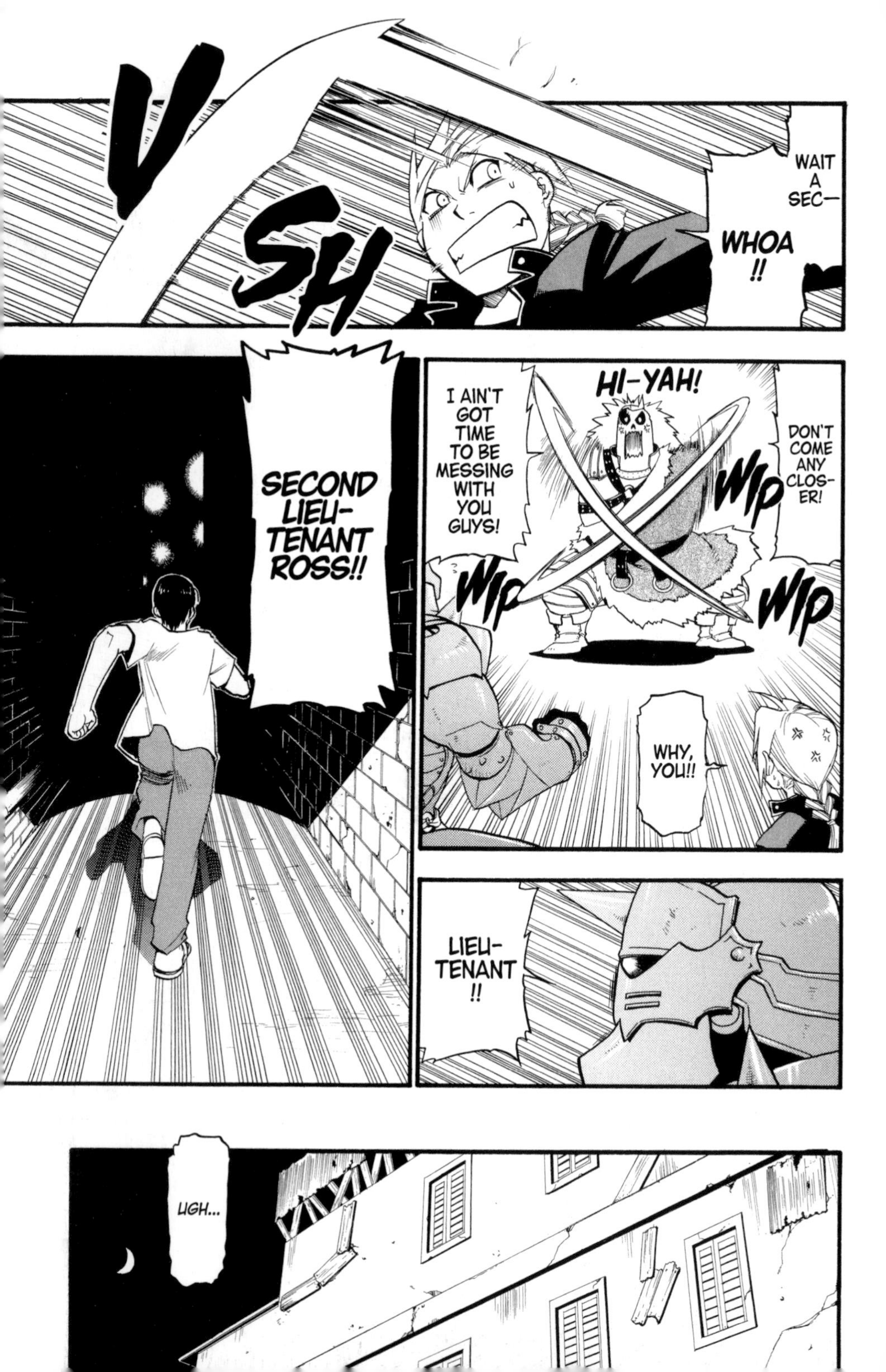
WAIT A SEC—
WHOA !!
VSH
DON'T COME ANY CLOS-ER!
HI-YAH!
I AIN'T GOT TIME TO BE MESSING WITH YOU GUYS!
WIP
WIP
WIP
WHY, YOU!!
LIEU-TENANT !!
SECOND LIEU-TENANT ROSS!!
UGH...

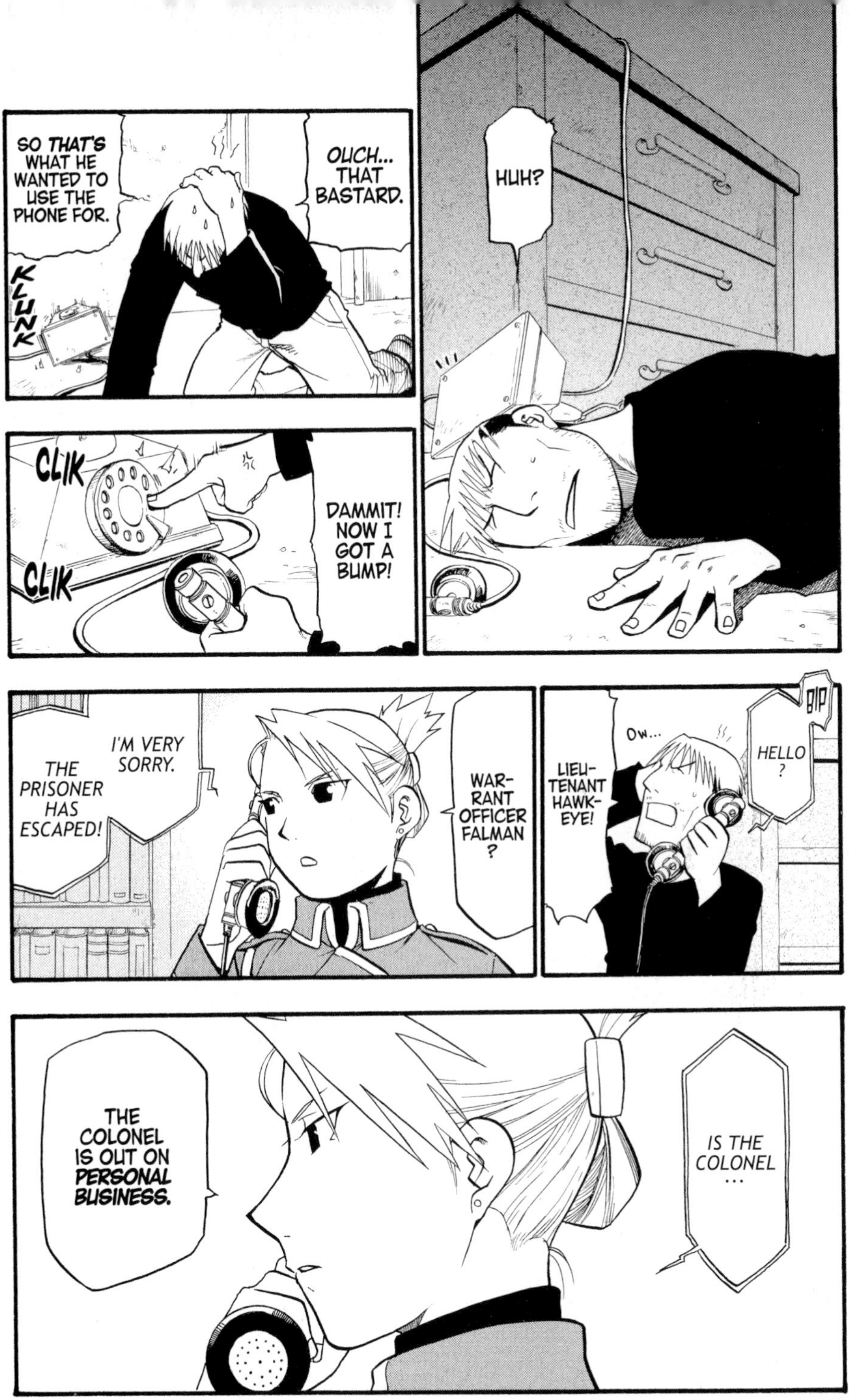
HUH?
OUCH... THAT BASTARD.
SO THAT'S WHAT HE WANTED TO USE THE PHONE FOR.
KLUNK
DAMMIT! NOW I GOT A BUMP!
CLIK
CLIK
BIP
HELLO?
OW...
LIEUTENANT HAWKEYE!
WARRANT OFFICER FALMAN?
I'M VERY SORRY.
THE PRISONER HAS ESCAPED!
IS THE COLONEL...
THE COLONEL IS OUT ON PERSONAL BUSINESS.

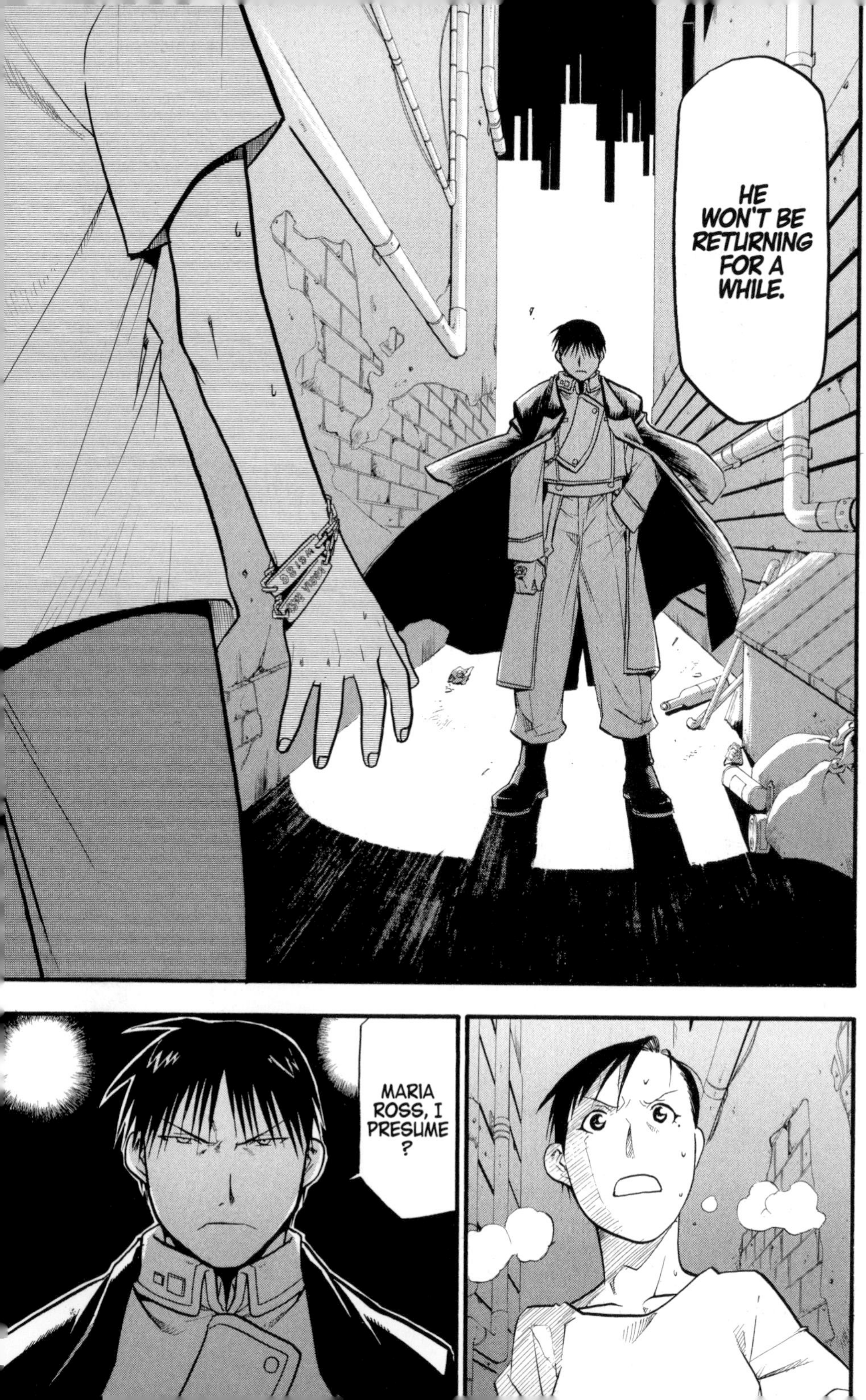
HE WON'T BE RETURNING FOR A WHILE.
MARIA ROSS, I PRESUME?

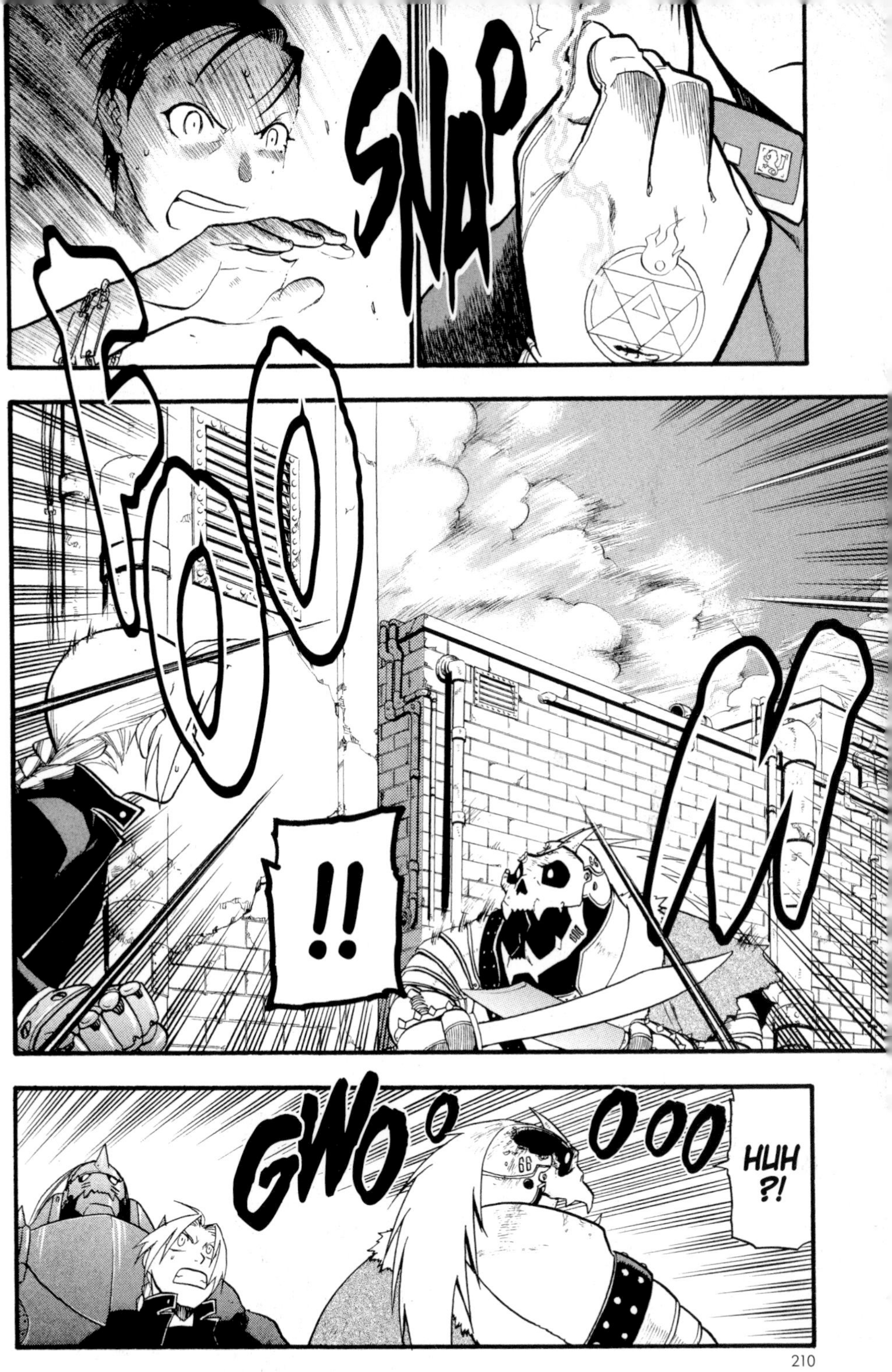
SNAP
FOOM
!!
HUH ?!
GWOOOOO

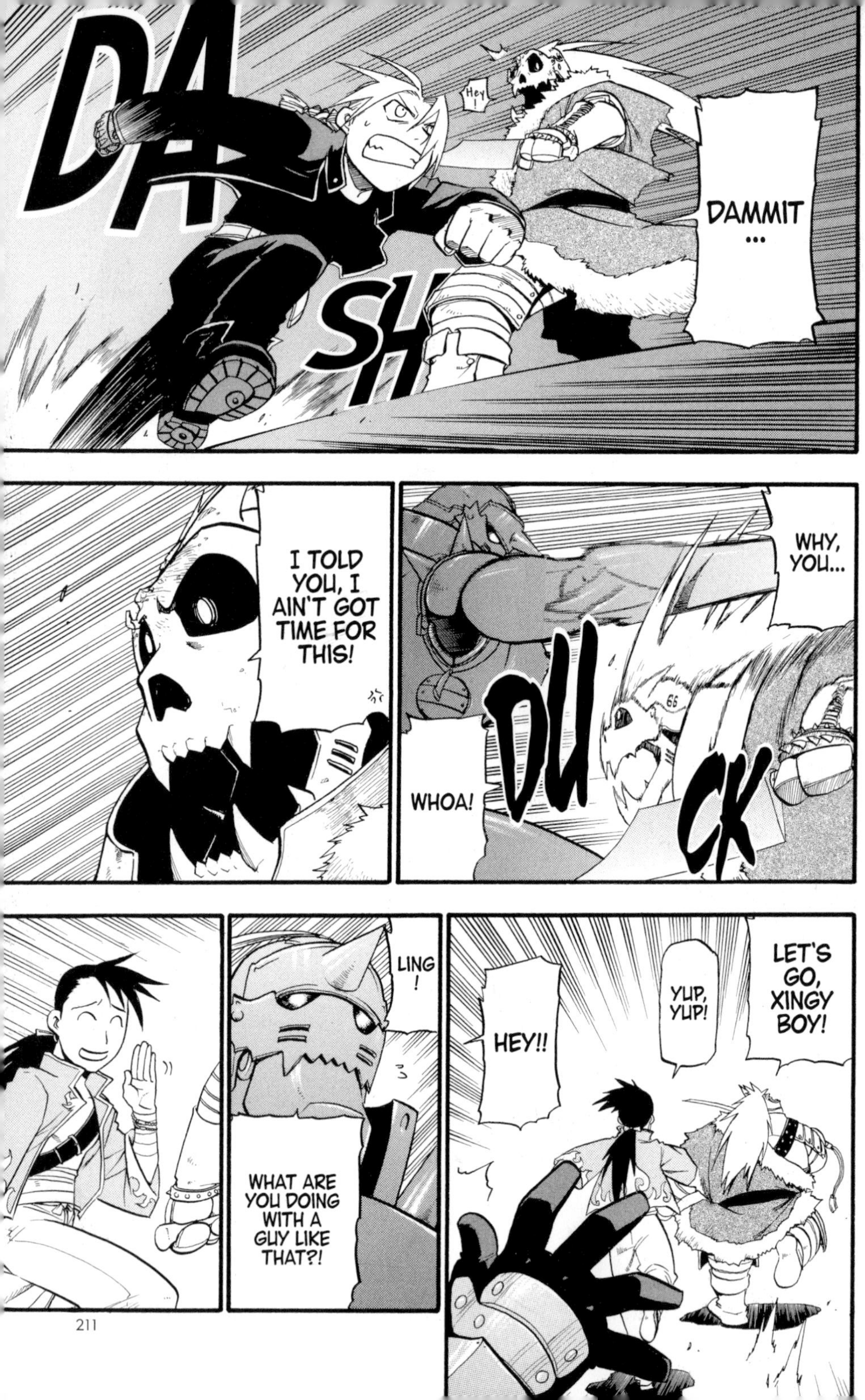
Hey!
DAMMIT...
DA
SH
WHY, YOU...
DU
CK
WHOA!
I TOLD YOU, I AIN'T GOT TIME FOR THIS!
LET'S GO, XINGY BOY!
YUP, YUP!
HEY!!
LING!
WHAT ARE YOU DOING WITH A GUY LIKE THAT?!

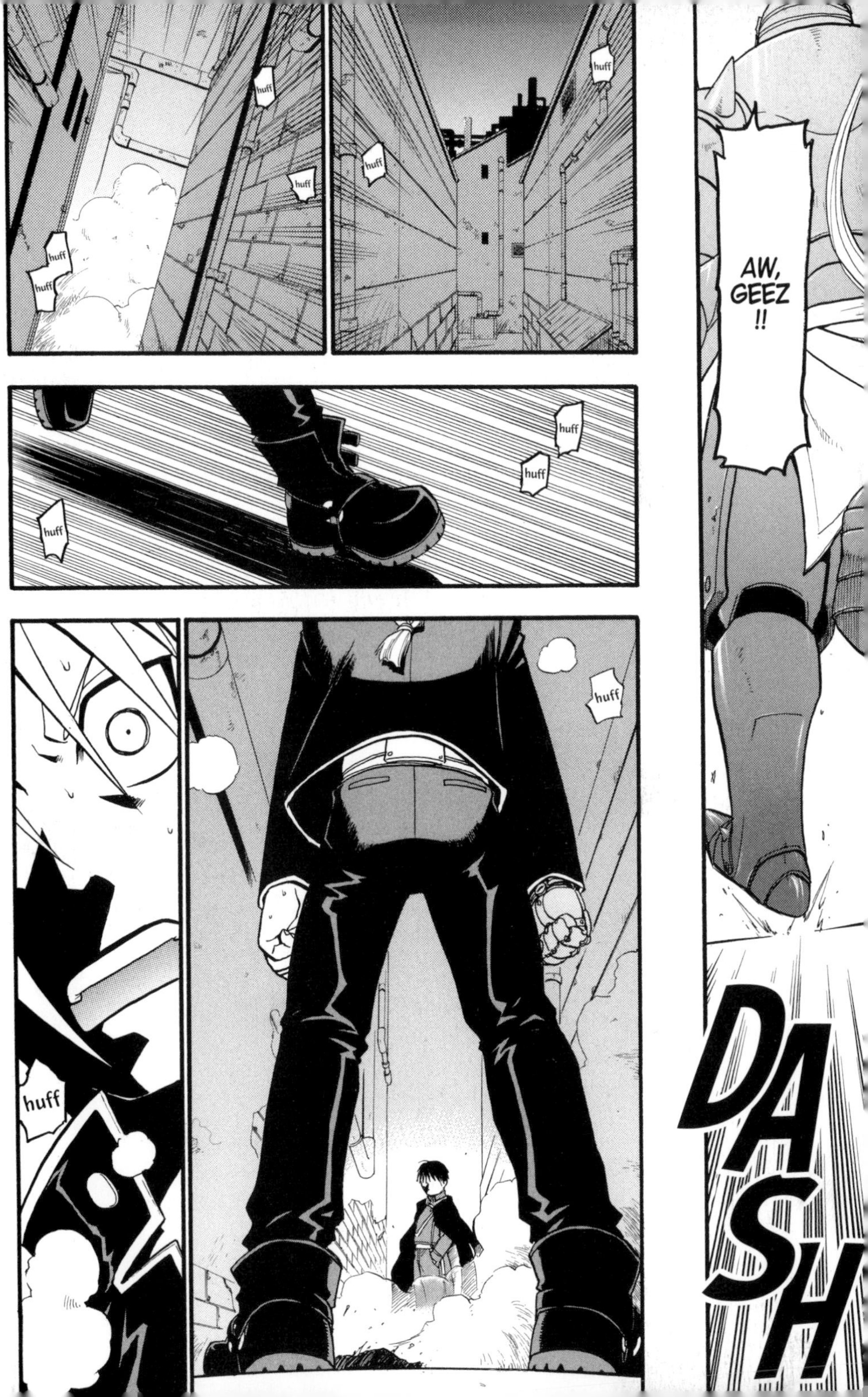
AW, GEEZ !!
DASH
huff
huff
huff
huff
huff
huff
huff
huff
huff
huff
huff
huff

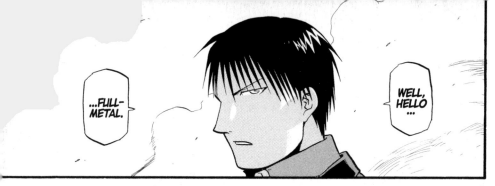

...FULL-
METAL.

WELL,
HELLO
...

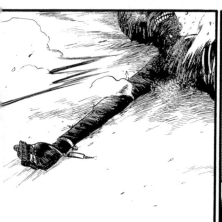

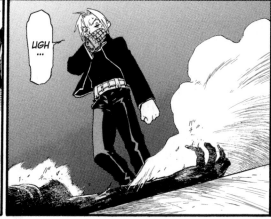

UGH
...

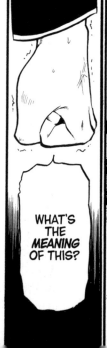

WHAT'S
THE
MEANING
OF THIS?

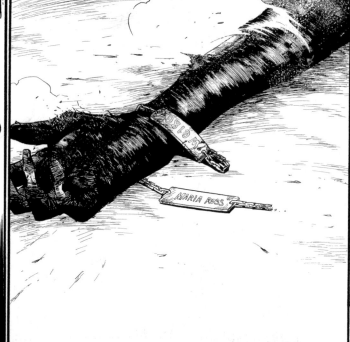

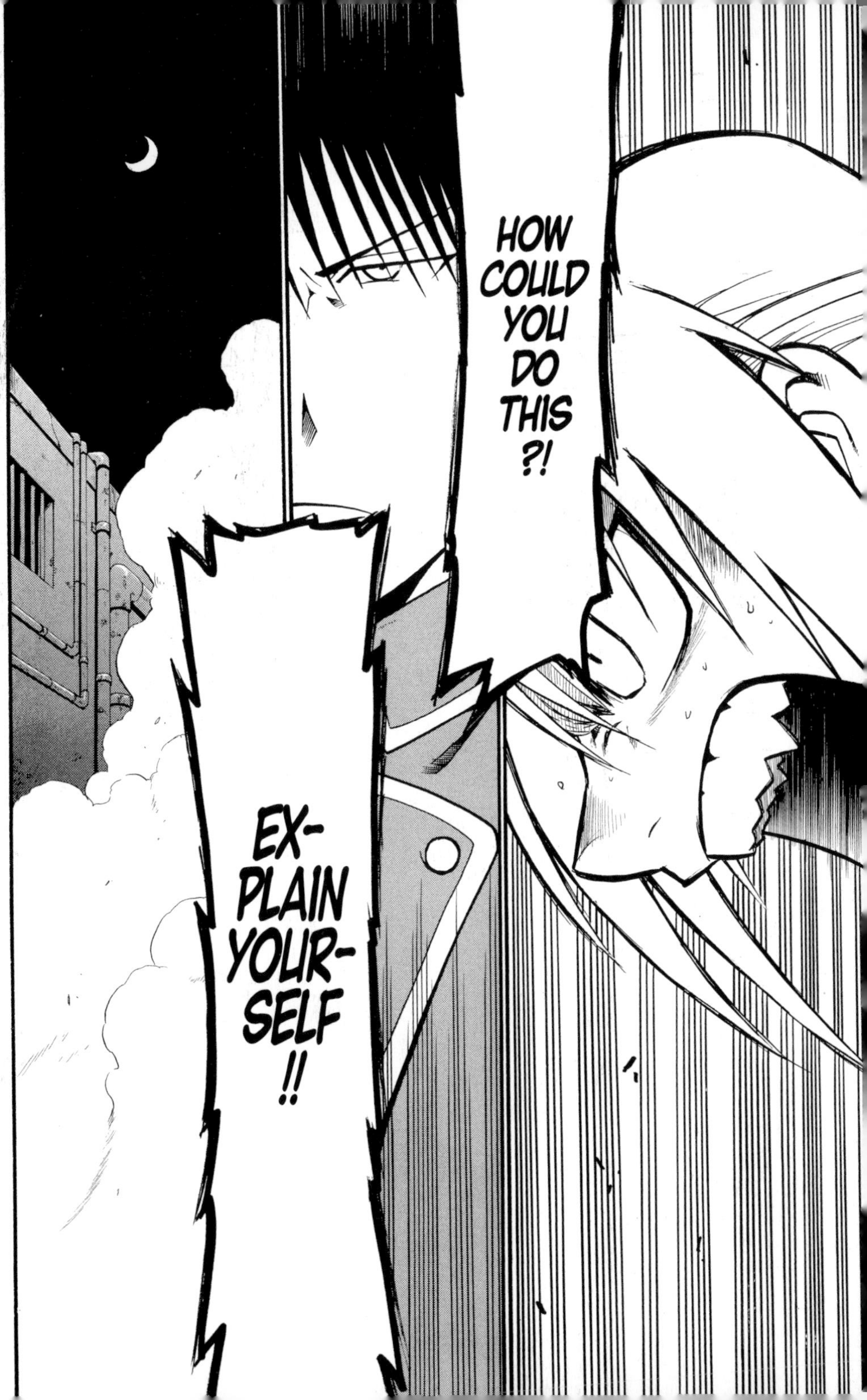
HOW COULD YOU DO THIS?!
EX-PLAIN YOUR-SELF!!

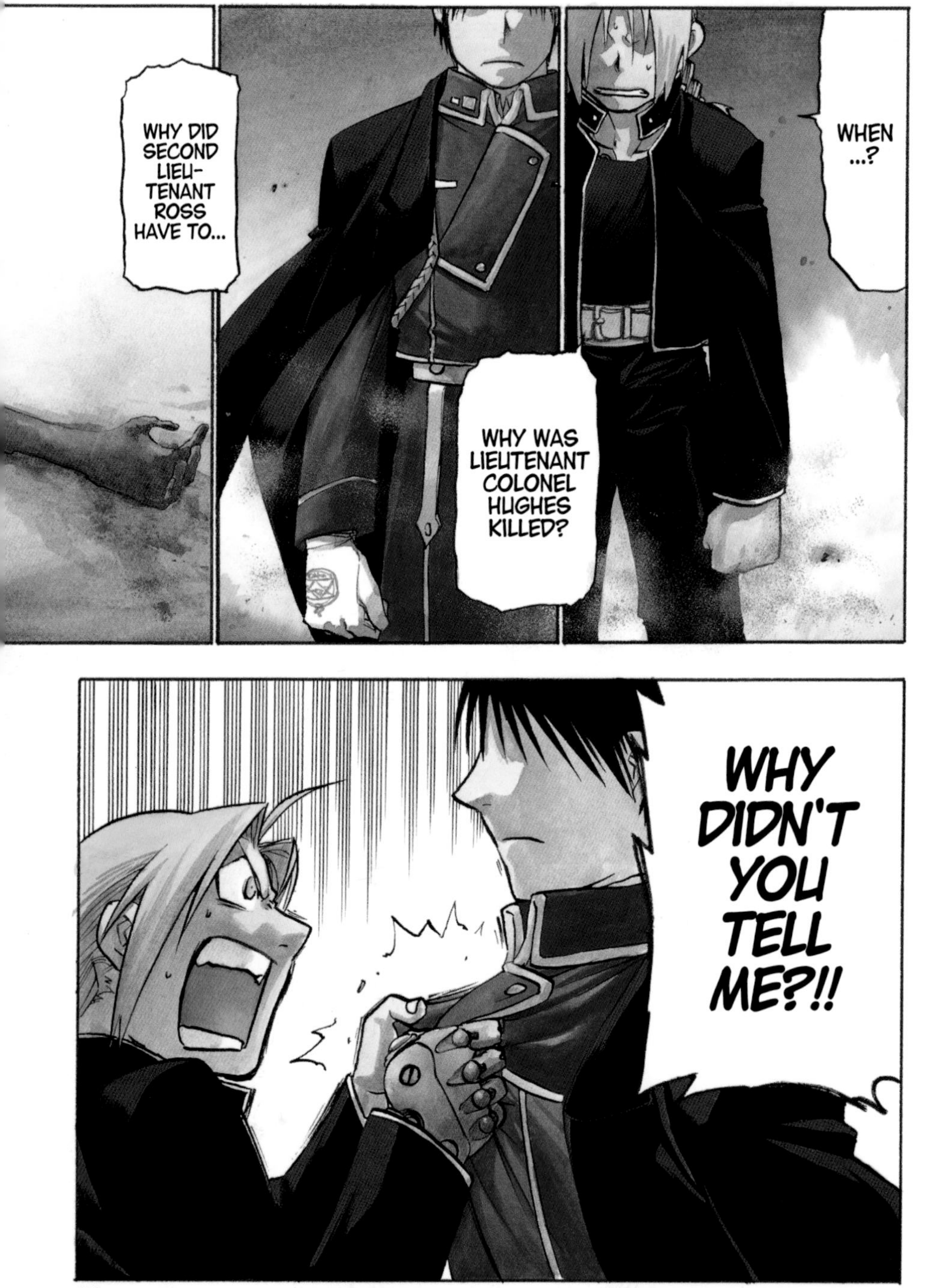
WHEN ...?
WHY DID SECOND LIEU-TENANT ROSS HAVE TO...
WHY WAS LIEUTENANT COLONEL HUGHES KILLED?
WHY DIDN'T YOU TELL ME?!!

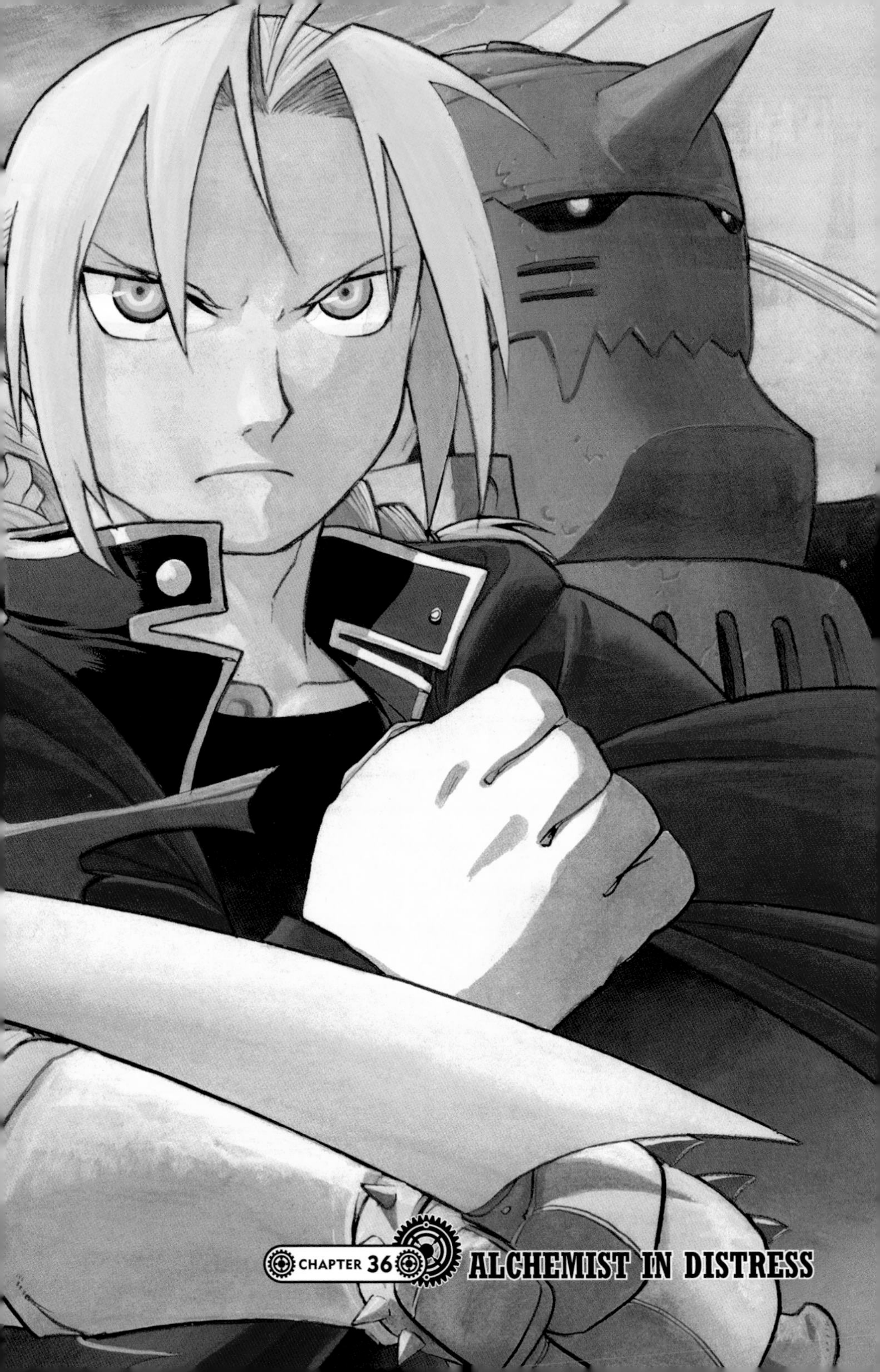
CHAPTER 36
ALCHEMIST IN DISTRESS

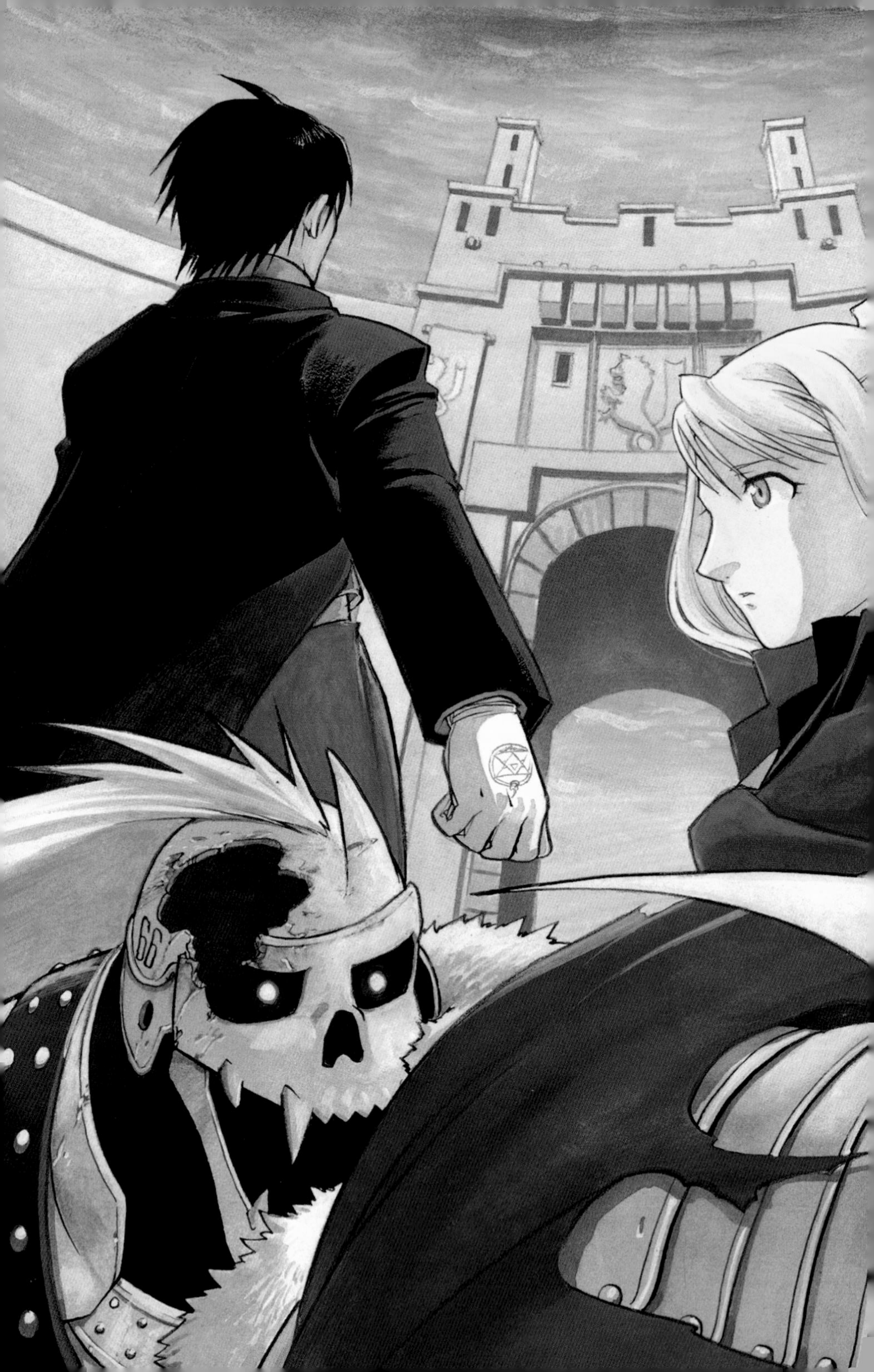
66

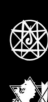

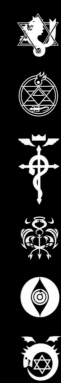

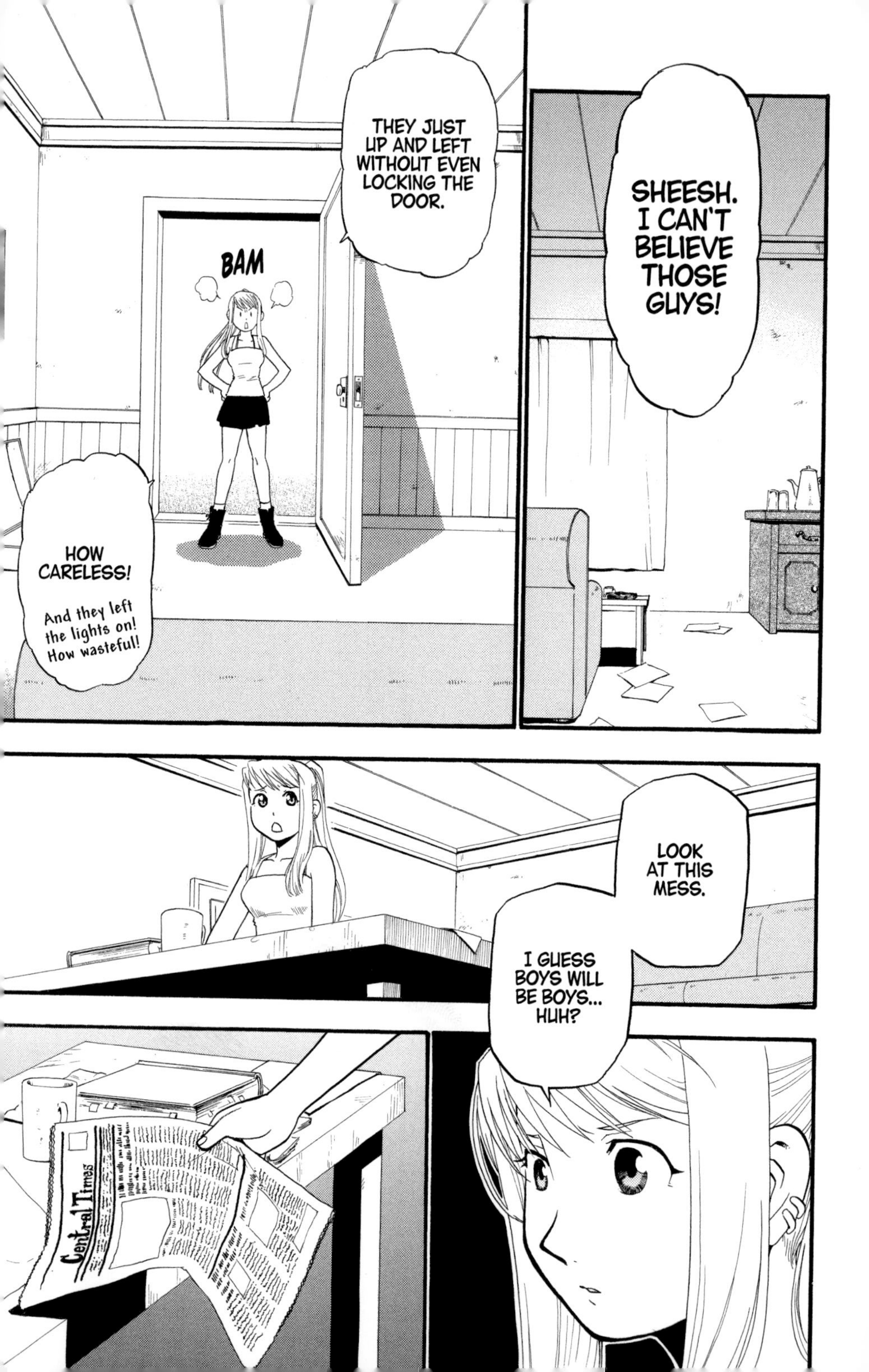
SHEESH. I CAN'T BELIEVE THOSE GUYS!
THEY JUST UP AND LEFT WITHOUT EVEN LOCKING THE DOOR.
BAM
HOW CARELESS!
And they left the lights on! How wasteful!
LOOK AT THIS MESS.
I GUESS BOYS WILL BE BOYS... HUH?
Central Times

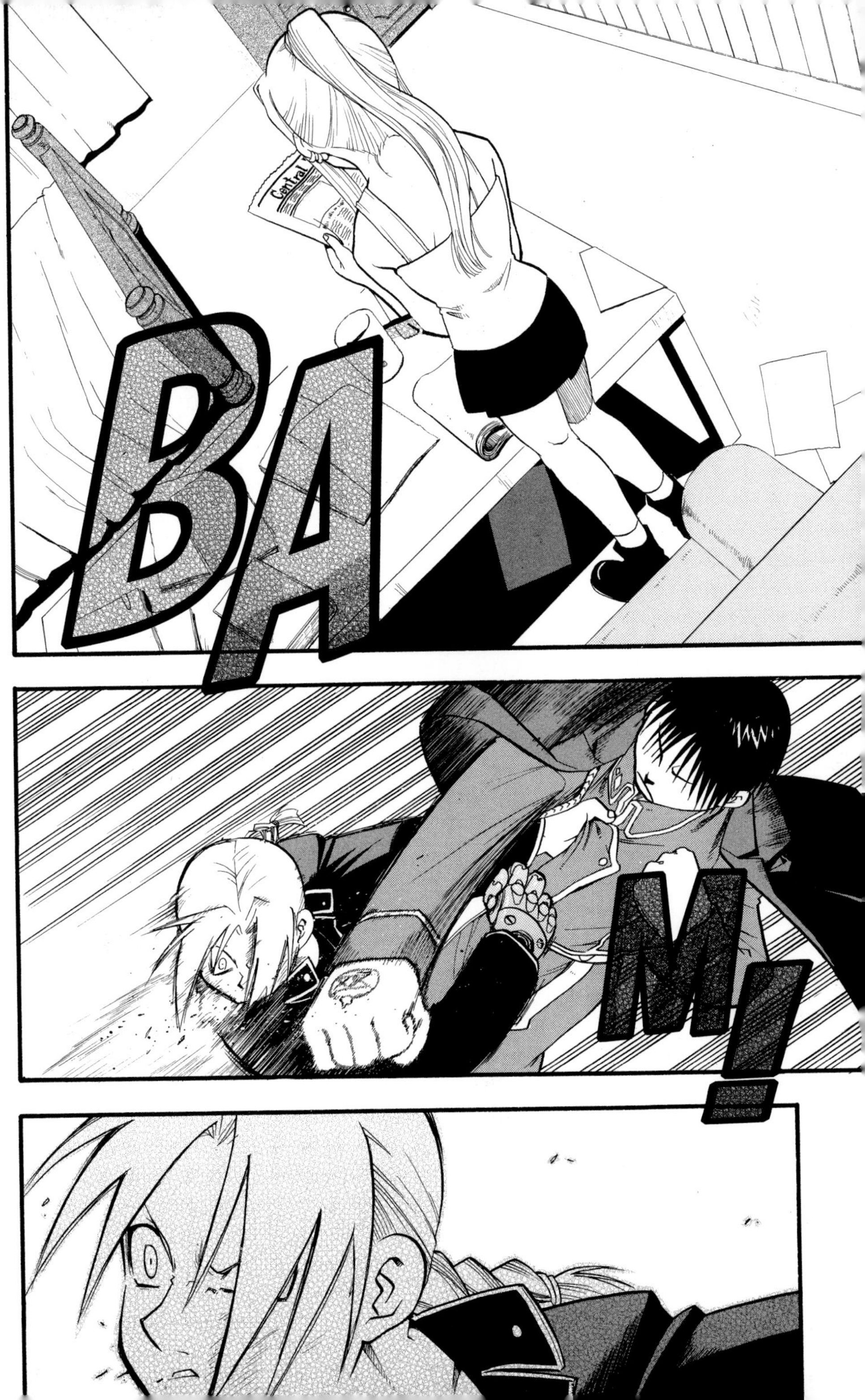
Central
BA
M!

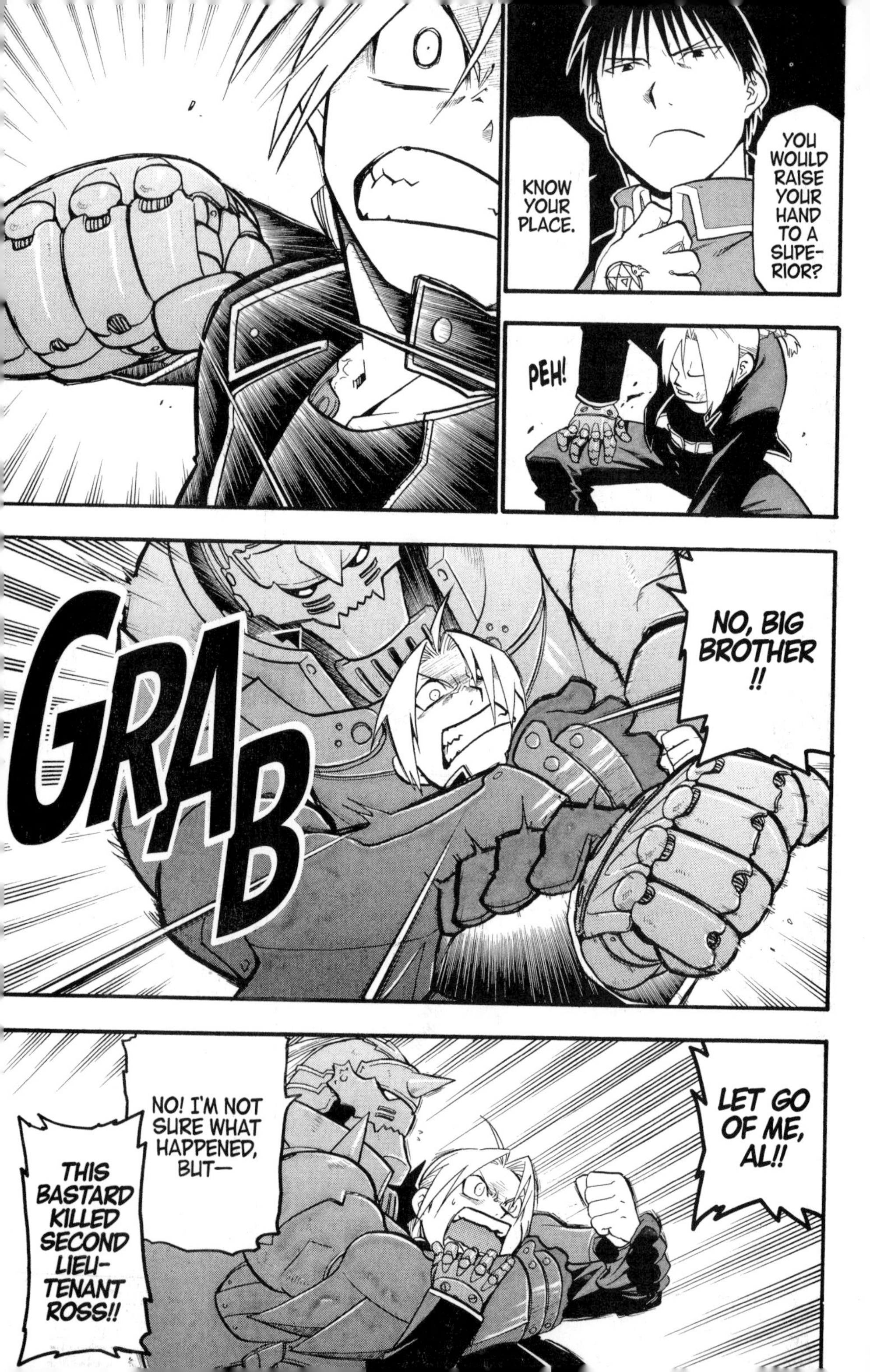

YOU WOULD RAISE YOUR HAND TO A SUPE-RIOR?
KNOW YOUR PLACE.
PEH!
NO, BIG BROTHER !!
GRAB
LET GO OF ME, AL!!
NO! I'M NOT SURE WHAT HAPPENED, BUT—
THIS BASTARD KILLED SECOND LIEU-TENANT ROSS!!

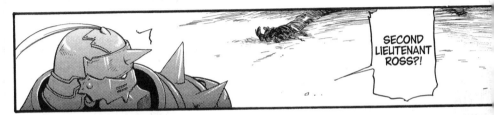

SECOND LIEUTENANT ROSS?!
WHAT'S THE MEANING OF THIS, COLONEL?
MARIA ROSS WAS CONVICTED OF MURDERING HUGHES. WHEN SHE ESCAPED FROM PRISON, OUR ORDERS WERE SHOOT TO KILL.
THERE'S NOTHING MORE TO SAY.
THAT DOESN'T EXPLAIN ANYTHING!!
I APOLOGIZE FOR KEEPING HUGHES'S DEATH A SECRET.
What is that?
Aah!!
WEEOO

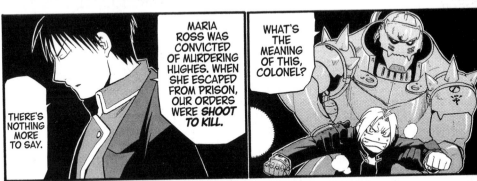

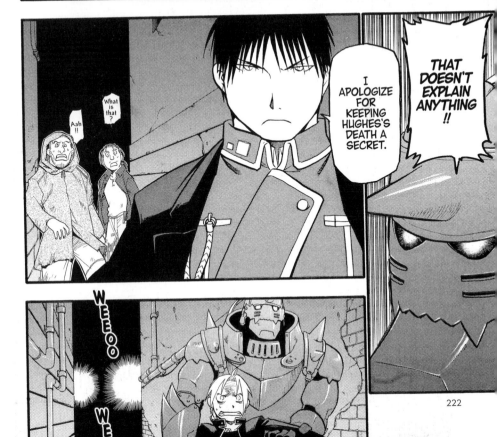

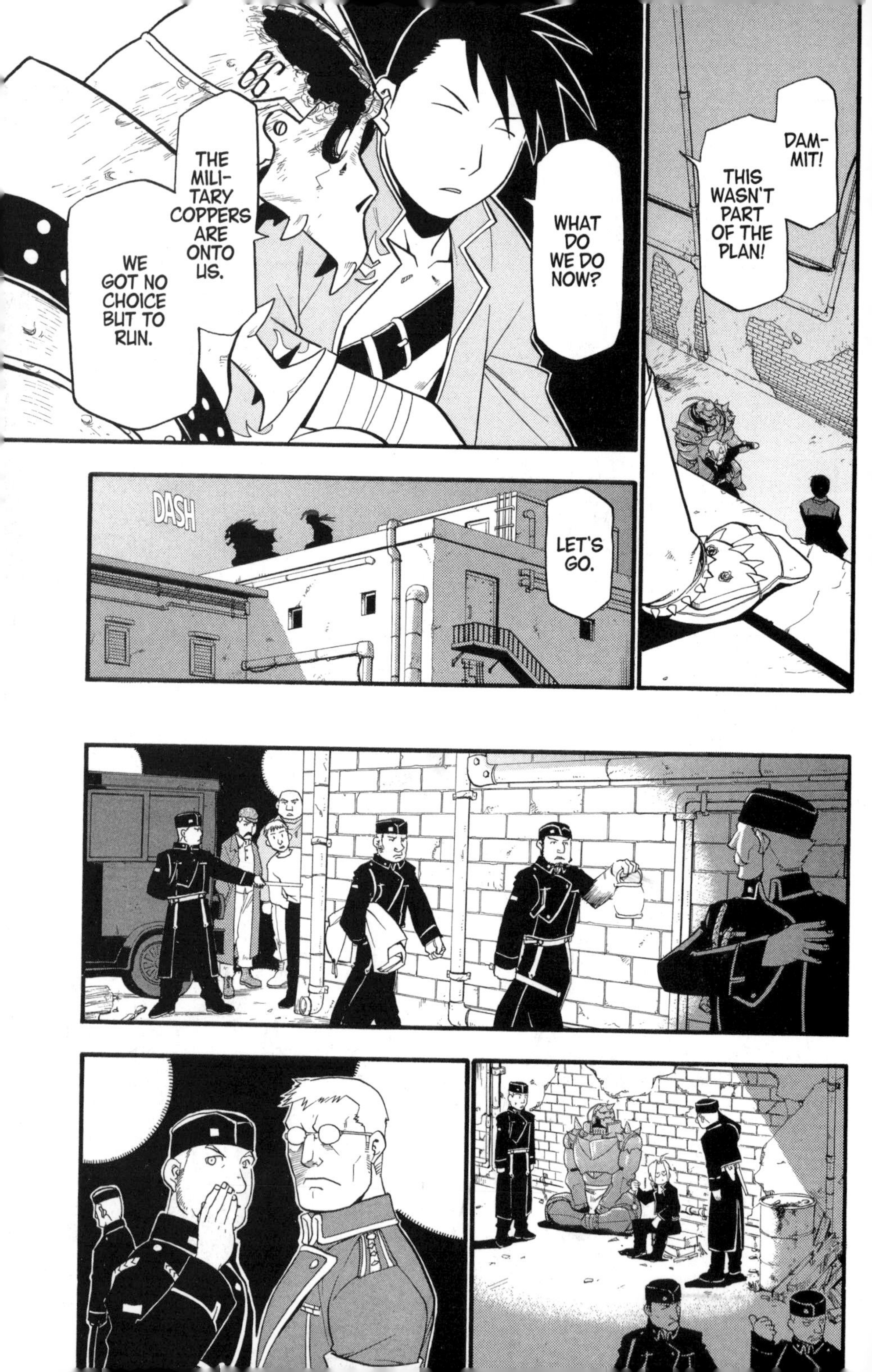
DAM-MIT!
THIS WASN'T PART OF THE PLAN!
WHAT DO WE DO NOW?
THE MILITARY COPPERS ARE ONTO US.
WE GOT NO CHOICE BUT TO RUN.
LET'S GO.
DASH

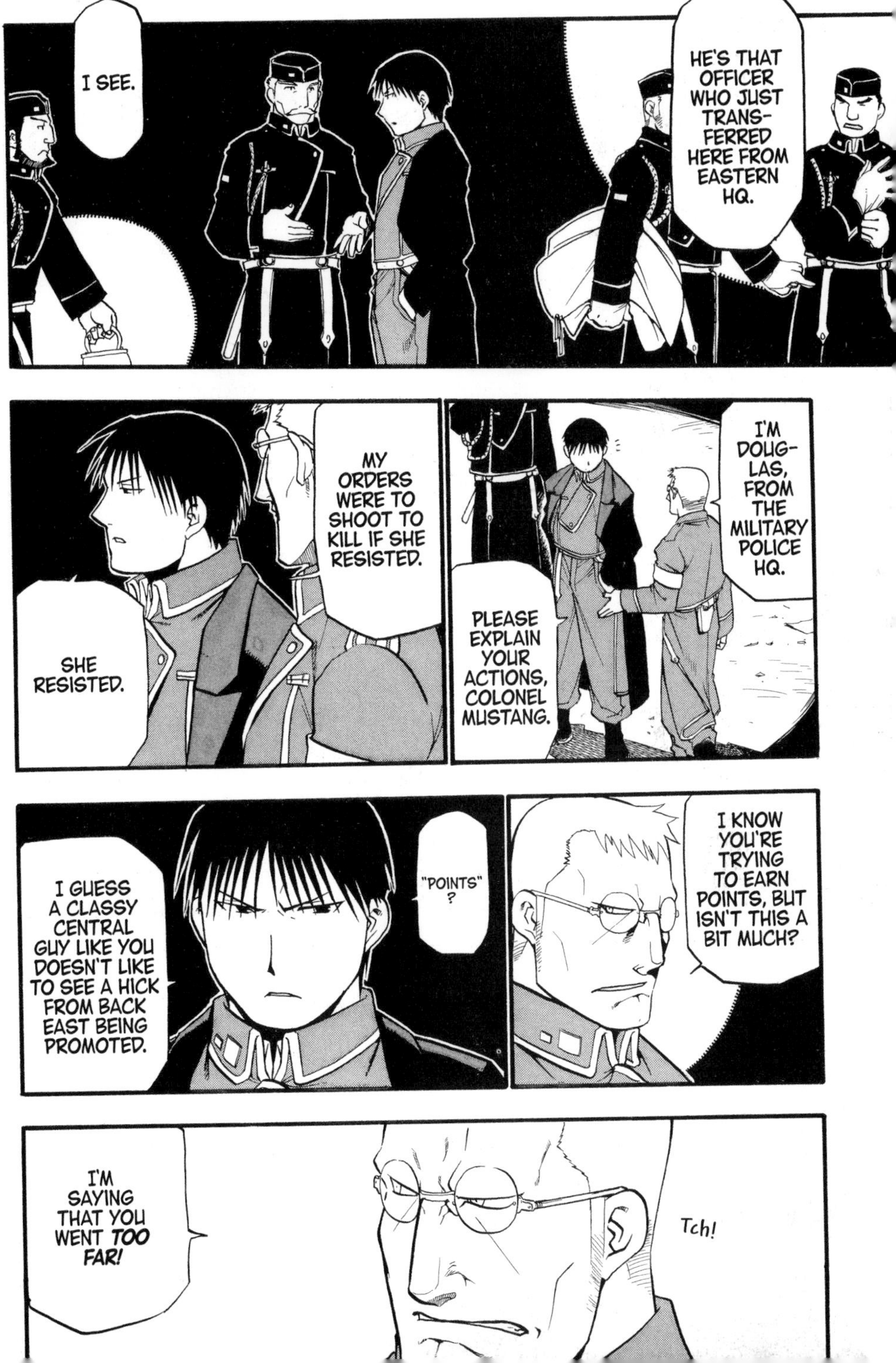
HE'S THAT OFFICER WHO JUST TRANS-FERRED HERE FROM EASTERN HQ.
I SEE.
I'M DOUG-LAS, FROM THE MILITARY POLICE HQ.
PLEASE EXPLAIN YOUR ACTIONS, COLONEL MUSTANG.
MY ORDERS WERE TO SHOOT TO KILL IF SHE RESISTED.
SHE RESISTED.
I KNOW YOU'RE TRYING TO EARN POINTS, BUT ISN'T THIS A BIT MUCH?
"POINTS"?
I GUESS A CLASSY CENTRAL GUY LIKE YOU DOESN'T LIKE TO SEE A HICK FROM BACK EAST BEING PROMOTED.
Tch!
I'M SAYING THAT YOU WENT ***TOO FAR!***

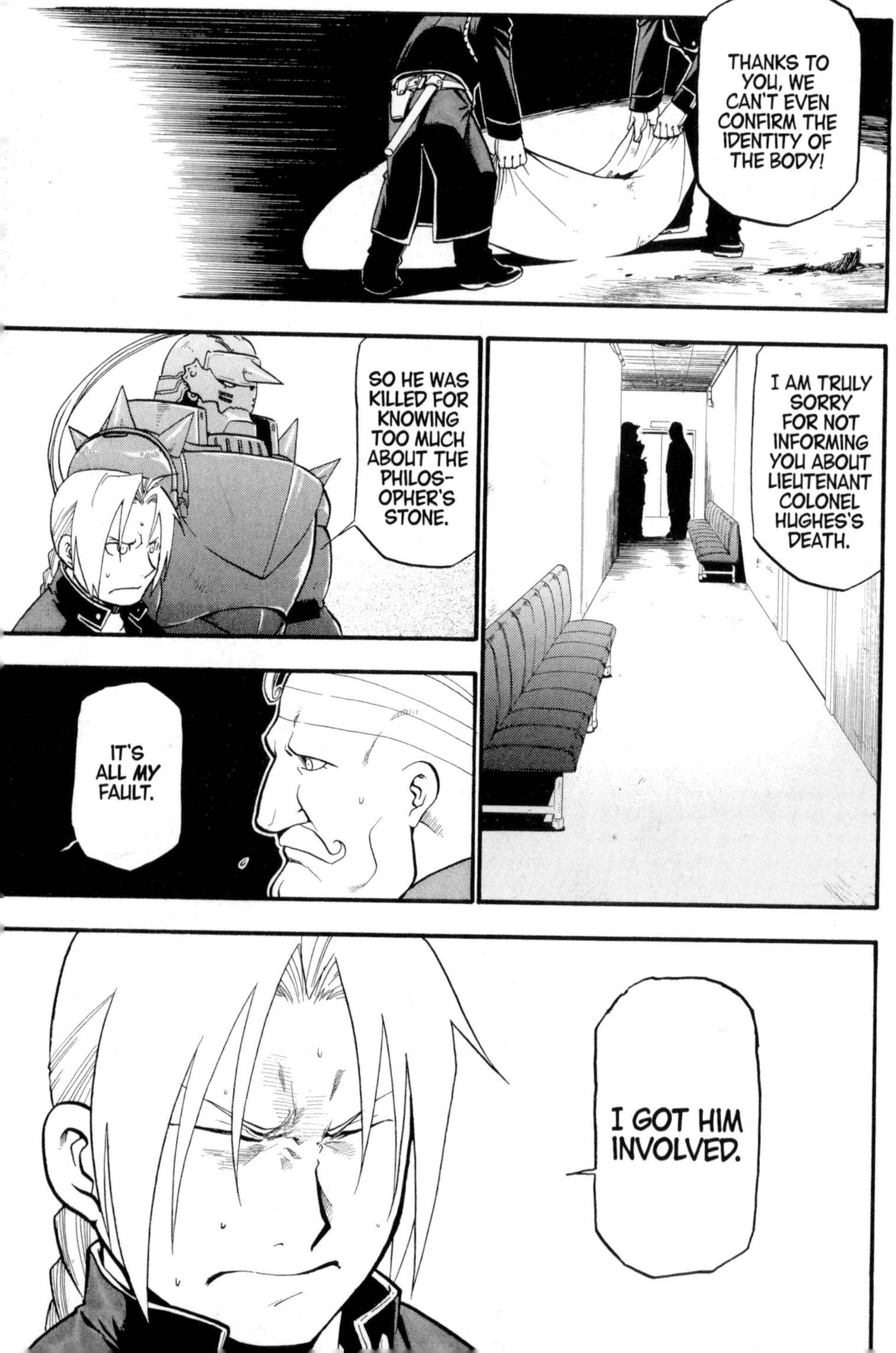
THANKS TO YOU, WE CAN'T EVEN CONFIRM THE IDENTITY OF THE BODY!
I AM TRULY SORRY FOR NOT INFORMING YOU ABOUT LIEUTENANT COLONEL HUGHES'S DEATH.
SO HE WAS KILLED FOR KNOWING TOO MUCH ABOUT THE PHILOS-OPHER'S STONE.
IT'S ALL MY FAULT.
I GOT HIM INVOLVED.

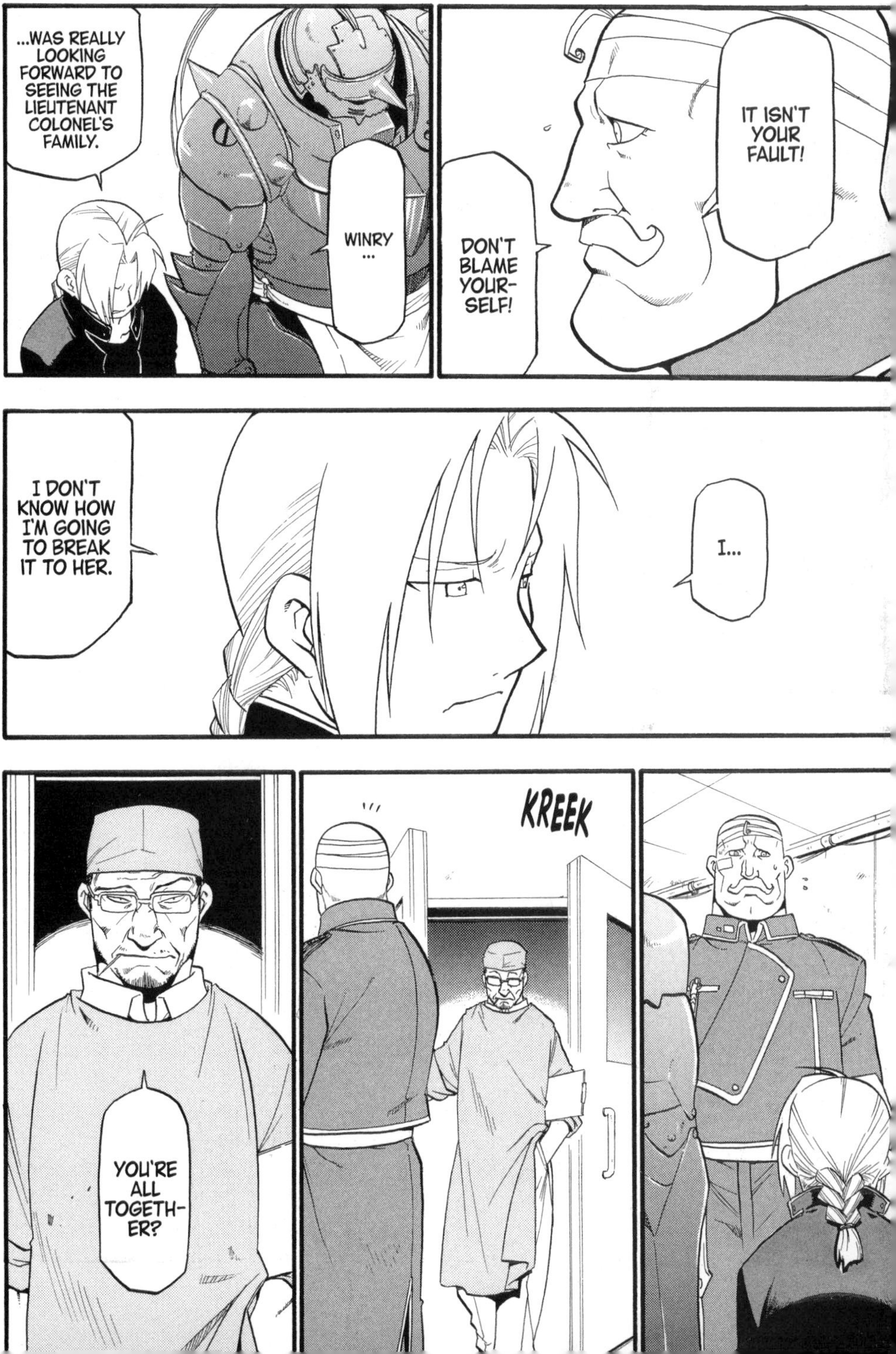
IT ISN'T YOUR FAULT!
DON'T BLAME YOUR-SELF!
WINRY ...
...WAS REALLY LOOKING FORWARD TO SEEING THE LIEUTENANT COLONEL'S FAMILY.
I...
I DON'T KNOW HOW I'M GOING TO BREAK IT TO HER.
KREEK
YOU'RE ALL TOGETH-ER?

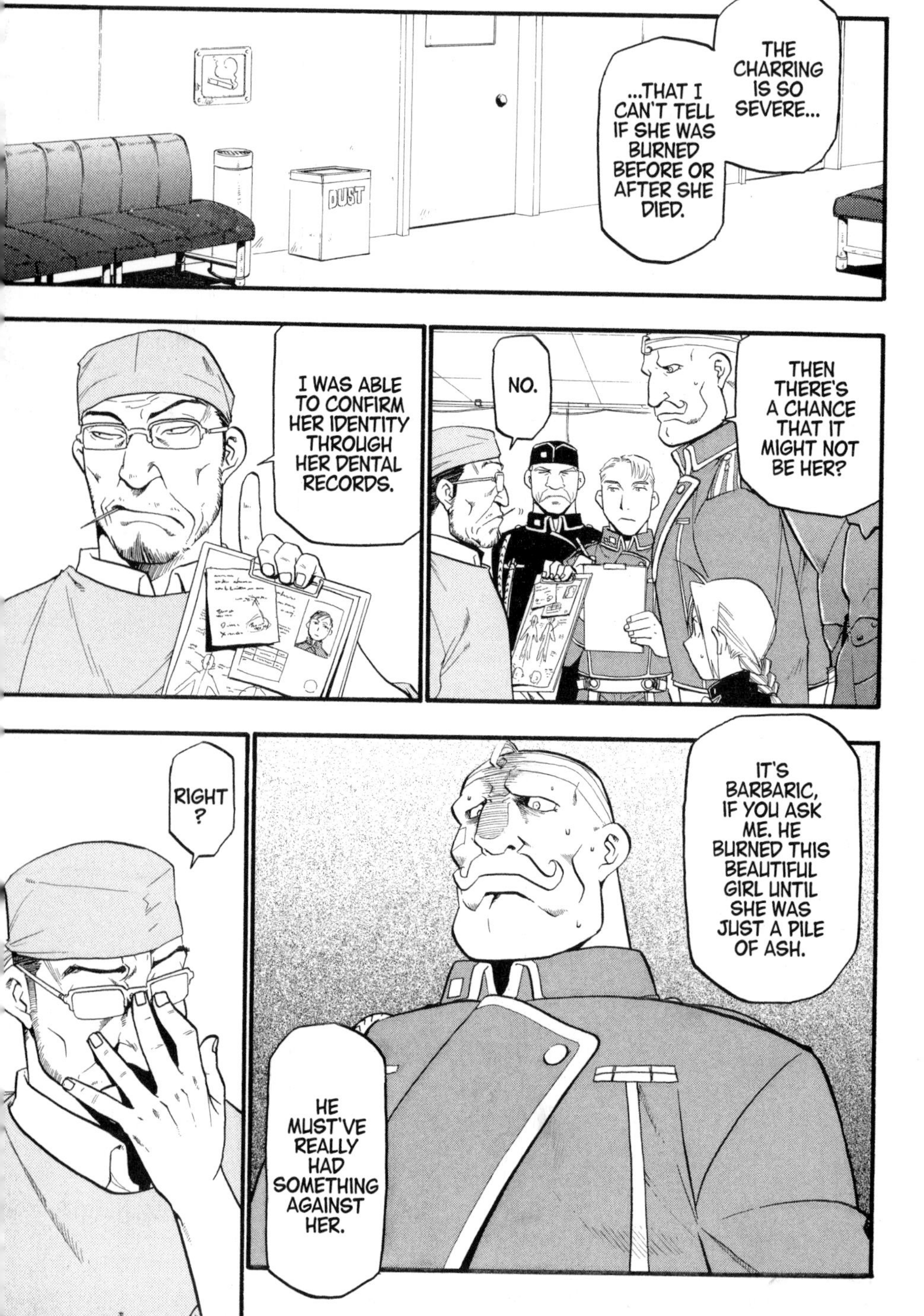
THE CHARRING IS SO SEVERE...
...THAT I CAN'T TELL IF SHE WAS BURNED BEFORE OR AFTER SHE DIED.
DUST
THEN THERE'S A CHANCE THAT IT MIGHT NOT BE HER?
NO.
I WAS ABLE TO CONFIRM HER IDENTITY THROUGH HER DENTAL RECORDS.
IT'S BARBARIC, IF YOU ASK ME. HE BURNED THIS BEAUTIFUL GIRL UNTIL SHE WAS JUST A PILE OF ASH.
HE MUST'VE REALLY HAD SOMETHING AGAINST HER.
RIGHT?

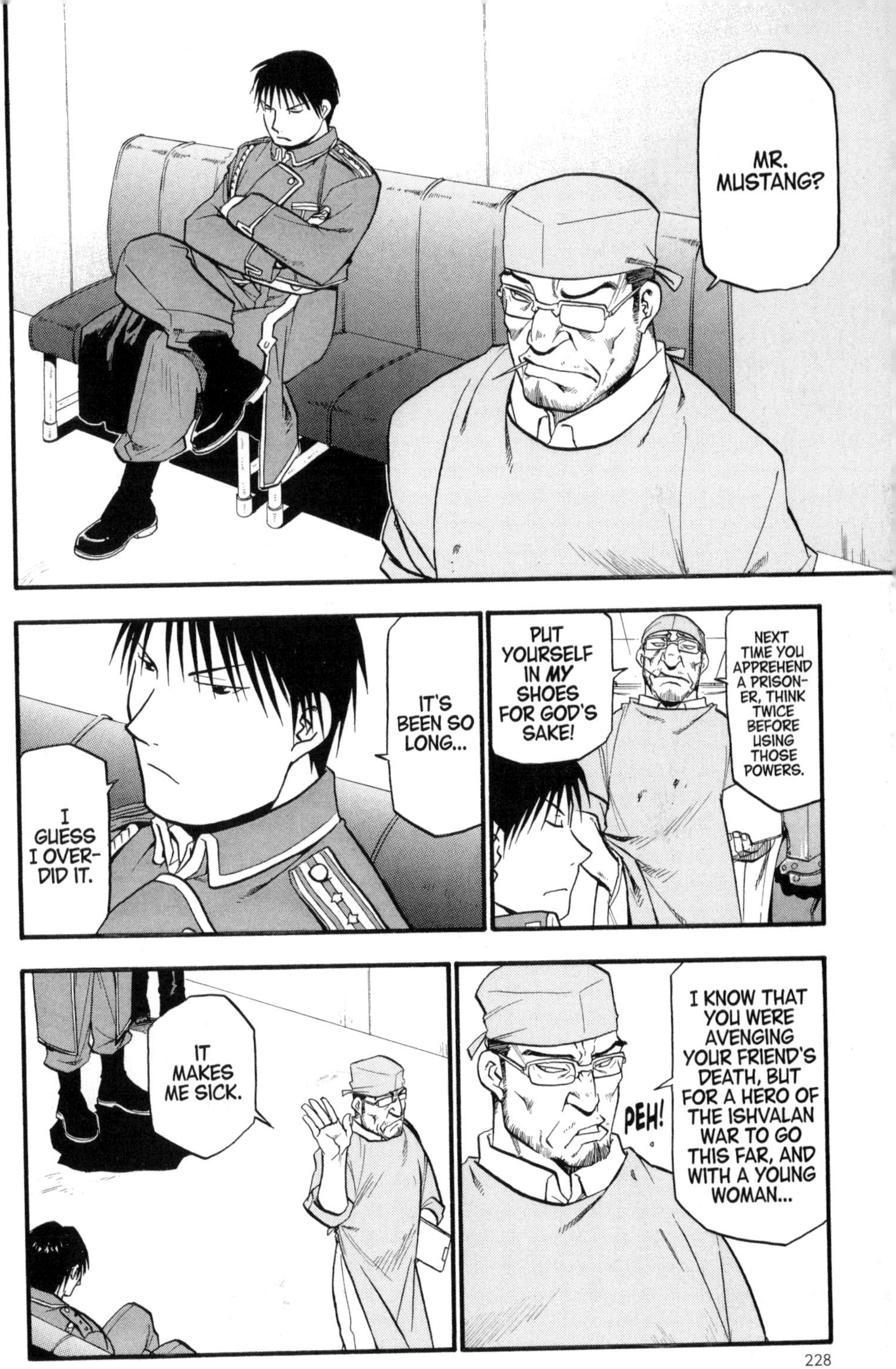
MR. MUSTANG?
NEXT TIME YOU APPREHEND A PRISONER, THINK TWICE BEFORE USING THOSE POWERS.
PUT YOURSELF IN MY SHOES FOR GOD'S SAKE!
IT'S BEEN SO LONG...
I GUESS I OVERDID IT.
I KNOW THAT YOU WERE AVENGING YOUR FRIEND'S DEATH, BUT FOR A HERO OF THE ISHVALAN WAR TO GO THIS FAR, AND WITH A YOUNG WOMAN...
PEH!
IT MAKES ME SICK.

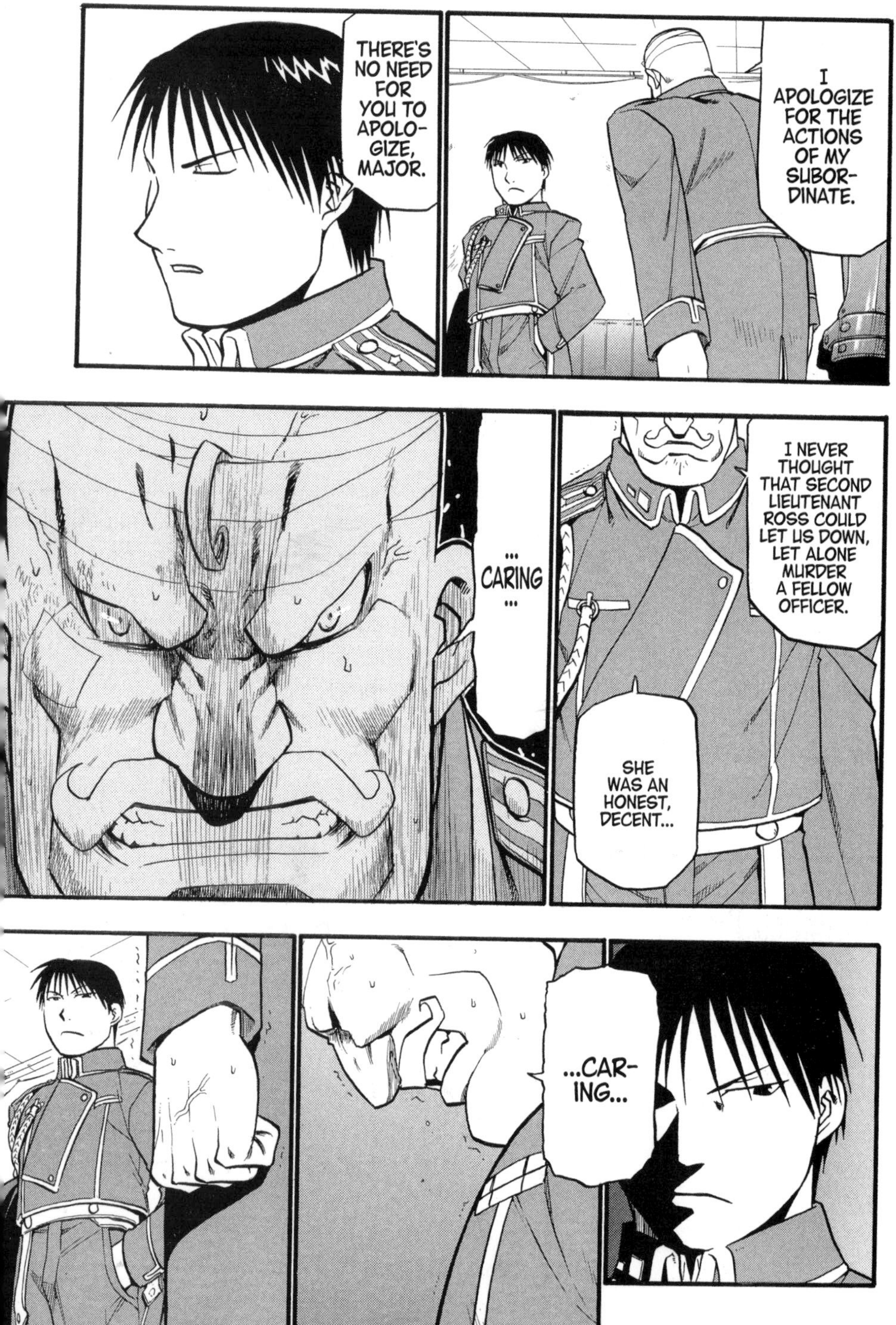
I APOLOGIZE FOR THE ACTIONS OF MY SUBOR-DINATE.
THERE'S NO NEED FOR YOU TO APOLO-GIZE, MAJOR.
I NEVER THOUGHT THAT SECOND LIEUTENANT ROSS COULD LET US DOWN, LET ALONE MURDER A FELLOW OFFICER.
SHE WAS AN HONEST, DECENT...
...CARING...
...CAR-ING...

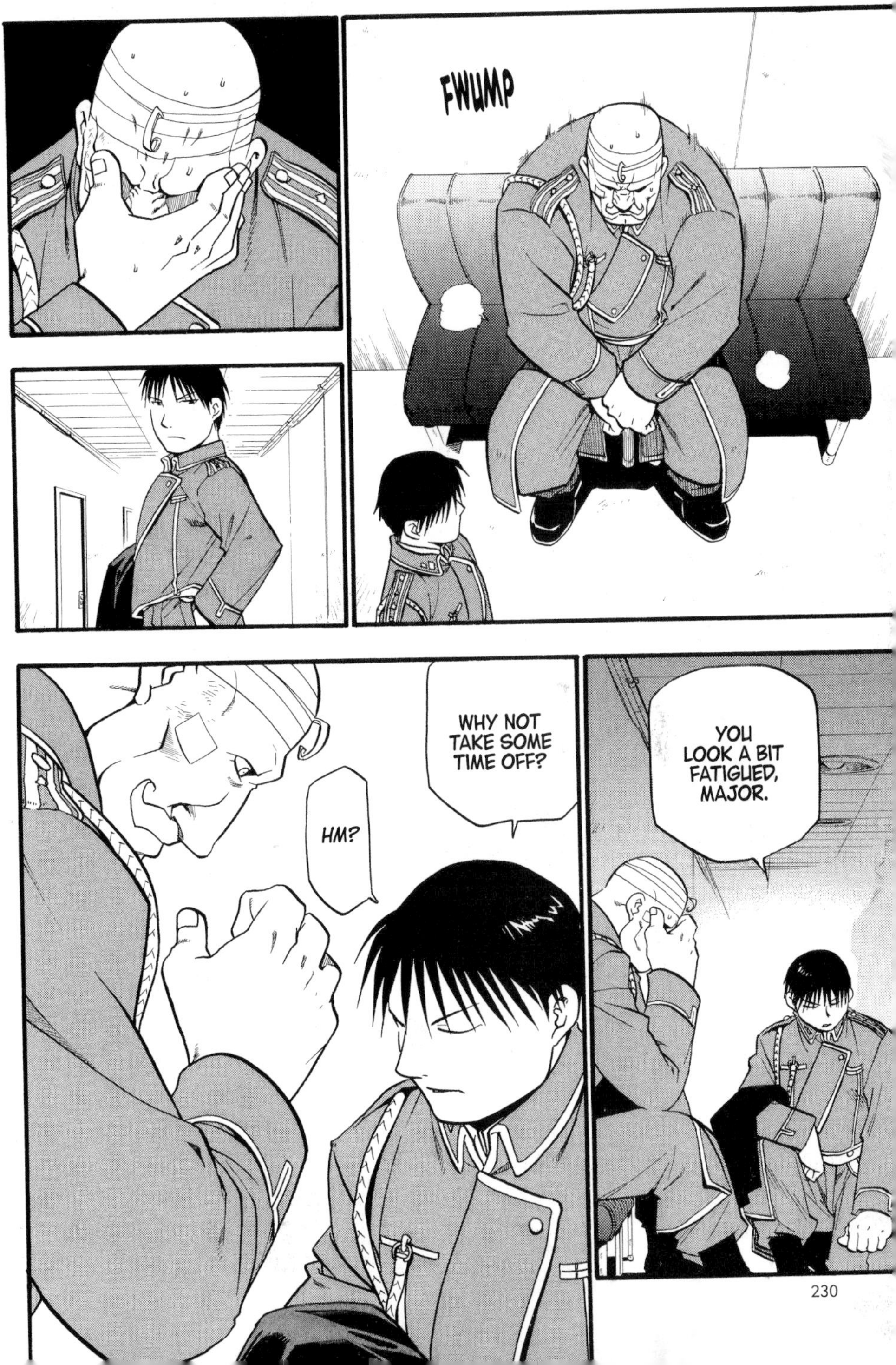
FWUMP
YOU LOOK A BIT FATIGUED, MAJOR.
WHY NOT TAKE SOME TIME OFF?
HM?

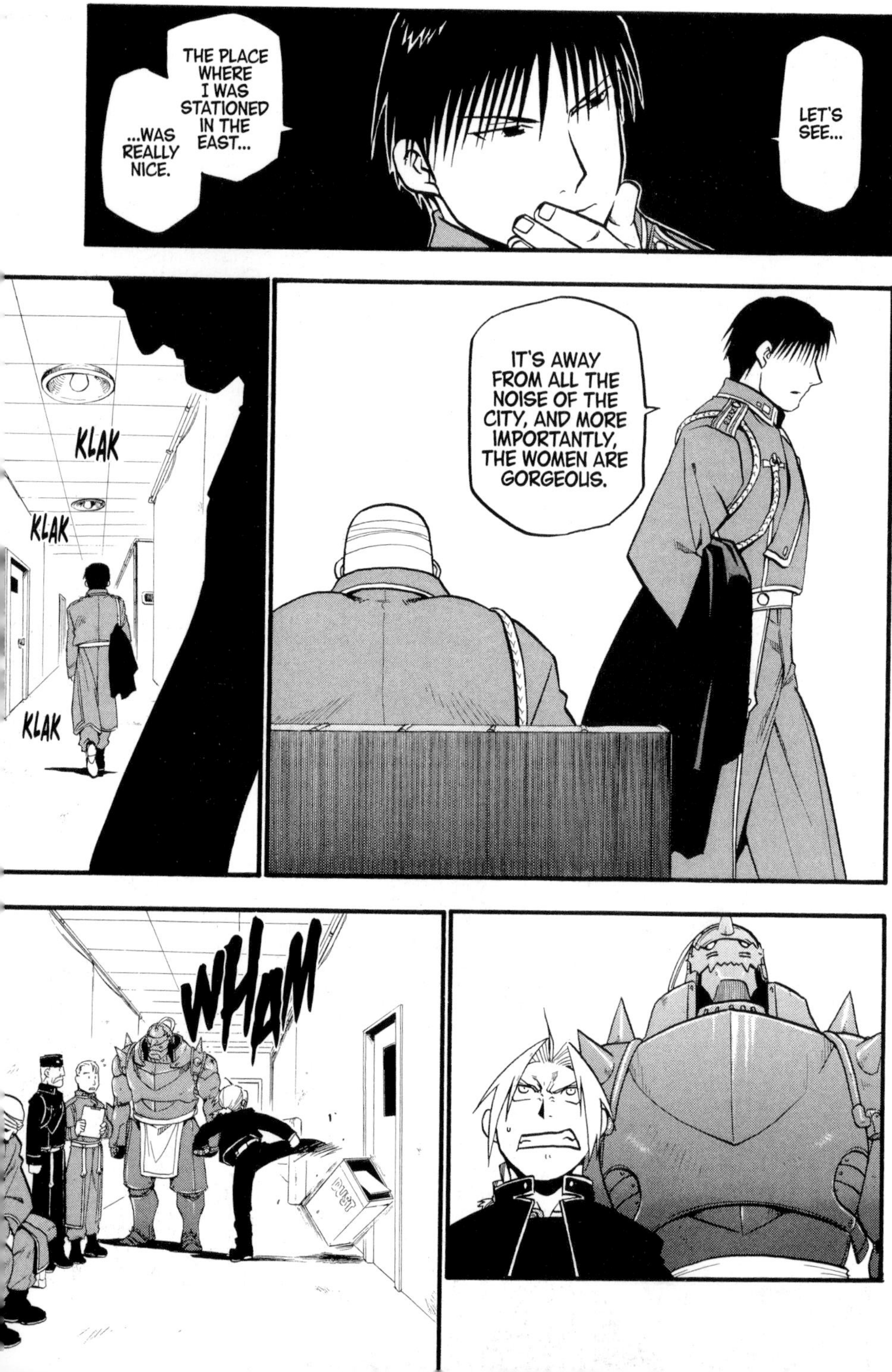
LET'S SEE...
THE PLACE WHERE I WAS STATIONED IN THE EAST...
...WAS REALLY NICE.
IT'S AWAY FROM ALL THE NOISE OF THE CITY, AND MORE IMPORTANTLY, THE WOMEN ARE GORGEOUS.
KLAK
KLAK
KLAK
WHAM

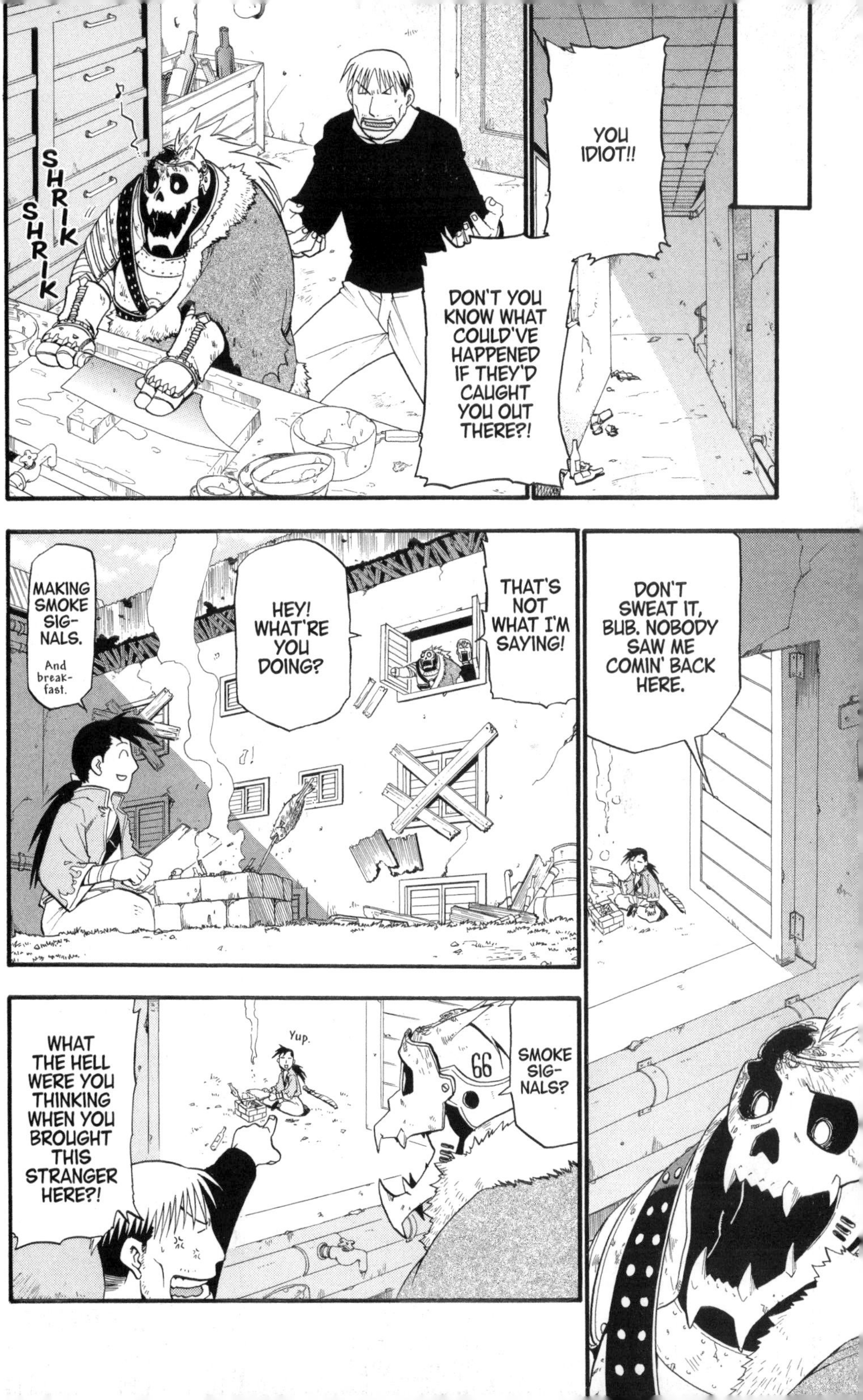
YOU IDIOT!!
DON'T YOU KNOW WHAT COULD'VE HAPPENED IF THEY'D CAUGHT YOU OUT THERE?!
SHRIK SHRIK
DON'T SWEAT IT, BUB. NOBODY SAW ME COMIN' BACK HERE.
THAT'S NOT WHAT I'M SAYING!
HEY! WHAT'RE YOU DOING?
MAKING SMOKE SIG-NALS.
And break-fast.
SMOKE SIG-NALS?
Yup.
WHAT THE HELL WERE YOU THINKING WHEN YOU BROUGHT THIS STRANGER HERE?!
66

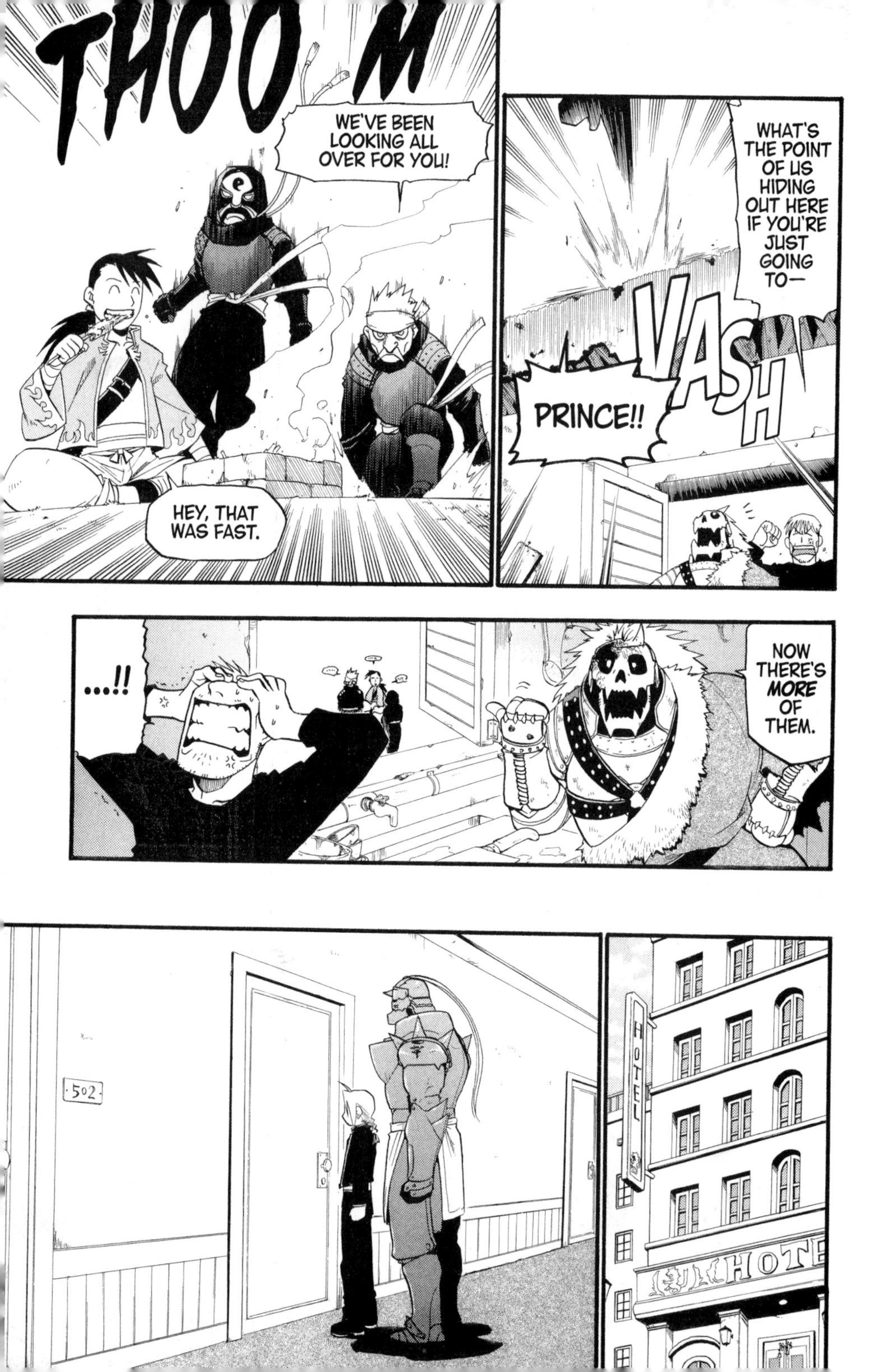
WHAT'S THE POINT OF US HIDING OUT HERE IF YOU'RE JUST GOING TO—
VASH
PRINCE!!
THOO M
WE'VE BEEN LOOKING ALL OVER FOR YOU!
HEY, THAT WAS FAST.
NOW THERE'S MORE OF THEM.
...!!
HOTEL
HOTE
502

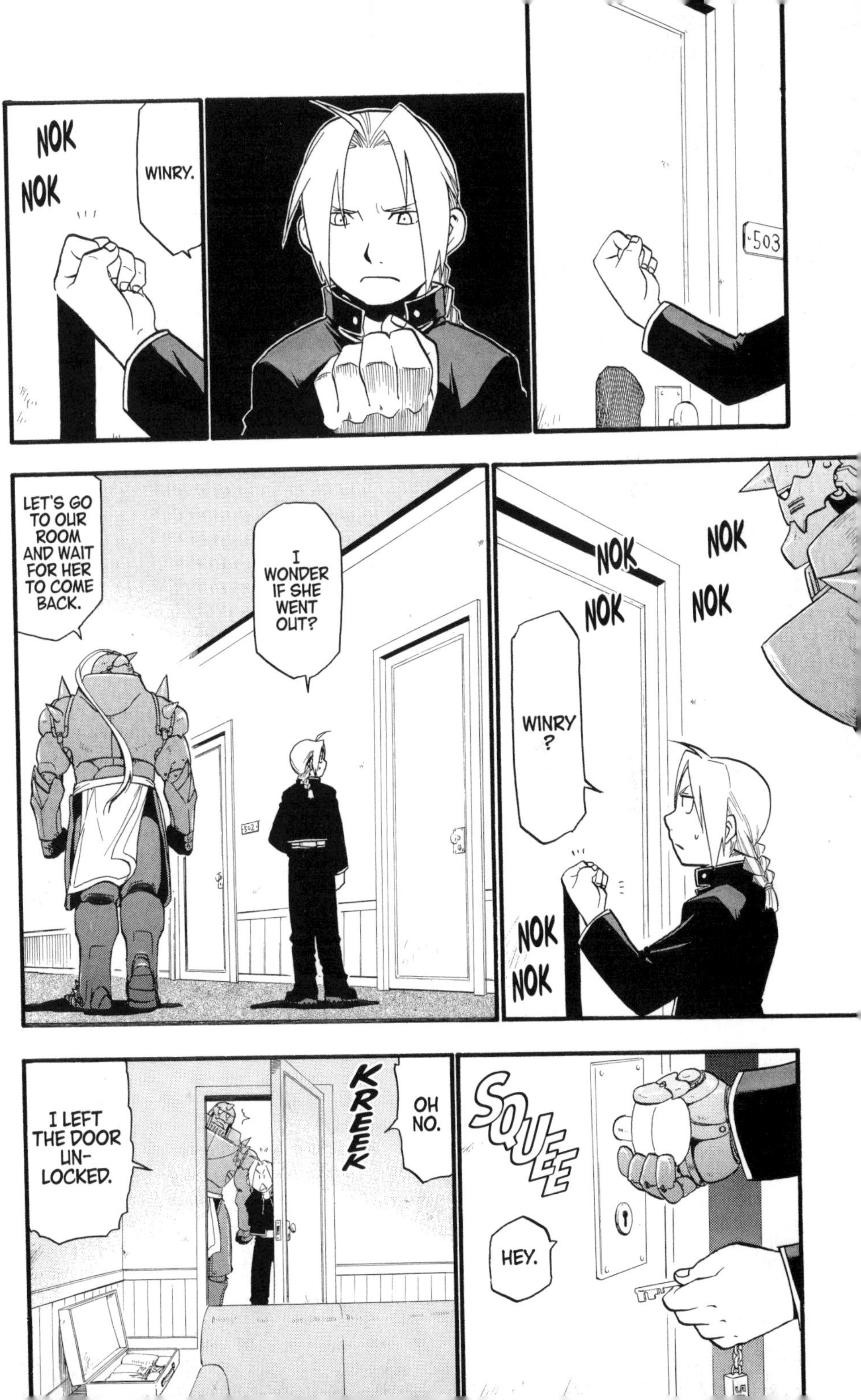
503
NOK
NOK
WINRY.
NOK
NOK
NOK
NOK
WINRY?
NOK
NOK
I WONDER IF SHE WENT OUT?
LET'S GO TO OUR ROOM AND WAIT FOR HER TO COME BACK.
SQUEE
HEY.
KREEK
OH NO.
I LEFT THE DOOR UNLOCKED.

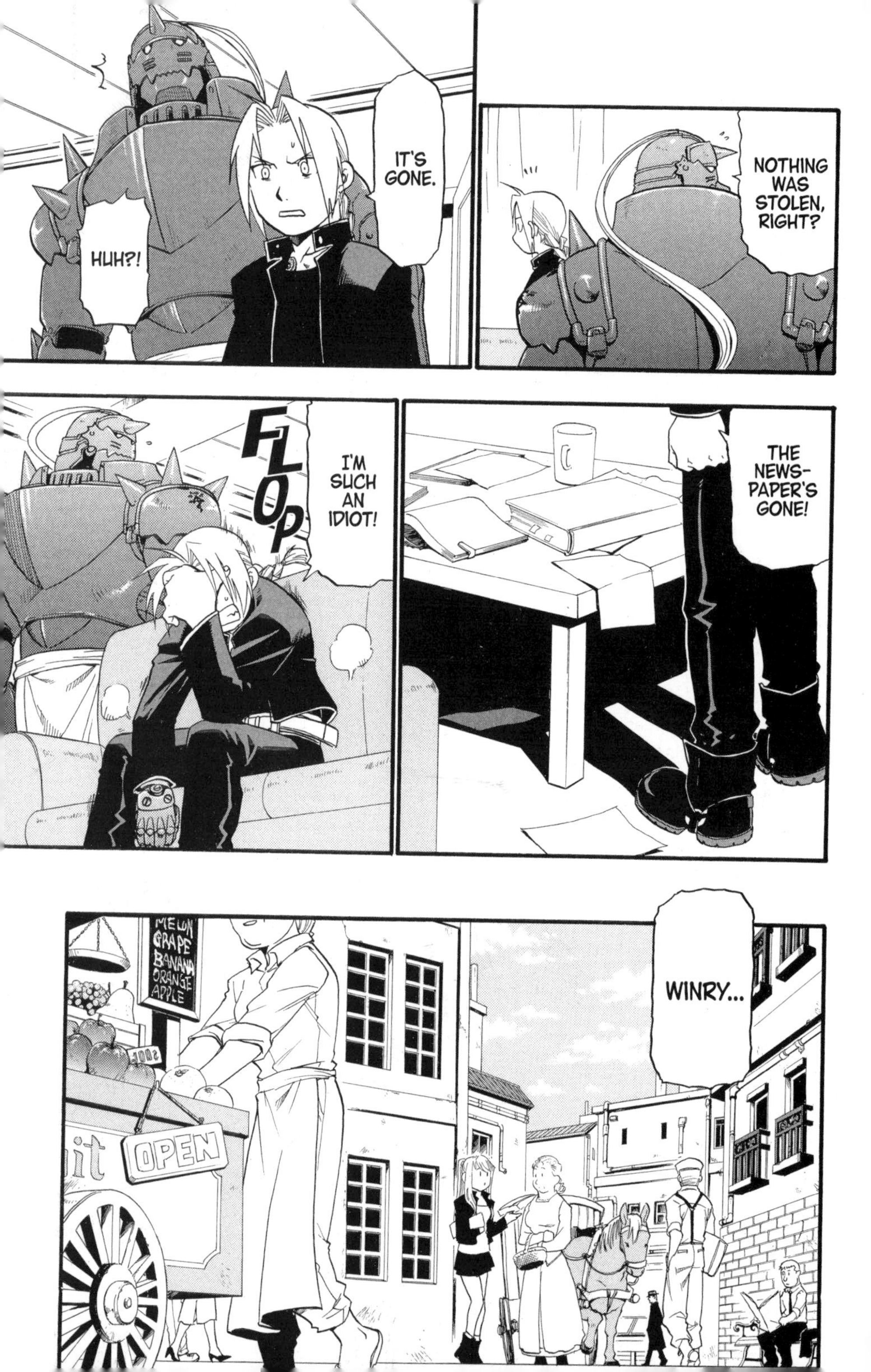
NOTHING WAS STOLEN, RIGHT?
IT'S GONE.
HUH?!
THE NEWS-PAPER'S GONE!
I'M SUCH AN IDIOT!
FLOP
WINRY...
MELON GRAPE BANANA ORANGE APPLE
OPEN

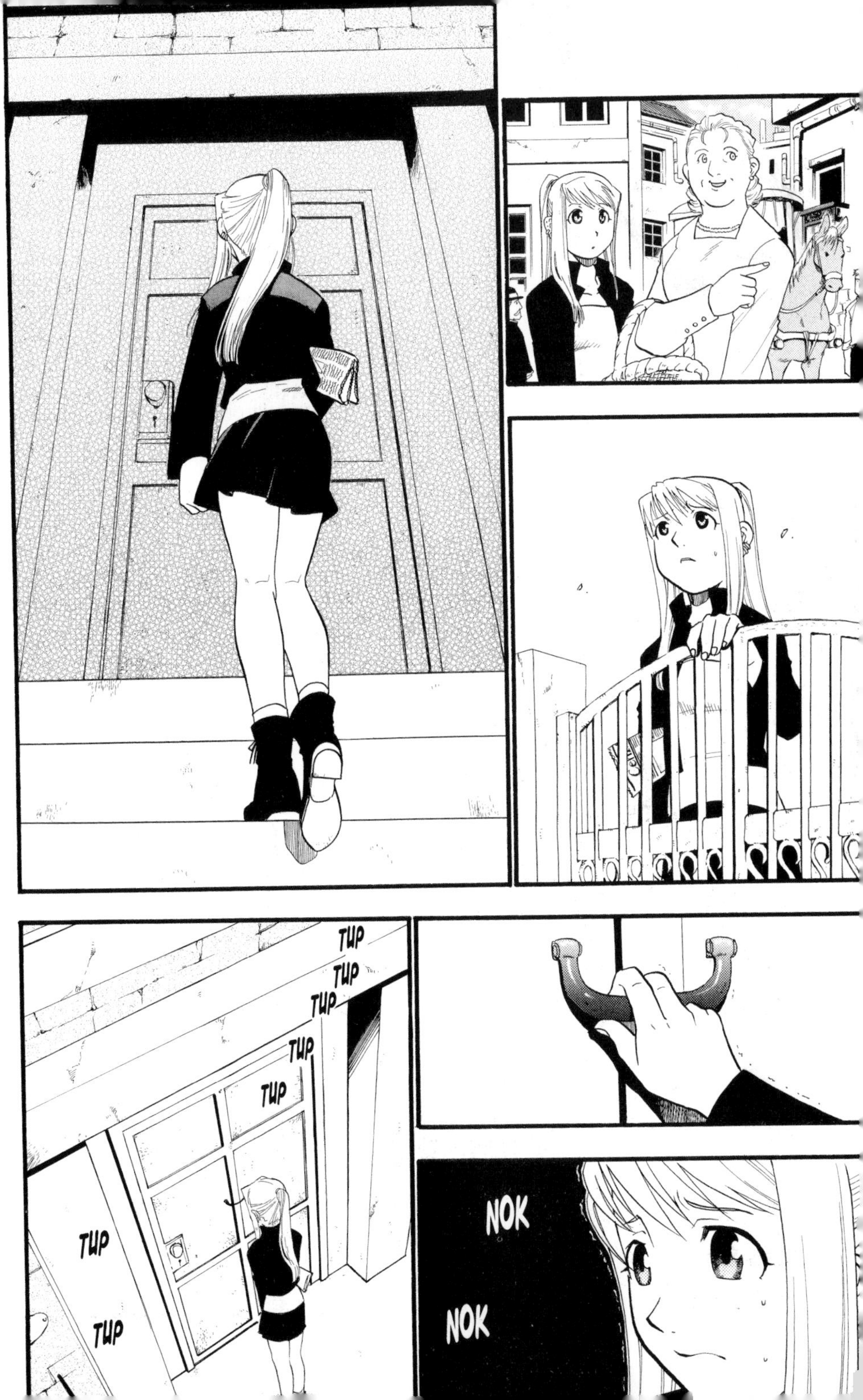
NOK
NOK
TUP
TUP
TUP
TUP
TUP
TUP
TUP

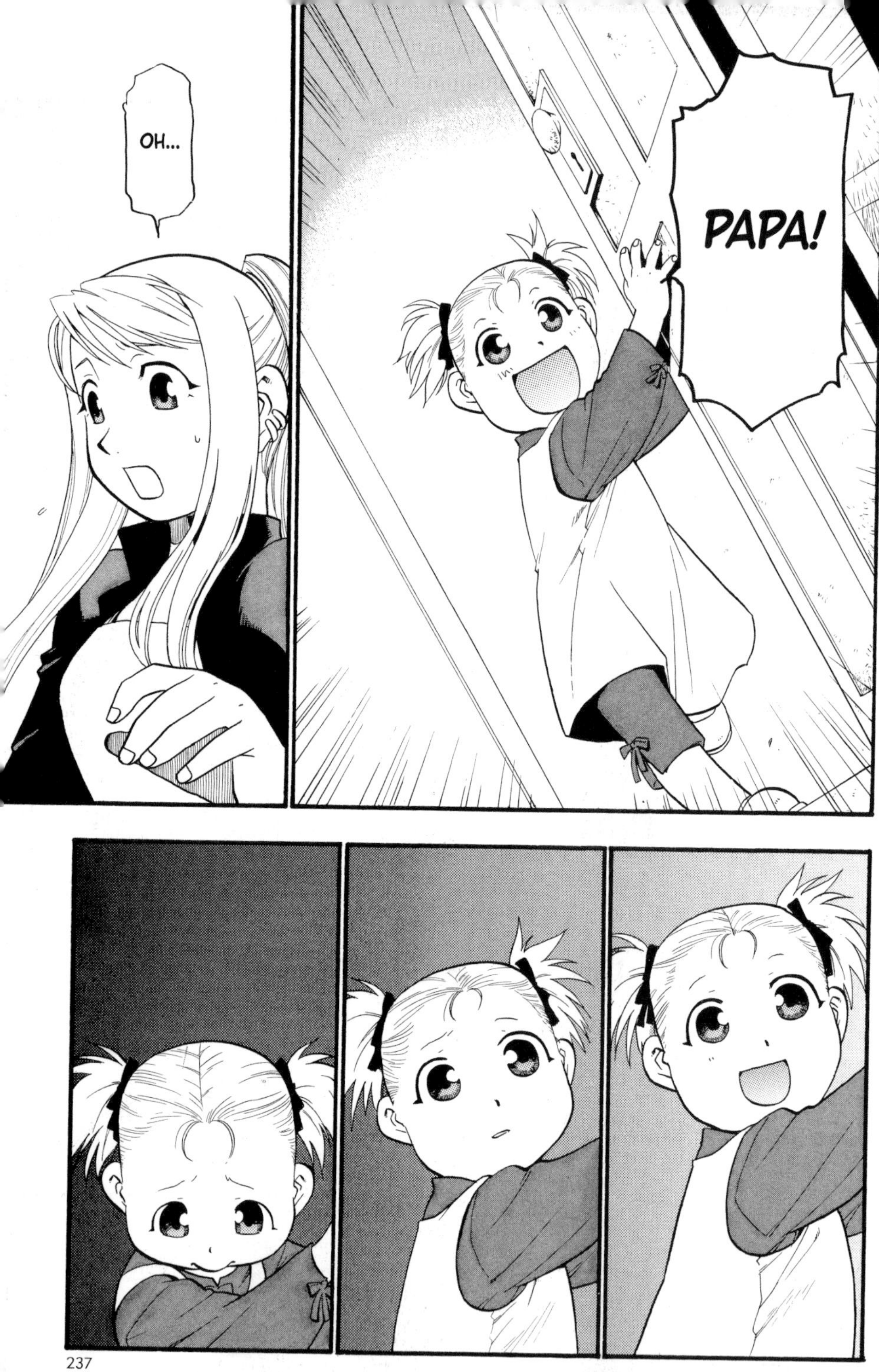
PAPA!
OH...

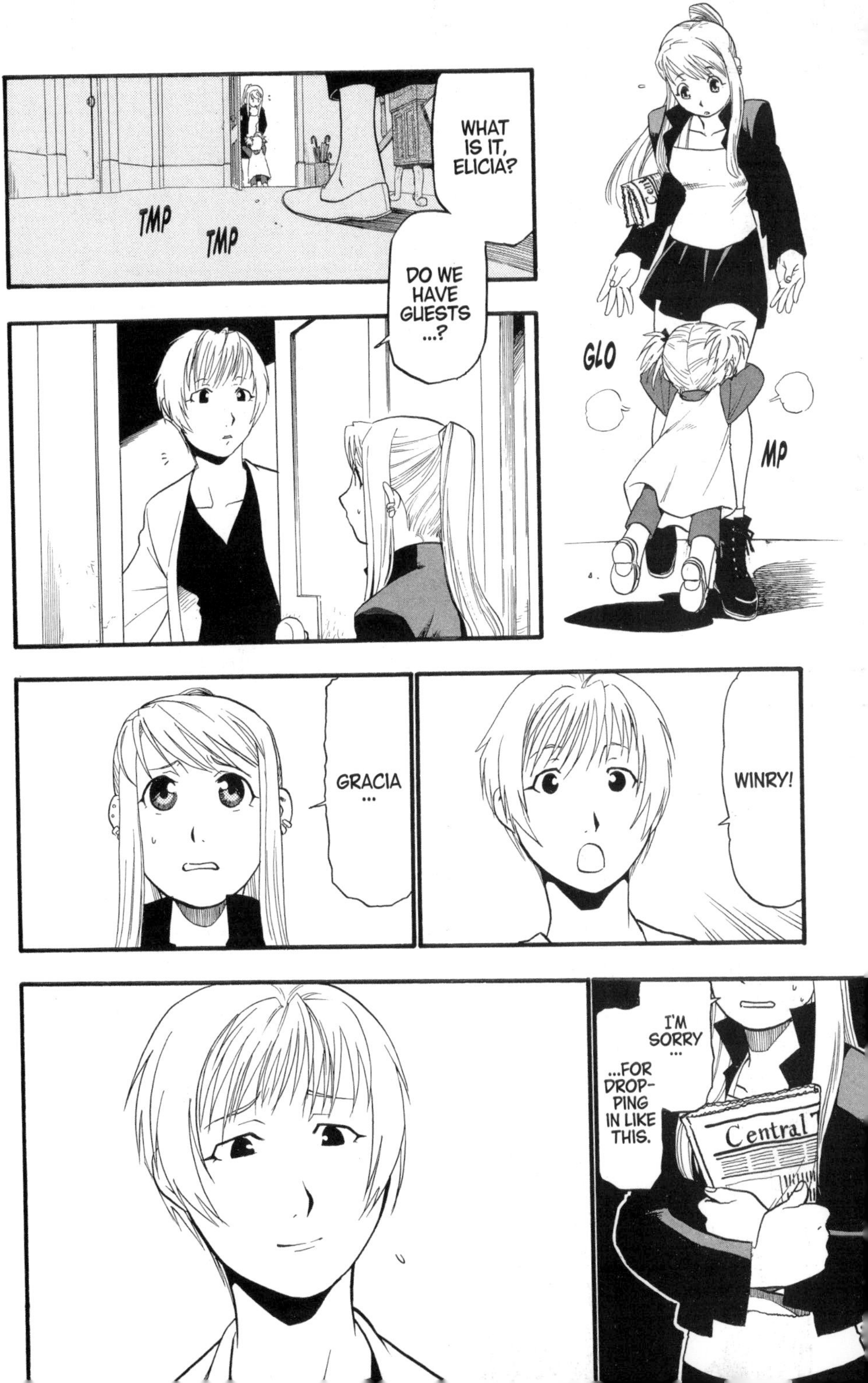
GLO
MP
WHAT IS IT, ELICIA?
TMP
TMP
DO WE HAVE GUESTS ...?
WINRY!
GRACIA ...
I'M SORRY ...
...FOR DROPPING IN LIKE THIS.
Central

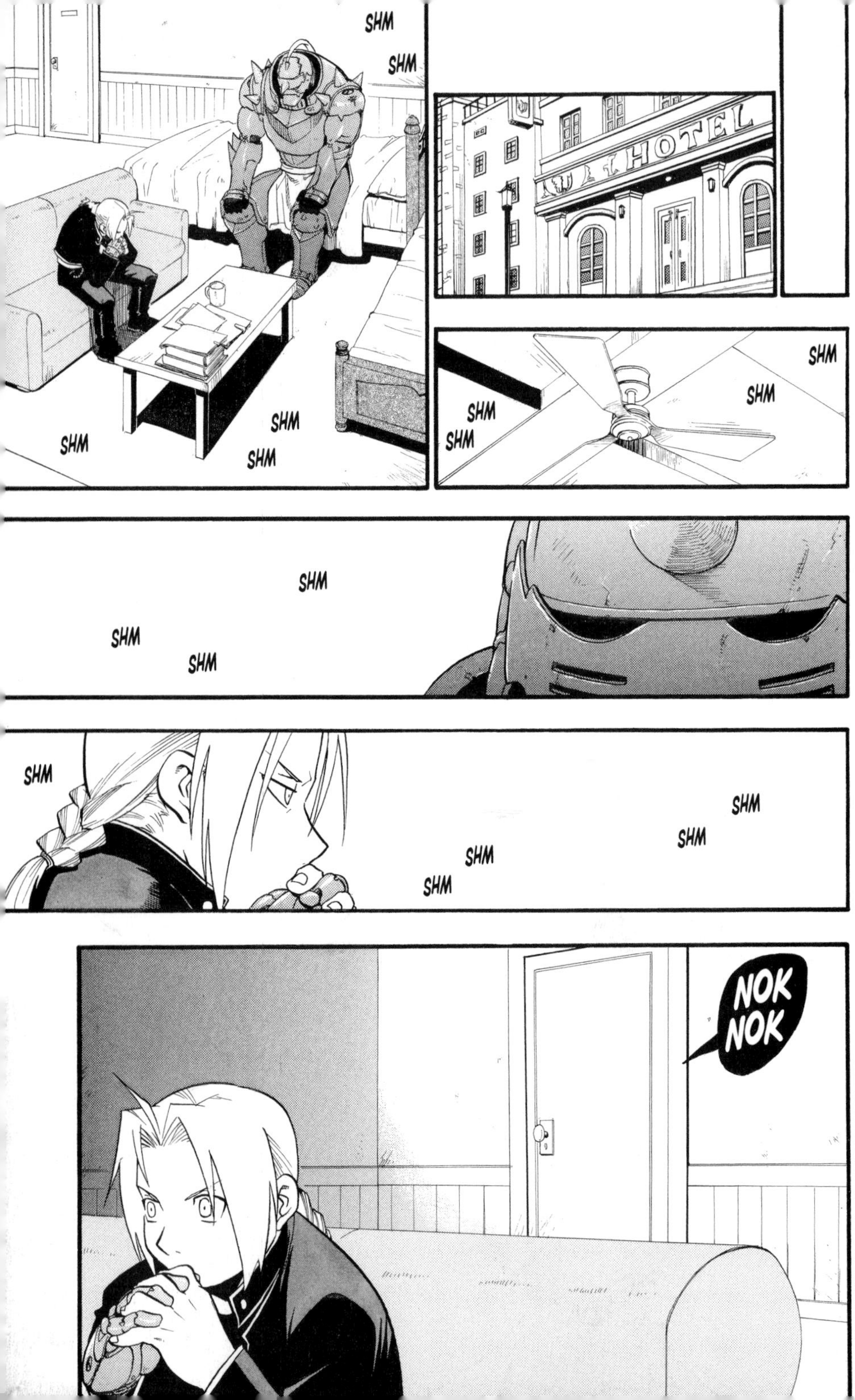

HOTEL
SHM
SHM
SHM
SHM
SHM
SHM
SHM
SHM
SHM
SHM
SHM
SHM
SHM
SHM
SHM
SHM
SHM
SHM
NOK NOK

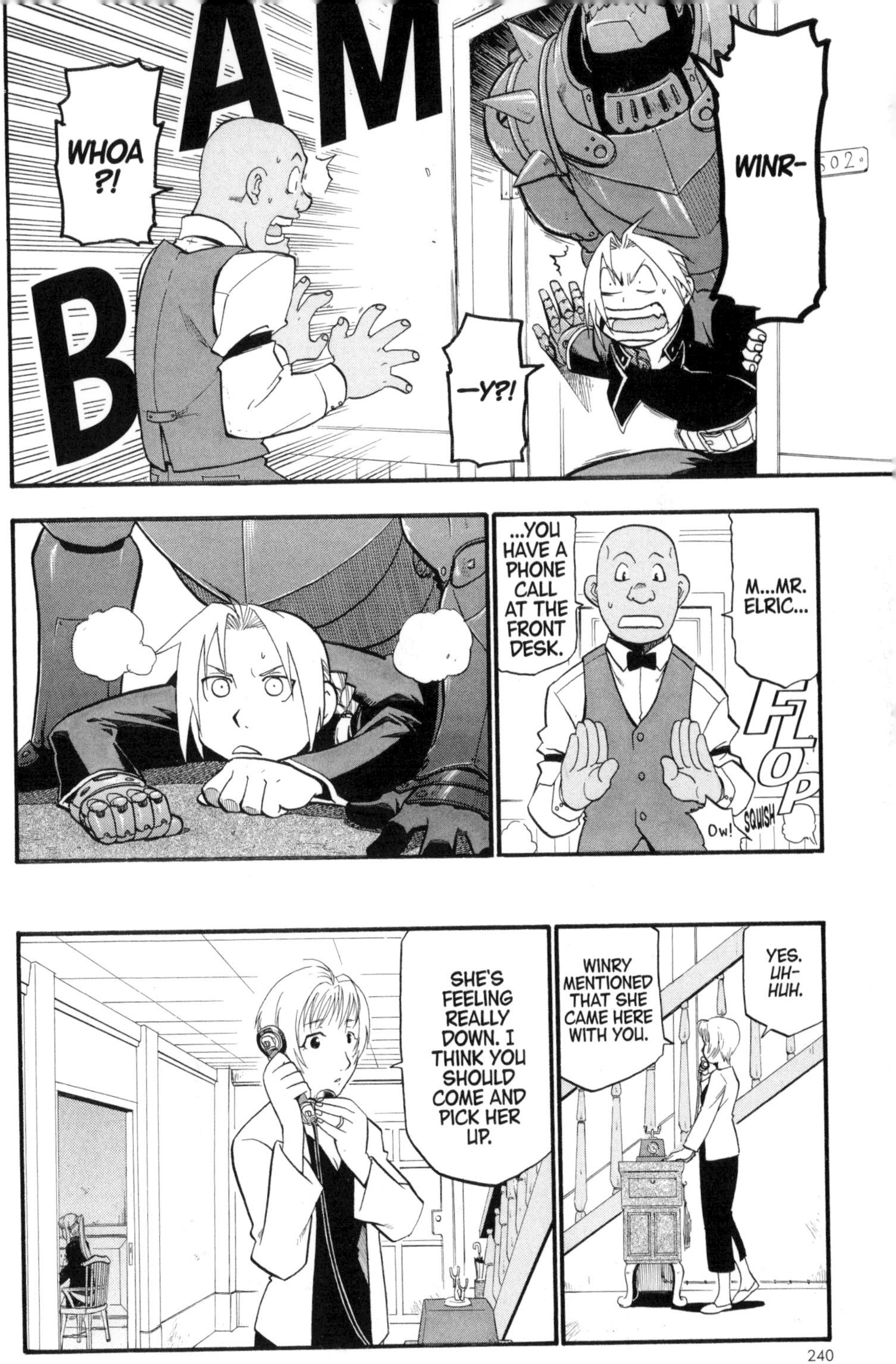
WINR-
502
—Y?!
BAM
WHOA ?!
M...MR. ELRIC...
...YOU HAVE A PHONE CALL AT THE FRONT DESK.
FLOP
SQUISH
Ow!
YES. UH-HUH.
WINRY MENTIONED THAT SHE CAME HERE WITH YOU.
SHE'S FEELING REALLY DOWN. I THINK YOU SHOULD COME AND PICK HER UP.

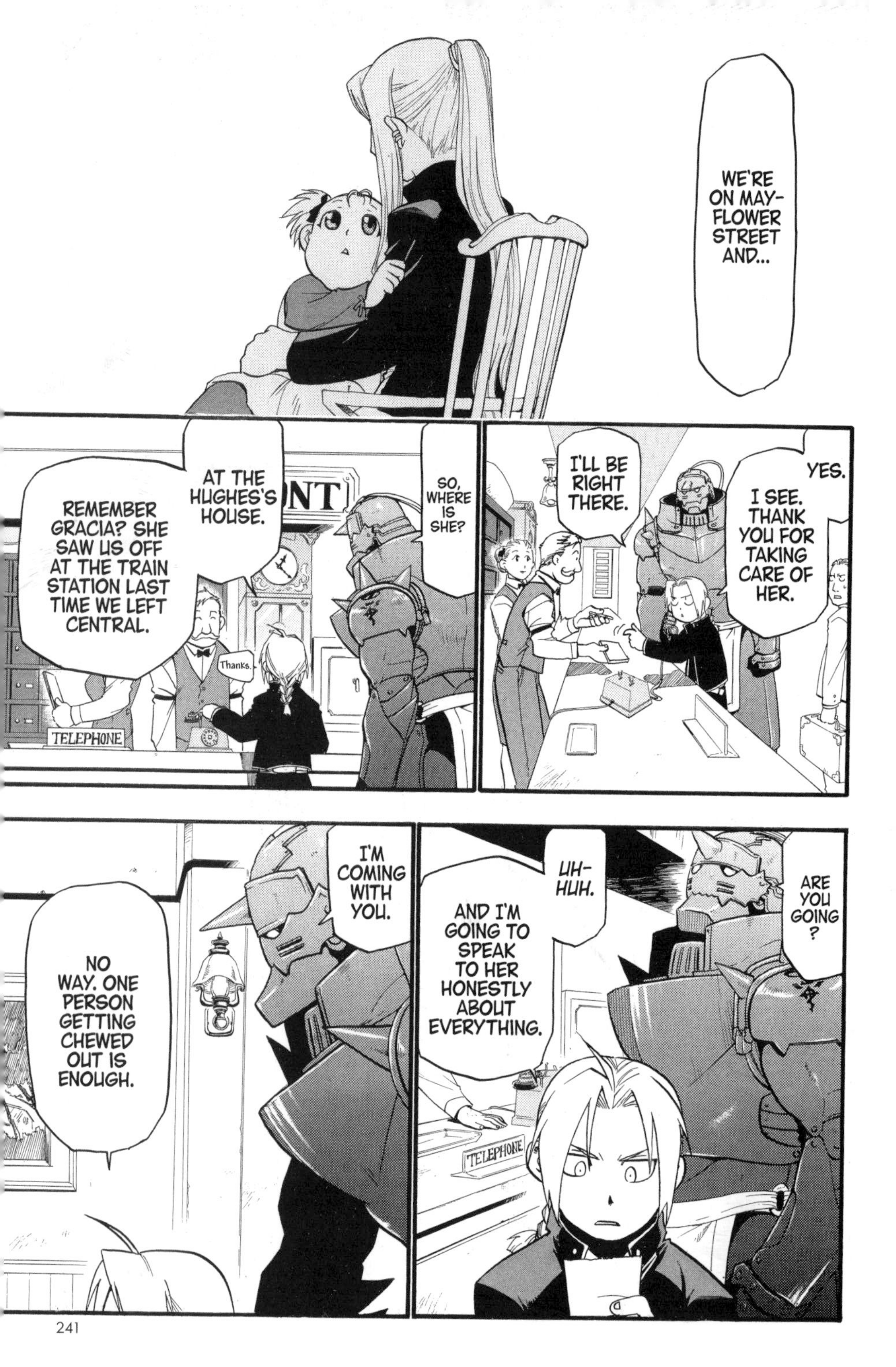
WE'RE ON MAY-FLOWER STREET AND...
YES.
I SEE. THANK YOU FOR TAKING CARE OF HER.
I'LL BE RIGHT THERE.
SO, WHERE IS SHE?
AT THE HUGHES'S HOUSE.
REMEMBER GRACIA? SHE SAW US OFF AT THE TRAIN STATION LAST TIME WE LEFT CENTRAL.
Thanks.
TELEPHONE
ARE YOU GOING?
UH-HUH.
AND I'M GOING TO SPEAK TO HER HONESTLY ABOUT EVERYTHING.
TELEPHONE
I'M COMING WITH YOU.
NO WAY. ONE PERSON GETTING CHEWED OUT IS ENOUGH.

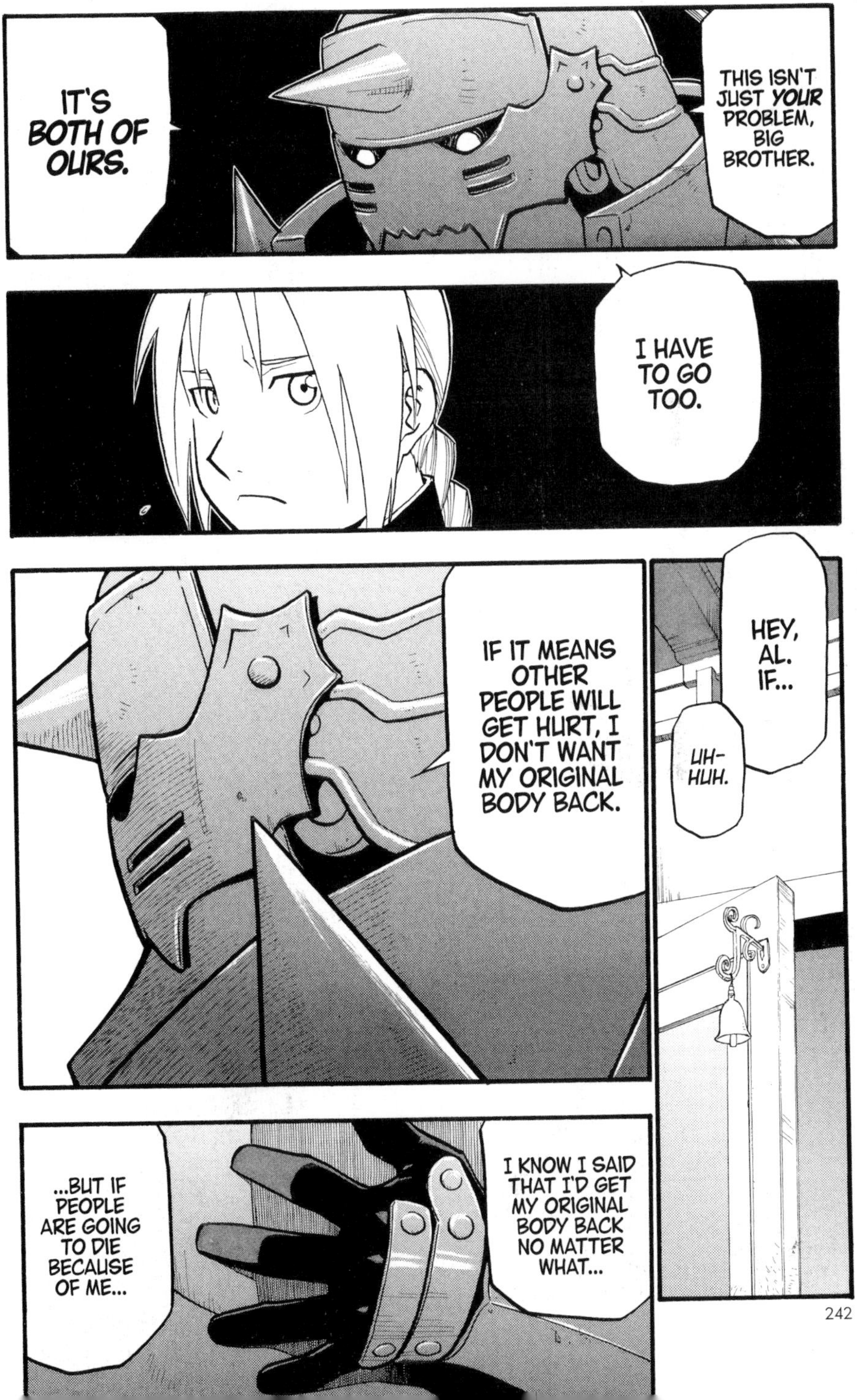

THIS ISN'T JUST *YOUR* PROBLEM, BIG BROTHER.
IT'S BOTH OF OURS.
I HAVE TO GO TOO.
HEY, AL. IF...
UH-HUH.
IF IT MEANS OTHER PEOPLE WILL GET HURT, I DON'T WANT MY ORIGINAL BODY BACK.
I KNOW I SAID THAT I'D GET MY ORIGINAL BODY BACK NO MATTER WHAT...
...BUT IF PEOPLE ARE GOING TO DIE BECAUSE OF ME...

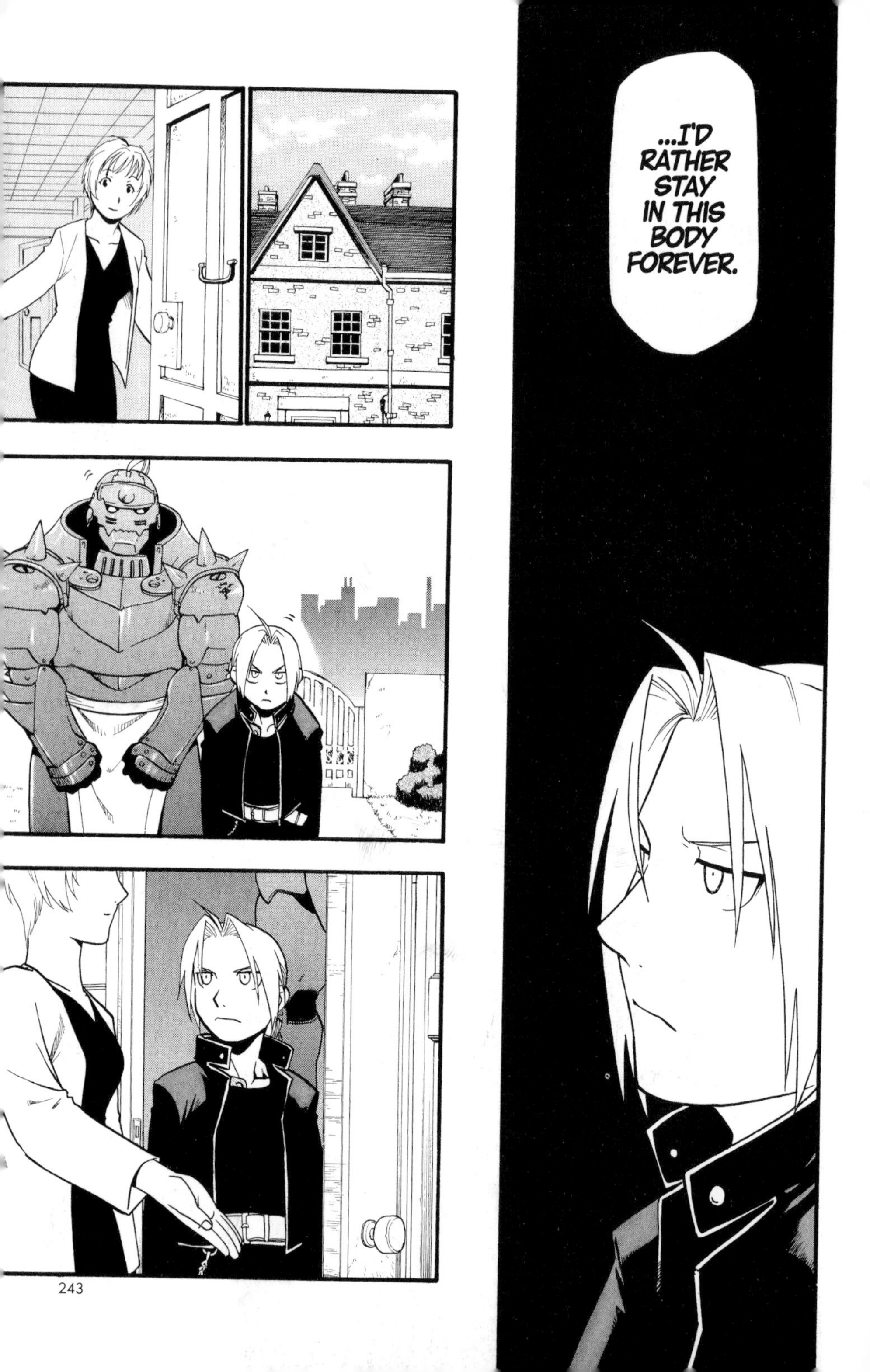
...I'D RATHER STAY IN THIS BODY FOREVER.

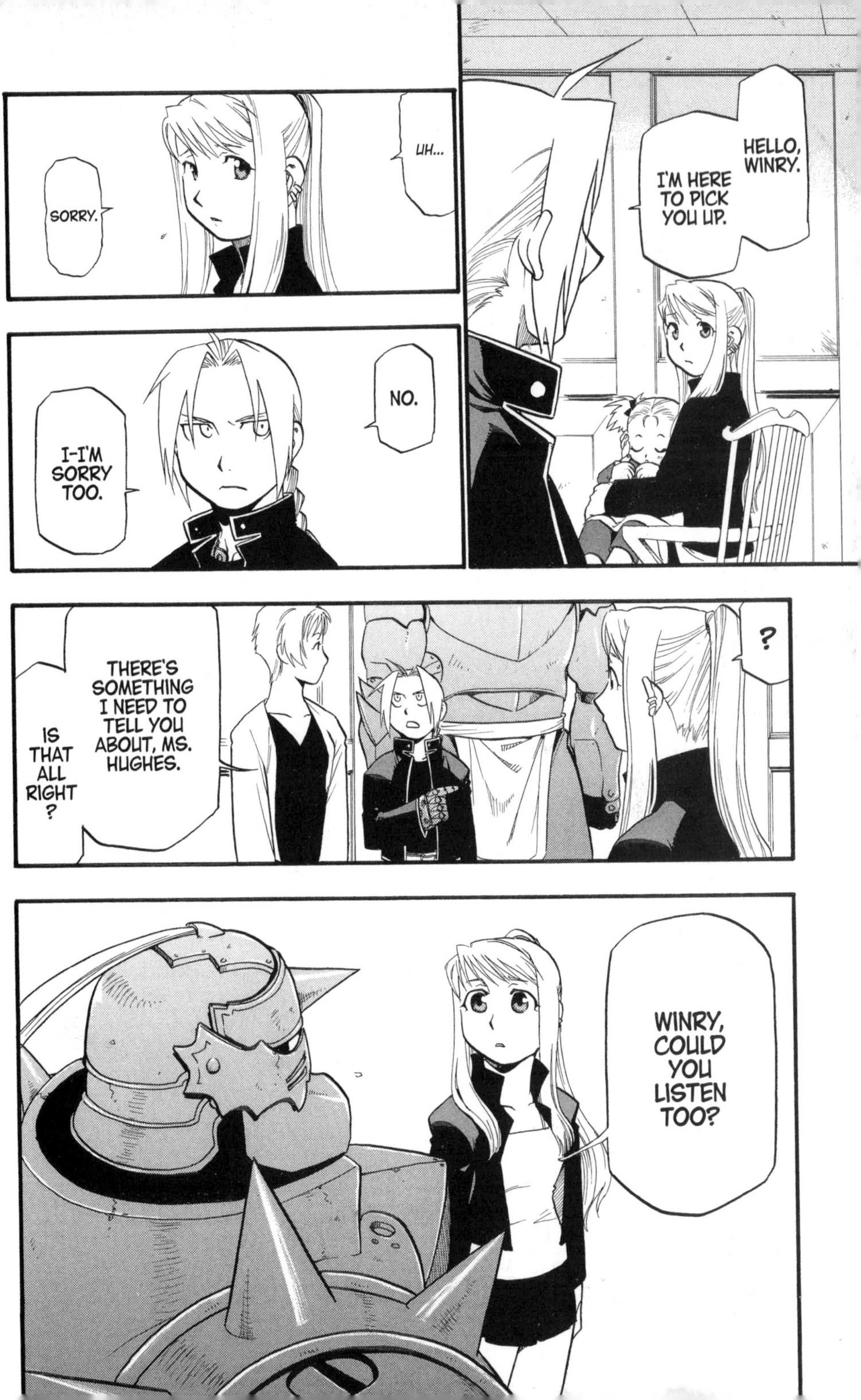
HELLO, WINRY.
I'M HERE TO PICK YOU UP.
UH...
SORRY.
NO.
I-I'M SORRY TOO.
?
THERE'S SOMETHING I NEED TO TELL YOU ABOUT, MS. HUGHES.
IS THAT ALL RIGHT?
WINRY, COULD YOU LISTEN TOO?

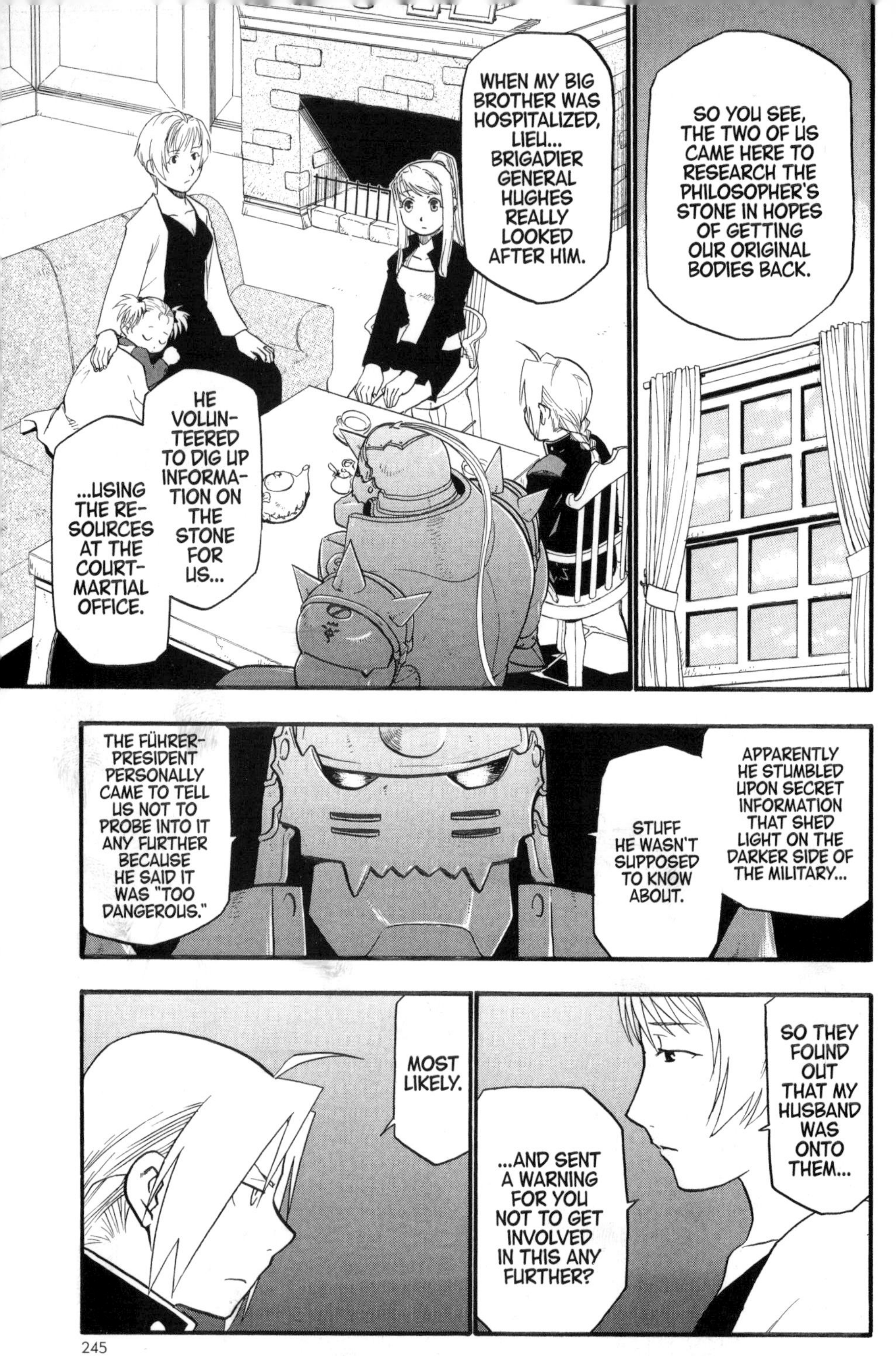
SO YOU SEE, THE TWO OF US CAME HERE TO RESEARCH THE PHILOSOPHER'S STONE IN HOPES OF GETTING OUR ORIGINAL BODIES BACK.
WHEN MY BIG BROTHER WAS HOSPITALIZED, LIEU... BRIGADIER GENERAL HUGHES REALLY LOOKED AFTER HIM.
HE VOLUNTEERED TO DIG UP INFORMATION ON THE STONE FOR US...
...USING THE RESOURCES AT THE COURT-MARTIAL OFFICE.
APPARENTLY HE STUMBLED UPON SECRET INFORMATION THAT SHED LIGHT ON THE DARKER SIDE OF THE MILITARY...
STUFF HE WASN'T SUPPOSED TO KNOW ABOUT.
THE FÜHRER-PRESIDENT PERSONALLY CAME TO TELL US NOT TO PROBE INTO IT ANY FURTHER BECAUSE HE SAID IT WAS "TOO DANGEROUS."
SO THEY FOUND OUT THAT MY HUSBAND WAS ONTO THEM...
...AND SENT A WARNING FOR YOU NOT TO GET INVOLVED IN THIS ANY FURTHER?
MOST LIKELY.

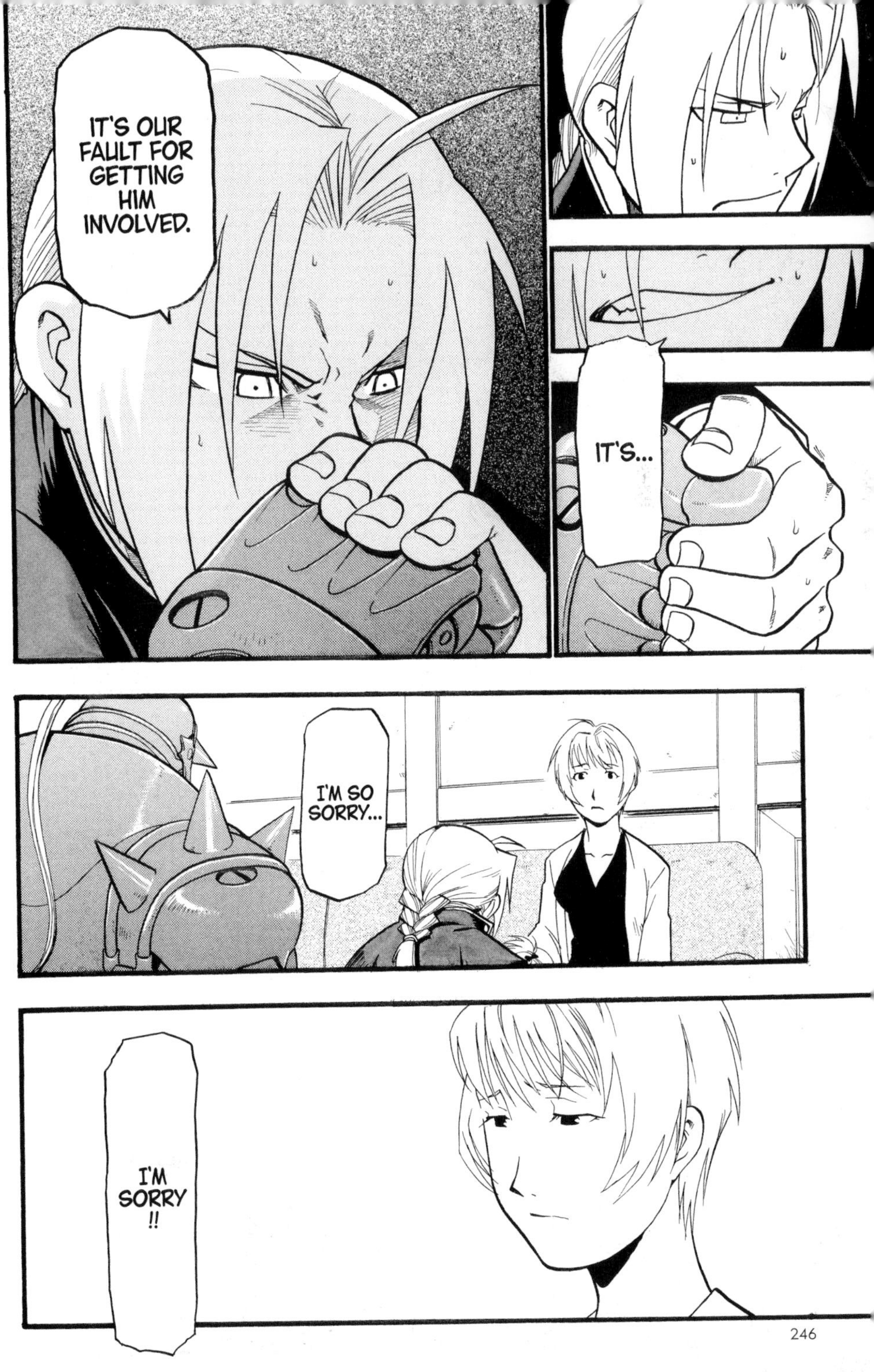
IT'S...
IT'S OUR FAULT FOR GETTING HIM INVOLVED.
I'M SO SORRY...
I'M SORRY !!

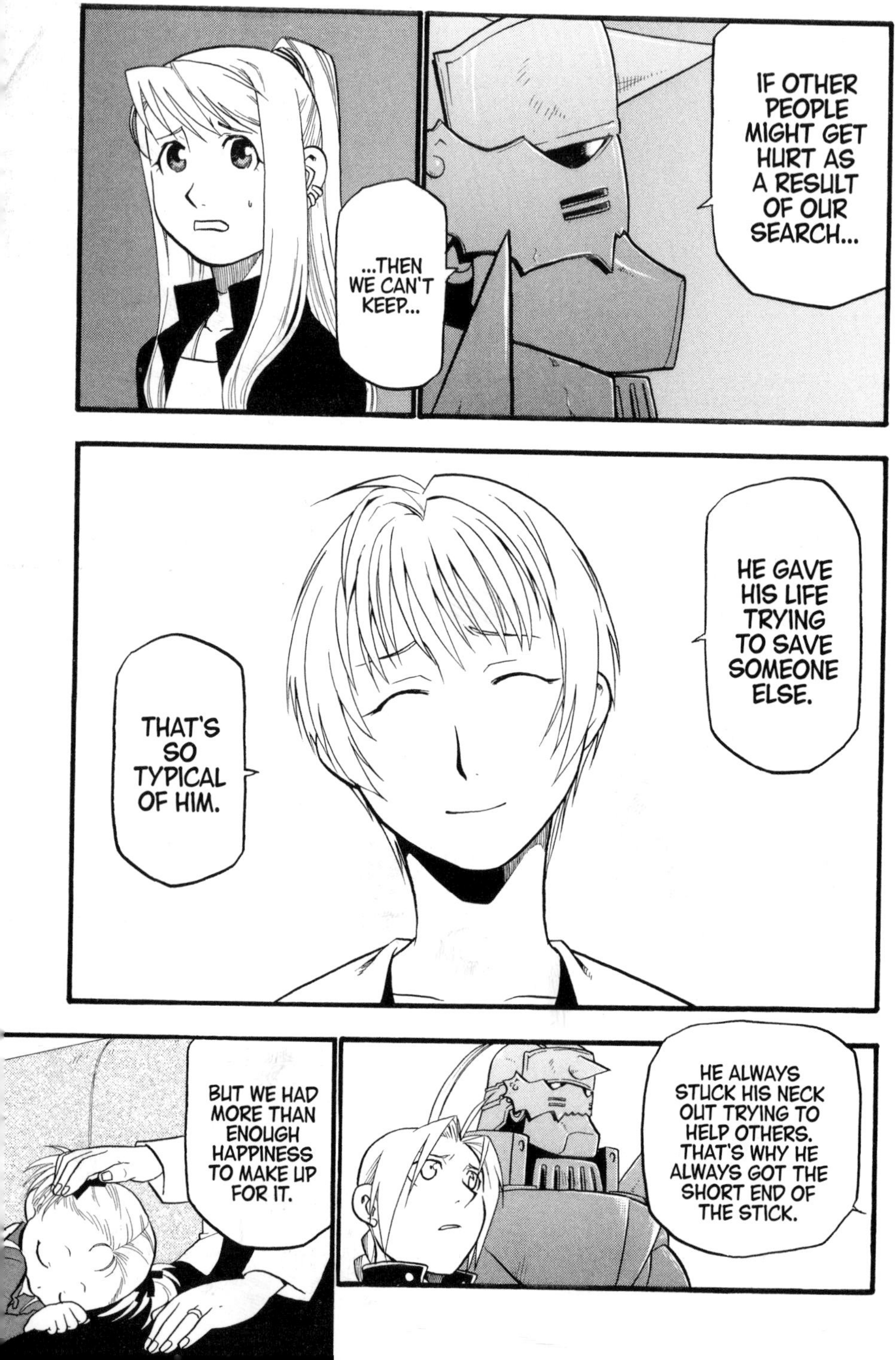
IF OTHER PEOPLE MIGHT GET HURT AS A RESULT OF OUR SEARCH...
...THEN WE CAN'T KEEP...
HE GAVE HIS LIFE TRYING TO SAVE SOMEONE ELSE.
THAT'S SO TYPICAL OF HIM.
HE ALWAYS STUCK HIS NECK OUT TRYING TO HELP OTHERS. THAT'S WHY HE ALWAYS GOT THE SHORT END OF THE STICK.
BUT WE HAD MORE THAN ENOUGH HAPPINESS TO MAKE UP FOR IT.

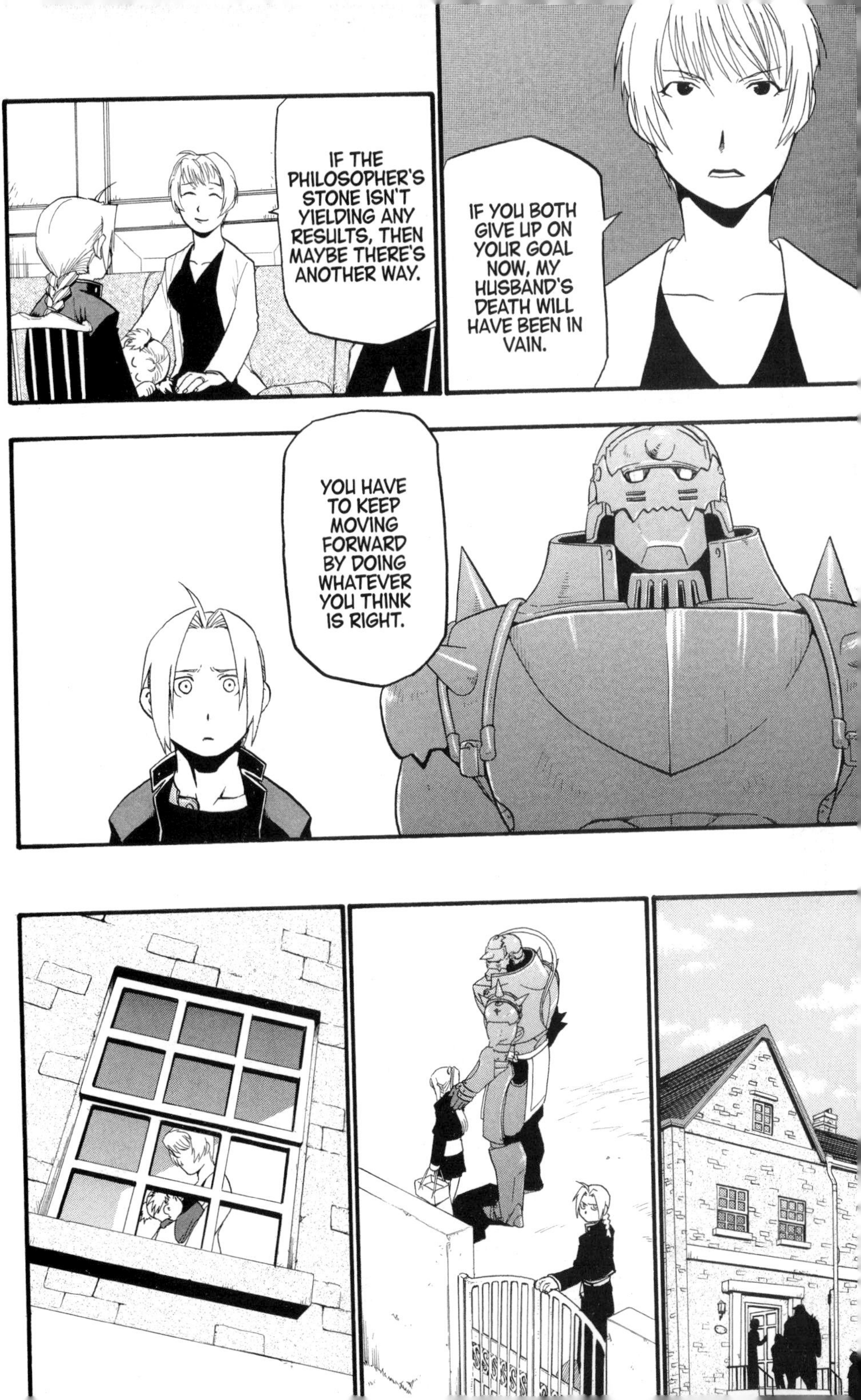
IF YOU BOTH GIVE UP ON YOUR GOAL NOW, MY HUSBAND'S DEATH WILL HAVE BEEN IN VAIN.
IF THE PHILOSOPHER'S STONE ISN'T YIELDING ANY RESULTS, THEN MAYBE THERE'S ANOTHER WAY.
YOU HAVE TO KEEP MOVING FORWARD BY DOING WHATEVER YOU THINK IS RIGHT.

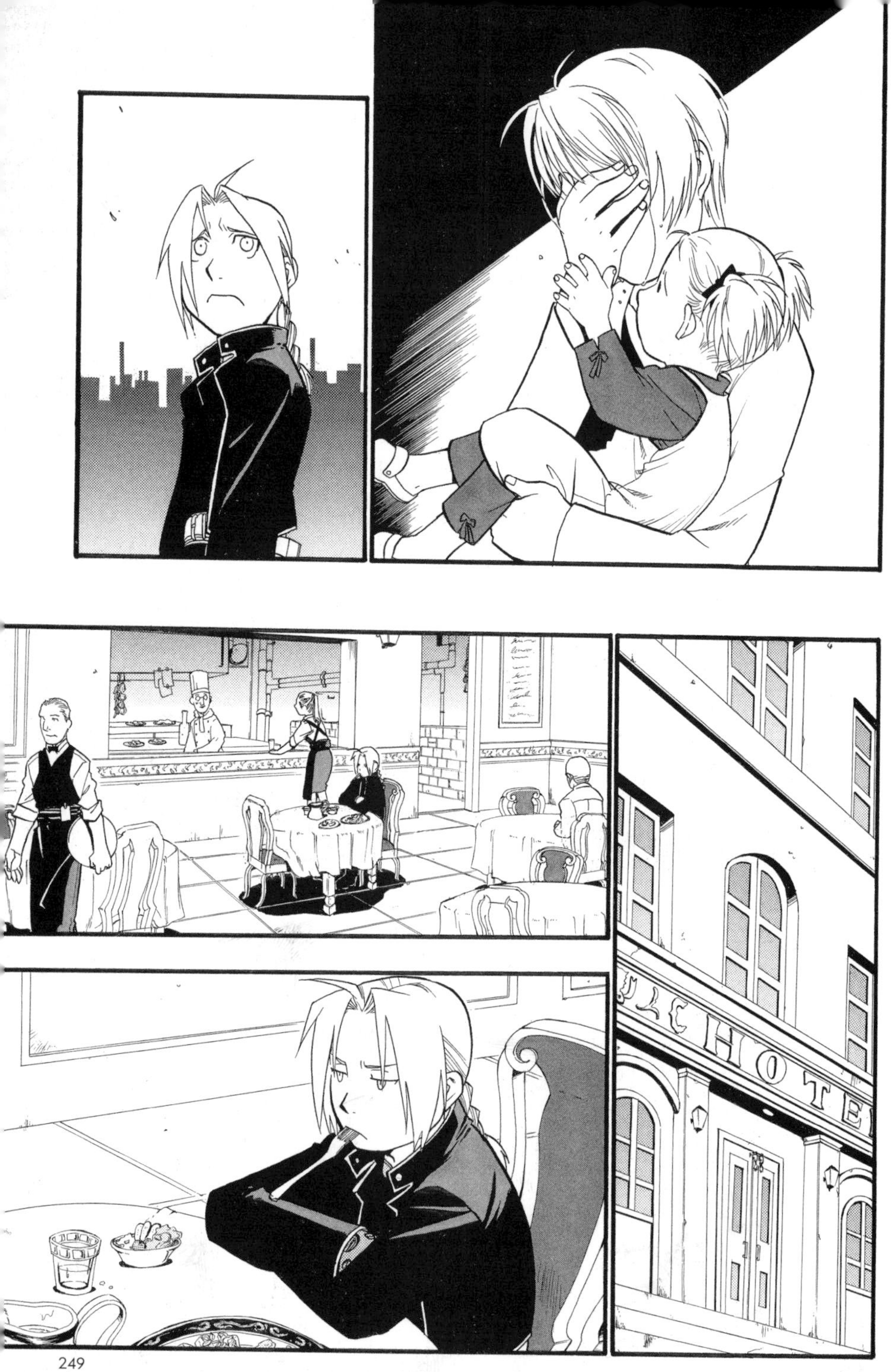
HOTE

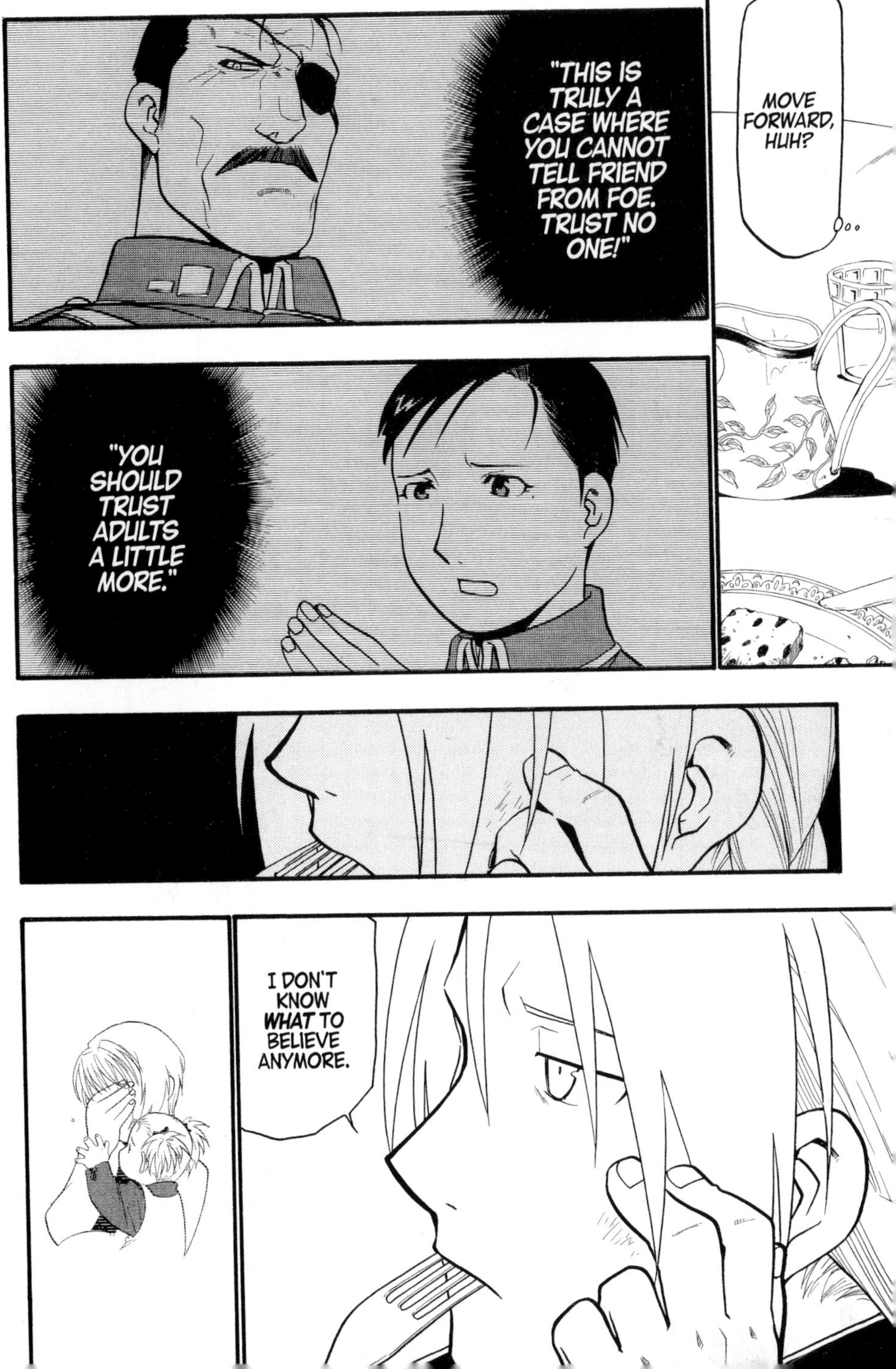
MOVE FORWARD, HUH?
"THIS IS TRULY A CASE WHERE YOU CANNOT TELL FRIEND FROM FOE. TRUST NO ONE!"
"YOU SHOULD TRUST ADULTS A LITTLE MORE."
I DON'T KNOW *WHAT* TO BELIEVE ANYMORE.

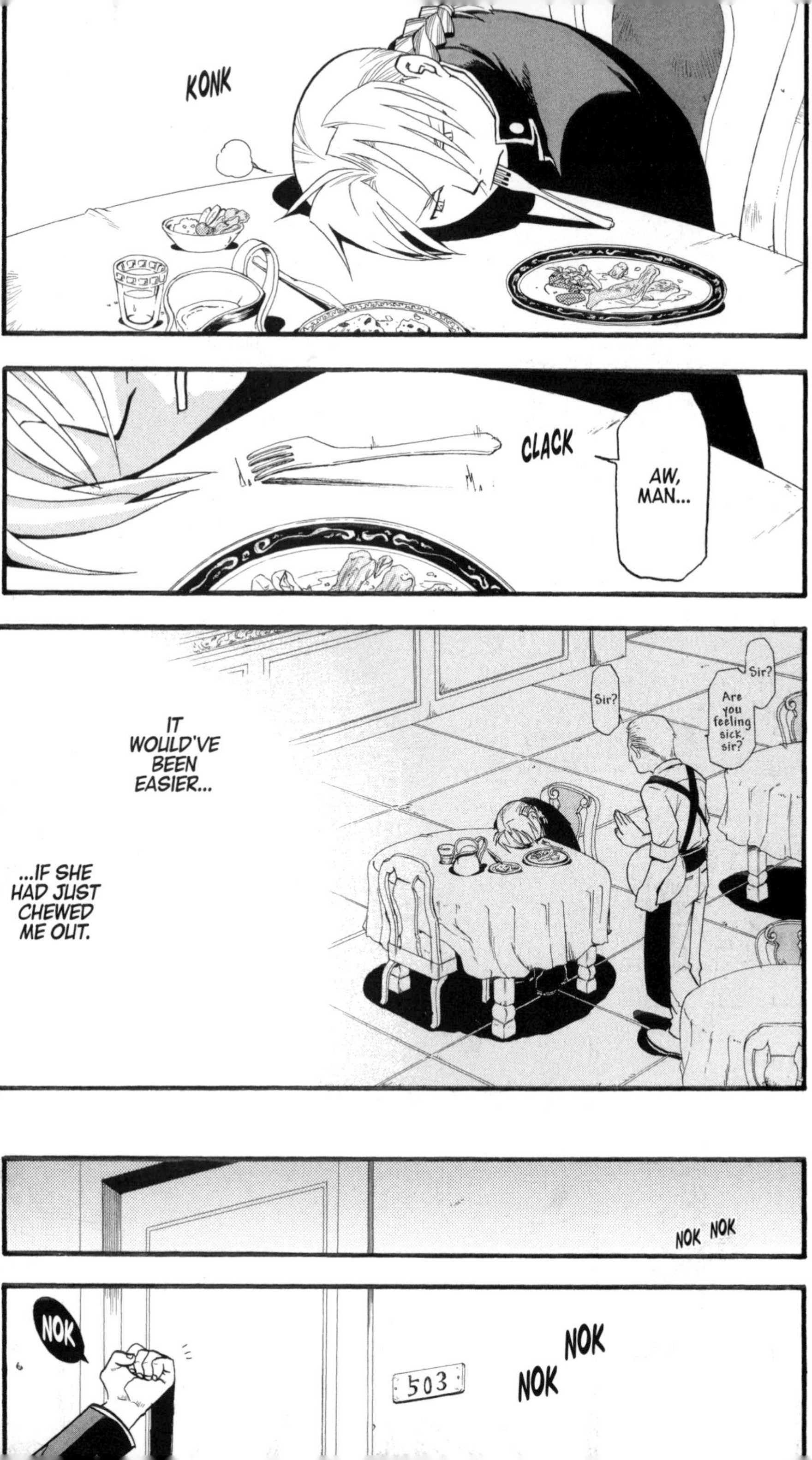
KONK
AW, MAN...
CLACK
Sir?
Are you feeling sick, sir?
Sir?
IT WOULD'VE BEEN EASIER...
...IF SHE HAD JUST CHEWED ME OUT.
NOK NOK
NOK
NOK
503
NOK

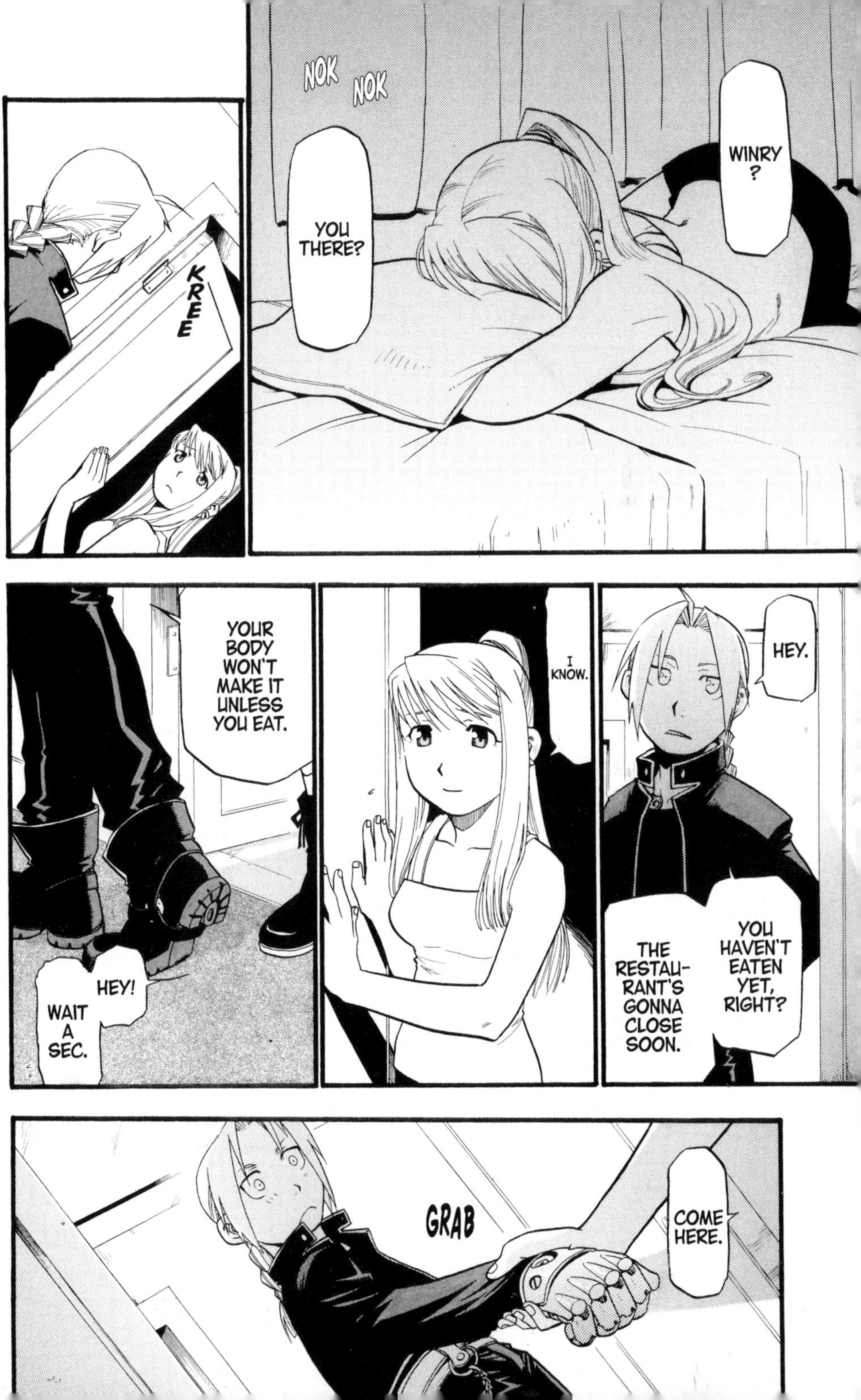
NOK NOK
WINRY ?
YOU THERE?
KREE
HEY.
YOU HAVEN'T EATEN YET, RIGHT?
THE RESTAU-RANT'S GONNA CLOSE SOON.
I KNOW.
YOUR BODY WON'T MAKE IT UNLESS YOU EAT.
HEY!
WAIT A SEC.
COME HERE.
GRAB

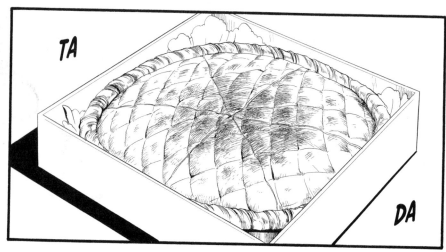

TA

DA

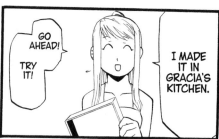

GO AHEAD!

TRY IT!

I MADE IT IN GRACIA'S KITCHEN.

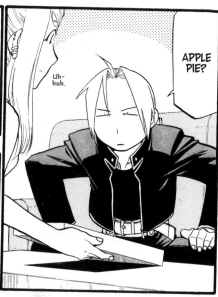

Uh-huh.

APPLE PIE?

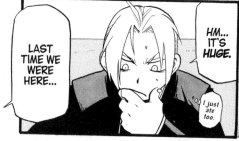

LAST TIME WE WERE HERE...

HM... IT'S *HUGE*.

I just ate too.

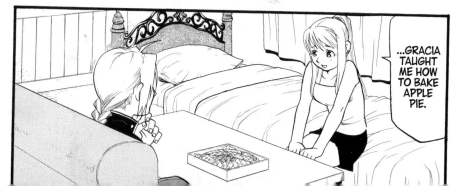

...GRACIA TAUGHT ME HOW TO BAKE APPLE PIE.

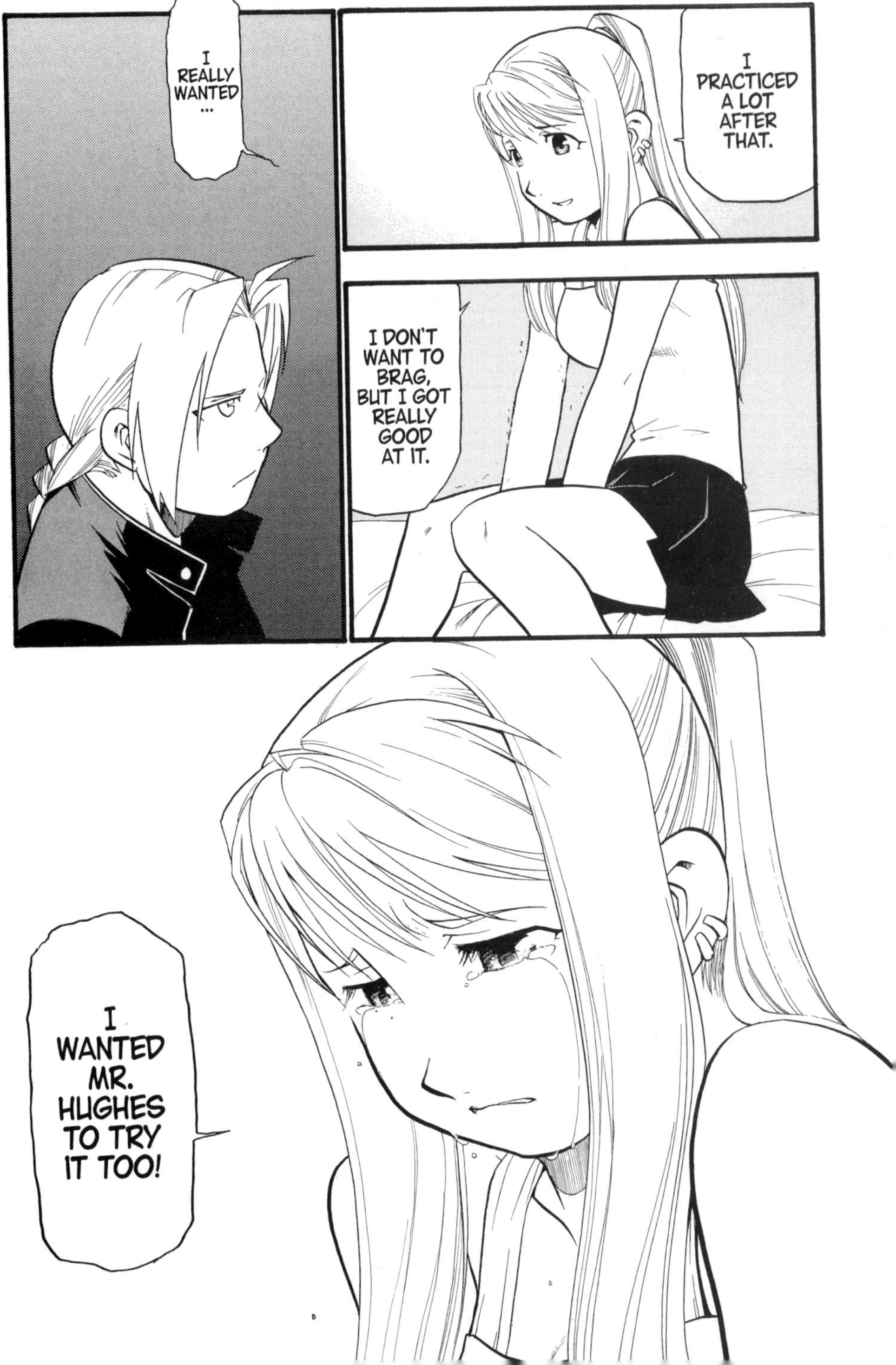
I PRACTICED A LOT AFTER THAT.
I DON'T WANT TO BRAG, BUT I GOT REALLY GOOD AT IT.
I REALLY WANTED ...
I WANTED MR. HUGHES TO TRY IT TOO!

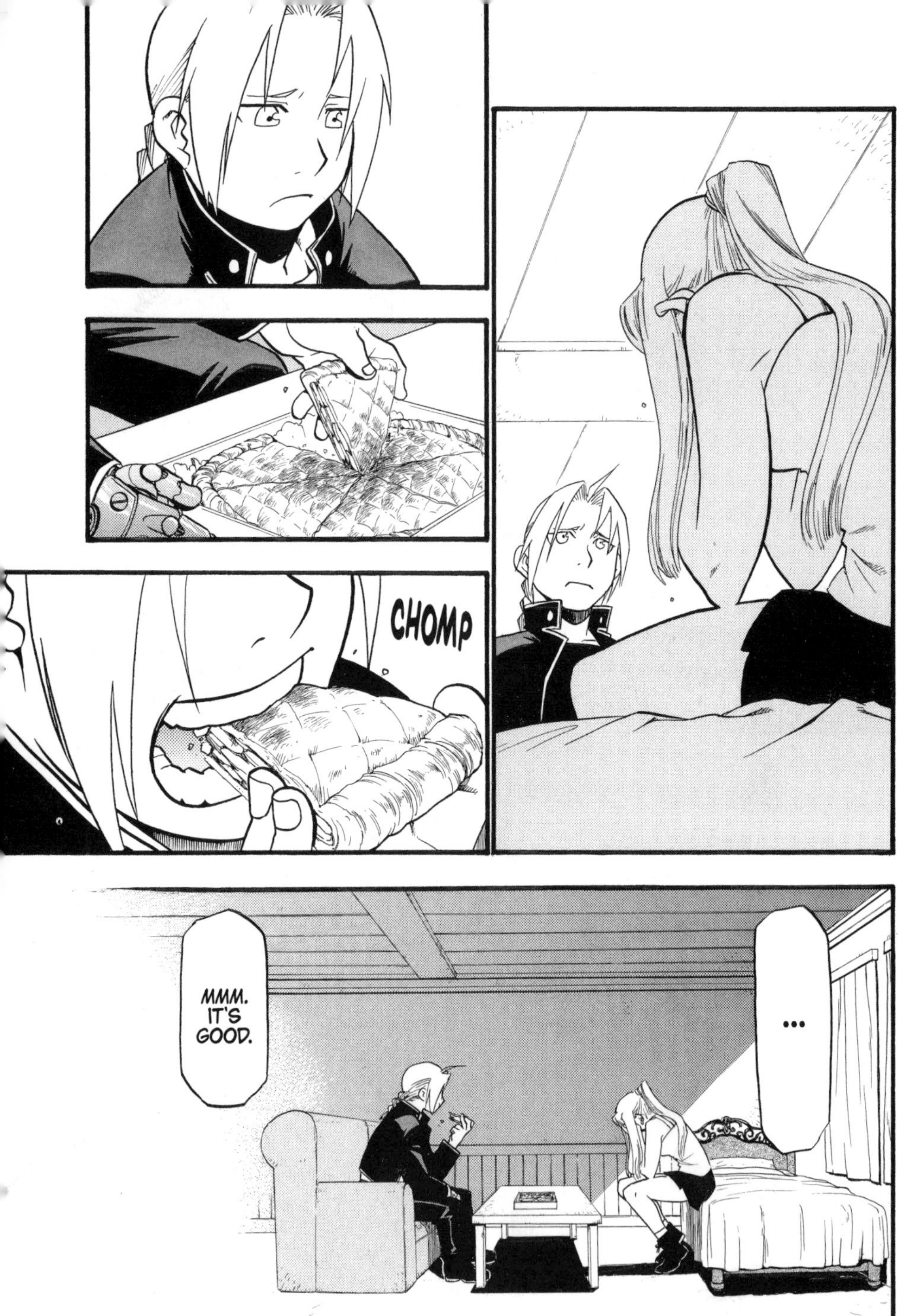
CHOMP
...
MMM. IT'S GOOD.

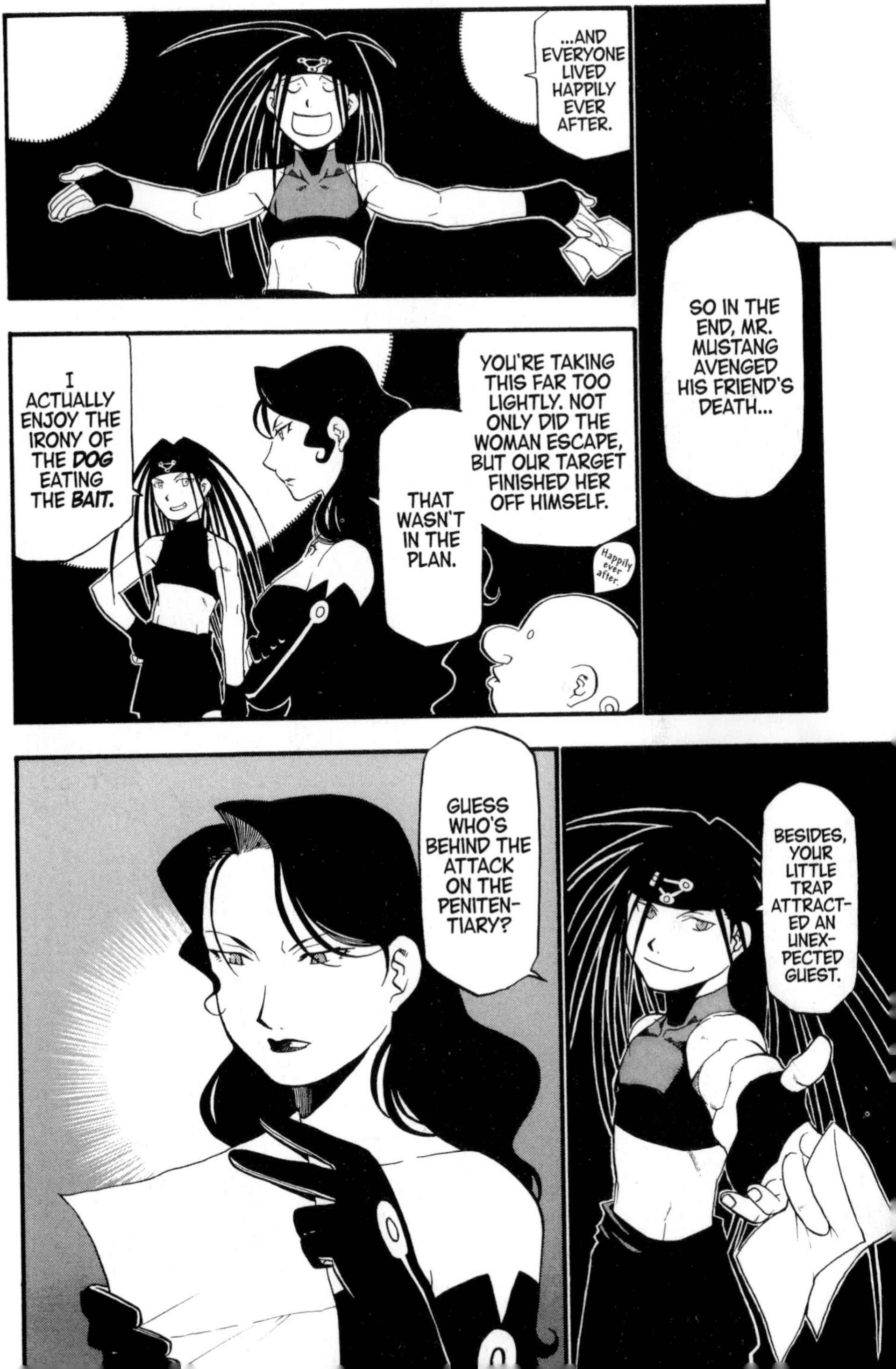
SO IN THE END, MR. MUSTANG AVENGED HIS FRIEND'S DEATH...
...AND EVERYONE LIVED HAPPILY EVER AFTER.
YOU'RE TAKING THIS FAR TOO LIGHTLY. NOT ONLY DID THE WOMAN ESCAPE, BUT OUR TARGET FINISHED HER OFF HIMSELF.
THAT WASN'T IN THE PLAN.
Happily ever after.
I ACTUALLY ENJOY THE IRONY OF THE **DOG** EATING THE **BAIT**.
BESIDES, YOUR LITTLE TRAP ATTRACTED AN UNEXPECTED GUEST.
GUESS WHO'S BEHIND THE ATTACK ON THE PENITENTIARY?

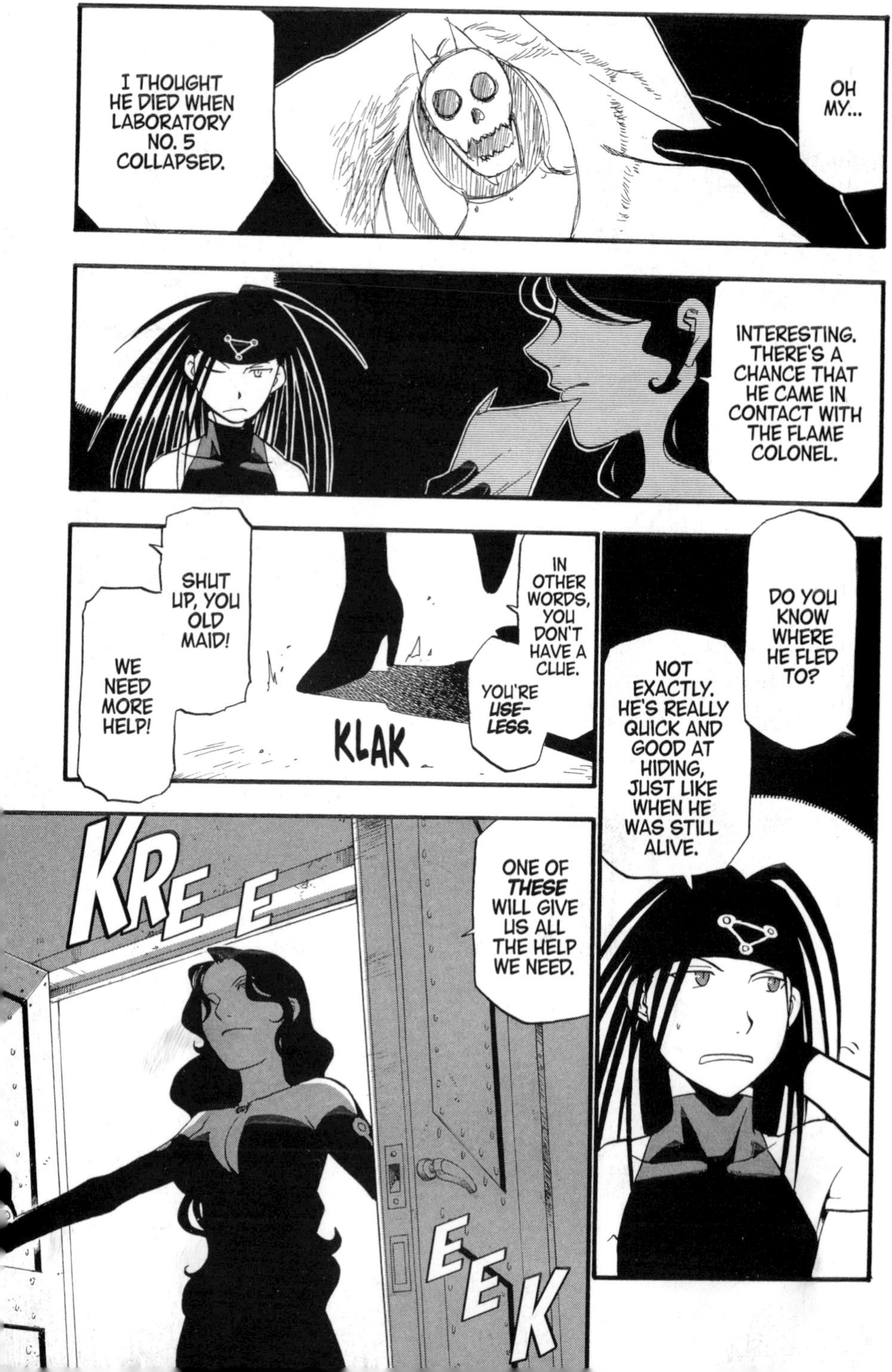
OH MY...
I THOUGHT HE DIED WHEN LABORATORY NO. 5 COLLAPSED.
INTERESTING. THERE'S A CHANCE THAT HE CAME IN CONTACT WITH THE FLAME COLONEL.
DO YOU KNOW WHERE HE FLED TO?
NOT EXACTLY. HE'S REALLY QUICK AND GOOD AT HIDING, JUST LIKE WHEN HE WAS STILL ALIVE.
IN OTHER WORDS, YOU DON'T HAVE A CLUE.
YOU'RE USE-LESS.
KLAK
SHUT UP, YOU OLD MAID!
WE NEED MORE HELP!
KREE
ONE OF THESE WILL GIVE US ALL THE HELP WE NEED.
EEEK

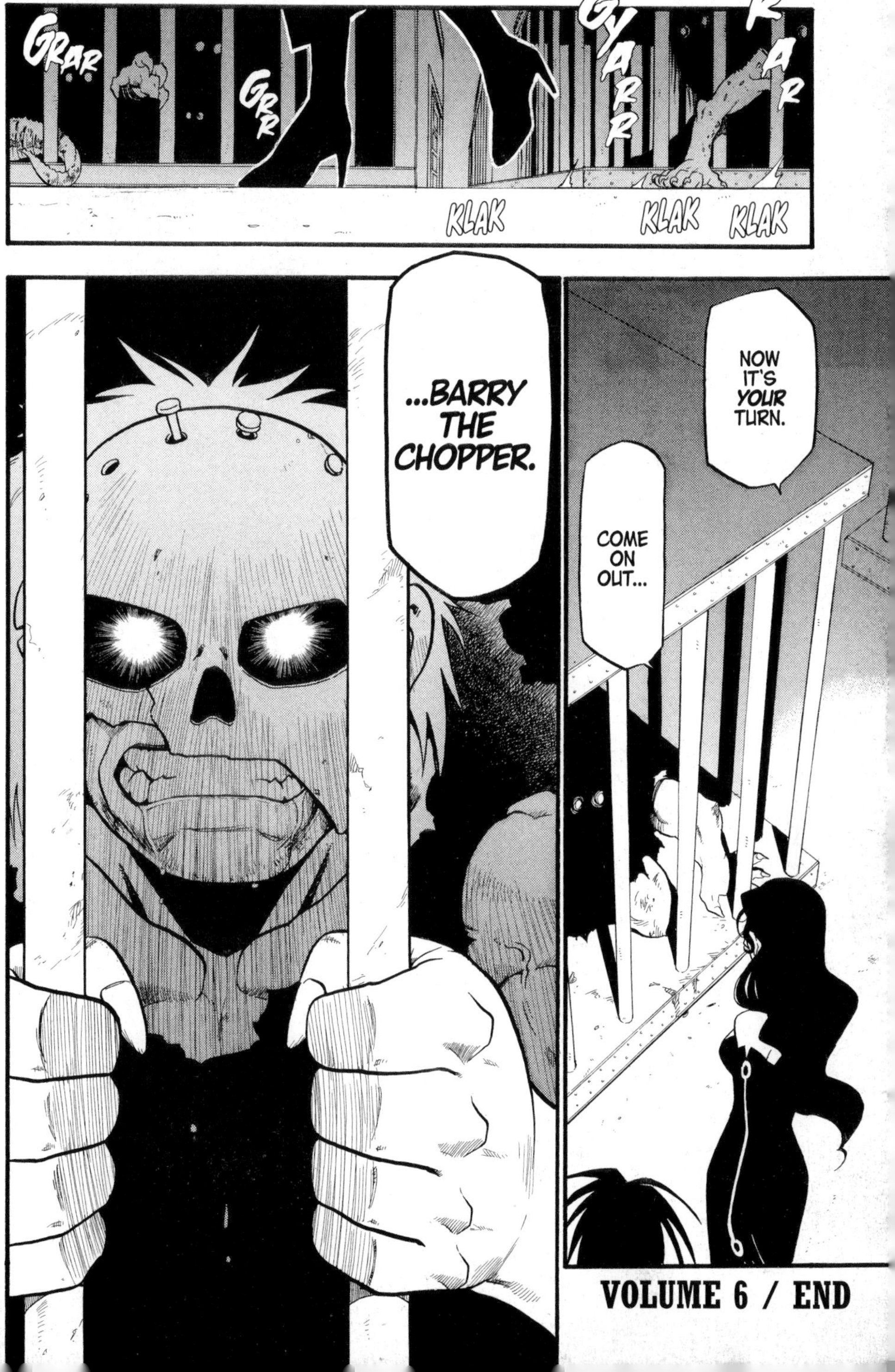
RAR
GYARRR
GRR
GRAR
KLAK
KLAK
KLAK
NOW IT'S YOUR TURN.
COME ON OUT...
...BARRY THE CHOPPER.

VOLUME 6 / END

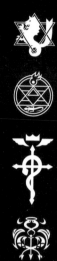

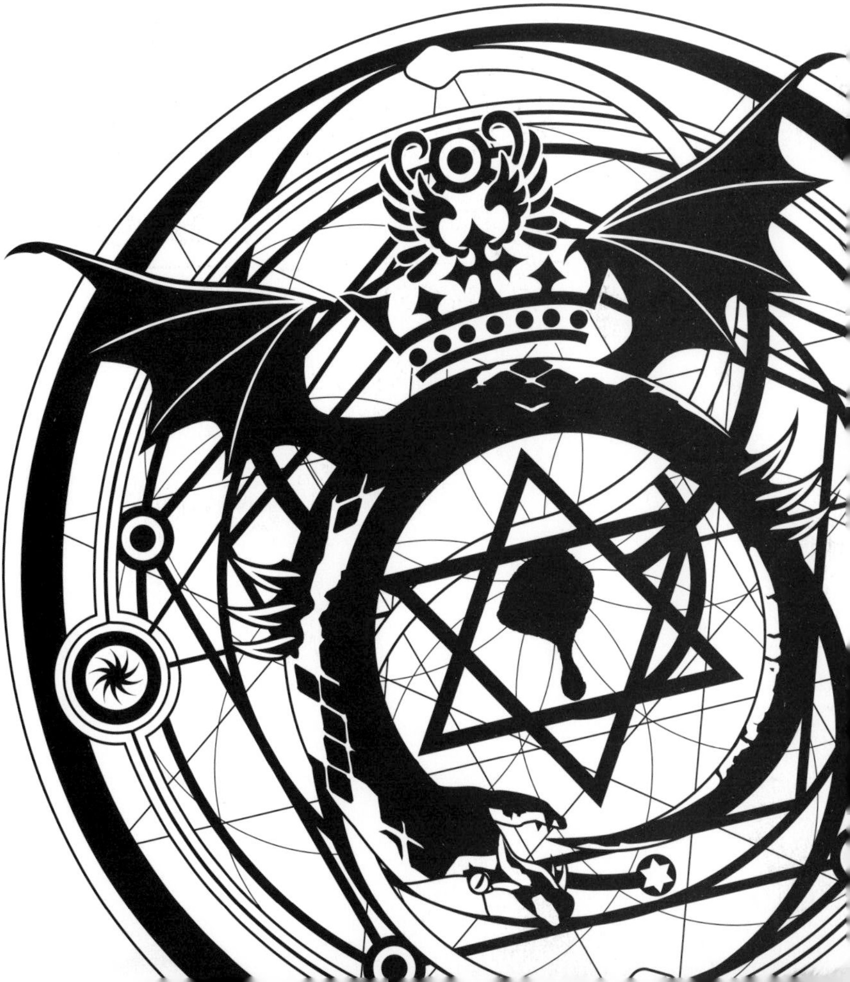

FULLMETAL ALCHEMIST

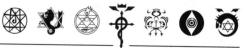

CONCEPT SKETCHES

06

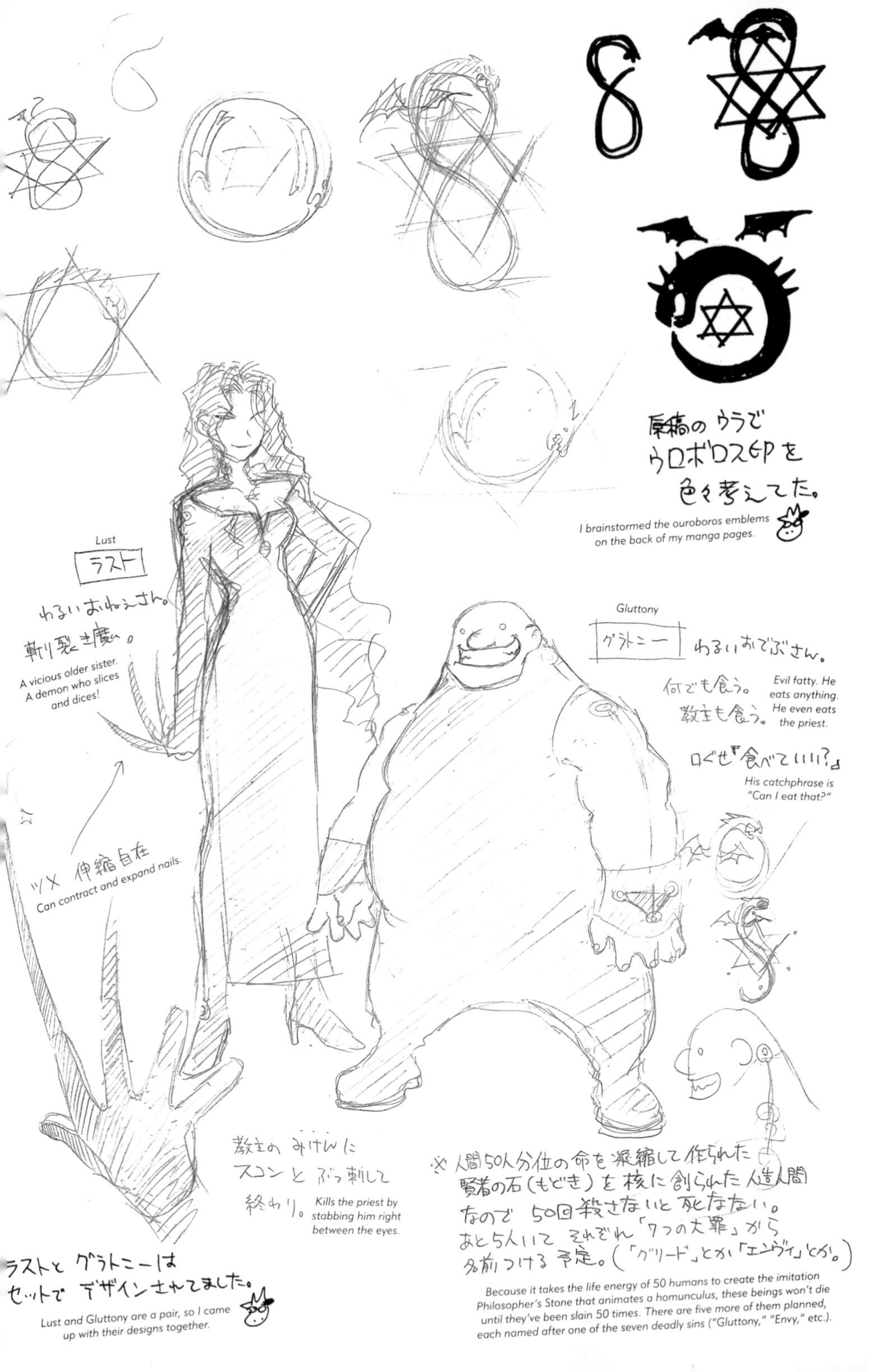
原稿のウラで
ウロボロス印を
色々考えてた。
I brainstormed the ouroboros emblems on the back of my manga pages.
Lust
ラスト
わるいおねえさん。
斬り裂き魔。
A vicious older sister. A demon who slices and dices!
ツメ 伸縮自在
Can contract and expand nails.
Gluttony
グラトニー
わるいおでぶさん。
何でも食う。
教主も食う。
Evil fatty. He eats anything. He even eats the priest.
口ぐせ『食べていい?』
His catchphrase is "Can I eat that?"
教主の みけんに
スコンと ぶっ刺して
終わり。
Kills the priest by stabbing him right between the eyes.
※人間50人分位の命を凝縮して作られた
賢者の石(もどき)を核に創られた人造人間
なので 50回殺さないと死なない。
あと5人いて それぞれ「7つの大罪」から
名前つける予定。(「グリード」とか「エンヴィ」とか。)
Because it takes the life energy of 50 humans to create the imitation Philosopher's Stone that animates a homunculus, these beings won't die until they've been slain 50 times. There are five more of them planned, each named after one of the seven deadly sins ("Gluttony," "Envy," etc.).
ラストとグラトニーは
セットでデザインされてました。
Lust and Gluttony are a pair, so I came up with their designs together.

Sloth Initial Design

A big fellow, he's meant to resemble Frankenstein's monster.

←スロウス 初期案

でかい男、
フランケンシュタインな
イメージだった。

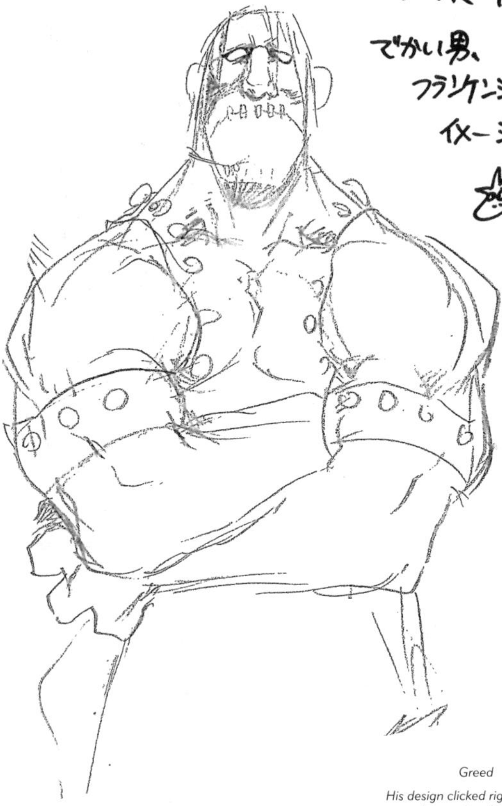

Greed

His design clicked right from the start. Except that the placement of his ouroboros mark changed.

グリード →

最初から
かっちり
デザインが
決まっていた。

ウロボロス印の
場所がちがう
くらいかな。

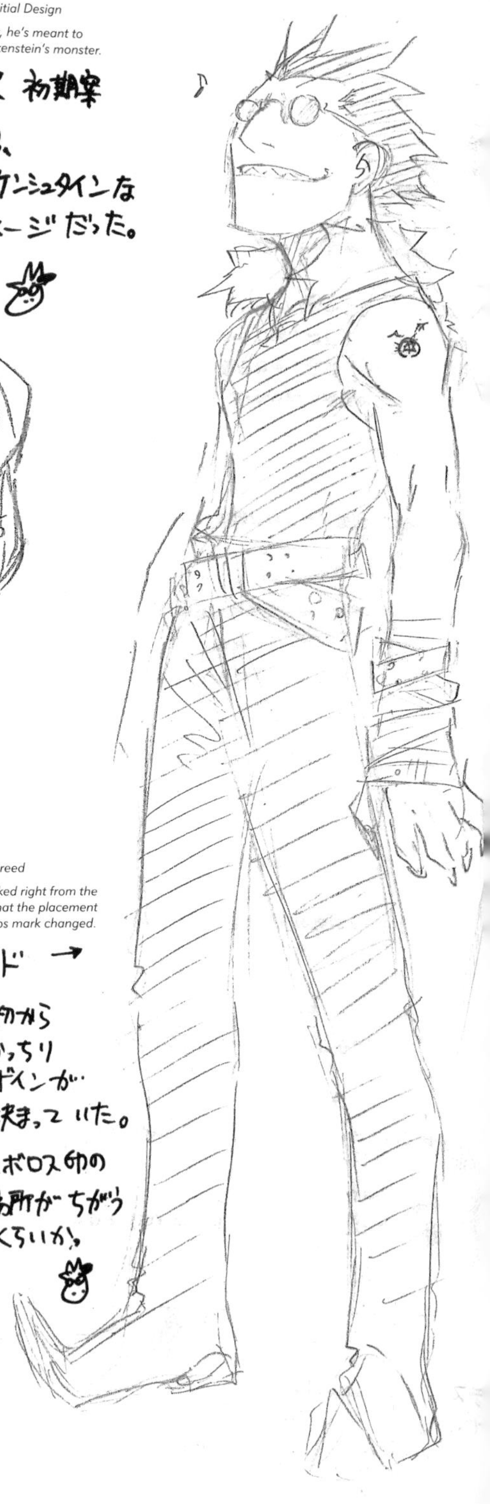

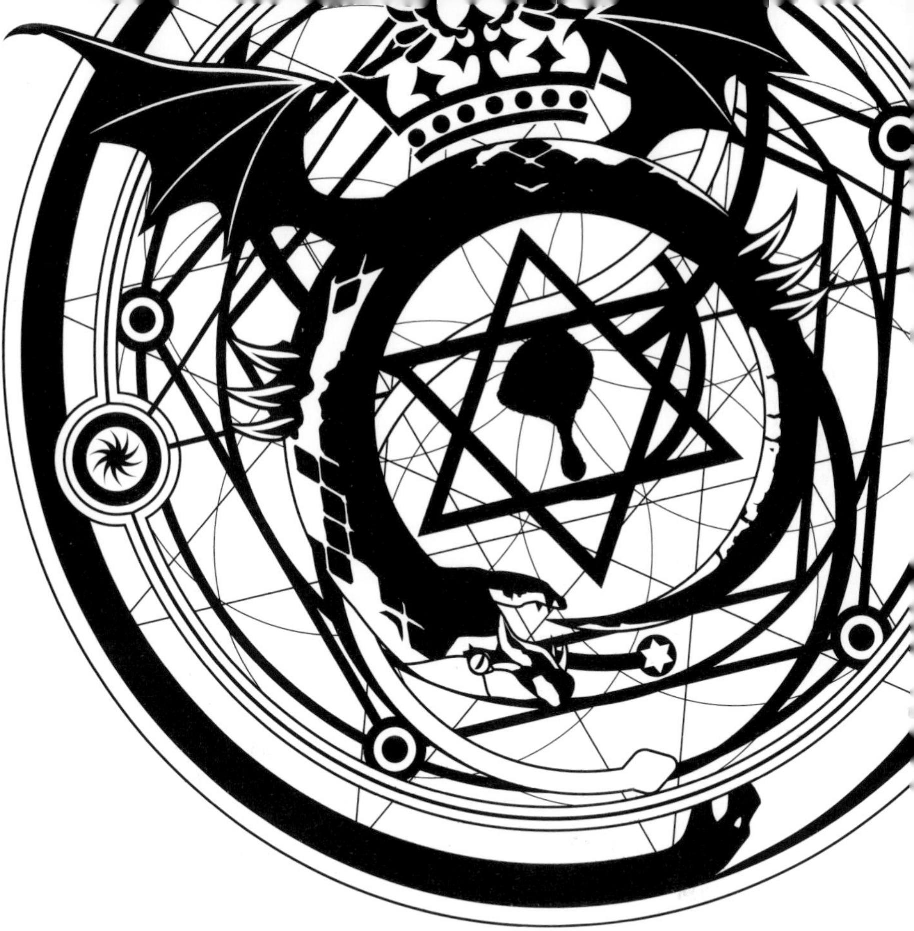

ABOUT THE AUTHOR

Born in Hokkaido, Japan, Hiromu Arakawa first attracted attention in 1999 with her award-winning manga *Stray Dog*. Her series *Fullmetal Alchemist* was serialized from 2001 to 2010 with a story that spanned 27 volumes and became an international critical and commercial success, receiving both the Shogakukan Manga Award and Seiun Award and selling over 70 million copies worldwide. *Fullmetal Alchemist* has been adapted into anime twice, first as *Fullmetal Alchemist* in 2003 and again as *Fullmetal Alchemist: Brotherhood* in 2009. The series has also inspired numerous films, video games and novels.

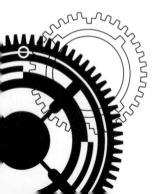

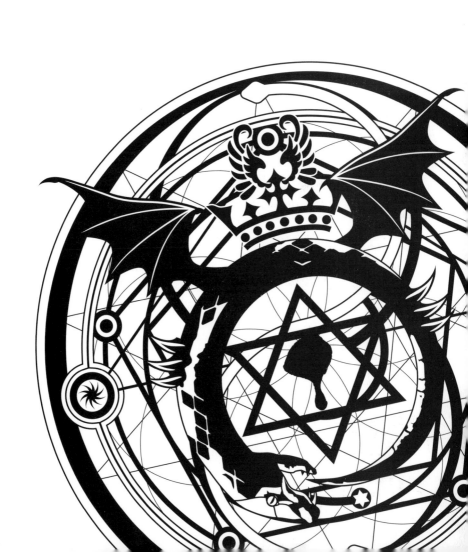

FULLMETAL EDITION

FULLMETAL ALCHEMIST

VOLUME 06

Story and Art by HIROMU ARAKAWA

Translation: AKIRA WATANABE
English Adaptation: JAKE FORBES
VIZ Media Edition Editor: URIAN BROWN
Touch-Up Art & Lettering: STEVE DUTRO
Design: ADAM GRANO
Editor: HOPE DONOVAN

FULLMETAL ALCHEMIST KANZENBAN vol. 6
© 2011 Hiromu Arakawa/SQUARE ENIX CO., LTD.
First published in Japan in 2011 by SQUARE ENIX CO., LTD.
English translation rights arranged with SQUARE ENIX CO.,
LTD. and VIZ Media, LLC. English translation © 2019 SQUARE
ENIX CO., LTD.

Printed in Canada

Published by VIZ Media, LLC
P.O. Box 77010
San Francisco, CA 94107

10 9 8 7 6 5 4 3 2 1
First printing, August 2019

viz.com

This is the last page.

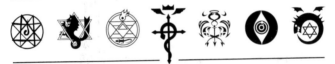

Fullmetal Alchemist reads right to left.

WITHDRAWN